AF380000

THE LONG 1980s

Editors
Nick Aikens
Teresa Grandas
Nav Haq
Beatriz Herráez
Nataša Petrešin-
  Bachelez

Contributors
Nick Aikens
Henry Andersen
Zdenka Badovinac
Barış Gençer
  Baykan
Hakim Bey
Manuel Borja-Villel
Rosi Braidotti
Boris Buden
Cristina Cámara
Jesús Carrillo
Bojana Cvejić
Luc Deleu
Diedrich
  Diederichsen
Nazım Hikmet
  Richard Dikbaş
Corinne Diserens
Ayşe Düzkan
Merve Elveren
Charles Esche
Marcelo Expósito
Božidar Flajšman
Annie Fletcher
Diana Franssen
June Givanni
Lisa Godson
Teresa Grandas
Nav Haq
Beatriz Herráez
Lubaina Himid
Lola Hinojosa
Antony Hudek
Tea Hvala
Gal Kirn
Neža Kogovšek
  Šalamon
Anders Kreuger
Elisabeth Lebovici
Rogelio López
  Cuenca
Geert Lovink
Amna Malik
Pablo Martínez
Lourdes Méndez
Aleš Mendiževec
Ana Mizerit
Alexei Monroe
Meriç Öner
Nataša Petrešin-
  Bachelez
Bojana Piškur
Marta Popivoda
Carlos Prieto del
  Campo
Pedro G. Romero
Rafael Sánchez
  Ferlosio
Igor Španjol
Chris Straetling
Luís Trindade
Erman Ata Uncu
Jelena Vesić
Mar Villaespesa
Vladimir Jerić Vlidi
Ana Vujanović

Valiz, Amsterdam
L'Internationale

www.valiz.nl
www.internationaleonline.org

THE LONG 1980s

CONSTELLATIONS OF ART, POLITICS AND IDENTITIES

A Collection of Microhistories

CONTENTS

PART 3
PROCESSES OF IDENTIFICATION

PART 3.1
HYBRIDITY AND ANTI-IMPERIALISM

PART 3.2
BODIES PUT UP A FIGHT

PART 4
NEW ORDER

PART 4.1
CAPITAL AND ITS CRISES

PART 4.2
1989

THE LONG 1980s

CONSTELLATIONS OF ART, POLITICS AND IDENTITIES

An Introduction

Friends, citizens, subjects, travellers: we welcome you to our book. With the title *The Long 1980s: Constellations of Art, Politics and Identities*, we would like to offer you a multitude of perspectives and histories from, and on, the period of the eighties.

The core question: why the eighties? It is primarily because in analyzing the eighties, we identify many of the genealogies of our present moment. We look retrospectively here to a period of profound change in the world. A period that is still fresh within the living memory of many people, and that has had a lasting influence on our civil society, culture, politics, ecology and economics. If we consider just a few of the central events and narratives of that period — we might take, for example, the redrafting of the socio-economic rulebook defined by the neoliberal ideology of Ronald Reagan and Margaret Thatcher, the end of the Cold War following the collapse of the Soviet Union, the beginnings of the institutionalization of multiculturalism, not to mention the invention of the World Wide Web — we identify the catalysts of seismic shifts on a global scale. These are but a few of the better-known manifestations, amongst many others that took place at a more local or regional level, that still determine many of the practices, counter-practices and ideological partialities of today. Many of the facets that comprise the crisis of the Western world order that we are currently experiencing can be directly traced to things that occurred in the eighties. For this reason, we decided to make a book about it.

What else was happening as these paradigmatic shifts were taking place? We zoom further into the territories of Europe, the broad geo-political focus within which this book situates itself, and we see seismic changes during this period. To the south, dictatorships in Portugal and Spain transitioned to capitalist democracies, resulting in a consensus-based politics that was often blind to the recent past. In Turkey, the decade began with a military coup and the subsequent reformulation of the constitution, which would have a profound effect on all aspects of governance and everyday life. In former Yugoslavia, the death of Tito and the demise of socialism precipitated the nation's eventual disintegration into war, genocide, and the emergence of new geo-political frontiers. To the west, the formation and rapid proliferation of neoliberalism would have a profound effect on how governments and their publics came to view one another, heightened by the situation of deep economic recession. Within and against these contexts the voices, bodies, and ideas of new subjectivities emerged. Subjectivities that were articulating their position through the constituent identities of gender, sexuality, and race. The appearance of feminist, post-dictatorship, postcolonial and queer politics in the eighties, for example, and their manifestations within the spheres of art and culture bear testament to many of the constellations — of art, politics, and identities — that we describe as the sub-title of the book.

As you will get to see, it is, in fact, many of these latent or counter-narratives that we felt were significant to foreground, understanding that historical consciousness varies greatly across time and space. Over half the contents of this book is given over to case studies — 70 in total — that as a collective body of case studies might be seen to comprise an atlas of alternative practices, sitting in parallel to the dominant arc of history, whether challenging, mirroring, or deflecting it. It has been important to see that alternatives existed, particularly in that era when Thatcher resolutely told those forced to listen in the Western and Anglo spheres, not only that there wasn't an alternative, but that society didn't even exist at all. Yet the reality was that both alternatives and societies did exist, and still do in fact, bringing us to the heart of the many struggles and contradictions that define the early part of the twenty-first century. The supposedly definitive worldview that we remember has been unravelling. This book is about many of those that either did not want to accept it or saw it coming, and who used the situation to create spaces of solidarity, imagination, and invention. The eighties was a long decade, so much so that we decided to define it as being more like 20 years — roughly speaking from 1975 to 1995 — in recognition of the fact that a definitive decade is too blunt a method for defining the many faces of a complicated and pivotal era. It has helped us in our attempt to form a more complex portrait of this long decade.

The case studies presented comprise a collection of stories, facsimiles, and images from various spheres of creativity, such as arts, activism, or social movements — and they often have a local or national character. These inspiring, ground-breaking stories have often never been translated in any other language or are little known outside the frame of contemporary art history or beyond national borders. How to produce new narratives by weaving these stories together, was the question we faced when structuring the book. We have organized the case studies in four units, larger chapters whose titles are the result of numerous editorial musings and internal debates about ethics and humour, and draw aspirations from various cultural references and from specific case studies mentioned in the publication. Within each of them we identified keywords that relate to the material presented, and from those we arranged two subchapters. The first chapter 'No Alternative?' appropriates Margaret Thatcher's infamous maxim and explores the numerous ways cultural practitioners were offering alternative spaces and formats to the emergent neoliberal order. This section is divided into the sub-sections 'Autonomous Zones' and 'Broadcast Yourself'. The second chapter, 'Know Your Rights', looks at the cultural and activist practices that were responding to the wave of forms of cultural and political oppression in the eighties. As such, it is composed of the sub-chapters 'Ecologies and Anti-Militarism' and 'Civil Liberties'. The third chapter, 'Processes of Identification', is framed around the sections 'Hybridity and Anti-Imperialism' and 'Bodies Put Up a Fight', looking at the manifold ways subjectivities and identities were articulating themselves through culture and at the intersections of emergent forms of racial and sexual politics. The last chapter, 'New Order', closes the publication with 'Capital and Its Crises' and '1989'. It addresses the decade's new regime — in terms of the rapid accession of neoliberal politics as the perceived only game in town, but also as a new conception of, or blindness to, the concept of history itself. The book ends with a series of case studies from the decade's final year.

The opening tone for the book is set by two acclaimed writers and theorists, Rosi Braidotti and Diedrich Diederichsen, whose contributions speak from their own positions and lived experience of the long eighties and what the era represented for their own theoretical endeavours. In her essay, titled '"It will have been the best of times: thinking back to the 1980s"', Braidotti examines the significant moments and places in the epochal analysis that this selection of essays, documents, and case studies seeks to put forward, revealing certain strands of her philosophical studies in a first-person contribution. She reflects on the critiques of orthodox Marxism and the subsequent appearance of new forms of leftist positions, the fall of the Berlin Wall and the upsurge in conservative ideology, as well as the consolidation of the neoliberal economy. This is interlaced with a consideration of how different discourses were migrating across fields forming new philosophical currents and creating a setting where historical acceleration appears as all but inescapable. Similarly for Braidotti, the issue of representation — both political and aesthetic — and its limits appear as the central problematic marking the time period. What exactly can be said and by whom?

The second opening essay, titled 'From Anti-Social-Liberal Punk to Intersectional AIDS Activism: (Sub-)Culture and Politics in Eighties Europe', sees Diedrich Diederichsen sketch a pathway combining political, social, and aesthetic aspects from the eighties. Diederichsen draws on historical sources that not only refer to spheres of discourse and theory, but also stem from the music culture of that period, particularly the punk movement. He analyzes and interrelates fields of experience that belong to diverse categories creating a polyphonic approach to the decade's political struggles, the transformations at the heart of critical theory and their relationship to artistic practices and youth culture. By tracing the minutiae of a generation characterized by disenchantment and nihilism, the theorist parses a complex, multifocal map, creating a global lens through which to view the decade.

This book is the result of a long period of research and programming across museums and universities in Europe. Over the course of the five-year programme 'The Uses of Art', partners within the L'Internationale confederation[01] presented a number of exhibitions that examined the eighties from different social, political, and cultural contexts, exploring the many different counter-narratives that we felt might offer an alternative reading of our recent past. These varied from looking at specific groups or movements to new tendencies in artistic practice, as well as the emergence of different forms of activism within the context of states in processes of radical transition.[02] In the majority of these exhibitions, the

01   L'Internationale is a confederation of six modern and contemporary art institutions. L'Internationale proposes
      a space for art within a non-hierarchical and decentralized internationalism, based on the values of difference and
      horizontal exchange among a constellation of cultural agents, locally rooted and globally connected. It brings together
      six major European art institutions: Moderna galerija, Ljubljana; Museo Nacional Centro de Arte Reina Sofía, Madrid;
      Museu d'Art Contemporani de Barcelona, Barcelona; Museum van Hedendaagse Kunst Antwerpen, Antwerp; SALT,
      Istanbul and Ankara, and Van Abbemuseum, Eindhoven. L'Internationale works with complementary partners such as
      Middlesbrough Institute of Art (MIMA), Liverpool John Moores University, Stiftung Universität Hildesheim and KASK/
      University College Ghent School of Arts, along with associate organizations from the academic and artistic fields.
02   Details of all the activities focused on the eighties as part of the 'Uses of Art' programmes can be found in the
      colophon of the book.

various curators and institutions were addressing the eighties from localized perspectives, deliberately using the investigation into microhistories to point to wider societal changes. Indeed, interestingly for many of us involved in working on the eighties, we arrived at this time period independently from our L'Internationale colleagues in other parts of Europe. Each of us had identified the eighties as a moment of significance in understanding our respective recent histories as well as the genealogy of our current moment. Yet, many of these exhibitions and investigations remained — and drew their strength from — their specific locality.

In this respect, the opportunity to place the different microhistories from our respective research on the eighties in dialogue has been one of the main motivations behind the book. Significantly, it has also allowed us to consider many ideas and stories that were not part of our respective exhibitions. It is an opportunity for us as editors — and you as readers — to start to forge connections and affinities between the extraordinary collection of case studies, ideas and events that took place. Many of these connections are addressed in the collection of twelve larger essays that form a major component of the grouping. However, we hope many more constellations will emerge as readers visit and revisit the pages of the book. Our intention here is not to draw equivalences between the contexts. Rather, by placing these case studies in dialogue, we hope they may start to offer an alternative means of navigating Europe's recent history that foregrounds the individuals and localities involved but connects them to similar struggles and desires which they might have hitherto been unaware of. By bringing these stories into convergence within a book, rather than presented through our respective typical bourgeois institutions, we might begin to forge a sense of a complexified collective history that extends across the streets, cities, and organizations of Europe. This collective history, in which a plurality of narratives and identities are implicated, might offer us some help in understanding our present moment and how we arrived where we are, as well as the necessity of forging a future together, no matter how hard and distant that might sometimes feel.

The long journey in making this book would not have been possible without the vision and trust of many people. You, readers, will not necessarily be familiar with all these names, but these are several colleagues and friends that we would very much like to thank for their collaboration and support. We would like to thank Merve Elveren at SALT and the independent researcher Erman Ata Uncu, both from Istanbul, and Adela Železnik at Moderna galerija, Ljubljana, for their invaluable contribution in bringing together much of the content of this book. Steven ten Thije is a colleague that we must thank most graciously for being the tireless water-carrier of the L'Internationale confederation. Thank you Steven. We thank all of the many contributors to this book for sharing so eloquently your knowledge through the many texts and images that comprise your essays and case studies. Two gatherings are also important to acknowledge: 'When Were the 1980s?', a symposium organized by Ana Bigotte Vieira, Luís Trindade and Giulia Bonalli in Lisbon in 2015, where the editors of this book presented their research and with it the idea of this shared project was born. Secondly, the seminar '1980s — The Multiple Origins of Contemporary Art in Europe Today', organized by Nataša Petrešin-Bachelez and Steven ten Thije at KASK/ School of Arts of University College Ghent in 2016, where a number of authors of this publication were brought together. Lastly, we would like to thank our many colleagues in our respective institutions and across the confederation. This book is the outcome of the many conversations we have shared. We recognize that the possibility to work together and exchange ideas over a sustained period of time and across cultural contexts is precious and something not be taken for granted. We hope it may continue long into the future.

So, with that, dear readers we introduce this book *The Long 1980s*. We hope you will discover stories, histories and herstories that enrich your understanding of the entangled relationship between art, politics, and identities from the eighties, and that we all are living with today.

The editors
Nick Aikens, Teresa Grandas, Nav Haq,
Beatriz Herráez, Nataša Petrešin-Bachelez

'IT WILL HAVE BEEN THE BEST OF TIMES: THINKING BACK TO THE 1980s'

Rosi Braidotti

NOT JUST *ANY* AGE OF TRANSITION

Looking back to the eighties from the context of 2017 is like staring at a golden era from the edge of the abyss. So much has happened since, not all of it positive, and although the eighties paved the way for the violent world we inhabit today, they felt very different. Consider the context of the eighties: the elections of Margaret Thatcher in the UK in 1979 and of Ronald Reagan in 1980 in the USA set the stage for a conservative ideological onslaught, which brought neo-liberal economics and the Christian-driven American Right to the core of Anglo-American politics. A massive reaction against Marxism as the platform for activism, theory and political organizing was set in motion. The long-term implications of the historical defeat of Communism, heralded by the conservative ideologue Fukuyama as nothing less than 'the end of history'[01] were and still are momentous, both in Europe and elsewhere. For instance, the 1989 Soviet withdrawal from Afghanistan enabled the build-up of Islamist opposition that consolidated both the Taliban and Bin Laden's power base in the region. 'Post-communism' bred neo-colonial relations, in a global era of perpetual warfare, both in the Balkans and in the Gulf area.

As I argued elsewhere,[02] the eighties were an age of philosophical transition as well. In 1979, the high priest of the radical libertarians Herbert Marcuse died, followed in 1980 by the towering figure of Jean-Paul Sartre, and by the psychoanalyst Jacques Lacan in 1981. Other thinkers who were closer to us as teachers also died prematurely: Nicos Poulantzas committed suicide in 1979 and Roland Barthes died in an accident in 1980. Also in that year, Louis Althusser, who had been mentally ill for some time already, strangled his wife and was locked away in a criminal asylum. With the death of General Tito, also in 1980, the crisis of Western European Marxism became officially, while a greater portion of the world's youth was far more upset about the assassination of John Lennon, in New York, which took place the same year. 'Lennon, not Lenin!' had been a rallying cry for the revolutionary youth throughout the previous decade and it became even more poignant as the effects of that radicalism came into sharper focus.

01

Francis Fukuyama, *The End of History and the Last Man* (New York: Simon & Schuster, 1992).

02

Rosi Braidotti: 'Introduction', in *After Poststructuralism: Transitions and Transformations*, vol. 7, *The History of Continental Philosophy* (Durham: Acumen, 2010).

In this context, France, which will offer the framing of this text, continued to strike a different political and intellectual note, with the election of the socialist François Mitterrand to the presidency in 1981. Throughout the eighties, Paris provided the world forum for progressive and left-wing critiques of Soviet Communism and for the elaboration of alternative forms of political radicalism. France functioned as an avant-garde observatory that focused on the world-changing events taking shape all around. For instance, as early as 1980, the French writer Marguerite Duras, who, as a member of the communist anti-Nazi resistance in her youth was a close friend of Mitterand's, foresaw the fall of the Berlin Wall. She wrote enthusiastically about the Polish trade-union Solidarity's strikes in the Gdansk shipyard, led by future Nobel Peace Prize winner Lech Walesa. In the period between 1973 and 1978, another future Nobel Peace Prize winner, Alexander Solzhenitsyn, published the *Gulag Archipelago*, which he had written in secrecy in the USSR, in three volumes in Paris. It provided the definitive account of Stalin's death camps and the final statement about the failure of Soviet Communism and became a point of reference for poststructuralist philosophers' critiques of Marxist philosophy. Last but not least: Ayatollah Khomeini, the political leader of the Iranian Islamist revolution of 1979, lived in exile in Paris in the years preceding the fall of the Shah. The progressive politics as well as intellectual life of the eighties were dominated by the multiple energies emanating from Paris.

The speed and intensity of these convulsive events could not fail to affect the idea and the place of Europe, the legacy of the colonial and fascist past, in a changing geo-political world order. As the former West developed a more acute awareness of its colonial and postcolonial legacy, the critiques of Eurocentrism became a central concern, which connected to the poststructuralist discussions about the legacy of Enlightenment humanism and new forms of cosmopolitanism. These developments also hand an impact on the political project of the European Union (EU), which embarked on an expansion process[03] in the midst of the post-communist/postcolonial conjunction. I will return to this.

PARIS, JE T'ADORE

French philosophy, with its combination of theoretical exuberance and political passions, provided an embarrassment of intellectual riches that made it the key intellectual horizon for my generation. Paris at the time was, philosophically speaking, simply the most exciting place on Earth. While I enrolled for my postgraduate degree at the Sorbonne in what they called 'History of systems of

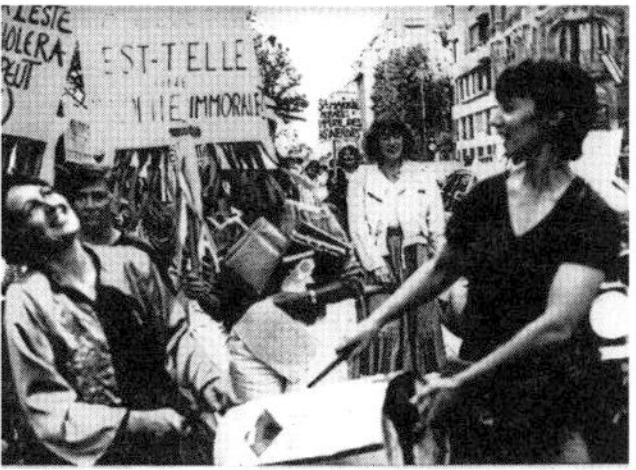

Demonstration in solidarity with American women after the election of Ronald Reagan, Paris, 30 June 1982. Front row, holding a drum, from left to right: Rosi Braidotti, Oristelle Bonis. A few rows behind them: Danielle Haase-Dubosc

03

The Maastricht Treaty was signed in 1992, the same year as the North American Free Trade Agreement (NAFTA), while the World Trade Organization (WTO) is set up in 1995.

thought', which was related to Foucault's Chair at the Collège de France, I savoured everything the city had to offer intellectually. The radical university of Vincennes hosted some of the best minds of the day: Hélène Cixous, Jean-François Lyotard and Gilles Deleuze, to name but a few. The Collège de France starred Roland Barthes, Pierre Bourdieu and Michel Foucault, whose magisterial courses on bio-power are forever engraved in my mind. Luce Irigaray held seminars in makeshift locations after Lacan expelled her from his 'École freudienne' for excessive independence of mind. It was not until I started attending Deleuze's seminars at the marginal university of Vincennes, however, that I discovered the complexities of listening to a genius: that was what great philosophy in the making was all about.

Philosophically, I related mostly to the branch of poststructuralism known as the 'line of immanence', which runs through Spinoza, Nietzsche, Foucault and Deleuze, as opposed to the 'line of transcendence', which runs through Kant, Derrida, Levinas. This tradition of critical thought inspired my own attempts to rearticulate a radical sense of materialism, embodiment, and accountability. By bringing back the marginalized tradition of political Spinozism, moreover, the materialist branch of poststructuralist philosophy in the eighties also redefined the question of political praxis in terms of ethical agency.

Developments in feminist theory also played a formative role in my development, and that of the decade. The Lacanian psychoanalytic feminist movement was at the centre of the scene, notably the 'psychanalyse et politique' group of Antoinette Fouque — who set up the Éditions des femmes and edited the magazine *Des femmes hebdo* (1982). Luce Irigaray, being *persona non grata* to the Lacanians, ran her own independent seminars and collaborated with several feminist collectives of Paris, notably *Sorcières* and *Histoires d'Elles*. Simone de Beauvoir was still very active and her group gathered round the journal *Les Temps Modernes*, which from 1973 devoted a special section — 'Chroniques du sexisme ordinaire' — to feminist issues. Julia Kristeva, Michèle Montrelay and Marcelle Marini were teaching groundbreaking classes at Paris VII, as did historian Michelle Perrot. There was a strong group of feminist sociologists around Christine Delphy but they hardly taught. In 1981, they founded the interdisciplinary social sciences journal *Questions féministes* (later *Nouvelles questions féministes*), which included Monique Wittig for a while.

In Paris in 1981–1982, I also crossed paths with great American academic feminists like Kate Stimpson, Nancy Miller, Domna Stanton, Joan Scott and Naomi Schor, who came to Europe and were carefully following the new developments in France in that period and translating them into English. They were part of

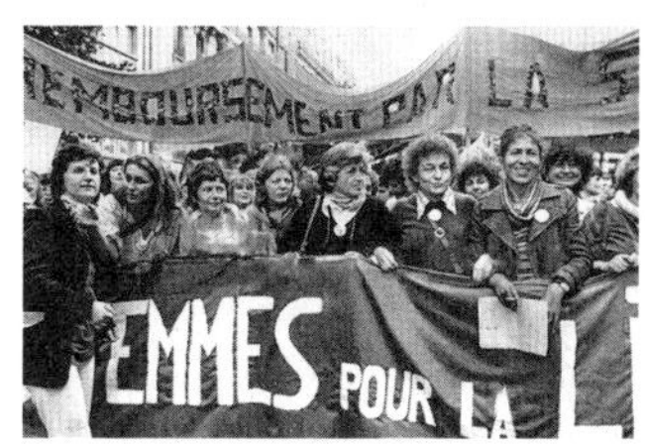

National Pro-Abortion Women's March, 6 October 1979. From left to right: Martine Storti, Sophie Chauveau, Luce Irigaray; Simone Iff, Huguette Bouchardeau, Maya Surduts. Behind Maya, in the second row: Christine Buci-Glucksman

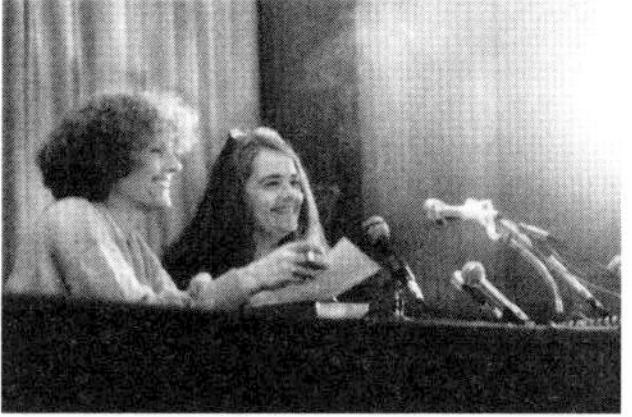

Press Conference on the Iranian Revolution, La Mutualité Hall, Paris, 1979. Feminists petitioning the new regime for women's rights. From left to right: Delphine Seyrig, Kate Millett

a wave of American academics who were especially taken with the psychoanalytic and semiotic aspects of the new groups and translated and exported these to the USA. This was to produce the 'Franco-American disconnection' (Stanton 1980), which would make 'New French Feminism' (De Courtivron and Marks 1980) into a global phenomenon[04]. It could not fail to affect French women themselves. Some were turned into stars, notably Cixous, Kristeva and Irigaray, who, incidentally, are not at all native French, Cixous being a Jewish Algerian; Kristeva Bulgarian and Irigaray Belgian. Others however felt dispossessed and misrepresented; there was widespread concern about misleading interpretations of the concept and theories involved and the risk of depoliticizing them.

The orchestrated import of French ideas into the USA, which made 'traveling theories' (Said 1978) into an established practice and turned the task of translation into a new discursive political economy, also opened up a new academic market, mostly in literary theory, comparative literature, cultural and gender studies and film theory. The impact of French thought on international feminist theory and practice was nothing short of an epistemological revolution.[05] In the mid-eighties, as the notion and the politics of difference moved centre stage,[06] American feminism plunged into the 'sex wars' that would divide its radical wing.[07]

Philosophy departments however took a clear and explicit distance from these fashionable trends and closed ranks. From 1980 to 1995, the public debate around the critical legacy of the seventies grew more bitter and contested. The rise of Reagonomics and Thatcherite authoritarianism installed a climate of right-wing political backlash, which could not fail to attack the credibility of European and especially French poststructuralist theories. These were dismissed by the political Right as being both relativistic and a sign of wishy-washy liberalism. Their hostility continued to grow throughout the nineties as the 'theory wars'[08] (Sprinker 1995; Neilson 1995; Butler and Scott 1992) raged through American universities, fuelled also by the rise of the religious Christian Right. By 1995, the game was over and the counter-offensive against poststructuralism was well in place (Gallop 1997; Spivak 2003). Nonetheless, the inspirational power of French theories, feminist and other, remained high and affected the most critical and creative minds of that generation of academics.

Deleuze was one of the first to comment on this hasty and fallacious historical dismissal of critical radicalism in both politics and philosophy.[09] Targeting the fame-seeking narcissism of the *nouveaux philosophes*, Deleuze stressed the political conservatism of their practice, which reasserted the banality of individualistic self-interest, in keeping with the neoconservative political liberalism of that era. Deleuze stressed instead how his

04

Jane Weinstock and I published a critical review of this phenomenon in 1980.

05

See the Milan Women's Bookstore Collective (1990); Adriana Cavarero (1990); Herta Nagl-Docekal and Herlinde Pauer-Studer (1990), and Andrea Maíhofer (1995); Celia Amorós (1985); Maria Isabel Santa Cruz et al. (1994) and Henrietta Moore (1994).

06

Eisenstein and Jardine 1980; and Frye 1996.

07

Vance 1984.

08

See Jeffrey Williams, ed., *PC Wars: Politics and Theory in the Academy* (New York: Routledge, 1994).

09

Gilles Deleuze, 'On the New Philosophers (Plus a More General Problem)' and 'May '68 Didn't Happen', in *Two Regimes of Madness: Texts and Interviews 1975–1995* (New York: Semiotext(e), 2006).

own critical philosophy laboured to avoid and critique the arrogance of that universalizing posture. Other leading philosophers such as Lyotard, Dominique Lecourt, and the gay activist Guy Hocquenghem, also took a clear stand against the trivialization and self-serving dismissal of the spirit of radical philosophy by a new generation of opportunistic intellectual entrepreneurs.[10]

The Trans-Atlantic disconnection that dominated our philosophical horizons also shaped the academic careers of my generation. We — the graduate students of a field of feminist research that formally did not yet exist — witnessed the genesis of a new system of import-export of ideas that gave us a foretaste of cultural globalization. We could also see glaring disparities not only in the selection of which French thinkers were being translated into English, but also in the speed of publication of these translations.[11] We watched the meteoric rise of Derrida and Foucault in the USA and wondered why Deleuze was left behind.[12] As a consequence, today we know that it is historically but also theoretically impossible to speak of French feminist theory without implying the Trans-Atlantic nexus and that these theories essentially belong to the English-speaking world (Oliver 2000; Cavallaro 2003).

THE TIME-BOMB OF RADICAL PEDAGOGICS

The generation of feminists situated between 1980 and 1995 was the first to enjoy the institutional presence of supportive and talented women teachers and supervisors, many of whom were feminists themselves, such as Genevieve Lloyd, Seyla Benhabib, and Luce Irigaray. The effects of the actual, physical presence of women lecturers in philosophy departments beginning in the seventies throughout the eighties cannot be stressed enough. The influence of these progressive teachers on my generation of radicalized younger women philosophers engaged in feminism was to be everlasting. But, much as we enjoyed thinking back through our mothers, we were far from dutiful daughters.

The eighties generation sought to challenge the false universalism of philosophical thought as being a form of particularism: it protected male, white privileges and inflated them to transcendental proportions. I and my peer groups focused on highlighting the difference that feminist philosophers can make to the actual practice of the discipline. In the longer term, many of us actually left philosophy as an institutional site and contributed to the creation of new interdisciplinary fields.[13] Being pioneers in women's studies, we were given the chance to develop institutional, pedagogical, and methodological structures that operationalized the full potential of non-dialectical and anti-hierarchical

10

See Jean-François Lyotard and Jacob Rogozinski, 'La Police de la pensée', *L'Autre Journal 10* (1985); Dominique Lecourt, *Les Piètres penseurs* (Paris: Flammarion, 1999); published in English as *Mediocracy: French Philosophy Since the Mid-1970s*, trans. Gregory Elliott (London: Verso, 2001); Guy Hocquenghem, *Lettre ouverte à ceux qui sont passés du col Mao au Rotary* (Marseille: Agone, 1986). *The nouveaux philosophes* will later strike a political alliance with the French right-wing politicians, like Sarkozy.

11

For instance, Julia Kristeva's work appeared fast in English: *About Chinese Women* (originally published in 1974) came out in 1977, *Desire in Language* (originally published in 1969) in 1980, the *Kristeva Reader* in 1986. Hélène Cixous was slightly behind, with the 1976 translation of 'The Laugh of the Medusa' (originally published in 1975) and the 1986 translation of *The Newly Born Woman* (co-written with Catherine Clément and originally published in 1975); *The Book of Promethea* (originally published in 1983) in 1991, and the *The Hélène Cixous Reader* in 1994. Luce Irigaray, however, lagged behind, with the double translation of both *Speculum of the Other Woman* (originally published in 1974) and *This Sex Which is Not One* (originally published in 1977) in 1985, *The Ethics of Sexual Difference* (originally published in 1984) in 1993, after which the speed picked up somehow.

12

The linguistically oriented movement, inspired by Jacques Lacan, Jacques Derrida and Roland Barthes, was centred at the Yale school of literary theory; see

difference. In so doing we ended up altering the very theoretical premises of emancipatory feminism from which we had started, innovating on content and concepts. We also started canonizing a firm corpus of feminist scholarship that institutionalized the idea of collective teamwork as a key collaborative method. As Joan Kelly argued,[14] feminism carried a double-edged vision that combined oppositional consciousness with deep empowering creativity. The affirmative element within the feminist recomposition of knowledge is one of my generation's lasting theoretical legacies.

The core of my philosophical interest, like for so many in my generation, coalesced around questions of identity, responsibility, becoming a subject of both knowledge and transformative politics or praxis. The main issues I engaged with were: how can we think with and on behalf of the excluded, the marginalized, the 'missing people'? What concepts and methods can help us do justice to the social and intellectual experiences and knowledge of those that have received no recognition in the language and institutional practice of conventional wisdom? What is the appropriate language in which to express silences and regenerate missing voices? The politics of discourse and the limits of representation became crucial concerns. So much of our collective embodied experience — as women, gays, pacifists, leftists — seemed somehow pitched against what was discursively acceptable or even sayable.

In 1988, I accepted an experimental new academic position at the university of Utrecht. So I left Paris to set up an interdisciplinary women's studies department and devise a new curriculum. Working in a feminist academic environment, in an interdisciplinary, intellectually cutting-edge and politically progressive — if not downright transgressive — context had its advantages. Radical pedagogics now became the basis for my institutional practice. The price to pay for such daring experiments, however, was to accept my distance from the institutional practice of philosophy. This new focus, though not without some pain, allowed me to liberate my own philosophical thought from a number of institutional habits. I became nomadic as a deep conceptual level as well as an existential condition.

EXTRA-MURAL PHILOSOPHY

In the same period, the French were also experimenting with new institutional structures. With the privilege of hindsight, it is clear that throughout the eighties, in response to both external prompts and internal dynamics, the practice of philosophy in Paris expanded towards activities that were outside the established institutions of the discipline. If the interdisciplinary university

Barbara Johnson (1980, 1998), Shoshana Felman (1993), Marjorie Garber (1997). The pioneers of French feminist theory in the US were Domna Stanton (1987); Nancy Miller (1986); Alice Jardine (1985); Naomi Schor (1987); Catharine Stimpson (1989) and Joan Scott (1999). Gayatri Spivak expanded it to postcolonial theory. Interest in Deleuze did not take off till the early two-thousands.

13

See my chapter with Judith Butler: 'Out of Bounds: Philosophy in an Age of Transition', in Braidotti, ed., *After Poststructuralism*, pp. 307–335.

14

See Joan Kelly: 'The Double-edged Vision of Feminist Theory', *Feminist Studies* 5, no. 1 (1979), pp. 216–227.

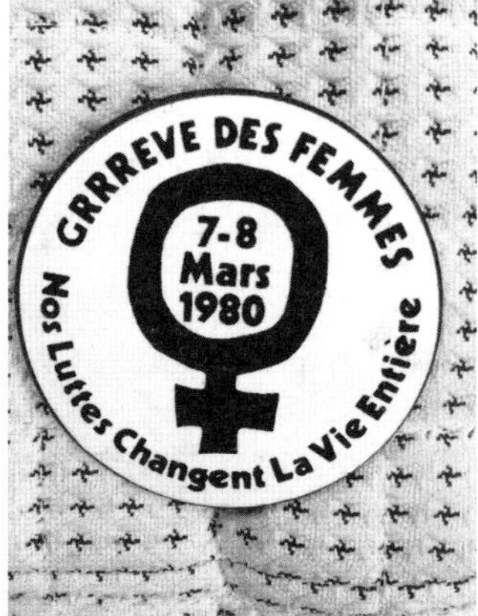

The official badge of the National Women's Strike, 8 March 1980

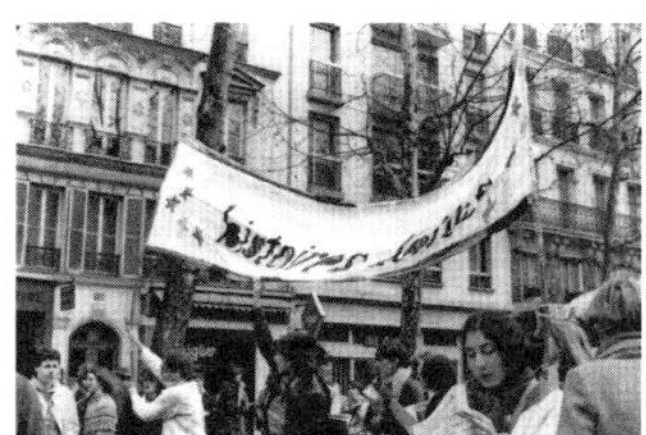

National Women's Strike, 8 March 1980. Holding the 'Histoires d'Elles' banner from left to right: Wendy Spinks, Katy Hamilton-Baillie

of Vincennes had provided the politicized model for the radical knowledge and training institution of the seventies, the Collège international de philosophie, founded in 1983 by Châtelet, Derrida, Faye and Lecourt, with the support of President Mitterand, embodied the vision and inspiration of the eighties. These extramural trajectories brought philosophy closer to real life. This approach continued the activist dispositions of the sixties and seventies, but also reflected a new culture that was becoming more informed by the arts, media and popular culture.

Intellectual, even theoretical meetings took place in cafes, at conferences, in feminist collectives, at gay and lesbian political meetings, anti-war rallies and demonstrations, in editorial boards, bars, community radio stations, in music and film festivals. Often framed by transnational contexts, philosophical thinking moved beyond the specific 'sites' of legitimate institutionalization to produce the possibility of thinking critically and creatively, bringing philosophy in the world. Although it was formatted and framed by reason, thinking was an outward-bound, external, and often reactive activity, driven by forces and affects that acted independently of the rational will. This was important to us, both as philosophers and as feminists and gay and lesbian activists.

The collective character of philosophical thoughts in general and the trans-individual character of so many knowledge claims that I shared with others became central to my work. All the more so as I belong to an 'intermediary generation' that witnessed some key moments in the history of feminism: respectively the rise of the 'feminism of difference' in Paris, its re-implantation in the USA and the 'sex wars' in the USA. Having been the first generation of philosophers who studied with great feminist teachers, we also gained some first-hand experience of institutional gender politics. This also taught us bitter lessons from the start: feminist philosophers were not always well received in philosophy departments and were only occasionally supported by institutional means and funds. They often had to find other venues for seminar activity and collective discussions. And even today, academic philosophers tend to practice mono-disciplinary purity and to withdraw support from interdisciplinary approaches that would situate the task of thinking philosophically anywhere outside academic departments of philosophy. The objections to women's, feminist, queer, cultural and media studies are upheld. As these interdisciplinary programmes are more developed in the USA than in Europe, this leaves many European radical philosophers even more homeless.[15]

French philosophers have a long established tradition of intervention in social, cultural, and political life, as public intellectuals, social critics, and activists. The likes of Jean-Paul Sartre

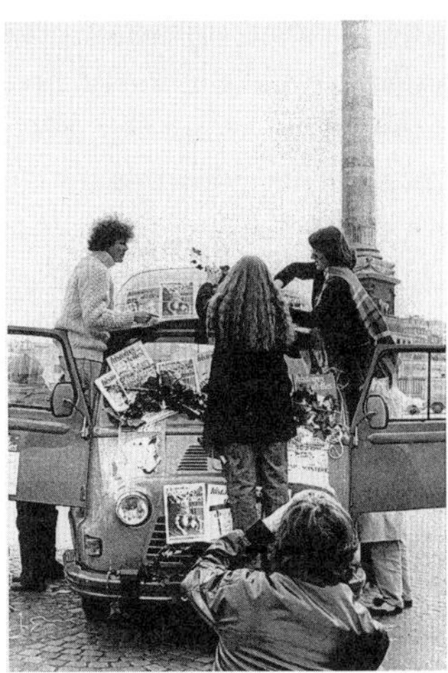

National Women's Strike, 8 March 1980. The 'Histoires d'Elles' van at the Bastille. From left to right: Wendy Spinks, Jane Weinstock (with her back to camera), Rosi Braidotti

15

The positive side of this situation, however, is that it contributes to the diaspora of philosophical ideas, which is generative, spreading them across the spectrum of society. As a result, philosophical reflection is no longer confined to academic settings, but has a broader reach |into the world and hybrid cross-pollinations occur whether the institutions like them or not. Think, for instance, of the role that philosophical thinking plays in human rights struggles, in non-governmental organizations such as Médecins sans Frontières, in Amnesty International, Human Rights Watch, and Greenpeace. Consider also how many philosophical thinkers have made significant contributions to critical legal theory in recent years.

and Simone de Beauvoir stand high in this tradition, lending their support to a variety of crucial causes such as decolonization, socialism, antiracism, feminism and pacifism. They also founded alternative journals and publication venues, such as *Les Temps modernes*, *Questions feminists* and the daily newspaper *Libération*. There was, however, a difference in the scale and mode of engagements of the philosophers who came after the existentialist generation. They intervened on questions of justice, human suffering, responsibility, economic and social sustainability, and global belonging, making use of visual culture and media and reflecting on its meaning, but they did so less in the name of an engagement with Marxist or any other ideology than as an end in itself. They prioritized the critical analysis of power relations at both the macro and the micro levels as the main task for philosophers and brought into focus issues of sexuality, identity and cultural subjectivity.

Michel Foucault and Gilles Deleuze[16] both captured the post-Marxist spirit of the times when they posited the emergence of a new function for the philosopher as public intellectual. If the contrast with the received Hegelian model of the universalistic philosopher as rational guardian of the moral development of mankind (the gender is not a coincidence) is easily drawn, the difference from the engaged or 'organic' intellectual of the previous generation of Gramscian and existential thinkers requires more cautious phrasing. As Foucault and Deleuze put it:

> At one time, practice was considered an application of theory, a consequence; at other times, it had an opposite sense and it was thought to inspire theory ... In any event, their relationship was understood in terms of a process of totalization. For us, however, the question is seen in a different light. The relationships between theory and practice are far more partial and fragmentary. ... the relationship which holds in the application of a theory is never one of resemblance. ... Practice is a set of relays from one theoretical point to another and theory is a relay from one practice to another. ... A theorizing intellectual, for us, is no longer a subject, a representing or representative consciousness. ... Representation no longer exists; there's only action—theoretical action and practical action which serve as relays and form networks.

Coherent in their practice, the poststructuralists predicate philosophy in the plural and move it toward social, political, and ethical concerns. They see themselves as 'specific' intellectuals, providers of critical services, analysts of the conditions of possibility of discourse, working with ideas that are also programmes

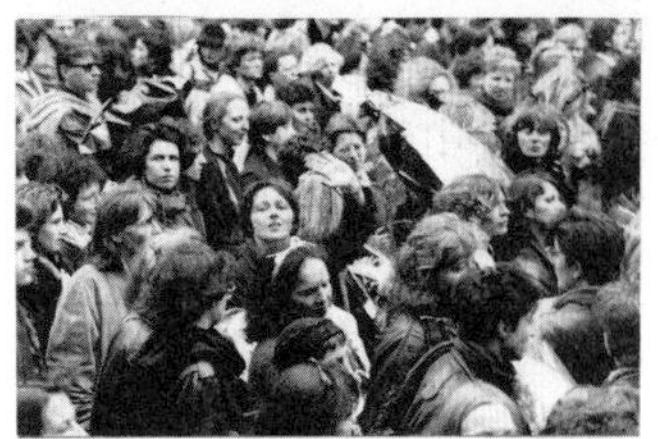

Simone de Beauvoir's Funeral, 19 April 1986. In the centre, waving (at her brother): Rosi Braidotti. Next to her: Marie-Jo Bonnet

16

See Michel Foucault and Gilles Deleuze, 'Intellectuals and Power', in *Language, Counter- Memory and Practice*, ed. Donald F. Bouchard (Ithaca, NY: Cornell University Press, 1977), pp. 205–207.

for action rather than dogmatic stockpiles of beliefs. This style is 'problematizing' in its radical empiricism, or anti-universalism, and in the awareness of the partiality of all philosophical statements. As a result, the kind of philosophy that emerged in the late eighties was on the edge of institutionalization, embodying what Foucault called 'permanent critique'. Because of this radical commitment to philosophy and its outsides, training as philosophers while being activists at that point in time actually meant having to ask fundamental questions such as: Why think? How can we connect the practice of thinking to larger social and ethical concerns? How can we resist the negative and oppressive aspects of the present? What is philosophy all about and how can it help us lead politically useful, socially productive, and morally adequate lives? These questions resonated loudly with my feminist concerns and passions.

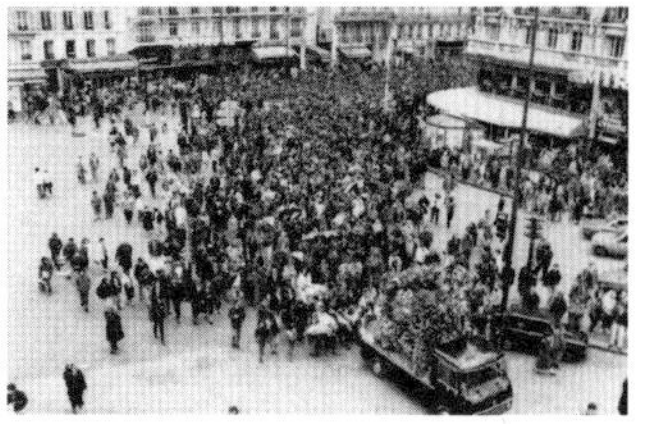
Simone de Beauvoir's Funeral, 19 April 1986

What attracted me to poststructuralism is that it was also one of the most effective answers to the decline of modernist utopias, mostly Marxism and various master narratives of politics. This kind of thinking made it not only possible but also necessary to connect the task of philosophy to the challenges coming from contemporary social movements—mostly those associated with feminists, gay and lesbian rights, environmentalists and peace activists, racial and ethnic minorities in the context of postcoloniality. I went on to develop the nomadic ethics of affirmation into a collective political practice that challenges the dominant representation of the subject of knowledge and develops the yet unrealized potential of multiple possible becoming.

WHAT IS EUROPEAN ABOUT CONTINENTAL PHILOSOPHY?

As I indicated earlier, the landmark date of 1989 also brought the question of Europe further onto the foreground. For one thing, it challenged the discursive equation of 'Europe' with 'French theory', which had been forged in the USA and caused a violent backlash in both countries. Secondly, it fostered the emergence of more Europe-wide perspectives. This changing historical context also played a part in rendering feminist philosophy especially complex in this period. The fall of the Berlin Wall in 1989 and the expansion of the European Union, as well as the new wave of wars that emerge in the period (the first Gulf War, the Falklands War, and the Yugoslav and Balkans War), had a major impact on the development of continental and transnational feminism. The most immediate effect however, was the expansion of feminism both east and west of the former border, granting more visibility to feminist philosophers from former Eastern Europe. In the former East, mainstream and feminist philosophical voices could finally get a wider audience, generating a philosophical renewal. I cannot stress enough the importance of original political thinkers, such as Belgrade-based Žarana Papić, whose work on nationalism and subjectivity remains fundamental. Daša Duhaček provides important analytical insights into Eastern European radical feminism as a critique of the patriarchal aspects of the Yugoslav communist state. The Croatian Rada Iveković, now based in Paris, challenges narratives that assume the centrality of a Western philosophical perspective by adopting a broadened, antinationalist and postcolonial perspective. But the phenomenon is so vast and rich that it deserves a fuller treatment than I can grant it here.

The late eighties in Europe were a period of political hope and of great expectations about the future of the European Union. As I stated explicitly in *Nomadic Subjects*, my awareness of what it means to be European — as opposed to holding an intellectual position on the issue — emerged from the experience of becoming a migrant in Australia. I was a European with Europe in exile, Europe in migration— the category 'European' became thinkable just as it lost its self-evidence. I think I became aware of my Europeanness in this moment of distance, of dis-identification, of loss, of taking my departure from that location. I carried that back with me when I returned to Europe via Paris.

And this was a very formative moment, when I became aware not only of the contingent nature of identity, but also of the extreme complexity of something that we could call European subject positions. Philosophically, as my work focused more on the project of decentring the subject and the practice of critical theory, race and postcolonial philosophical studies became more and more important. The critique of Eurocentrism evolved as the counterpart of the rejection of the universalizing powers of self-reflexive transcendental reason. The self-aggrandizing gesture that positions 'Europe' as a concept that mobilizes and enhances the higher human mental faculties has to be defeated, regrounded and held accountable.

More specifically it has to be read alongside the devastating historical phenomena that have been central to the alleged civilizing mission of the European 'mind': colonialism, racism, fascism. It was clear to me that recognizing this complex historical legacy meant to hold Eurocentric 'reason' accountable for its real-life effects in the world, while also acknowledging the great achievements of our culture. This was the beginning of wisdom and also of historical lucidity. As Glissant and Balibar argue, it is also the end of a self-replicating sense of ignorance about those 'others' who constitute such an integral part of European culture, including philosophy.

The early awareness that so many of my favourite philosophers were foreigners, migrants, exiles, grew into the project of returning European critical theory to its nomadic spirit. Another Europe is possible, one that rejects the imperial posture and its arrogant pretensions and accepts its new historical role as a significant peripheral. So, becoming accountable for my Europeanness coincided with my becoming aware of the impossibility of being one, in the unitary sense of the term. Becoming nomadic seemed the most appropriate option for an antinationalist, antiracist, non-Eurocentric and Europe-based feminist philosopher.

BEYOND

So hold me, Mom, in your long arms.
...
In your automatic arms. Your electronic arms.
In your arms.
So hold me, Mom, in your long arms.
Your petrochemical arms. Your military arms.
In your electronic arms.
Laurie Anderson, *Oh Superman*, 1981

Laurie Anderson was basking in the streets of the Latin Quarter when I was studying there — she is one of my intellectual heroines — both musically and politically. Her work proves that the posthuman sensibility was always already in the picture for my generation. As Donna Haraway published her paradigm-shifting text 'A Cyborg Manifesto' in 1985, a more creative but equally critical gaze fell upon the ongoing cybernetic revolution and its consequences for economic globalization in the era of the Anthropocene. The process of biogenetical recoding of reproduction, which began in 1978 with the birth of the first test-tube baby, Louise Brown, culminated with the cloning of Dolly the sheep in 1996, while the Human Genome Project was officially launched at the end of the eighties.

These scientific and technological advances accelerated the theoretical process of questioning the very status of what counts as human. Reflections on humanism — Western and non-Western — on posthumanism and post-anthropocentrism increased not only within philosophy, contributing to the so-called 'ethical turn', but also in trans-disciplinary areas, or studies, like gender, queer, transnational, postcolonial and environmental studies. The convergence of these powerful reflections on humanism and anthropocentrism (Braidotti 2013) encouraged many to acknowledge that thinking is not the prerogative of humans only,

but that it actually takes place in the world. The relational ontology of the neo-materalist branch of poststructuralism, notably
the creative neo-Spinozism of Deleuze, triggers and sustains the
posthuman elements of our contemporary condition. Retrospectively, I would say that dealing critically with multiple 'supermen' of
all kinds and denomination, in order to cut them down to size, has
been one of the contributions of my generation. Because I know
that Anderson is right when she sings: 'when love is gone, there's
always justice. And when justice is gone, there's always force.'

And when there is force, there's always the collective pursuit of affirmative becoming.

FROM ANTI-SOCIAL-LIBERAL PUNK TO INTERSECTIONAL AIDS ACTIVISM

(SUB-)CULTURE AND POLITICS IN EIGHTIES EUROPE

Diedrich Diederichsen

For me, the eighties start with punk, in the broadest sense, above all in the intersection where something became conceivable that wasn't conceivable before. Punk historians enjoy arguing about which musical expression was the first to earn the title of punk: was it the Sex Pistols in 1977 London, the Ramones in 1976 New York, or even the proto-punk of The Stooges in 1968 Detroit? That's not significant for me. Punk, just like the international year 1968, was a cultural intersection that took place all over the world, and it wasn't the private property of the global north-west. But while it is striking that with the events of 1968 a type of youth revolt took place in the same year all over the world — even if the objectives in Prague, Mexico City, Tokyo and Paris would have been described differently — punk managed to take place completely variably, at any time between 1968 and 1989. I have a friend who explains how punk changed everything in Orange County in 1984 and another friend who insists on 1975 from the perspective of Ann Arbor, Michigan. If the eighties started with punk, they are not a long or a short decade, but one that — as opposed to '45 or '68 or even '89 — always started at a different time and frequently kept starting over and over again.

NOT A LEFTIST FUTURE

Punk stood the idealistic, optimistic, future-oriented, progressive perspective of the 1968 movement on its feet. But unlike the Marx quote alluded to here, these feet weren't necessarily materialistic ones. It could just as easily refer to a pessimistic, nihilistic, sceptical, regressive contact with the ground. Punk was almost always associated with intensification. The generation of the '68 movement was accused of being too soft and inconsequential, too willing to compromise and too pragmatic; the opposite of which was often being impatient, highly charged and often ready to use violence. With this allegation, all that remained to be seen was whether they shared the premises of the '68 movement: many varieties of punk were actually left-wing anarchistic, as official interpretations often described them. People turned against the established New Left that had arrived in institutions and had now become teachers, politicians and opinion makers, towards the RAF, the Red Brigades, the ETA, and squatting. But there were also many different varieties of punk that no longer wanted anything to do with any of the values. And it was more or less clear that Black Flag, who sang *No Values* and the Sex Pistols, who referred to *No Feelings*, still belonged to the leftist punks. Other types of rejection were more fundamental, and therefore also more compatible with a new right-wing movement, which was slowly starting to form.

HYPER-ETHICS

Punk was much stricter than previous movements. People were no longer able to join a movement by simply adopting its ideas and the basics of body language. It was now about personal integrity, which is why a certain criticism quite rightly recognized an ethical fetishism, which the magazine *New Musical Express* dubbed 'rockism': an authenticism of self-invocation and self-overburdening that experienced its hyper-existentialist climax in punk rock, constantly seeking and condemning 'selling out', 'betrayal' and the 'poser'. The vast majority of those punks stayed loyal to the anarchistic scene during the seventies; a small number ended up becoming neo-Nazis and football hooligans, and some of those with bourgeois parents ended up in art school.

ANTI-SOCIAL-LIBERAL

Punk culture represented an anti-social-democratic revolt in every respect, of course against various types and forms of social democracy, but also against the alliance of '68 and trade unions in social democracy and, above all, the various social-liberal coalitions that reigned in many European countries during the seventies. Politicians such as Bruno Kreisky, Olof Palme, Willy Brandt, Harold Wilson, and later James Callaghan and Joop den Uyl not only represented the decade in which Europe was stronger under social-democratic influence than ever before or after. They were also socialist/social-democratic leaders of workers' parties who, albeit often hesitantly, made common cause with the culturally rebellious children of the bourgeoisie and their ideas of emancipation, which were often individualistic or hedonistic, as well as with the new social movements associated with them, such as feminism. The seventies were characterized by the combining of leftist class struggles with cultural revolution, or, to put it in the words of Boltanski and Chiapello, the short-term coalition of 'social critique' that had almost come to an end and was already doomed, but had not yet been neoliberally defeated, with the 'artistic critique' of the followers of the '68 movement, which had not yet become entirely individualistic. Punk responded to the symptoms of removing the plausibility of these constellations in a variety of ways, usually by sinking its teeth right into them. The coming together of 'liberal' positions, as expressed in the dissolution of the ban on abortion and the criminality of homosexuality, for example, with social democratic/socialist ones had something of an echo of the May '68 constellation in the governments mentioned (student-based, anti-consumerist anarchistic, wanting to become allies with the workers and their call for prosperity and participation). It was an unusual historic combination that couldn't be responded to with a single counter-movement and could, at the same time, be seen as an adjustment for the survival of leftist projects. Around the year 1980, it were the social democratic etatists rather than the liberal parts of the alliance that were weakened, but punk zeroed in on the state and spent the next decade painting the encircled A over every hammer and sickle. More importantly than the seriousness, passion, and the hyper-ethical rigour and existentialism with which this unilateral hatred of the state was practised, was the fact that punk virtually screamed out to be immediately separated from other movements or opposing interpretations. The flood gates had been opened. It is telling that in Simon Reynolds' influential chronology of the stylistic diversity phenomenon referred to as post-punk, which left punk rock far behind artistically in terms of creativity, the first post-punk bands come before historical punk rock, chronologically speaking: [01] punk rock was like a black historical hole without any substance, simply a massive blow, or shock, that made the decade explode in every possible unforeseeable direction.

[01] Simon Reynolds, *Rip It Up and Star Again: Post-Punk 1978–1984* (London: Faber & Faber, 2005).

THE CASE OF THE NEOLIBERAL DICE

One such explosion wasn't an explosion at all, but a curious standstill. With the decoupling of social democracy and a liberalism that had stopped being anything other than an economic (neo-)liberalism, with the end of Keynesian social democracy in the west and a type of communism in Southern-Europe that had become 'more pragmatic' — so-called Eurocommunism, which, besides Italy, arose mainly in the post-fascist democracies of Spain and Portugal —as an indicator for a disruption to a rigidly formed Eastern Bloc, the die had been cast. The premises of the Cold War were called into question and the economic momentum of an EU that was slowly coming to an agreement about a common currency generated another gravitational force that would ultimately lead to the events of 1989. Until then, no one had seen them coming: at least no one where I lived and spent a lot of time during the eighties, the old Federal Republic of Germany, New York, Madrid and London, expected that the Iron Curtain would ever fall. We were also strangely disinterested in it. As leftists, we didn't exactly stand in solidarity with Solidarity, we thought of it — with punk columnist Julie Burchill in *The Face* — as an 'anachronistic' embodiment of an old workers' subjectivity.

BAUDRILLARD

Along with Jean Baudrillard, even back then, many believed themselves to be in a cold post-historical Western eternity, in which passions and depth could no longer exist, only merciless transparency:

> For something to have meaning, there must be a scene … a minimum of illusion … Without this strictly aesthetic, mythic and ludic dimension, there is not even any scene of the political, where something might cause a stir … the events of Biafra, Chile and Poland, of terrorism or inflation, or of nuclear war. We are given an over-representation of them by the media, but not the true picture. All this is simply obscene for us, since through the media it is made to be seen without being gazed at.[02]

In 1981, two years before these lines were published, Blixa Bargeld explained as a case in point in an interview with *Spex*, that contrary to the old classic leftists, he wasn't able to develop solidarity with the struggles in El Salvador and Nicaragua, because 'I don't even know if El Salvador really exists — perhaps it's an invention of the *Tagesschau*'.[03] Baudrillard didn't mean invention, but instead, precisely because we are so enlightened and the world so transparent, we're no longer able to perceive it as existent, as a different counterpart. While we shared Félix Guattari's[04] belief in the early eighties that the media were engaging in a type of 'semiotic poisoning' (while in the East they were still simply telling lies), for Baudrillard, this poisoning wasn't about twisting or masking the truth, but about the total visibility of the truth achieved by the media, which made its dramatization (also as a requirement of politics) impossible. This theory, which was in many regards problematic and anti-progressive, often nostalgic for traditional gender relations, once again became popular, but for less than it was worth, vulgarized to the mere complaint that we live in a world of intensely circulating signs that aren't connected to reality in any way: everything is a simulation of the media. It wasn't until 1987 that Group Material organized the 'Anti-Baudrillard' symposium, documented by the magazine *File*:[05] in the books published in the English-speaking world as *Simulations* and *The Political Economy of the Sign*, Baudrillard abandoned

02

Jean Baudrillard, *Fatal Strategies* (Munich: Matthes & Seitz, 1991), p. 78.

03

Blixa Bargeld, interview in *Spex* no. 9, 1981.

04

Félix Guattari, 'Wunsch und Revolution: Ein Gespräch mit Franco Berardi (Bifo) und Paolo Bertetto', trans. by Alice Tetley-Paul (Heidelberg: Verlag Das Wunderhorn, 1978), p. 71.

05

Group Material, 'Anti-Baudrillard', *File* 28, part 1, 1987, pp. 109–119.

the idea that art could be a place for critical examination. There's certainly not a role for political art in Baudrillard's openly anti-socialist hyper-scepticism, but there's not a role for any form of political engagement either; the reason for declaring him, in particular, as an enemy was certainly related to the fact that in the generally anti-political artistic practices of the early eighties, he was one of the most influential theorists to be actually received in the artistic world.

NEO-SITUATIONISM

This theory boom, specific to art, also has equivalents in the humanities faculties of Europe, which paid with a vacuum of engagement for the disappearance of the leftists of the '68 movement and their absorption into green parties and the peace movement. However, in the course of the decade in which the self-abolition of the left was being masochistically pursued by means of projects like the anti-rationalist 'critique of reason' — an umbrella term for the convergence of interest in non-European cultures that had come about ethnologically/anti-imperialistically with an anti-leftist scepticism towards any type of enlightenment and modernism — at some point it emerges that besides the failed 'long march through the institutions' and the other orthodox forms that constituted the '68 movement (against which punk directed itself so vehemently), there were still developments waiting to be (re)discovered. During the Group Material symposium, one of the artists who normally referred to Baudrillard, the Neo-Geo painter Peter Halley, explained that he has rediscovered the 'Situationalists' through Baudrillard. The symposium agreed that the 'Situationalists' were important. In the same year, I was also involved, together with Albert Oehlen, in an edition of the journal *Durch*,[06] published in Graz, which was largely devoted to the Situationists. The expert Roberto Ohrt, whose vast monograph on the Situationists entitled *Phantom Avantgarde*[07] was published the following year, was extremely helpful. A short time later, SI exhibitions followed in Boston and Paris. Greil Marcus published *Lipstick Traces*,[08] in which Situationism is assigned a major role as the broader context of punk, and specifically European punk. By the end of the decade, the movement that had been mostly forgotten since the mid-seventies, was on its way to becoming what it is today: a canonical, key subject area in academies. As of 1990, Guy Debord's notion of the 'spectacle' once again represents everything that had, until 1980, been called the 'culture industry' and that hadn't existed or had disappeared in the fog of the notions of 'simulation' during the eighties.

06

Durch 3/4 guest editor Albert Oehlen (Graz: Kunstverein, 1987).

07

Roberto Ohrt, *Phantom Avantgarde: Eine Geschichte der Situationistischen Internationale und der modernen Kunst* (Hamburg: Nautilus, 1988).

08

Greil Marcus, *Lipstick Traces (on a Cigarette)* (Cambridge, MA: Harvard University Press, 1989).

In the eighties, three basic emotions prevailed instead: the feeling of unreality (for which the various theories of simulation, for example, as well as the continuation of Marxist cultural criticism later accounted), the sense of a standstill (the return of conservative politicians to power, the replacement of historical-political narratives and narratives related to class struggles with ecological, geo-philosophical and Gaian-esoteric narratives), and the looming apocalypse (people could sense the end of the Cold War, but could only imagine it as the end of the world and as a nuclear confrontation between the blocs, also inspired by ecological fantasies). All three sentiments can be traced back to the fact that the whistle had already been blown to mark the end of the Cold War in historical-philosophical spheres; its time was over. However, the decisive goal (Gorbachev) had not yet been scored. The match had gone into extra time.

INDUSTRIAL

How could a resistance against these poorly understood sentiments be organized on an aesthetic level? The aggression of punk and its aesthetic siblings in so-called *Wilde* or *Heftige Malerei* (Wild or Fierce Painting), as it was blossoming in various parts of Europe, from Spain to Germany, in horror films and aggressive performance art (from Minus Delta to La Fura dels Baus) was, above all, gestural. It took place in a limited cultural area and was aimed at a slightly older section of the public, which took part in the same culture. It was an exodus without an exact destination. The next steps were more permanent. The simultaneously armoured, equipped, and aggressive, but also artificial and invented, cyborgian body of industrial music on the one hand and synth-pop on the other, weren't gestural and weren't communicative; with them, or in them, you could live in a state of depression enjoyed with a great deal of pathos, as well in a state of apocalyptic seriousness. But they also unleashed something: sexuality freed itself from the liberation; in the electric beats, the clanging marches in minor keys, the tattooed, muscular bodies — initially mainly of men — it escaped from the rule that the sexual liberation should have been a liberation 'to nature', as was the heterosexual norm among hippies and members of the 1968 movement. Instead, what Félix Guattari told Franco 'Bifo' Berardi in 1978 became true: 'we'll establish a model of man and woman in a completely artificial manner'.[09] That was the industrial body, which before the realization that manifested itself in the nineties was often associated

09
Guattari, 'Wunsch und Revolution', p.71.

with Judith Butler, that there's no such thing as natural bodies. Meanwhile, various ideas and ideals of artificiality were circulating. To break with the more or less essentialist idea of feminity conceived by differential-feminism was rare among feminists of the seventies, but this changed at the turn of the decade, when performance artists such as Karen Finley and Johanna Went, punk performers such as The Slits, X-Ray Spex, Lizzy Mercier Descloux, and authors such as Kathy Acker, as well as many others, did the groundwork on new 'artificial' bodies — to use the terminology of the time — including those of women. However, these were less geared towards a relatively uniform, very particular mixture of sound, material and atmosphere than the industrial scene.

WE'VE GOT A BIGGER PROBLEM NOW [10]

If punk was a gesture, then it was strongly determined by what it was directed against. As described, this was the social liberality of the seventies. The tragedy of punk was that its opponents were shot in the back from the other side of the battlefield. Were we guilty of the seizure of power by Helmut Kohl, Maggie Thatcher, Ronald Reagan, and so on? How would the uprising look now, after having tried to develop a modernized form of symbolic counterforce that has now made way for a much more old-fashioned central power (and the failure to see the modernity of this new conservatism was of course another misjudgement: an old misunderstanding that the politically reactionary positions are, on the whole, regressive).

BRITISH BLACKNESS

Punk didn't come about on its own, at least not in Great Britain. In terms of organization as well as aesthetics, punk was associated with another youth revolt, namely that of young people of the Caribbean diaspora in the United Kingdom. The connection between these two youth cultures developed in a different way from earlier predecessors, which focused on negotiations, appropriations and projections. This had come about as the result of the slow loosening and blurring of racist segregation in the USA and later also had an impact in other parts of the world: for instance, when white British musicians, above all, were enthusing about rediscovering blues as blues rock around 1965, or when a West-German concert agency sent old, established African-American blues musicians such as Sonny Terry & Brownie McGhee or Sam Lightnin' Hopkins on tour through Europe as the 'American Folk Blues Festival'.

[10] No one better articulated the political opposition towards the hippies and members of the '68 movement, which wasn't apolitical or right and didn't want to be, but instead made efforts to save leftist projects, than the Dead Kennedys with their song *California Über Alles*, which characterized the Green Governor Jerry Brown as a hippy fascist. When, a short time later, something much worse happened and Ronald Reagan became President of the USA, they give the song new lyrics and a new title: *We've Got a Bigger Problem Now*.

The white punk generation, initially decidedly white, with their rebellion envy aimed at non-white people, seemed, on the surface,
indifferent to the body politics of the African-American musical
influence.[11] Industrial artists such as Genesis P-Orridge declared
that it was important for them to stop defining themselves by
means of the blues.[12] In some respects, punk rock was anti-blues,
and not just in musical terms. In the daily idiom of the seventies,
the expression 'blues dance' referred to a slow, intimate, erotic
partner dance: the opposite of the aggressive pogo. But while
punk, to a certain degree, wanted to be 'white',[13] non-white culture in the punk setting was much more visible than black musicians were in blues rock. In the music of the seventies, a few
varieties of jazz aside, segregation largely prevailed: black musicians played soul, fusion and funk; white musicians played blues
rock, singer/songwriter music and prog rock. Punk wanted to do
away with black elements, but started a coalition with reggae music and, above all, musicians. It was rare that there were punks
who actually played reggae — The Clash, The Ruts, Stiff Little Fin-
gers — but as a sound and culture in the world of punk, reggae
was both present and often essential. In the so-called post-punk
culture (for example The Slits, The Pop Group, and chart acts such
as Culture Club), reggae also had a powerful musical influence.
But more importantly, blackness in and from Britain was perceived
differently by the mainstream culture in the rest of the world than
blackness from the USA during the sixties and seventies, as either
hero and/or victim stories. It became associated with specific
narratives (from the Caribbean leftism that arrived via Stuart Hall,
Linton Kwesi Johnson and others to Rastafari religion, and so on)
and not with an ahistorical, general state of being black; with history, instead of with skin colour. This had a huge influence on the
perception of 'race' and differences in the rest of Europe too. The
emergence of the extremely popular neo-ska bands The Specials,
The Beat, The Selecter, and Madness around the year 1980 oscil-
lated in an interesting way between an explicitly antiracist oc-
currence, which addressed the interplay and the joint visibility of
black and white musicians, and an ambiguous reception tradition,
as ska had often been the music of extreme right-wing skinheads
in Britain in the seventies.

FEAR OF A BLACK PLANET

European hip hop reception developed in two waves: hip hop first
came to Europe, doubly exotified, around 1983/1984. On the one
hand it was black, and on the other hand it wasn't interpreted
as a political statement and was more culturally associated with

[11]
'White Riot, I want a riot, white riot,
a riot of my own', sang The Clash.

[12]
At various points, e.g.: '... the roots
of blues and slave music has been
explored, and now we've done
industrial music. We have to go
beyond ...': in S. Alexander Reed,
*Assimilate: A Critical History of
Industrial Music* (Oxford: Oxford
University Press, 2013), p. 141.

[13]
Sometimes so much that a
critic such as Lester Bangs saw
manifest racism at work, cf. Lester
Bangs, 'White Noise Supremacists'
(1979), in *Psychotic Reactions and
Carburetor Dung*, ed. Greil Marcus
(New York: Alfred A. Knopf, 1987),
pp. 272–282.

stories from the ghetto of the South Bronx: drugs, urban decay, violence. When politicized hip-hop emerged in the late eighties with Boogie Down Productions, Public Enemy and so on, followed by so-called 'conscious' rappers such as A Tribe Called Quest, as well as brilliantly aggressive nihilists such as Just-Ice or Schoolly D, this changed to a second wave of reception. Now the European fans started to apply a hermeneutic approach. White, French high school students started reading up on the history of the Black Panther Party and the Nation of Islam, Basque activists wanted to find out if Public Enemy were in solidarity with leftist Basque nationalism (answer: no, they're white too). At the same time, something much more important was going on: the huge influence of hip hop culture on the one hand, and the increasingly individualized, biographized, and significantly less stereotyped black presence in art and mainstream culture on the other hand, provided a template with which non-white youths in big cities all over continental Europe could identify during the eighties.

YOUTH MOVEMENTS AND THEIR INTERPRETATION

It wasn't only European fans of African-American music who started diving into questions of interpretation, which hadn't been the case with the international exchange of stories of liberation from the sixties and seventies. Young people who wanted to become part of a movement or style that carried forward what previous subcultural orientations such as punk, hippie, mod, and so on, had achieved, also had to start interpreting themselves or, in words often used in connection with paradigmatic eighties superstars such as Madonna: *invent themselves*. Magazines such as *i-D* and *The Face* in Great Britain, so-called lifestyle magazines in German-speaking countries such as *Wiener* in Austria and, later, *Tempo* in Germany were based on the dialectics between readability and opacity of youth and street fashion. The idea shared by all of these magazines, as well as a critical way of thinking that extended far beyond them, was the notion that the connection between behaviour, appearance and political/cultural convictions, which underpinned hippies as well as punks, would remain a stable factor in the interpretation of cultural developments. In the new situation of the eighties, you just have to read a larger number of youth cultures, which only differ in the details, much more carefully. The counter-idea, namely that new romantics, psychobilly, neo-mods, crusties, and grebos weren't historical cultural movements, but merely pop music trends that often only related to three or four bands and should be read as artistic statements rather than social ones, didn't catch on. Too much semiotic effort had been spent and implemented against an old sociology, which was deaf to the expressiveness of youth fashions, to study the socio-political themes and conflicts of the present on the *Gesamtkunstwerk* of the youth cultural habitus. During the eighties, this became a defining motive that pervaded everything from academia to the tabloids.

NON-SIMULTANEITY AND MOVIDA

While such feelings of unreality and a world in decline affected the most varied of art forms and schools of thought during the eighties in countries such as Great Britain, the Netherlands, Germany, and France, and events like the Chernobyl nuclear accident seemed to confirm the apocalyptic mood, completely different moods prevailed elsewhere. The fact that people in Madrid in the eighties didn't spend any time thinking about the doom and gloom affecting northern Europe, as disseminated by the likes of Joy Division and The Cure, Andrei Tarkovsky and Lars von Trier, had nothing to do with the cliché of *Völkerpsychologie* of north/south differences. The sense of an unlimited new beginning, a history that is to be completely scrapped, not a 1968 that needs to be half-defended and half-overcome, and the availability of technologies for self-invention that extended far beyond fashion and youth culture, especially in the politics of sexuality and drugs, resulted in the story of the endless hedonistic nights of the La Movida Madrileña in Madrid, often rumoured to be a cliché: the excess and ecstasy-filled precursor to the British rave stories from 1988 and the techno nights in Berlin after the fall of the Berlin Wall. At that time in Madrid, I came across many, often queer, reinventions of American, rather than British, models of counterculture: psychedelic and greaser punk from the sixties, reconstructed motorbike and proto-hippy sentiments, carefully restored electric organ sounds from the late sixties, gay and non-gay psychobilly creations, lots of sunglasses after dark, The Cramps: a strong likeness to the French enthusiasm for the US, in the same way that the New Rose label celebrated it in the eighties. At the same time and in the same neighbourhood was Latino disco, already so focused on endlessness like nothing else in the mid-eighties, Chicago House aside. Just like in the rest of Europe, bright graffiti sprung up everywhere in the city; the dry political slogans that had been painted on walls during the sixties and seventies were replaced quite aptly with bright slogans in the eighties, which often only alluded to the artist. That was the case all over Europe; in Madrid and Italy the designs weren't taken from the influential African-American graffiti artists from the hip-hop culture, but from urban anarchism. The main symptom of this, derived from punk, was a historical non-simultaneity.

INDIE AND SELF-ORGANIZATION

One thing that was blossoming and thriving everywhere was the alternative and self-organized small-scale capitalism or para-socialism of the countercultures, encompassed emblematically in the term 'indie', which initially referred to new organizational forms in the record industry, but soon also came to include cinema, the off-spaces of visual arts, and alternative print products called fanzines. There had always been independent record labels and film companies, but the criterion for their specialization was either local culture or music for which it wasn't worth using bigger production and distribution methods, or a sensitive or illegal product, or one with a bad reputation, such as pornographic or horror films. However, an independent movement emerged in the eighties, which claimed a special status in political terms on the one hand, and in artistic terms on the other: more politically radical and more artistically uncompromising, to a certain extent as a response to the critique of a 'semiotic poisoning' of the mass media, for which the blunted language of ideology criticism had long since failed to suffice. There had to be places where 'we' could develop our own language. Paradoxically, this was highly successful. One reason why critique of ideology almost disappeared in the eighties as a discourse was that it became practical. The identification with these products combined political and ethical with aesthetic components in a non-trivial way: productive dilettantism, acoustic arte povera, aggressive humour. From Rough Trade in London to Recommended Records in Switzerland, Crammed in Italy and Zickzack in Germany to Plurex in the Netherlands, these organizations, eager to take responsibility in political and aesthetic terms, sprung up all over the place. The long-term problem wasn't the 'selling out' to the major companies, as the moralization and hyper-ethics of the punks would have it, but the inability paired with a structural impossibility of organizing sales and planning for a market. Rough Trade didn't fail due to a lack of interest, but as a result of too much interest. The Smiths were too successful, but the distribution network could not be built for only a few acts. The result was that the majors took over distribution again and that the indies were absorbed into the companies as small market development units and production departments. By the end of the eighties, 'indie' was a generic terms in the media department stores that emerged at that time and were expanding significantly (before the MP3 crisis and subsequent crises).

DIEDRICH DIEDERICHSEN

The new political model didn't come from Europe; it originally emerged from the USA. If people had still been aware in 1975 that gay and lesbian rights, class struggles, and antiracism, by whatever name, belonged together, they'd forgotten it again by 1985. People kept on doing something or depoliticized something else. At best, people perhaps still agreed that whatever it was they were doing went against the establishment, the system of power. To 'build a counter-power' was also a statement of the late RAF in the eighties. Michel Foucault, responsible for the notion of 'counter-power', became one of the first victims of AIDS. As the public started to agree that the victims of AIDS belonged to certain so-called risk groups, a new type of politics came about, a new notion of political action, which still doesn't have a proper name today, but which has taken the place of political engagement since the late eighties. The risk groups were: male homosexuals, Haitians (all), drug users who used and shared needles; somewhat less: heterosexual women (who have sex with someone from one of the aforementioned groups); less still: heterosexual men (who have sex with women, who have sex…— I don't think this ever happened). The obscenity of these group names and the anticipation or reconstruction of their epidemically relevant connections was so infamous that it became clear that the 'power' no longer worked the way it used to, *divide et impera*, but only across divides, but extremely exact divides. When, in his *Postscript on the Societies of Control*, a very important text in the nineties, Gilles Deleuze shows that control doesn't consist of police officers asking to see identity cards, but instead of sometimes being let in with an identity card and sometimes not, you then have the formula for being sorted into risk groups. It was a logical next step for the people stigmatized in that way to join forces. The politics of the future had to become intersectional. That term was first used by Kimberlé Crenshaw in an essay in 1989,[14] and she developed the theory behind it for the first time in 1990.[15] While she didn't refer specifically to AIDS, the unrelated arbitrariness of the categories at play in AIDS and their influence on decisions relating to life and death constitute a forward-looking model for intersectional politics, which must not be restricted to obvious coalitions, but that on the other hand has to prevent people from falling in love with their identity, supposedly embodied in a homogeneous way, too much. It wasn't by chance that the involuntary intersectionality of anti-AIDS activism also brought about artistic formats that still determine debates about political art to this day.

14

Kimberlé Crenshaw, 'Demarginalizing the Intersection of Race and Sex: A Black Feminist Critique of Antidiscrimination Doctrine, Feminist Theory and Antiracist Politics', *University of Chicago Legal Forum* I (1989), article 8, pp. 139–167 (1989).

15

Kimberlé Crenshaw, 'Mapping the Margins: Intersectionality, Identity Politics, and Violence Against Women of Color', *Stanford Law Review* 43, no. 6 (July 1991), pp. 1241–1299. Women of Color at the Center: Selections from the Third National Conference on Women of Color and the Law.

1. NO

ALTERNATIVE?

INTRODUCTION

Nav Haq

It was in an article published by the *Daily Telegraph* newspaper on 22 May 1980 that British Prime Minister Margaret Thatcher wrote her renowned statement: 'There's no easy popularity in what we are proposing, but it is fundamentally sound. Yet I believe people accept there is no real alternative', four of the last five words subsequently being shortened to its most oft-quoted form 'There is No Alternative' (or TINA). It was a clear statement of intent to position neoliberalism as the new worldview that there was no escape from — the dismantling of welfare state society, to be replaced by a vision emphasizing the socio-economic emancipation of individuals driven by free-market capitalism. But what of those that did not buy into this ideology or were failed by it, and how did they respond?

In the sphere of alternative culture across the societies of Europe, social groups, activists, and cultural practitioners were involved in various forms of self-organization, looking to create new modes for community, art, media, education, political economy, and ownership. The first chapter of this book considers numerous examples of those that created the spaces for these alternatives. Its two subchapters 'Autonomous Zones' and 'Broadcast Yourself' provide the case studies for many of these counter-cultural movements of the eighties, and the various strategies they employed to provide alternative messages and media to those of the mainstream, in their own cultural contexts. They are primarily examples of initiatives seeking positions of autonomy, outside of state and market forces.

Three longer essays are included in this chapter, each offering reflections on the means and motivations employed by those organizing alternative movements. Media theorist Geert Lovink considers how self-published magazines by the squatters' movements in both Amsterdam and Berlin opened up a more communitarian understanding of space and ownership, as well as a counter economy based on self-sufficiency. Writer and curator Jelena Vesić and media researcher Vladimir Jerić Vlidi describe a trajectory of the term 'alternative' within the sphere of political conservatism, moving from its negative connotation in the eighties through to positive connotations with the present-day emergence of the so-called 'Alt-Right'. Asking what is actually 'alternative', she considers the case study of *TV Galerija* in Belgrade as an example of an autonomous space for culture that sat in opposition to market logic. And Manuel Borja-Villel, Director of the Museo Nacional Centro de Arte Reina Sofía, calls for a radical reorientation of museum structures to counter the neutralizing effects of neoliberalism, through the empowerment of their publics.

In the subchapter 'Autonomous Zones' an excerpt from philosopher Hakim Bey's seminal manifesto *Temporary Autonomous Zones* describes the formation of spaces that elude formal structures of control, allowing for their own autonomous logic. The idea of the 'temporary autonomous zone' was influential in phenomena such as the rave movement, arguably Europe's last big youth movement that opened up an ambiguous kind of 'third space' of experience outside of state and market forces during recession-era Britain and Belgium, as well as being influential in the squatters' movement, further described in this subchapter by Diana Franssen. In the context of Spain, Beatriz Herráez discusses the work *Arquitectura Prematura* (Premature Architecture), that formed architectural propositions for autonomous spaces in response to the institutionalization of culture, including a proposal for a camouflage for squatted buildings. And Nazım Hikmet Richard Dikbaş writes on BİLAR Corporation, which under the conditions of post-coup dictatorship in Turkey provided alternative education in Ankara, Izmir, and Istanbul on social sciences, politics, economics, and media. Their activities are best described with their statement: 'Democracy can be best attained and furthered through the maintenance of critical thought and the free flow of culture and ideas.'

Other practices described here are examples of self-organized artistic work seeking to address disenfranchisement with the status quo. Teresa Grandas writes on the activities of Taller Llunàtic (The Lunatic Workshop), who in the context of post-dictatorship Spain were an example of a countercultural collaborative practices that confronted the conservatism of society with provocative images, including those of the violent or erotic kind. Antony Hudek describes the art space Montevideo in Antwerp, which was a key venue for experimental art for the generation following that of the post-war avant-garde and before the emergence of formalized institutions for contemporary art in Belgium. Whereas Alexei Monroe looks at the organigram created by the group Neue Slowenische Kunst (NSK) in Slovenia, which mirrors that of a totalitarian regime, in consideration of the group's strategy of 'over-identification' with power.

The second subchapter, 'Broadcast Yourself', provides several case studies of events and organizations that utilized the new potentialities of media and self-practice. Three exhibitions are discussed. Cristina Cámara describes 'La imagen sublime' from 1987, a key exhibition of video art that highlighted the emergence of new media technologies in Spain. Similarly, Diana Franssen discusses the 1985 event 'Talking Back to the Media' in Amsterdam that provided artistic deconstructions of television media, often through strategies of parody. Henry Anderson provides analysis of Jef Cornelis' film *De langste dag* (The Longest Day) (1986), which was broadcast live on television, the opening of the renowned exhibition 'Chambres d'amis' in Ghent, using the production values of a major sporting event. With Cornelis' critical perspective on the hermeticism of contemporary art, *De langste dag* possesses a tension of 'publicness', between his interest in television as mass media and this particular exhibition renowned for literally entering the space of people's homes. And June Givanni reflects on the Black Film workshops, taking place when filmmaking became part of the emancipatory project of black and minority ethnic groups during the era of civil unrest in early-eighties Great Britain.

Other case studies provide examples of alternative practices that used print media as a core component of their activism. Merve Elveren discusses the magazine *Sokak* (Street), which offered information rarely seen in mainstream media, including for example on the representation of different groups in Turkish society such as the LGBTQ community and the Kurdish minority, alongside legal advice and commentary on subcultural activity in Turkey. Anders Kreuger dissects some of the activities of Club Moral in Antwerp. Run by Anne-Mie Van Kerckhoven and Danny Devos, Club Moral was at once an art space and a noise band, and also generated the radical alternative magazine *Force Mental*. Ana Mizerit recalls the Youth Day poster scandal in Yugoslavia, when the New Collectivism faction of NSK won a poster competition after submitting a design based on one used historically for Nazi propaganda. Our aim for this section is to provide some key examples of artists and activists who felt the necessity to invent spaces for alternative ideas, ways of living and for challenging dominant positions of power.

1.1 AUTONOMOUS

Dissent And The
Neoliberal Condition
1980s

The Temporary
Autonomous Zone,
Ontological Anarchy,
Poetic Terrorism
1985

Rave
1985–1995

Squatters
1980

Montevideo
1981–1984

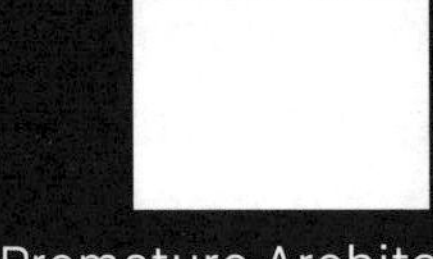

Premature Architecture
1984–1992

The Phlegm of Taller
Llunàtic
1977–NOW

ZONES

Neue Slowenische Kunst
1986

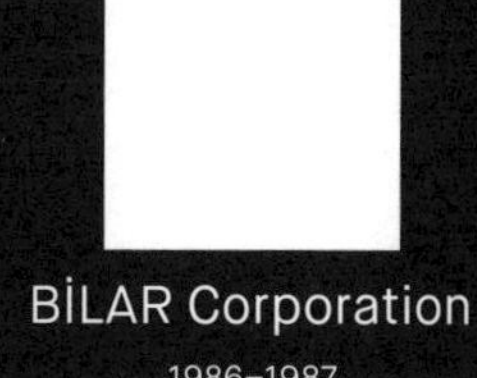

BİLAR Corporation
1986–1987

DISSENT AND THE NEOLIBERAL CONDITION

Manuel Borja-Villel

I

The truth is that it would seem risible to imagine our colleagues elsewhere, from Acconci to Dibbets and from Oppenheim to Graham, earnestly striving to convince us of the fact, for example, that thanks to them Picasso or Miró will be demystified and people's admiration of them will come to an end, in the way that has been done here. Or that with Conceptualism the 'scams' of the dealers and museums will be smashed.
Or that there will necessarily be a rethinking of commodification, with all the socio-political consequences that must ensue; and that there will be an end to the contradictions which derive from current artistic practice.

Antoni Tàpies, 'Arte conceptual aquí' (Conceptual Art Here), *La Vanguardia*, 14 March 1973

Finally, the most surprising thing is the weight of adjectives, the emotional and paternalistic tone, the mythic conception that we sense here of 'art' and the 'artist' and the need to justify the artist's position and activity by attacking a certain artistic practice, on account of the fact that it exposes the contradictions of the cultural medium in which 'the artist and his work' are deployed (without questioning even for a moment the structures that engender them and at the same time sustain them).

Grup de Treball, 'Documento-respuesta a Tàpies' (Response Document to Tàpies), *Nueva Lente*, 21 November 1973

Excerpted from a pair of texts that Antoni Tàpies and the Grup de Treball wrote in 1973, these quotes bear witness to the dispute in which they confronted one another that same year, and which marked a point of inflection in Spanish art. Controversies like this one, born of the irreconcilability of their respective approaches to art and politics, were very frequent at the time. It was not only Tàpies and the Grup de Treball that squared up to each other. In the early days of the Transition, major mutual differences were also expressed by art critics such as Juan Manuel Bonet, Quico Rivas or Francisco Calvo Serraller. Beyond Spain's borders, examples multiplied. In 1982, the social historian of British art T.J. Clark had a heated exchange with the American theorist Michael Fried, whom he accused of being a formalist; in 1984, Thomas McEvilley, William Rubin and Kirk Varnedoe engaged in an intense and extended argument over the exhibition '"Primitivism" in 20th-Century Art: Affinity of the Tribal and the Modern', curated by the latter two at MoMA, New York. A glance at the periodicals archives shows us a time that now seems far distant, in which positions in the field of culture were stated, argued and defended. Disagreement and confrontation have not been the exception in the modern world, but consubstantial with it. For evidence that this is so we need only look back to the successive 'combats' between champions of the old and the modern, and of the abstract and the figurative, or the supporters of a committed art and the upholders of art for art's sake. Artists such as Adrian Piper, Michael Asher, Philippe Thomas and Marcel Broodthaers have made capital works of the discussion and the lecture, but in light of the present absence of debate, despite the fact that the conversation and the dialogic have become important rhetorical figures in contemporary art, it is quite clear that we are in another era.

Our society is by definition agonistic, and however much intellectual dissent may have receded into the background, it is hardly credible that the discordance of ideas and attitudes should disappear without further ado. The many and multitudinous demonstrations and protests of all kinds that occupy our streets and squares testify to that. That being said, information today is largely channelled through the Internet, which is one of our privileged modes of sociability. We know that no institutional form is ever neutral. Far from it. They all favour certain behaviours and hinder others. On the social networks, interaction with others was originally intended to be limited to following, to appending a 'like', but it could be said that our subjectivity is now exclusively dependent on the number of followers we are capable of engendering. What this would encourage is not so much debate as consensus and affiliation, which are often prefabricated.

Could it be that there is no longer anything to discuss? Or that we have arrived at a kind of Arcadian state in which all the various artistic and political stances are reconciled with equanimity, without antagonisms of any kind? The first possibility would be that of a society in which judgement no longer has any function. The second is unlikely, given that we live in a world in which the communication industries, with their slogans, and their lowest version, sensationalist journalism, are so abundant. But perhaps we should look to a third possibility, one that is no less problematic: the lack of confrontation can also point to complicity or, what is worse, the avoidance of asking questions so as not to be questioned.

The situation in the realm of culture has been and is similar to that of other instances of the political. Caught up as they were in internal troubles, not to mention scandals of various kinds, during the eighties and nineties many entities lost their capacity to represent the people, to benefit rather than to benefit *from* the populace. The need to come up with new forms of organization and mediation, both in the museum and in society as a whole, became acute. As a result, the end of the millennium witnessed the emergence of new forms of mobilization and resistance. In much the same way that in the nineteenth century, the crisis of 1848 evidenced the fact that the bourgeoisie no longer represented the emerging social classes and that these would be organized on the basis of new political formations, the long eighties represented a period of wide-ranging reaction, whose end was marked by the irruption of the anti-globalization movements.

As we have seen, art has not been left untouched by the mutations that have overtaken the political in recent decades. At the same time as the market took off in an inflationary surge, the critical tendency in contemporary art intensified. If Jung or Freud were the theoretical references of many artists of the thirties and fourties, in much the same way theoreticians, intellectuals, philosophers or political scientists such as Toni Negri, Félix Guattari, Chantal Mouffe, Ernesto Laclau, Judith Butler and many others who question the *status quo* have increasingly constituted the *koiné* of current art since the eighties. A rapid review of the biennials and big international exhibitions shows that this is the general trend. The trouble is that the critical variable of these initiatives is mainly confined to content. They often lack the smallest element of self-reflection or awareness of the conditions of production in which that content appears. An exhibition, a collection or museum not only exist in relation to the history of art, they are also political acts in that they are public interventions, even if, as Georges Didi-Huberman reminds us, the actors themselves are ignorant of the fact.

With the justification of a supposed anti-idealism and the vanishing of the Subject, notions such as those of public sphere, critical space or class antagonism tended to disappear from view and, indeed, to be considered unnecessary. Throughout the eighties and nineties we witnessed the emergence of multiple political subjectivities (ethnic, gay, ecological, feminist, religious...). In the majority of cases, however, this multiculturalism has tended rather to celebrate the diversity of styles and differences serving essentially to sustain a subterranean One, in which any radical and antagonistic productive difference is obliterated; in other words, a suppression of difference in favour of a whole that is the container of the multitude. This suppression has no doubt been served by the exclusion of public space: that common place in which plural identities can converge and act as antagonists, and which forms the basis of any democratic project.

In the eighties, we were faced with the evident logic that every act of rebellion, at least as it had been conceived by modernity, ends up being assimilated by the system. As Julia Kristeva commented at the time, there was a lot of talk — as there is again today — of the return of fascism, of religious fundamentalism, of nationalism. But these phenomena are no more than short-lived outbreaks — let us hope — in our societies of brutal archaic diseases that democracy will end up neutralizing. The real threat, now as then, comes from a system that tends to schematize singularity — albeit in a way as perverse as that theorized and proclaimed by certain proponents of multiculturalism — and to deprive individuals of their psychic specificity. In today's society, what is exceptional about human beings is at risk of being debased and trivialized. Everyone seems to accommodate and adapt to a standardized hierarchy of the expected personal image. Culture as critical rebellion, as a liberating element, is in danger of disappearing as it is transformed more and more into a product ready to be consumed.

The purpose of culture today is thus highly problematic. We have been living for four decades now in a post-historical, post-democratic society, in which any kind of modern revolution seems as infeasible, as unviable as the idea of an artistic or intellectual vanguard located outside of society and capable of liberating and guiding us towards some desired goal. The theoretical intellectual opined and established a criterion, so that the uncultivated reader knew what to believe. It is hardly surprising, then, that throughout modernity men and women of letters have come forward to debate, not only about culture, but also about politics. Hannah Arendt and Jean-Paul Sartre are examples of this attitude. However, apart from the occasional philosopher with a fondness for the role of television personality enlightening us as to our situation, it would seem that the condition of intellectual has lost whatever relevance it once had. This explains the pessimism of those who see the culture of our time as lacking commitment to itself, and their nostalgia for other times. But the contemporary world is theatrical. The author tends to disappear in the interstices of texts and hypertexts and we the public are asked to complete the stories and make them our own. The idea of an author who might show us the way is, therefore, unthinkable. Of course, this does not mean that all options are equal, but rather that in their multiplicity they 'antagonize' each other and compete for a power that is situated in the discursive sphere. In addition, the consumers know what they want, having been told a thousand times by the communication industries. And what they are looking for is not so much a revelation of the truth as the attainment of their desire. Never has a time been so little disposed towards prophets as ours. Those who act and those who fight are no longer represented, hence the crisis of the institutions. Those who speak and act are a multitude in which, in Foucault's words, 'there's only action — theoretical action and practical action which serve as relays and form networks'. Actions are now small-scale, in a multiplicity of sites, in the power of the crowd.

     II

The museum has, until quite recently, been a contradictory place that has functioned simultaneously as both apparatus of the State and war machine. It has constituted a paradoxical heterotopy: as an archive, its primary task was to preserve; as an exhibition, its purpose was to show. It has dedicated itself to education and social reform, at the same time as it has grown from the plunder of successive colonies, while concealing the fact. It has been a space for study and recollection, yet it has contributed to the abovementioned theatricalization of the world. As Umberto Eco and Isabella Pezzini suggested in their recent book *El Museo*, this is a discontinuous space in the continuity of society.

The opening of the Centre Georges Pompidou in 1977 inaugurated a period of incessant construction and expansion of museum spaces dedicated to contemporary art, a process consolidated in the nineties. Contemporary art, which had hitherto occupied a more or less marginal position, began to be extensively collected and to enjoy a relative centrality in the cultural life of the new globalized world. The museum had ceased to be the temple of the muses and become an instrument in the service of the enhancement of the city and a dynamic energizer of the economy. The eighties were also the period of the culture wars, a highly virulent phenomenon in the United States during the Reagan administration — it will suffice to recall here the scandal surrounding the cancellation of the Mapplethorpe show at the Corcoran Gallery in Washington, D.C. in 1989, and its consequences for the economic sustainability of that institution. It would seem that this was the decade in which the autonomy of art institutions vis-à-vis markets began to be undermined. The museum was required to behave like a firm: to bow to the laws of marketing, to present clear objectives and financial results and not to get involved in scandals that might raise doubts about its 'respectability', that is, its corporate identity.

In 1984, in his now legendary article 'Museums, Managers of Consciousness', Hans Haacke alerted us to what was then coming to be a general trend: the desire to manage museums as if they were companies. In 1988 Thomas Krens was appointed director of the Solomon R. Guggenheim Foundation, and although (with the exception of Bilbao) his franchise system was a failure, his neoliberal approach came to be seen as exemplary. Krens was at once both a symbol and a symptom of a wider political and economic state of affairs. In the mid-seventies, capital began to dominate every aspect of human life, the citizen became an entrepreneur and the cold abstract management of the economy and of our lives usurped the place previously reserved for politics. The public was identified with the consumer and it was accepted that the purpose of an art centre was to generate an unlimited number of spectacular events that would make it financially and politically profitable, even if the artistic experience was now to be largely a matter of brand recognition.

Michel Foucault affirmed, with regard to Nietzsche, that history becomes effective only to the degree that it introduces discontinuity into our very being. In its discontinuity, the museum acquires meaning when it attaches greater importance to the process than the results. It is not a question of the museum speaking for others, but of it providing the means of empowering those who gather around it.

THE TEMPORARY AUTONOMOUS ZONE, ONTOLOGICAL ANARCHY, POETIC TERRORISM

Hakim Bey

Hakim Bey, otherwise known by his real name Peter Lamborn Wilson, is an American author best known for advocating anarchist ideologies that were formed in response to his perception of American imperialism at the time, as well as his subsequent experiences of tribal and anti-colonial cultures in Lebanon, India, Pakistan, and Iran during the sixties and seventies. In particular, he has promoted the idea of the Temporary Autonomous Zone: the creation of spaces that form their own social and political logic based around the collective dynamic, and therefore independent of formal means of control. These ideas were influential not just for those participating in the anarchist scene, but also in alternatives movements such as rave in the eighties and nineties. His book *T.A.Z.: The Temporary Autonomous Zone* was published by Autonomedia in 1991, but its first chapter 'Chaos: The Broadsheets of Ontological Anarchism' was first published in 1985 by Grim Reaper Press. These two sections have been selected from 'Chaos: The Broadsheets of Ontological Anarchism'.

POETIC TERRORISM

Weird dancing in allnight computer banking lobbies. Unauthorized pyrotechnic displays. Land-art, earth-works as bizarre alien artifacts strewn in State Parks. Burglarize houses but instead of stealing, leave Poetic-Terrorist objects. Kidnap someone & make them happy.

Pick someone at random & convince them they're the heir to an enormous, useless & amazing fortune — say 5000 sq. miles of Antarctica, or an aging circus elephant, or an orphanage in Bombay, or a collection of alchemical mss. Later they will come to realize that for a few moments they believed in something extraordinary, & will perhaps be driven as a result to seek out some more intense mode of existence.

Bolt up brass commemorative plaques in places (public or private) where you have experienced a revelation or had a particularly fulfilling sexual experience, etc.

Go naked for a sign.

Organize a strike in your school or workplace on the grounds that it does not satisfy your need for indolence & spiritual beauty.

Graffiti-art loaned some grace to ugly subways & rigid public monuments — PT-art can also be created for public places: poems scrawled in courthouse lavatories, small fetishes abandoned in parks & restaurants, xerox-art under windshield-wipers of parked cars, Big Character Slogans pasted on playground walls, anonymous letters mailed to random or chosen recipients (mail fraud), pirate radio transmissions, wet cement...

The audience reaction or aesthetic-shock produced by PT ought to be at least as strong as the emotion of terror — powerful disgust, sexual arousal, superstitious awe, sudden intuitive breakthrough, dada-esque angst — no matter whether the PT is aimed at one person or many, no matter whether it is 'signed' or anonymous, if it does not change someone's life (aside from the artist) it fails.

PT is an act in a Theatre of Cruelty which has no stage, no rows of seats, no tickets & no walls. In order to work at all, PT must categorically be divorced from all conventional structures for art consumption (galleries, publications, media). Even the guerrilla Situationist tactics of street theatre are perhaps too well known & expected now.

An exquisite seduction carried out not only in the cause of mutual satisfaction but also as a conscious act in a deliberately beautiful life — may be the ultimate PT. The PTerrorist behaves like a confidence-trickster whose aim is not money but CHANGE.

Don't do PT for other artists, do it for people who will not realize (at least for a few moments) that what you have done is art. Avoid recognizable art-categories, avoid politics, don't stick around to argue, don't be sentimental; be ruthless, take risks, vandalize only what must be defaced, do something children will remember all their lives — but don't be spontaneous unless the PT Muse has possessed you.

Dress up. Leave a false name. Be legendary. The best PT is against the law, but don't get caught. Art as crime; crime as art.

ART SABOTAGE

ART SABOTAGE strives to be perfectly exemplary but at the same time retain an element of opacity — not propaganda but aesthetic shock — appallingly direct yet also subtly angled — action-as-metaphor.

Art Sabotage is the dark side of Poetic Terrorism — creation-through-destruction — but it cannot serve any Party, nor any nihilism, nor even art itself. Just as the banishment of illusion enhances awareness, so the demolition of aesthetic blight sweetens the air of the world of discourse, of the Other. Art Sabotage serves only consciousness, attentiveness, awakeness.

A-S goes beyond paranoia, beyond deconstruction — the ultimate criticism — physical attack on offensive art — aesthetic jihad. The slightest taint of petty ego-icity or even of personal taste spoils its purity & vitiates its force. A-S can never seek power, only release it.

Individual artworks (even the worst) are largely irrelevant — A-S seeks to damage institutions that use art to diminish consciousness & profit by delusion. This or that poet or painter cannot be condemned for lack of vision, but malign Ideas can be assaulted through the artifacts they generate. MUZAK is designed to hypnotize & control — its machinery can be smashed.

Public book burnings — why should rednecks & Customs officials monopolize this weapon? Novels about children possessed by demons; the NYTimes bestseller list; feminist tracts against pornography; schoolbooks (especially Social Studies, Civics, Health); piles of NY Post, Village Voice & other supermarket papers; choice gleanings of Xtian publishers; a few Harlequin Romances — a festive atmosphere, wine-bottles & joints passed around on a clear autumn afternoon.

To throw money away at the Stock Exchange was pretty decent Poetic Terrorism — but to destroy the money would have been good Art Sabotage. To seize TV transmission & broadcast a few pirated minutes of incendiary Chaote art would constitute a feat of PT — but simply to blow up the transmission tower would be perfectly adequate Art Sabotage.

If certain galleries & museums deserve an occasional brick through their windows — not destruction, but a jolt to complacency — then what about BANKS? Galleries turn beauty into a commodity but banks transmute Imagination into faeces and debt. Wouldn't the world gain a degree of beauty with each bank that could be made to tremble... or fall? But how? Art Sabotage should probably stay away from politics (it's so boring)–but not from banks.

Don't picket — vandalize. Don't protest — deface. When ugliness, poor design & stupid waste are forced upon you, turn Luddite, throw your shoe in the works, retaliate. Smash the symbols of the Empire in the name of nothing but the heart's longing for grace.

1985

SQUATTERS

Diana Franssen

In the second half of the seventies, the squatters' movement in the Netherlands really gained momentum. In 1980, this culminated in an unprecedented explosion of protest that put squatting at the centre of political and public debate. During this period, squatting grew into a social movement that spoke out against the shortage of affordable and social housing.

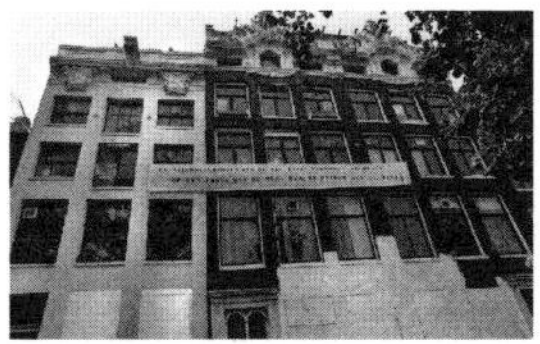

Groote Keijser, Amsterdam, Summer 1980. Photo: Rob Hameeteman

The squatters' movement was diverse. On the one hand, they tried to improve living conditions by influencing decision-making through actions such as street festivals. On the other hand there was more direct and politicized activism. This led to outright confrontation of the radicalized squatters movement — motivated by housing shortage, speculation in the housing market and a failing government — with prime-minister Dries van Agt of the Christian-Democratic party (CDA). The actions became harder under the influence of the Militant Autonomen Front (MAF), a coalition not endorsed by everyone in the squatters' movement.

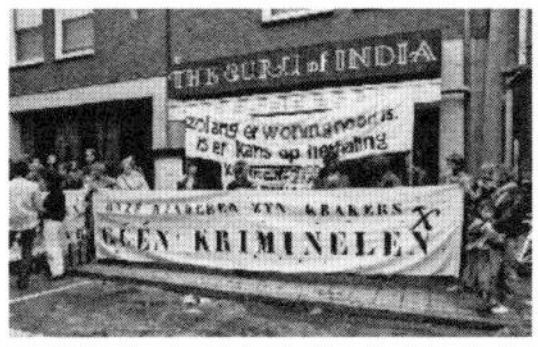

'Maffe mammies' in action, eviction Vogelstruys, Amsterdam 1980. Photo: Rob Hameeteman

The most famous militant struggle took place during the coronation of Queen Beatrix on 30 April 1980, with the slogan 'Geen woning, geen kroning' (No housing, no coronation). The coronation day, conceived for the establishment as a showcase of their pomp and power was, for the squatters, the ideal stage to vent their frustration and anger. For one day, the streets of Amsterdam turned bloody and violent in scenes rarely seen before or since.

The twentieth century in the Netherlands has been dominated by the idea of 'maakbaarheid' (social engineering), a concept that has transformed through the successions of different socio-political realities. While the first half of the century was marked by social engineering as a modernist, progressive conception of society (the realization of the welfare state), a shift occurred between 1970–1985 toward the 'emancipated citizen', inspiring civil participation as a form of social engineering.

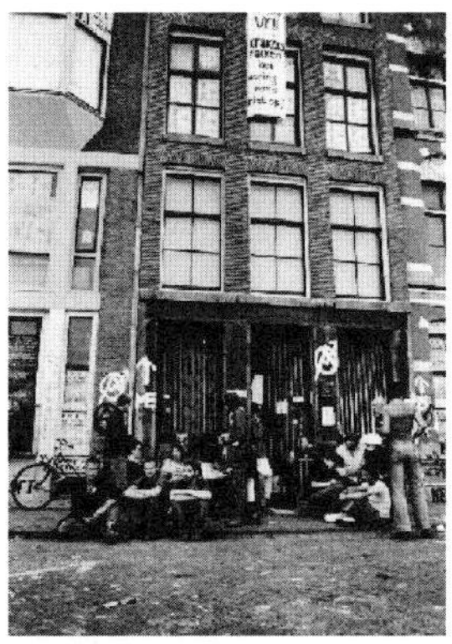

Squatters at Prins Hendrikkade, Amsterdam, 1980. Photo: Rob Hameeteman

The early eighties increasingly confronted the state with an articulate and highly critical civil society, with strong viewpoints on women's and gay rights, housing issues and nuclear energy. Social engineering as a bottom-up practice also became increasingly visible in the urban space, where squatters slipped into vacant buildings, not only due to a shortage of dwellings, but also to elude bureaucratic structures of control and create new forms of living. The proliferation of a DIY mind-set and the experimentation

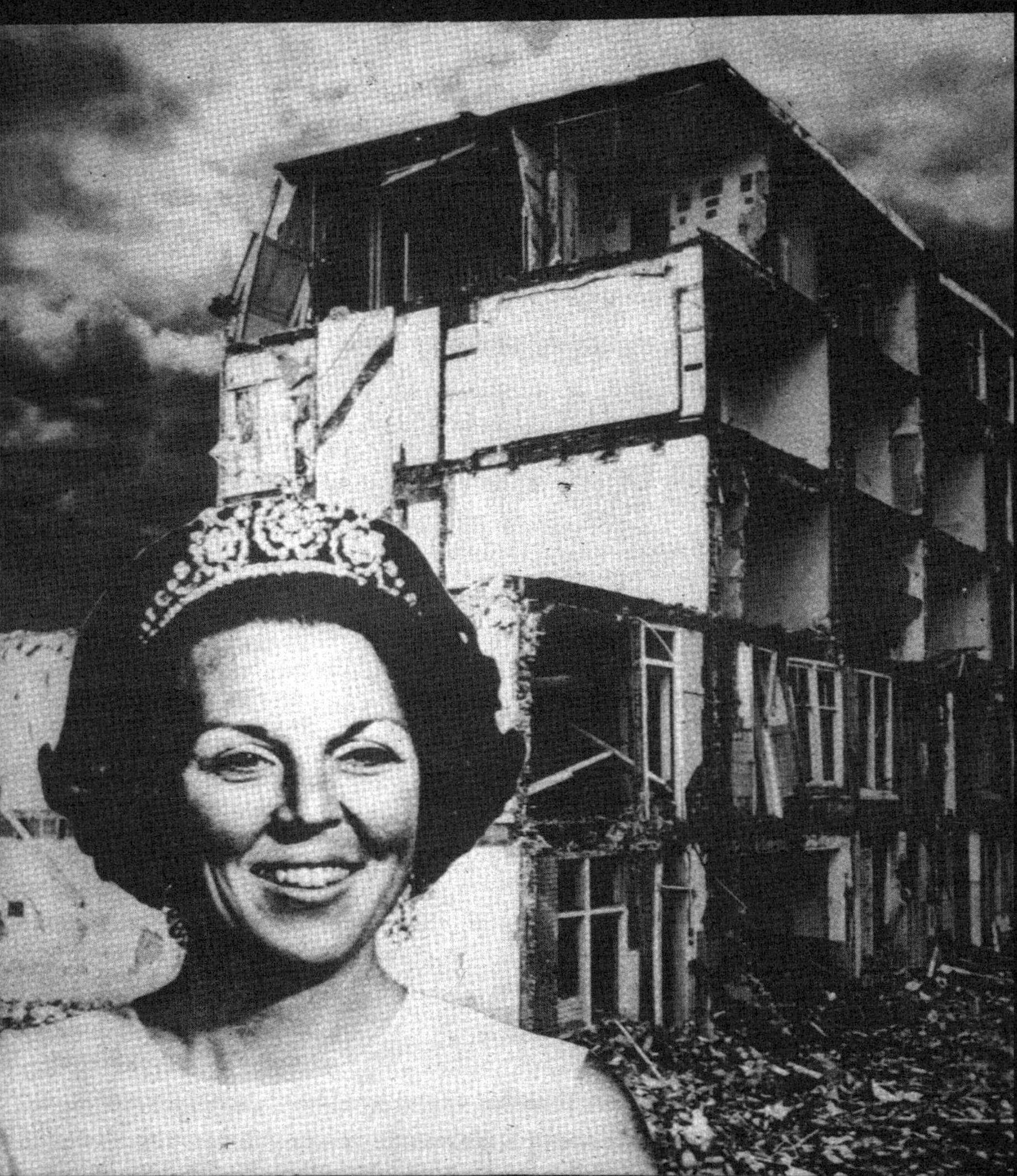

Geen woning, geen kroning (No Housing, No Coronation), 1980, poster

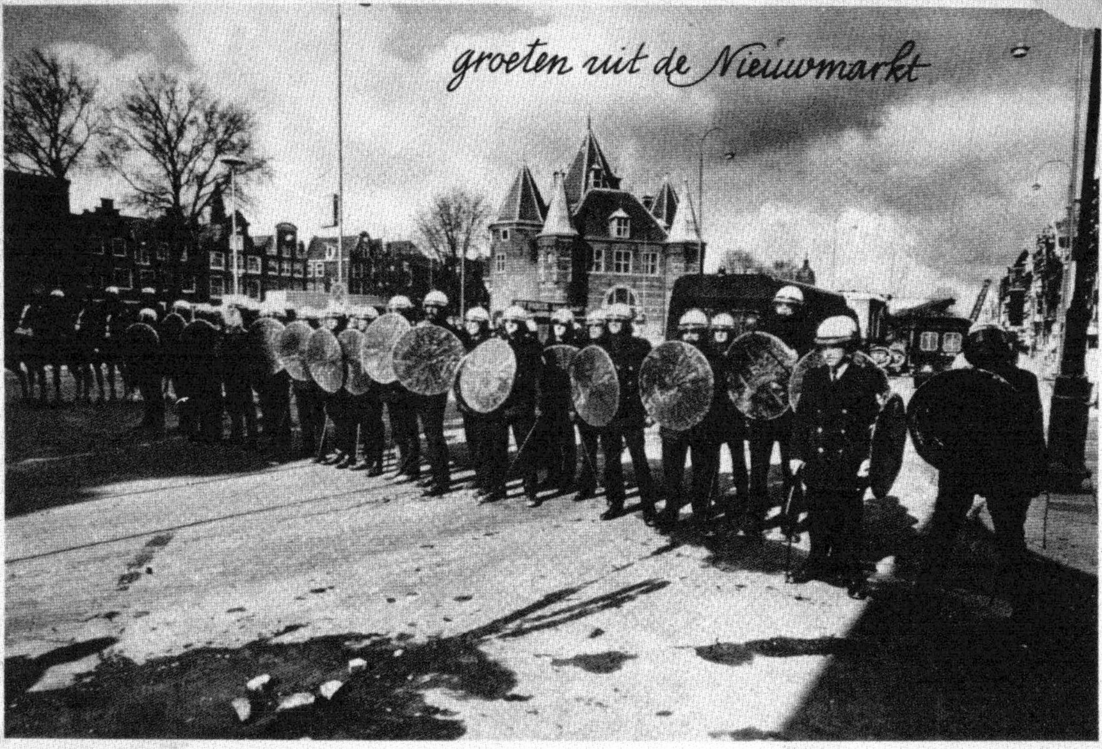

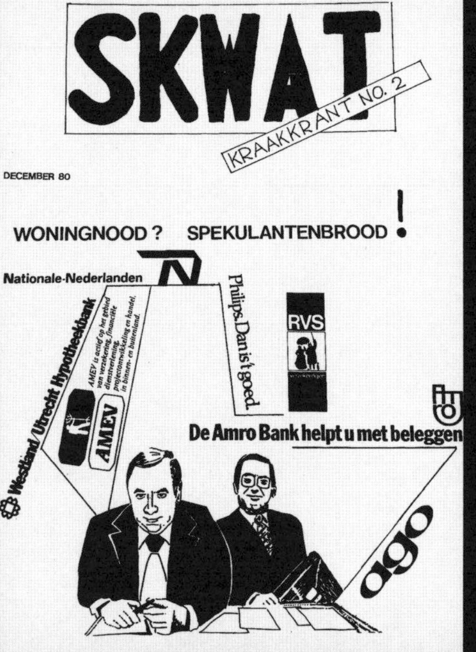

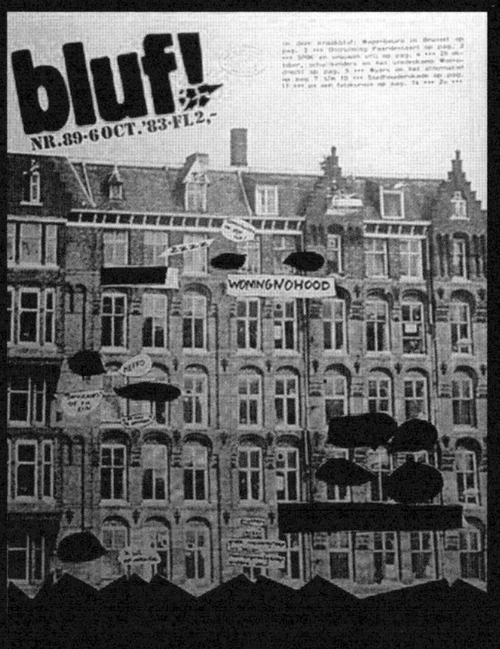

Groeten uit de Nieuwmarkt (Greetings from the Nieuwmarkt), *Het Parool*, 1975

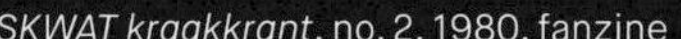

SKWAT kraakkrant, no. 2, 1980, fanzine

Bluf!, no. 89, 1983, fanzine

with alternative forms of cultural production such as pirate radio stations, television and printed media (*Bluf!*), testified to the belief that squatting was a more 'autonomous way' of life that could give more freedom.

It was a position that was lost under the government of prime minister Ruud Lubbers (also of the Christian-Democratic party CDA), who was elected in 1982 and remained in power for over a decade. Under Lubbers, societal debates became more depoliticized, and the Netherlands evolved toward a more closed society in which not civil society but market forces increasingly influenced decision-making.

The national deficit caused by the economic crisis in the seventies, and the so-called *Dutch disease* had led to enormous inflation rates, decreasing industrial production, soaring unemployment, and rising social security costs.[01]

The government responded by diminishing the power of trade unions and breaking down the welfare state. Simultaneously, government intervention was reduced through decentralization, deregulation, and privatization, and new measures were taken to stimulate the economy.

While the squatters' movement, supported by neighbourhood activists, had emerged as a force to put the shortage of affordable housing on the political agenda (save-the-city-motivation), and to engineer countercultures in autonomous spaces outside of institutions (free-space-motivation), the initial mobilizing force rapidly lost its militant character, and declined in the latter half of the eighties.

01

The term 'Dutch disease' was coined by *The Economist* magazine in 1977. The magazine analysed a crisis taking place in the Netherlands following discoveries of vast natural gas deposits in 1959. The newfound wealth and massive export of gas caused the Dutch guilder to rise sharply, making export of all non-oil products less competitive in the world market. Unemployment rose and capital investment in the country dropped. 'Dutch disease' became widely used in economics to describe the paradoxical situation where seemingly good news, such as the discovery of large oil reserves, turns out to have a negative impact on a country's broader economy.

PREMATURE ARCHITECTURE
ISIDORO VALCÁRCEL MEDINA

Beatriz Herráez

Isidoro Valcárcel Medina (1937) is regarded as one of the foremost figures of conceptual art in Spain. His work has evolved since the sixties, when the country was ruled by a dictatorship and international contemporary art movements arrived in a fragmented and distorted form. The imbalance resulting from his forced estrangement to the places where many of his contemporaries developed their work had direct effects on IVM's work and the way in which he understood artistic practice. His works posed a challenge at the heart of a time that it would be difficult to pigeonhole in current strategies of the use of anachronism; IVM's subtle irony can be viewed as responses to the enthusiasm of those movements imported from the production centres of culture, movements which were far removed from the time and place of his own activity. IVM seems aware that the repetition of the same must be shown, time and again, as singular innovation. This prompts him to seek his own working models, carefully put together to wholeheartedly reject any nostalgic attitude and seemingly pointing towards premeditated failure, a lack of intent opposed to that which is persistently promoted as a 'reality principle'*: the resolve to domesticate our sensibility in common places.

Between 1984 and 1992, IVM worked on the series *Arquitectura Prematura* (Premature Architecture). This consists of technical drawings that — as urban responses to specific situations such as those generated by the institutionalization of culture, the expansion of precarious settlements on city fringes, and the rise in unemployment and the appearance of the figure of the jobless person — challenge the roles of institutions such as the museum and the job centre. These designs are constructions that make no claims to be utopian but 'are carriers of news items that are known by everyone beforehand, because they are self-evident', obvious or 'confirmed through their good sense'. IVM's architectural works, voluntarily distanced from any correlation between the avant-garde and architecture, and aware of the unexpected effects of functionalism and its planning of 'cemeteries of reinforced concrete', are premature because they are ahead of their time.

*

All sentences in quotation marks reproduce the words of the artist compiled in the exhibition catalogue *Ir y venir de Valcárcel Medina* (Come and Go by Valcárcel Medina) edited by José Díaz Cuyás (Barcelona: Fundació Antoni Tàpies etc., 2006), except for the reference to 'cemeteries of reinforced concrete', from *Internationale Situationniste* 3 (1959).

This series of projects includes *Okupa y Resiste* (Occupy and Resist), a camouflage system for squatted buildings, in which a façade in the form of a stage set is superimposed on, and conceals the facades of the occupied properties, keeping the authorities oblivious to what is happening inside, or preventing eviction; *Colonia de chabolas* (Community of Shacks), an emplacement of junk dealers for which he proposes a system of trailers and prototypes for single-family homes that interact with the environment of rubbish tips, adapting to the changes in the terrain; and *Museo de la ruina* (The Museum of Ruin), built from the outside, it prevents any visitor or worker from passing through — 'A building which, unable to hold its own weight and heading towards ruin, will slowly deteriorate until it collapses'.

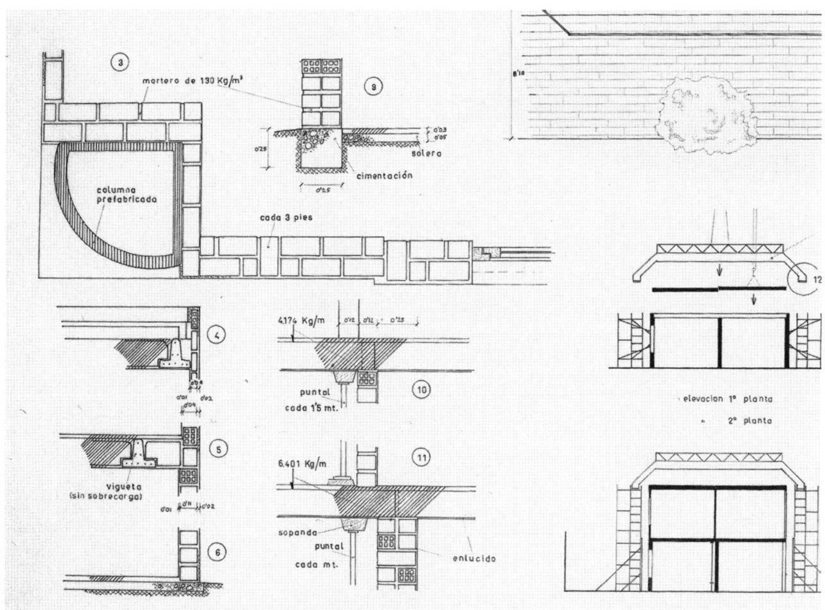

Museo de la ruina (The Museum of Ruin), Madrid, 1986, architecture, tracing paper, 145×71 cm. Courtesy Isidoro Valcárcel Medina / Arxiu Fundació Antoni Tàpies

Other public anti-institutions from the series include *Edificio para parados* (Building for the Unemployed), where people on benefits can circulate in a kind of Kafkaesque drift, and are kept busy inside a space that outwardly has no entrance and no exit; *Torre para suicidas* (Tower for Suicides), which 'has all the necessary spaces for those who want to end their life, without the bothersome reuse of monuments, skyscrapers, train tracks, lakes, bridges and other structures whose urban consideration is noticeably altered by such transformations of use'. The artist draws a comparison with the Viaduct in Madrid, known as a popular suicide spot onto which the City Council fitted a large methacrylate glass screen as a deterrent, 'covering up the certainty of suicide, in exchange for seeing the horizon all blurred'. These are just some of the works of 'obvious' resistance produced by IVM in the eighties.

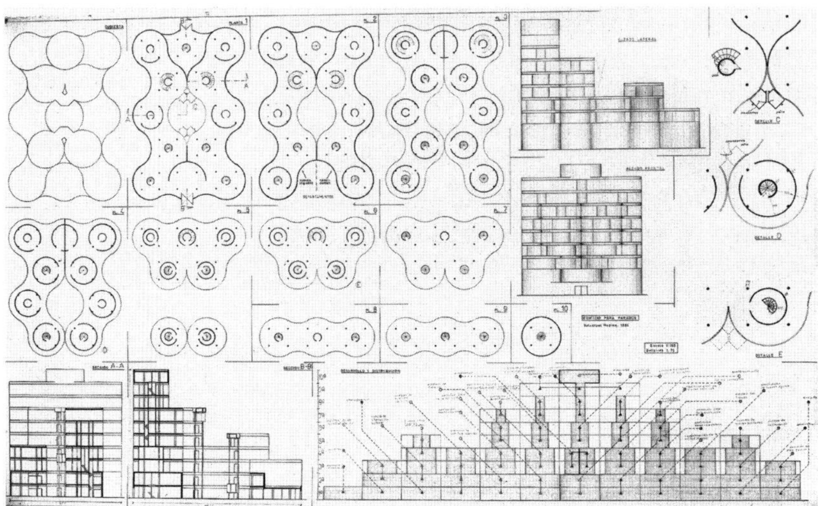

Edificio para parados (Building for the Unemployed), Madrid, 1984, architecture, tracing paper, 146,5 × 89,5 cm. Courtesy Isidoro Valcárcel Medina / Arxiu Fundació Antoni Tàpies

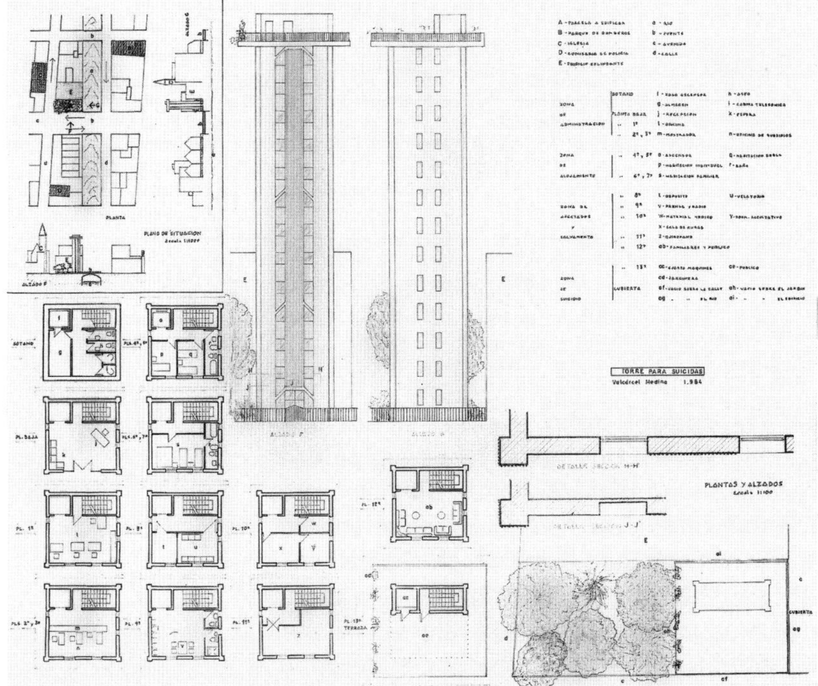

Torre para suicidas (Tower for Suicides), Madrid, 1984, architecture, tracing paper, 84.5 × 74.5 cm. Courtesy Isidoro Valcárcel Medina / Arxiu Fundació Antoni Tàpies

RAVE

Nav Haq

Rave culture from the eighties and nineties could be considered as being Europe's last major youth movement. During this period of profound social and political change, rave, in its various guises, reverberated around the continent from its epicentre of Great Britain, Belgium and Germany. As an alternative movement, it enacted a desire to be autonomous, with a belief in tolerance and experimental living, all built around the latent energy of electronic music. As a music-based culture, it embraced self-practice, invention and unbridled creativity, arguably leading to the densest period in history for the diversification of music.

Regularly drawing many thousands of participants, raves themselves have been theorized as 'temporary autonomous zones' — spontaneously organized concentrations of people and musical energy that eluded formal structures of control. Though embodying both dystopian and utopian impulses, raves possessed some extraordinary qualities, transgressing such social factors as race and class. For young people in Berlin attending illegal clubs, rave music contributed to a sense of a new beginning after the fall of the Berlin Wall.

Rave culture was built around 'electronic music', often made through improvisations with both the existing and emergent technologies of the day. The music itself possessed a distinct new aesthetic that redrew the boundaries of music. Each locale developed its own rave music culture, evolving countless forms of acid house, techno, hardcore, jungle and beyond. The 'cut-and-paste' sampling of rave (audio and visual) is also now seen as a typical facet of postmodern culture. It could arguably be described as the most intense period for the diversification of music in history. Ultimately, this unbridled creativity is what brought out the energetic feeling of rave.

Alongside the emergent technologies, there were also social, political and economic conditions of the moment that led to the advent of rave. Following the decline of industrialism, and the birth of neoliberal ideology that formulated a relationship between the capitalist free-market and the state. For those who felt failed by both the market and the state, particularly during this era of deep recession, raves opened up a third kind of space. It was a spontaneous, autonomous movement that formed its own logic based on the collective, in opposition to the atomization of neoliberal individualism. The desire for an alternative life or culture was the drive, built around the latent energy of electronic music, and the combination of electronic music and narcotics, more specifically ecstasy, proved to be particularly potent.

In a situation of moral panic, governments across Western Europe legislated to criminalize rave culture. The UK's Criminal Justice Act of 1994 being the first and most visible example, followed eventually by legislation in Belgium, France and elsewhere. This legislature outlawed public gatherings of a certain size, duration and volume, famously describing music as 'the emission of a succession of repetitive beats'. For many of the generation involved, it was considered a key moment in the erosion of civil liberties. Rave culture was inhibited due to its ambiguous place outside of neoliberal ideology, existing autonomously of both market and state forces.

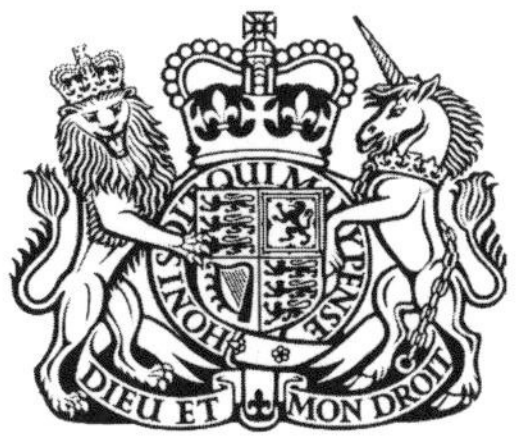

Criminal Justice and
Public Order Act 1994

1994 CHAPTER 33

Part V

Public Order: Collective Trespass or Nuisance on Land

Powers in relation to raves

63   Powers to remove persons attending or preparing for a rave

(1) This section applies to a gathering on land in the open air of 100 or more persons (whether or not trespassers) at which amplified music is played during the night (with or without intermissions) and is such as, by reason of its loudness and duration and the time at which it is played, is likely to cause serious distress to the inhabitants of the locality; and for this purpose—

    (a)   such a gathering continues during intermissions in the music and, where the gathering extends over several days, throughout the period during which amplified music is played at night (with or without intermissions); and

    (b)   "music" includes sounds wholly or predominantly characterised by the emission of a succession of repetitive beats.

(2) If, as respects any land in the open air, a police officer of at least the rank of superintendent reasonably believes that—

    (a)   two or more persons are making preparations for the holding there of a gathering to which this section applies,

    (b)   ten or more persons are waiting for such a gathering to begin there, or

    (c)   ten or more persons are attending such a gathering which is in progress,

he may give a direction that those persons and any other persons who come to prepare or wait for or to attend the gathering are to leave the land and remove any vehicles or other property which they have with them on the land.

(3) A direction under subsection (2) above, if not communicated to the persons referred to in subsection (2) by the police officer giving the direction, may be communicated to them by any constable at the scene.

(4) Persons shall be treated as having had a direction under subsection (2) above communicated to them if reasonable steps have been taken to bring it to their attention.

(5) A direction under subsection (2) above does not apply to an exempt person.

(6) If a person knowing that a direction has been given which applies to him—

    (a)   fails to leave the land as soon as reasonably practicable, or

    (b)   having left again enters the land within the period of 7 days beginning with the day on which the direction was given,

he commits an offence and is liable on summary conviction to imprisonment for a term not exceeding three months or a fine not exceeding level 4 on the standard scale, or both.

(7) In proceedings for an offence under this section it is a defence for the accused to show that he had a reasonable excuse for failing to leave the land as soon as reasonably practicable or, as the case may be, for again entering the land.

(8) A constable in uniform who reasonably suspects that a person is committing an offence under this section may arrest him without a warrant.

(9) This section does not apply—

    (a)   in England and Wales, to a gathering licensed by an entertainment licence; or

    (b)   in Scotland, to a gathering in premises which, by virtue of section 41 of the Civic Government (Scotland) Act 1982, are licensed to be used as a place of public entertainment.

(10) In this section—

"entertainment licence" means a licence granted by a local authority under —

    (a) Schedule 12 to the London Government Act 1963;

    (b) section 3 of the Private Places of Entertainment (Licensing) Act 1967; or

    (c) Schedule 1 to the Local Government (Miscellaneous Provisions) Act 1982;

"exempt person", in relation to land (or any gathering on land), means the occupier, any member of his family and any employee or agent of his and any person whose home is situated on the land;

"land in the open air" includes a place partly open to the air;

"local authority" means—

    (a) in Greater London, a London borough council or the Common Council of the City of London;

    (b) in England outside Greater London, a district council or the council of the Isles of Scilly;

    (c) in Wales, a county council or county borough council; and

"occupier", "trespasser" and "vehicle" have the same meaning as in section 61.

(11) Until 1st April 1996, in this section "local authority" means, in Wales, a district council.

64　Supplementary powers of entry and seizure

(1) If a police officer of at least the rank of superintendent reasonably believes that circumstances exist in relation to any land which would justify the giving of a direction under section 63 in relation to a gathering to which that section applies he may authorise any constable to enter the land for any of the purposes specified in subsection (2) below.

(2) Those purposes are—

    (a)　to ascertain whether such circumstances exist; and

    (b)　to exercise any power conferred on a constable by section 63 or subsection (4) below.

(3) A constable who is so authorised to enter land for any purpose may enter the land without a warrant.

(4) If a direction has been given under section 63 and a constable reasonably suspects that any person to whom the direction applies has, without reasonable excuse—

    (a)　failed to remove any vehicle or sound equipment on the land which appears to the constable to belong to him or to be in his possession or under his control; or

    (b)　entered the land as a trespasser with a vehicle or sound equipment within the period of 7 days beginning with the day on which the direction was given,

the constable may seize and remove that vehicle or sound equipment.

(5) Subsection (4) above does not authorise the seizure of any vehicle or sound equipment of an exempt person.

(6) In this section—

    "exempt person" has the same meaning as in section 63;

    "sound equipment" means equipment designed or adapted for amplifying music and any equipment suitable for use in connection with such equipment, and "music" has the same meaning as in section 63; and

    "vehicle" has the same meaning as in section 61.

65　Raves: power to stop persons from proceeding

(1) If a constable in uniform reasonably believes that a person is on his way to a gathering to which section 63 applies in relation to which a direction under section 63(2) is in force, he may, subject to subsections (2) and (3) below—

    (a)　stop that person, and

    (b)　direct him not to proceed in the direction of the gathering.

(2) The power conferred by subsection (1) above may only be exercised at a place within 5 miles of the boundary of the site of the gathering.

(3) No direction may be given under subsection (1) above to an exempt person.

(4) If a person knowing that a direction under subsection (1) above has been given to him fails to comply with that direction, he commits an offence and is liable on summary conviction to a fine not exceeding level 3 on the standard scale.

(5) A constable in uniform who reasonably suspects that a person is committing an offence under this section may arrest him without a warrant.

(6) In this section, "exempt person" has the same meaning as in section 63.

66   **Power of court to forfeit sound equipment**

(1) Where a person is convicted of an offence under section 63 in relation to a gathering to which that section applies and the court is satisfied that any sound equipment which has been seized from him under section 64(4), or which was in his possession or under his control at the relevant time, has been used at the gathering the court may make an order for forfeiture under this subsection in respect of that property.

(2) The court may make an order under subsection (1) above whether or not it also deals with the offender in respect of the offence in any other way and without regard to any restrictions on forfeiture in any enactment.

(3) In considering whether to make an order under subsection (1) above in respect of any property a court shall have regard—

   (a)   to the value of the property; and

   (b)   to the likely financial and other effects on the offender of the making of the order (taken together with any other order that the court contemplates making).

(4) An order under subsection (1) above shall operate to deprive the offender of his rights, if any, in the property to which it relates, and the property shall (if not already in their possession) be taken into the possession of the police.

(5) Except in a case to which subsection (6) below applies, where any property has been forfeited under subsection (1) above, a magistrates' court may, on application by a claimant of the property, other than the offender from whom it was forfeited under subsection (1) above, make an order for delivery of the property to the applicant if it appears to the court that he is the owner of the property.

(6) In a case where forfeiture under subsection (1) above has been by order of a Scottish court, a claimant such as is mentioned in subsection (5) above may, in such manner as may be prescribed by act of adjournal, apply to that court for an order for the return of the property in question.

(7) No application shall be made under subsection (5), or by virtue of subsection (6), above by any claimant of the property after the expiration of 6 months from the date on which an order under subsection (1) above was made in respect of the property.

(8) No such application shall succeed unless the claimant satisfies the court either that he had not consented to the offender having possession of the property or that he did not know, and had no reason to suspect, that the property was likely to be used at a gathering to which section 63 applies.

(9) An order under subsection (5), or by virtue of subsection (6), above shall not affect the right of any person to take, within the period of 6 months from the date of an order under subsection (5), or as the case may be by virtue of subsection (6), above, proceedings for the recovery of the property from the person in possession of it in pursuance of the order, but on the expiration of that period the right shall cease.

(10) The Secretary of State may make regulations for the disposal of property, and for the application of the proceeds of sale of property, forfeited under subsection (1) above where no application by a claimant of the property under subsection (5), or by virtue of subsection (6), above has been made within the period specified in subsection (7) above or no such application has succeeded.

(11) The regulations may also provide for the investment of money and for the audit of accounts.

(12) The power to make regulations under subsection (10) above shall be exercisable by statutory instrument which shall be subject to annulment in pursuance of a resolution of either House of Parliament.

(13) In this section—

"relevant time", in relation to a person—

(a) convicted in England and Wales of an offence under section 63, means the time of his arrest for the offence or of the issue of a summons in respect of it;

(b) so convicted in Scotland, means the time of his arrest for, or of his being cited as an accused in respect of, the offence;

"sound equipment" has the same meaning as in section 64.

MONTEVIDEO

Antony Hudek

Montevideo represents one of the most significant chapters in Antwerp's recent cultural past, despite the brevity of its existence (June 1981–September 1984). Founded by Annie Gentils and Stan Peers, and the artist Hugo Roelandt, the largely self-funded contemporary art space filled a void in the Antwerp and Flemish art worlds of the early eighties. Antwerp had played a major role in supporting and promoting radical contemporary art in the late sixties and seventies, with such galleries as Wide White Space and X-One, and the publicly funded International Cultural Centre (ICC). By the late seventies, however, the city had lost its contemporary art lustre, much of it in favour of Brussels, despite the continued efforts of the ICC (where Gentils was working at the time) and rare exceptions (Ruimte Z in Borgerhout). It took the opening of new commercial art galleries in the early eighties (Zeno X, Cintrik) and, crucially, the appearance of Montevideo, to place Antwerp back on the European contemporary art map.

Gentils' frame of reference was less Antwerp's heyday of the late sixties and seventies than the late fifties and early sixties, when her father, Vic, as part of the G58-Hessenhuis group, co-organized significant exhibitions in Antwerp's Hessen House, bringing major international artists to Antwerp. More immediate impulses that led Gentils to co-found Montevideo was a decisive trip to the US in 1979 with her friend, the Antwerp artist Anne-Mie Van Kerckhoven. The two discovered the music and performance scenes in New York and Los Angeles, experiencing first-hand the work of Chris Burden and the punk and emergent No Wave scenes (James Chance in particular). This exposure to the musical and performative trends in the US, as well as to the experimental music pursued in Brussels at the time (at the now legendary club Plan K, and through the pioneering label Les Disques du Crépuscule), made a strong mark on Montevideo's early programming.

On 6 June 1981, Montevideo opened in a large, abandoned late-nineteenth-century warehouse in the old port of Antwerp. For the equivalent of about 50 euros a year, Gentils and Peers rented three sections of the building (approximately 2000 square metres) from the city of Antwerp. (The other eight sections were also rented out to artists and a video production organization). The unheated industrial space, with its cobblestone floor and natural light streaming through skylights, suited Gentils' and Peers' ambition to create an unstructured environment where music, dance and art could converge, and that could also serve as a lively social hub for the city's artists and international visitors. The opening exhibition set the tone: the Antwerp artist turned scientist Luc Steels made a large-scale laser installation that cut across the entire space of Montevideo. The next show, in December 1981, saw the architect and artist Luc Deleu place a full-size crane on its side, an installation that served as a backdrop for a very crowded New Year's party featuring Jacques Chapon's Rasta Connection.

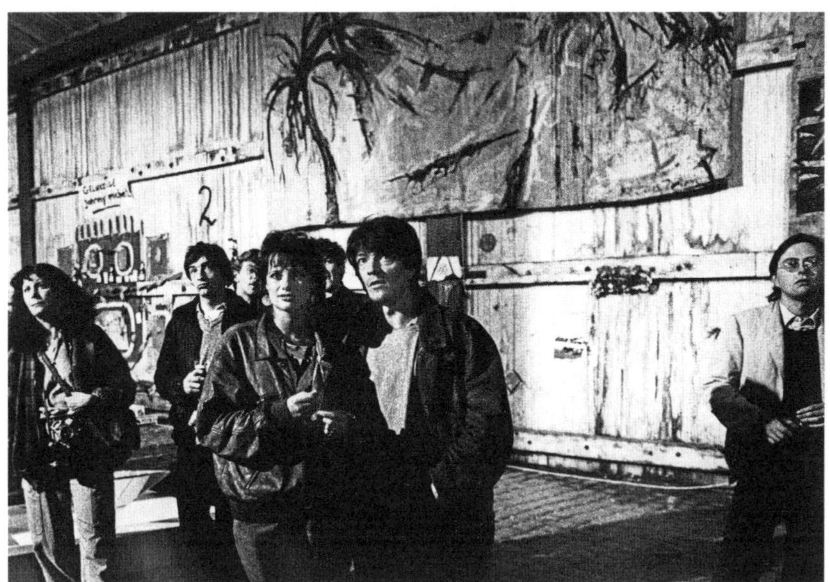

Opening of 'Marchandises, 5 millions de tonnes de marchandises livrées chaque année' (Merchandise, 5 Million Tons of Cargo Shipped Annually), April 1983, live broadcast Antwerp–Ghent–Amsterdam, *IJsbreker* television documentary by Jef Cornelis. Courtesy Annie Gentils Montevideo Archive. Photo: Elisabeth Lemahieu

1984

In 1982, Montevideo began producing more substantial exhibitions, in addition to frequent music and performance events (by, among others, Club Moral, Ria Pacquée and the radical Belgian ensemble AKT — Ivo van Hove, Karl Desloovere and Jan Versweyveld). One of the first exhibitions at Montevideo was an ambitious display of holography by the artist Ludo Mich, at the time an international advocate of the medium. The first major group exhibition at Montevideo, and the first accompanied by a catalogue (designed by Peers), took the history of the building as inspiration. 'Marchandises, 5 millions de tonnes de marchandises livrées chaque année' (Marchandises, 5 Million Tons of Cargo Shipped Annually, 1983) offered an up-to-date survey of contemporary art in Antwerp, including artists such as Guillaume Bijl, Deleu, Pacquée, Roelandt, Van Kerckhoven, Guy Rombouts and Wout Vercammen.

1981

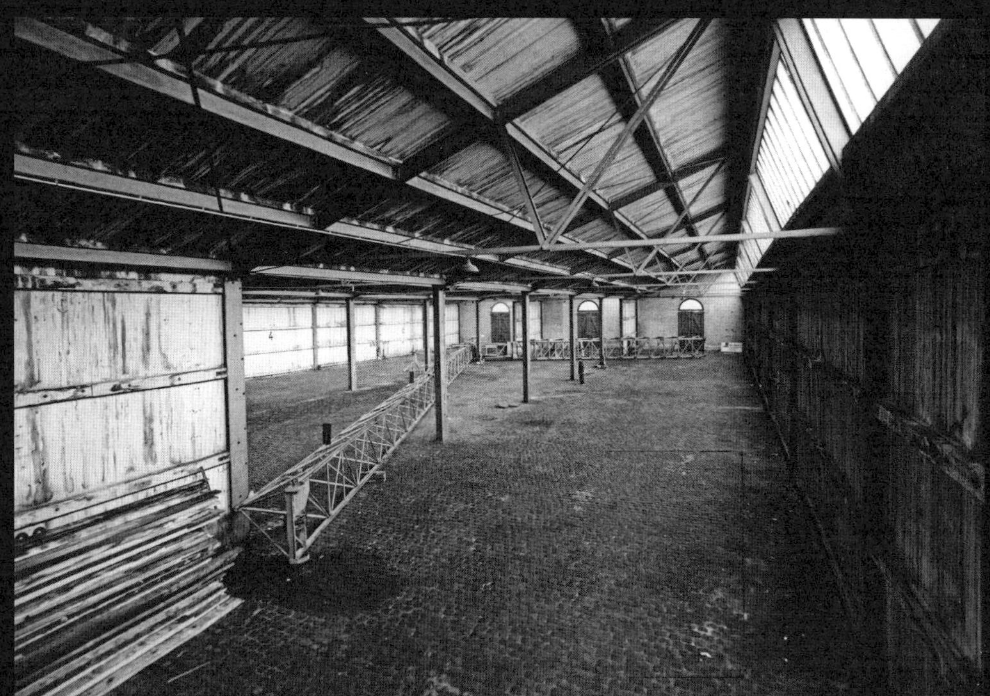

Luc Deleu, *Schaal en perspectief* (Scale and Perspective), December 1981. Courtesy Annie Gentils Montevideo Archive. Photo: Benny Urban

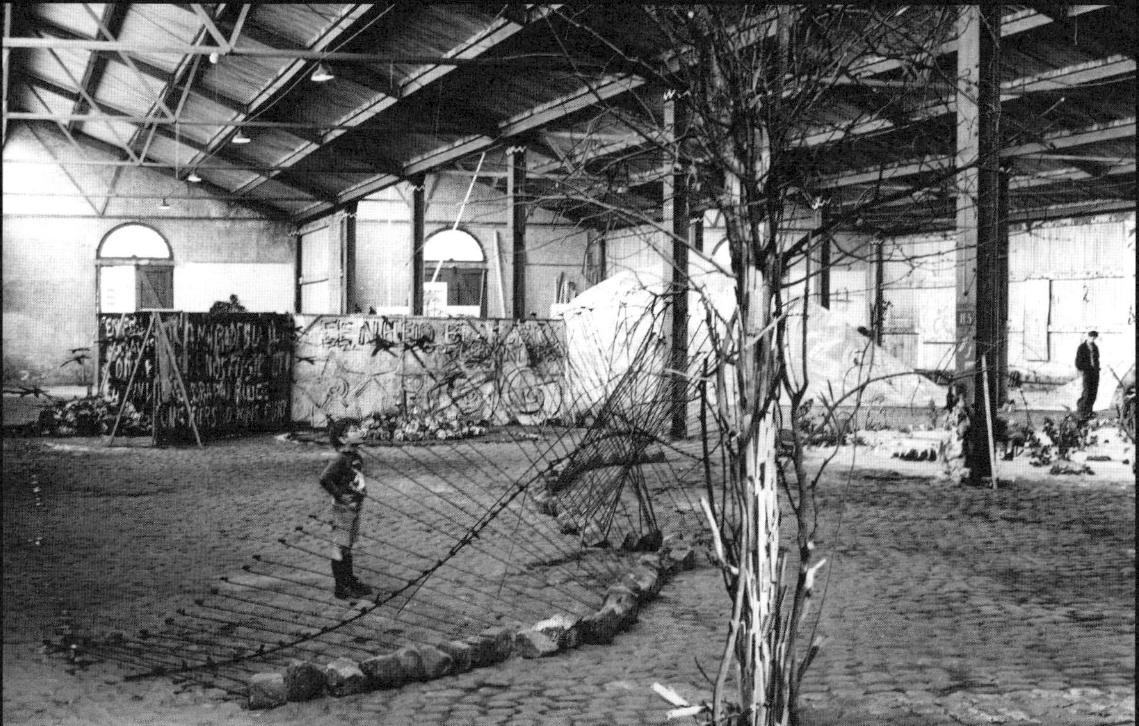

'De eerste chauvinistische — La première chauviniste' (The First Chauvinist), April 1984. Installation view of works by Fred Eerdekens, Ann Veronica Janssens & Monika Droste and Claude Yande. Courtesy Annie Gentils Montevideo Archive

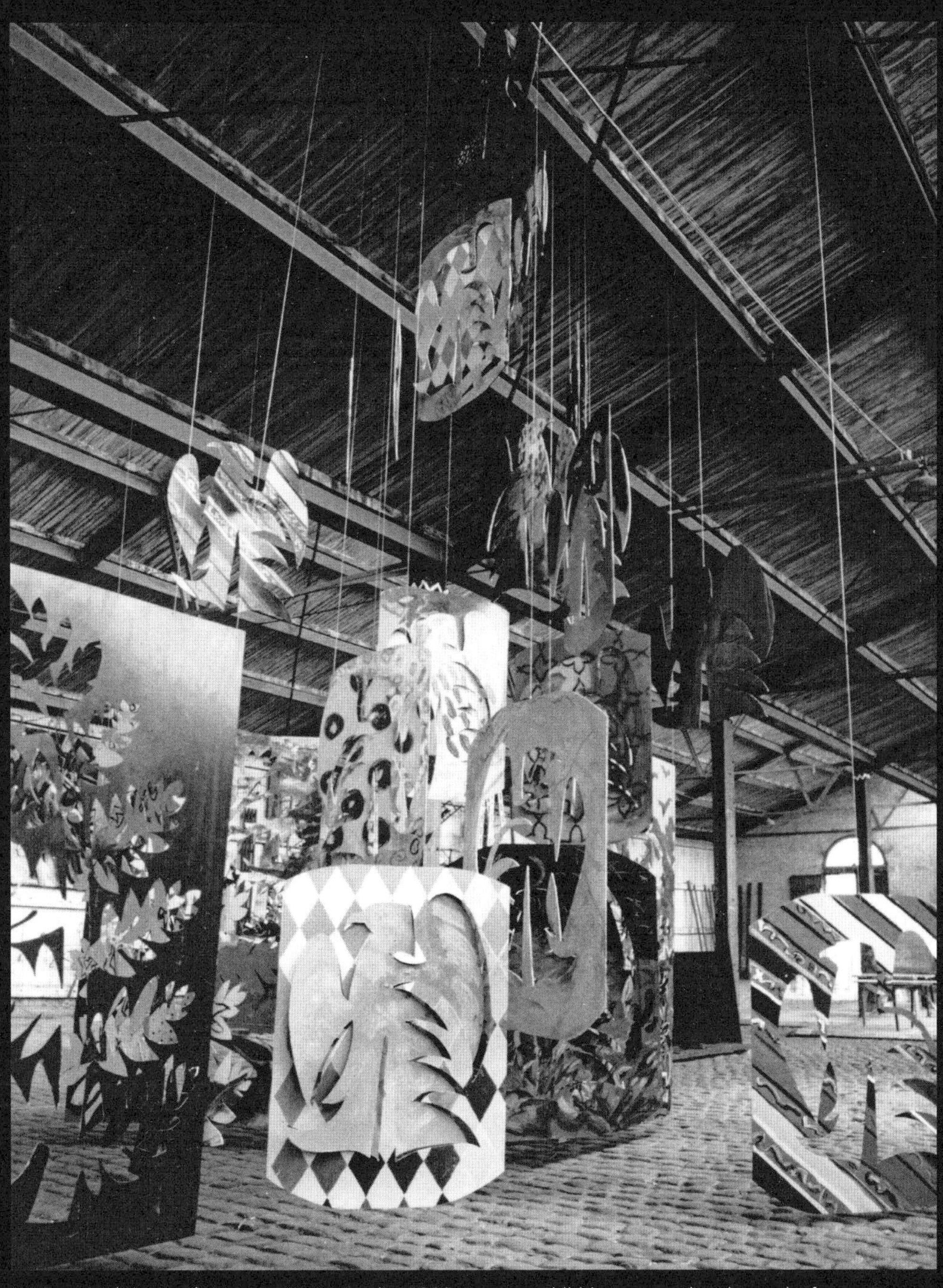

'Diagonale' (Diagonal), 11 June–25 September 1983. A group exhibition presenting the work of approximately forty international artists. Installation view of work by Horst Glasker. Courtesy Annie Gentils Montevideo archive. Photo: Stan Peers

Three more major group exhibitions followed, each accompanied by a catalogue designed by Peers: 'Diagonale' (Diagonal, part of the 1983 Middelheim Biennial), 'De eerste chauvinistische – La première chauviniste' (The First Chauvinist, 1984) and Montevideo's final show, 'Torens van Babel' (Towers of Babel, 1984). By the end of 1984, Gentils and Peers found themselves unable to carry on without additional support from the City of Antwerp, which was denied. In 1985, the port authorities reclaimed the Montevideo warehouse, which ever since has been sitting idle, falling prey to more degradation and weeds with each passing year.

For their research and support the author would like to thank Annie Gentils, Stan Peers and the MA Film Studies and Visual Culture of the University of Antwerp, Class of 2016: Tirsa van der Kleij, Shana Peulinckx, Emma Priem, Jasper van Quekelberghe and Bram Vroonland.

NEUE SLOWENISCHE KUNST

Alexei Monroe

Neue Slowenische Kunst (NSK) was created in Ljubljana in 1984 as a platform to develop and transmit a set of ambivalent artistic techniques, first associated with the controversial group Laibach (at that time banned from performing in Slovenia). Laibach allied with the painters' group IRWIN and theatre group Scipion Nasice Sisters to create an artistic formation that would overshadow and contribute to the disintegration of the Yugoslav state and later emerge as a borderless artistic 'State in Time'. One of the key motifs supporting Neue Slowenische Kunst as *Gesamtkunstwerk* and one cause of the fascination and alarm that NSK works still provoke was the organigramme. It depicted real NSK groups, units designed to mimic state institutions and abstract principles. These elements appeared in a seemingly totalitarian hierarchical command structure. Its projection of the contaminated aesthetic ideal of a totalitarian state was partly based on an aesthetic appreciation of this mode and an awareness that others might respond to it aesthetically as a work of (state) art. While it was strategic and conceptual, it was also intuitive and poetic. Unlike nationalist projects based on ideal, shadow-less projections of nation states, NSK's projection of a future state consciously incorporated the totalitarian shadow that modernist state structures incubated.

Laibach's embryonic 1982 version[01] introduced terminology and concepts that would later appear in the collective NSK versions ('Immanent Consistent Spirit', 'Projective Assembly', et cetera). Functioning initially as a stylized internal planning document, it illustrates the organigramme's role in projecting into the future an influence the artists did not yet actually possess.

Another variant was used as part of the symbolic propaganda representing the collective NSK performance *Krst pod Triglavom* (1986). Besides appearing in print and on posters, this black-and-white version appeared on the inner lid of New Collectivism's *Suitcase for Spiritual Use*, a series of elaborate decorative panels in the shape of a cross that unfolds from within a fur-lined suitcase.[02] The appearance and subsequent development of the organigramme (to which new groups were added as NSK expanded) signalled its intention to confront state and society with a radically alternative structure that challenged the present order.

01

Reproduced on p. 463 of Zdenka Badovinac, Eda Čufer and Anthony Gardner, eds., *NSK from Kapital to Capital: Neue Slowenische Kunst: An Event of the Final Decade of Yugoslavia* (Cambridge: MIT Press, 2015).

02

See www.delo.si/znanje/izobrazevanje/kabinet-cudes_3.html (accessed 15 January 2017). Other photographs of the suitcase do not show the organigramme and it is not clear at precisely which point it was added.

Like so much of NSK's state-centred art, the organigramme was designed with the 'actually existing' and increasingly dysfunctional Yugoslav state structures in mind. It confronted them with an 'immanently existing' proto-state in totalitarian form. It was intended to provoke, captivate and infiltrate and it destabilized elements of the state that were opposed to it while seducing others, above all the Slovenian socialist youth organization ZSMS, whose officials commissioned NSK to produce posters and even invited Laibach to perform at the 1987 ZSMS Congress in Celje. While conservative elements in Slovenia and Yugoslavia used NSK as one of many pretexts for populist-authoritarian mobilization, ZSMS used it to radicalize its self-image and propel it away from what it saw as inherently authoritarian socialist orthodoxy.

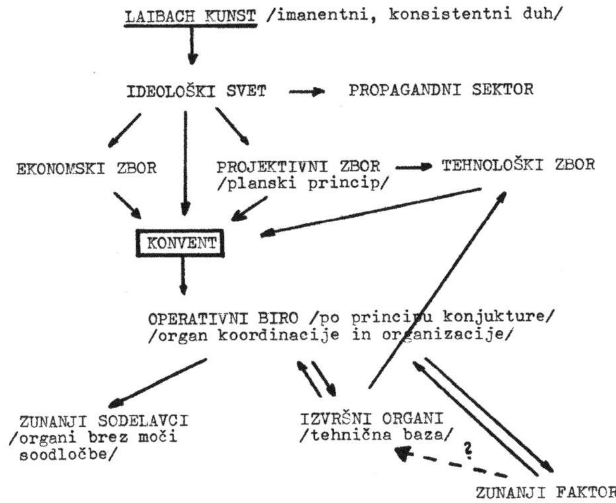

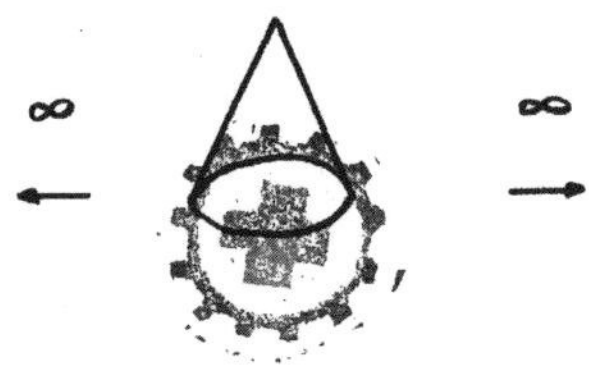

Laibach Kunst, *Organigramme*, 1982, typescript on paper, 30 × 21 cm.
Courtesy Moderna galerija, Ljubljana

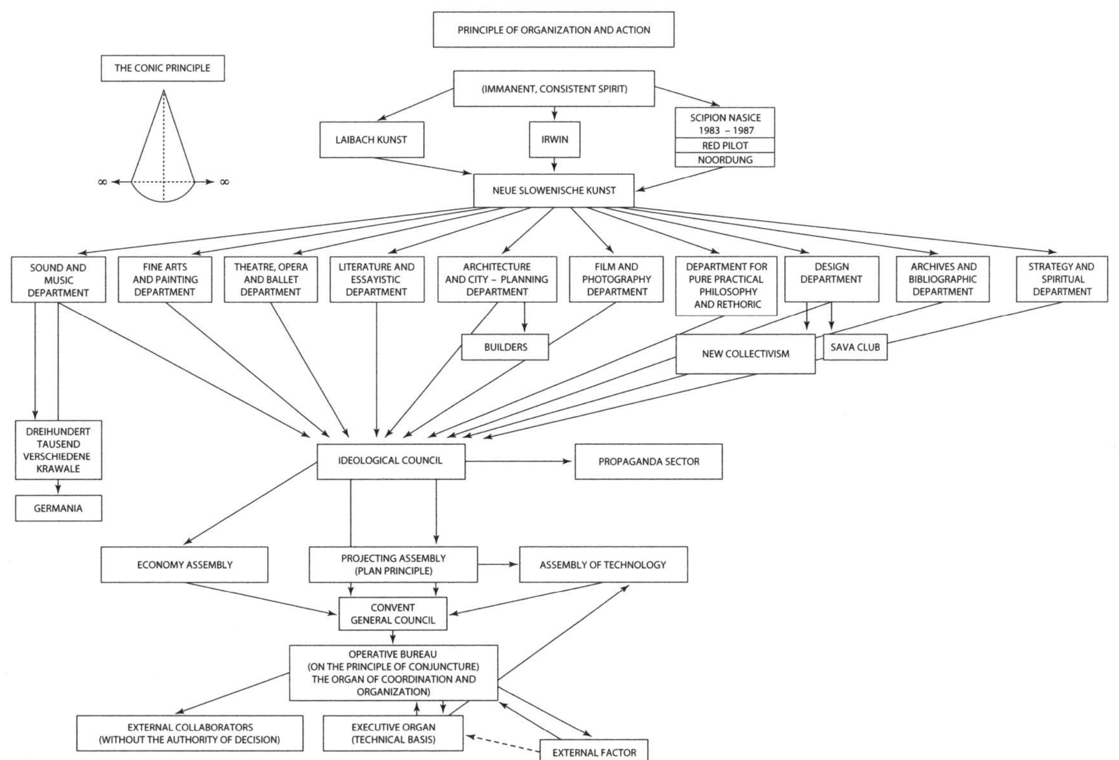

Neue Slowenische Kunst, *NSK Organigramme*, 1986(–1992). Layout: Laibach and New Collectivism

A more elaborate variant showing newly-created bodies such as Red Pilot was included as a poster with Laibach's *Krst pod Triglavom* LP,[03] which confusingly bore the caption 'Der NSK Koffer für geistigen Gebrauch' (*Suitcase for Spiritual Use*). The organigramme's suggestively totalitarian form combined with the German language used in this version activated another set of meanings outside of Slovenia, accentuating the threat that many perceived the structure to embody. This version featured in the 1989 BBC documentary *Rough Guide to Ljubljana*[04] and, together with a slightly later English version, helped transmit the illusion of NSK as a shadowy mass political art movement, rather than a small group of Slovenian artists actually concerned with aesthetic construction and rigorously questioning 'actually existing' power structures.

03

See www.discogs.com/ Laibach-Krst-Pod-Triglavom-Baptism/release/505022 (accessed 15 January 2017).

04

See www.youtube.com/ watch?v=J6n9-dA94d8 (accessed 15 January 2017).

THE PHLEGM OF TALLER LLUNÀTIC

Teresa Grandas

To talk of countercultural practices in the Spanish state during the eighties means to refer to stances of resistance and subversion against the established order, some materializing in opposition to Franco's dictatorship, others surfacing well into the ensuing democracy as a position taken up in opposition to new circumstances. The 'normalizing' will of the Transition to democracy, which gave precedence to a smooth passage and with no radical ruptures from the previous regime, blurred the outlines of many break-away impulses and had a greater inclination towards the integration of art and culture inside a new institutional system, and conventionality shaped by mercantilism. In the face of demands from the new art market and the appearance of spaces heeding to a consumer notion of a markedly conservative artwork, Taller Llunàtic (The Lunatic Workshop) is a clear example of insubordination towards political and cultural power, of resistance against a move into new circuits of production, perpetually denying, rejecting, and refuting. Taller Llunàtic emerged in Mallorca as an open group aligned with the publication *Neón de suro*, and was initially made up of Josep Albertí, Bartomeu Cabot, Lluis Maicas, and Jaume Sastre from 1979 to 1988. Yet by the late eighties, only the first two remained, and their activity continues to this day. The artistic context in Mallorca in the seventies was fiercely conservative, and, therefore, the group was widely shunned, sharing a mutual confrontation with the political, social and cultural situation, a critique of the commodification of artworks, and the questioning of their importance with a significant precursor: the Criada 74 group (1974–1977).

Taller Llunàtic disjoints artistic conventions by questioning the cornerstones of the art object and the system underpinning it. In the face of intolerance over difference, it is characterized by a multi-disciplinary collective practice encompassing actions, performances, exhibitions, videos, manifestos, magazines (most saliently *El Correu de Son Coc*), publications and self-publications, anti-artistic exercises coming together in a transgression of the limits of art and social conventionalism, aspiring to stand back from the ever-more-established ordinariness and mediocrity in politics, society, and culture, and the mechanisms of power that

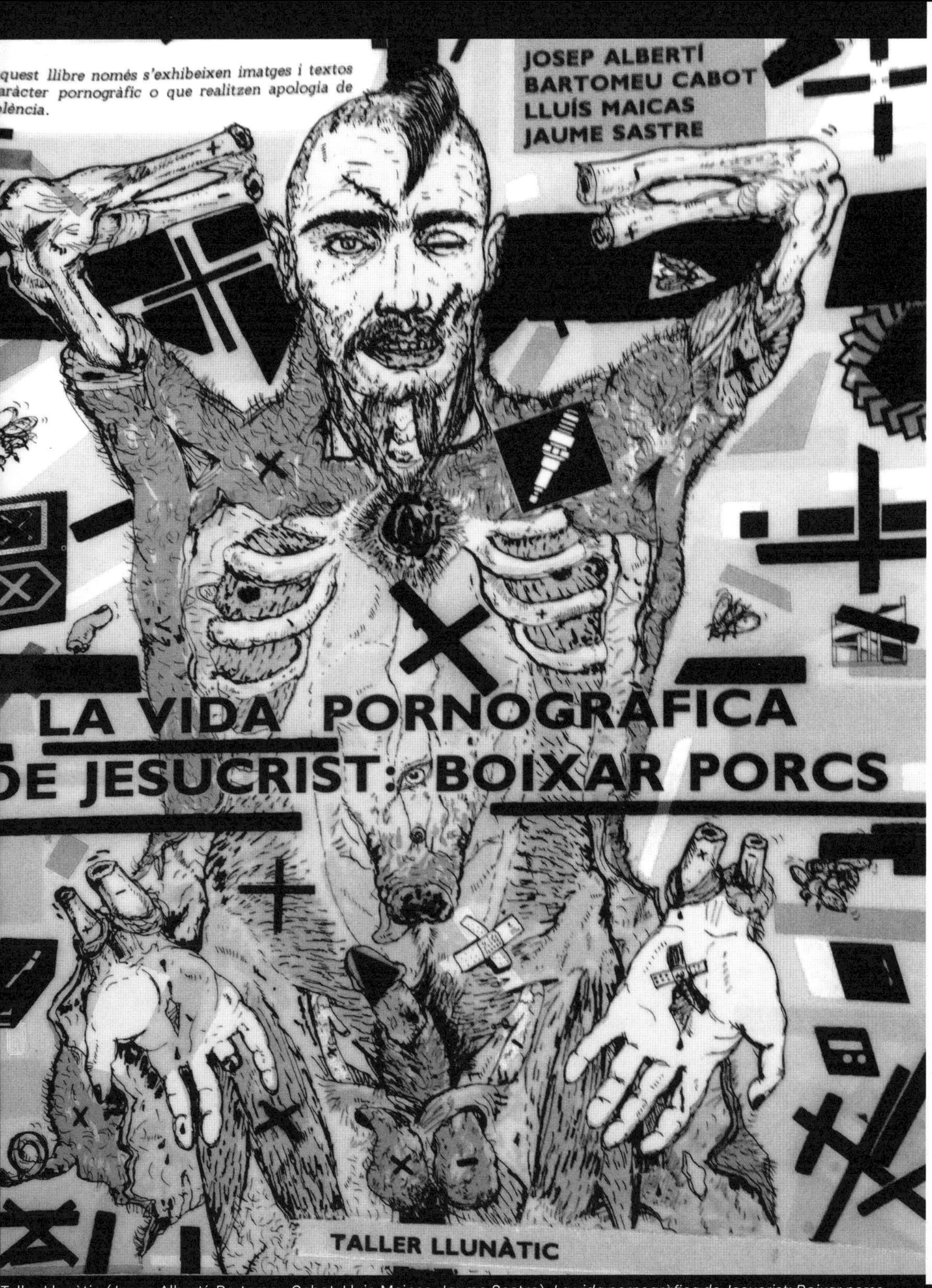

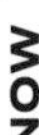

Taller Llunàtic (Josep Albertí, Bartomeu Cabot, Lluis Maicas, Jaume Sastre), *La vida pornogràfica de Jesucrist: Boixar porcs* (The Pornographic Life of Christ: Shagging Pigs), Ciutat de Mallorca, 1985, book cover

govern them. The art establishment and institution are understood as instruments of neutralization and destruction, and against this backdrop they unleashed a subversion which, despite being initially manifested in the humour and parody of the essence of art, of its enshrinement and agents, became, through the passage of time, increasingly more radical, moving towards the self-exclusion of artistic conventions through scathing irony and unhinged aggression. The use of arresting colours and highly arresting visual images are catalysts which blast away established notions by using eroticism, pornography, violence, provocation, insults, and impertinence, modes of rejecting the models and conventions of a society which does not respond to expectations.

'We spit out orgasms on the neurotic tidiness of civilized people', Josep Albertí wrote in 1977 inside a large penis. It is the vindication of the scatological, of effluvia and bodily excretions, spaces of outbursts and emancipation issuing forth from orifices, disobeying what is socially acceptable and the limits of art in Bataillean excess. Titles such as *La vida pornogràfica de Jesucrist: Boixar porcs* (The Pornographic Life of Jesus Christ: Shagging Pigs), or *el retrato del artista meando sobre la Virge* (Portrait of an Artist Peeing on the Virgin), *Violación del Redentor* (The Rape of the Redeemer), *Jesuxoricidi* (Jesuxorcide), *El clítoris de Elmo Sonnier* (The Clitoris of Elmo Sonnier); themes like sodomization, depravation, sacrilege, degeneration, pornography; motifs such as clitorisses, penises, whores, forbidden sexual pleasures. This, therefore, is how Taller Llunàtic prescribes its work, a kind of 'degenerate art' which calls for tradition and the artifices which demarcate our collective behaviour to be spat on. Insubordinate and unruly, in 1986 they proclaimed:

> Promiscuity, jubilee, eclecticism, the euphemism of freedom as an excuse for not bloodying hands (YES, THE REPRESSION OF FREEDOM!) dominate today's art and desperately call for the need to surgically treat these traumatic dimensions in order to put an end, once and for fucking all, to the whole sickly sap. In a nutshell, nip the damage in the bud.
>
> Taller Llunàtic: *La vida pornogràfica de Jesucrist: Boixar porcs*

BİLAR CORPORATION

Nazım Hikmet Richard Dikbaş

It's called remembering. In other words, creating the past: despite all the interruptions of facts and chronologies.

1   What could be an alternative method in higher education? What is absent in higher education in the arts, social sciences and philosophy in Turkey? What other examples, from the past or from the international scene, can you think of? Whenever these questions are asked, whenever these topics come up, and when it is my turn to say something, I always come up with the same example, which I remain passionate about: I tell its story, trying to remember the striking details, to revive that experience. I end up saying much more than I initially planned; yet nevertheless I always regret that I may have missed something in formulating it into a narrative, a story, a *good memory*.

2   It is perhaps fitting, that it is a student, and not one of the founders or 'teachers' of BİLAR who writes this text. One of BİLAR's aims was to re-establish the intergenerational flow of information and experience, viciously cut off by the military coup of 12 September 1980. And it did this in a remarkably elegant manner: not by attempting to restage the seventies, or the political, literary and artistic vitality of that decade, but by bringing together a group of intellectuals who had lived through the coup, and whose fields of interest had expanded further over that time with the youth of the early nineties. For this group of intellectuals this was a way to tell their own circles, and the rest of the world, 'we are here and we stand strong', and it also provided us, the youngsters, with self-confidence by presenting us with a set of diverse tools of knowledge. BİLAR was a whole, consisting of its teachers and students and it learned socialist feminism from Gülnur Savran and Orhan Koçak who told the story of İkinci Yeni, one of the most influential movements in poetry in the Republican era. It invited as guest Ece Ayhan, with his intellectually sealed and aesthetically defiant brand of poetry, that sent much-appreciated shockwaves through the classroom. İskender Savaşır gave an introduction to psychoanalysis, explaining that it was impossible to deal with the subject matter from a single viewpoint, and had us make presentations.

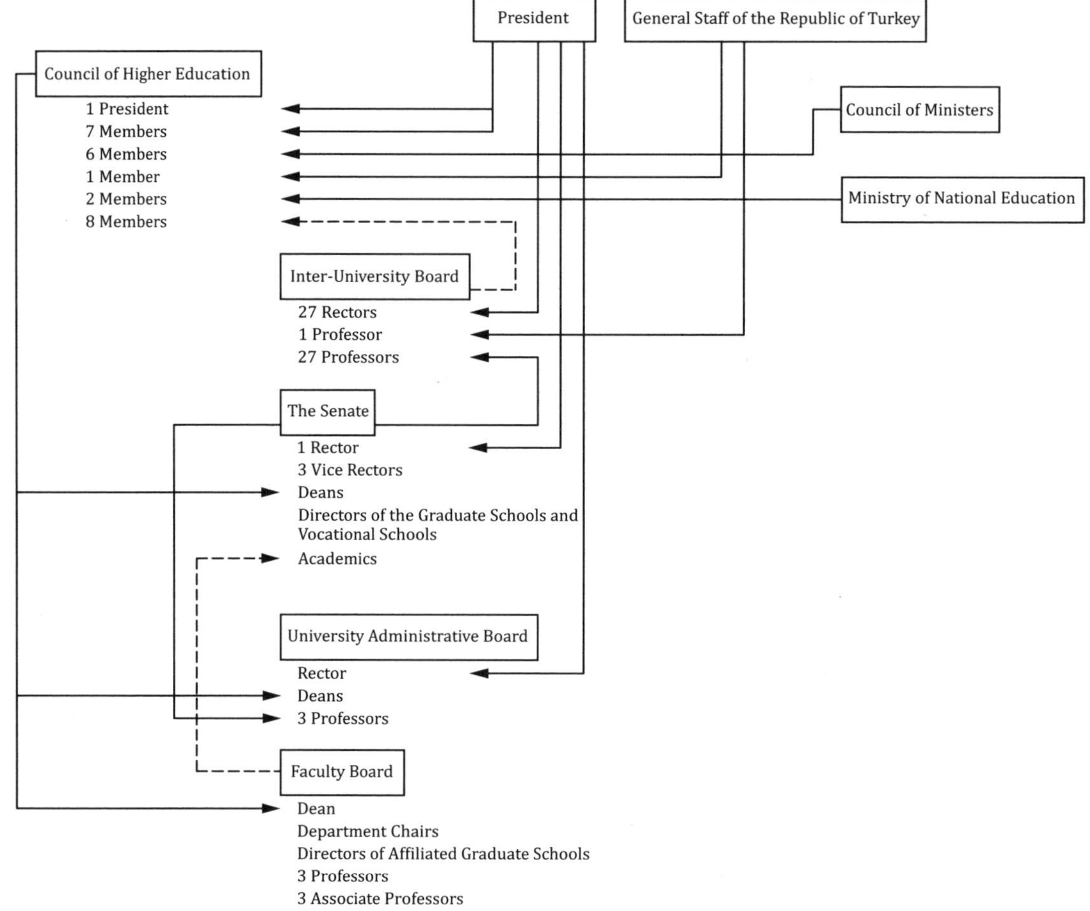

Diagram of educational structure

3   Comparing BİLAR's academic staff with the best universities in Turkey today would put them to shame — yet even that uneven comparison holds no longer. Over the last couple of years, universities in Turkey have become further depleted with the widespread and continuing dismissals of the Academics for Peace. BİLAR's educational atmosphere is a distant dream in any university, private or public, in Turkey today. At BİLAR's entrance, on Zambak Street, just off İstiklal Street, you did not present an ID, you weren't body-checked, and you did not pass through a turnstile. And BİLAR was free. Today's students may be taken aback by that last revelation, so let us repeat: there was no charge. Besides, I could get there by walking 20 minutes from my shared-student-flat, and I was devastated when I missed a single class. It was a place where I could listen to those who spoke, and where my comments or questions were heard.

I. Turkiye'de Siyaset

1. Anayasalar, Rejimler, Demokrasi   2x3   Bulent Tanor

        Iliski: Kuruldu
        Ne dedi: Hayir; Yucel'inkinde "Insan Haklari"
                   ve de mesgul; Saglam'i onerdi.

2. Secimler ve Siyasal Katilim   2x3   Sirin Tekeli

        Iliski: Kuruldu
        Ne dedi: 4 saati icin olabilir; Ahmet Kotil'den
                   de yararlanilabilirmis bu konuda (Golge
                   Adam'dan iliski kurulacak -telefonunu
                   bilen?

3. Partiler, Dernekler, Sendikalar   2x3   Fadil Kocagoz

        Iliski: Kurulmadi (Izmir, 115465 veya Yeni
                   Gunden)
        Ne dedi: ???

4. Devlet, Ordu, Ozgurlukler   2x3   Cemil Oktay

        Iliski: Kuruldu
        Ne dedi: Yeni baslik onerdi -Turk Siyasal Uslubu
                   Cercevesinde Devlet, Ordu ve
                   Ozgurlukler;
        Zaman: Pazartesi 16:00 dan sonra, hafta sonu

5. Siyaset ve Egitimde Laiklik   2x3   Gencay Saylan

        Iliski: Kurulmadi -telefonunu bilen?
        Ne dedi: ???

6. Hukuk Rejimindeki
    Anti-Demokratiklikler   2x3   Cetin Ozek

        Iliski: Kuruldu
        Ne dedi: Evet; ayrica 4'e de talip oldu.
        Zaman: 20 Kasim-15 Aralik donemi disinda

II. Karsilastirmali Siyaset

7. Tarih Boyunca Devlet - I   2x3   Sirin Tekeli
8. Tarih Boyunca Devlet - II   2x3   -   -

        Iliski: Kuruldu
        Ne dedi: Cengiz Arin'in zaten Nail'in programinda
                   benzerini yaptigindan tekrara gerek
                   gormedigini belirtti; tekrar notlarina
                   donmesi, hazirlanmasi vakit alirmis

Draft syllabus. Archive: Gülnur Savran

That was the secret of BİLAR. The gaze of the speaker / critic / poet / writer / filmmaker / philosopher / lecturer, or whoever was in charge of a presentation and had prepared it with the utmost dedication — that was how we felt — was turned towards the class, the audience, the students. This was the most striking gesture: Particularly in those courses I tried not to miss, the way the speaker turned towards the room, the listeners, a nod of encouragement, an arm lifted to trigger debate, eyes opened wide in curiosity, a smile expecting a question or a comment. The effort to create, or in fact, force a platform of debate meant everything to us. This was the only way to give birth to new tools and methods: This approach is what we have the least of today, yet it is what we, desperately, need most.

1.2 BROAD–CAST

Autonomy, Revolt and the Imagination to Leave the Stage
1980s

1984: The Adventures of the Alternative
1984

Black Film Workshops
1983–1995

'Talking Back to the Media'
1985

Jef Cornelis'
The Longest Day
1986

Club Moral
1981–1993

YOUR–
SELF

'A political poster must
be like a blow into an
open wound'
1987

AUTONOMY, REVOLT AND THE IMAGINATION TO LEAVE THE STAGE

READING *BLUF!* (AMSTERDAM) AND *RADIKAL* (BERLIN)

Geert Lovink

Berlin Slogonomics: 'Glauben, gehorchen, sterben' — 'Du hast keine Chance, aber nutze sie' — 'Radikal sein heisst, das Übel an der Wurzel packen!' (Radikal); 'In Gefahr und größter Not bringt der Mittelweg den Tod.' (Alexander Kluge); 'Wir sind die Terroristen und grüssen die Touristen.'(Kischstrasse 5); 'Alle Macht den Ratten' — 'Ich möchte ein Eisbär sein im kalten Polar, dann müßte ich nicht mehr schrei'n.' (Grauzone); 'Lebe Liebe Lache' — 'Sonderzug zur Endstation' (Abwärts); 'Ein Lachen wird es sein, das euch beerdigt!' (Peter-Paul Zahl); 'Hört auf zu heulen, es hat gerade erst angefangen.' — 'No tears for the creatures of the night, my eyes are dry, goodbye.' (Tuxedomoon).

Movements are not history. The past is history. The questions of 1981 are today's questions; the present and past tense are interchangeable. The post-punk era is dark: Mondays are the worst. We are in an ice age where neo-liberalism takes command, struggling to keep heroin at a distance. We've gone beyond stagnation and breathe in as we go into free-fall. The decline is surreal, so much waste to play with. The post-war reconstruction period is over. The welfare state and its class compromises are being buried alive. What's announced is the security state, the state of war, with brand new nuclear weapons. It's 1984. Then suddenly the reality of an imagined movement. Hear the cry of self-determination, to leave history aside, as we decide, together. It is time to consider the art of appearance, disappearance — and reappearance.

The Berlin-based monthly *Radikal* and the Amsterdam weekly *Bluf!* were 'movement papers' from the early eighties, both with a circulation of around 3,000 copies. Both came out of the squatter's movements of the time. What is most striking about them is their strategy. The assumption here is that movements are not weather phenomena: 'Alle reden vom Wetter. Wir nicht' ('Everyone talks about the weather. We don't') as the pre-anthropocene poster of the SDS (Social Democratic Student Union) stated. Movements are products of contradictions in society that cannot be absorbed by existing institutions. They do not just come and go, like violent revolts, but are social, collective entities created through a collective will. The question 'what's to be done' was — and still is — a real one.

Movements come into existence when we utilize the hermeneutic tools at hand to unfold space and stretch time so we create the conditions for events to take place. A chain of events materializes in time. This could explain why thirty to forty years later, in an accelerated world that structurally lacks time, there are less and less social movements. They simply no longer have the necessary intervals (the time from A to B) to unfold.

In the current social media regime we are running after the facts. The increase of (global) connectivity has not lead to synchronicity. This can only happen if we liberate ourselves from the real-time regime and create local spaces of exception.

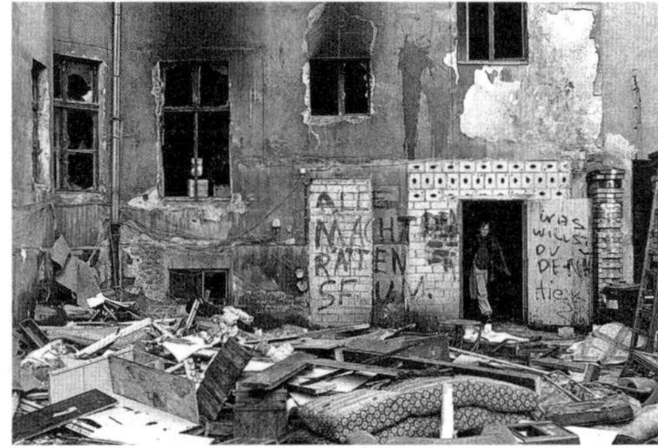

Geert Lovink in an evicted punk squat, West Berlin, December 1983

Previously, the creation of a movement was not a mysterious enterprise yet there weren't handbooks either. There was a shared mythology, how to manoeuvre, how to express anger and frustration and turn it into collective action. Movements were not parties with members and central committees. They were celebrated as amorphous entities: liquid, on the move, facing repression as their true enemy. In the eighties, movements were bodies in time. The question of strategy rarely arises today because movements rise and fall so quickly. Discussions used to have consequences. In comparison to forty years later, movements had more time to evolve, to grow and recover after confrontations, regroup, come back in order to, inevitably, fall apart and dissipate into society through a multitude of practices.

The main protagonist is the rebel, the one who has already said no, and starts to act in small units: the group, collective, scene, tribe, hood. The downside is the ghetto character of the movement. Revolution and the fight for freedom are not events, but processes. Once a movement manifests itself, and survives its first confrontations, it needs time to grow. The question is: in which direction? How to defend what has been built up? Revolt is a fact. It is time to deny a dialogue with power.

There was a reservoir of disenfranchised subjects struggling with economic recession, fuelled by a critical mass of experiences that were passed on from one rebel generation to the next, from neighbourhood initiatives to anti-Vietnam war structures to Situationist remnants. Debates were not 'talk fests' but discursive clashes — with consequences. Both magazines were not academic, although they found space for theoretical reflection. Both cities struggled with a broad disillusion with 1968 celebrity cult and anti-intellectual attitudes (with Amsterdam the pragmatist and

West-Berlin the theoretician, and both with a punk edge). Activists read these magazines not just for the news or comments on mainstream press, but also to find out what was discussed within the movement: the available options, the tendencies and overall mood.

Radikal classified itself as a 'clandestine' newspaper, comparing itself with less-known internal news channels such as Charlie Kaputt, Agit 883, FIZZ, Langer Marsch and INFO-BUG.[01] *Radikal*, from its inception in 1976, was tied to the tradition of the radical left, the revolutionary tradition of Marxist-Leninism. It is probably best placed in the tradition of the undogmatic 'spontaneous left' that operated outside the dogmatic political parties' leftovers (so-called K-Gruppen or communist groups), while also close to the remainders of the 'Spassguerrilla'[02] (Fun Guerrilla) traditions and its ironical tactics aimed at playful provocations of power and seventies tribal wisdom, ascribed to American Indians. This was mixed with a more rigorous, activist wing, linked to the writings of Toni Negri, that was in search of 'militant creativity'.

An important difference between the German and Dutch scenes at the time was the absence of 'armed struggle' in the Netherlands, resulting in a more playful, satirical relationship with the authorities. In contrast, West-Germans were exposed to a repressive police state that tried, on numerous occasions, to persecute squatters and protesters as 'criminal' organizations, from the confrontation at the nuclear power plant Brokdorf, the mass arrests in Nuremberg to large protests against Startbahn-West at Frankfurt airport. Autonomous movements often stood in solidarity with those in jail, including the Red Army Faction and members of the 'revolutionary cells'. Another important difference was the scepticism shown towards 'the alternative' and the moralistic reform mentality of the Greens and the peace movements that protested against the latest generation of nuclear weapons, a critique forwarded by authors such as Henryk Broder, Wolfgang Pohrt, Eike Geisel and others writing for *Konkret* magazine.

The *Bluf!* weekly was founded in late 1981 in Amsterdam after two years of riots and the occupation of thousands of houses and apartments, which created a critical mass of young unemployed students who would also become active in anti-nuclear, ecological, anti-militarist and feminist movements.[03] Both magazines brought together the radical wings of 'new social movements' beyond the New Age synergy of the 'rainbow coalition'. Squatting is not just about the politics of (social) housing, affordable rents and living in shared houses, but about a radical politics that is put into practice.

Both *Bluf!* and *Radikal* functioned through self-organized infrastructures: independent printing press collectives, photo-

01

See the German Wikipedia entry: https://de.wikipedia.org/wiki/Radikal_(Zeitschrift).

02

https://en.wikipedia.org/wiki/Spa%C3%9Fguerilla. The book *Spassguerilla* appeared in 1984 (reprint Münster: Unrast Verlag, 1993) and was widely read in radical circles at the time.

03

Disclaimer: more on the first two years can be found in the political science (University of Amsterdam) MA thesis of Geert Lovink and Eveline Lubbers (in Dutch), August 1983, *Bluf! 't Moet kunnen: Een skriptie over een bewegingsgebonden alternatief weekblad*, URL: www.worldcat.org/title/bluf-t-moet-kunnen-een-skriptie-over-een-bewegingsgebonden-alternatief-weekblad/oclc/65575098. I was one of the founders of *Bluf!*, together with Eveline and others. I left the editorial collective mid-1983 to live in a squat in West-Berlin where I mingled with the scene around *Radikal*, shared an apartment with a few of them in Kreuzberg in mid-1984 before returning to Amsterdam to work on Adilkno, the group that later wrote *Cracking the Movement* (1990), a history of the Amsterdam squatters movement. I continued to contribute to *bluf!* until it was dissolved, for instance with an essay in the 1983 Christmas issue on the doom and gloom culture of decay inside the Berlin squatters movement, including more theoretical contributions.

graphers (and their darkrooms), an editorial office housing electric typewriters, typesetting machines and early personal computers that were all linked to a network of voluntary sellers distributing the papers at demonstrations, in concert halls, bars, bookshops, and record stores. This was part of a wider network of self-governed spaces such as theatres, restaurants, food stores, cinemas, cafes, bicycle repair shops, neighbourhood equipment rentals, including free radio stations. The structure of the newspaper was aimed at embodying the ethos of the social movement — the magazines were run as part of a 'counter-economy' that did not depend on subsidies or donations and thus needed a sizable movement in order to sustain itself.

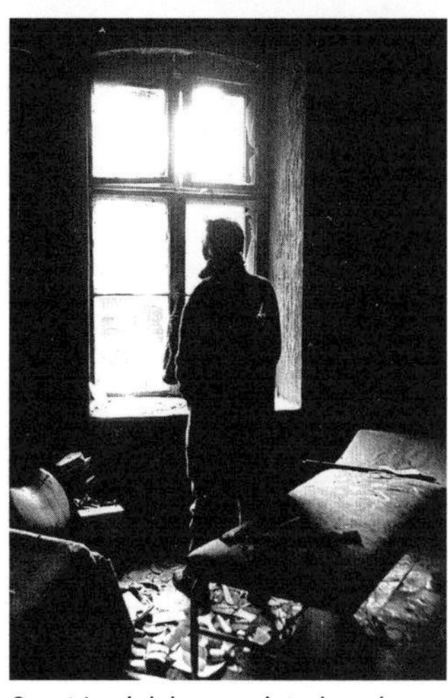

Geert Lovink in an evicted punk squat, West Berlin, December 1983

Both newspapers reported the sabotage of electricity poles taken down in protest against nuclear energy, wrote about anti-fascist attacks against extreme-right demonstrations, about Berlin riots on May 1, stolen NATO documents, tactics how to identify police infiltration, a press release about a burned down IKEA store, an attack on the Turkish consulate last Wednesday, the rise of right-wing neo-nazi parties, unemployment and the right to be lazy, on protests against Ronald Reagan, about the dire situation in Northern Ireland and Central America. What also united *Bluf!* and *Radikal* is the literary genre of the strategic contributions, published under pseudonyms, a mix of analytical essays and opinion pieces that all asked 'what is to be done?'. These were usually released in between large-scale events, following evictions and riots or in the build-up to demonstrations. The strategy paper tries to map a constellation of opinions and shared feelings about the state of the movement, and where to take it next.

It is easy to date the two magazines through their anti-aesthetic style: fast, rough, ugly, amateur-like, unfinished. The hasty sketches look rather childish, expressing a refusal to grow up; unlike the underground quasi-avant-garde styles of punk and New Wave, both of which had a strong presence in the movement, yet whose aesthetics never dominated. Punks were an identity sub-group, much like radical gays or lesbians. If anything, punk could be qualified as a deep, dark hippie style (in contrast to the trippy 1967 flower power aesthetics, stripped of its dream-like utopian layers, using typesetting and scissors, those final years before the arrival of DTP and Photoshop. The non-design was not used to convince a broad public or attract followers. Anger at society was real and did not have to be communicated. It was neither about the medium nor the message. What mattered were direct actions and the inevitable confrontation that followed.

Both magazines are aware of the 'technological revolution' that is about to start with the introduction of personal computers. Just listen to Abwärts' 1980 song *Computerstaat*. A 1984 position paper of the 'Revolutionary Cells' on the rise of unemployment, flexible contracts and the shortening of the work week speaks of 'cybernization, precaritization, forced labour' and the 'way to Silicon Valley'. The flip side of the welfare state-in-demise is a security state that channels its information flows through fibre-optic cables. The result is the transparent citizen who is powerless to hide secrets. The existing mainframe computers are not embraced as a liberating tool. Neither is the PC, which is dismissed as a not so independent 'terminal'.

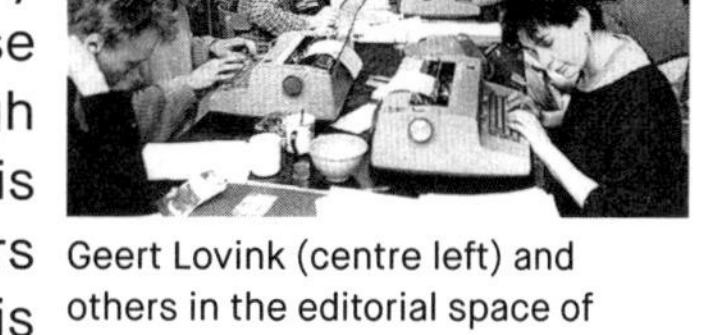
Geert Lovink (centre left) and others in the editorial space of the squatters' weekly *Bluf!*, Van Ostadestraat 233, Amsterdam, 1982

The strategy papers can also be read as contemplations on how to organize one's life. If the personal is political and vice versa, how to integrate all these desires and demands into one radical design?

A paradigmatic turning point in the long farewell to Marxist frameworks in the history of *Radikal* would be the publication of an interview that three members of the *Radikal* collective had with the French theorist Jean Baudrillard, who visited West-Berlin in late January 1984. Throughout the seventies, translations of Baudrillard's texts were published by Merwe Verlag in their infamous pocketbook series. In 1982, the intellectuals in Berlin were shell-shocked by the publication of the German edition of *Symbolic Exchange and Death*. A central theme of the edition was to outdo simulation and develop strategies for a movement beyond appropriation, reform and the spectacle of resistance. The title of the interview is 'Death of the Political Subject', following what *Radikal* had already discussed as the 'death of the movement' numerous times in 1982–1983. What was so shocking about Baudrillard's revelations? What is questioned is the primacy of the political subject that is in control, together with others, of the direction and destiny of the movement. Take out the political subject and what is left is objective, ironic moves in which the larger social entity ('the movement') is no longer in charge. The Düsseldorf band Fehlfarben's call to arms, played at so many demonstrations from loudspeakers on an audio truck, 'Keine Atempause, Geschichte wird gemacht, es geht voran' (No breathing space, history is being made, we're making progress), suddenly fell to pieces. The earlier insight of Michel Foucault, that there was only power, no counter-power, let alone 'Keine Macht für Niemand' (No power for no-one) was already problematic enough (yet still manageable). If there was no outside, then resistance would become an integral part of power. In that sense, power became omnipresent and impossible to tackle — hidden, even in the smallest of gestures, in words, sentences and subconscious moves. In reference to the 1979 revolution in Iran (and its backlash), Foucault had remarked on the 'impossibility of revolt'. The 1980–1981 riots in Zurich, Berlin, and Amsterdam, the militant protests against nuclear energy in West-Germany, France, and the Netherlands, had all proven that uprisings were all too real. But what if no one is in charge? What happens when a movement loses track, stagnates, yet doesn't know how to stop? In other words: how can we free ourselves from the historical obligation to continue forever? It was no coincidence that the central slogan of the Dutch squatters movement was: 'Kraken gaat door!' (Squatting continues) and that the international squatting symbol, based on the Indian sign for 'continue', came from Amsterdam. How can a movement otherwise deal with setbacks such as evictions of its strategic sites other than by announcing it will be back?[04] It will only return if it is able to regain its energy.

The interview with Baudrillard centres on the impossibility of continuity. Revolts occur and disappear, seemingly without consequence. The question of the media has not led to an answer as it only provides the possibility for an endless return of the same talking heads. Events do not need to be politically motivated in order to occur. Against the subject strategy Baudrillard proposes that we walk over to the other, to the object. How can resistance go faster than the speed of light, go slower than the absolute inertia of the barricade, the act to no longer move at all? The six-page transcript reads like a polite conversation that refuses to spark. The German radicals try hard to integrate the French discourse into their own but ultimately fail. The encounter ends with Baudrillard stating that it is 'all a question of immanence. Maybe I prefer to move around in an immanent world where I no longer have transcendental hopes and everything happens within the irony of an objective game. I understand, this may not be comforting...'[05]

The 'Baudrillard' issue nos. 126–127 appeared by the time that a long trial against two of the alleged *Radikal* publishers, Benny Härlin and Michael Klöckner, ended. The editorial group struggled with the dissolution of collective structures in the movement, an increased awareness of the simulacrum of 'media reality' that implicated the magazine itself and a desire to escape the logic of state repression. By early 1984, there was a growing awareness that the paper had become a myth of its own.

The question had already been posed by Michel Foucault when he stated that 'revolts are fireworks, launched in the darkness of power. The moment they light up they've vanished.'[06] What's the goal of (making) history? How can crowds obstruct the pitfalls of inevitable history as an endless cycle of hope and disillusion?

We should allow ourselves to be wiped out, remove the tracks after we've used them and see activism as the perfect crime. That was the 1984 question. How can a movement in decline,

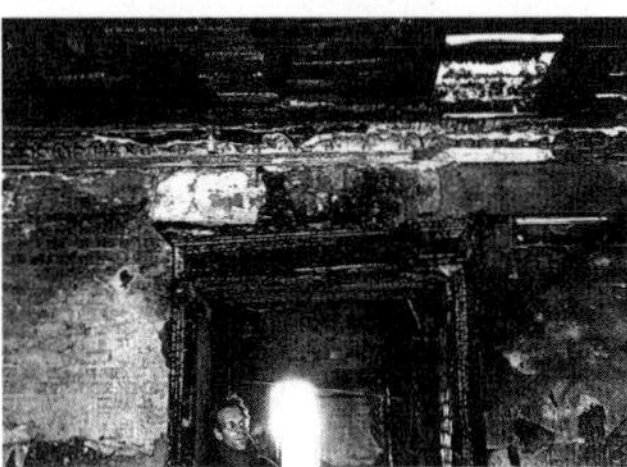

Geert Lovink in an evicted punk squat, West Berlin, December 1983

04

This is already the key issue of the April 1981 *Radikal* nos. 90–91 (subtitle: 'magazine against a controlled movement') with the headline 'Bewegung Kaputt?' In line with Elias Canetti's thesis in *Crowds and Power* (1960) we could say that the crowd grows fast and climaxes quickly, yet it takes a much longer time to disappear entirely. There is a consensus that the Berlin squatters movement disintegrated in 1983–1984 when parts were legalized and the remaining houses were evicted, without the possibility to squat new ones. A Wikipedia overview of all houses occupied in the first wave in West-Berlin (1980–1981) and the second wave in East-Berlin (1990) can be found here (in German): https://de.wikipedia.org/wiki/ Wikipedia:WikiProjekt_Autonome_ und_Hausbesetzer-Bewegung.

05

Radikal nos.126–127 (March/April 1984), p. 11.

06

Quoted in *Radikal* no. 100 (January 1982), p. 13, as part of an strategy papers entitled 'Standstill is the End of Movement' as part of the 'autonomy debate'.

having celebrated its events, its heroic moments of confrontation and lived episodes of subversion, disappear gracefully? How can we exit the stage before things get ugly and not repeat the mistakes of the 1968 generation that got caught up in factions, New Age escapism, ugly reformism and market fundamentalism? The fascination with the end is not morbid. It is a way to look for new beginnings. This is summarized in the slogan 'In the beginning there's the end, otherwise the new would be the old.'

Here we end this short treatise on the political metaphysics of (dis)appearance. *Bluf!* disappeared, after 6,5 years, in April 1988, closing itself rather than waiting for Dutch authorities to close it down as it had attempted to do one year earlier. Its closure happened after the Amsterdam squatters scene had itself fallen apart in violent struggles between the remaining wings.[07] *Bluf!* metamorphosed into various initiatives, one of them being the Ravijn publishing house. *Radikal*, on the other hand, ironically, failed in this respect. The magazine brand was passed on. After the famous court case in 1983–1984, numerous new editorial collectives took over but they lacked strong roots in a social movement. *Radikal* turned into an ideological tool within factions of the 'autonomous movements'.

Squatting is occupying space. It remains a powerful act. However, today's movements, if they want to be visible at all, will have to find ways to occupy time. It's only then that the question of disappearance can be addressed. How can we stretch time? Is the disruption of real-time regimes sufficient and what is the most effective approach? Is slow politics the only option? Maybe the creation of social movements is no longer a viable strategy in the twenty-first century. And if so, what do short-term revolts have to offer? Wouldn't that require a form of ultra-Leninism, coordinated by hyper-aware, well-prepared decisionist units, organized networks that take over the second a system collapses? If Blanquism 2.0[08] is conspiratorial and not our preferred option, then how could we otherwise instigate a radical change of time-space coordinates? Let's update Hakim Bey's Temporary Autonomous Zone for today to bring together space and time: the Occupied Temporality Networks.

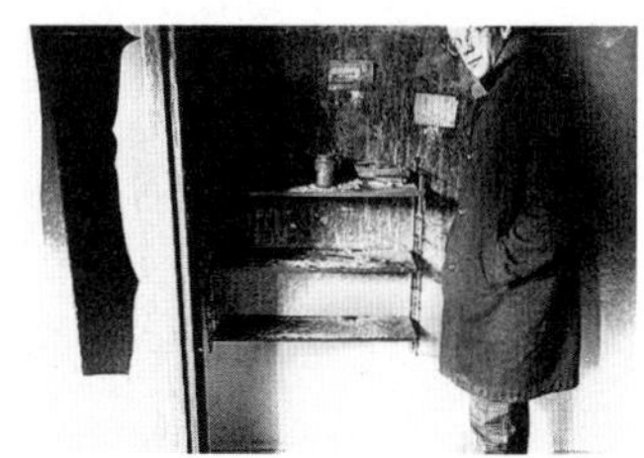

Geert Lovink in an evicted punk squat, West Berlin, December 1983

07
See the chapter 'Collapsing New Buildings' [Einstürzende Neubauten] in Adilkno, ed., *Cracking the Movement, Squatting the Media*, Brooklyn, NY: Autonomedia, 1994, pp. 185–229.

08
See: https://en.wikipedia.org/wiki/Blanquism. In this age of digital surveillance the rise of offline and extramedial conspiratorial cells seems inevitable. Blanquism does not believe in the theory of the revolutionary subject (such as the working class, the precariat, minorities etc.) as prime actor and acts in a secretive manner.

SOKAK

Merve Elveren and Erman Ata Uncu

The Turkish weekly magazine *Sokak* (Street), under chief-editor Tuğrul Eryılmaz, began with a dissident editorial policy that was an alternative to mainstream journalistic practices. A total of 32 issues were published, from August 1989 to April 1990. Reflecting the struggles of unrepresented and marginalized social groups during repressive post-coup times in its stories, *Sokak* was one of the first periodicals to offer space for the expression of identity politics in Turkey. With regard to its take on issues such as minorities, political convicts, or new developments in public space, the magazine stood apart from its left-leaning or socialdemocratic contemporaries, since its focus remained on the stories of individuals rather than on the relevant legal processes. An editorial team was employed in southeastern Turkey, which was a unique practice in the eighties. Thanks to the contributions made by this local team, *Sokak* managed to establish a distinctive tone that was manifest in such headlines as 'Dear judge, take me into custody: A woman's life in south-eastern Turkey' or 'There isn't one editor-in-chief that could survive (Kurdish magazines)'.

Frequently addressing LGBTQ individuals and feminists in its articles, *Sokak* was the first of its kind in the Turkish-language press to bring the issues of sexuality and gender into the public debate. In reports from Pürtelaş — an Istanbul neighbourhood where transgender sex workers were systematically subjected to police violence throughout the eighties — state violence, city planning and identity politics were bridged. Furthermore, lesbians, gays and feminists were frequently featured in the magazine in such news items as 'Up-rise of lesbian existence: As told by socialist-feminists' or 'Therapy for gays: Wish we had the same'.

The focus on new modes of public demonstration and on minority issues was in accordance with the magazine's overall humoristic approach, also evident in its layout. With a young readership in mind, *Sokak* fashioned a zine-like, DIY approach to design, supported by vignettes. These vignettes were used in each issue, and printed with references to the pressing topics of the day. For instance, during the presidential election campaigns of 1989, *Sokak* featured a sticker that read 'My candidate for presidency against all evil is Batman' with the picture of a half-naked male model wearing a Batman mask. Other vignettes included 'Stay 24' with a James Dean photograph, 'Turkey is a free land'

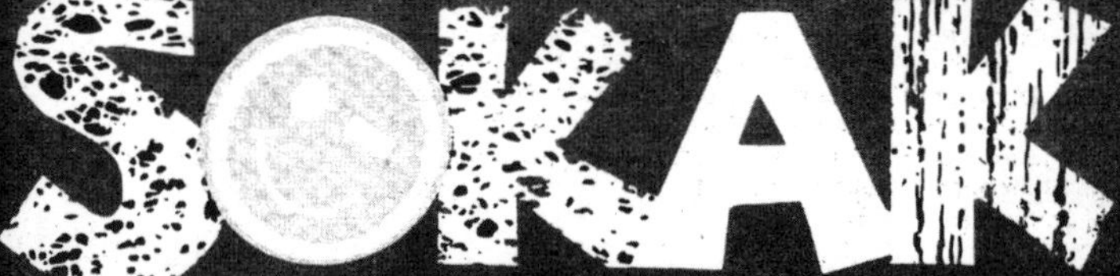

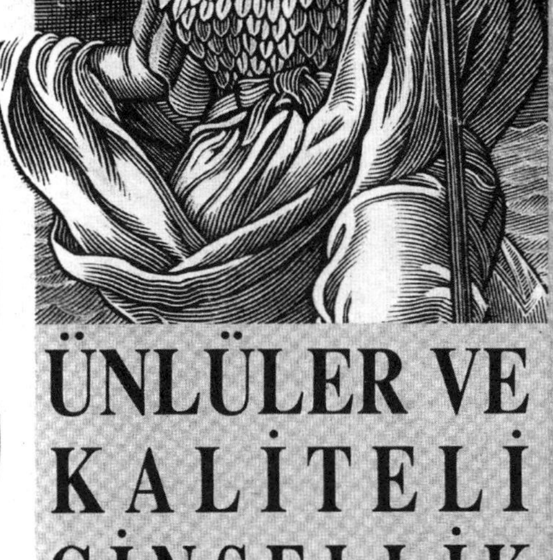

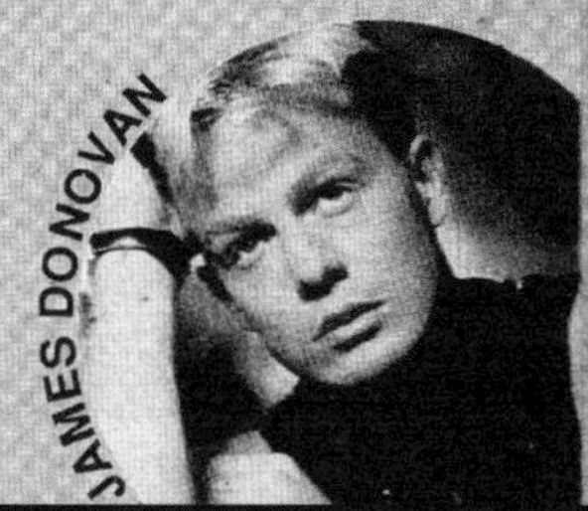

Sokak (Street) year 2, no. 11, 18–24 March 1990. Archive: Tuğrul Eryılmaz, Murat Öneş and Nilgün Öneş

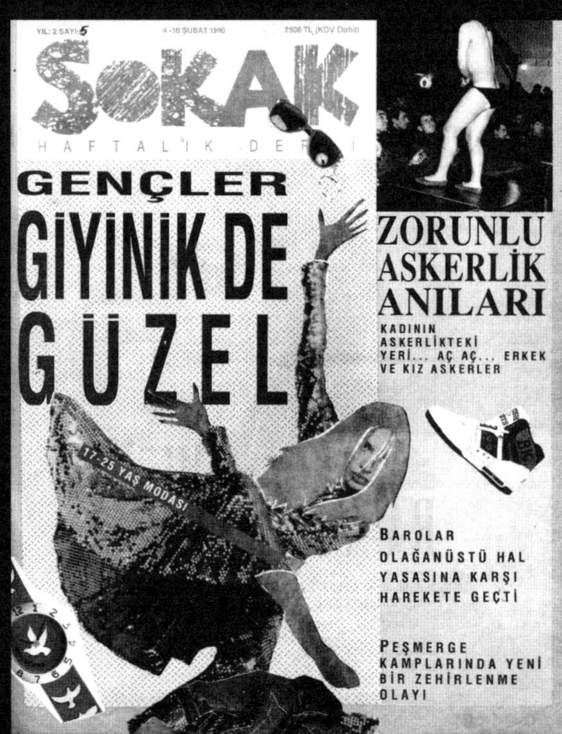

Sokak (Street) year 2, no. 5, 4–10 February 1990. Archive: Tuğrul Eryılmaz, Murat Öneş and Nilgün Öneş

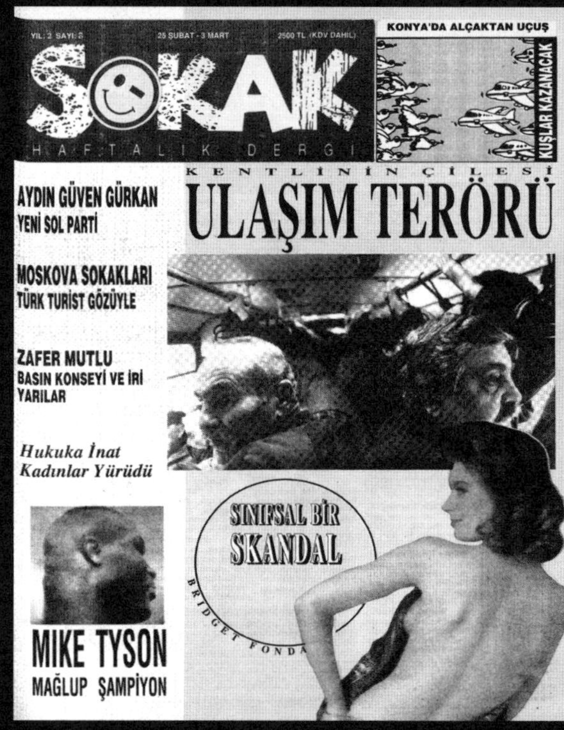

Sokak (Street) year 2, no. 8, 25 February–3 March 1990. Archive: Tuğrul Eryılmaz, Murat Öneş and Nilgün Öneş

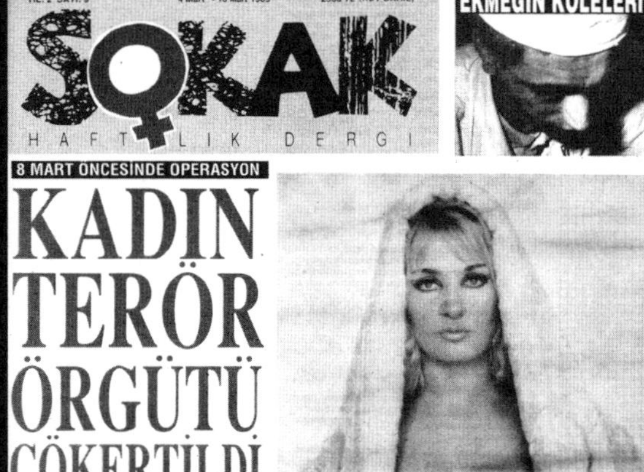
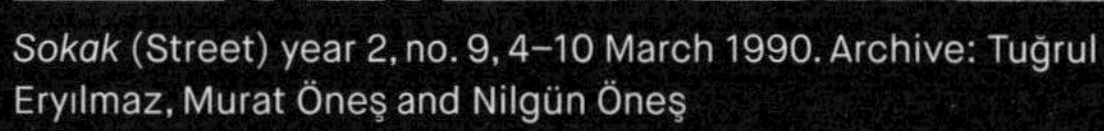

Sokak (Street) year 2, no. 9, 4–10 March 1990. Archive: Tuğrul Eryılmaz, Murat Öneş and Nilgün Öneş

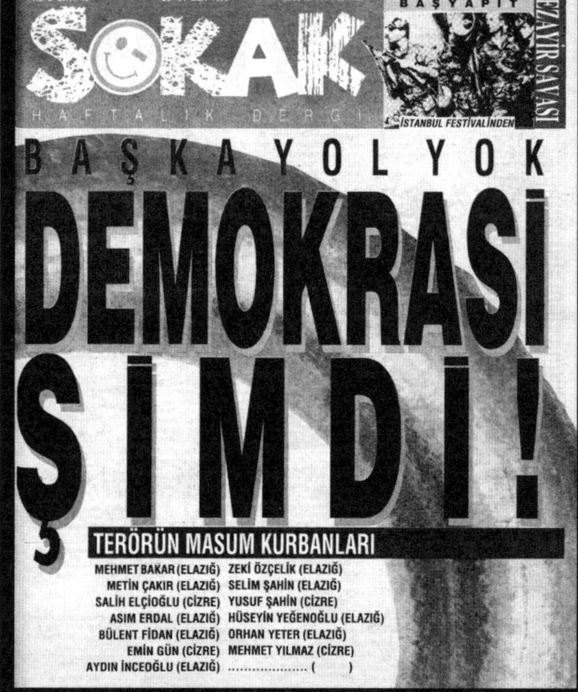

Sokak (Street) year 2, no. 12, 25–31 March 1990. Archive: Tuğrul Eryılmaz, Murat Öneş and Nilgün Öneş

on April Fools' Day, 'Don't tap my phone', and 'Romanian bear eats his own people, USA bear eats Panama' in December 1989.

Extensive use of humour was intended to attract younger readers. The goal of reaching younger people could also be discerned in the choice of subject matter. A good example is 'The University Board Game', featured in the October 1989 issue. Simulating a university student's first day at school, this board game gave such directions as 'The university is the property of the State. You are, too. If you do not agree, quit both this game and the university' or 'Have you ever considered begging? Or working as a prostitute, a gigolo?'

The magazine's young-adult-oriented editorial policy was also noticeable in its coverage of popular culture alongside political matters. Featuring pieces on rock stars, underground dance culture, or comics in addition to 'serious' issues such as feminism, minorities and political lawsuits, *Sokak* also paved the way for removing the distinction between high culture and subcultures in the Turkish-language press.

'A POLITICAL POSTER MUST BE LIKE A BLOW INTO AN OPEN WOUND'[01]

Ana Mizerit

The now legendary case of the notorious project that addressed the public sphere and caused a collision between the ruling ideology and an artistic statement, was the 1987 action of New Collectivism (Novi kolektivizem, NK), the propaganda department of the art collective Neue Slowenische Kunst (NSK), now known as the 'Poster Scandal'. The conflict, which grew into a political scandal, was successful thanks to mimicry intensified by suggestive provocation and shock. The case is considered a classic example of NSK's artistic strategy, not without parallels in the newly-founded civil movements of the eighties.

The crucial difference lies in how NSK reflected the situation. Instead of open opposition and attack they employed an apparently affirmative strategy without apparent critical distance, which Slavoj Žižek described with the concept of over-identification. They did internalize the language of the regime with excessive engagement, which, in the case of NSK, showed as being over-bureaucratic, over-national, and over-totalitarian.

Like the other NSK groups, New Collectivism employed the retro method, i.e. eclectically tapping into various spaces and times, which resulted in a newly constructed montage of *partial* objects with radically provocative and also contradictory contents while maintaining the ambiguity of (not) understanding images. This same strategy was used in the notorious political 'Poster Scandal', which became an example of a battle that the Slovene alternative scene fought against the state, and won. New Collectivism chose an image of repeating a trauma to respond to the annual repetition of the Youth Day festival, a celebration aimed at perpetuating the myth of the unity of young generations as the future mainstay of socialist welfare in Yugoslavia.

The proposal that won the anonymous competition for the Youth Day poster was submitted by Studio NK/New Collectivism and was in reality a remake of *The Third Reich: Allegory of Heroism*, a painting by Richard Klein, one of the favourite artists of the Nazi regime. The only elements that were changed in the image of an archetypal Aryan hero were the symbols: the German eagle was replaced with a dove of peace, the Nazi flag with a Yugoslav one,

01

One of the New Collectivism's statements in response to the attacks because of the Youth Day poster, written in 1987 on the Proclamation (Razglas) poster, issued after the poster scandal as an explanation of their strategy and actions.

the torch with a relay baton, while the typography used was the same as that in the newspaper *Slovenski poročevalec* published on the day of the liberation of Ljubljana at the end of the Second World War. The committee of the Union of Socialist Youth of Slovenia (ZSMS) sent the poster to Belgrade, where the celebration was to take place. Not long after that, one of the leading Yugoslav newspapers published an article describing the surprising similarity with the Nazi poster noticed by a member of the public. What followed was political hysteria, media lynching, police interrogations, and criminal charges, which were subsequently dropped. The members of New Collectivism defended themselves with a term they coined themselves, the retro-garde as an artistic creative approach.

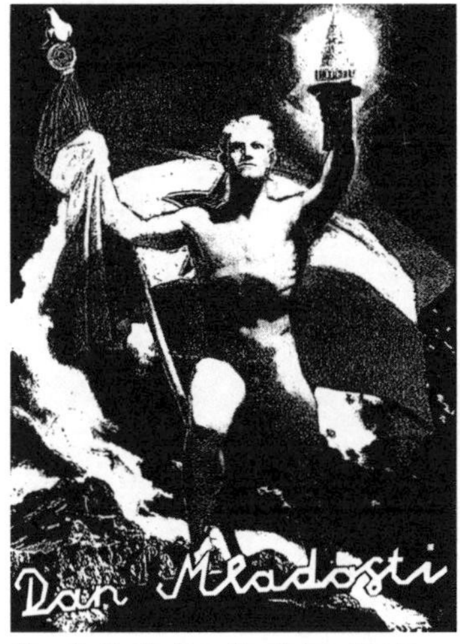

New Collectivism, *Youth Day Poster*, 1987

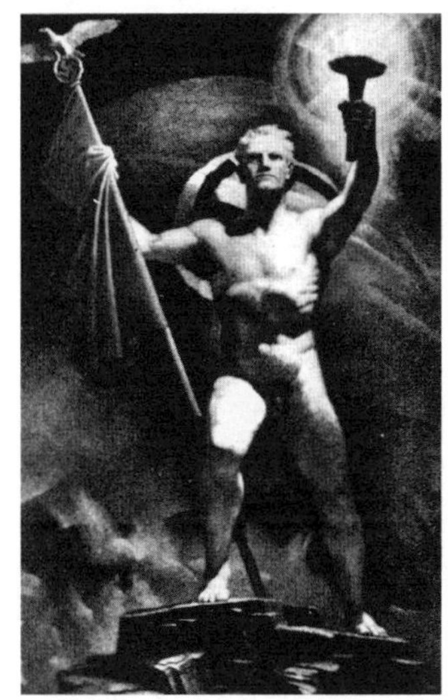

Richard Klein, *The Third Reich: Allegory of Heroism*, 1936

The artistic action became really effective with this disclosure, since the accusations against New Collectivism demonstrated the evident unease of the Communist Party, which, by choosing New Collectivism's poster as the most appropriate one, showed that it was what it chose. Indeed, even more so: the Party became an 'external collaborator' of sorts by directly contributing to the end result. Although the poster was never printed as intended, the scandal was so far-reaching that the poster ended up being reproduced in millions of copies of newspapers. This, in a way, completed the mission of the poster both in terms of its mass production and public access. The calls to abolish the Youth Day festival, first heard in Slovenia in the mid-eighties, were heeded; after 43 years, Youth Day saw its last celebration that year.

Ко је и због чега наиван

● Руководство омладине Словеније повлачи плакат, али одбија оцене о смишљеном потезу и наводној акцији против Штафете младости

(Љубљана, 1. марта) — Овде се после подне састао Секретаријат Председништва Републичке конференције ССО Словеније да би још једном размотрио ситуацију која је настала након открића неких југословенских листова да је предложени плакат за Дан младости плагијат плаката својевремено израђеног у нацистичкој Немачкој.

Као што је познато синоћ је Председништво Републичке конференције ССО Словеније одлучило да се плакат повуче, а Секретаријат се данас само још договорио о томе на који начин и какве ставове заступати на састанцима ко-

ЗА СВАКУ ОСУДУ

Бележимо два мишљења из Марибора. — Чрт Месарич, председник Градске конференције ССРН, каже:

— То је увреда за Словенију и за све напредне и поштене Словенце. Срамота је да се тако нешто догоди, да се једна ликовна група може тако да понаша. Такво понашање и такав плакат доприносу заустављању процеса демократије. На овај начин ни у ком случају не може се говорити о демократизацији друштва, не може се говорити о оправданости таквих мишљења и размишљања, јер нормалан и поштен човек, Словенац, грађанин Словеније и Југославије, радник, самоуправљач, сигурно тако не размишља. Овакав плакат је за сваку осуду, нанео је велику штету Словенији и Словенцима, свима нама у Југославији.

Матија Гјеркиш, секретар Међуопштинског комитета СК Марибора:

— Кад сам чуо за овај плакат, видео га на телевизији, морам рећи да је то за мене био прави шок. То је срамота, то је нешто чега би се требало стидети сви поштени Словенци. Изјава из штаба ССО Словеније, односно првог председника, била је исувише шкрта, и ми тиме не можемо бити задовољни. Чудно је да ликовна група која је радила на том плакату може једноставно мимо свих да ради шта хоће, да пласира своје „болесне" идеје за Дан младости, да их нуди Словенцима, целој Југославији. Сада је питање како и шта урадити да „поправимо" ову срамоту међу свим народима Југославије.

С. Ф.

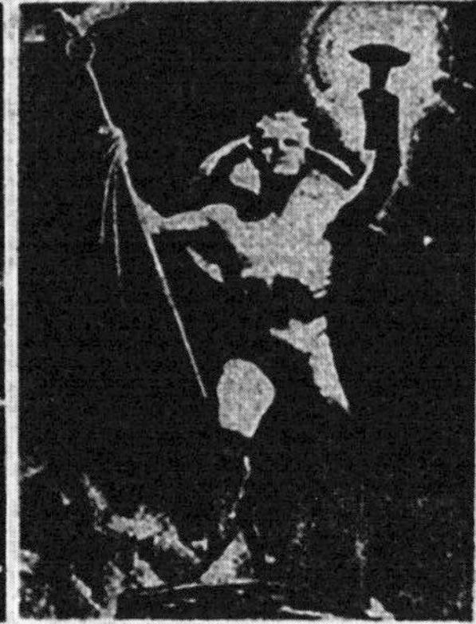

ПОЗАДИНА ЈЕДНЕ НАМЕРЕ: Усвојени плакат за Дан младости и репродукција дела Рихарда Клајна „Трећи Рајх"

ји ће се сутра и прекосутра одржати у Савезној конференцији ССОЈ у Београду.

У синоћној расправи је потврђено да је напрт плаката заиста настао из поменуте подлоге, али су одбачене оцене и инсинуаци-
је да се ради о некаквом „новом фашизму" и неодговорном односу према Дану младости и Штафети. Посебна пажња била је посвећена „квалитету" који је почео да окружује омладинску организацију Словеније: „стално је неко напа-
да и оптужује најтежим квалификацијама, па је стално у позицији да се брани. Тако је, рецимо, на синоћној седници руководилац Марксистичког центра РК ССО Словеније

НАСТАВАК НА 2. СТРАНИ

Clipping from *Borba*, 2 March 1987

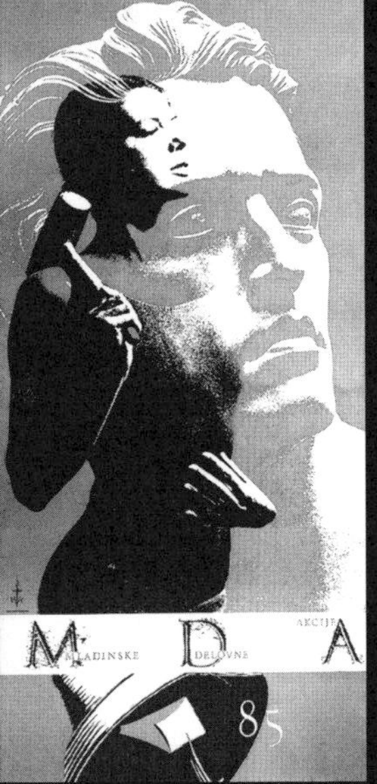

Neue Kunsthandlung / New Collectivism, *Youth Work Brigades*, 1984, poster, offset, 150×68 cm

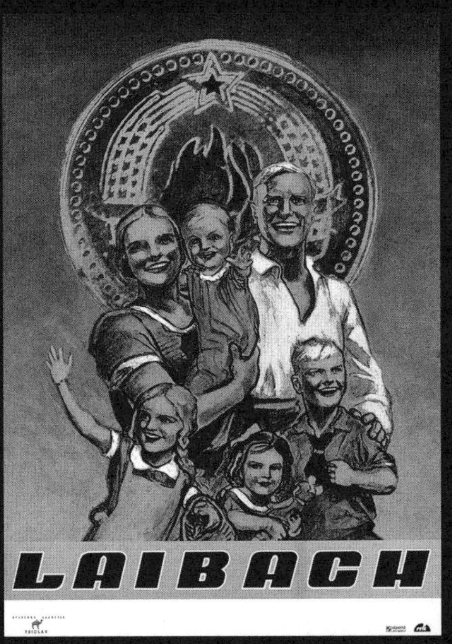

New Collectivism, *Sympathy for the Devil*, 1989, poster, offset, 93×67 cm

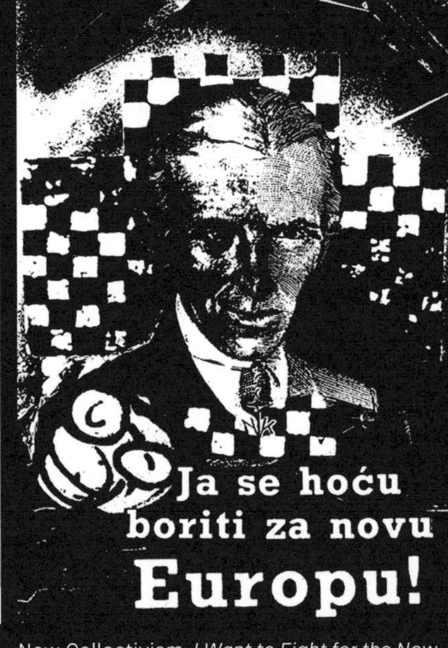

New Collectivism, *I Want to Fight for the New Europe*, 1991, war poster, silkscreen, 100×70 cm

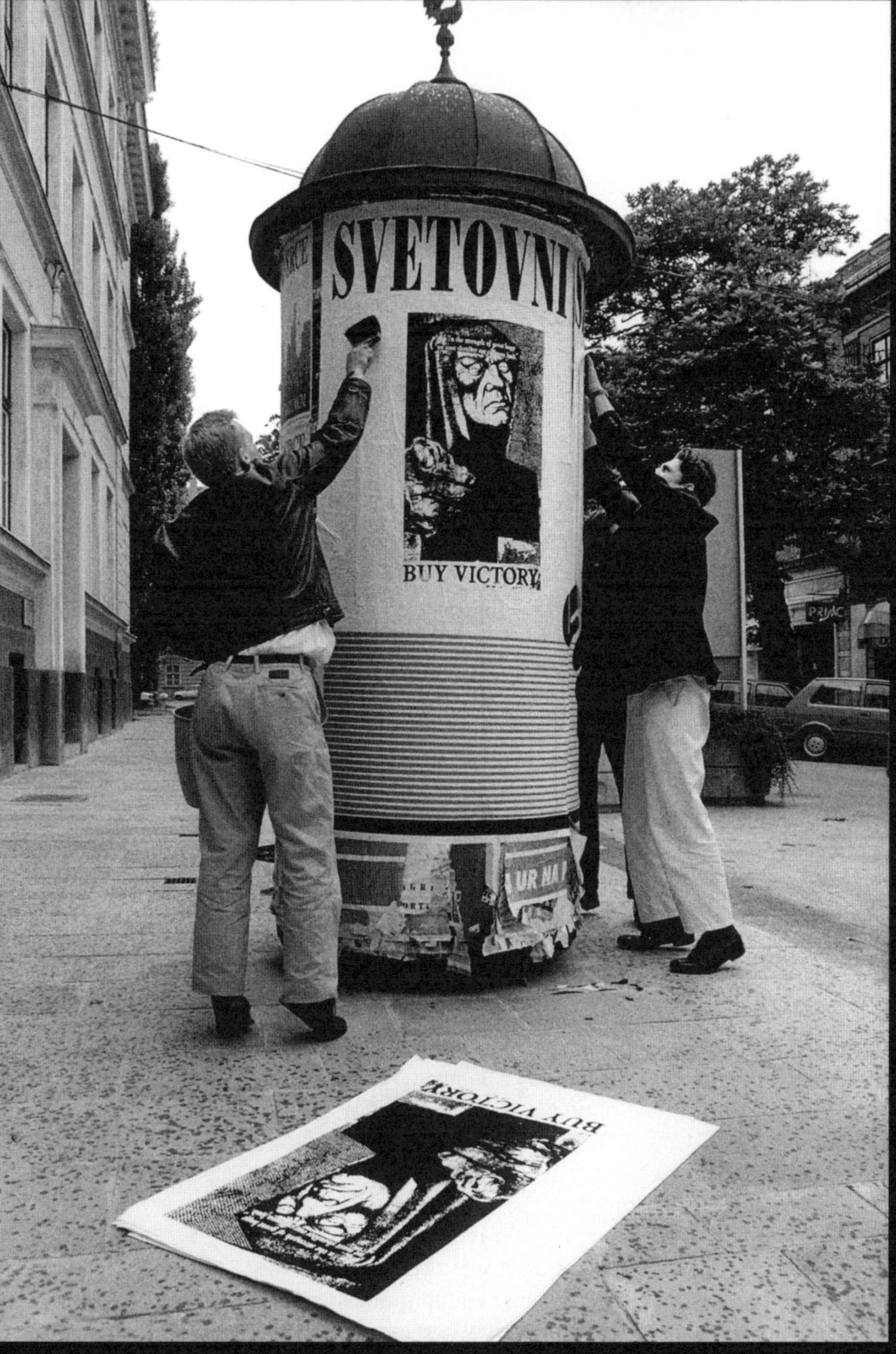

New Collectivism, war posters action during the Ten-Day War in Slovenia, 28 June 1991.
Photo: Barbara Čeferin

CLUB MORAL
MORAL AND MENTAL IN ANTWERP

Anders Kreuger

> Mental rotation.
> Depth versus the picture-plane.
> Naive versus sophisticated.
> Mental folding.
> Time versus distance.
> Spatial cognition.
> Anne-Mie Van Kerckhoven in *Force Mental rvstd* 12 (1985) [01]

Back in 1981, the two young Antwerp-based artists Anne-Mie Van Kerckhoven (AMVK, b. 1951) and Danny Devos (DDV, b. 1959) opened a space for concerts, exhibitions and other collective events in a factory building in the Borgerhout area. Run by and with and for artists, Club Moral functioned as a physical space until 1993. It championed hard-edge aesthetics and shock-and-awe politics, flash-lighting some of the darkness that enveloped polite society in the Catholic Low Countries at the time — and perhaps still does. Nowadays, Club Moral is the brand name for the activities that the two artists, who also live together, undertake jointly, primarily concerts.

In 1982, AMVK and DDV also founded *Force Mental*, a magazine 'for excesses of all kinds'. They explicitly stated that they would publish 'extreme expressions of all persuasions' although 'the ideology doesn't have to be ours'. Fifteen issues were printed until 1988, and a 16th issue appeared online in 2005. A facsimile edition of these 602 pages of text and image, for which AMVK's graphic design is a unifying and electrifying constant, was released in 2010 under the title *Force Mental rvstd*.

For readers today, *Force Mental* is a remainder of vintage Club Moral, but also a reminder that the dilemma at the heart of this two-faced endeavour is more intractable than ever. The 'soft mainstream' of the left-wing seventies is comparable to that of the liberal twenty-tens. To break out of demoralizing compromise with the predominant order, we must take a radical mental stance against business-as-usual, however attractive it may seem from the point of view of peace and mutual understanding. To avoid the degradation of revolutionary or reactionary violence, we must take a radical moral stance against extremism, however attractive it may

01

'Ons feuilleton, episode nr. 12', in *Force Mental rvstd*, ed. Danny Devos and Anne-Mie Van Kerckhoven (Antwerp: Club Moral, 2010), p. 379.

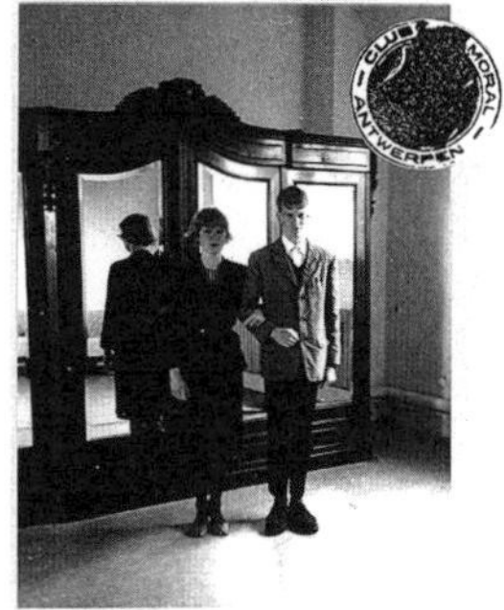

Anne-Mie Van Kerckhoven and Danny Devos, 1981.
Photo: Geli Weyler

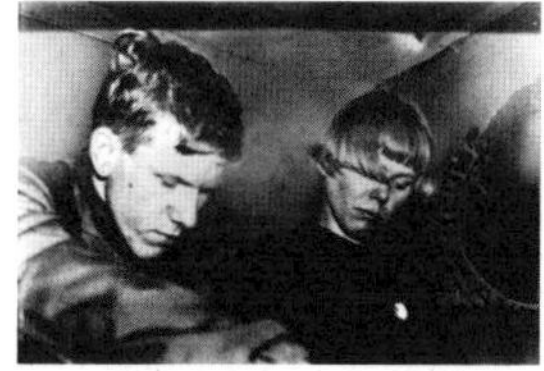

Club Moral performing, 1984.
Photo: Frank Heirman

seem from the point of view of political and aesthetic expediency.

But when is our critique more radical? When we place extreme and provocative phenomena within explanatory (and therefore necessarily ideological) frames? Or when we present them as uncommented cut-outs from contemporary life? Whichever route we choose, we must always be attentive to detail: aesthetically and politically, morally and mentally.

AMVK had been involved with the three first issues of the journal *Data*, supported by the Universitaire Instelling Antwerpen (a predecessor of Antwerp University). DDV joined her for the fourth issue. It was to be independently financed and dedicated to the 'New Right', with, among other things, a contribution by William Bennett, who founded the band Whitehouse in London in 1979 and claimed to be playing 'the most violent music of the New Right'. After missing the deadline, Bennett submitted a text written as a cut-up paraphrase of a manifesto from Britain's National Front — possibly to critique himself and others, more probably driven by an urge for aestheticized political provocation that was very much 'in the air'. *Data* had folded in the meantime. AMVK and DDV founded their own journal instead.

In *Force Mental* no. 10, 1984, DDV wrote:

June 1982, the first issue is out. Out of interest, and loyalty to Bennett, his piece 'The Struggle for a New Musical Culture' is published, although with an editor's note: 'This article is written for *Data*, a magazine that would have had as its 1st theme: New Right.' Only a few days after the outcome of *Force Mental* 1, the reactions turn loose: Scandal! Club Moral publishes a pamphlet by the National Front, they support the New Right organizations.[02]

AMVK and DDV possibly valued the catharsis of calamity over the comfort of commentary and consistency. This was probably a mistake. They were judged for it, but they persisted with their deliberately jarring activities, together and in their separate careers, and have won over many of their initial detractors — precisely through their uncompromising, self-consuming radical criticality. The work of these two artists constitutes an ongoing revolutionary transgression against the 'politeness' of a society whose very identity is that it has consistently resisted reform.

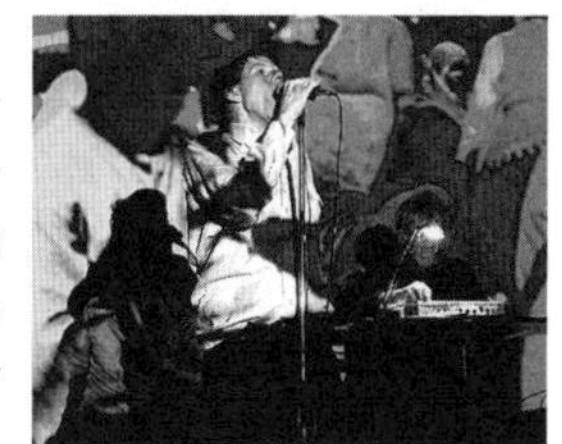

Club Moral performing, 2010
Photo: Christine Clinckx

02

Ibid., p. 306 (the English has not been edited.)

1984: THE ADVENTURES OF THE ALTERNATIVE

Jelena Vesić and Vladimir Jerić Vlidi

After 'post-truth' being The Word of the Year 2016, the 2017 arrival of 'alternative facts' comes as the natural element, as another corresponding 'alt' product of what wants to be called 'alt-right'. This is expected — normal — continuation of the process through which the very concept of 'alternative' seems to be appropriated and twisted beyond recognition, to outline today *precisely this one worldview that does not allow for any alternative than itself*. The debate on the trajectory of 'alternative' towards 'alt-' is mostly concerned with examining the role of the rising power, sophistication and 'uncontrollability' of media, and with the sense of diminishing ability of formal democracies to address this, or any other problem.

The process of deconstructing alternative was similar to what happened with words such as *avant-garde, revolution, modernism*, and many others that used to be the building blocks of so-called 'grand narratives' of (mainly) the previous century and. This path would indeed be outlined by media, especially television, and by various different 'happenings of the people', both a late remnant of an avant-gardist 'totalitarian dream' of synchronizing society in the joint motion forward, and an early reminiscent of the 'alt-' sentiment of today.

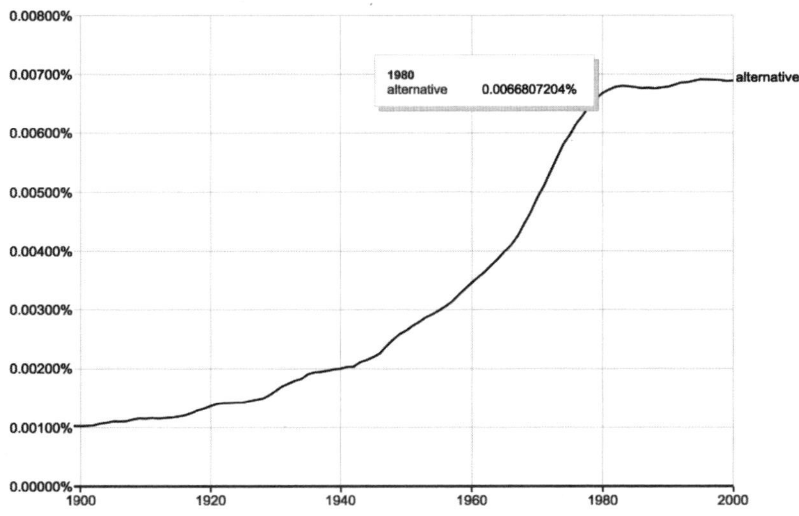

Graph: Google Ngram Viewer: [alternative], 1900–2008 in English, goo.gl/JMCgUB

ALTERNATIVE EIGHTIES

It is not hard to locate the arrival of the Alternative to the global stage at the very beginning of eighties (NGram). The changes brought by the shiny and colourful decade had a dazzling effect;

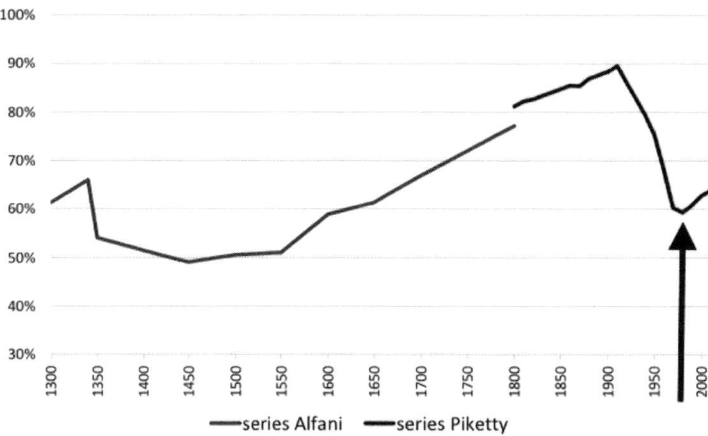

Guido Alfani, 'The Top Rich in Europe in the Long Run of History (1300 to Present Day)', 15 February 2017, VoxEU.org, http://voxeu.org/article/europe-s-rich-1300

after observing the media spectacle of entertainers acting as politicians and society turned into an exposition of lifestyle, everything from the seventies backwards appears as dull, grey, or explicitly in black-and-white, as the washed-out image distant from any meaning it may re-acquire today.

The first of the paradoxes that came as the integral part of 'alternative turn' was its ability to operate as 'non-ideological ideology'. The term came with internal contradictions already built-in; the Alternative as presented by Reagan and Thatcher was construed as the vessel to introduce the 'impossible' blend of religion and opportunism, a neoconservative ideology enwrapped in the principles of neoliberal market (de)regulation (the contradiction of using *neo* and *liberal* in regard to *capitalism* being another element of inverse logic of this construction). But the 'great communicators' themselves added the additional layer of opaqueness (deregulating the very sense of meaning), by communicating 'alternative' in negative or paralogical terms (e.g. as Thatcher's 'no alternative', or Reagan's 'the only alternative').

Over time, similarly to the effect observed in politics where the rejection of the firm and fixed idea of political left brought to the fore the relative and 'pragmatic' but futile concept of the 'the left of centre', those Alternatives that prevailed abandoned the visionary (and 'obsessively elaborated') ideas of avant-garde in favour of positioning themselves always relative to a concrete situation. But once there had been other options; some specific political and economic circumstances would produce the autonomous and 'alternative' alternatives, characterized by their meta-position of being alternatives both to the own social constellation and their global inspirations.

'The death of Ian Curtis, the death of Joseph Broz Tito, and the death of Yugoslavia.' — Laibach on what triggered their artistic activities in eighties.[01]

The eighties began: in the West, Reagan and Thatcher were 'born'; in Yugoslavia, Tito died. The sentiments had to be different, but what these events had in common was their motion towards the search for alternatives, about to acquire an unmatched speed, or, with all implications of the word, an *acceleration*. The tranquil 'End of History' soon to be (semi)enthusiastically announced in the West in Yugoslavia and elsewhere would result in another painful and devastating 'birth of history' (which, seemingly, 'had no alternative').[02]

One of the distinct phenomena in Yugoslavia to mark the seventies transitioning towards the eighties, and (neo)avant-garde giving way to alternative could be found in the specific use of mass media. The formation and the subsequent popularity of the eighties alternative scene gravitated around the emergence of the New Wave, a complex cultural phenomenon heralded by the Yugoslav music scene involving design, photography, theatre, magazines and the ultimate form of video. As the computer expert and writer Bruno Jakić underlines, Yugoslav local subcultures were 'more than a mere emulation of their Western analogues'. He defines the New Wave scene as the blend of 'social critique, music, and arts with the occasional use of home computers', establishing the analogies between the alternative and subcultures ('distinct subculture of meetings, radio shows, music, and parties').[03] Alternatives were using the same infrastructure as (neo)avant-gardes before them; most of the bands, artists, writers and other participants of the New Wave emerged trough the cultural centres, festivals, youth and students clubs and journals that were developed during the seventies (or after 1968) under the principles of 'democratization of art', 'artistic/academic autonomy', 'new art practices' and '(workers) self-management'.[04]

CURATING TV: 'RADICAL (CON)TEMPORALITY' OF TV GALERIJA

One of the paradigmatic figures to bring the principles of 'democratization of art' to the mass media was Dunja Blažević, whose work in the context of Yugoslavia and more specifically in the context of Belgrade was already symbolic for her experiments in the field later to be recognized as curating (at the time, by its very actors it was termed as 'applied critique', signifying a different

01

Vinko Peršić, 'Laibach: Mi smo SS masovne, popularne kulture' ('Laibach: We are the SS troopers of mass, popular culture'), *Novi List* 15 August 2011, www.novilist.hr/Scena/Glazba/Laibach-Mi-smo-SS-masovne-popularne-kulture.

02

The alliance of what would be probably recognized today as 'single-issue' activist groups (dedicated to human rights, gay rights, ecology, or peace activism, etc) that grew to become the political force to formally trigger the process of the dissolution of Yugoslavia emerged in Slovenia in the early eighties around the *Mladina* (Youth) political weekly and Radio Študent (both financed by the State). It was known as 'Alternative', frequently written with a capital A.

03

Bruno Jakić, 'Galaxy and the New Wave: Yugoslav Computer Culture in the 1980s', in *Hacking Europe: From Computer Cultures to Demoscenes*, ed. by Gerard Alberts and Ruth Oldenziel (London: Springer, 2014), pp. 107–128.

04

More in Branislav Jakovljević, *Alienation Effects: Performance and Self-Management in Yugoslavia, 1945–91* (Ann Arbor: University of Michigan Press, 2016).

approach to exhibition practice and showing art). She arrived at the scene in the early seventies as the editor of the visual arts programme of Belgrade's Students Cultural Centre (SKC) — the institution established as a result of 1968 as an 'institution-movement' — and created a platform for development of New Art Practices and rethinking their links with historical avant-gardes.[05]

In the early eighties Blažević turned to television. While terrestrial television in the West was just past its recent peak and had recorded the most watched terrestrial broadcasts ever—and was already starting to give way to various more competitive and personalized offerings from cable TV providers, thus shifting the power and the control over programming to marketing depart-ments—television in Yugoslavia was still viewed and operated as a public asset controlled by policies and editors. TV Belgrade being at the time the only TV station in Serbia, Blažević's editorial work at the *Other Art* show [06] presented the possibility of intro-ducing the attitudes and ideas of artistic (and political) avant-gardes to the widest audiences possible.

In 1984 Blažević continued with the unique television format of *TV Galerija* (TV Gallery). Consisting of discussions and interviews, reportage, artworks and movies and especially of the growing form and format of video, it was broadcasted monthly until 1991 to produce around 90 shows (only about 20 have been discovered in the archives so far). Frequently referencing Gerry Schum and his *TV Gallery* as a pioneering project in the field of curating media,[07] Blažević did not repeat his conceptual approach to 'curating TV'; in line with her affiliations with engaged art she would rather use television as a kind of 'pedagogical enterprise':

> ... I started presenting the videos — first it were only excerpts of the various video works and I acted as some sort of a presenter-pedagogue. ... As our programme was running for years and gained its own audience, I started playing ever longer segments, because people had already been used to video, and I could play integral pieces. In the end, I cut out the introduction altogether, because I thought that the audience already had the required knowledge. Then I started the production with the artists.[08]

Blažević was able to present the show on art (and around art) on the national TV network with a degree of artistic autonomy in using the mass media that remains as the rare exception from the rule and a thing that was then, as it would be now, 'impossible'. As the sovereign author of the programme she was independent in choosing the topics and the guests. Importantly, by strategically negotiating a slot at the very end of the late-night

05

See: Prelom kolektiv, 'The Case of Students Cultural Centre in 1970s', www.prelomkolektiv. org/eng.PPYUart.htm. Interview with Dunja Blažević, 'SKC and New Cultural Practices', in *SKC and Political Practices of Art*, ed. Prelom Kolektiv, pp. 81–84, www. prelomkolektiv.org/pdf/catalogue. pdf.

06

Perhaps the very name of the show referenced the influential concept of the Other Line of Yugoslav art by Ješa Denegri, art theorist and critic and a frequent guest of the show — the hypothesis recognizes the art that represents *the continuum of breaks* from some of the ever dominant 'bourgeois' artistic tendencies.

07

'The TV gallery only exists in a series of TV transmissions, that means TV Gallery is more or less a mental institution, which comes only into real existence in the moment of transmission by TV.' Gerry Schum in a letter to Gene Youngblood, 1969, www.eai.org/ supporting-documents/837.

08

Interview with Dunja Blažević (WHW/kuda.org/SCCA/pro.ba), *Political Practices of (Post)-Yugoslav Art: Retrospective 01*, ed. by Jelena Vesić and Zorana Dojić (Belgrade: Prelom kolektiv, 2010), p. 160.

umbrella show, she did not have to conform the content to strict programming, and the exact duration of the broadcast would depend on if the guests or the host decided to enter into longer discussions, or if it was decided to present longer footage.

Another part of the strategy was to address the problem of 'mass' in mass media: the possibility of *TV Galerija* having too low a rating for national TV coverage and being seen as bourgeois-elitist (in the then dominant rhetoric of socialism) or non-sustainable (in the contemporary rhetoric of capitalism). Referencing both the existing (the current socialist policies) and the new (the emerging language of civil society), Blažević claimed the neo-avant-garde art community to be a 'cultural minority' which, as all other recognized minorities at the time, was guaranteed its right to public expression. This change in articulation perhaps most clearly reflected the shift from the avant-gardist topics of engaged art, of radical democratization and frontality, characteristic for the art of the seventies, to the problematic of minorities and of 'rights-based' social activism, more characteristic for the alternative politics of proto-civil society of eighties, that would emerge in the full sense only with post-socialism, with the end of Yugoslavia and the rise and professionalization of the civil democracies in the newly-formed nation states.[09]

The sentiment of the times is probably best explained by one of the actors of Yugoslavia's alternative scene of the eighties, Rastko Močnik, who in his recapitulation concludes that alternatives were entrapped in the vain hope that opening the new political horizons would not undo the achievements of the past, and by the same stroke capture the future in the perpetual present:

> The structures such as [social] welfare state, public education and similar are being preserved through the permanent class struggle, and are not achievements that could be considered as 'this Is what we made so far and we can only progress further'. That was my attitude towards socialism in the 1980s, and it was very wrong, I would say. My colleagues and I … were thinking further, about what should come next, about freedom of expression, freedom of association, how to prevent the bureaucratization of self-management, about personal and cultural issues, and so on. That was how the 1980s went — the worse it was getting with economy, the better it was with human rights.[10]

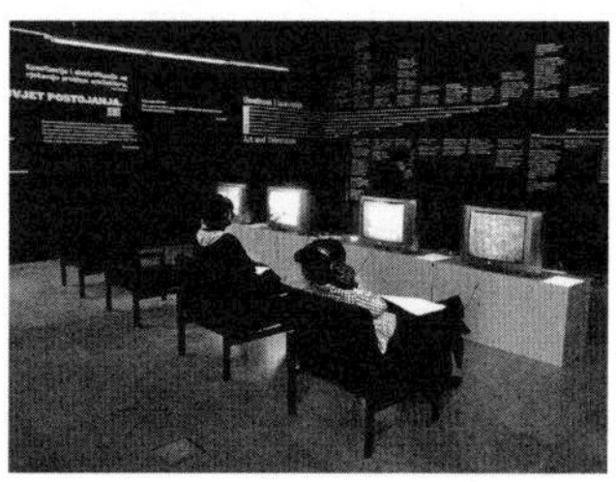

New Media Center_kuda.org, *TV Galerija* (TV Gallery), 'Political Practices of (Post-)Yugoslav Art: Retrospective 01', Museum of Yugoslav History, Belgrade, 29 November–31 December 2009, video archive. Photo: Vlidi

09
For further analysis of the causal connections between the minority politics, new social movements and Alternatives overarched by the concept of 'radical democracy' (Laclau, Mouffe) and gradual rejection of socialist politics and class-based political struggle, see: Ozren Pupovac, 'Springtime for Hegemony: Laclau and Mouffe with Janez Janša', *Prelom* 8/9 (2006), pp. 115–136. In this study, Pupovac also underlines (using the Yugoslav, or more precisely Slovenian example) how heterogeneous political subjectivity of 'civil society'/radical democracy of the eighties that led to the end of socialism and establishing of capitalist democracies in former Eastern Europe and former Yugoslavia has been resolved in reaching the homogenous nationalist consciousness ever since the nineties.

10
Jelena Vesić and Vladimir Jerić Vlidi, interview with Slovenian sociologist, theorist and political activist Rastko Močnik, 'There is No Theory without the Practice of Confrontation', *Red Thread Issue* 4 (2017) http://red-thread.org/en/article.asp?a=75.

ALT-COEXISTENCE OF ALTERNATIVES — TV GALERIJA VS. DYNASTY

The same year the *TV Galerije* was launched and after considerable (public) discussion on the values of such Western TV programmes displaying the opulence and banality of the rich, involving both the warnings it would 'corrupt socialism' and enthusiastic letters by the audience to the editors asking for the show, in mid-1984 Radio Television Belgrade started broadcasting the famous American soap-opera *Dynasty*, which became so popular it was 'emptying the streets'. The imagery of 'capitalism that never was' in the West would get to shape the 'capitalism to be' in many post-socialist countries, including Yugoslavia. Soon after, the TV offering was about to expand to broadcasting spectacular populist speeches by various 'larger than life' characters complemented by the endless production of national and historical mythology, opening the space towards the nineties for the equally endless row of TV prophets, 'teleshops', the explosion of lifestyle and celebrities, leading to the never-ending era of soap operas and *reality politics* of the two-thousands. This is probably common for many other cultural alternatives of eighties: in the era of 'new mysticism' to come, (following its own avant-gardist tendency) art was being ever more demystified. But in 1984, the Alternative was (still) promising a world in which both *TV Galerija* and *Dynasty* can and will exist side by side.

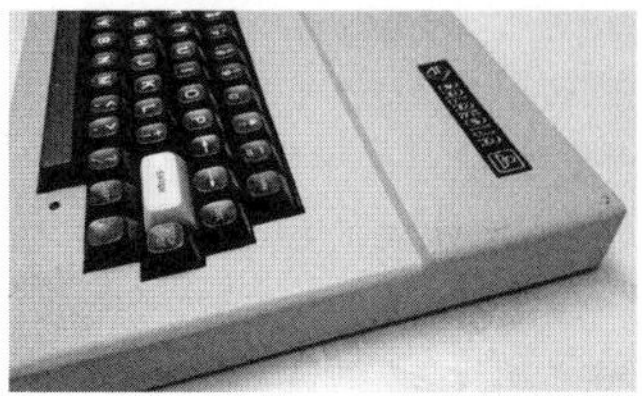

Galaksija computer (from the collection of Voja Antonić, 2017). Photo: Vlidi

HERE'S THE ALTERNATIVE: NO PATENTS, NO COPYRIGHT

At the very end of 1983 and the beginning of 1984, the famous Apple 'Big Brother' ad announced several great transformations. This, unlike most of the other alternative motions of the decade, was a campaign against the Old Corporations and only indirectly implicated the State. In what today reads as a cynical anecdote, Apple made the move on behalf of the people against the massive corporate force of IBM, because of 'intrusion of privacy'.[11] In the spectacular commercial, directed by Ridley Scott, the smashing of the central screen by the young hammer-wielding heroine liberates the technology and puts it at the disposal of the people stuck in the Orwellian, grey and obedient world. It manifested the arrival of a particular form of individualism that would be expressed by everyone's inherent creativity once the interface towards the complex and cumbersome computing machinery is being resolved.

Less obvious was that the creativity about to be expressed would foster the emergence of the unprecedented industry that in less than two decades would globalize and monopolize the world,

[11]

David Burnham, 'The Computer, the Consumer and Privacy', *New York Times*, 4 March 1984, www.nytimes.com/1984/03/04/weekinreview/the-computer-the-consumer-and-privacy.html.

determining almost all aspects of life and work and giving new corporations more control and power with less accountability than IBM could even dare to dream of back in 1984. This was probably also not obvious at the time to the very actors of the computer scene themselves, who have seen their rise from the 'garage' — a place soon to become a mythical source of alternative, DIY, 'self-propelled' and 'independent' artistic propositions and technical innovation — as a sort of a genuine bottom-up, emancipatory and horizontal motion. 'Garage' would come to symbolize the 'guerrilla tactics' that brought to the fore the entire field of alternative music and media, the entire spectre of emerging technology, the sense of time spent together in alternative communities, the figures of 'entrepreneur' and 'hacker' (evolving to become today 'the philosophers of our times') …

'WHY NOT RUN ON 'MORE THAN 100%'?

Although in 1960 it was one of only six countries to successfully develop its own mainframe computer (CER-10),[12] in the eighties Yugoslavia was lagging behind in the wave of advancing personal computing. As the living standard crumbled, the most significant obstacles were high prices of Western products and components, and the laws barring private import of any significant amount of goods (the attempt by State to halt the outflow of foreign currency under the pressure of crisis). Voja Antonić, a young and self-thought engineer, addressed both problems. As elsewhere, the new technology was introduced by the old, and computers arrived carried by the magazines and radio. The potential of Antonić's invention was entangled with the enthusiasm of computer publicist Dejan Ristanović and radio host Zoran Modli — and the spirit of New Wave.

By 'hacking' the processor and optimizing the code,[13] Antonić came up with a complete and feasible solution for self-building a microcomputer using only the affordable components available on the Yugoslav market. The instant acceptance and appeal of Galaksija (Galaxy), named after the popular science magazine where it was presented as a DIY project in January of 1984, was a consequence of both its innovative design and how the machine was distributed; Galaksija was offered as a do-it-yourself kit. Beating the wildest estimations, at least 8,000 people wrote to order or to confirm building their own computer, and magazine editor Ristanović, who also helped in writing Galaksija code, saw the print run of the special issue 'Computers in your home' quadruple to 120,000 copies.

12
Jelica Protić and Dejan Ristanović, 'Building Computers in Serbia: The First Half of the Digital Century', *ComSIS* 8, no. 3 (June 2011), pp. 549–571, p. 563, www.doiserbia.nb.rs/img/doi/1820-0214/2011/1820-02141100021P.pdf.

13
Voja Antonić, 'Hacking the Digital and Social System', Hackaday.com, 3 August 2015, http://hackaday.com/2015/08/03/hacking-the-digital-and-social-system.

Zoran Modli, the host of the Ventilator 202 radio show, had already experimented with broadcasts from various different locations such as cultural and youth clubs, concert venues, book-shops and streets, and, being a licensed commercial pilot, in 1981 he was allowed to run the very first live radio broadcast while flying a small Cesna airplane over Belgrade. He stated that this was his 'attempt to demystify the ideas of radio and airplane'.[14] As a part of his mission to 'give the power of technology to the "ordinary guy on the street"' the software for Galaksija, along-side software for the other then popular platforms and very early versions of digital 'zines', would be shared in what was to become a regular slot of the show by being broadcasted in the form of 'noise' over the radio waves to be recorded on compact cassettes and then loaded into the computers of the listeners.[15]

Galaksija appeared as the complete solution to introduce personal computers to the general public by using the existing infrastructure at almost no costs. It offered the alternative concept on many levels, and towards various different constellations; it presented an alternative in regard to the policy of the Yugoslav State that at the time restricted the import of technology; it presented an alternative proposition in regard to the history of technology, by the early introduction of an integrated video processor and using more than 100% of programme memory; it used a 'wireless transfer' of data in 1984. Insisting on the principles of DIY and sharing through giving the blueprint to the public and even making copy protection difficult at the level of hardware, it presented an alternative to the concept of developing personal computing relying on the regime of patents and copyright.[16] The DIY approach also meant that no two units looked the same, expressing the skill and aesthetics of their makers-owners.[17] Perhaps most importantly, it presented a massive and systematic educational campaign: the interest and knowledge in building and improving hardware and software could be exchanged and transferred between experts, enthusiasts, and population in a public, self-maintained and 'organic' way.

Later, Antonić would go on to produce dozens of different projects that would be offered as public domain. However, the progressive tendencies of the early computer scene (described as 'elitist, a part of the culture of alternative music and art, but not driven by political motives'[18]) would not be reproduced; as the Galaksija project faded away, the computing industry would become based on imports and experts, Yugoslavia would soon disappear 'without alternative', and the computer scenes of newly created nation-states would follow the dominant trends of nineties 'without history'.

14
Source: Zoran Modli, 'Ventilator 202', http://modli.rs/radio/ventilator/ventilator.html.

15
This is not the first time such things were done — for example, the Dutch radio show *Hobbyscoop* broadcasted software since 1977 (see Frank C.A. Veraart, 'Transnational (Dis)Connection in Localizing Personal Computing in the Netherlands, 1975–1990', in Alberts and Oldenziel, *Hacking Europe*, pp. 25–48, p. 30), and in the early eighties a lot of radio stations in Europe were beaming the other-worldly squeeking sounds of software, while the DIY launch of the machine through the press was inspired by how the Altair 8800 home computer was presented in the US via the *Popular Electronics* magazine in the mid-seventies. What was probably unique was combining this, and more, into the social and media environment creating the 'Galaksija ecosystem' that is public and self-sustainable.

16
Jakić, 'Galaxy and the New Wave', pp. 120–121.

17
'The Galaksija computers, all identical by the design of their electronics, were delivered without a casing. As a result, most Galaksija computers looked different, some were without even a case.' (Jakić, 'Galaxy and the New Wave', p. 120).

18
'"The development of independent Yugoslav software through the exchange of cassette tapes, radio broadcasts, and transcriptions was similar to that in the Netherlands. But in Yugoslavia, the autonomy was hard wired. The architecture of the locally produced kits and computers was such that the software protection, either backed hacked from the US standards or locally produced, had to be removed before it could be installed. The thriving

'Alternate History' aficionados (who usually spend their time pondering questions like 'what would have happened if the Aztecs had resisted Spanish colonization?') have devoted significant time to speculating about an alternate reality in which the Galaksija exceeded Western models in popularity during the 1980s, saved Yugoslavia from dissolution and made inexpensive microcomputer kits available to the Third World.[19]

Lily Lynch

Perhaps the absence of avant-gardes and of left politics *en masse* — the source of much of the present-day sense of loss and disorientation — can be explained by the disappearance of its material substrate of the future. For the 'alt-' forces the future is merely the opportunity for rearranging of what is formerly known as history, for the eternal re-writing and re-visioning of the 'better past', as in contemporary slogans of 'taking *back* control' over something or making it 'great *again*'; the past re-enacted only with 'facts adjusted' to meet the certain ideological premise.

In their alternative practices, *TV Galerija* and Galaksija both acknowledged the past, disregarded the present and looked straight into the future. Their proposition was to face the growing complexity of technology and of media, not to hide it. In the *alternate reality* where such propositions were given the future, surely the people would have other problems to worry about; but it would be, on many levels, an entirely different world. 'I never patented anything',[20] stated Voja Antonić, while Dunja Blažević underlined: 'I was not limited with "TV minutes". That was the first thing that I fought for.'

hacker scene in Yugoslavia was elitist, participated in a culture of alternative music and art, but was not driven by political motives.'" ('Introduction: How European Players Captured the Computer and Created the Scenes', in Alberts and Oldenziel, eds., *Hacking Europe*, pp. 1–21, p. 17).

19
Lily Lynch, 'Galaksija, cult Yugoslav DIY computer from the 1980s lives on', *Bturn* 4 December 2011, http://bturn.com/4614/galaksija-do-it-yourself-computer.

20
Source: http://bif.rs/2012/06/voja-antonic-pronalazac-novinar-i-publicista-postoji-nesto-jace-i-od-ljudske-gluposti.

BLACK FILM WORKSHOPS

June Givanni

'Race relations' in eighties Britain were characterized by the struggles of previous decades: equal rights and justice; representation; human and citizenship rights. These were closely linked to black theatre, art, music, dance, film, and publishing. The sectors were inter-connected and supportive, rooted in the Caribbean Artists Movement, and the activist movements led by New Beacon Books, Bogle L'Ouverture, the Institute of Race Relations, Race Today, and others. The decade was characterized by the 1981 and 1985 uprisings across Britain, which placed questions of discrimination high on the political agenda (e.g. Black Audio Film Collective won the Grierson Award for their groundbreaking *Handsworths Songs*).

Black independent filmmakers were working in a difficult commercial marketplace.[01] One of the first organizations operating in the pre-workshop environment was the Black Media Workers Group. The Association of Cinematograph, Television and Allied Technicians Film Union and the British Film Institute were key supporters of the independent film sector. Channel 4 was launched with a remit to provide innovative broadcasting. The three institutions developed a model of integrated practice (production / distribution / educational activities) through the 'Workshop Declaration' under which franchised workshops would receive commissions, salaries and equipment.

Following their strategic Third Eye Film Festival (1983) and Seminars on Black and Third Cinema (1983 and 1984), the Greater London Council's negotiation with the key funders led to the recognition of four franchised black film workshops: Black Audio Film Collective, Sankofa, Ceddo and Retake, including the provision of funding from Channel 4. Between them the workshops produced bodies of work that explored filmic, documentary and representational languages, through their modes of collaboration and production.

The Declaration required workshops to focus on ethnic diversity and local issues. Retake, the first Asian Film and video collective to be franchised under the ACTT Workshop Declaration wrote: 'Our documentary films have been produced as a response to the needs of the community involving community consensus from research to actual issues to be included in the programmes.' The community was also central to Ceddo. 'It is in the area of exhibition and seminars that we can develop a forum for an exchange

01

Horace Ové, Lloyd Reckord, Lionel Ngakane, Frankie Diamond Jn,; Nii Kwate Owoo, Colin Prescod, Menelik Shabazz, Kuumba Productions (Imruh Bakari and Henry Martin), Penumbra Productions (H.O. Nazareth) and others.

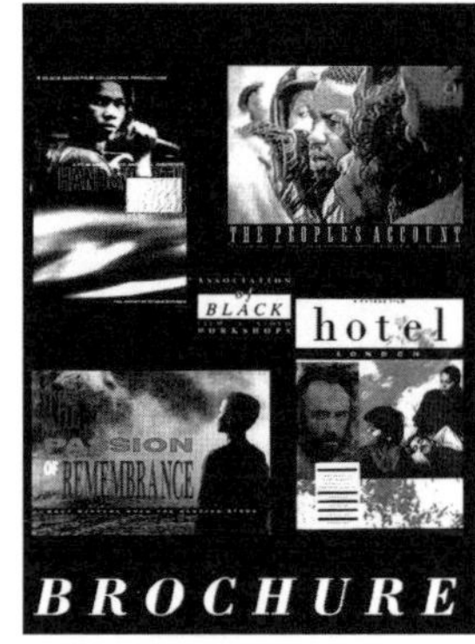

Association of Black Workshops, 1985–1986, brochure. Featuring both franchised and unfranchised UK Black Workshops, with introduction by Jim Pines

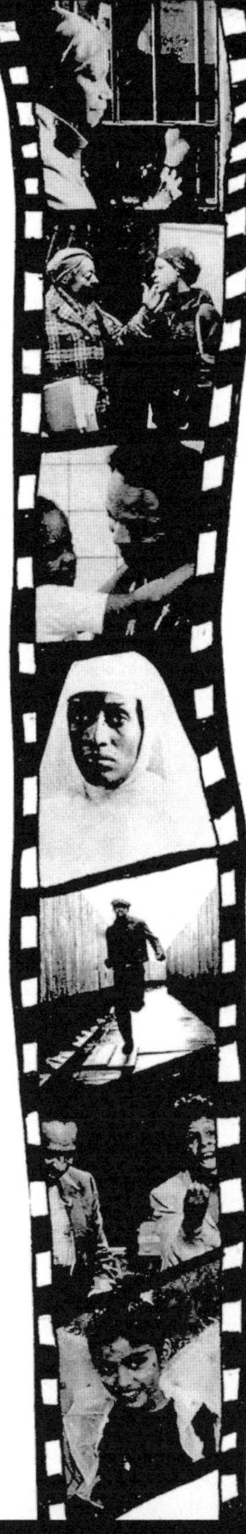

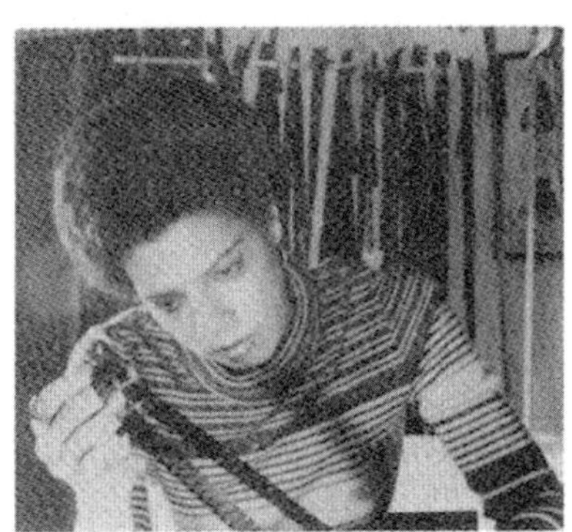

Black Film Festival

COMMONWEALTH ARTS CENTRE

presents

BLACK FILM FESTIVAL

1st-13th FEBRUARY 1982
From 7.00 p.m.

Commonwealth Institute
Kensington High Street
London W.8

Tickets:

£1.50 and £1.00 Students, OAP's and Children
Box Office: 01-602-3252 Ex 214/221

Commonwealth Institute Black Film Festival, 1982. The programme featured films from black American and UK filmmakers.
Organizers: Jim Pines and Parminder Vir

between ourselves, the community and other filmmakers on ideas of race, gender and Third World Cinema and spread the creative and political awareness of the visual media.'[02] Women film makers within the workshops played a significant role in shaping the political consciousness and in the wider achievements of the four workshops.[03]

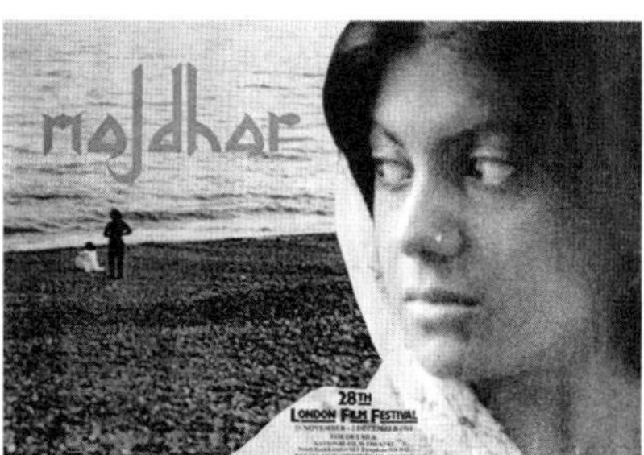
Poster for *Majdhar*, Retake Film, director: Ahmed Jamal, 1984

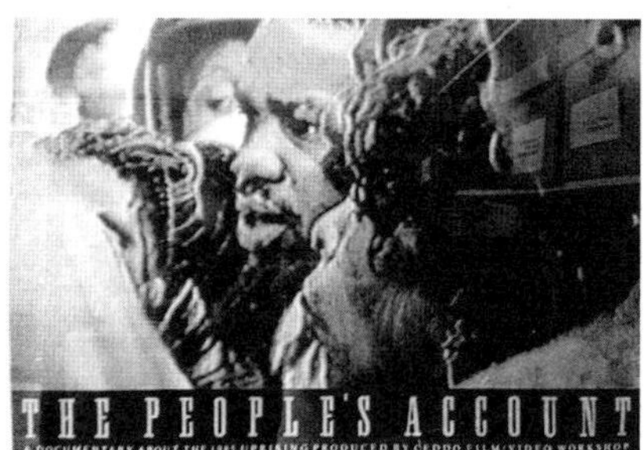
Poster for *The People's Account*, Ceddo Film/Video Workshop, director: Milton Bryan, producer: Menelik Shabazz, 1985

In 1985, Ceddo's *The People's Account* documented the Broadwater Farm riots. Under the advice of the Independent Broadcasting Association, Channel 4 did not broadcast the film due to its depiction of the police as racist. Jim Pines stated:

> The general problem seems to turn on the whole question of official discourses regarding black-related situations, and the struggle for many black independent practitioners to somehow subvert these discourses while at the same time seeking relatively unimpeded access to the main exhibition and broadcast outlets. It involves a process of breaking the established boundaries of legitimacy.[04]

Kobena Mercer wrote that such approaches to documentary practice 'perform a critical function of providing an alternative version of events so as to inform, agitate and mobilise action'.[05]

Who killed Colin Roach? (1983), Sankofa's first film, addressing the death of a young black man in police custody, was a film that caught the mood, anger, and political perspectives of the time '... I made it a priority to create the space for them to articulate an alternative point of view to the official reconstructions which were being pronounced by the dominant media.'[06] Mercer has referred to this generation of 'cinematic activists' as ... 'being engaged with the cultural struggle that takes place within the "domain of image-making" through self-conscious cinematic strategies'.[07]

02

Association of Black Workshops brochure.

03

Maureen Blackwood, Martina Attille and Nadine Marsh-Edwards in Sankofa; Lina Gopaul, Avril Johnson, and Claire Joseph in Black Audio Film Collective; Dennis Elmina Davis, Valerie Thomas, June Reid and Sukai in Ceddo.

04

Introduction to ABW, ibid.

05

Kobena Mercer, 'Diaspora Culture and the Dialogic Imagination: The Aesthetics of Black Independent Film in Britain' in *Black Frames: Critical Perspectives on Independent Black Cinema*, ed. by Mbye Cham and Claire Watkins (Cambridge: MIT Press, 1988), pp. 50–61.

06

Jim Pines, 'Territories: Interview with Isaac Julien', *Framework: The Journal of Cinema and Media* 26–27 (1985), pp. 2–9.

07

Kobena Mercer, *Welcome to the Jungle: New Positions in Black Cultural Studies* (London: Routledge, 1994).

'TALKING BACK TO THE MEDIA'

Diana Franssen

In the eighties, commercial TV multiplied its audience through satellite, cable, special channels, community access, and through changes and developments in both hardware and approach. Mass media started to fragment, becoming less monolithic. Artists were responding to these developments by appropriating and re-purposing media techniques and strategies.

In 1985, Amsterdam hosted the festival 'Talking back to the Media'. It was organized by a group of international artists, most of them based in Amsterdam, who gathered under the name Artists Talking Back to The Media: Aart van Barneveld, Max Bruinsma, Ulises Carrión, David Garcia, Sabrina Kamstra, Sebastián López, Raul Marroquin, Rob Perrée, and Marijke de Vos. 'Talking back to the Media' showed the work of artists who used mass media to deconstruct and critique the 'reality' presented by these media. Many works parodied the medium of television, using and subverting its strategies.

During the festival, Amsterdam's streets, theatres, airwaves, and artist spaces were involved in showing content. Video pro-grammes were hosted in the evenings at Time Based Arts; film screenings took place at Kriterion cinema with films by Chris Marker, Barbara Bloom, Yvonne Rainer and Valie Export; and the Shaffy Theater staged a try-out of the play titled *Het houten zwaard* (The Wooden Sword) by Dick Hauser. Posters were produced by Barbara Kruger, Klaus Staeck, and John Baldessari. VPRO Radio broadcasted two live shows of sound art curated by Max Bruinsma and Ulises Carrión. The newly launched cable TV service Kabel Televisie Amsterdam (KTA) aired four hour-long programmes of video works and interviews, something that would not have been possible over traditional airwaves. The artist initiative Aorta exhibited photographs in a selection of artists reacting on mass media, including Victor Burgin, Nan Goldin and Lydia Schouten, selected by Sebastián López and Rob Perrée. Artist space De Appel organized artists' interviews, lectures and round table conversations with General Idea, Barbara Kruger, Hans Haacke, and others.

'Talking Back...' not only meant responding to mass media, but also deploying its modes of distribution, making these visible and audible in the city, a place where media controls culture. The festival drew on the whole scope of electronic and mass media,

Research into the festival by Camie Karstanje and Brigitte Bélanger, commissioned by De Appel Foundation and LIMA, Amsterdam.

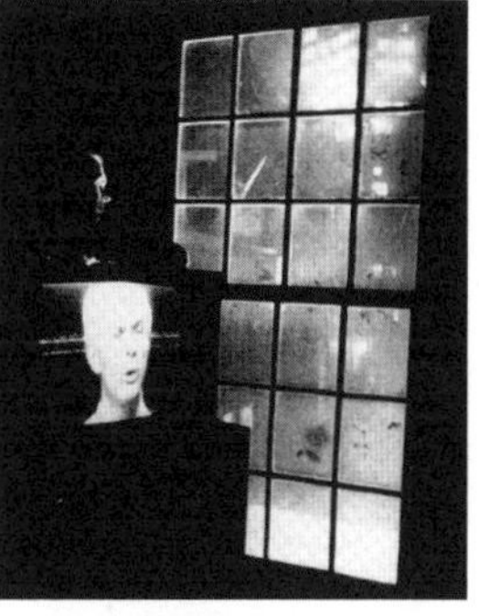

Instituut Houtappel, *Haft und Urteil*, 1981

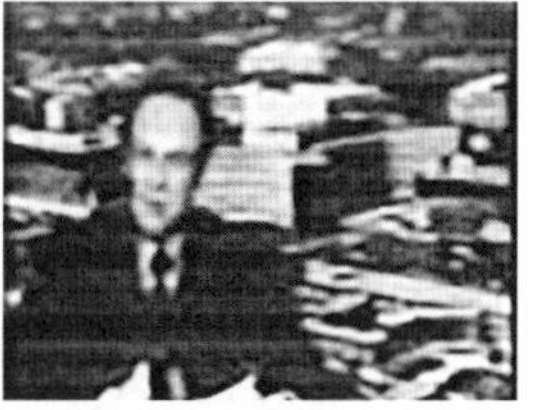

Raul Marroquin, *Fandangos Evening News*, 1977, video still

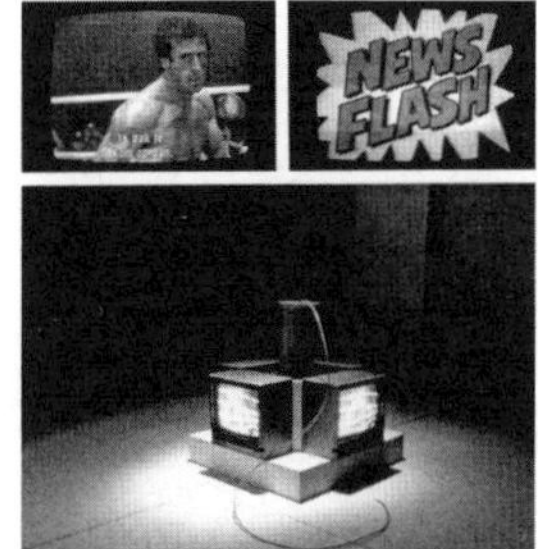

Servaas, *Are You Afraid of Video?*, 1984, installation and two Screenshot. Courtesy: Stedelijk Museum, Amsterdam

Talking Back to the Media, 1985, catalogue cover

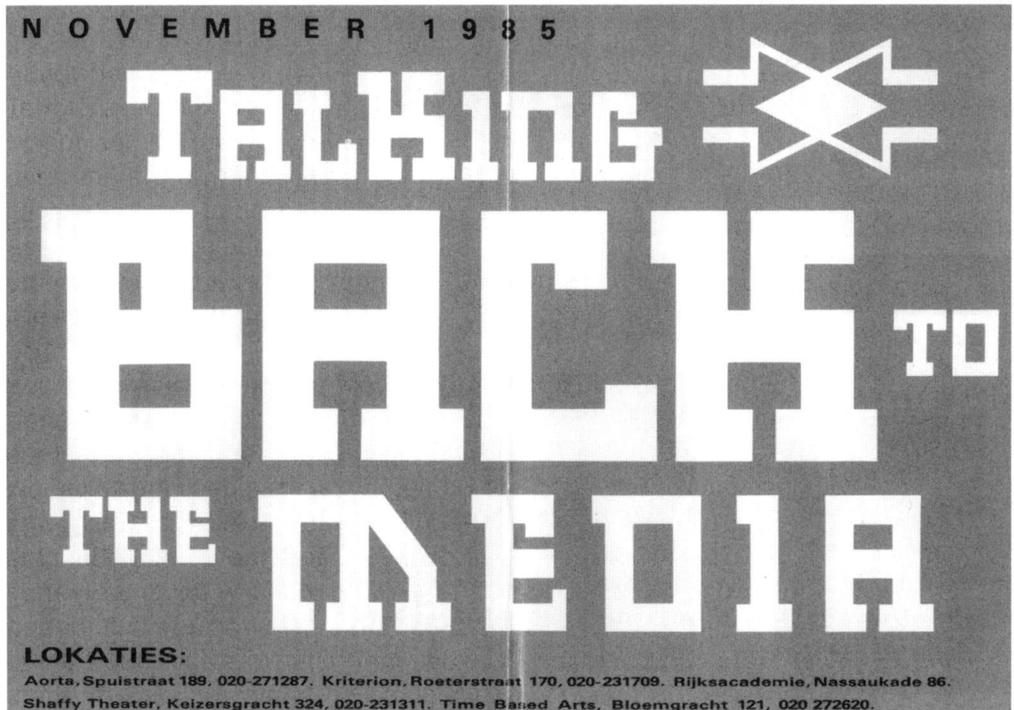

Talking Back to the Media, 1985, flyer

by its language, its use of media channels and by commissioning works. This result of this extensive collaboration between artists, art institutions and artist' initiatives had a significant influence on Dutch video and media art. Eventually, a network around the medium was built, exhibition spaces opened and self-published magazines such as *Mediamatic* were published, all drawing on different forms of counterculture.

In his contribution to the festival's publication, Sebastián López put forward a theoretical basis for the festival. He drew on Jean Baudrillard and structuralism, analysing media culture in terms of a 'language of images', and characterized television as 'the imperialism of a reading system'.[01] In motivating the locations for the festival he states:

> The idea of the autonomy of artistic practice is still being maintained by the use of 'aurical' locations (museums and art galleries) and formalist criticism. Works of art were and still are categorized in an *in-out* relationship: either *in* the institution which consecrates them as art works, or *out* in the open field of the non-sacred, that is on the street and into the media: to put them in the risky context where they can no longer control their work.[02]

01

Sebastián López, 'Constructie De-Constructie', in *Talking Back to the Media*, eds. Sabrina Kamstra et al. (Amsterdam: Stichting Talking Back to the Media, 1985), pp. 6–9.

02

Ibid., p. 8.

'LA IMAGEN SUBLIME'
VIDEO ART PRACTICES IN SPAIN

Cristina Cámara

'La imagen sublime: Vídeo de creación en España (1970–1987)' (The Sublime Image: Creative Video in Spain) was the first video creation retrospective mounted in Spain. Organized in 1987 at the Centro de Arte Reina Sofía, which had only opened the previous year, and curated by Manuel Palacio, its importance lay in its efforts to unite and select in order to recount the history of the medium, which, with differing fortunes in the seventies and eighties, was still searching for its own place. The show was part of one of the main lines of work defined from the very beginning of this art centre's inauguration, the exhibition 'Procesos: cultura y tecnología' (Processes: Culture and Technology, 1986), and denoted modernity's resolute will to programme, focusing on art made from technological supports.

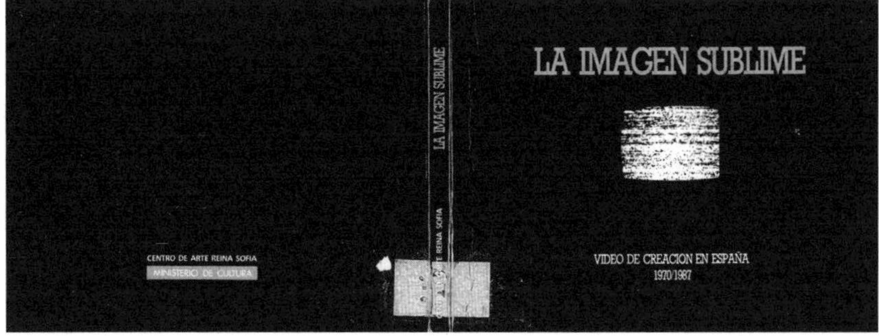

La imagen sublime: Vídeo de creación en España,1970–1987 (The Sublime Image: Creative Video in Spain, 1970–1987), Museo Nacional Centro de Arte Reina Sofía, Madrid, 1987, exhibition catalogue. Photo: Joaquín Cortés / Román Lores

The exhibition, centred exclusively on single-channel works, revolved around two spaces. The first was an exhibition space, which screened thirty-nine films selected in different blocks and sessions, displayed 'a graphic history of Spanish video' by way of photographic documents, posters of encounters, shows and festivals, and featured a document service with an ambitious, and previously unpublished, bibliographical overview as reference material. The second space was in the auditorium, with video screenings, shown thematically, and the organisation of encounters and round-table discussions. The programme 'Time Code', also presented inside this second space, was a

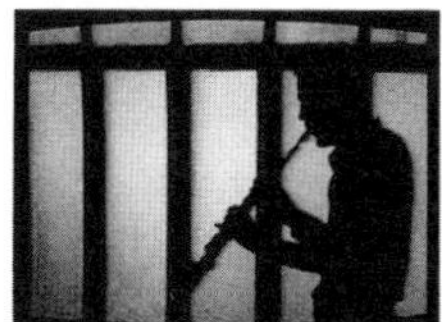 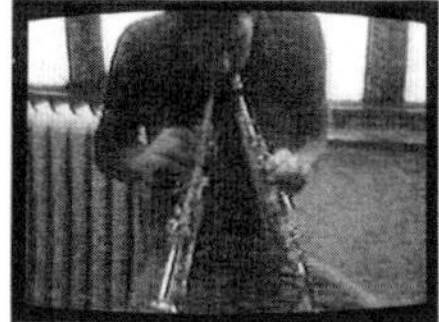 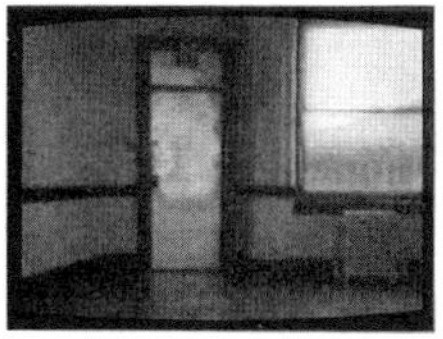

Si en España hubiese un debate sobre si el vídeo es cine personal o experimental con medios electrónicos, **Indian Circle** formaría parte indisoluble de las prácticas que alimentaran la discusión.
Al igual que algunas de las mejores películas de cine experimental de hace una veintena de años, **Indian Circle** basa su grandeza en el agotamiento de todas las posibilidades de análisis y observación de un espacio, en este caso un austero, casi vacío, "loft". Es una nueva experiencia de percepción del espacio, pero también del tiempo, pues en el plano único que constituye la cinta no funciona el concepto de duración ni el de diégesis, pese a que existan cambios de ritmo en una especie de sucedáneo de *racords*.
Los movimientos de cámara son el principal protagonista. Sin embargo ésta, con velocidad variable, ora enfocando algún objeto, ora abandonando al libre albur el foco, siguiendo

panorámicas horizontales o verticales, de derecha a izquierda o de izquierda a derecha, encuadrando el suelo, el techo, las paredes, no es la única presencia, también hay un hombre en el "loft": un músico, Peter Van Riper, que con sus músicas y sonidos y desplazamientos en el mismo espacio cerrado establece una dialéctica respecto a los movimientos de la cámara. Peter Van Riper toca uno o dos clarinetes, una caracola marina, frota dos piñas, hace música vocal..., se mueve. A veces, la cámara se detiene, y el músico calla, reforzando una cierta sensación de ansiedad, pero inmediatamente uno o ambos reinician la actividaù. Consumada toda la instrospección, a la cámara sólo le queda el contracampo imposible −"el espacio detrás de la ventana"− del cuadro fílmico. Hacia allí dirige su ojo, pero un fundido da por concluida la experiencia, hacía ya rato que la habitación estaba en silencio.

INDIAN CIRCLE (1982)

Vídeo: EUGENIA BALCELLS.
Música: PETER VAN RIPER, incluyendo el tema "Wire somels" de TERRY FOX.
Duración: 30'.
Color: NTSC.
1982.

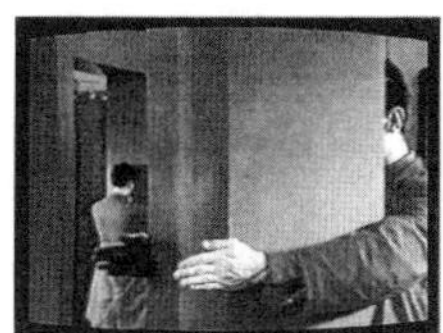 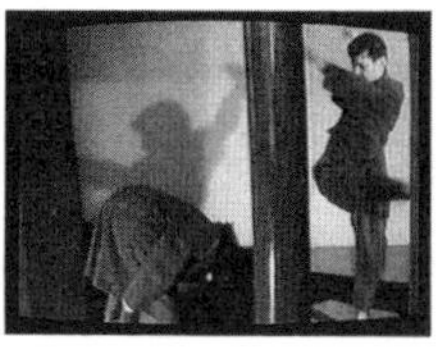 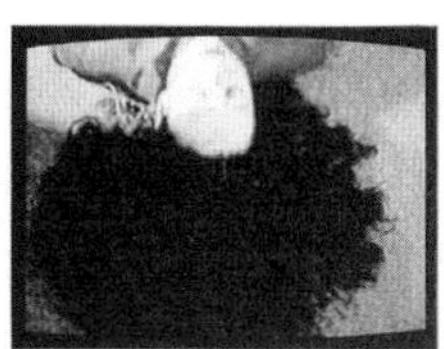

El vídeo es siempre movimiento, puede que en la pantalla se exhiba una imagen estática, pero el flujo de electrones no ceja su incansable movimiento. Los autores de **Infinito 5** remarcan esta característica en el mismo inicio de la obra: imagen fija en blanco y negro de una acción de Pedro Garhel y Rosa Galindo en Arco-85, origen del trabajo videográfico, la imagen no llega nunca a tomar movimiento, pero paulatinamente va aumentando su autorreferencialidad a base de ir modificando la textura frente a nuestros ojos: vemos cómo el cuadro de la imagen atraviesa la pantalla y progresivamente se va incorporando el color.
Excelente comienzo para un trabajo sobre el espacio escénico, como es **Infinito 5**, muy probablemente el más pertinente acercamiento a la dicotomía campo-contracampo realizada en el vídeo español.
Para ello, los autores utilizan las sombras, la iluminación, el color, las apariciones y desapariciones de campo utilizando las esquinas como lugar privilegiado para la composición de las perspectivas, pero también para disgregar y destruir la idea de espacio videográfico.

Es cierto que la planificación a veces resulta incomprensible, sobre todo en el uso de los primeros planos (sin duda, su utilización es siempre una cuestión moral); y que se tiene la impresión que de las ralentizaciones y algunos *zooms* responden más a la lógica tecnológica del medio que a una necesidad expresiva, pero no son obstáculos suficientes para empañar el soberbio trabajo sobre el espacio.
Según avanza la cinta asistimos a una seudoprogresión en la ficción del encuentro de ambos accionistas, las falsas perspectivas dificultan la coincidencia. Al fin logran conocerse cinco posturas antes de desaparecer, quizá definitivamente, la mujer. Posteriormente siguen buscándose, pero la dificultad se acrecenta, pues el espacio se ha revestido de espejos que reproducen y multiplican sus imágenes. En el último plano parece que se acercan, la imagen se repite en uno de los espejos que falsea, una vez más, toda distancia. Un congelado oportuno deja el final infinito.

INFINITO 5 (1985)

Realizador: ANTONIO CANO.
Performers: PEDRO GARHEL, ROSA GALINDO.
Música: DEPOSITO DENTAL.
Fotografía: LUIS CARLOS GONZALEZ.
Equipo vídeo: JAVIER G. VADILLO.
Espacio: ENRIQUE HERRADA.
Vestuario: ALICIA BELMONTE.
Arquitecto jefe de producción: JUAN GOMEZ.
Ayudante producción: ANTONIO MARIN.
Secretario producción: EDUARDO LUDEÑA.
Sobre una idea original de: PEDRO GARHEL, ANTONIO CANO.
Producción: COAM.
Duración: 9'.
Madrid, 1985.

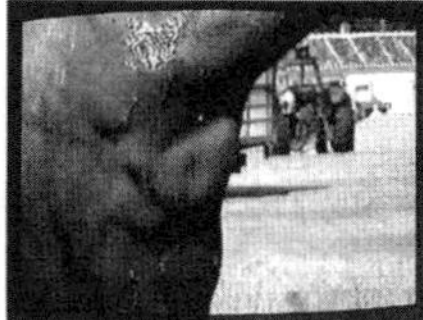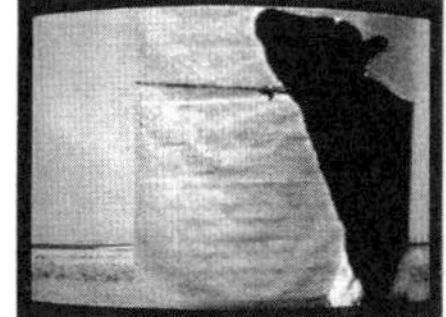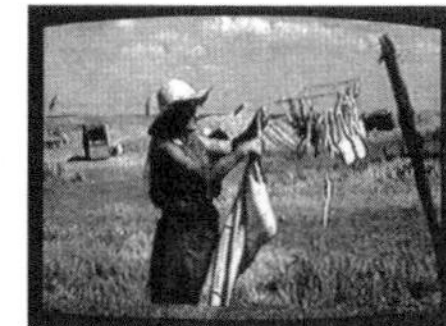

Pornada es la suma de muchos aciertos. En primera lectura es un documental; documental aunque los autores sepan que nada es inocente en la manera de grabar y que no existen documentos que no sean subjetivos. **Pornada** es un documental rabiosamente subjetivo sobre una determinada zona de la meseta norte en la provincia de León; es un vídeo paisajista, tal como a veces se denomina a aquellas obras en las que el paisaje cumple el papel de protagonista.

No es fácil realizar un vídeo paisajista sobre la meseta, porque este subgénero se alimenta de las posibilidades fotográficas de la cámara y, desde luego, resulta difícil, por repetido, fotografiar la meseta sin caer en lo ya visto. Codesal y Rodríguez lo solventan con una soberbia composición plástica, escrutan el paisaje mesetario con despaciosas panorámicas, con planos cargados de sentidos muy connotativos, con la luz, con las sombras. También es difícil captar el tempo de las tierras baldías, de las paredes agrietadas, del verano inacabable, del no tener nada que hacer. Los autores lo resuelven con un montaje productor de sentido, tan inusual en vídeo, capaz de fijar las imágenes en la conciencia por acumulación de fragmentos discontinuos de sujetos y de objetos.

Pero **Pornada** es una combinación infrecuente de metáfora y metonimia. Metáfora de una sociedad rural que desaparece con imágenes de animales literalmente empapelados o a punto de ser arrasados por tractores, de la dificultad de la comunicación con imágenes de comunicaciones telefónicas imposibles, pues al fin y al cabo no hay más que un aparato en todo el pueblo. Metonimia en el uso de la banda sonora, del caballo de cerámica incrustado en una segunda imagen dentro del cuadro, que relincha en off. **Pornada** incorpora una nueva forma de ver imágenes en el vídeo español que obliga a "lavarse los ojos después de cada mirada".

PORNADA (1985)

Realización: RAUL RODRIGUEZ, JAVIER CODESAL.
Operador: JAVIER LOPEZ IZQUIERDO.
Con la participación de: TEYO RODRIGUEZ, FELISA RODRIGUEZ, ELENA RODRIGUEZ, JUAN DANIEL RODRIGUEZ.
Edición: M.L.V. POSPRODUCCION.
Duración: 22'.
1985.

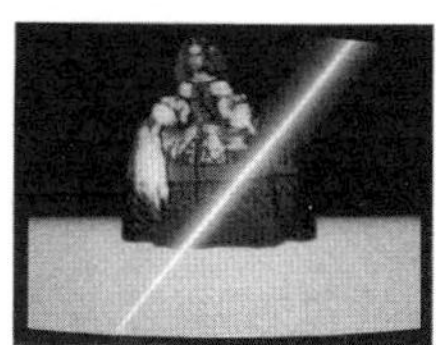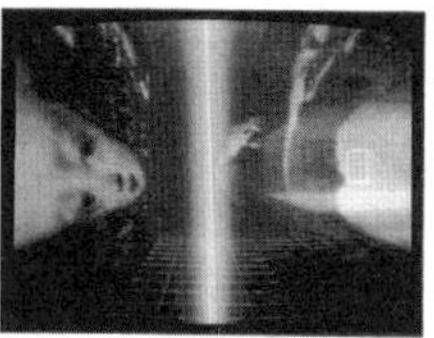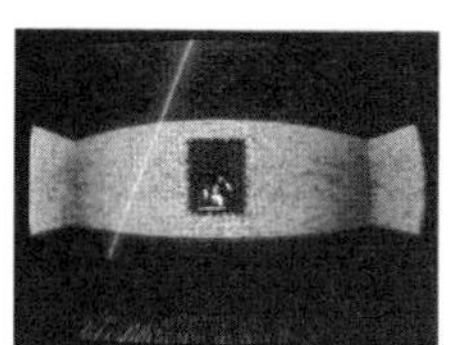

Si hubiera que buscar algún tipo de especificidad en la imagen electrónica, no cabe duda de que debería rastrearse en las relaciones que establece con el uso de la tecnología. En este contexto, el hecho de que **Menina** sea la primera obra española de creación grabada íntegramente por ordenador, no es lo más importante; mucho más interesante es preguntarse por su participación en los debates sobre los cambios sociales y sensoriales que se inician con la imagen digital.

Que Juan Carlos Eguillor emplee como referencia para su trabajo el cuadro velazqueño de "Las meninas", precisamente aquél en el que, por vez primera en la historia de la pintura, se intenta la representación del espacio pictórico fuera de campo, no es ni mucho menos accesorio para las transformaciones espacio-temporales producidas por la imagen digital. La imagen digital subvierte todas las reglas clásicas de representación; no remite, ni re-presenta, a ninguna imagen que no sea ella misma; no existe un espacio imaginario del que procedan las distintas imágenes, no existe, pues, el juego entre espacio-campo y fuera-de-campo en el que han basado su grandeza los más sobresalientes directores de cine; todo está grabado con anterioridad, y late en la imagen que vemos, las transiciones se realizan teniendo como unidad básica el *pixel* y no el fotograma; el tamaño de los objetos no responde a ninguna ley de perspectiva, y se vuelve completamente relativo en relación con el decorado. Por fortuna, todo esto, y mucho más, se encuentra en **Menina**.

Todo es gratuito en el menú de efectos digitales de **Menina**, no existe producción de sentido en el viaje a ninguna parte que se realiza en la cinta (tanto es así que no se sabe con certeza cuándo se inicia el retorno); pero precisamente eso es lo que nos gusta y lo que la hace contemporánea, ¿o no estamos, acaso, en los tiempos de la ausencia de un poder legitimador y de la clausura de la experiencia del yo único?

MENINA (1986)

Producción: FUNDESCO.
Diseño y dirección: JUAN CARLOS EGUILLOR.
Productor ejecutivo: FELIX B. LIZARRALDE.
Imagen generada por computador ATC.
Director técnico: VICENTE AGUSTI.
Programación: FELIX BERGES, JORGE CRESPO, JUAN RAMON TORAN.
Música original: RAMON FARRAN.
Director de posproducción: LUIS GOMEZ CORNEJO.
Edición: MARIANO ANTORANZ.
Técnicos de posproducción: FERNANDO OLMO, PEDRO PAGES, JOAQUIN GARCIA.
Operador cámara: SANTIAGO GOMEZ.
Secretaria de producción: ITZIAR DE CASTRO.
Duración: 13'.
1986.

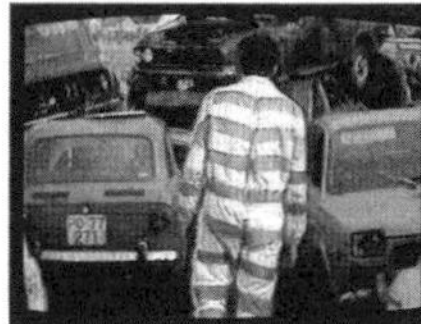 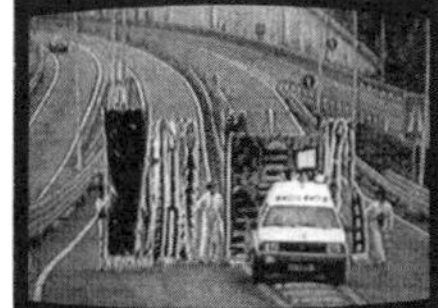 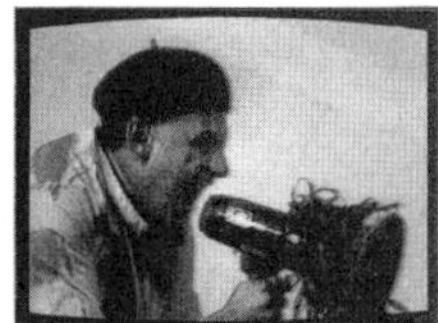

Salvamento e Socorrismo es la mejor ilustración de textos en vídeo que se ha realizado en España. Y, por supuesto, no se trata de nada peyorativo sino muy al contrario, la fórmula más eficaz para desarrollar un trabajo audiovisual distinto (y contemporáneo) al de las adaptaciones literarias del cine.

Es cierto que **Salvamento e Socorrismo** cuenta con el valor añadido de la actuación del propio Antonio R. Reixa, sin ningún tipo de duda, el mejor *showman* del vídeo español y el único protagonista que puede recibir el nombre de tal de nuestra videografía. Reixa tiene aptitudes para cumplir el papel –tan necesitado– de una estrella (local) del vídeo; al menos del modo que Michael Smith o William Wegman lo son en el vídeo norteamericano. Quizá ese fuese un camino para salir de la crisis de

creación que atenaza al último vídeo mundial y conseguir algo que parece tan difícil para el soporte magnético como es una original técnica de representación.

Desde otro punto de vista, **Salvamento e Socorrismo** es una realización extremadamente sencilla, pese a su exuberancia y barroquismo; a veces peca de una cierta gratuidad en la utilización de limitadas técnicas de posproducción (ralentizaciones, saturaciones de color), pero en otras se consigue un excelente ritmo visual únicamente mediante plasmación visual de las poesías de Reixa. Y, sobre todo, los guiños. Esa "acción" de fumarse un cigarro en la calle, ese recital de poesía en una sala vacía, esa entrevista al niño que lee "Pravda", ese negro que baila la muñeira, pertenecen a lo más productivo del vídeo español.

SALVAMENTO E SOCORRISMO (1985)   105

Guión y dirección: A. R. REIXA.
Producción: VIDEOESQUIMAL PRODUCCIONS.
Realización técnica: CARLOS AMIL, ANTONIO SEGADE.
Edición: XAVIER F. VILLAVERDE.
Productores: MODESTO ROMAN, XAVIER LEYTE COELLO, A. R. REIXA.
Maquillaje: MARA COSTAS.
Música: OS RESENTIDOS.
Producción y sonido: FRANCISCO TRINIDAD.
Decorados y vestuario: MENCHU LAMAS, ANTON PATIÑO.
Colaboraciones: X. L. SUAREZ CANAL, ALICIA ZAPATERO, F. XAVIER OCAÑA, RAFAEL OJEA, MANUEL ABAD, JULIAN HERNANDEZ.
Actores: RUBEN LOSADA, XAVIER FERNANDEZ SOTO, ALBERTO L. TORRADO, A. R. REIXA, GABRIELA FERNANDEZ, MIGUEL COSTAS, MODESTO ROMAN, TANIA RODRIGUEZ PINO, ANTELA RODRIGUEZ CID.
Duración: 40'.
1985.

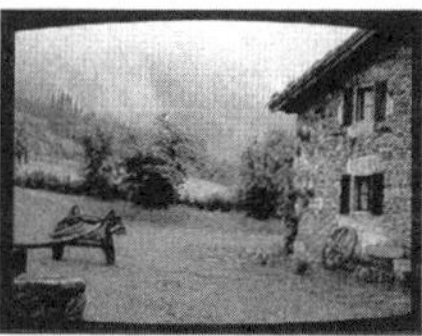 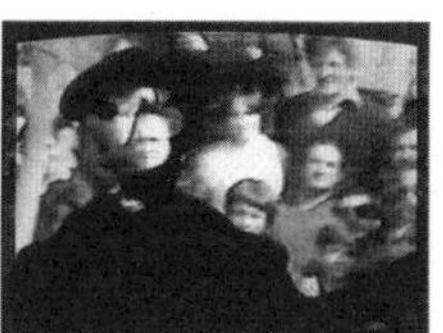 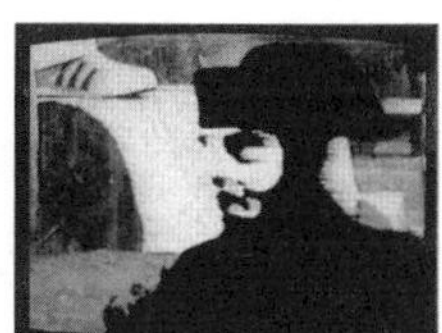

Existe una coincidencia artística entre las investigaciones de algunos de los pioneros del videoarte como Nam June Paik y el concepto de *atentado*, columna vertebral del trabajo artístico de De Vargas. La primera gran aportación del videoarte fue aceptar que el ruido también es una señal. Paik invirtió diodos, destrozó cables, conectó transistores diversos en su propósito de crear imágenes nunca vistas. De Vargas, por su parte, ha aplicado desde hace más de diez años el concepto de *atentado* al conjunto de sus trabajos (pintura, escultura, cine, vídeo, etc.) como forma de definir su relación con la creación y experimentación artística. Precisamente, las características del *atentado* como una intervención permanente convierten en final provisional todas las obras de De Vargas.

Canciones vascas sigue el esquema de destrucción paulatina que el autor propone en gran parte de su trabajo. En la cinta asistimos a un comienzo en el que todavía pueden distinguirse algunas imágenes figurativas hasta llegar al final (provisional) en el que el ruido de imagen y sonido se constituye en la "materialidad" de la obra; *atentado* tanto a las condiciones de percepción como al mismo proceso de creación. Sin embargo, De Vargas incluye en **Canciones vascas** un elemento dramático importante sobre las imágenes de un concurso de *aizkolaris*, incorpora las siluetas de un guardia civil y un vasco (con boina y bayoneta) que pelean hasta morir. De la combinación (dialéctica) de estos dos factores surge el resultado; probable metáfora sangrante de una sociedad crispada.

CANCIONES VASCAS (1980/84)   117

Realización: RAMON DE VARGAS.
Duración: 16'35''.
1980/84.

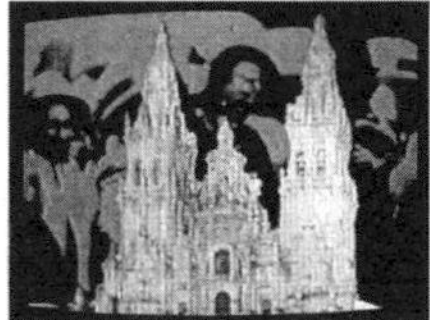 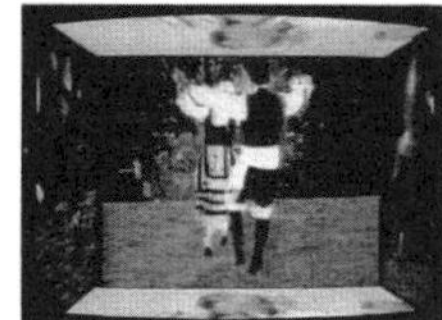 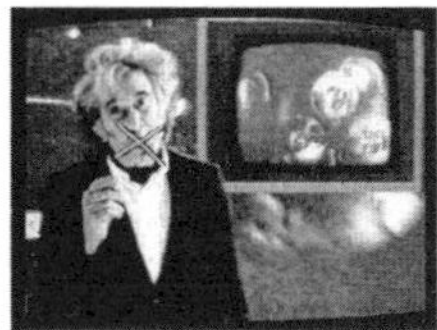

ALICIA EN GALICIA CANIBAL (1987)   125

Guión, dirección, realización: XAVIER F. VILLAVERDE.
Música: OS RESENTIDOS.
Letra: ANTON REIXA.
Argumento: ANTON REIXA, XAVIER F. VILLAVERDE.
Posproducción: JOSE MANZANO, JULIO CHORRO, JORGE MALVAR.
Iluminador: ANTONIO SEGADE.
Cámaras: ALBERTO SEGADE, ANTONIO SEGADE.
Director de arte en edición: JAVIER BARRIONUEVO.
Vestuario: ISAAC PEREZ VICENTE, PGBLLAS.
Peluquería, maquillaje: EQUIPO MARA COSTAS.
Director de producción: FRANCISCO CASAL.
Producción: CARMEN DE MIGUEL, MODESTO ROMAN, GONZALO BELTRAN.
Script: MILAGROS VARA.
Intérpretes: ROSA FERNANDEZ, EZEQUIEL, BELEN NEGREIRA, ANTON GUITIAN, ANDRES VILLA, JUAN GOBERNA, CARMELA PENAS, ENRIQUE COSTAS, ALFONSO AGRA, ISABEL CAMPOS, CARMEN PORRAS, ALBERTO COBIRTA, TANIA y ANTELA RODRIGUEZ, JULIA, SILVIA y PAULA PEREIRA, GONZALO BELTRAN, JULIA COSTAS, MARIA FERNANDEZ, MARIA RODRIGUEZ, XOSE FERNANDEZ, EUGENIA FERNANDEZ, CARLOS ALONSO.
Colaboración: VIDEO REPORT (Posproducción), CECISA, TVG, TVE (Centro regional de Galicia), ARQUIVO DA IMAXE (Xunta de Galicia).
Patrocinadores: U.I.M.P., XUNTA DE GALICIA, GRABACIONES ACCIDENTALES.
Producción: XAVIER VILLAVERDE ASOCIADOS.
Duración: 11'. 1987.

La imagen sublime: Vídeo de creación en España, 1970–1987 (The Sublime Image: Creative Video in Spain, 1970–1987), Museo Nacional Centro de Arte Reina Sofía, Madrid, 1987, exhibition catalogue.
Photo: Joaquín Cortés / Román Lores

co-production between European TV producers which saw Spain's public-service broadcaster Televisión Española participate with a piece by Xavier Villaverde.

The selection was formulated around three different times during the brief history of the medium in Spain. The first was in the early seventies, with works made within conceptual practices by the likes of Antoni Muntadas, Francesc Torres, Antoni Miralda, and Juan Navarro Baldeweg, as well as *Primera muerte* (First Death, 1970), the first video work produced in Spain by Silvia Gubern, Àngel Jové, Jordi Galí and Antoni Llena. Although the work is indexed in the exhibition catalogue and leaflet, it doesn't appear to have been screened due to issues with the copy (according to Àngel Fernández Santos, a technician at the Museo Reina Sofía).

A second time-period focuses on the late seventies and early eighties, with the arrival of the first post-production companies and new teams which, under the auspices of the German Institute, allowed some groups, primarily from Barcelona but also from Madrid, to work on the first production by Pedro Garhel in 1979. The San Sebastian International Video Festival also took place around this time, with editions in 1982, 1983 and 1984; under the direction of Guadalupe Echevarría, it represented a turning point in the dissemination and institutional promotion of the video medium in the Spanish state. Names such as Eugènia Balcells, Juan Carlos Eguillor and Antonio Cano, well-known figures on the international scene, attended the Festival and were represented through the display of some of their most recent works in the exhibition.

The third period was represented through the most recent works, from 1985 to 1987, by pre-eminent artists on the scene, such as the aforementioned Juan Carlos Eguillor, Xavier Villaverde and Pedro Garhel, as well as Javier Codesal, Antón Reixa, José Ramón da Cruz and José Montes-Baquer, who had all participated in the scores of festivals and video programmes that cropped up throughout the decade, for instance the Madrid National Video Festival, Zaragoza Video, the Catalonia Video Creation Show and Virreina: Els dilluns vídeo. By and large, the said artists had a background in image studies and tapped into video as the sole channel of artistic expression, with many of them, once the eighties boom was over, working professionally in the TV, advertising and film industries.

The tapes were bought during the creation of the Museo Nacional Centro de Arte Reina Sofía, not to become part of the holdings of its collection, but for its documentation department, viewed as a suitable place for their conservation. Following on from the debates and reflections which materialized in the eighties, video finally found its place in the museum, and not on television or in commercial circuits.

JEF CORNELIS' *THE LONGEST DAY*

Henry Andersen

De langste dag (The Longest Day), coordinated by director Jef Cornelis (b. 1941) for the Belgian television network BRT, was commissioned to cover Initiatief '86; an amalgam of several large-scale public art exhibitions taking place in and around the city of Ghent, most notably 'Chambres d'amis', curated by Jan Hoet, who invited 58 Belgian and international artists to make work in private houses throughout the city. Broadcasting on 21 June 1986, presenter Chris Dercon asked: 'Can art support live television?' The question comes roughly two minutes into the more than six hour live broadcast *De langste dag*.

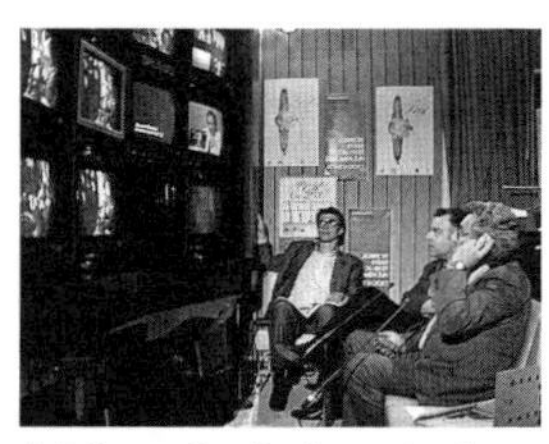

Jef Cornelis, *De langste dag* (The Longest Day), 1986, video still, 6:14:48 hours. Control Room

By 1986, Jef Cornelis had already established himself as a broadcaster of contemporary art with the programme *Zoeklicht* (Searchlight), a series of small filmed vignettes focusing on exhibitions of contemporary art, both in Belgium and abroad. After making films on large-scale exhibitions in Venice, Kassel, and Sonsbeek in the seventies, the director took a very critical stance to the art world, considering it 'remote, critical [and] ambiguous', and largely stopped broadcasting on contemporary art altogether.

Cornelis' response to the broadcast commission was already notable for its sheer scale. He employed all of the considerable technical facilities, staff, and budget of BRT to cover the art event 'as if it were a football match', even using two helicopters to give

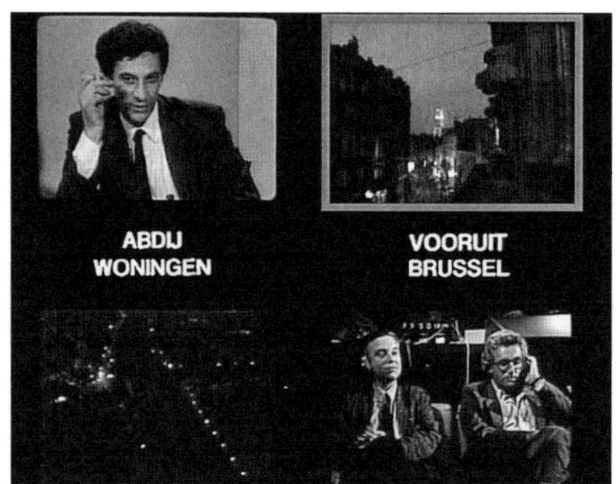

Jef Cornelis, *De langste dag*, 1986 (The Longest Day), video still, 6:14:48 hours. Jan Hoet in discussion with commentators Germano Celant and Denys Zacharoloulos

an overhead view of the proceedings and to move two teams of mobile camera operators about the city. Formally, *De langste dag* quoted almost exactly from the language of large-scale sports broadcasts such as that of the Tour de France. In a central control room, three commentators (Germano Celant, Denys Zacharopoulos, and Chris Dercon) narrated and discussed the proceedings and also held live interviews with several artists 'on-the-ground' via radio connection. Throughout the broadcast, the camera cut to a phone room, and viewers were invited to dial in with questions or remarks for the artists and hosts.

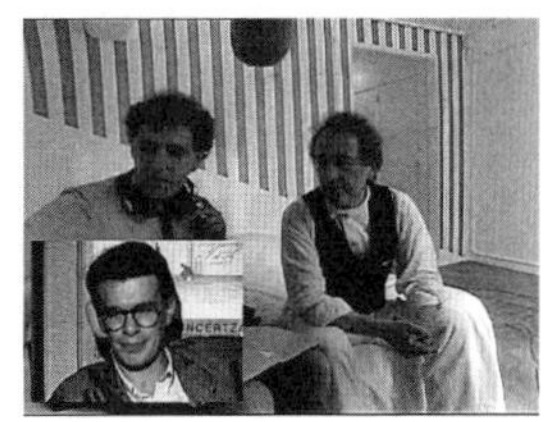
Jef Cornelis, *De langste dag* (The Longest Day), 1986, video still, 6:14:48 hours. Daniel Buren in discussion with Chris Dercon

As with many of Cornelis' films covering large-scale art events (*Documenta 4*, *Documenta V*, *Sonsbeek buiten de perken*, et cetera), there is a strong undercurrent of criticism in the director's relationship to the event. This criticism is voiced not only by the artists and commentators who question the theatricality and scale of Initiatief '86, but by Cornelis' editing choices as well. At one point, Cornelis again made use of the picture-in-picture device to overlay a speech from Minister of Culture Patrick De Waele with artists Jef Geys and Panamarenko, who watch a live-feed of the speech as they eat a meal of grilled salmon and champagne. Commentator German Celant described the overlay as 'an extra-ordinary event … only possible through TV'.

What makes *De langste dag* such an unwieldy cultural document is both the chaotic energy of its 'liveness', and its own self-conscious reflection on the medium of live-to-air television. Behind its impressive scale and ambition, *De langste dag* was largely motivated by an earnest question about the responsibility of art to a broader public, and what role television might play in such an exchange. Indeed, we may see Cornelis' documentary as a very different response to Hoet's curatorial demand for 'Chambres d'amis'. For Hoet, the invitation to international artists to make work for a selection of private houses in Ghent was a way to wrestle art away from the museum and confront it with the domestic sphere. In *De langste dag* too, art was brought into the private homes of the people of Ghent, but in a way that was decidedly riskier and more democratic than that of the exhibition itself. Art entered homes and interacted with its public via the markedly domestic technology of television.

Rather than offering art to its viewers, *De langste dag* offered art for consumption by television. Contemporary art was made to interface with a medium that is radically different in terms of its economy of image and its relationship with its audience. It shows how the ideas of contemporary art travel when they are turned into images and made to adhere to the rapid pace of live television.

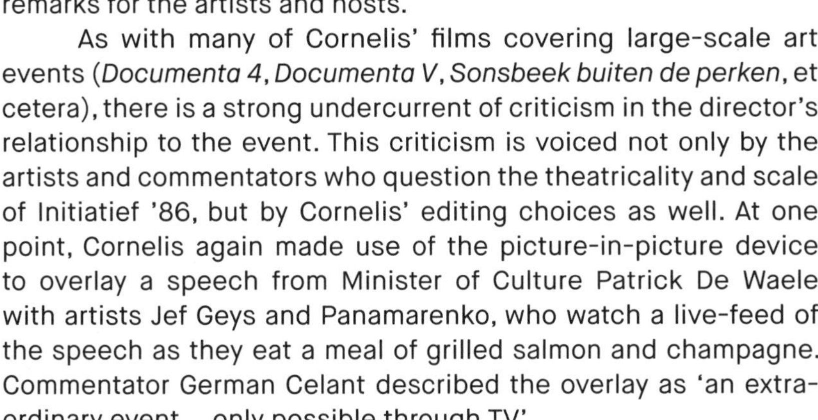

1986

2. KNOW YOUR

RIGHTS

INTRODUCTION

Beatriz Herráez

In the introduction to this book, Diedrich Diederichsen establishes a direct link between the eighties and punk, a counterculture movement bound to the discontent and critical spirit of a generation, and sparked by the dismantling of the welfare state initiated by the new conservative policies at the time. The chapter 'Know Your Rights' borrows its title from a well-known track by the British punk band The Clash. The song functions as an anthem that also profoundly reflects an epoch in which the deployment of neoliberal policies caused numerous civil rights secured in the previous decades to progressively diminish. Therefore, the forms of opposition in this new geopolitical map often operated on the flipside of the optimism that defined the outlook of struggles that surfaced in the preceding decades, thereby relinquishing a revolutionary perspective that sought to tighten its grip on radical social and political transformation. In the face of preceding models, the eighties would be characterized by the inception of different forms of collective mobilization, paying heed to multiple struggles, including new feminisms, gays and lesbian rights, or anti-war and environmental movements.

Following the structure of the publication, 'Know Your Rights' is divided into two subchapters entitled 'Ecologies and Anti-Militarism' and 'Civil Liberties'. The first starts with Lisa Godson's essay on the environmental protests that took place in different enclaves around Europe (the UK, Turkey, Ireland…). The issues touched upon by the historian include a look at the actions carried out by Greenpeace, and the anti-nuclear and environmental campaigns that took place in this period, setting forth an analysis of the relevance of their effects on the processes of political transformation in Central and Eastern Europe. Taking Godson's theories as a point of departure, the chapter explores case studies such as the Women's Movement of Greenham Common Women's Peace Camp, by Annie Fletcher, the march of a group of women protesting at nuclear weapons being sited at an army base in England; the reproduction of the Orbanist Manifesto (1980), whereby Luc Deleu explores the environmental responsibility of architecture and urbanism practices; the visibility work of the Radical Democrats in Turkey regarding environmental issues, as well as those related to religion, feminism, anti-war and the LGTB movement written by Bariş Gençer Baykan; and the repercussions and demands of militant publications engaged with activism and civil rights such as *Razmerja* (Relationships), from Slovenia, by Božidar Flajšman, and Spain's *El viejo topo* (The Old Mole) reflected on by Pablo Martínez. This first subchapter concludes with two cases that spotlight the momentum gained by the anti-war movement in the same period. On one side, through the reflection on the insubordination movement in Spain within the framework of the country joining NATO and the European Union, by Carlos Prieto del Campo, and on the other, via the campaign 'No to compulsory military service' advocated in Turkey through an appeal published by *Sokak* (Street) magazine and the *Güneş* newspaper. Between 1989 and 1990, *Sokak* featured a section also called 'Know Your Rights', a space focused on decrying the restrictions and rights violations in the country, by Merve Elveren and Erman Ata Uncu.

The second chapter, on 'Civil Liberties', opens with the theorist Gal Kirn's essay on the transformations of Socialist Civil Society in eighties Yugoslavia, underscoring the contradictions brought about by a particular convergence of elements from both the Communist and Capitalist regimes. The emergence of civil society, the 'democratic reinvention' of territory, and the nationalist-liberal shift that occurred in the latter years of the decade are some of the points put forward. With regard to Slovenia, Kirn links the demand for democratic reforms with artistic practices and the work of collectives that were the rudiments of organized political groups, those that would promote the struggles and demands aligned with the LGTB movement, trade union movements and the peace movement. Tied in with the context expounded by Gal Kirn, the case studies completing this passage address the fights for freedom of thought, expression and the press; the Article 133 of the Penal Code of the Socialist Federal Republic of Yugoslavia, 'sanctioning the act of speaking out against or criticizing the authorities (...), written by Neža Kogovšek Šalamon; the 'Petition of Intellectuals'(1984), a text with 1,256 signatures, which included prominent cultural and academic figures in the country and was addressed to the Prime Minister of Turkey, by Merve Elveren and Erman Ata Uncu; and the text about the film *Rocío* (1980), banned in Spain in 1981 and branded by its detractors as a form of political pamphlet and as anticlerical, a contribution by Pedro G. Romero. The passage concludes with the study of another audiovisual essay, *Handsworth Songs*, the feature-length film produced in 1986 by the Black Audio Film Collective in the aftermath of the riots and protests in the Handsworth area of Birmingham, by Nick Aikens.

In the third essay of this chapter anthropologist Lourdes Méndez explores the emergence and fragmentations of the feminist movement in Spain in the eighties through a passage that analyzes its demands throughout history — the right to vote, sexual and reproductive rights, equal pay. Making mention of the twofold oppression women have been subjected to, 'as workers and as women', Méndez points to the forgetfulness from which these struggles have suffered, in addition to feminism's risks of institutionalization and the application of neoliberal policies, which increases the inequality that stems from positions of sex/gender, class and race, in the words of the author. Moreover, two case studies by Teresa Grandas are framed inside Spain: the first concerns the Danger to Society and Social Rehabilitation Law implemented in 1970 to persecute behaviour deemed 'anti-social' (of, for instance, drug addicts, beggars, homosexuals), and not fully abolished until 1995, followed by the construction, at the beginning of the nineties, of new forms of political and activist subjectivity from gay and lesbian groups (Radical Gai and LSD) and their mobilization during the AIDS crisis, written by Jesús Carrilllo. These activist practices are set in conjunction with the birth of the LGBT community scene in Slovenia, strongly articulated around cultural initiatives, discussed by Igor Španjol. The coda to the chapter lies firstly with artist Sunil Gupta's work *'Pretended' Family Relationships* (1988), a photographic series that explore multi-racial gay relationships and offer a response to the British law known as Clause 28 banning the 'promotion of homosexuality', by Nick Aikens, and secondly with the exhibition '100%' (1993), the first exhibition organized in a museum in Spain that featured the exclusive participation of female artists, denouncing their invisibility, written by Beatriz Herráez.

2.1 ECO—LOGIES

Environmental Protest in
Europe in the Eighties
1980s

Greenham Common
1981–2000

Orbanist Manifesto
1980

El Viejo Topo
1976–1982

Insubordination in Spain
1980–1990

ANTI-MILITARISM

Razmerja and Ecology

1982–1984

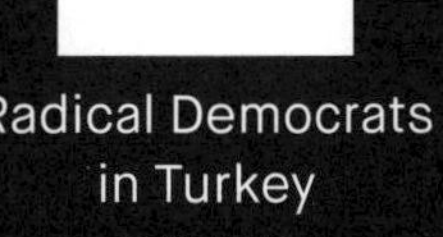

Radical Democrats
in Turkey

1985–1989

ENVIRONMENTAL PROTEST
IN EUROPE IN THE EIGHTIES

Lisa Godson

This essay seeks to provide an overview of aspects of environmental protest in the eighties, with case studies of particular groups, actions, and areas. It involves elements of radical action, institutionalization, state-sponsored violence, global environmental problems and a concern with local pollution issues that often connected with distant corporate or political power-bases. While certain issues that had been central to the environmental movement for over a century remained significant, in the first half of the decade the nuclear arms race was the backdrop against which some of the most profound protests took place. In particular regions, including Central and Eastern Europe and the Basque Country, environmental action also worked as a vehicle for claims to greater political autonomy and nationalism. The end of the decade saw the further institutionalization of environmentalism, not least through the stimulus of the European Union, but also a high point for environmental activism, not least in the Eastern bloc.[01]

Although difficult to describe in unitary terms, environmentalism (in some European countries 'ecologism') is typically considered to have its roots in the mid-nineteenth century. This mainly relates to conservation movements founded during the classical phase of modernity in response to the impact of industrialization and urbanization on the environment. More overtly political elements also responded to the effects of Inclosure legislation, such as the Commons Preservation Society (CPS), founded in England in 1865, and one of the first environmental organizations in Europe.[02] The concerns of the CPS were often expressed in anti-enclosure protest activities in its early days. By the eighties it mainly functioned as an advisory or advocacy body that informed more radical actions such as squatting and occupations, for example by publishing the definitive *Rights of Way: A Guide to Law and Practice* (1983) and through its involvement with the Common Land Forum (1986) which endorsed greater public access rights to commons.[03] Despite government commitment to implement the recommendations of the forum, this was stymied by the lobbying of powerful private land-owning interests, a response that was echoed in other European countries under economically right-wing governance: in Britain, legislation was not implemented until the 2000 Countryside and Rights of Way Act. Other regions of Europe in the eighties saw the continuation of traditional rights of access or 'freedom to roam', in particular the Nordic countries of Iceland, Sweden, Finland and Norway.[04]

In the eighties, the CPS and other long-established European bodies promoted rights of access to the environment as a shared amenity (for example for recreational walking), but the broader concept of 'the commons' and 'commoning' involving activities antithetical to capital was more fulsomely taken up by others,

01

For a series of case studies on environmental protest in individual countries in the European Union see Christopher Rootes, ed., *Environmental Protest in Western Europe* (Oxford: Oxford University Press, 2003).

02

See Ben Cowell, 'The Commons Preservation Society and the Campaign for Berkhamsted Common, 1866–70', *Rural History* 13, no. 2 (2002), pp. 145–161.

03

See Christopher P. Rodgers et al., *Contested Common Land: Environmental Governance Past and Present* (London: Routledge, 2012).

04

See Thomas H. Beery, 'Nordic in Nature: Friluftsliv and Environmental Connectedness', *Environmental Education Research* 19, no. 1 (2013), pp. 94–117; Hans Gelter, 'Friluftsliv: The Scandinavian Philosophy of Outdoor Life', *Canadian Journal of Environmental Education* 5, no. 1 (2000), pp. 77–92.

including intellectuals on the left, for example the influential Marxist historian Peter Linebaugh. With groundwork made towards this concept and a reclamation of its historic roots in the eighties, the discourse of 'the commons' became more widely spread following the collapse of the Soviet Union at the end of the decade when 'it became possible to think of communism without the totalitarian state'.[05]

A more overt aspect of environmental campaigns and protests in the eighties connects to the deleterious effects of noxious substances spawned by intense industrial, agricultural and fishing methods. In some ways, this was a continuation of concerns first fully articulated in the sixties, for example through the ground-breaking work of Rachel Carson, author of *Silent Spring* (1962).[06] While unevenly expressed in the preceding decades, by the eighties protests tended to figure environmental concerns as an aspect of human rights, expressed variously in terms of access to ethically managed natural resources, land rights, political autonomy and freedom from the nefarious impact of political and corporate greed.

GREENPEACE

The non-governmental Greenpeace (founded 1971) was one of the most significant environmental protest groups of the eighties. It generated a number of linked organizations of the same name in the seventies that were brought together as 'Greenpeace International' in 1979. During the eighties, the organization expanded greatly; branches were established throughout Europe and the world. Greenpeace undertook key actions focused on the transport and dumping of toxic waste and the protection of sea-life, most prominently through their opposition to commercial whaling. Their tactics included direct confrontation and 'ecotage', a concept popularized by Edward Abbey's novel *The Monkey Wrench Gang* (1975) and *Ecotage!* by Sam Love and David Obst (1971). Among their civil disobedience tactics was the piloting of their own fleet of vessels to carry out protests or directly intervene to protect the environment. For example, in the early eighties Greenpeace took a series of direct actions against Spanish whaling, and in 1982 the Greenpeace ship *Sirius* sailed into the port of Leningrad and released 2000 helium balloons protesting nuclear testing by the USSR. These actions could be perilous: in 1983, four Greenpeace divers were contaminated by radiation whilst attempting to block a discharge pipe at Sellafield nuclear reprocessing plant in Cumbria in North-West England that was releasing more than 10 million litres of radioactive water into the sea every day. Greenpeace was fined £50,000 and the

05

Peter Linebaugh, *Stop Thief! The Commons, Enclosures and Resistance* (Oakland: PM Press, 2014), p. 5.

06

See Mark Hamilton Lytle, *The Gentle Subversive: Rachel Carson, Silent Spring, and the Rise of the Environmental Movement* (Oxford: Oxford University Press, 2007).

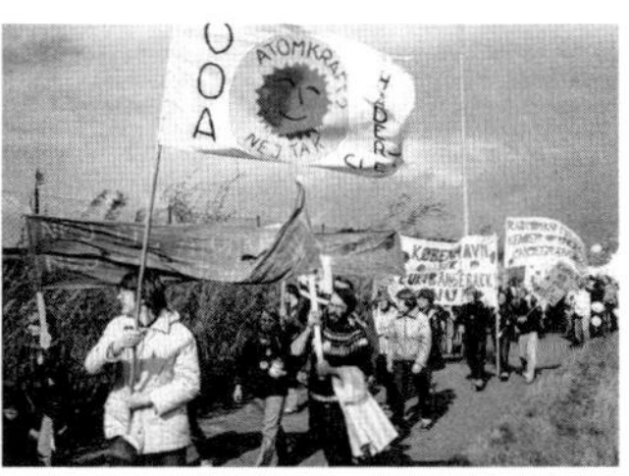

Protest march to Barsebäck nuclear power station, Sweden, 1980. The banner to the front shows the Smiling Sun or 'solmærket', which was designed by the Danish student Anne Lund and became used as a symbol against nuclear energy. Photo: Søren Rud

government-owned British Nuclear Fuels Limited (BNFL) was granted a permanent injunction against the organization. BNFL was later found guilty on four criminal charges for the discharge.[07]

In 1985, activists sailed the Greenpeace vessel *Rainbow Warrior* to the Pacific Ocean to engage in actions related to nuclear testing, including the evacuation of islanders from Rongelap Atoll, which had been contaminated by radioactivity from historic American activity, and to lead a flotilla to protest against French testing in the area. While in Auckland harbour in July 1985 the ship was sunk by explosive devices attached to its hull by French intelligence agents from the Direction Générale de la Sécurité Extérieure, causing the drowning of the Dutch photographer Fernando Pereira. The resulting political fall-out in France, nicknamed 'Underwatergate' by some, obscured the broader significance of European exploitation of the Pacific region for nuclear-political ends.[08]

ANTI-NUCLEAR PROTESTS

In the eighties, protests against nuclear weapons were broadly cast as part of an international peace movement for which environmental rights were foundational, with protest against the nuclear energy industry more specifically focused on ecological threat. In general, anti-nuclear protests were often coloured by assumptions about the role of humans as stewards of nature. For example, the activist Angie Zelter described the abolition of nuclear weapons as one element in the struggle to solve 'the pressing social and environmental crises that threaten the whole web of life on our fragile planet'.[09]

The seventies had seen a détente in the Cold War, with a number of Strategic Arms Limitation Talks (SALT) and subsequent treaties aimed at arms control, particularly SALT I (1972) and SALT II (1979). However, following the invasion of Afghanistan by the USSR in December 1979, the USA did not ratify SALT II. Indeed, the Soviet-Afghan War (December 1979–February 1989) was a significant factor in elevating Cold War tensions particularly in the first part of the eighties, including the resumption of the nuclear arms race involving the development and stock-piling of weapons. In late 1979, members of NATO had approved the deployment of US GLCM cruise missiles and Pershing II nuclear weapons in Europe, galvanizing protest in the following years.

The most intense and sustained European protest of the eighties was around the Royal Air Force (RAF) base at Greenham Common in Berkshire, England, a storage site for cruise missiles. As detailed by Annie Fletcher (see 'Greenham Common' elsewhere

07

See Luther J. Carter, *Nuclear Imperatives and Public Trust: Dealing with Radioactive Waste* (London: Routledge, 2017, originally published 1987).

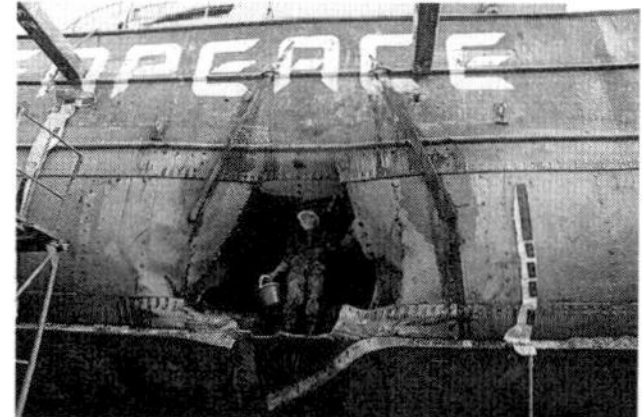

Greenpeace *Rainbow Warrior* ship after being attacked by French secret agents in Aukland Harbour, 10 July 1983

08

For a contemporary analysis, see Steve Sawyer, 'Rainbow Warrior: Nuclear War in the Pacific', *Third World Quarterly* 8, no. 4 (1986), pp. 1325–1336.

09

Angie Zelter, 'Trident Ploughshares Support for Decommissioners', in *If I had a Hammer … Decommissioning the War Machine*, ed. EDO Decommissioners (WordPress, 2009).

in this volume), the first iteration of the Greenham Common Women's Peace Camp was in September 1981 when the group Women for Life on Earth marched to the base and a small number of women chained themselves to the perimeter fence; in the months following, a series of woman-only camps were built around the base and other camps were established around other European bases. Vestigial camps were still at Greenham Common up to two decades later, but the time of most concentrated activism and occupation was in the eighties, as the last missiles were removed in 1991. The Greenham activists carried out a series of well-documented actions including the encircling of the facility by tens of thousands protestors on two successive occasions in 1983 and breaking into the base numerous times, powerfully represented by imagery of women dancing on the missile silos on New Year's Eve, 1982. As one commentator noted, this frequent breaching of the base amounted to 'rather more than a symbolic point about the supposed impressive security conferred by the weapons'.[10] Alongside that evental history of the protest was the importance of daily endurance by such a 'great range of diverse but mostly ordinary and representative women'[11] in the often harsh conditions of camp life over long periods of time (see Fletcher, 'Greenham Common' in this volume).

The International Relations scholar Catherine Eschle has identified six interlocking, often overlapping, discourses used to describe anti-nuclear activist women, labelling them as maternalist, anti-violence, culturalist, materialist, cosmopolitan, and cosmological in character.[12] Of this schema, the cosmological offered the most elaborated environmental discourse, and 'mobilized gendered imagery as part of its holistic conception of the universe and the role of humans within it', drawing on a self-conscious ecofeminism 'in critiques of a dualistic masculine worldview involving separation from and mastery over nature'.[13] Despite charges of promoting a biologically determinist gendered reading of the environment, more recent scholarship has revisited ecofeminism and its key texts as sensitive to contingencies and contexts.[14]

The force of the peace mobilization of the early eighties was evident in October 1982 when nearly 3 million people protested in cities throughout Europe including Rome, Vienna, Stockholm, Paris, and Dublin 'to protest nuclear missile deployments and to demand an end to the arms race'[15] with the largest single protest in the Dutch city of the Hague. This was the biggest mobilization of peace protests in European (and human) history until the protests against the war in Iraq in February 2003.

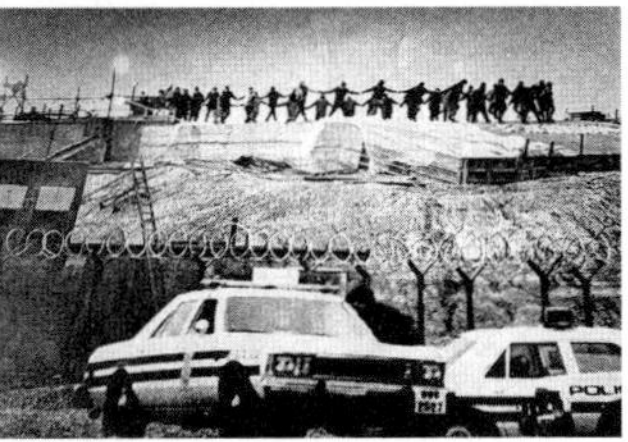

Greenham Common protest, dancing on the silos at dawn, New Year's day, USAF air base, Berkshire, 1 January 1983. Photo: Raissa Page

10
Mary Midgley, 'Shouting Across the Gulf', *London Review of Books* 6, no. 19 (1984), pp. 7–11, p. 8.

11
Ibid., p. 8.

12
Catherine Eschle, 'Gender and the Subject of (Anti)Nuclear Politics: Revisiting Women's Campaigning against the Bomb', *International Studies Quarterly* 57, no. 4 (2013), pp. 713–724.

13
Eschle, 'Gender and the Subject of (Anti)Nuclear Politics', p. 717.

14
See for example Joan Cadden, 'Focus: Getting back to the Death of Nature: Rereading Carolyn Marchant', *Isis* 97, no. 3 (2006), pp. 485–486.

15
David Cortright, Peace: *A History of Movements and Ideas* (Cambridge: Cambridge University Press, 2008), p. 148.

In communist Central and Eastern Europe (henceforth Eastern bloc), both anti-nuclear campaigns and protest about local environmental issues were significant in the eighties, and ultimately played an important role in the political transitions of 1989/1991.

The European Nuclear Disarmament Campaign (END, founded 1982) was largely based in western Europe and became important in backing unilateral initiatives and supporting the work of dissidents in the Soviet Union and its east-central European satellite states. Their strategy in fostering a 'détente from below' meant the building of close relationships with the Hungarian Dialogue Group, Charter 77, the Moscow Trust Group, and other intrepid anti-nuclear forces in the East.[16] The aspiration of the END to work in pan-European solidarity was sometimes seen as naïve by those living under oppressive regimes. This was not least because of suspicion of utopian sloganeering to a population inured to aspirational exhortations by repressive regimes. END's idealistic focus on 'peace' at the expense of recognizing everyday suffering and regional difference was viewed as naïve, particularly in the area of environmental destruction. This was forcefully expressed by Czech dissident and writer Václav Havel in his 'Anatomy of a Reticence' (1985), written, according to a note by the author, to be delivered at a peace conference in Amsterdam in his absence. Havel contrasted the Western peace activist to a citizen of his own country who

> can have absolutely nothing to say about the possible conversion of a large tract of his homeland into a desert for the sake of a bit of inferior coal … since he cannot protect even his children's teeth from deteriorating due to environmental pollution, since he cannot even obtain a permit to move for the sake of his children's teeth and souls from northern to southern Bohemia, how could he influence something on the order of some sort of 'Star Wars' between two superpowers? All that appears so terribly distant to him, as far beyond his influence as the stars above.[17]

The importance of environmental activism as a mobilizing agent for populist protest against Eastern bloc regimes is widely recognized. Prior to the mid-eighties, individual governments paid little heed to the environmental consequences of enforced industrialization, with production quotas taking precedence over health and environmental considerations, often in service to centralized power. The resulting life-threatening pollution and disastrous environmental conditions have been characterized thus:

16

Lawrence Wittner, *Confronting the Bomb: A Short History of the World Nuclear Disarmament Movement* (Palo Alto: Stanford University Press, 2009), p. 165.

17

Václav Havel, 'Anatomy of a Reticence' (1985) available at http://www.vaclavhavel.cz/showtrans.php?cat=eseje&val=4_aj_eseje.html&typ=HTML (accessed 23 July 2017).

Villages in Czechoslovakia were black and barren because of acid rain, smoke, and coal dust from nearby factories. Drinking water from Estonia to Bulgaria was tainted with toxic chemicals and untreated sewage. Polish garden vegetables were inedible because of high lead and cadmium levels in the soil. Chronic health problems were endemic to much of the region.[18]

Many of the ecological movements that emerged across the Eastern bloc in the eighties were connected with the political drive for democracy, with unsatisfied demands for an improved environmental situation leading to insistence on widespread political change. Examples include the 'phosphorite war' in Estonia involving a campaign in the late eighties against the opening of new phosphorite mines in Virumaa, figured as the catalyst for Estonian independence; intensive campaigns by Hungarian activists against the construction of the proposed Gabčíkovo-Nagymaros dam on the Danube River, which ignited more general political opposition; the activities of Bulgaria's Ecoglasnost group; the Slovak Union of Landscape and Nature Protection, perhaps the only important current of opposition before 1989;[19] the Latvian Popular Front's exposés of petrochemical poisoning on the Daugava River; the actions of the Polish Ecological Club (PKE), 'widely recognized as being the first legally established independent, non-profit, environmental non-governmental organization in the former socialist block countries of Central and Eastern Europe'.[20]

The single most important, and catastrophic, environmental catalyst towards political action was the Chernobyl disaster. Shortly after midnight on 26 April 1986, a badly designed reactor at the nuclear power plant in Chernobyl in the then Ukrainian Soviet Socialist Republic of the Soviet Union exploded, leading to highly radioactive fallout across an extensive region including the western USSR and Europe. In the aftermath of the explosion, a news blackout was imposed, with 'Soviet paranoia and secretiveness about anything to do with industrial accidents, military matters and nuclear power' making the confusion worse.[21] The disaster eventually necessitated widespread evacuation and projections of tens of thousands of excess deaths from radioactive contamination, and is seen as both a key factor in the eventual demise of the Soviet Union and as galvanizing environmental protest in the broader region. Again, in the wake of Chernobyl there was a conflation of independence and environmental movements, for example in Lithuanian protests against the Ignalina nuclear power station, which played an important role in the struggle against centralized authority in Moscow,[22] and protests in Armenia against the Medzamor nuclear power plant and the Nairit

18

Mary Ann Cunningham, 'Eastern European Pollution', in *Environmental Encyclopedia*, ed. Marci Bortman and Peter Brimblecombe et al. (Michigan: Thomson Gale, 2003, 3rd edition), pp. 407–409, p. 407.

19

Petr Jehlička and Tomas Kostelecky, 'The Development of the Czechoslovak Green Party since the 1990 Election', *Environmental Politics* 1, no. 1 (1992), pp. 72–94.

20

Polish Ecological Club, http:// zb.eco.pl/gb/18/pke.htm (accessed 1 September 2017).

21

Zhores Medvedev, 'Chernobyl: A Catalyst for Change', in *Milestones in Glasnost and Perestroyka: Politics and People, Volume 2*, ed. Hewett and Victor Hansen (Washington DC: Brookings Institute, 1991), pp. 19–30, p. 23.

22

Jürgen Salay, 'Environment and Energy in the Baltic Countries', in *Economic Policies for Sustainable Development*, ed. by Thomas Sterner (Dordrecht: Springer Science and Business Media, 1994), pp. 113–131.

Chemical Factory.[23] But more than anything, the effects of the Chernobyl disaster emphasized the transnational, even global, characteristics of ecology.

LOCALIZED PROTEST IN THE FACE OF HASTENED GLOBALIZATION

Of course, concerns about the ill effects of industrialization were not confined to the Eastern bloc, and the eighties saw numerous protests throughout Europe against local environmental threats. This was often in regions that were undergoing hastened process-es of modernization and globalization, for example through the encouragement of multi-national corporations to set up manu-facturing or processing facilities in previously 'under-industri-alized' areas. One such example was in Spain, where fishermen protested against the establishment of a plant on the northwest Atlantic coast by the Canadian mining and manufacturing com-pany Alcan Aluminium Limited over fears of ground-water pollu-tion, and another in Ireland where local groups became adept at stalling and protesting planning decisions from the mid-seventies into the eighties.[24]

The attitude of the Irish government in this period has been characterized as 'jobs versus environment'[25] and in areas of high unemployment and 'under-development' there was often a heavy social penalty for protestors. This meant dissenting voices were often lone individuals drawing attention to personal suffering rather than as members of an established environmental group, as in the disturbing case of the Hanrahan family which received worldwide coverage.[26] They were dairy farmers in County Tipperary whose family, neighbours, and livestock suffered inexplicable health problems following the opening of a chemical plant by the American pharmaceutical company Merck Sharp & Dohme one mile up-wind from the Hanrahan farm. In one of the longest civil cases in Irish history during which the Hanrahans lost the land they had farmed for seven generations due to their legal costs, they were finally awarded compensation. The Hanrahan case doubtlessly mobilized opposition to other major corporations building chemi-cal plants in Ireland, for example through protests against Merrell Dow and Sandoz, and tensions between a government keen to encourage foreign direct investment and local populaces fearful of the ill effects of weakly regulated industry persisted.

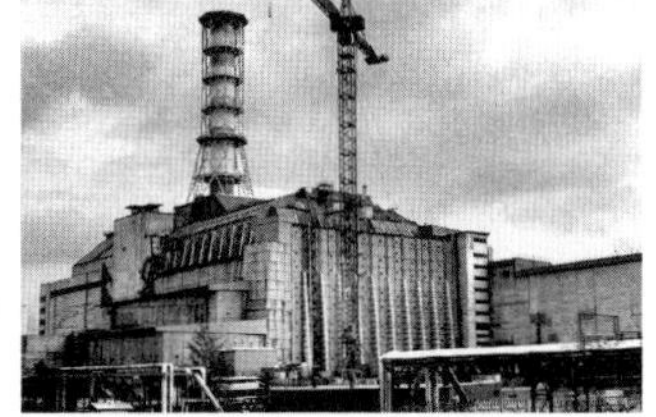

Aftermath of the explosion in the nuclear reactor, Chernobyl, April 1986

23

See Magnus Andersson, 'Environment and Transition in Eastern Europe', in *Change and Continuity in Poland's Environmental Policy* (New York: Springer, 1999), pp. 3–19.

24

For a contemporary perspective, see H. Jeffrey Leonard, *Pollution and the Struggle for the World Product: Multinational Corporations, Environment, and International Comparative Advantage* (Cambridge: Cambridge University Press, 1988).

25

Seán MacConnell, 'A Decade Fighting a multinational', *Irish Times*, 16 March 2006.

26

See for example Doug Payne, 'A Long Toxic Way to Tipperary', *New Scientist* 5 January 1991, available at www.newscientist.com/article/mg12917501-100-a-long-toxic-way-to-tipperary/ (accessed 30 August 2017); Jerry O'Callaghan, *The Red Book: the Hanrahan Case against Merck, Sharp and Dohme* (Dublin: Poolbeg, 1992).

The course of environmental issues in Turkey was marked by the policies ushered in following the military coup and subsequent junta of 1980–1983. Environmental activism and politics were affected by the interaction of globalization processes and domestic issues and the start of a move away from the state-centric modernity that had dominated post-Ottoman Turkey.[27] While the 1982 Constitution recognized the environmental rights and duties of all Turkish citizens and the State (Article 56), this was rarely operationalized in practice and the eighties saw the planting of a number of environmental problems seeded by a developmentalist imperative. Turkey was subject to a hastened phase of neo-liberal modernization by a government keen to embrace a free market model including large-scale infrastructural projects, often to the detriment of the local environment.

[27] Gabriel Ignatow, 'Globalizations and the Transformation of Environmental Activism: Turkey since the eighties', *Globalizations* 5, no. 3 (2008), pp. 433–447, p. 437.

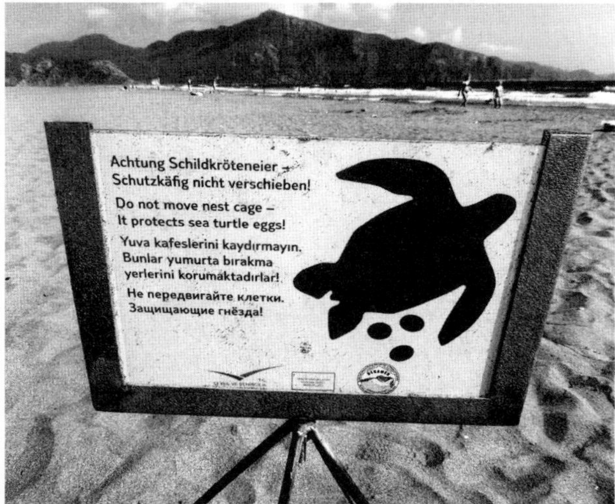

Sign on Iztuzo 'Turtle' Beach, South West Turkey, one of the main breeding grounds for Loggerhead Sea Turtles and site of conflict between environmentalists and developers at various times since the eighties

In general, the approach to the environment was a techno-managerial one that engendered later problems, for example in terms of fishing where the government subsidized a fleet that could compete with other Mediterranean countries; with poor regulation this led to problems of over-fishing and pollution in subsequent years. While environmentalism was in the hands of state actors in the early years, the eighties saw the development of civil society and the rise of new social movements, including environmentalist groups.[28] As with Central and Eastern Europe in the same period, environmentalism was tolerated by the government, as it was perceived as apolitical and unthreatening

[28] See Aimilia Voulvouli, *From Environmentalism to Transenvironmentalism: The Ethnography of an Urban Protest in Modern Istanbul* (Oxford: Peter Lang, 2009), in particular Chapter 5.

to the established political order. Most activism focused on issues of locally-unwanted-land-use (LULUs) especially regarding energy, tourism and urban planning projects that threatened green areas,[29] such as the campaign against the development of Iztuzu beach, a nesting site for loggerhead turtles in the South-West. The late eighties saw the burgeoning Bergama movement against gold mining in Western Turkey that politicized environmentalism in the country into the nineties and beyond.[30]

[29]

Baran Alp Uncu, *Within Borders, Beyond Borders: The Bergama Movement at the Junction of Local, National and Transnational Practices*, PhD thesis (London School of Economics, 2012), p. 102. Available at http://etheses.lse.ac.uk/498/1/Uncu%20Within%20borders%2C%20beyond%20borders.pdf (accessed 12 August 2017).

[30]

See Çiğdem Adem, 'Non-State Actors and Environmentalism', in *Environmentalism in Turkey: Between Democracy and Development?*, ed. Fikret Adaman and Murat Arsel (Hants: Peter Lang, 2005), pp. 71–86.

ORBANIST MANIFESTO, 1980

Luc Deleu

Until we can start evacuating our planet on a massive scale, or importing goods from space, we will need to fulfil all our needs with what is found here on Earth — apart from the (required) solar energy and possibly other (unacknowledged, but equally vital) space energy.

One-third of the world population is undernourished. This implies that we would have to expand our existing arable land by over 30% to satisfy our actual needs. Besides intensifying food production per square metre, we could make a huge effort to transform deserts, steppes and wastelands into arable land. But we will also need to utilize as much 'free space' in our conurbations as possible for food production. All the more so because if anything, we should strive to save our jungles, forests, woodlands and other nature areas and even expand them into reserve areas.

If we choose to accept these priorities, in theory this means there are hardly any opportunities left to us to expand our conurbations in terms of surface area. This in turn puts considerable pressure on our living conditions. If we wish to guarantee maximum residential comfort for all, we will need to create far greater efficiency in the organization of our living environments than has been achieved up to this point. We will need to focus more strongly on the polyvalent use of urban spaces. In this critical phase, the best solution would be for everyone to organize his living situation on an individual basis, according to his personal preferences, resources, options and limits. This can be seen as analogous to the entirely decentralized organization of a plant community (*phytocoenosis*), in which every specimen bears full responsibility within the limits and opportunities offered by its station. On the other hand, we should set strict requirements for the macro-structures of legal entities (organized groups of individuals such as corporations, private limited liability companies, associations, pressure groups, etc.) in order to balance the macro-level impact and land use of such entities with the micro-level impact and land use of individuals within the ecotope (environmental effects and *biocoenosis*[01]). Once again, we can observe an analogous arrangement in nature, in which the biological equilibrium is best served by an ecosystem that comprises a large number of species, as this leads to more diverse effects on the individual species. On the other hand, in a system in which there is a limited variety of species,

[01] Community of all living organisms.

this equilibrium is more easily upset, which may even result in the proliferation of a particular species (plague).

Inconvenient and unnecessary elements need to be dumped (i.e. shot into space with a rocket). The remaining elements need to be stacked as clearly and compactly as possible (while making sure that these entrepots can be used for a variety of functions). As all communities (*anthropocoenosis*,[02] *zoocoenosis*,[03] *phytocoenosis*, *microcoenosis*[04] and *mycocoenosis*[05]) are closely interconnected, we will have to be very careful not to smother one in favour of the other. To this end, we need to limit pollution to a bare minimum and recycle as much materials as possible. We will need to be particularly efficient when it comes to recycling organic waste, which can be used to replenish our arable land. This way, we will be able to conserve the maximum amount of biogenic matter (which is necessary for *phytocoenosis*).

Fortunately, we have a major spatial reserve in the form of our oceans and seas (whose *biocoenoses* are in a critical state). This reserve is twice as large as the surface on land. For example, the Earth's entire population could be accommodated on one million 40,000-tonne cruise liners. Indeed, if the number of ships were increased to two million, their residents would even be fairly comfortable. The entire population of Belgium could find a perfect mobile home for themselves on five thousand 40,000-tonne liners.

02
Human community.

03
Animal community.

04
Bacterial community.

05
Fungal community.

Luc Deleu, *Proposal for Total Disuse of Public Lighting: Orbanic Idea for Antwerp*, ink on paper, 118×108 cm. Courtesy M HKA, photo: M HKA

It is my modest hope that the picture of 'momentaneous times' that I have outlined above brings home the importance of adopting a new 'orbanist' perspective to town planning and architecture. In 'momentaneous times', town planning and architecture work according to orbanist priorities. The aesthetic priorities and stylistic elements of 'non-momentaneous times' are no longer relevant in a situation of DIY architecture and self-made cities, in which the built-up environment is codetermined by each individual citizen.

Indeed, in 'momentaneous times', the urbanist architect (orbanist) fulfils an entirely different role altogether. Just as the (pictorial) function of painting (in Western art) changed profoundly after the invention of photography, town planning and architecture (orbanism) have presently undergone a change of function and meaning. A key aspect of the 'momentaneous' orbanist's current profession is providing 'information' (reduction of uncertainty). The orbanist is a medium, a trendsetter and/or the town jester, etc. He designs, publishes, performs, exhibits, realizes or plays around, and so on.

His new ideal is 'free space'. Instead of focusing on infrastructures that define the Earth's space and make it more one-dimensional, the orbanist now utilizes ultrastructures that increase this space without limiting its wide range of potential uses.

Today's orbanist is a theoretician first and foremost — one who in rare cases is able to realize his visionary models that outline how to structure our planet's spaces.

Although it is a dynamic and evolving planet, as home to a constantly self-realising orbanism that is influenced by the actions of all its individual inhabitants, the Earth can constantly be considered completed in the 'momentaneous times'.

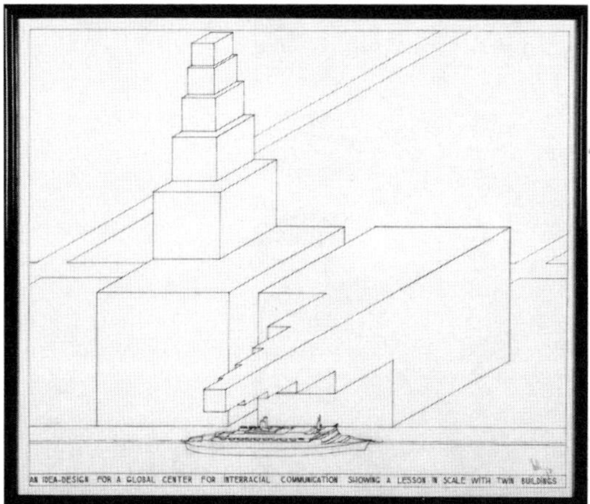

Luc Deleu, *An Idea-Design for a Global Center for Interracial Communication Showing a Lesson in Scale with Twin Buildings*, 1988. Courtesy M HKA, photo: M HKA

Luc Deleu / T.O.P. Office, *Proposals 1972–1980 Revisited 2002*. Courtesy Luc Deleu / T.O.P. Office

GREENHAM COMMON

Annie Fletcher

In the eighties the fear of nuclear war hung over everything. The Women's Movement of Greenham Common was a resistance movement that protested the decision to allow the American military to locate 96 nuclear cruise missiles at the RAF Greenham military base in Berkshire, England. As CND (Campaign for Nuclear Disarmament) campaigner Annie Tuncliffe noted at the time 'People were looking for a focus for their anxieties, and Greenham was it'.[01] What became known as the Greenham common peace camp, which lasted almost two decades, began with an anti-missile march from Cardiff to the RAF Greenham base on the 5th of December 1981 by the group Women for Life on Earth. They delivered a letter to the Base Commander, which stated 'We fear for the future of all our children and for the future of the living world which is the basis of all life'. When the military refused to acknowledge the letter the women chained themselves to the fence and refused to withdraw. They subsequently set up an impromptu peace camp that drew widespread publicity and support. The first blockade of the base occurred in May 1982 with 250 women protesting — 34 arrests were made.

On 29 September 1982, the women were evicted by the local District Council but within days set up a new camp nearby. While men joined in the initial protest and blockade in February 1982, it was decided it should be a women's only protest. Much of the rhetoric and symbols employed were expressed in terms of motherhood and the responsibilities of caring for future generations; nappies, toys, wool and ribbons were tied to the fence in contrast to the aesthetics of the base itself as a distinctly male and militarized space. As Susanne Moore explained: 'Women could use their identity as carers and mothers to say, this is about the future safety of our children. We weaponized traditional notions of femininity.'[02]

Informal networks between women began to be deployed as a way of strengthening the movement — 30,000 women responded to a chain letter sent out in December 1982 resulting in 'Embrace the Base' where women joined hands around the base. On 1 April 1983, 70,000 protesters formed a 23 km human chain from Greenham to Aldermaston and the ordnance factory at Burghfield. In December 1983, another 'Embrace the Brace' included 50,000 women. Sections of the fence were cut and hundreds of arrests were made.

01

www.theguardian.com/
artanddesign/2016/may/06/
greenham-common-
protest-1981-remembered
(accessed April 2017).

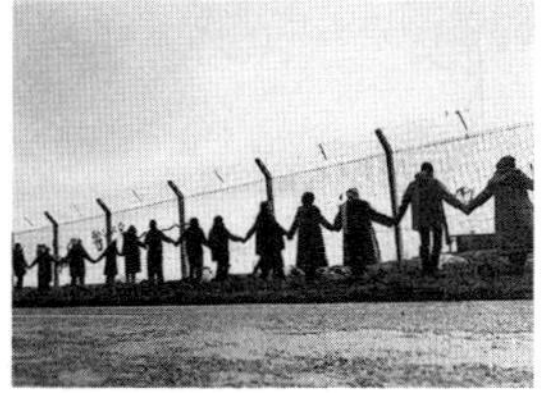

Yellow Gate Women, 2008, a documentary about the women's anti-nuclear protest at Greenham Common by Concordia Media, 2008, director: Margaretta D'Arcy, film still

02

www.theguardian.com/
uk-news/2017/mar/20/
greenham-common-nuclear-
silos-women-protest-peace-
camp (accessed April 2017).

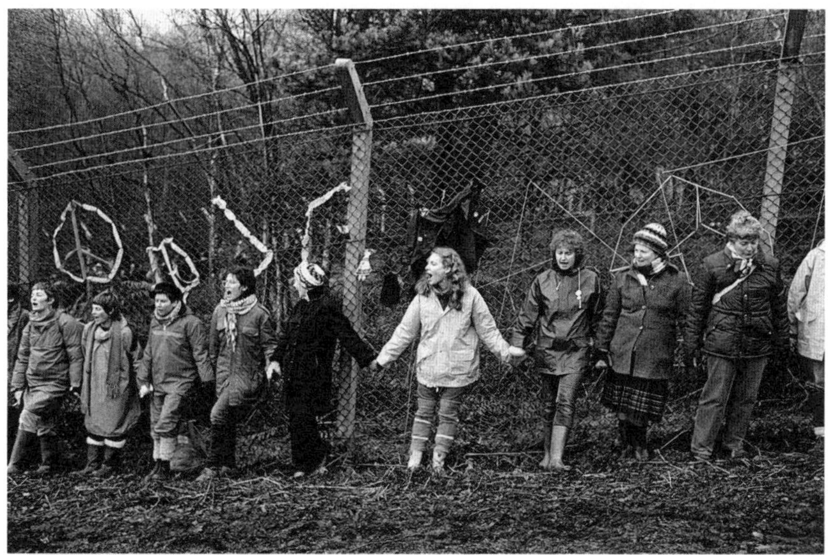

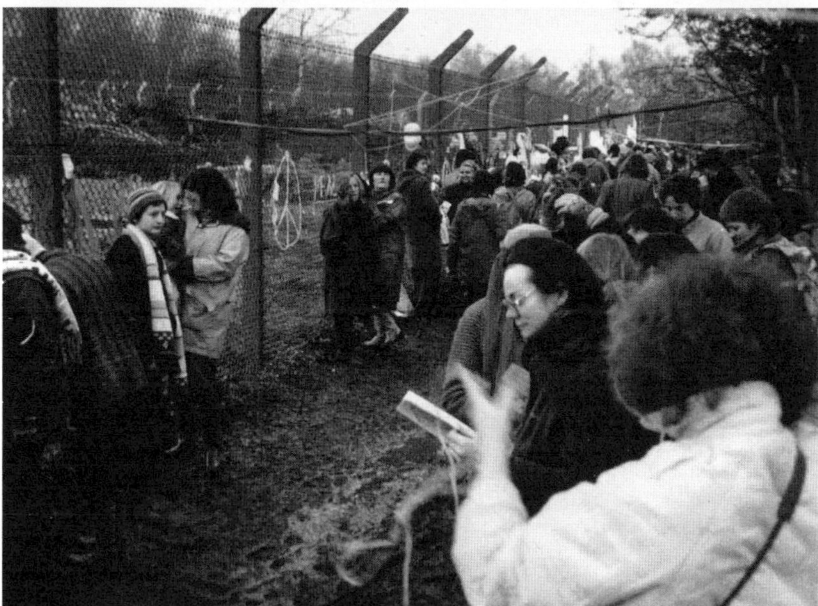

Women join hands around the fence of Royal Air Force Station Greenham Common near Newbury, Berkshire

Media attention prompted the creation of other peace camps at more than a dozen sites in Britain and elsewhere in Europe. Throughout the protest, many strategies were developed: physical blockades and disruption of the barrack itself, long term occupation, spectacular and joyful public actions and legal challenges. Nuclear convoys were blockaded and disrupted. Yet conditions at the camp were harsh — the police and military intimidation was rife. Dwellings were often destroyed and had to be rebuilt.

The camp self organized along non-hierarchical lines refusing essentialising messages beyond their determination to ban the bomb. It was divided into nine smaller camps at various gates around the base. The first was called Yellow Gate and others included Blue Gate with its New Age focus, Violet Gate with a religious focus, and Green Gate, which was women-only and did not accept male visitors. There was a vast cross section of intergenerational women, many of whom were politically active for the first time. Expressions of feminism, gendered relationships to family, domesticity and public life, nature and reproduction, and spirituality and religion were all explored. Many women spoke of it as a moment of cultural, social and importantly 'public' politicial learning.

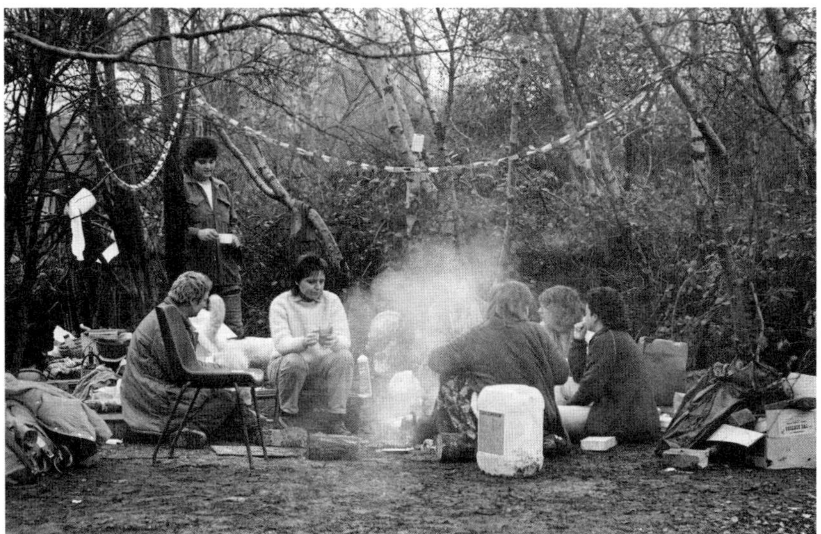

Women prepare for Christmas at Peace Camp at Royal Air Force Station Greenham Common near Newbury, Berkshire, 14 December 1985. The camp was established to protest against the decision of the British government to allow American cruise missiles to be sited at the air base

Greenham Common affected the lives of many women. It changed the public perception of their roles within public and political life. In December 1987 Ronald Reagan and Mikhail Gorbachev signed the Intermediate-Range Nuclear Forces Treaty, bringing an end to cruise missiles. In August 1989 the first missiles left the base and the final missiles were flown back to the USA along with the USAF personnel in 1991–1992.

RADICAL DEMOCRATS IN TURKEY

POLITICAL ICEBREAKERS IN THE MID-EIGHTIES

Bariş Gençer Baykan

In the mid-eighties, Radical Democrats in Turkey worked hard to place LGBT issues, ecology, anti-militarism and atheism in the national spotlight. It was a taboo-breaking struggle for freedom and democracy in the aftermath of a coup d'état. The political trajectory of İbrahim Eren, the leader of the Radical Democrats party, was quite significant in the formation of the group. In the mid-seventies, he worked with the Workers Party of Turkey and he was an environmentalist activist in İzmir, monitoring the pollution in the Gulf of İzmir, protesting the cement factory and also maintaining a support group for lesbians and gays in the city under a local NGO, Aegean Environment Health Association, founded in 1978. The association was closed after the coup and Eren went abroad and lived in Italy, France and Germany. Impressed by the successes of Partito Radicale in Italy and Die Grünen in Germany in general elections, he decided to launch a similar initiative that might help coalesce social movements in Turkey. Back in Turkey in 1985, he was among the founders of the Social Democracy Party but was

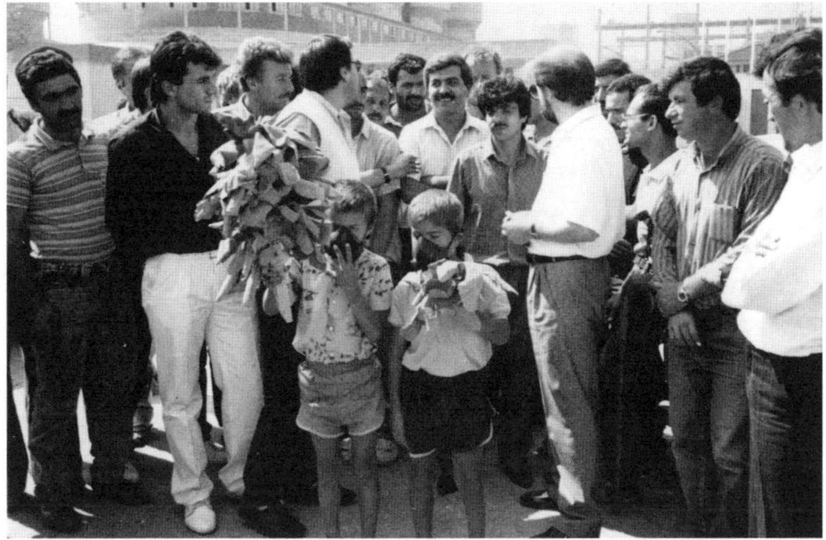

Radical Democrat Green Party, Akçimento cement factory protest, 24 March 1988. Archive: İbrahim Eren

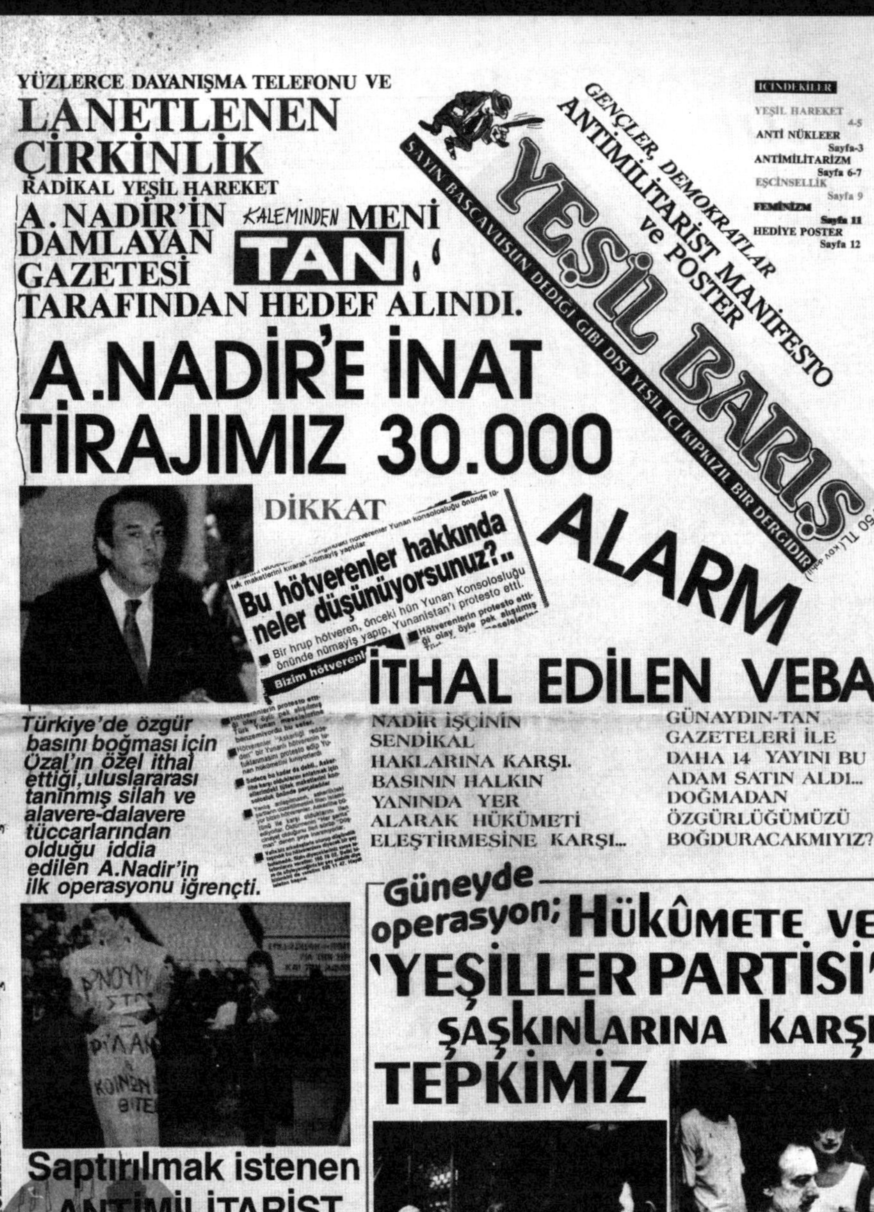

Yeşil Barış (Green Peace) no. 2, July 1988. Archive: İbrahim Eren

THE LONG 1980s

disappointed by the weak emphasis on democratic struggle and left the party with a group of like-minded activists. In June 1987, they formed an association called Environmentalist Green Peace, an attempt seen as the first step of a political party in the making. It tended to be an umbrella organization for environmentalist, feminists, LGBT, anti-militarists and atheists. In practical terms, though, their political struggle was mainly based on two pillars: First, they consistently fought the discrimination and harassment of LGBT people. In their view, the crackdown on prostitution was used as a pretext for harassing gay/transgender people. In April 1987, they launched a hunger strike against escalating police violence, the first public protest on LGBT issues. A group of writers, artists and public intellectuals supported the hunger strike and national and international media attention made it harder to suppress the dissents. The second pillar was the environmental struggle. They raised awareness on the extinction of species, protested the planned nuclear power plant on the Mediterranean coast and tried to close down a cement factory near İstanbul. They protested the demolishment of a Byzantium Basilica in İstanbul's historical peninsula and destruction of historical heritage. The Radical Democrats were the first to introduce the concepts of anti-militarism and conscientious objection in a country where militarism is deeply rooted in culture. Furthermore, they campaigned against the prohibition of the Kurdish language. Although the LGBT faction was a minority, the entire movement was pejoratively labelled as 'gay movement/party'. Activists have been intimidated, threatened and jailed. Even the progressive movements and alternative media turned a blind eye to this radical democratic movement.

Between 1988 and 1989, they published six issues of the journal *Yeşil Barış* (Green Peace), with a circulation of around 20,000 copies. In line with the internal factions, regular sections were devoted to 'Gay Liberation', anti-militarists, feminists and atheists. Some theoretical discussions on 'Red/Green' or 'Socialists/Radicals' dichotomies could be found frequently. In November 1988 they launched the initiative for a Radical Democrat Green Party. The draft programme criticized capitalism and authoritarian socialism and denied the social democratic concepts of 'participative democracy, representative democracy and civil society'. It advocates for a fundamental democratic green party by referring to rising green movements in Germany, Spain, Italy, Hungary and Poland. Nevertheless, the anti-authoritarian and autonomous character of the group undermined the basis of a legal party and they also lost activists to the newly founded Green Party. The movement disbanded over the debates regarding local elections in March 1989.

RAZMERJA AND ECOLOGY

Božidar Flajšman

In the early eighties, following the demise of President Josip Broz Tito, the circumstances in Yugoslavia became increasingly oppressive as the country slid deeper and deeper into economic and political turmoil. Largely controlled by the regime, the mass media did not broach subjects we were interested in or concerned about. Among the few exceptions were student and youth newspapers and magazines, published not only in Ljubljana but also in the periphery. The most critical and influential among the youth papers was *Razmerja* (Relationships) published in Metlika, a town in Bela Krajina, the south of Slovenia. It raised such controversial subjects as suppressed histories (e.g. the trials against some of the survivors of the Dachau concentration camp), free elections, the one-party system, the Yugoslav People's Army, trade unions, ecology, urban construction on the highest-quality soil, the Youth Day celebration as a ritual dedicated to the deceased president, the struggles of individual companies, the Romany issue, and issues related to art and culture.

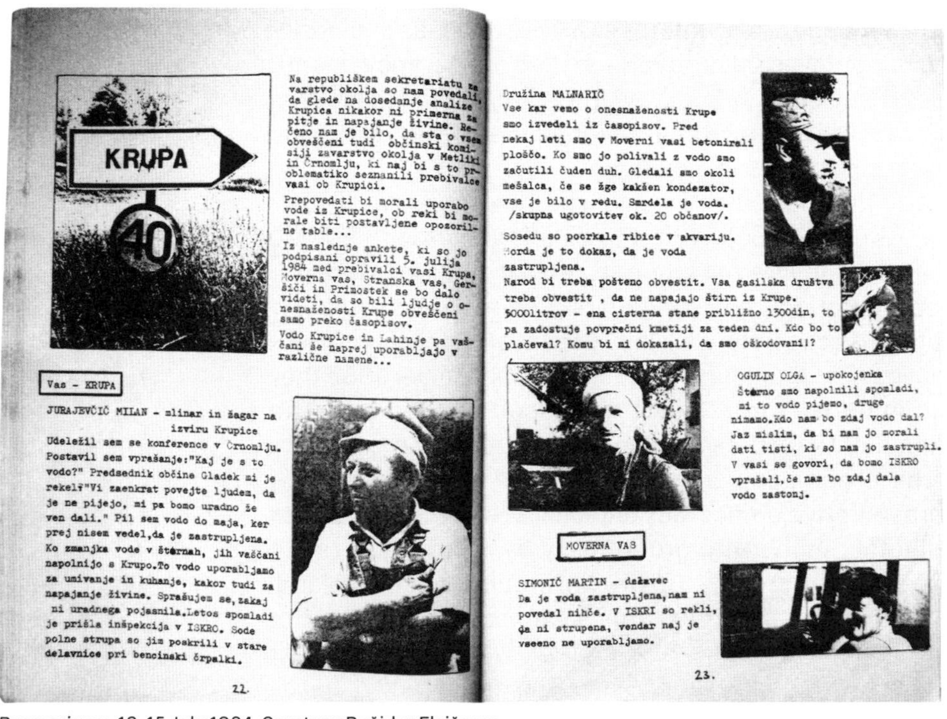

Na republiškem sekretariatu za varstvo okolja so nam povedali, da glede na dosedanje analize Krupica nikakor ni primerna za pitje in napajanje živine. Rečeno nam je bilo, da sta o vsem obveščeni tudi občinski komisiji zavarstvo okolja v Metliki in Črnomlju, ki naj bi s to problematiko seznanili prebivalce vasi ob Krupici.

Prepovedati bi morali uporabo vode iz Krupice, ob reki bi morale biti postavljene opozorilne table...

Iz naslednje ankete, ki so jo podpisani opravili 5. julija 1984 med prebivalci vasi Krupa, Moverna vas, Stranska vas, Geršiči in Primostek se bo dalo videti, da so bili ljudje o onesnaženosti Krupe obveščeni samo preko časopisov.

Vodo Krupice in Lahinje pa vaščani še naprej uporabljajo v različne namene...

Družina MALNARIČ

Vse kar vemo o onesnaženosti Krupe smo izvedeli iz časopisov. Pred nekaj leti smo v Moverni vasi betonirali ploščo. Ko smo jo polivali z vodo smo začutili čuden duh. Gledali smo okoli mešalca, če se žge kakšen kondezator, vse je bilo v redu. Sardela je voda. /skupna ugotovitev ok. 20 občanov/.

Sosedu so pocrkale ribice v akvariju. Morda je to dokaz, da je voda zastrupljena.

Narod bi treba pošteno obvestit. Vsa gasilska društva treba obvestit , da ne napajajo štirn iz Krupe. 5000litrov - ena cisterna stane približno 1300din, to pa zadostuje povprečni kmetiji za teden dni. Kdo bo to plačeval? Komu bi mi dokazali, da smo oškodovani!?

OGULIN OLGA - upokojenka

Štarno smo napolnili spomladi, mi to vodo pijemo, druge nimamo.Kdo nam bo zdaj vodo dal? Jaz mislim, da bi nam jo morali dati tisti, ki so nam jo zastrupli. V vasi se govori, da bomo ISKRO vprašali,če nam bo zdaj dala vodo zastonj.

JURAJEVČIČ MILAN - mlinar in žagar na izviru Krupice

Udeležil sem se konference v Črnomlju. Postavil sem vprašanje:"Kaj je s to vodo?" Predsednik občine Gladek mi je rekel?"Vi zaenkrat povejte ljudem, da je ne pijejo, mi pa bomo uradno že ven dali." Pil sem vodo do maja, ker prej nisem vedel,da je zastrupljena. Ko zmanjka vode v štarnah, jih vaščani napolnijo s Krupo.To vodo uporabljamo za umivanje in kuhanje, kakor tudi za napajanje živine. Sprašujem se,zakaj ni uradnega pojasnila.Letos spomladi je prišla inšpekcija v ISKRO. Sode polne strupa so jim poskrili v stare delavnice pri bencinski črpalki.

SIMONIČ MARTIN - dažavec

Da je voda zastrupljena,nam ni povedal nihče. V ISKRI so rekli, da ni strupena, vendar naj je vseeno ne uporabljamo.

22.   23.

Razmerja no. 12, 15 July 1984. Courtesy Božidar Flajšman

Official distributors did not dare take on *Razmerja*, so the paper was sold in an activist manner: in the streets, by mail, in restaurants and bars, in hardware and appliances stores, and in some larger bookstores. Formally, the paper was published under the auspices of the Metlika branch of the League of Socialist Youth of Slovenia. Between 1982 and the end of 1984, one special and 13 regular issues were published, the former dedicated in its entirety to the ecological disaster in the Krupa River in Bela Krajina, which had been polluted with polychlorinated biphenyls (PCB) by the Iskra company, thus damaging the health of the local population. In 1983, an analysis of the water and sediments in the Krupa showed the limit value of PCB had been exceeded by 300 times. We were the first to notify the Slovene public of this ecological disaster, in detail and objectively. The big newspapers either shied away from reporting on the issue, or else published misleading information. Because of the reaction of the political authorities and scientists working for the regime who tried to cover up this ecological crime, we formed a close alliance with the affected people living by the Krupa. Together with them we met with the government of the Republic of Slovenia and demanded that immediate and effective action be taken. This led to pressures from the republican political bodies who accused us of discrediting the achievements of the revolution and postwar development, and portraying our society as undemocratic. Because of such criticism, some of us turned to the Russell Tribunal (also known as the International War Crimes Tribunal), or rather its then president Vladimir Dedijer. Alenka Bizjak, Božidar Flajšman, Dušan Plut, and Zoran Hočevar gathered material for the tribunal, entitling the document 'Ecological Geno-cide' and presenting it at a protest meeting held at the Faculty of Arts in Ljubljana on April 26, 1985. Representatives of the tribunal Vladimir Dedijer and Rudi Rizman attended the meeting, where we put forward our suggestion that it convene a special session to address the issue and ramifications of ecological genocide in the modern world, and the perilous practice of multinational corpora-tions exporting environmentally harmful technologies to the un-derdeveloped world. Dušan Plut and I presented in detail the dire case of the Krupa, drawing further attention to similar cases in Slo-venia, Yugoslavia, and around the world. This case was instrumen-tal in triggering the development of the ecological movement and the subsequent formation of the Green Party of Slovenia. With its civil-society activism, *Razmerja* eventually managed to persuade the authorities to clean up the Krupa River. In light of the above we can claim that *Razmerja* played a pioneering role in the sphere of ecological activism in Slovenia, and greatly boosted the develop-ment of environmental awareness.

Ekipa Razmerij je obiskala nekaj institucij, ki so bile s
strani Republiškega komiteja za varstvo okolja določene
kot nosilci nalog za reševanje ekološke katastrofe "PCB v
Krupi". Da bi prikazali, kako pristojni rešujejo ta pri-
mer, smo zbrali nekatere dokumente, ki so povezani z zas-
trupitvijo Krupe.

Dve stvari nikakor ne gresta skupaj.

Medtem ko se odgovorni "prizadevno dogovarjajo v navidez-
nem začaranem krogu", seveda v skladu s predpisi in zako-
ni, da bodo nekoč lahko sprejeli odloke - pa ostajajo o-
groženi ljudje ob Krupi osamljeni in prepuščeni sami sebi.

Zastrupljenega območja ni moč reševati v pisarnah, četudi
po samoupravni poti.

Ali bi v primeru vojne tudi čakali na mobilizacijo ljudi
in sredstev do redne skupščinske seje ali letne konference
štaba civilne zaščite?

      Bili smo na sestanku krajevne skupnosti
      Semič, bili smo na skupščini občine Čr-
      nomelj, obiskali smo tovarno kondenza-
      torjev ISKRA Semič, bili smo na upravi
      inšpekcijskih služb v Novem mestu, šli
      smo na zavod za socialno medicino in hi-
      gieno v Novem mestu, bili pa smo tudi v
      Ljubljani in se oglasili na pristojnih
      republiških komitejih in zavodih. Pred-
      vsem pa smo se pogovarjali z ljudmi v
      vasi Krupa, v Stranski vasi, v Moverni
      vasi, Semiču, Geršičih, Primostku itd.
      V Metliki smo imeli namen obiskati pred-
      sednika izvršnega sveta občinske skupš-
      čine, vendar je bil na dopustu.

      Slikovnega materiala v tej številki ni
      veliko. Film, na katerem je bila posne-
      ta kopica sogovornikov in aktualnih pri-
      zorišč, smo izgubili nekje na območju
      novomeškega kapitlja. Pravzaprav smo ga
      pozabili skupaj s "flešem" na škarpi p-
      red zavodom za soc. medi in hig.. Pošte-
      nega najditelja oz. tatu, ki ni vedel,
      kaj krade, obveščamo, da je "fleš" izpo-
      sojen, da smo ga dolžni vrniti, na fil-
      mu pa ni golih bab. Poslušaj, če vrneš
      oboje, boš dobival Razmerja eno leto b-
      rezplačno!

Vse pogovore je opravila ekipa v sestavi: Rudles Vlašič,
Andrej Vidic, Neno Jelenčič, Sonja Bezenšek, Leon Gregor-
čič, Božo Flajšman. Sestanku KS Semič sta prisostovala še
Jani Bevk in Duška Vraničar.

3.

BILO NAS JE **13**

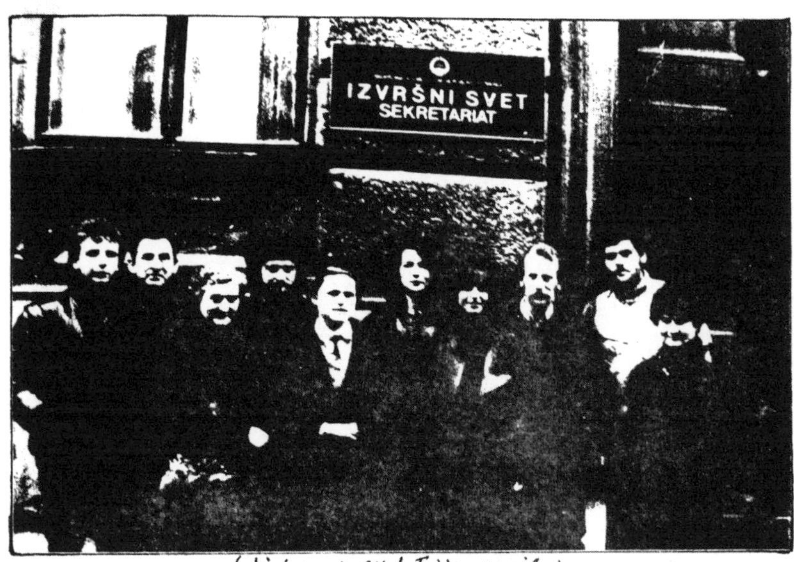

/ tj. 6. nov. 84 / Trije manjkajo

Zaradi prepočasnega reševanja onesnažene reke Krupe in po kapljah curljajoče pomoči vaščanom ob Krupi in Lahinji, je delegacija neposredno prizadetih krajanov 6. novembra 84 obiskala republiški izvršni svet.

To so bili Jože Per, Franc Oven, Irena Per, Tončka Mihelčič in Marija Janežič. Pridružili so se jim predstavniki Razmerij Neno Jelenčič, Božo Flajšman, Sonja Bezenšek, Seka Badovinac in Leon Gregorčič. Od Zveze društev za varstvo okolja v Sloveniji pa so bili zraven Angela Bratko, Neža Exel in Vladimir Krivic.

Ker je delegacija prišla nenajavljena, je bilo spočetka nekaj protokolarnih težav, vendar jo je že po nekaj minutah sprejel podpredsednik IS tovariš Frlec. Krajani so mu izročili pismo, ki ga objavljamo na strani 28. Prav tako objavljamo zapisnik razgovora s tov. Frlecom. Razgovoru sta se pridružila tudi republiška sanitarna inšpektorica tovarišica Hitijeva in predsednik republiškega komiteja za zdravstvo tovariš Miklavčič.

Prav tako objavljamo na strani 30. zapisnik s sestanka posebne republiške komisije, ustanovljene zato, da bi reševanje ekološke katastrofe steklo bolj organizirano, hitreje in z večjim uspehom kot doslej.

25.

Bezek, Mirjam. 'Obsojen uvodnik zadnjih Razmerij.' *Dolenjski list* 7 February 1985.

Flajšman, Božidar. 'Ne dramijo le katastrofe.' *Delo* 26 March 1985.

—.'Komisija za spremljanje onesnaženosti Krupe: Pomirjajoče in zavezujoče ugotovitve.' *Delo* 14 December 1985.

—.'Krupa: ali res blatenje stroke?' *Dolenjski list* 16 January 1986, p. 9.

—.'Pomirjajoče in zavezujoče ugotovitve: Poštni predal 29.' *Delo* 18 January 1986, p. 16.

—.'Pusti crknit Belokranjce: Po tem, kar se dogaja, bi tudi na ta način lahko razložili kratico PCB.' *Dolenjski list* 6. November 1986, p. 8.

—.'Je v Beli krajini ogroženih nekaj tisoč ljudi?: Poročilo iz ZDA.' *Dolenjski list* 29 January 1987.

—. *Vizualna ekologija: Ekološki nagovori vidnih sporočil*. Ljubljana: Univerza v Ljubljani, Akademija za likovno umetnost in oblikovanje, 2006, p. 105–109.

—. *Podobe časa: Metlika na razglednicah*. Metlika: Mestna skupnost Metlika, 2015, pp. 134–135.

'Kaj mislimo in hočemo: Uredniški konzilij Razmerij odgovarja predsedstvu skupnosti borcev.' XIV divizije. *Dolenjski list*, 21 February 1985.

Komisija za koordinacijo strokovnega dela pri reševanju problematike onesnaženosti Krupe. 'O Krupi in ureditvi razmer; šest vprašanj prebivalcev ob Krupi in odgovor komisije za koordinacijo strokovnega dela pri reševanju problematike onesnaženosti Krupe.' *Delo* 26 March 1985, p. 9.

Nevarna (metliška) razmerja, TV 15, glasilo *ZB*, 24 January 1985.

Plut, Dušan. 'Belokranjske vode: Novo mesto.' *Dolenjski muzej* 1988.

—, Álenka Bizjak, Božidar Flajšman, Zoran Hočevar. *Ekološki genocid, gradivo za protestni shod na Filozofski fakulteti v Ljubljani*, 26 april 1985.

Rogelj, Silvestra. 'Proizvodnja kondenzatorjev je močno onesnažila Krupico.' *Delo* 12 June 1984.

Roter, Zdenko. *Padle maske*. Ljubljana: Sever & Sever, 2013, pp. 347–348.

Pucelj, Gregor. 'Russelovo razsodišče se bo lotilo ekoloških genocidov.' *Delo* 29 April 1985.

Razmerja, glasilo OO ZSMS Metlika, št. 12, 15 July 1984, št. 13, 29 November 1984 in posebna številka posvečena aferi Krupa, 24 August 1984.

Razmerja odgovarjajo, TV 15, glasilo *ZB*, 21 February 1985.

Rizman, Rudi. *Izzivi odprte družbe*. Ljubljana: Liberalna akademija, 1997, pp. 268, 273.

Stališča s seje sveta za informiranje pri OK SZDL Metlika z dne 31 January 1985 glede vsebinske zasnove Razmerij — glasila OO ZSMS Metlika ter skladnost dosedanjih številk z vsebinsko zasnovo.

Zajc, Srečo. 'Russel brani Krupo.' *Mladina* 9 May 1985.

EL VIEJO TOPO

Pablo Martínez

The near-forty-year regime Spain remained under through the designs of Francisco Franco's dictatorship, which cemented violent, corrupt and authoritarian state structures, had a major impact on the shaping of subjectivities, controlling not only the production and distribution of thought but also behaviours and forms of social relations. The scant flow of any theory differing from those imposed by the National Catholic dictatorship through censorship forced critical thought to clandestinely perforate the surface in Spain, for instance with publications such as *Realidad* and *Cuadernos de Ruedo Ibérico*, which articulated domestic ideological resistance from outside its borders. Although some magazines began to introduce aspects of post-'68 cultural and social revolution in the latter years of the dictatorship (*Star* and *Ajoblanco* in 1974, *Ozono* in 1975), it wasn't until 1976 that diverse publications appeared with outwardly political content that broke away from Francoism. In October 1976, in Barcelona the first edition of the magazine *El Viejo Topo* (The Old Mole) came into being, and developed across two eras: the first spanned the transition-to-democracy period (1976–1982), while the second started in 1993 and continues in the present day.

In its first phase, the *El Viejo Topo* was key to the development of thought found in the critique of culture and daily life, with aspirations towards the Gramscian idea of the construction of a historical bloc which could propel real transformation (with a sky-high distribution and average print run of 35,000 copies, which sometimes reached 50,000). The magazine would play a key role in ushering in debates which resisted social control and sought to take apart the repressive machinery of the regime — not surprisingly, the aftermath of Francoism in moral-bound legislation would spill out of the dictatorship (Adolfo Suárez, in power between 1976 and 1981, had close ties to Opus Dei). In its contribution to the construction of a new society which eschewed the Church's moral control, running through the state, and in constructing one with new values, *El Viejo Topo* took on some of the most radical approaches opposed to inheriting the regime. Its early editions featured articles like Teresa Ingles' 'Lesbianismo y feminismo' (Lesbianism and Feminism), or the interview '¡Todos somos bisexuales!' (We're All Bisexual!) conducted by Secretari del Front d'Alliberament Gai de Catalunya (the Catalan Liberation Front) without revealing its identity for fear of the reprisals stipulated in the Danger to Society and Social Rehabilitation Law of 1970, and still in force until 1979 in reference to homosexuality. Articles were also published which championed a reframing of the state's psychiatric institution and introduced the debate around the possibilities of alternative psychiatry outside the mental institute. The magazine took a stance on the prison situation, serving as a spokesperson in the demands of COPEL (the Coordinator of Prisoners in Protest, which, created in 1976, called for amnesty for social prisoners whose imprisonment was the result of laws such as the Danger to Society Law), and outlining the situation of repression in the Basque Country. These themes all intersected political and militant practice, not only in the period of democratic transition, but also with an impact on the development of social movements in the eighties. Its editions do not recount the literal nature of the events that occurred, given the insertion of radical thinking is more often forward-looking, and unfurls images of what is possible, or alters awareness.

Ideologically, *El Viejo Topo* gave rise to a unique space of debate, its pages calling upon nihilistic libertarian and radical thought in the social critique of Marxist orthodoxy.

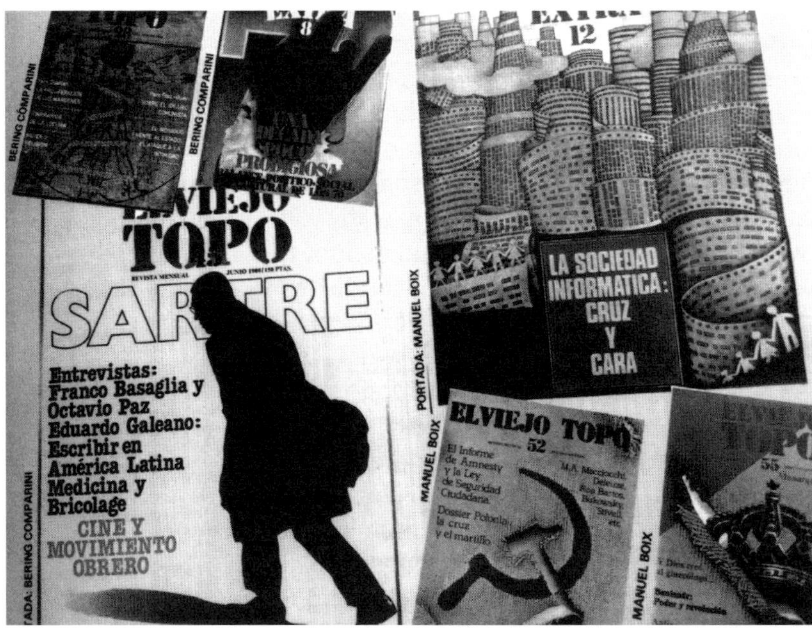

Image from the book *El Viejo Topo: Treinta años después* (The Old Mole: Thirty Years After), Ediciones de Intervención Cultural / El Viejo Topo, Madrid, 2006, p. 29

INSUBORDINATION IN SPAIN

AUTHORITARIAN SOCIALIST MODERNITY AND WIDESPREAD ANTAGONISTIC DISOBEDIENCE

Carlos Prieto del Campo

The insubordinate movement in Spain, or rather, the movement against compulsory national service and any other obligatory alternative civilian service, was, during the nineteen-eighties, the first genuinely post-Francoist mass movement. Firstly, because it unmasked the authoritarian nature of the project of socialist modernity decided upon by political elites from the party system, by those responsible for the Transition to democracy in Spain after the fascist dictatorship. Secondly, because it afforded a precise demarcation of the elites' pact and the recently constructed party system, which in this instance was demonstrated paradigmatically and was aware of other equally authoritarian manifestations in the economic, social and cultural policies of the first democratic governments, in the organization of state terrorism by the GAL[01] throughout the eighties, and in Spain joining NATO and the European Union in 1986. And thirdly, because to thousands of citizens it cast out a progressively large-scale strategy of civil disobedience and sabotaged the model of authoritarian regulation in this political alternative, culminating in its abolition in 2001 by the Partido Popular (People's Party); a model of civil disobedience which would anticipate the struggles in the years to come of disobeying the crisis, combating evictions and austerity, and confronting the inescapable hollowing out of democracy by the Spanish and European elite after the 15M anti-austerity movement.

01

State-sponsored death squads to fight ETA.

The PSOE's (Spanish Socialist Workers' Party) approach and the Partido Popular's final handling, from 1996 onwards, of the right to conscientious objection were both authoritarian, anti-democratic and repressive.

Firstly, because they proceeded from the hypothesis that national service *should be* compulsory and a political critique contesting its existence and obligatory nature, citing substantive reasons with respect to the origin, role and behaviour of the army over previous decades (the Civil War) or years (the authoritarian transition to democracy overseen from the early seventies), were issues that went beyond the content of democratic right and the content of that which was stipulated in Article 30 of the Spanish Constitution of 1978, which acknowledged the right to conscientious objection.

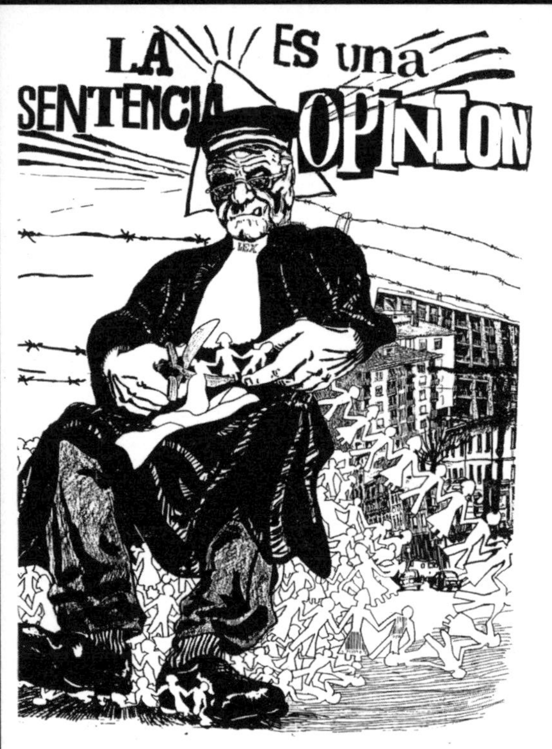

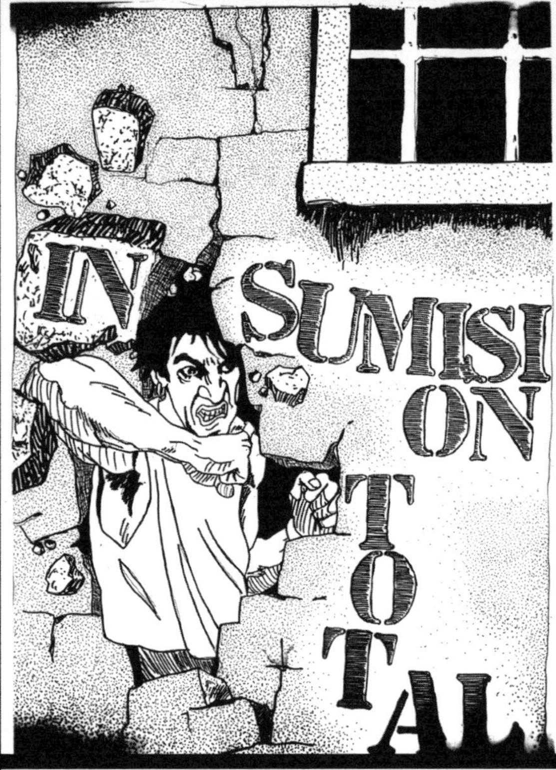

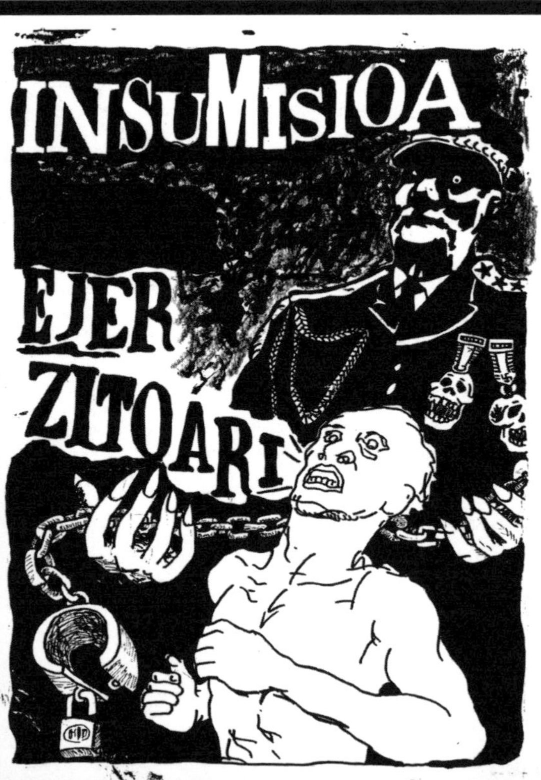

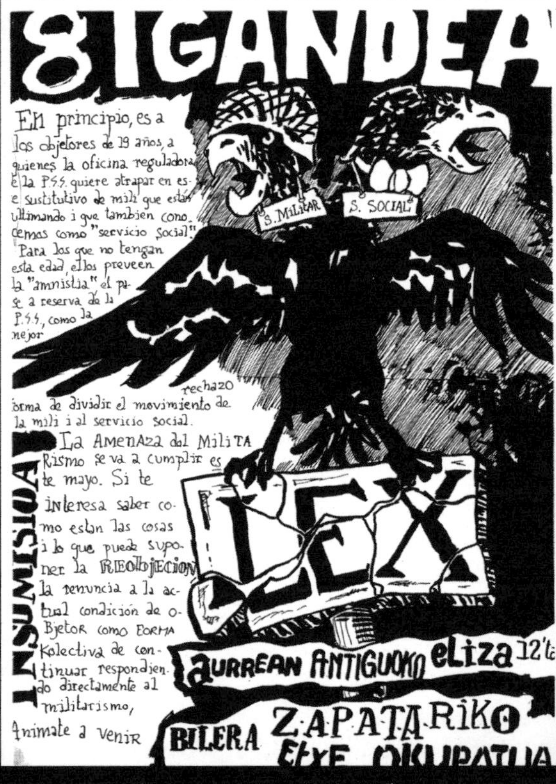

Insumisión (Refusal of military service posters), c. 1980–1998. Courtesy Detritus (Detritus Aranburu Eguizábal)

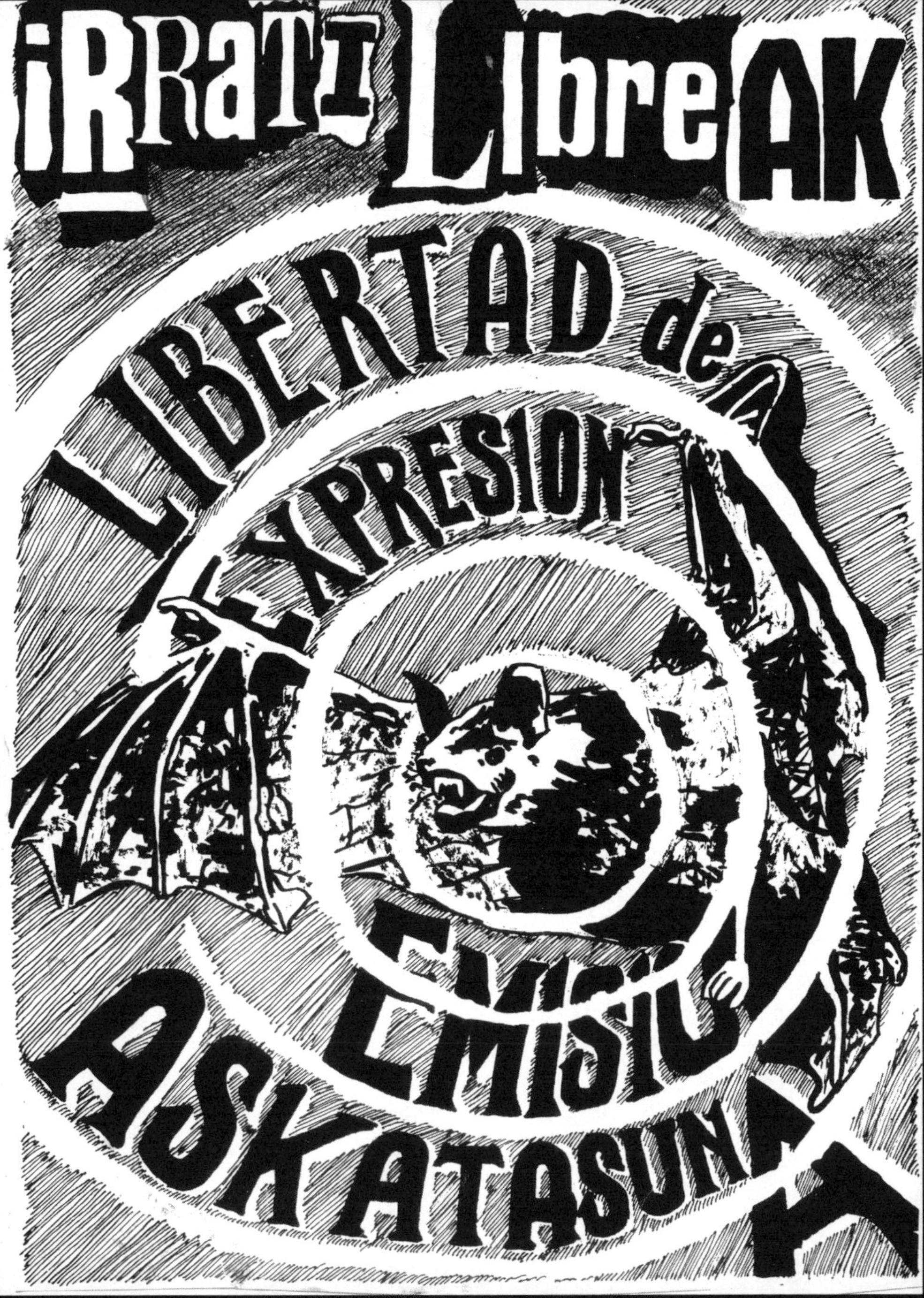

1990

1980

Libertad de expresión (Freedom of Speech / Free Radio Station), c. 1980–1998, poster. Courtesy Detritus
(Detritus Aranburu Eguizábal)

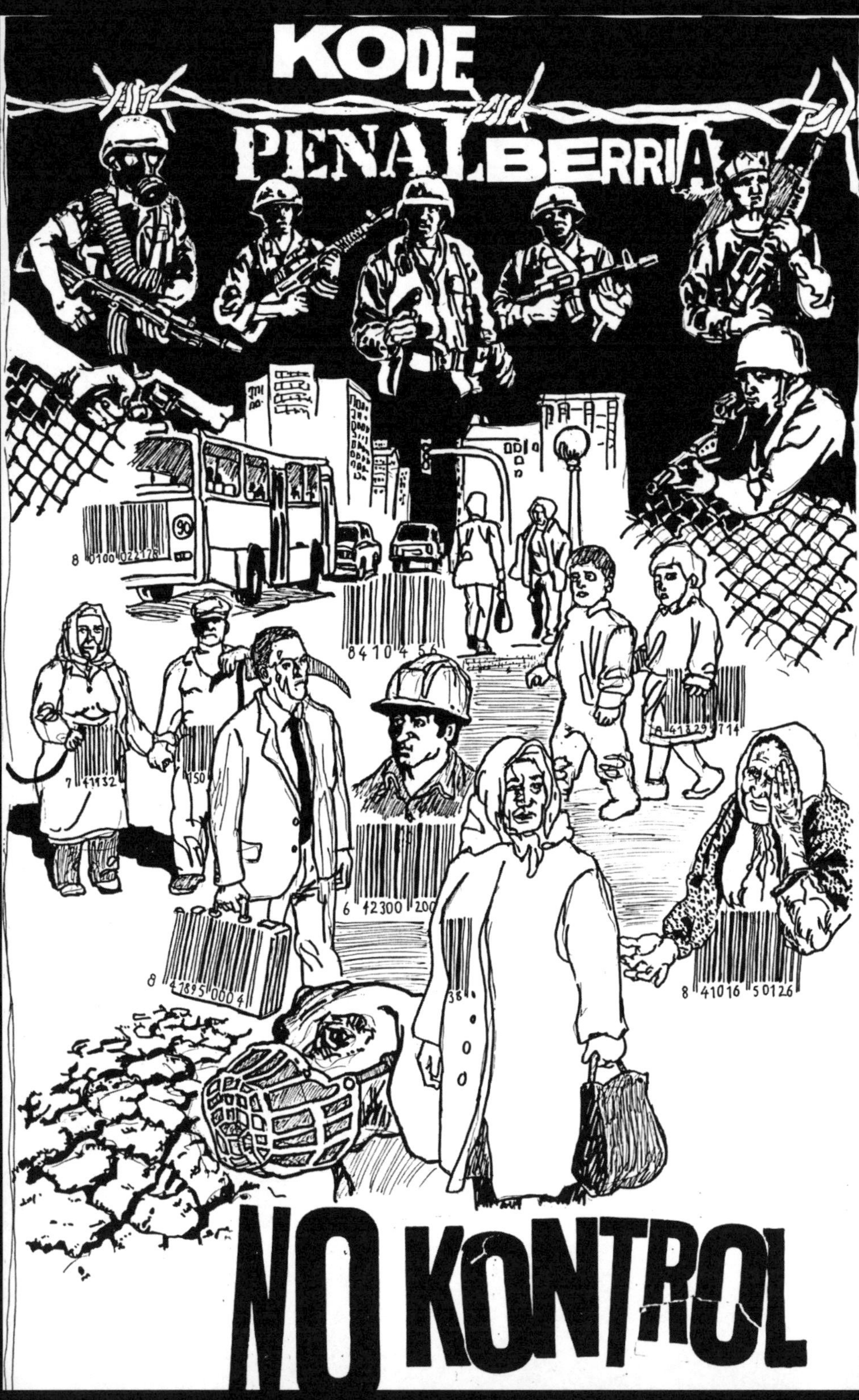

No Kontrol, c. 1980–1998, poster. Courtesy Detritus (Detritus Aranburu Eguizábal)

Secondly, because national service during the early years of a fledging and ailing democracy was from an outmoded, violent and dangerous institution in the very materiality and day-to-day of those who carried it out, for it obliged tens of thousands of young people every year to receive second-rate military training in an army still structured from its Francoist origins, degrading and humiliating in its management and treatment of troops and unappealing within the new constitutional framework.

Thirdly, because they set out from the hypothesis that in being obligatory by nature and non-objectionable as a radical expression of democratic deficit it must be offset by imposing an alternative civilian service which would run on longer, by some distance, than the length of military service and was as much lacking in content and truly progressive social purpose as it was poorly managed and subject to the corresponding penal and disciplinary system (a four- to six-year minimum prison sentence), inventing the imposition of an obligation where it denied the extension and intensification of a right.

Against the backdrop of this crackpot, repressive, reactionary, and obsolete legislative matrix, a movement of mass insubordination broke out, protean and multifarious in its disobedience over the eighties and nineties and never allowing the legal model to become stabilized at any point, obliging the government to permanently dodge and skip forwards to repressively freeze the situation. Attempts to dissuade the non-fulfilment of national service by imposing a bureaucratic and absurd alternative civilian service in a society still riddled with sky-high rates of unemployment, and in need of the construction of a sturdy welfare state proceeding from the dissipation of social rights handed down from the dictatorship, forced the Spanish state to finally change tack and definitively professionalize the armed forces at the end of the twentieth century.

'NO TO COMPULSORY MILITARY SERVICE'

Merve Elveren and Erman Ata Uncu

In Turkey, conscientious objection to military service became a public matter in January 1990 with the call by Tayfun Gönül, who was a medical doctor and a frequent contributor to the alternative weekly magazine *Sokak* (Street). Together with *Sokak*, *Güneş* newspaper announced the 'No to compulsory military service' campaign to support Gönül's declaration. Democratic socialists, feminists, students, publishers, and conservative writers demonstrated their support; however, Gönül, along with the editors-in-chief of *Sokak* and *Güneş*, were tried with the charge of 'alienating the public from military service'. And in the following issues *Sokak* included articles on being against military service, criticizing the concept of 'professional military', mentioned by Gönül in his campaign text.

CALL FOR CAMPAIGN
NO TO COMPULSORY MILITARY SERVICE

[...]

If there truly is something called 'freedom of conscience', if people cannot be forced to act against their personal conscientious convictions as long as they do not directly harm others, and if States have recognized this 'freedom', then they have to find other ways than 'compulsory military service' to form their armies.

In cases where carrying out military service or joining the army is against the conscientious convictions of a person, no force whatsoever can impose the obligation of 'compulsory military service' upon such a person. This right, which has become especially widespread after World War II, and has increasingly become an inseparable part of human rights, is known as the right to 'Conscientious Objection.' The right to conscientious objection is required by natural law, and the State of the Republic of Turkey has implicitly recognized this right by signing the Universal Declaration of Human Rights as well as via the 1982 Constitution.

If the State is sincere in this recognition, then it must act to change the laws and regulations stipulating compulsory military service.

A person's conscientious conviction can be formed by very different factors. For instance, some may object to taking up arms or taking part in a military organization because their religious beliefs require it, if they are Christian, Buddhist, Taoist or a Jehovah's Witness. Others may reject military service for a non-religious, political reason, for instance because they are pacifists and are against all forms of violence, or anarchists who are against all forms of tyranny and institutionalized violence. A radical Muslim who considers himself the soldier of Allah may not want to serve the secular State. A revolutionary socialist who is against the bourgeois army, or a member of another nation who defines the army of the ruling nation as a colonialist power, may reject military service.

Then again, one does not necessarily have to have such radical political views and/or religious beliefs. A liberal, a social democrat, and even a conservative may consider the presence of the army useful and necessary, but also feel that his own personality is not compatible with military service, and that the army should be made up of professional soldiers.

Conscientious objection can also be based on entirely practical reasons. A person may not want to depart from his partner, or suspend his scientific career, or take a forced break from the business he has established.

And all these people live in this society. They cannot be considered non-existent. The current implementation of the State of the Republic of Turkey acts as if these people do not exist, and forces them to act against their personal conscientious convictions by imposing 'compulsory military service'. This is a serious human rights violation.

We call upon those who share similar thoughts to exercise their RIGHT TO RESIST against this human rights violation. As part of this campaign, from now on, we will on the one hand focus on exposing militarism in order to change laws and regulations related to military service, while on the other hand we will try to create and foster concrete solidarity among victims.

Tayfun Gönül

Sokak (Street), year 1, no. 1, 7–13 January 1990. Archive Tuğrul Eryılmaz, Murat Öneş and Nilgün Öneş

ZORUNLU ASKERLİĞE

1990'ların dünyasında özgürlük arayışlarının giderek artacağının ipuçları var. Özgürlük ve tabular, birbirleriyle asla bağdaşamayacak iki kavram. Yıkılması gereken tabuların başında da ordu ve militarizm geliyor. Militarizm, bütün insan ilişkilerinde tahakkümü ve sistematik şiddeti meşru gören, olumlayan, toplumun bütün dokularına sinmiş bir hastalık. Bu yüzden insanlık özgürlük arayışında militarizmle hesaplaşmak zorunda.

Ordu, Türkiye'de bir tabu. Üstelik şimdiye kadar pek dokunulmaya cesaret edilemeyen bir tabu. Hepimiz askeri marşlarla, cafcaflı bayram kutlamalarıyla büyüdük. Kendi tarihimizi, fetihçi, asker bir millet olduğumuzu ve bunun erdemlerini vazeden, resmi tarihin ağzından öğrendik. Ordu, bütün politik çekişmelerin ötesinde saygın bir konumdaydı.

12 Eylül'le birlikte ordunun bu konumu sarsıldı. Sivil politik güçler kendi açılarından militarizmi eleştirmeye başladılar. Kuşkusuz bu eleştiri ordunun darbe yapma geleneği ile sınırlıydı.

Ancak, artık ortada çok daha önemli bir gerçek var. Militarist değerler, basında açıkça dile gelmese de, yer yer alay konusu olmaya başladı. Gençler artık geniş ölçüde askere gitmek istemiyor.

Askere gitmeyenin erkek sayılmadığı dönemler geride kalmak üzere. İnsanlar artık askerlikten kurtulmanın yolları üzerinde ciddi ciddi kafa yoruyorlar.

Dünyanın bütün orduları, kendi varlık nedenlerini yurt savunması kavramının arkasına gizlenerek meşrulaştırırlar. Eğer herkes savunmadaysa kim saldıracaktır, o zaman? Gerçek ise ordunun sistematik şiddet ve yok etmeye yönelik bir örgütlenme olduğudur. Her ne kadar güç dengeleri ve hükümet politikaları zaman zaman frenleyici olsa da her profesyonel askerin kafasında bir fatih olmak yatar. Bu yüzden, kalıcı bir dünya barışı orduların olduğu koşullarda mümkün değildir.

Savaş gerekçesiyle varlığını meşrulaştıran ordunun asıl işlevi ise "barış" dönemine ilişkindir. Ordu, bir ülkedeki statükoyu korumakla yükümlüdür her şeyden önce. Statüko ise, o toplumdaki tahakküm ilişkilerinin bütünüdür. Yönetenlerin yönetilenler, mülk sahiplerinin mülksüzler, erkeklerin kadınlar, egemen ulusun diğer uluslar üzerindeki tahakkümüdür statüko.

Ve en sonu ordu bir eğitim kurumudur. Herkese uniforma giydirir, kişiliksizleştirir. Emirlere mutlak itaati öğretir. Kendi astlarına emretme yeteneği kazandırır. Var olan makinenin çarklarının dönmesi için kişiyi kendi yaşamından vazgeçecek ölçüde duygusuzlaştırır, mantıksızlaştırır, robotlaştırır. Otoritelerin tanımladığı bir "düşmanı" yok etmeyi, farklı olana nefretle bakmayı öğretir.

İnsanların özgürlük arayışı, "Ben devletim, canımın

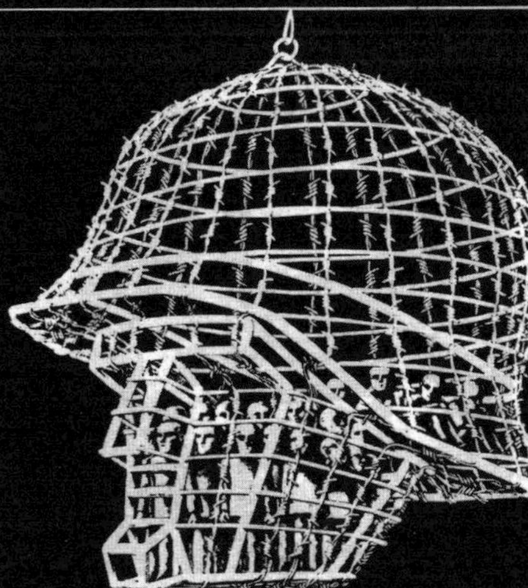

Amnesty International
(Uluslararası Af Örgütü)'nden

TAYFUN GÖNÜL

Sokak dergisi, Tayfun Gönül'ün
"Zorunlu Askerliğe Hayır"
kampanyasına sayfalarını açtı.
Kampanyaya katılmak
isteyenleri mesaj ve 60 satırı geçmeyecek (mümkünse)
mektup, yazı ve katkıları için
Yamalı Bohça PK 10'a yazabilir.

istediğini yaparım" demeyi giderek güçleştiriyor.

Eğer bir "vicdan hürriyeti" varsa, insanlar başkalarına doğrudan zarar vermemek koşuluyla kendi vicdani kanaatlerine aykırı davranmaya zorlanamazlarsa ve devletler de bu 'hürriyeti' kabul etmişlerse, artık kendi ordularını oluşturmanın "zorunlu askerlik hizmeti" dışında yollarını bulmak zorundalar.

Askerlik yapmanın, orduya katılmanın kişinin vicdani kanaatlerine aykırı olduğu durumda hiçbir güç bu kişilere "zorunlu askerlik" yükümlülüğünü dayatamaz. Özellikle İkinci Dünya Savaşı'ndan sonra yaygınlaşan ve giderek insan haklarının ayrılmaz bir parçası olan bu hakka "Vicdani red" hakkı diyoruz. Vicdani red hakkı doğal hukukun gereğidir ve Türkiye Cumhuriyeti Devleti imzaladığı İnsan Hakları Bildirgesi'yle ve 1982 Anayasası ile bu hakkı zımnen kabul etmiştir.

Eğer bu kabulünde samimiyse yapması gereken zorunlu askerliği öngören yasa ve yönetmeliklerini değiştirmektir.

Kişinin vicdani kanaati çok değişik etkenlerle oluşabilir. Örneğin kimileri Hristiyan, Budist, Taoist, Yehova Şahidi olduğu için dini inancı gereği eline silah almayı ve askeri örgütte yer almayı reddebilir. Ya da din dışı bir nedenle, politik olarak, şiddetin her türüne karşı bir pasifist, tahakkümün bütün biçimlerine ve kurumlaşmış şiddete karşı bir anarşist olabilir. Kendini Allah'ın askeri sayan bir radikal Müslüman olabilir ve laik devlete hizmet etmek istemeyebilir. Veya burjuva ordusuna karşı çıkan bir devrimci sosyalist, egemen ulus ordusunu sömürgeci bir kuvvet olarak niteleyen bir başka ulusun bireyi olabilir.

Böylesi radikal politik ve dini inançları da olması gerekmez. Ordunun varlığını gerekli ve yararlı gören, ancak kendi kişiliğinin askerlikle bağdaşmadığını ordunun profesyonellerden oluşması gerektiğini düşünen bir liberal, bir sosyal demokrat hatta bir muhafazakar olabilir.

Ayrıca, vicdani kanaat, tamamen pratik nedenlerden de kaynaklanabilir. Kişi belki sevgilisinden ayrılmak, ya da bilimsel kariyerine ara vermemek, kurduğu işi yarıda bırakmamak istiyordur.

Ve bütün bu insanlar, bu toplumda yaşamaktadır. Yok sayılamazlar. TC Devleti şu anki uygulamasıyla bu insanları yok saymakta ve "zorunlu askerlik hizmetiyle" onları vicdani kanaatlerine aykırı davranmaya zorlamaktadır. Bu ağır bir insan hakları ihlalidir.

Benzer düşünenleri bu insan hakları ihlaline karşı DİRENME HAKKINI kullanmaya çağırıyoruz. Kampanyada bundan sonra bir yandan militarizmin teşhiriyle birlikte askerlikle ilgili yasa ve yönetmelikleri değiştirmeye yönelirken diğer taraftan mağdurlar arasındaki somut dayanışmayı yaratmaya ve geliştirmeye çalışacağız. ▲

Sokak (Street) year 2, no. 1, 7–13 January 1990. Archive: Tuğrul Eryılmaz, Murat Öneş and Nilgün Öneş

EVDE OTURURKEN

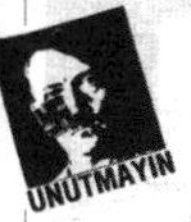

HAKLARINIZI BİLİN

Sokak (Street) year 1, no. 1, 27 August–3 September 1989.
Archive: Tuğrul Eryılmaz, Murat Öneş and Nilgün Öneş

ÇOCUKLUĞUNUZU YAŞARKEN

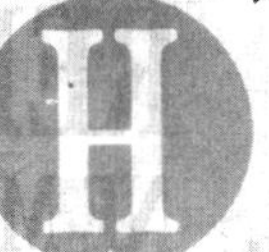

HAKLARINIZI BİLİN

10 EYLÜL 1989 SOKAK

Sokak (Street) year 1, no. 3, 10–16 September 1989.
Archive: Tuğrul Eryılmaz, Murat Öneş and Nilgün Öneş

TRAVESTİLER

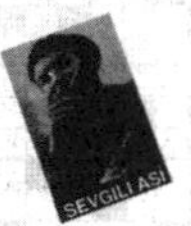

HAKLARINIZI BİLİN

Sokak (Street) year 1, no. 7, 8–14 October 1989.
Archive: Tuğrul Eryılmaz, Murat Öneş and Nilgün Öneş

'KNOW YOUR RIGHTS'

Merve Elveren and Erman Ata Uncu

Between 1989 and 1990, *Sokak* (Street) magazine published a section carrying the same title as The Clash' 1982 song *Know Your Rights*. Prepared in clear and accessible language by İştar Gözaydın, it was the first magazine page in Turkey centred on 'rights', which aimed to promote democratic citizenship and awareness of legal restrictions and constitutional violations of the period. Some titles from this section include: 'Know your rights at the police station', 'Know your rights when you are walking on the street', 'Women, know your rights against your men', 'Know your rights when traveling', 'Know your rights on your way to military service', and 'Tenants, know your rights.' After the closure of *Sokak*, contributors to this page became the founding members of the Helsinki Citizens' Assembly.

KNOW YOUR RIGHTS WHEN YOU ARE AT HOME

You are a student and you are sharing an apartment with some friends. Your neighbours are constantly watching you and take it upon themselves to interfere with those who go in and out of your place. They even come to your door and ask for your father's phone number. Clearly, you feel uncomfortable. What do you do?

If you are an adult over 18, this concerns you and only you, not your relatives. First off, tell this to your neighbours in nice words. Continue to live your life as you wish, unless you disturb your neighbours with noise or garbage. Anyway, they cannot do anything in legal terms. The rest depends on your courage in life.

Sokak [Street], year 1, no. 1, 27 August–3 September 1989. Archive: Tuğrul Eryılmaz, Murat Öneş and Nilgün Öneş

KNOW YOUR RIGHTS WHEN LIVING YOUR CHILDHOOD

Your neighbour Aunty Ayşe constantly screams out of her window: 'Keep it down, 'Don't play with the ball', and so on. Desperately, you go and play in another garden, but this other lady pours cold water on you, and the janitor pops your ball.

Obviously, it is your right to play games, but you have to do it without disturbing others. In turn, Aunty Ayşe should not stamp her feet in rage against your modest enthusiasm. If she simply screams at you, try to express yourself in nice words. But if some aunty pours water on your head, don't surrender, because she 'causes [you] bodily pain' (Article 456 of the Criminal Code). If the janitor pops your ball, he 'deliberately damages [your] property' (Article 516 of the Criminal Code). Both acts are considered crimes according to the Turkish Criminal Code and can carry a prison term of 6–12 months and 1–3 years, respectively. Your mother or father should put pressure on aunty by proposing to go to the Court of First Instance, and the janitor by going to the Court of Peace.

Sokak (Street), year 1, no. 3, 10–16 September 1989. Archive: Tuğrul Eryılmaz, Murat Öneş and Nilgün Öneş

TRANSVESTITES, KNOW YOUR RIGHTS

You are over 18. You have already decided upon your sexual preference. You are neither a homosexual who prefers relationships with people of the same sex, nor a transsexual who has had gender reassignment surgery. You are a transvestite with your feminine look, feminine attitude and demeanour. Is it possible for you to document your choice in the framework of the Turkish system of law?

According to the application of Turkish law, only the identities male or female can be entered into the gender slot on identification cards. As required by Article 46 of the Law on Populations, 'changes' can be confirmed by a court decision. You can apply to the Court of Justice to try this.

Sokak (Street), year 1, no. 7, 8–14 October 1989. Archive: Tuğrul Eryılmaz, Murat Öneş and Nilgün Öneş

2.2 CIVIL

Policing the Crisis, The People's Account and *Handsworth Songs*
1978–1986

'Pretended' Family Relationships, Sunil Gupta
1988

Rocío (1980), 88 minutes, Tangana Films
1980

The Danger to Society and Social Rehabilitation Law

AIDS, Sexual Dissidence and Biopolitical Activism
1990

'100%'
1993

The Feminist Movement in Nineteen-Eighties Spain
1980s

LIBERTIES

The Birth of the Gay
Scene in Slovenia
1984

Contradictions of the
Socialist Civil Society in
Nineteen-Eighties
Yugoslavia
1980s

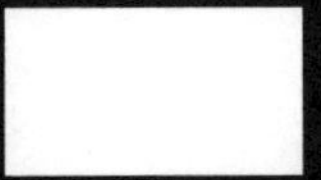

Verbal Delict
1981–1987

'Petition of Intellectuals'
1984

CONTRADICTIONS OF THE SOCIALIST CIVIL SOCIETY IN NINETEEN-EIGHTIES YUGOSLAVIA

Gal Kirn

A BRIEF INTRODUCTION TO SOCIALIST YUGOSLAVIA

Yugoslavia was the federative and revolutionary entity founded during WW2 at the time of fascist occupation and brutal — also civil — war. The Yugoslav partisans were the only political formation open to all nations and nationalities and they organized an effective resistance that liberated large proportions of territory as early as mid-1941. They were one of the few resistance movements that liberated itself from the fascist occupation under their own steam. The partisan struggle triggered a social revolution that was characterized by huge popular support and the empowerment of workingclass people. Also, it continued with other means after the split with Stalin in 1948: firstly in the rise of workers' self-management and secondly, in a rupture with the regional politics, which brought Yugoslavia on the path of non-alignment (Kirn 2015).

The self-management path produced a series of unforeseen effects: a relative freedom in the fields of culture (Djurić and Šuvaković 2003) and economy (Samary 1995), and political pluralism within a party that also conducted market reforms. The latter weakened federal institutions and self-managed planning, while giving priority to market rationality that integrated the Yugoslav economy into the global market. This resulted in the gradual dismantling of the inter-republican solidarity model, substitution of federal funding by commercial banks, fiercer competition among socialist enterprises, while it also intensified conflicts among workers and non-workers, and the emergence of wildcat strikes and student protests. In short, Yugoslav socialism was not a stable social form but rather a transitory and contradictory formation that combined capitalist and communist elements.

The exhaustion of partisan politics was a result of multiple discontents and a longer internal process that can be identified with the failure of market socialism (Samary 1988) and a waning of the ideological legitimacy of the League of Communists. Externally, the integration into the global market came at the price of intensified competition and harsh austerity programmes of international monetary organizations throughout the eighties (Magaš 1993). However, all these macro-economic and geopolitical causes[01] do not provide us with a complete answer to the break-up of Yugoslavia. This article argues that the emergence of civil society did not as such deliver the final 'political' blow to socialist Yugoslavia, but actually engaged in various struggles, with often contradictory and even opposing demands. The hypothesis highlights that the politico-economic crisis first underwent an intensified democratic (re)invention that aimed to reform and democratize socialism, while towards the eighties hegemonization of the civil society was conducted by nationalist-liberal forces.

[01] For a detailed overview see Ramet 2005.

Unquestionably, socialist civil society is not to be idealized as a kind of harmonious island that initiated the democratic change that led to a democratic state, while it is also not to be demonized as a kind of Western conspiracy that, through civil society, sponsored the break-up of Yugoslavia. Rather, socialist civil society was undergoing — just like the whole social formation — major contradictions and antagonisms. Civil society cannot be isolated from a deeper transformation of the economy and the state apparatus that took place in the light of neoliberal restructuring of capitalism, and socialism.[02] Furthermore, the story of the bloody break-up of Yugoslavia came at the peak of European integration processes. 25 years later, the European Union faces major challenges and an internal crisis, while the whole post-Yugoslav region is undergoing drastic economic and political upheavals, which are not so dissimilar from those in the eighties.

02
The young Marx already claimed that the bourgeois separation is based on the free and abstract citizen who participates in public life and is equal in front of the law (state), while it obfuscates the class struggle within civil society, where bourgeois and worker enter into an 'equal' contractual relation.

EMERGENCE OF THE *DEMOCRATIC* CIVIL SOCIETY

To bracket the complexity of the history of twentieth-century socialist revolutions one can argue that the revolutionary take-over of power did not result in either the disappearance of the state nor in the emergence of the civil society as communists had projected; while the history of Yugoslav socialism can also show that the state and civil society never completely merged with one another, as totalitarian studies suggest. Even if the politics of Yugoslav social self-management proclaimed to spread social property and workers control from production to reproduction, there were strong confrontations and many political issues.

In the eighties, the socialist civil society and workers' opposition in the whole Eastern bloc explicitly targeted communist parties and their leaderships (the state) that allegedly represented the working class (in civil society). In the case of Yugoslavia, the eighties brought a deep democratization process, which was not without ambivalences and regressions. The whole period is summed up by theorist Maja Breznik:

> In retrospect, we see that punk actually was a detonator of the democratic revolution of the eighties, since the political transformation only supervened the social transformation where punk had such a central role ... the nationalist and separatist political forces which democratically took the power, arrested, at least temporarily, the transformation by diverging it into the nation-building and the restoration of capitalism on neo-liberal premises.

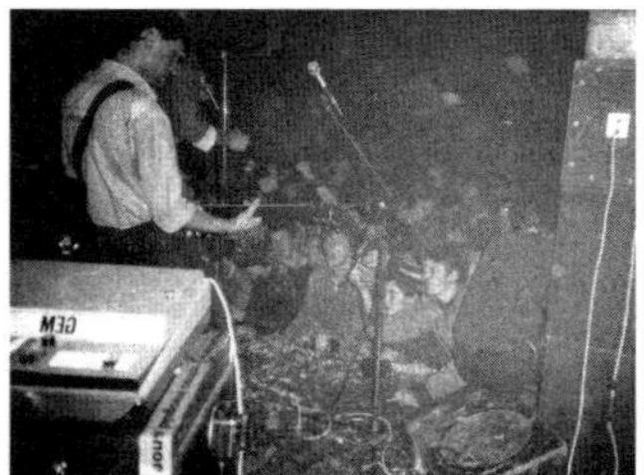

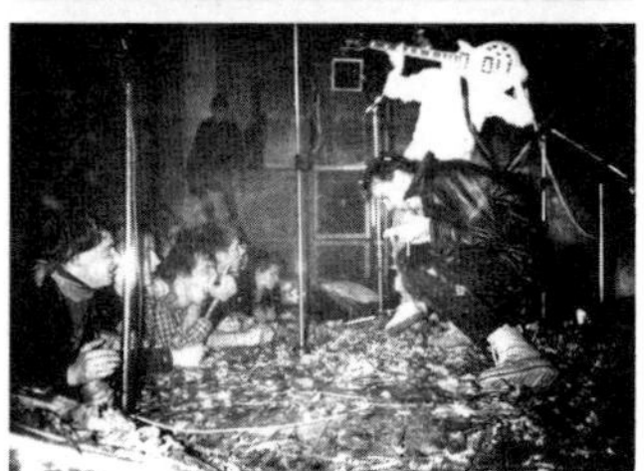

Punk band Termiti performing in Ljubljana, 1981. Photo: Matija Praznik

How did the reactionary tendency hegemonize the democratic transformation and, as Breznik rightly points out, wheel it into 'nation-building' and 'the restoration of capitalism on neo-liberal premises'? The early eighties saw a major destabilization through economic discipline from austerity packages to the rise of unemployment and high inflation. The ideological legitimacy of the socialist leadership crumbled, since it could not keep the fundamental promises of the social(ist) contract.

Due to the relative prosperity and advantages that the socialist republic of Slovenia had vis-à-vis other republics, the civil society was first born there in the early eighties. This was the time of the veritable democratic reinvention that consisted of progressive theoretical, artistic, and political practices and groups. Ironically, despite avant-garde being deemed historical and out-dated, it was precisely art collectives and punk, most notably, that can be ascribed the major role in the early democratization process. From the very start, punk was deemed as dangerous, anarchic, and even fascist by the ideologues of the League of Communists and severe reactions by the police could be seen as a trigger that made the tiny art scene into a popular site with the youth and urban scene. The initial 'artistic' phase was followed by more organized and politicized groups that demanded democratic reforms of the existing socialism. Those groups wanted to broaden the political space and include new rights and although their voice was not taken seriously at first, it then could no longer be ignored in a long series of protests, actions, performances, proclamations, and strikes. These groups were heterogeneous and expressed diverse demands, but it is important to state that their aim was not to undermine the general politico-economic orientation and independent path of socialism and the Yugoslav project. They were however extremely critical towards all ideological sacred cows and they targeted the power structures, corruption of socialist leadership, and authoritarian laws within Yugoslav society.

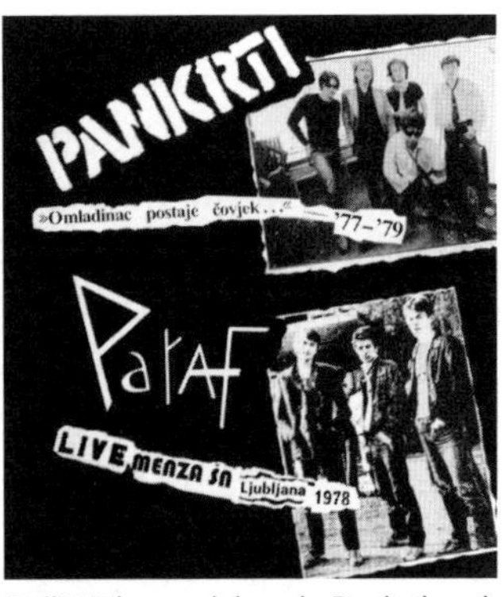

Split LP by punk bands Pankrti and Paraf, cover

The Association of Socialist Youth (ZSMS) was a subsidiary socialist organization and part of the political state apparatus, which would usually provide major cadres for the League of Communists. However, in the eighties, it began to openly challenge the course of the federation and the republic's leadership. There were many other important groups that were organized in a coherent and continuous way for the first time: LGBT movement, ecological movement, women's movement, peace movement, and workers' movement (strikes). Those groups, formally social and cultural 'associations', articulated different demands: from recognition of new political, social, and economic rights/equality of minoritarian groups, rejection of the death penalty and demilitarization that would end the forced conscription (freedom not to serve the army) to a workerist demand for the improvement of working conditions and higher wages. Some of these struggles were very successful: the freedom of journalism and communication was expanded and the death penalty was abolished by the end of the eighties. However, despite the fact that many of these groups remained very active and initiated fresh debates both outside and within the party apparatus, the early eighties did not see a major political event that would result in what Mouffe and Laclau (1985) named a 'chain of equivalences'. The latter denotes a political logic that brings together very different demands, which may catalyse into a more general political organization that would challenge the socialist system. A parallel existence of alternative spaces, journals, discourses of the progressive civil society gives the impression that it was successful in creating a 'critical public'.

Furthermore, the conservative and nationalist groups gathered around the (Catholic) Church were still marginal at that time. The latter became the largest civil society actor with an established institutional and financial network that gradually was also mobilized by ideological means. Already in 1987, assessing ideological work and actions of the church and their civil representatives, political theorist Tomaž Mastnak spoke of the danger of 'totalitarianism from below'. Though until the late eighties, the church was not as influential and the major political demands and actions came from the progressive side of the political spectrum. This was apparent from lively public debates in the weekly magazines such as *Mladina* (Youth) and more specialized theoretical journals (*Nova revija, Problemi, CKZ, Tribuna*), artistic magazines and Radio Student. There was a renaissance in publications of theoretical and political treatise in the early eighties — also the famous Ljubljana circle/encounter of critical Marxism and psychoanalysis took shape in that time. In addition, art groups such as Neue Slowenische Kunst, Borghesia, Marina Gržinić/ Aina Šmid and others catapulted themselves into the midst of Yugoslav politico-artistic space, soon to be 'exported' to the West as a variation of neo-avant-garde art. Many artist groups took a conscious decision to intervene in the sacred ideological kernels of then existing socialism, at times stirring major controversy, most notably with the New Collectivism poster affair. The avant-gardist group re-designed a Nazi poster about heroism and won the competition for the major official Youth Day in Yugoslavia. This act made the group instantly famous. However, many art groups/ artists performed subtle twists in aesthetical forms and thus contributed to the reinvention of utopian and avant-garde promise. I argue that their encounters with a theoretical and political scene made a lasting impact on the democratization of socialism.

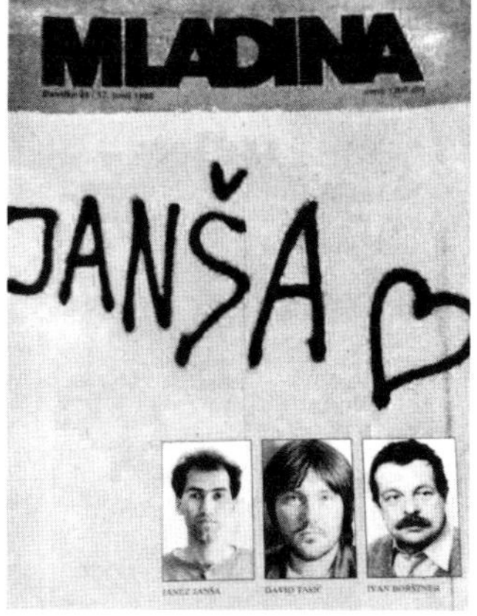

Mladina weekly, 17 June 1988, cover

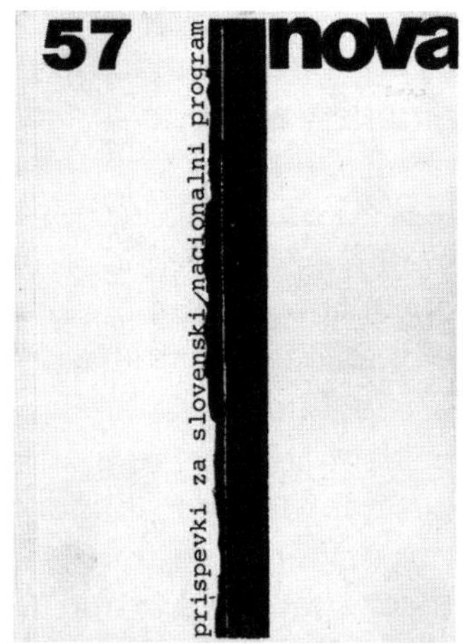

Nova revija, Prispevki za slovenski/ nacionalni program no. 57, January 1987

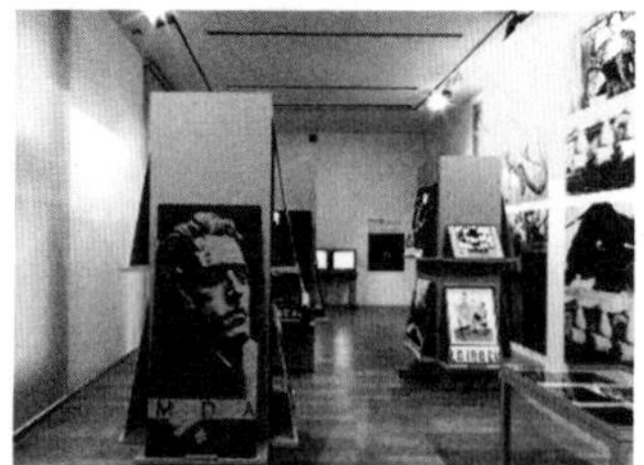

New Collectivism, *Youth Work Brigades* poster at exhibition, 1984

These diverse civil-society, artistic, and political movements appeared in other regions of Yugoslavia as well, but with varying intensities at different times.[03] Even with the events at the end of the eighties and the tragic war that ensued, we should not forget that the laboratory and experiences of this intense period happened thanks to the relative openness of the then existing socialism and the active engagement of diverse collectives. One could say that there was a strong influence of democratic civil society on the existing official self-management apparatus. If the existing infrastructure permitted political and cultural associations access to space and funding, then the civil sphere influenced and pushed the ideology and institutions of self-management towards democratic reforms. This period showed that another *democratic socialism* was possible, and even practiced it in a relatively successful way.

NATIONALIZATION OF THE CIVIL SOCIETY AND RISE OF THE NATION-LIBERAL STATE

Turning to the later part of the eighties, one should keep an eye open for the deepening of the economic crisis and the fierce struggles within the state apparatuses for domination, which resulted in a political crisis of the federation and nationalistic tendencies within republican leaderships. This did not remain unechoed within civil society. The demands for a deep democratization of socialism were joined by demands for a confederation of Yugoslavia and prioritization of republics, which would eventually become an open defence of independent nation-states. Also, there were increasing demands for a free market society with private property, which confirmed liberalism as the major political option through the strengthening of civil society. But the story of resonance between socialist reformers and liberals came to an end, or rather was further weakened with the rise of nationalist ideology. There were at least three major political events in the period from 1987–1989 that had a huge impact on the withering away of Yugoslavia and on the implementation of the model 'one nation one (liberal) state'. These events resulted in a fast decline of the democratic civil society.

Let us start in 1987, which could be seen as the major departure for nationalism, which was practically banned by Yugoslav political and legal practice. It is important to first settle some accounts with a now recurring ideological cliché, namely that nationalism was a matter of *Lumpenproletariat* and an ignorant rural faction. This is a typical class-racist position evoked by many liberal voices and critics of civil wars from the nineties, who could

03

I would not like to give the impression that Slovenia was very exceptional in the eighties, however one has to highlight Slovenia's relative economic privilege compared to other regions: there was basically no unemployment, while some regions had as much as 25–30%; there was an economic growth despite the austerity; and Slovenia had much political influence within the federation.

not explain the bloody turn of events from the allegedly democratic heaven of the eighties. Since nationalist deviations have to do either with the artificial entity of Yugoslavia or with the rural faction and backwardness, the democratic and liberal side of civil society and transitional elite could wash their hands of responsibility. But in fact, it was as early as 1987 that nationalist platforms came into existence with the push of the majority of intelligentsia in different republics. Many academics in Slovenia (57th issue of right-wing *New Review*) and in Serbia (Serbian Academy of Sciences and Arts) drafted and promoted national memoranda. Building the national mythologies of the 1000 years old yearning of small nations to become independent, nurturing the image of eternal enemies of each nation and of sacred places to be reconquered — all this had two precise aims: the formation of independent nation-states and the disintegration of Yugoslavia. The memoranda and theoretical treatises of this and subsequent journals would analyse the historical viability of independence from different angles: legal, economic, political, and cultural. Since the official League of Communists still operated within the socialist horizon and federal institutions, the major agency of independence came on the agenda of civil society.

The theoretical promotion of the dream of independence reached the masses, or acquired material form during the so-called JBTZ affair in Slovenia in 1988. Four people, journalists and political activists, were arrested by the military police and brought before a military tribunal because they wanted to publish military secrets on possible manoeuvers of the Yugoslav people's army in the event of disintegration. The judicial process — as was the habit in military tribunals — was conducted in Serbo-Croatian, which was the *lingua franca* of the federation, while defendants insisted upon their right to answer in Slovenian and thus refused to answer. After being convicted, a massive uprising and solidarity gestures of tens of thousands of people took place in front of the prison. Those imprisoned became national heroes overnight. In the months that followed, different manifestations brought together cultural and political groups, and people from all over Slovenia: it was time for a Slovenian spring. This uprising soon played out in the old cliché of minorities and small republics fighting against the dirty and alienated centre (Belgrade), The initially democratic civil society now became predominantly nationalistic.

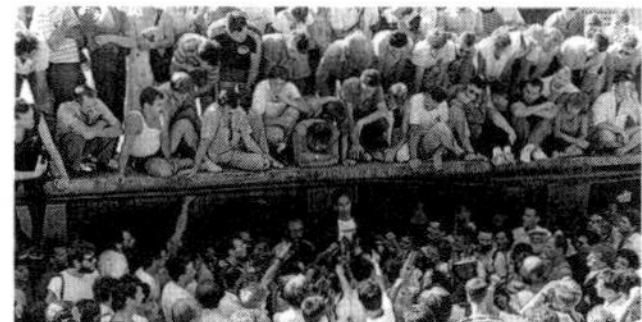
Roška, JBTZ trial, 1988

Secondly, not long after the JBTZ affair, the economic situation in Kosovo exploded. It should be noted that throughout the eighties, the autonomous region of Kosovo became a Third World of Yugoslavia. The dismantling of inter-republican solidarity and austerity politics also affected the region with the most mineral wealth in Yugoslavia: Trepça's huge mining complex that

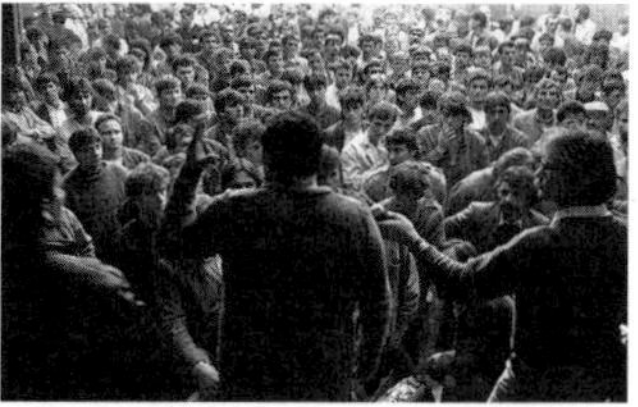
A strike in Labin, 1987

employed more than 20,000 miners in the early eighties became a hotbed of strikes. This culminated in the major miner strike of February 1989, which was one of the most dramatic and arguably longest underground strikes in world history, lasting eight days. The strike ended with more than 180 miners hospitalized and pro-Milošević Albanian leaders sacked. At that point it was seen as a temporary victory of the working class. However, Milošević's plan to take over power within the Serbian League of Communists, and later within the federation backfired: Milošević's leadership not only revoked a constitutional right to regional autonomy for Kosovo, but also organized a major nationalist event in support of his political movement in Kosovo, 600 years after Serbian aristocracy lost their rule to the Ottoman Empire. This step and further nationalization of the political leaderships obfuscated the central antagonism in Kosovo and underdeveloped parts of Yugoslavia, the one of economic and class issues that workers and the strike were highlighting. The struggle of miners in Kosovo was immediately translated into the signifiers of nationalism: Slovenian and Croatian people supported Albanian miners, who were undergoing Serbian aggression. This event became a catalyst of internal struggles in the federation and in the demise of the communist political elite.

Within the Slovenian context this development meant that parts of the old socialist elite and political bureaucracy entered into a democratic transition — despite their differences — together with other emerging political parties and civil-society agents that called for Slovenian independence. This what is usually referred to as the high peak of the Slovenian spring but was actually already the symbolic death of civil society. The latter was over-shadowed by another, more spectacular death of the major enemy: socialist Yugoslavia with its corrupted socialist elite and evil centre, but also the dissolution of the federative constitution that implied equality of nations and nationalities, inter-republican solidarity, and social property that gave way to private property. Thus, the ideological struggle at the end of the eighties became anti-Yugoslav and anti-communist.[04] Democratic civil society died, paradoxically, when its mission of free democratic elections was accomplished, while at the time this meant that class struggles were hegemonized by a nationalist and liberal ideology. Civil society ceded its political infrastructure, 'human resources', and past experiences to new political parties, which *en masse* tended towards the centre or right-wing political spectrum. These new political parties aspired to liberal democracy, while they were all nationalist. From this moment on civil society's space for real alternatives became inscribed on neoliberal TINA (there is no alternative), while the articulation of political difference and inter-penetration between

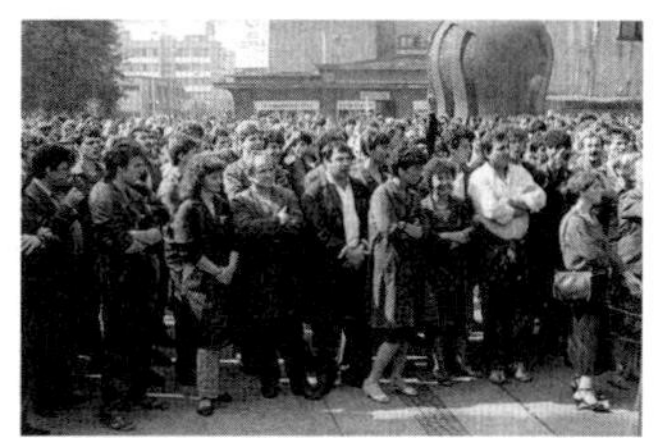

Worker's strike at TAM truck factory, Maribor, June 1988

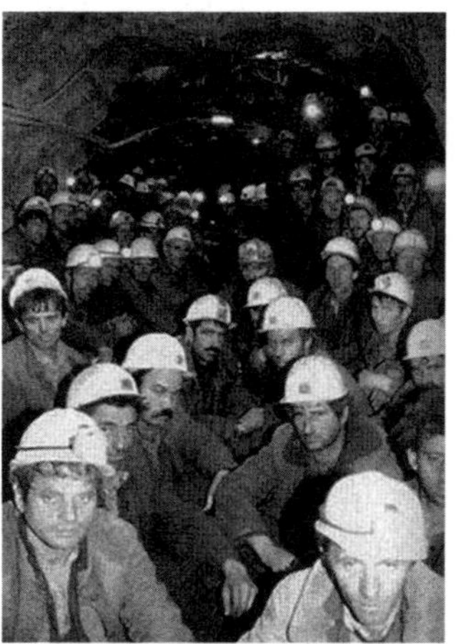

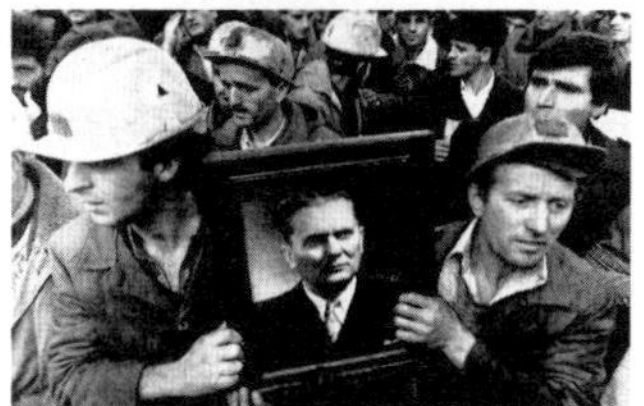

Trepça miner's strike. The biggest underground strike

04

It is noteworthy that Slobodan Milošević was a banker who was schooled in the West and started his career with an 'anti-bureaucratic revolution' that promoted technocratic and nationalist discourse.

art, politics and theory gave way to a political imaginary built on ethnically exclusive principles. The rest was confirmed by the nationalist victory: referenda for independence in 1990 and 1991 established new nation-states, which were recognized by large parts of the European community. Large parts of Yugoslavia were ethnically mixed, so the economic catastrophe of more than one region and toxic nationalisms were not signs of maturation that should be baptized by the 'international community' and emerging European Union. These political steps led to civil wars, exile and brutal impoverishment of 'Yugoslav' people, things that before 1987 were deemed by anyone as 'unimaginable'. The new coalition of liberalism (bankers, republican bureaucracy and technocracy) and aspiring nationalist elites dreamed of new 'nation-states', which resulted in wars.

THE YUGOSLAV EXPERIENCE RE-TRANSLATED INTO EUROPEAN HORIZONS

In Yugoslavia the liberal democratic transition went horribly wrong and resulted in civil wars, which happened for the first time on European soil since the end of WW2. Looking to contemporary situation of the periphery through the Yugoslav lenses, what can be learned or re-interpreted outside the cliché of TINA? Doesn't the Yugoslav scenario carry some resemblance to the Greek tragedy of the past few years? Syriza's election victory promoted a social-democratic programme and radicalized while receiving a clear message from below: a clear OXI ('No') to the troika's austerity could be compared to Yugoslavia's OXI to Stalin and the West after WW2. This was a historic moment not only for Greece, but for the whole of Europe. Real international solidarity would mean that the left in the entire European Union would organize general strikes and protests after the financial coup by the European political institutions. Instead, the troika could impose its own alternative: EITHER the periphery makes a strong neoliberal-austerity reform, OR we shall change your government. After the destruction of left alternatives we saw a media-supported struggle between neoliberalism and fascism within consolidated democracies in Europe.

There is a major split on the left about the future of Europe: on the one hand we had old romanticism of Europeanism, which geopolitically strengthens the position of the core countries, while on the other hand there are those who merely promote exit, which will not automatically save any of peripheral economies from global capitalism. If something was learned from the Yugoslav dissolution it is this: without a clear politico-economic programme, i.e.

how the country distributes wealth and defines production, fights poverty and austerity, neither the conservation of the status quo nor national independence can help to address the real causes. Any project that defies the neoliberal dictates should not align itself blindly with the nationalist project in local (language of the periphery's resentment) or European disguise (language from the core). Even if things are seen differently by the periphery and core countries, the progressive project — if linked to the word EXIT, be it Catalan, Greek, or Scottish — should carry an egalitarian and socialist promise. Otherwise, it is doomed to become just another capitalist class stratified society with the governing and much more dependent local elite vis-à-vis supranational forces. Emancipatory forces and imagination can avoid false exclusionary alternatives and evoke a third real alternative of popular emancipation that traverses, and goes beyond current Europe.

BIBLIOGRAPHY

Breznik, Maja. 'Solidarity, or What We Were Fighting For.' In *Management Tools: A Workbook for Arts Professionals in East and Central Europe*. Edited by N. Tomassi and B. Heer. New York: Arts International, 1995.

Djurić, Branka, and Misko Šuvaković. *Impossible Histories: Historic Avant-Gardes, Neo-Avant-Gardes, and Post-Avant-Gardes in Yugoslavia*. Cambridge, MA: MIT Press, 2003.

Kirn, Gal. *Partizanski prelomi in protislovja tržnega socializma v Jugoslaviji*. Ljubljana: Založba Sophia, 2015.

Laclau, Ernesto, and Chantal Mouffe. *Hegemony and Socialist Strategy: Towards a Radical Democracy*. London: Verso, 1985.

Magaš, Branka. *The Destruction of Yugoslavia*. London: Verso, 1993.

Mastnak, Tomaž. 'Totalitarizem od spodaj.' *Družboslovne razprave* 4, no. 5 (1987), pp. 91–98.

Močnik, Rastko. *Tri teorije*. Ljubljana: Založba / cf*, 1999.

Ramet, Sabrina. *Thinking about Yugoslavia: Scholarly Debates about Yugoslav Breakup and the Wars in Bosnia and Kosovo*. New York: Cambridge University Press, 2005.

Samary, Catherine. *Le Marché contre l'autogestion: L'expérience yougoslave*. Paris: Publisud etc., 1988.

VERBAL DELICT

Neža Kogovšek Šalamon

'Verbal delict' is the colloquial term used for the crime of 'hateful propaganda' as defined in the notorious Article 133 of the Penal Code of the Socialist Federal Republic of Yugoslavia. This was a crime sanctioning the act of speaking out against or criticizing the authorities, verbally or in writing. It was broadly defined, allowing the state authorities to prosecute any kind of expression of criticism by individuals, media and artists.[01] People punished under this provision were marked as 'political prisoners'.[02] The provision of Article 133 (1) read as follows:

> Any person who evokes or incites to, in writing, by leaflets, speech or in a different way: destruction of power of the working class or working people; unconstitutional change of the socialist self-governing social order; breaking of brotherhood and unity, and equality and equal rights of nations and ethnicities; overthrow social self-governance bodies or their executive bodies; resist against decisions of competent authorities or self-governance bodies important for security and development of socialist self-governing relations, security and defence of the state; or anyone who presents social and political circumstances in the state with an evil intent and untruthful manner, shall be punished with imprisonment from one to ten years.

According to the weekly *Mladina*, which was at the forefront of the fight against Article 133 in the eighties, 836 persons were prosecuted for verbal delict between 1981 and 1987.[03] The 'crime', which had been inspired by Soviet legislation, represented a serious threat to freedom of thought, freedom of expression and freedom of press. As the definition was written in a manner that allowed for a broad interpretation, it was not in line with the principle of legality. Indictments based on Article 133 became scarce by 1987. This was a result of not only the democratization process, but also of court battles concerning freedom of press led by lawyer Matevž Krivic.[04] Cultural associations, journalists, intellectuals and others became deeply involved in the resistance against Article 133 and called for its abolition. Surprisingly, in 1987 even the Public Prosecution informed the Executive Council of Yugoslavia about the problems that this crime is posing with regard

01

One example is the prosecution and conviction in 1981 of Serbian poet Gojko Đogo because of his collection of poetry titled *Vunena vremena* (Woolen Times). He was sentenced to two years of imprisonment by the District court in Belgrade. The supreme court lowered his sentence to one year. Citations: Michael Biggins, Janet Crayne, eds., *Publishing in Yugoslavia's Successor States* (New York, London and Oxford: Haworth Information Press, 2000), p. 109; http://riznicasrpska. net/knjizevnost/index. php?topic=244.0.

02

Jerneja Kos, 'T.i. "Verbalni delikt" v Sloveniji v osemdesetih letih', Diploma thesis, University of Ljubljana, Faculty of Social Sciences, 2004, p. 9.

03

Mladina no. 51, 9 December 1988, p. 9.

04

Rastko Močnik, 'Kaj je vse pomenil izraz "civilna družba"?', *Medijska Preža* December 2012, http:// mediawatch.mirovni-institut. si/bilten/seznam/43/ civilna-druzba/index.html#1 (3 April 2017). Mr. Krivic later became a judge of the Constitutional Court of the Republic of Slovenia.

to fundamental rights and proposed its revision.[05]

However, Article 133 was never repealed, but simply ceased to exist as the old federal penal code was replaced by the new penal codes by the successor states of the former Yugoslavia.

Because of negative experiences with prosecuting 'verbal delicts', the prosecution today is reluctant to prosecute other types of verbal crimes, including hate speech, defined as a crime of 'public incitement to hatred, violence and intolerance' in Article 297 of the 2008 Penal Code of the Republic of Slovenia. The incidents falling under this category are rarely prosecuted. One of the main reasons for this is the *legal opinion* of the Slovenian State Prosecutor's Office, which states that there is a need to ensure that only speech that actually threatens public order may be prosecuted.[06] In a world full of anti-Muslim and anti-immigrant sentiments this may soon present a similar problem as 'verbal delict' did under the previous regime.

05

Kos, 'T.i. "Verbalni delikt" v Sloveniji v osemdesetih letih', p. 13.

A badge designed by Matjaž Vipotnik in support of cancellation of Article 133 of the Penal Code of the Socialist Federal Republic of Yugoslavia, 1985

06

This legal opinion is available at: http://safe.si/ spletno-oko/pravno-stalisce- tozilstva-o-pregonu- kaznivega-dejanja-javnega- spodbujanja-sovrastva-nasi (3 April 2017).

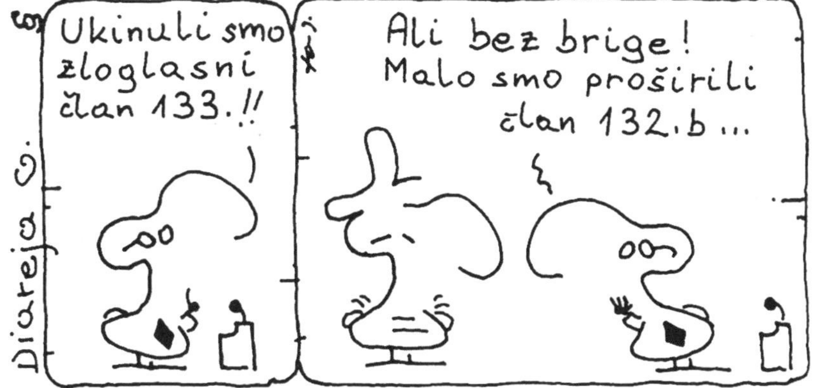

Tomaž Lavrič, *Diareja*, published in the magazine *Mladina*, Ljubljana, 1990. ('We abrogated the controversial Article 133!!'. 'But no worries! We slightly extended Article 132.b...') Courtesy the artist

1987

1981

'PETITION OF INTELLECTUALS'

Merve Elveren and Erman Ata Uncu

Widely known as the 'Petition of Intellectuals', the text 'Observations and Requests Pertaining to the Democratic Order in Turkey' was prepared collectively over a four-month period in 1984. Signed by 1,256 people and severely criticized by the Prime Minister Turgut Özal, the petition aimed to remove legal and practical limitations that prevent products of intellectual activity and art; to alter the structure of the Council of Higher Education (YÖK) in the direction of autonomy based on the principle of election; to call for press freedom. It was an action that had some of the strongest repercussions in the eighties, both because of its content, and because it was signed by a variety of figures ranging from the fields of popular culture to the intellectual sphere.

56 of the signees, who were accused of acting against the orders of the authorities under martial law, were acquitted on February 7, 1986. Following a report published in *Le Monde*, the petition began to attract attention abroad as well. A letter of support published on June 1 in Strasbourg by the Initiative for Solidarity, a group formed of Western intellectuals, was signed by more than 2,000 people.

March 5, 1984

Turkey is experiencing one of her gravest crisis, one from which she has not yet recovered. There is no doubt that all sections, levels and public servants of our society are jointly responsible for this great crisis. We Turkish intellectuals are fully conscious of the importance and priority of our shortcomings and responsibility. This consciousness bestows upon us the duty and the right to declare our views regarding the transition of our society towards a sound and secure order.

We find it necessary to state our views within the presently existing legislation and within that framework not constituting a criminal offense under Law No. 2969. Although we do not approve of these limitations, we are placed in the position of having to act within the said framework.

As citizens who have no purpose other than to fulfill their democratic responsibility, our sole support lies in the legitimacy, which we believe the people of our country will grant to our views. In this attempt, whose source of inspiration derives from the problems of our society, we have had no connection with any political milieu, establishment, organization or party whatsoever, inside or outside of Turkey, and existence of such a connection is unthinkable.

We enthusiastically believe that, by the use of rational methods, our society shall attain a bright future. In this belief and assuming our common responsibility, we exercise our constitutional right of petition to respectfully submit to the highest offices of the State our observations, thoughts and requests concerning the public.

OBSERVATIONS AND REQUESTS OF THE UNDERSIGNED PERTAINING TO THE DEMOCRATIC ORDER IN TURKEY

Democracy lives through its institutions and principles. If, in a country, the institutions, concepts and principles which form the basic elements of democracy are destroyed, it will become increasingly difficult to repair the damage.

To alienate democracy from its inherent values and institutions, to preserve it in form while emptying it of its contents, is as dangerous as it is to destroy it. Therefore we defend the view that the institutions, concepts and principles which support the structure of our state should be safeguarded and strengthened within a democratic environment.

Our people are worthy of all the human rights enjoyed by contemporary societies and they should possess them without exception. We consider it humiliating that our country should be reduced to the position of a state whose human rights guarantees are being debated in other countries.

The right to life and to live in human dignity is the primary goal of organized and social existence and it cannot be abolished in our era, on any grounds whatsoever; it is a natural and sacred right. In order for this right to achieve significance, people should be able to express and develop their thoughts freely, and to organize themselves accordingly. We believe that new and diverse thoughts conceived by the individuals of our society are not the reason for crises, as there have been efforts to show, but that they are necessary ingredient of social vitality.

Justice, which is the final refuge of human beings, also provides the main guarantee for living in human dignity. In a contemporary state where the rule of law exists, the effective means for fulfilling this is to refrain from obstructing in any way the search for justice, or from resorting to extraordinary courts and to unusual means of prosecution. We are of the opinion that the prolongation of extraordinary forms of government into periods considered normal is not compatible with the contemporary concept of democracy.

The limitation of citizens' rights without a court decision, the establishment of crimes by unilateral and incontestable administrative acts, the abrogation of people's political rights and the practice of making general accusations have all been instrumental in bringing about social disruption. It is not compatible with the concept of a State bound by the rule of law for certain acts not constituting a crime at the time they were performed — such as joining societies, cooperatives, foundations, professional chambers, unions and political parties, or expressing certain thoughts — to be labeled as criminal according to an opinion dominant at a later date.

The democratic system itself cannot be held responsible for the extensive acts of terrorism Turkey has undergone.

It is the undeniable duty of every organized society to fight against acts of violence. However, it is a basic attribute of the State to be bound by the rule of law in its fight against terrorism. The existence of terrorism can never be considered a justification for the State to resort to the same methods.

Torture, the existence of which has been proved by court decisions, is a crime against humanity. We fear that it may have become habitual for torture to be used as an extrajudicial, prior and primitive form of punishment. Furthermore, we consider as maltreatment and torture all prison conditions which exceed the purpose of limiting the prisoners' freedom.

Necessary measures must be taken to put an end to every kind of torture completely. The defense of the accused should begin at the same time as the inquiry and the accusation. If the principles of the rule of law are violated in all types of inquiry and prosecution, and such universal safeguards as the precept that "the accused is innocent until convicted" are disregarded, arbitrariness, especially in political cases, will become one of the basic elements of legal proceedings.

In consideration of the fact that all the levels of society share in the responsibility for terrorist acts, we believe it is necessary to stop the execution of death penalty verdicts already arrived at and to abolish capital punishment, with a view to totally eradicating the idea of the death penalty as a solution.

Believing in the universal truth that delayed justice is equivalent to injustice, we hold the view that the court proceedings continuing at present should be terminated as soon as possible.

Crimes are a result of social and political conditions. It must not be forgotten that the entire society bears responsibility for the turbulent period being experienced by Turkey. For these reasons and in order to contribute to social peace, we consider an extensive amnesty to be indispensable.

Politics, which is a way of separating good from evil and right from wrong in public life, means the participation of the entire society in government. The inevitable shortcomings of everyday politics, which may be seen in all countries, cannot justify the act of preventing anyone from serving society through politics, a way which should be open to all; nor of leaving this task to the monopoly of certain groups, a single person or certain persons. Politics cannot be reduced to the level of mere administrative decisions.

The National Will can only have meaning in systems where all sections of society have the right to organize freely. In countries where no one is prosecuted for his political convictions or philosophical ideas, where no citizen is censured for his religious beliefs, the Nation Will is the supreme power. Its legitimacy depends upon the attitude it takes towards the fundamental rights and freedoms.

All conditions which hinder the free determination of the will of the majority are antidemocratic. In the same way, the abolishment of fundamental rights, under the pretext of following the will of the majority, cannot be compatible with democracy.

Throughout the process of historic development the aim of democratic constitutions has been to protect the rights and freedoms of the individual. Legislation, under whatever name, which weakens the position of the individual in relation to the State, constitutes a deviation from democracy. In such cases constitutions, which should be the source of democratic life, become an obstacle to democracy itself.

Unions, professional organizations and associations, and above all, political parties are the indispensable pillars of democratic life.

It is as much the duty of professional organizations to protect their members' solidarity and economic interests as it is for them to be instrumental and influential, along with the political parties, in defending the democratic freedoms of individuals and groups and enabling them to participate in government. For this reason, we believe that the rights to organize and to participate should be granted the widest possible guarantee under constitutional provisions.

The existence of the elements of freedom, diversity and innovation in the life of a society is absolutely necessary for its future and its openness to development. Therefore, all products of thought should be protected and new proposals should be freely submitted to public opinion.

A free press is one of the fundamental elements serving to integrate the democratic order. Therefore it is imperative that the individuals of a society be kept informed about themselves in an independent, uncensored and multilateral manner; and that differing opinions and all kinds of criticisms be freely voiced and reflected in the press. It is only with such a press that a diversity in public opinion and democratic control of the government can be effected. For the same reasons we believe that the Turkish Radio and Television (TRT) should again become autonomous, as the first condition of its impartiality.

The main purpose of education is to produce freethinking people who are knowledgeable, skillful and productive. Conversely, it is not reconcilable with contemporary developments and with a pluralist democracy to try to create a single type of individual. Modern democracy aspires to form individuals who can look at the world through critical eyes.

Universities comprise the most educated section of society. To deprive them of their autonomy by claiming that they do not deserve to govern themselves implies a denial of the idea that democracy can function in our country. Placing all institutes of higher education under the authority of an over-powerful council whose members are all appointees serves as an obstacle to the proper education of young persons and to scientific research, and also creates great concern for the future of our country. Therefore we consider it necessary to alter the structure of Council of Higher Education (YÖK) in the direction of autonomy based on the principle of election.

We would like to emphasize that it is a requirement of civilization to remove the legal and practical limitations which prevent products of intellect and art from being created freely, and also to provide the same general guarantees to intellectuals and artists as are granted to all other citizens. A healthy social development requires that the creation and publication of all works art be free, that censorship which greatly restricts cultural activity be abolished completely, that no subject be considered taboo and that criminal liability be determined only by ordinary courts.

In the light of the above consideration and in full consciousness of our responsibilities towards our society, we most sincerely believe that contemporary democracy has an immutable essence, despite its different applications due to the special circumstances of various countries; that the institutions and principles which constitute this essence have been adopted by our nation; that legislation and practices which violate this essence should be abolished by democratic methods; and that, in this manner, we can overcome safely and soundly the crisis through which we are living.

Original text presented as in Aziz Nesin Archive

1984

ROCIO (1980), 88 MINUTES, TANGANA FILMS

A FILM BY FERNANDO RUIZ AND ANA VILA

Pedro G. Romero

In 1976, Fernando Ruiz and Ana Vila took over a cinema in Lisbon to organize the 1ª Mostra Internacional de Cinema de Intervenção, proceeding from the spirit of the Carnation Revolution. In Spain, the death of the dictator Francisco Franco had marked the start of a period of political uncertainty, and in this climate Ruiz and Vila made the decision to travel to Andalusia to begin putting together the documentary *Rocío*.

The Romería de El Rocío is a complex religious, cultural and sociopolitical phenomenon, to which anthropologists refer as a total social fact, an example of the economy of expenditure described by Georges Bataille in *The Accursed Share*. Fernando Ruiz, a resident of Almonte, the town where *El Roció* takes place, asserted: 'the film is an attempt to explain a phenomenon which had fascinated me since childhood'. With a Benjaminian-rooted dialectic use of images, Ruiz would unravel this populist phenomenon, leading him to renounce the atmosphere of social and political injustice, whereby conservative political powers and the Church use the liturgy of the celebration to enhance their power. As professor Hernández Díaz states in the opening sequences, 'images are broken to be irked; but they are also broken to be adored'.

Fernando Ruiz and Ana Vila began shooting the film, always a collective project, in 1976, swapping over directing and scripting roles. The photography of Víctor Estevão was key, and rooted in experience of counterculture film in which the camera optics confer the gestures of the subject matter being filmed. In 1979 a first edit was finished, with Salvador Távora composing the soundtrack, *Las manos* (The Hands), from his play *Herramientas* (Tools), giving shades of colour to a vague Andalusian nationalism. For its premiere in 1980, the film's running time was artificially extended with, according to Ruiz, overly didactic drawings and texts. It later won an award at the Seville Film Festival.

This early success sparked political concern in the most conservative quarters, with the film being condemned, on the same day as the attempted 23-F (23 February 1981) coup d'état, due to the defamation of José María Reales and the veiled accusation he ordered murders to take place in Almonte in 1936, during the fascist repression of the Civil War. Consequently, the film was seized, Fernando Ruiz was imprisoned and fined, sending him into bankruptcy, and the film was censored for distribution, cutting out a fragment which in truth was more of a signifier than significant. The politicized controversy surrounding the film spilled over into 1982, with the election victory of the socialists providing short-lived cause for hope for the film's directors, compounded by the neglect of their cause.

Following this betrayal, Ruiz decided to seek exile in Portugal, working odd jobs until 2005, when he reappeared to unveil his film in the show 'Vivir en Sevilla. Construcciones visuales, flamenco y cultura de masas desde 1966' (Living in Seville. Visual Constructions, Flamenco and Mass Culture Since 1966), held at CAAC in Seville. From that point, Associations for the Recovery of Historical Memory, the writings of Francisco Espinosa, the independent distribution by Hamaca, and José Luis Tirado's film *El caso Rocío* (The Rocío Case, 2013) would fuel the film's dissemination.

Yet the persistent clamour surrounding *Rocío* and its censorship conceals the huge political value of the work — paradoxically, its politicization sabotaged its political power; the aestheticization of politics over experience, the true politicization of art. The critical complexity and intensity of *Rocío* has the same scope as the object it depicts, and in *La seducción del caos* (The Seduction of Chaos, 1991) Basilio Martín Patino knew how to envisage the development of politics which were more liturgical than theological, in which the performance and its economy are dismantled from the inside, seizing the camera in the centre of violent episodes that for us are both subjection and liberation.

ROCÍO

Director .... Fernando Ruiz
Guión .... Ana Vila
Fotografía .... Vitor Estevao
Música Tema Rocío... Salvador Tavora
Montaje .... F. R. Vergara
                     Luciano Berriatua
Sonido .... Francisco Peramos
Color .... EASTMANCOLOR
Producción .... TANGANA FILMS
Productor ejecutivo... Vicente-Antonio Pineda
Distribución .... ECRAN DISTRIBUCION, S. A.

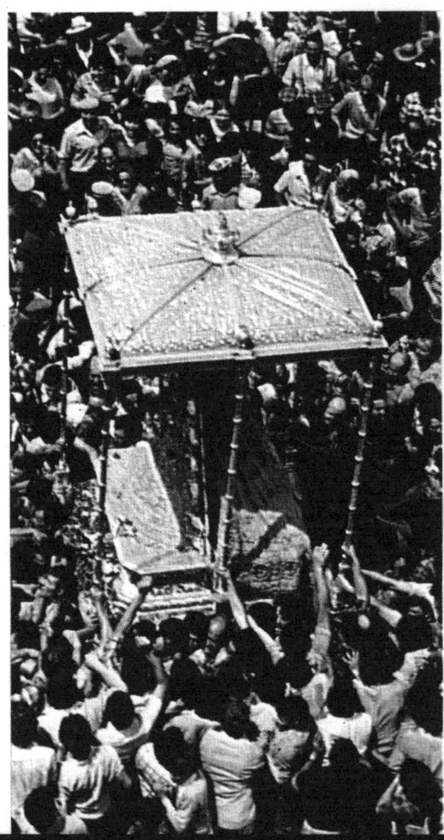

FRASES PUBLICITARI

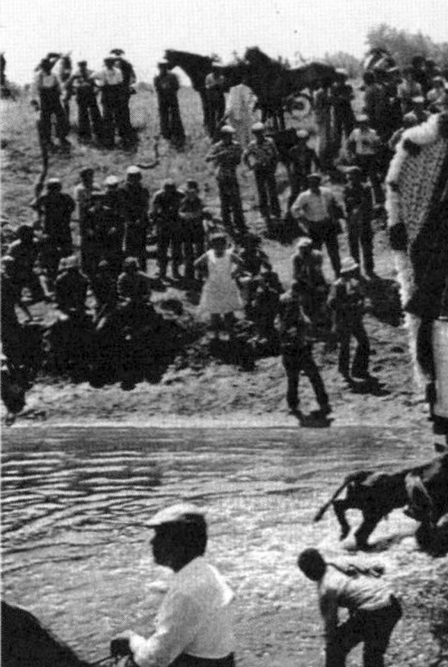

- Rocío es mito, esperanz
- Una rabiosa aspiración
- El alma y el sentir de u
- Rocío es la España que
- Un verdadero ritual de
- La mística del Rocío co
- Rocío es la primera pelíc

Avda. Alberto Alcocer, 46 dpdo. -

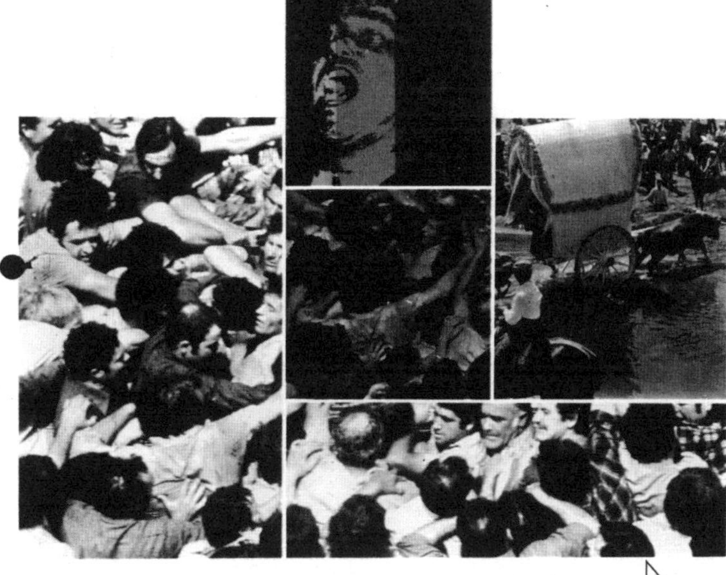

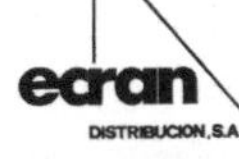

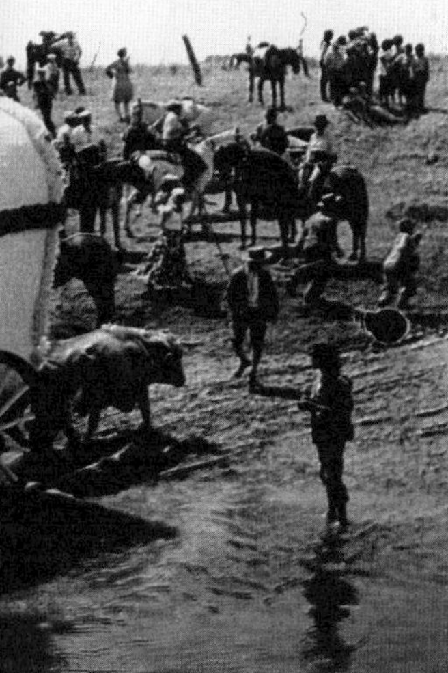

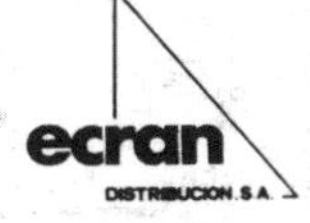

Flyer for film *Rocio*, 1980, director: Fernando Ruiz Vergara

POLICING THE CRISIS, THE PEOPLE'S ACCOUNT AND HANDSWORTH SONGS

Nick Aikens

In 1978, the first edition of *Policing the Crisis: Mugging, the State, Law and Order* was published. Edited by Stuart Hall, Chas Critcher, Tony Jefferson, John Clarke and Brian Roberts, it was a pioneering work of social science that emerged from the fledgling Centre for Contemporary Cultural Studies (CCCS), led by Hall at Birmingham University.

Taking the social phenomenon of 'mugging' in early seventies Britain as its starting point, it offered a critical analysis of the relationship between power embodied through the police, those marginalized by society — politically, economically, racially — and the way in which media were being mobilized to induce a sense of crisis. As the authors wrote, the book

> tries to examine why and how the themes of *race, crime* and *youth* — condensed into the image of 'mugging' — come to serve as the articulator of the crisis, as its ideological conductor. It is also about how these themes have functioned as a mechanism for the construction of an authoritarian consensus, a conservative backlash.[01]

The book is significant for two reasons. Firstly, for exposing the dangers 'when a ruling class alliance has achieved an undisputed authority' as was the case in Britain in the seventies.[02] And secondly, for its ability to place the phenomenon of mugging in a wider social context, reframing the question of law and rights within social divisions that implicated national identities, colonial relations and social cohesion.

The authors became interested in mugging when, in 1973, three boys of mixed ethnic origin were given sentences of ten and twenty years for 'mugging' a man on his way home, robbing and badly injuring him in Handsworth, Birmingham.[03] Handsworth was a residential area home to large African Caribbean and Asian communities and hit by high unemployment and poor housing. The extraordinary reaction to the mugging was a marker that Handsworth was a signifier for wider social tensions and conditions across communities, generations and those in power that would simmer throughout the seventies and eighties.

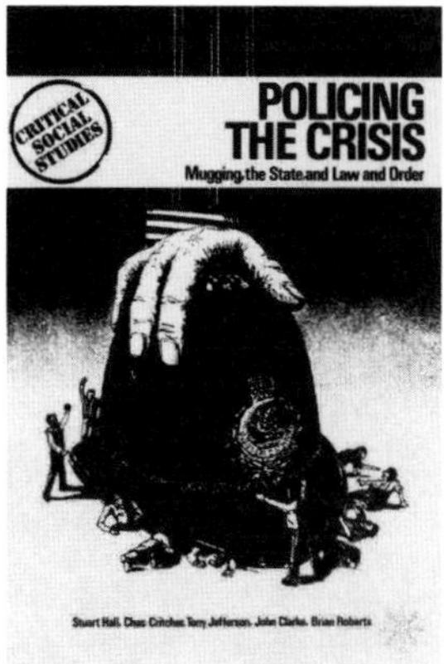

Stuart Hall et al, *Policing the Crisis: Mugging, the State and Law and Order* (London: Macmillan Education, 1978)

01

Stuart Hall, et al., *Policing the Crisis: Mugging, the State and Law & Order* (London: Pallgrave Macmillan, 2nd edition, 2013), p. 2

02

Ibid., xiv.

03

Ibid., p. 2.

Twelve years after the mugging in Handsworth, three major uprisings rocked Britain, in Handsworth, Brixton and Tottenham. These followed a series of uprisings in 1981 in cities across the UK. In 1985, the most explosive was in Tottenham, on the Broadwater Farm housing estate, which resulted in the death of PC Keith Blakelock as well as in hundreds of arrests and a number of prison sentences. In 1986, Ceddo Film and Video produced *The People's Account*, which was shot during and after the Tottenham uprising and includes interviews with residents, MP and Haringey Leader Bernie Grant, and other community activists. At the core of the film's message was the question of rights: the rights of those in Tottenham, Brixton, Handsworth and elsewhere to live without fear for their safety — as well as the right to speak and be heard.

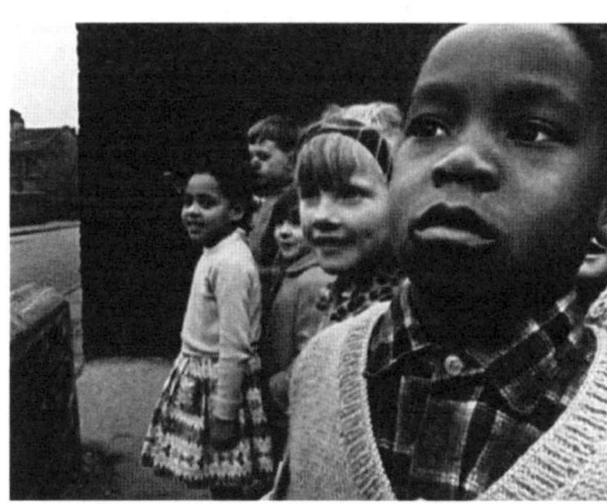
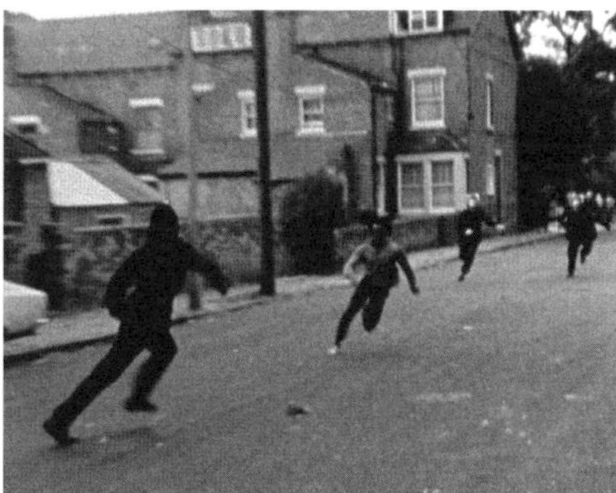

Black Audio Film Collective, *Handsworth Songs*, 1986, video transferred to HD. © Smoking Dogs Films; Courtesy Lisson Gallery

In 1986 Black Audio Film Collective produced *Handsworth Songs*, directed by John Akomfrah. The film, which was the collective's first major film piece, follows the 1985 uprisings in Handsworth. It weaves together sound (most powerfully illustrated by Mark Stewart and the Mafia's dub-refracted version of *Jerusalem*), media news reels, archival footage and a voice over, marking a more essayistic approach regarding the right to speak. Similarly, by drawing out historical trajectories and genealogies, dating back to the arrival of the Windrush Generation in Britain from the West Indies in the aftermath of the Second World War, *Handsworth Songs* locates the civil unrest of the eighties as part of a wider reflection on the articulations and ruptures inherent within the conditions of diaspora and society. In retrospect, *Handsworth Songs'* insistence on complexity can be seen as an alternative to the conservative impulses towards race, crime and 'integration' that are exposed in *Policing the Crisis*. And both insist on contextualizing questions of law, order and civil unrest within a wider set of historical relations.

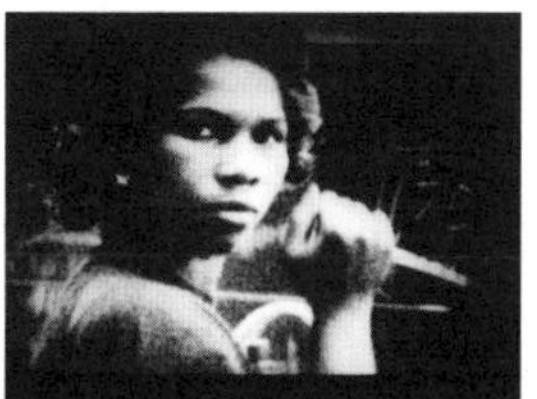
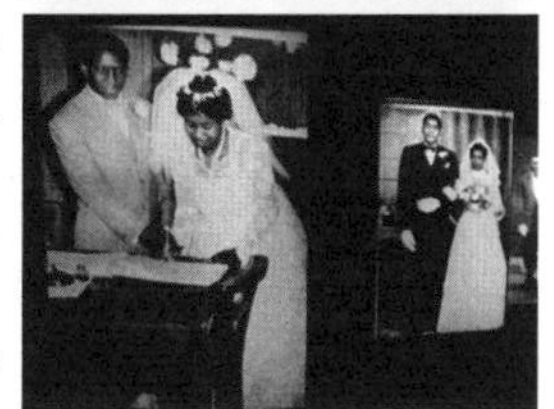

Black Audio Film Collective, *Handsworth Songs*, 1986, video transferred to HD. © Smoking Dogs Films; Courtesy Lisson Gallery

THE FEMINIST MOVEMENT IN NINETEEN-EIGHTIES SPAIN

EMERGENCE AND FRAGMENTATION

Lourdes Méndez

In the now long-standing history of the feminist movement, one constant is its apparent disintegration after gaining certain civil and political rights for women and its subsequent reappearance, either to resume the often unknown fights undertaken by its predecessors, or to begin new ones. This unknown is not the smallest paradox in a feminist movement which, in Europe, was virtually organized at the same time as the labour movement; in fact, well into the twentieth century the history of both movements was interwoven with agreements and disagreements. Disagreements between a labour movement made up of men and women who, despite being on the same page in their convictions as members of the same social class, failed to see eye to eye when certain female activists set out their own dual oppression: as workers and women. Disagreements caused by the little or no attention the labour movement, left-wing or far left parties, nationalist organisations and trade unions paid throughout history to women's demands, for instance the right to vote, sexual and reproductive rights, and equal pay. The verification of the structure of sexism that ran through both left-wing and right-wing organizations, through the labour movement and student movement, through First International in 1864, and the 1968 protests across different countries drove many women to organize themselves independently. This was done in single-sex groups so that women could fight for their rights from a feminist movement that, in Europe, took shape as third-wave feminism at the end of the sixties. The historicity of feminism raises the question of 'how the memory of such a significant movement, the recollection of its efforts, its intellectual and militant challenges, have managed to be erased with such ease' (Offen 2012, p. 31). Thus, erasing feminist struggles from memory contributes to its persistent classification as a 'new' social movement, of little use to understating its re-emergence at different times, or grasping the heterogeneous nature of a movement that reinvents itself time and again. In the seventies, states in western Europe, facing the resurgence of the feminist movement, were forced 'to create structures to take care of issues of equality between the sexes' (Dauphin 2010, p. 15). The expansive wave of this resurgence reverberated internationally when the UN established International Women's Year 1975. In Spain women obtained the right to vote in 1931 under the Second Republic (1931–1939), which also approved a divorce law, abolished the crime of adultery and approved wage parity between both sexes. Franco's death heralded the end of forty years of dictatorship (1939–1975) and enabled groups of women who had fought against both the Franco Regime and for women's rights to come out of hiding. It also enabled the legalisation of university women's associations, the seed of future study seminars on women and research institutes founded throughout the eighties.

Over fifty years have elapsed since, in the dying moments of Franco's dictatorship, female members of left-wing parties created feminist groups with ties to those parties; over forty since the first State Conferences of Women's Liberation were held in 1975, and since the Coordination of Feminist Organisations was established by the Spanish state in 1977; and thirty years since the beginning of the process to institutionalize feminism. Across this time span we have witnessed the endangerment of already-gained rights, and unmet expectations of reducing the inequalities between men and women promised in equality plans drawn up by organizations founded in the eighties, for example the Women's Institutes. Looking, in 2017, at the feminist movement of those years enables us to substantiate the path towards institutionalization laid by part of the movement, and the ground gained by neoliberalism, which has incited mutations worldwide, with one of the effects being the growing inequality arising from positions of sex/gender, and class and race/ethnicity. In addition to the economic effects, neoliberalism is part of 'the history of reactionary rhetoric' (Audier 2012, p. 616), advocating belligerent moral conservatism regarding women's sexual and reproductive rights, and a whole transformation capable of altering the legislative nature of sexual difference. Good examples of this belligerent conservatism are the vicious reactions in France to the same-sex marriage law passed in 2013, or in Spain, with the diatribes against family, marriage, women and maternity by representatives from the Catholic church which, protected by the Concordat,[01] has upheld a privileged relationship with successive governments from a Spanish state whose 1978 Constitution is declared non-religious.

BETWEEN THE STREET, INSTITUTIONS AND FRAGMENTATION

At the end of 1975 in Spain, which had just emerged from forty years of dictatorship, feminist groups (Moreno 1977) surfaced with ties to left-wing — communist and socialist — parties and unions, and, to a lesser extent, to the anarchist and Galician, Catalan and Basque nationalist organizations which had remained active in the fight against Francoism. These groups of feminist women, labelled 'dual militants' (Folguera 1988), would overcome ideological differences to set up platforms which, in 1977, the year in which a Constitution with only 'fathers' was being drafted, and the year that saw the first democratic elections take place, put forward a 'minimum common project resulting from the tensions between different feminist groups and political parties, some of which were close' (Frottie 2006, p. 81). The approval of the Constitution, still

[01]

The secular policies exercised during the Second Republic led the Holy See to consider the Concordat in decline. Franco's dictatorship reactivated it and, following Franco's death, the Concordats of 1976 and 1979 in force today were undersigned.

in force today, in 1978 included the beginning of equality between the sexes and non-discrimination on the grounds of sex or sexual practice among its articles. This was an undisputed achievement of an ever-more ideologically plural feminist movement, which, during the Second Feminist Conferences held in December 1979 in Granada, opposed difference and equality feminists and started 'to divide over the autonomy of feminism as a social movement and considered the issue of women's participation in political parties and state apparatuses' (Frottie 2006, p 82). The division also became apparent in the same year with the creation of the Feminist Party of Spain (Falcón 2012).

Although the institutionalization of a determined feminist political ideology already existed in other European Union countries, it began to crystalize in Spain[02] when, at the request of the Women and Socialism group, comprising feminist socialists which were members of the Partido Socialista Obrero Español (Spanish Socialist Workers' Party), pressure was mounting for this political party to use its absolute majority in Spanish Parliament to approve the creation of the Women's Institute in 1983. This organization, founded in the same decade in regional communities such as the Basque Country (Méndez 2006) and governed at that time from the centre-right Partido Nacionalista Vasco (Basque Nationalist Party), did not bring about the adhesion of the whole ensemble of associations making up the feminist movement. In fact, a large part of the movement was against its creation, viewing it as the start of a process to institutionalize feminism and under the belief no state could cope with the demands for the necessary radical transformation of society in order to put an end to patriarchy, classicism and sexism. These demands, put forth from certain feminist stances inside a movement which, after the break-up of egalitarians and differentialists, after the suspicion towards 'dual militants' that led to the creation, in many cities in the Spanish state, of Women's Assemblies which were autonomous from political parties, set in motion a new process of fragmentation which would create opposition between those who saw the institutional route taken in a positive light and those who radically rejected it. At Women's Institutes, not only were equality plans designed and based on internationally agreed and respected neoliberal policies in the interests of states, including the Vatican, there was also a drive towards associationism, promoting an 'NGO-ization' of women's and/or feminist groups under the assertion that women would thus have greater participation in sociopolitical life. What these organisations failed to mention was that this drive allowed them to exert control over such groups; control over the way in which, to develop their projects, they would request subsidies, thus becoming institutionalized groups that exist through public

02
The political strategies surrounding the institutionalization of equality feminism developed by the French and Spanish states offer interesting parallels, particularly during the term of office of the socialist François Mitterrand, who partially coincided with Felipe González' governments.

financing (Méndez 2008). This situation benefited Women's Institutes through the self-legitimation of their role and by nullifying potential feminist criticism over their proposals, the result of a consensus reached through consultation with associations. The biggest loser in this situation was a feminist movement which, in that decade, would splinter into multiple associations struggling to design common political ideologies. This fragmentation was not solely a product of the institutionalization process described, but also the situation facing the Spanish state, with Galicia, the Basque Country and Catalonia, nations with their own language and culture, fighting for independence through nationalist organizations with a strong female presence (Ugalde, 1996; Agra 2008). After Franco's death, and over the course of the eighties, nationalists with a left-leaning and feminist political sensibility created women's groups inside their organizations, reflecting upon their triple oppression as members of a nation, class and sex, and although they prioritized gaining national sovereignty, there was a need to jointly consider these three issues.

In a decade in which the number of organizations grew, in which political protest activism took to the streets, in which the institutionalization of feminism took root, in which nationalists introduced the triple oppression debate, the feminist movement had to address the heterogeneous nature of its political subject — woman/women. It had to debate how it affected the construction of a common feminist awareness of differences between women, the subjective experiences of identities of sex/gender, social class, race and ethnicity, hetero-normativity and sexual categories that structure the patriarchal and capitalist system. Acknowledging women's heterogeneity affected the only movement made up exclusively of women and compelled activists in higher education to attend seminars on women's studies created by feminist academics at certain universities. Therefore, as of 1983 there was one such seminar at the Complutense University of Madrid, a university which also approved the establishment of a Feminist Research Institute in 1988. Similarly, and despite the field of contemporary art not constituting a sphere of privileged action by feminist organizations, some Women's Assemblies[03] programmed — around the symbolic date of 8 March — exhibitions by women artists and talks which analysed their exclusion from the pages of canonical art history.

To tread over the uneven ground of the complex reality I am expounding, I am going to turn to two feminist slogans which, despite dating back to the end of the sixties, remain pertinent: 'my body is mine' and 'the personal is political'. By claiming the property of their bodies, feminists opened a can of worms, and not through demanding that democratic states acknowledge the

[03]
This was the case with the Women's Assembly of San Sebastián (Basque Country), which organized, in 1986 and 1987, exhibitions by women artists in a space granted by the San Sebastián City Council.

sexual and reproductive rights of their citizens, or through asking for sexual liberty. They opened it by shining a light on that which had been socially and politically concealed: domestic violence towards women, sexual harassment in the workplace, physical and psychological abuse, lesbophobia, homophobia, transphobia. Moreover, upon bringing to light issues such as lesbianism, pornography and prostitution, the feminist movement became fragmented. When lesbian feminists split off from the feminist movement to create their own organizations, they became visible in their status as a doubly oppressed collective and historical subject — because of their sex and sexual practices — and they decried the multiple effects of a hetero-normativity to which heterosexual feminists from the movement had paid little or no political attention. From the mid-eighties, Lesbian Feminist Collectives were springing up; they protested every 28 June and edited magazines such as *Nosotras que nos queremos tanto* (We Women Love Each Other So Much, Madrid), *El amor existe entre mujeres* (Love Exists Among Women, Euskal Herria), and *Tríbades* (Tribades, Barcelona). In 1985, almost at the same time as this fragmentation took place, a vote was passed, during an absolute majority government comprising a socialist party which was more mindful of the potentially adverse reactions by the right-wing powers and the Catholic church than women's rights and the widespread feminist demonstrations, to feebly decriminalize the voluntary termination of pregnancy under three scenarios: rape, the malformation of the foetus, and the psychological/physical danger to the mother. Just to be clear: decriminalization, not a right. A right that, after decades of feminist struggles, we finally obtained in 2010.

Let's now turn our attentions to the second slogan. Feminists from the seventies — still adhering to different political movements, still in disagreement over the main causes of women's oppression and, as a result, the ensuing disagreement over the strategies to develop a fight against them — were able to think like politicians about all those spheres in which they lived their lives and experiences. The slogan 'the personal is political' traverses the borders between Western states, encompassing egalitarian feminists, differentialist feminists, eco-feminists, and radical, liberal, materialist, socialist, anarchist, Marxist, nationalist feminists, laying stress on the fact that feminist struggles ran through every social struggle. The idea that feminism is transversal across every fight for emancipation was accepted by all 'classical', as it were, left-wing parties and social movements and by a plural alter-globalization movement comprising diverse organized groups which rejected neoliberal globalization or any form of inequality and discrimination. Nonetheless, feminists would not find reliable proof that such theoretical acceptance was going to materialize in practice, thereby leading them to reflect on how to attack a patriarchy that was so transversal in the 'old' and 'new' social movements.

A BRIEF FINAL NOTE

I have used the slogans 'my body is mine' and 'the personal is political' to finish sketching the milieu in which the eighties feminist movement in Spain operated for four reasons. The first, to demonstrate how demands such as the right to voluntary termination of pregnancy, which took decades to materialize, would form part of the political agenda of different generations of feminists. The second, to highlight the fact that one of the characteristics of the feminist movement is feedback, in each of its waves, among the struggles undertaken, the demands formulated, and the theorizations that protect them. The third, because it has enabled me to stress the early fragmentation of the feminist movement and to consider the emergence of new subjects whose demands would call for an overhaul of the feminist political agenda. And the fourth, to remember that each new feminist wave headed by young women who, despite often being unaware of past feminist struggles and the theories that go with them, have been born inside the framework of new social, sexual, political and academic realities made possible by their predecessors. It is this unawareness which is politically and intellectually damaging if we wish to image new forms of struggle, if we wish to keep on advancing to produce feminist knowledge. It is imperative for us to combat this unawareness, for us to restore, in every way, the long-standing history of the feminist movement and its theoretical and political achievements.

Agra Romero, María Xosé. 'O pensamento feminista en Galicia.' In *Diccionario Enciclopedia do pensamento galego*, pp. 450–475. Vigo: X. de Galicia/CCG, 2008.

Audier, Serge. *Néo-libéralisme(s). Une arché-archéologie intellectuelle.* Paris: Grasset, 2012.

Dauphin, Sandrine. *L'État et les droits des femmes: Des institutions au service de l'égalité?* Rennes: Presses Universitaires, 2010.

Falcón, Lidia. *La pasión feminista de mi vida.* Barcelona: Intervención Cultural/El Viejo Topo, 2012.

Folguera, Pilar. 'De la transición política a la democracia: La evolución del feminismo en España durante el periodo 1975–1988.' In *El feminismo en España: dos siglos de historia*, pp. 111–131. Madrid: Pablo Iglesias, 1988.

Frottie, Brigitte. 'L'égalité des sexes en Espagne comme enjeu politique dans le processus de democratisation.' *Politique Européenne* 20 (2006), pp. 75–98.

Méndez, Lourdes. 'Administrando la desigualdad entre los sexos: ¿Los estudios de género a la deriva?' In *El doble filo de la navaja: Violencia y representación*, pp. 169–187. Madrid: Trotta, 2006.

— 'Entre la calle y las instituciones: Nuevos desafíos para un feminismo globalizado.' In *La Igualdad no es una Utopía*, pp. 204–2011. Madrid: Thomson/Aranzadi, 2008.

—'Feminismos en movimiento en el Estado español ¿Re-ampliando el espacio de lo político?' *Revista Andaluza de Antropología Social* 6, 2014, pp. 11–30.

Moreno, Amparo. *Mujeres en lucha: El movimiento feminista en España.* Barcelona: Anagrama, 1977.

Offen, Karen. *Les féminismes en Europe, 1700–1950.* Rennes: Presses Universitaires, 2012.

Ugalde, Mertxe. 'Notas para una historiografía sobre Nación y diferencia sexual.' *Arenal: Revista de Historia de las Mujeres* 3, no. 2 (1996), pp. 217–256.

Valiente, Celia. 'El feminismo institucional en España: El instituto de la Mujer, 1983–1994.' *Revista Internacional de Sociología* 54, no. 13 (1996), pp. 163–204.

THE DANGER TO SOCIETY AND SOCIAL REHABILITATION LAW

Teresa Grandas

A society of discipline is built around devices which regulate habits and productive process to ensure its rules are abided by via mechanisms of inclusion and exclusion; or what Hardt and Negri described as the disciplinary power of biopolitics, prescribing normal behaviours and penalizing deviant behaviour, setting out the limits of thought and action in the process. Power is wielded as control and stretches across consciousness and bodies, or social relations through an imposed regime which neutralizes, deactivates, and prevents any hint of an imposed order being rebutted; a legal apparatus which defines the fabric of political subjects as dangerous.

Once the Spanish Civil War was over, Franco declared himself 'the Leader of Spain by the grace of God'. This direct affiliation with the divine power bore direct relation to the Catholic church's regime, and, more importantly, to its most reactionary strands, which came to be called National Catholicism, and which would determine an official moral code established by both censorship and repression. The hegemony of the Catholic church determined public and private life, with religion the doctrine behind the legislation. This was the context which saw the state approve, on 4 August 1970, the Danger to Society and Social Rehabilitation Law, a law which acted against any behaviour deviating from the norms of good conduct and based on the probability of posing a social risk or danger. The cases of endangerment included: habitual vagrants and ruffians; homosexual acts; the exhibition, trafficking or approval of pornography; prostitution; habitual begging and drunkenness; drug addiction, or the trafficking or consumption of drugs; morally perverted under 21s abandoned by their families; the sick and mentally deficient who are a menace to the community. Rather than sentences, the law implemented estrangement, control and detention, and applied convictions that could be established through legal channels due to their threat to the public order. Security measures established either detainment in custody or re-education centres, or arrest, and enabled the re-imprisonment of offenders who, having been freed, were unable to find work, and made redemption through community service or the right to parole, reprieve, or amnesty nigh on impossible.

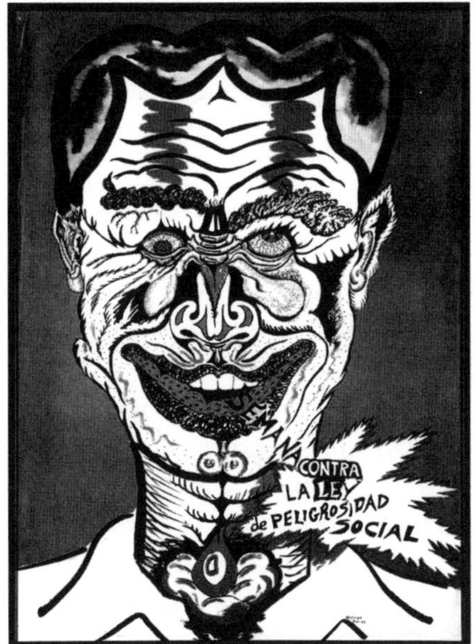

Manolo Quejido, *Semana contra la Ley de Peligrosidad Social*, 1977, poster, lithograph on paper, 1977. MNCARS Collection

This law was inherited from the Law of Vagrants and Miscreants (1933), the only Republican law to remain in existence through the Franco regime, but was promulgated from different criteria. After the Second Republic was declared, there was an amnesty that also affected ordinary prisoners and, in an environment defined by social instability, it sought to prevent crime and anti-social behaviour. It was modified by the dictatorship in 1954 to punish homosexuality and in 1970 it made way for the new Danger to Society and Social Rehabilitation Law, which acted on individual freedom and collective rights. The system exerted restrictive, repressive, debilitating, and demonizing control over dissenting ideologies and behaviour, establishing structural control which conditioned the daily life of citizens from all walks of life. The law came from an intolerance towards every departure from the established order, whilst revealing a moral imposition, control, censorship, and repression, not only politically but also morally and psychologically. It was an example of repressive technology through the state apparatus of dissidence, an arbitrary instrument of the control and regulation of social life. Surprisingly, it survived well into the democracy, and was rescinded, partially, in 1989, before being fully abolished in 1995. Although its repeal saw the records of those brought before the courts destroyed, it did not mean they were pardoned, and the belated nature of these rulings reveals the ongoing inertia that ran though the transition to democracy in Spain.

AIDS, SEXUAL DISSIDENCE AND BIOPOLITICAL ACTIVISM

Jesús Carrillo

In the context of the unceasing crisis of artistic and political imaginaries, new generations of artists, activists and academics have realigned their gazes towards the fragmentary and oft-forgotten movements which, in the early nineties, came together in resistance against the process of sexual normalization in Spain.

A first attempt to research and archive began in 2003 inside a more general exercise to contest the hegemonic narratives of Spanish art which made up the ambitious project *Desacuerdos. Sobre arte, políticas y esfera pública en el arte español* (Disagreements: On Art, Politics and the Public Sphere in Spanish Art). Within this framework, Carmen Navarrete, María Ruido and Fefa Vila connected the use of 'queer' adopted by the LGTB movement at the start of the nineties with the emergence of a new kind of political subjectivity. This narrative reflected the promiscuity of a group of dissidents from the feminist orthodoxy and the pro-rights movement of homosexuals who, from the early nineties, were consciously mobilizing themselves through biopolitical assumptions. A group of young gays and lesbians shared, under the provocative title of Radical Gai and LSD, respectively, their dissatisfaction with the status quo defined in the early decades of democracy, moving beyond, through their gestures and actions, the limits of increasingly normalized and commercialized private and public spaces.

The AIDS crisis would spark their mobilization against a system which, in its management of the disease, evinced the violence concealed in normalizing and supposedly inclusive discourses. Far from becoming an isolated cell of sectarian demands, they would come across other groups rebelling against the system, with whom they shared lifestyles and political and aesthetic references points.

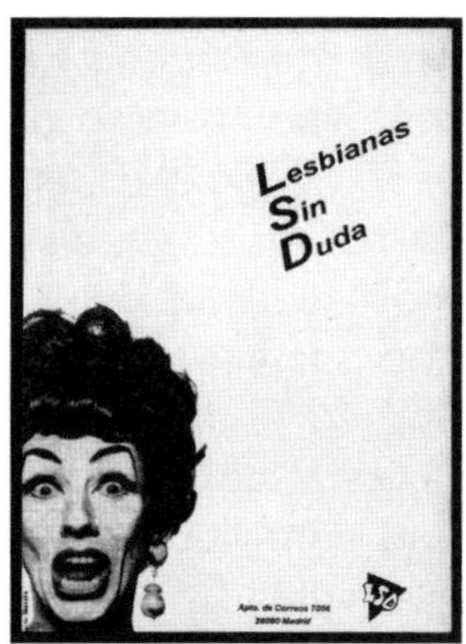

LSD, *Lesbianas Sin Duda*, poster, 90 × 31 cm. Courtesy ¿Archivo queer? (Centro de Documentación del MNCARS). Creative Commons BY-NC-ND

The disrepute of conventional modes of symbolization and the search for a new radical imagination to re-bind politics and life would make art a suitable space for action by this amalgamation of non-conformists. Proceeding from similar premises to those in ACT UP, Radical Gai and LSD deployed a field of operations which was aesthetically and politically undifferentiated, with interventions on the streets, in the classroom, and in bars, parties and protests, places where the personal and public were inextricably linked.

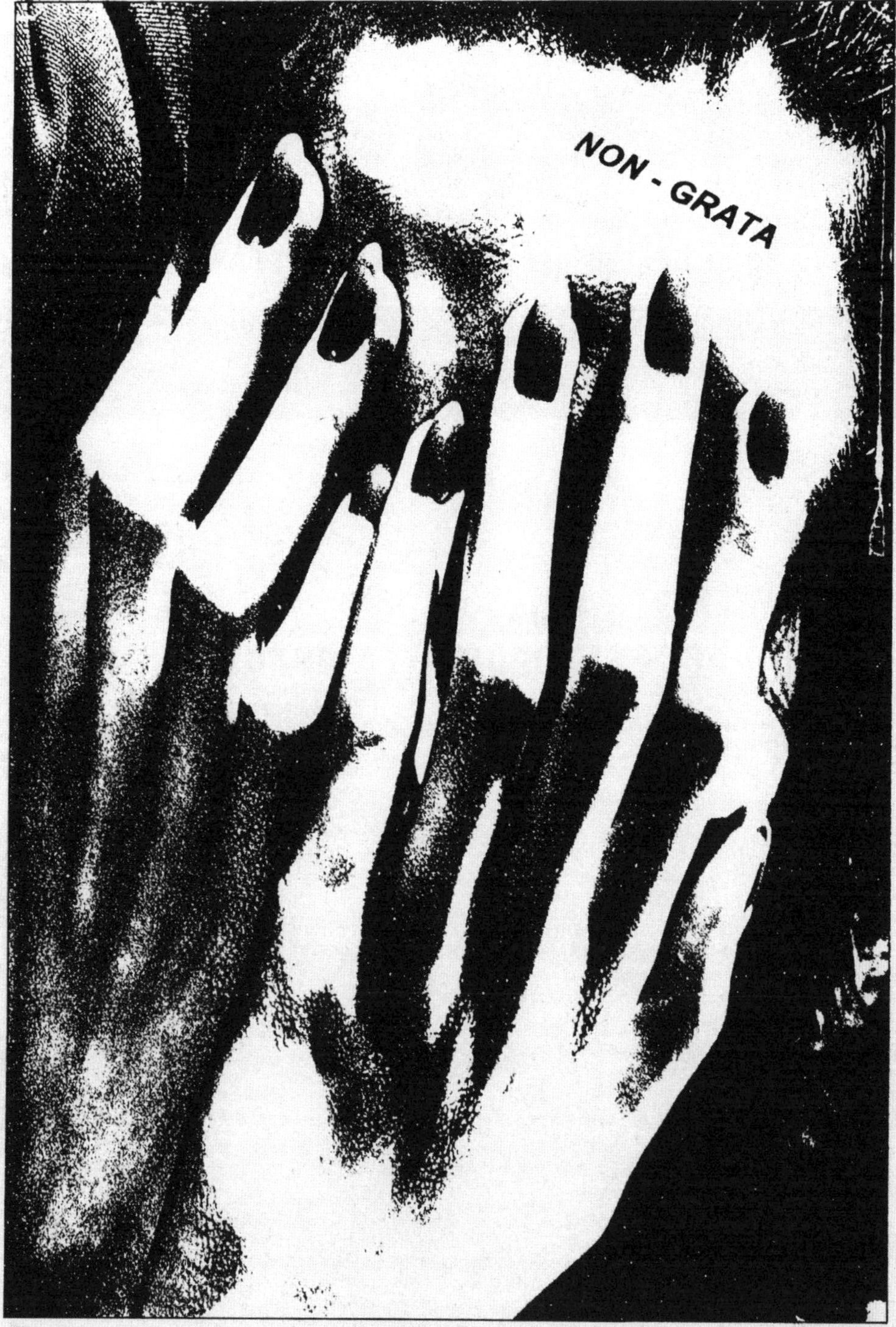

LSD, *Non grata* no. 4, 1994, fanzine. Courtesy ¿Archivo queer? (Centro de Documentación del MNCARS), Creative Commons BY-NC-ND

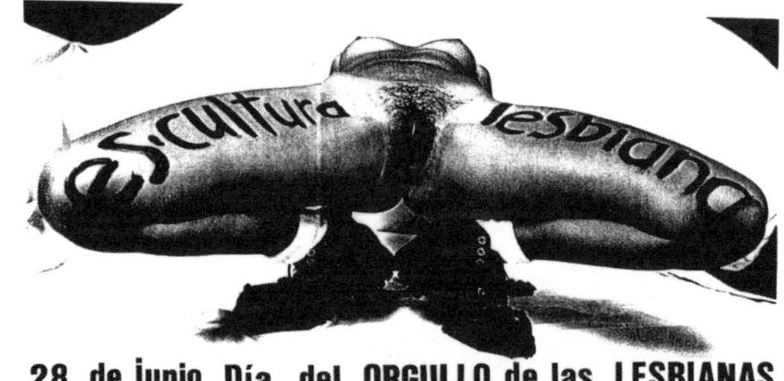

LSD, Lesbianas sudando deseo mani (Lesbians Sweating Out Mani Desire), 28 J, Tirso de Molina-Sol: 28 de junio, día del orgullo de las lesbianas (28 June, Lesbian Pride Day), 199?, poster, 31×90 cm. Courtesy ¿Archivo queer? (Centro de Documentación del MNCARS), Creative Commons BY-NC-ND

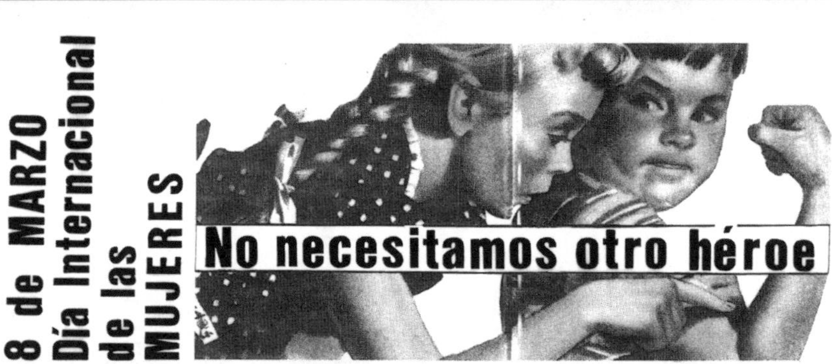

LSD, *8 de marzo, día internacional de las mujeres no necesitamos otro héroe* (International Women's Day Doesn't Need Another Hero), 199?, poster, 31×90 cm. Courtesy ¿Archivo queer? (Centro de Documentación del MNCARS), Creative Commons BY-NC-ND

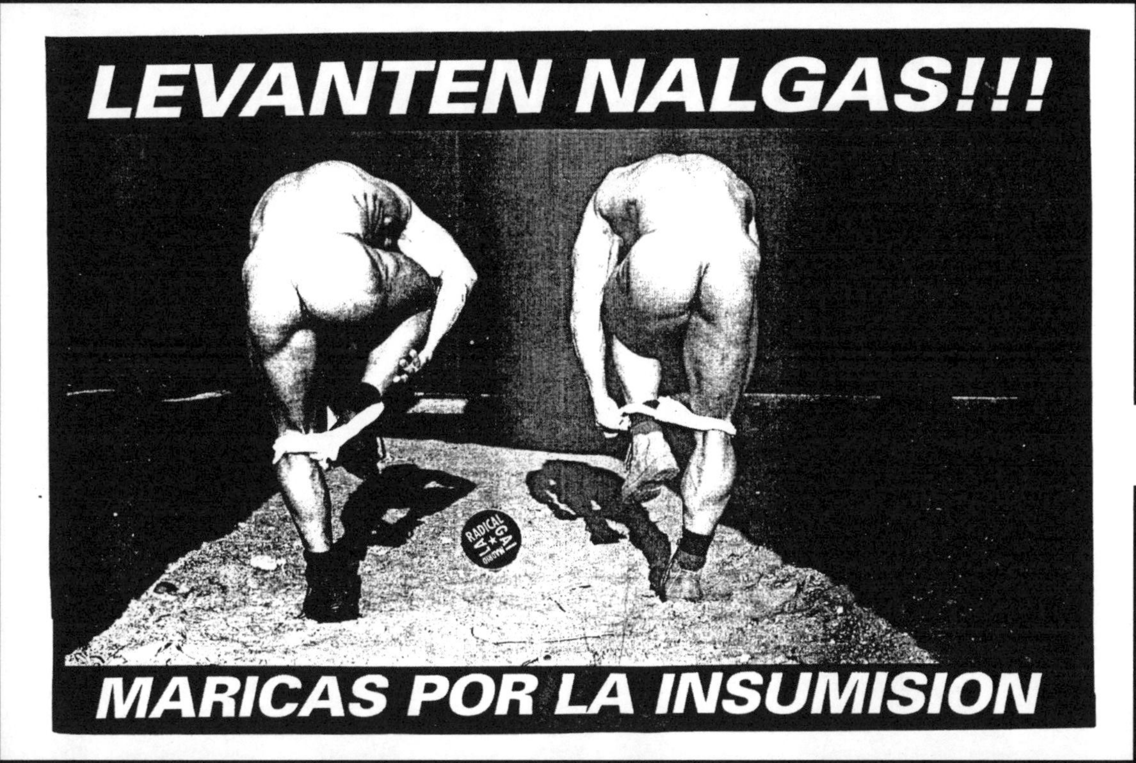

La Radical Gai, *Levanten nalgas maricas por la insumisión* (Queer Arses Rise Up in Insubordination), 199?, poster, 30×42 cm. Courtesy ¿Archivo queer? (Centro de Documentación del MNCARS), Creative Commons BY-NC-ND

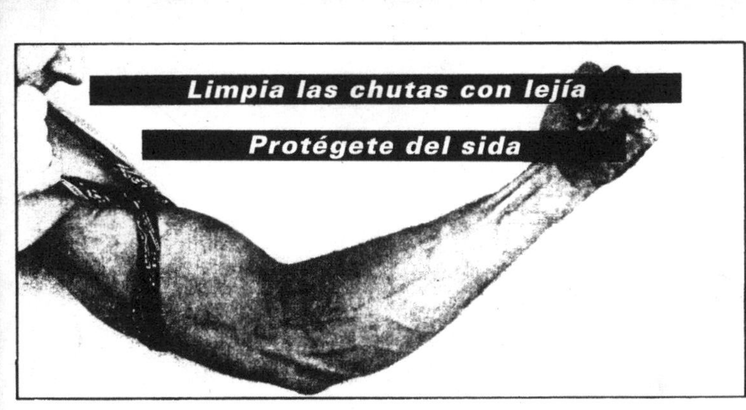

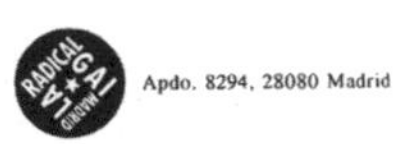

La Radical Gai, *De un plumazo* (At a Stroke) no. 3, 1994, fanzine, p. 28. (Limpia las chutas con lejía. Protégete del SIDA. Alguien tendrá que hacer la prevención) (Clean Those Needles with Bleach. Protect Yourself Against AIDS. Someone Will Have to Take Precautions). Courtesy ¿Archivo queer? (Centro de Documentación del MNCARS), Creative Commons BY-NC-ND

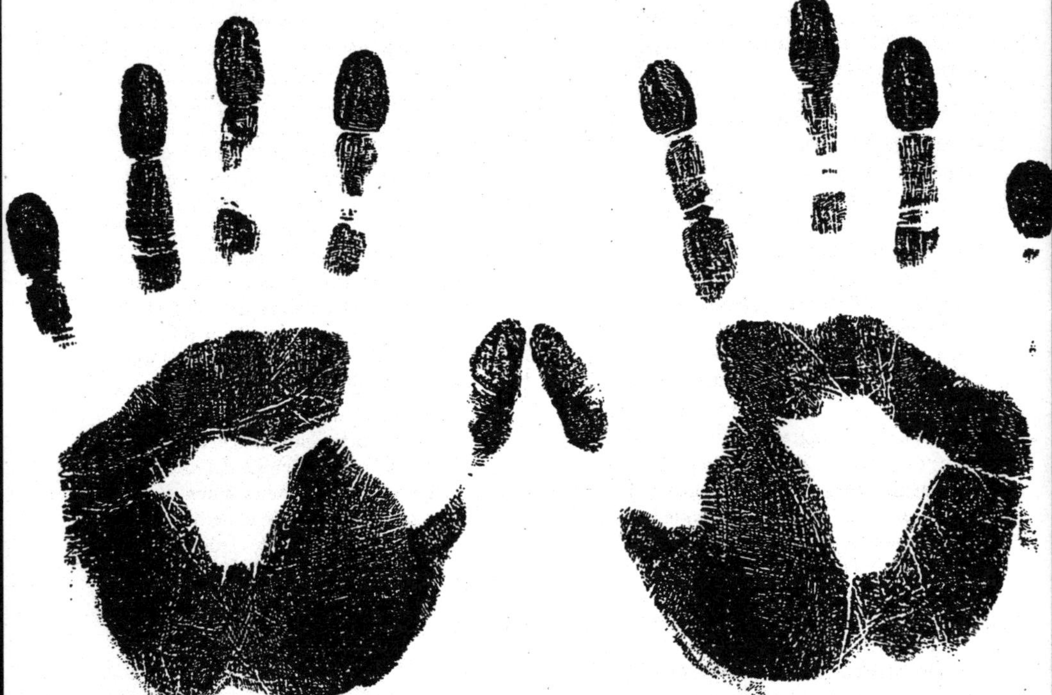

La Radical Gai, *De un plumazo* (At a Stroke) no. 4, 1995, fanzine, p. 25 ('El ministerio de Sanidad tiene las manos manchadas de sangre') (The Hands of the Ministry of Health Are Blood-Stained). Courtesy ¿Archivo queer? (Centro de Documentación del MNCARS), Creative Commons BY-NC-ND

Early attempts to archive artistic-activist LGTB practices did not come about by chance. At the start of the new millennium, when neoliberal ideology was plain for all to see in its hostility, there was a pressing need to find reference points for a new political subjectivity. The fervent citizen demonstrations in 2003 seemed to demonstrate the right conditions for such eager democratic reactivation, and at that particular time the *Desacuerdos* project managed to articulate a strategic alliance between activists, artists, researchers and progressive institutions.

Almost ten years on, since 2011, the initiatives to revisit the watershed of relationships between art and activism, produced as the eighties moved into the nineties, are proliferating. In 2013, the exhibition 'Mínima resistencia. Entre el tardomodernismo y la globalización' (Minimal Resistance: Between Late Modernism and Globalization) displayed, for the first time inside the Museo Reina Sofía, LSD and Radical Gai placards, posters and publications as part of the project 'The Uses of Art'.

In parallel, the same museum welcomed the research residency *Anarchivo sida* (AIDS Anarchive), developed by Aimar Arriola and Nancy Garín. It analysed the artistic-political practices which unfolded around AIDS and their radical incommensurability within the traditional notion of archive and museum. Finally, a group of researchers, activists and former members of Radical Gai and LSD — Lucas Platero, Fefa Vila, Andrés Senra and José Luis Carrascosa — with the collaboration of the Museo Reina Sofía Documentation Centre through Guillermo Cobo, conceptualized and brought to life other forms which could take on an archive with the capacity to consider a new artistic and political subjectivity.

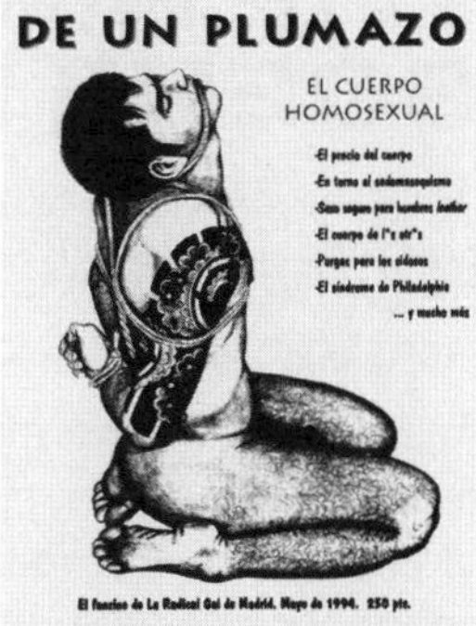

La Radical Gai, *De un plumazo* (At a Stroke) no. 3, 1994, fanzine, p. 1. ¿Archivo queer? (Centro de Documentación del MNCARS). Courtesy ¿Archivo queer? (Centro de Documentación del MNCARS), Creative Commons BY-NC-ND

1990

THE BIRTH OF THE GAY SCENE IN SLOVENIA

Igor Španjol

At the turn of the eighties, the proliferation of contemporary international cultural movements and the opening of urban centres of culture for the young brought new ideas and a search for other channels of political and cultural work and forms of artistic production. It was a time of 'the alternative scene', the largest mass cultural movement in Slovenia to date. Common to all of this heterogeneous production was a revolt against the cultural hegemony of the time; the political system, on the other hand, allowed such critique to project an image of tolerance. Within the alternative scene, exciting and influential cultural and social scenes developed, owing primarily to the activities of the youth culture centres and clubs.

The people involved in 'the scene' saw their activities as a social practice intrinsically embedded in a specific space and social relations. The aim was to establish a position of difference from the mainstream cultural policies and the ruling ideology, to win a place for the alternative artistic practices and gain social recognition; a comprehensive intermediate space and field of action with specific production relations and ways of self-organization and inclusion. Just how intense the cooperation between the agents and spaces became is perhaps best illustrated by the example of the event Magnus Homosexuality and Culture.

In 1984, the Magnus festival inaugurated the first openly organized gay and lesbian movement, not only in Yugoslavia, but in the whole of Eastern Europe. Events included screenings of gay-themed films, debates, exhibitions and DJ nights. The fourth Magnus Festival was supposed to take place in the spring of 1987. However, a political and media campaign was launched against the organizer, framing the planned festival as an 'international congress of homosexuals'. Social Council and Health Inspection Service have concluded that 'the Congress should be prohibited, since the risk groups from all over Europe will pose a serious risk of the spread of AIDS'. The festival was first postponed to the autumn, but in that form no longer occurred.

Later on, the festival was over, but the efforts to keep the film festival running never stopped. Therefore the Ljubljana LGBT Film Festival is one of the oldest in Europe. Later that same year, a gay section Magnus was officially established as part of the Student

Cultural and Art Centre ŠKUC. The ŠKUC lesbian section was set up in 1987 and was the first lesbian group in Eastern Europe. In addition to cultural, artistic and scientific productions, the purpose of both was to fight against all forms of discrimination. These organizations are still active in many areas, devoting most of their time to culture, the arts and various media while recently they have also been politically active, focusing on socialization, health and creating safe places.

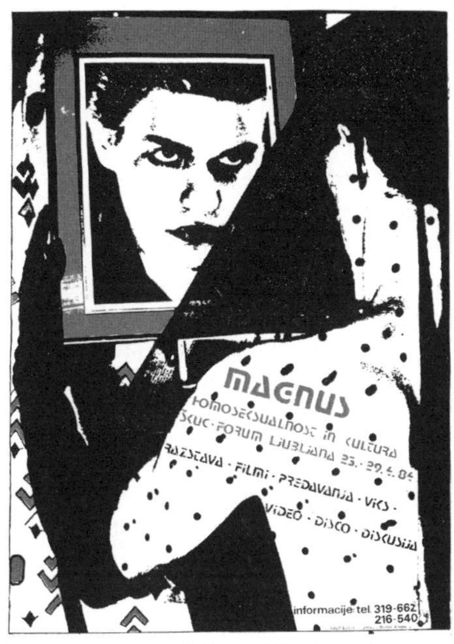

Homosexuality and Culture, 1984, festival poster,
design: Aldo Ivančić, Dušan Mandić

With its multimedia programme, Disco FV was one of the main meeting points and venues for subcultural production and alternative art. Forced into changing location several times — (Disko Študent at the Student Campus (1981–1983), Dom mladih (Youth Centre) at Zgornja Šiška (1983–1984), K4 at Kersnikova Street in Ljubljana (1984–1985) —, it became a symbol of the alternative scene's fight for its place. Led by the FV, a multimedia group of a number of colleagues, it was characterized by the production of a narrowly profiled themed programme, and it served as the producer and motor of the development of photography, music, film, video, multimedia projects, performances, installations, Xerox technique and graffiti.

The Disco FV team brought new technologies into the field of culture and hosted the gay club. Later on, the gay nights on Saturdays in K4 no longer represented the 'scene' as a whole, as had been the case at Šiška.

'PRETENDED' FAMILY RELATIONSHIPS, SUNIL GUPTA

Nick Aikens

> In the late eighties a very interesting idea emerged in a roundabout way that lesbian and gay relationships were not real, or not as real as heterosexual relationships.[01]
>
> Sunil Gupta

On the left of each of Sunil Gupta's photographs with collage is an image of a mixed race gay couple. To the right of the portrait an extract from poems, written by Gupta's then partner Stephen Dodd are collaged on. Next to this are cropped black-and-white images of protests and gatherings on the streets of London. Gupta began the series *'Pretended' Family Relationships* as a means to explore multi-racial gay relationships in Britain under Thatcher's government of the eighties. Whilst Gupta was working on the series, the British government introduced a clause in a Local Government Bill that banned the 'promotion' and teaching of the acceptability of homosexuality as what it termed '"pretended" family relationships'. The bill came to be known as Clause 28 and was met with what Gupta describes as a 'vigorous response' from the gay community.[02] The clause affected local groups working with gay communities who were forced to cease or limit their activities, or to apply self-censorship. Within the arts, it had damaging ramifications. It curtailed funding possibilities and venues became reluctant to include work that would run counter to the clause's demands. Clause 28 remained on the statute books in Scotland until 2000 and in the rest of the UK until 2003.

Gupta's series is a pointed response to Clause 28 and the spectre of racist homophobia in eighties Britain. It is also a thoughtful investigation into the question of representation, both in political and documentary terms. Mixed race gay couples were invisible in the public sphere in eighties Britain. Photographing male and female couples (this was the first time Gupta had included lesbians in his images) both on the streets of London and in their homes was a way to invert that invisibility. Similarly, by making the proportions of each piece the same as a 35mm-frame Gupta, and then filling that frame with different elements (a portrait of a couple, a text and a cropped image) he unsettles the assumption that the documentary photographic image can represent either

01

Sunil Gupta, *Pictures From Here* (London: Autograph Books, 2003), p. 56.

02

Ibid.

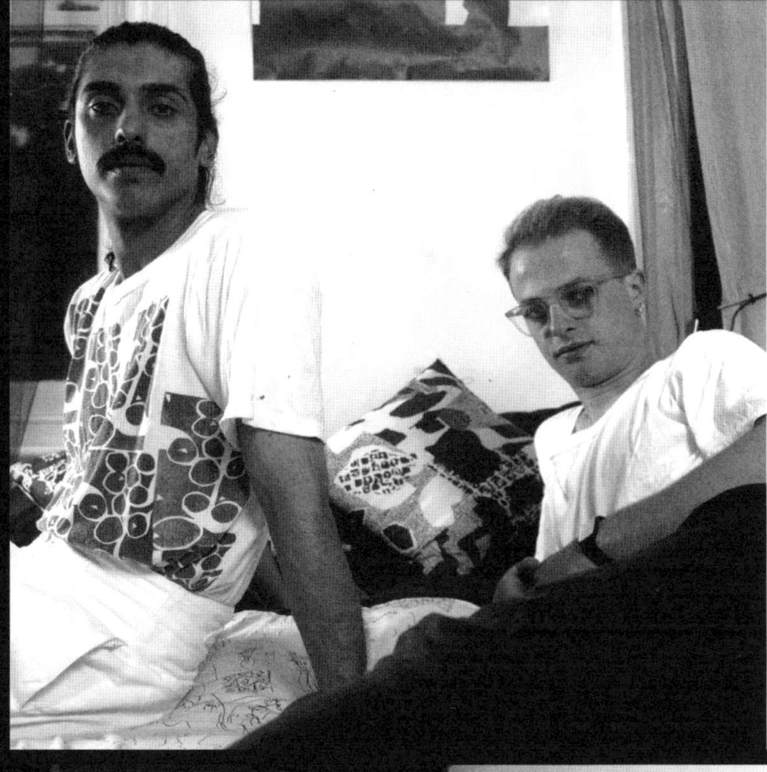

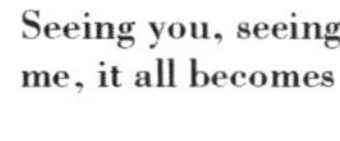

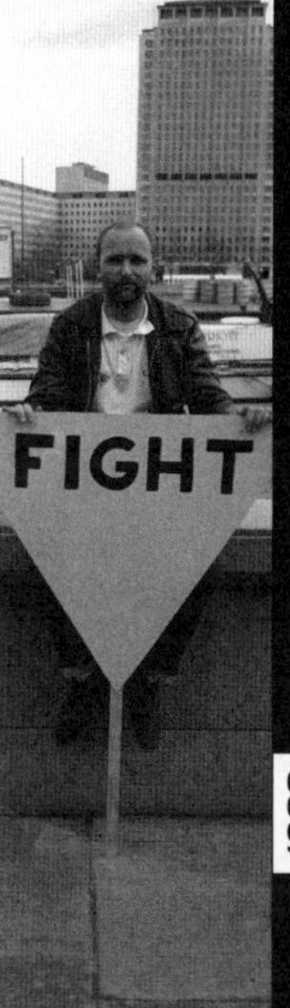

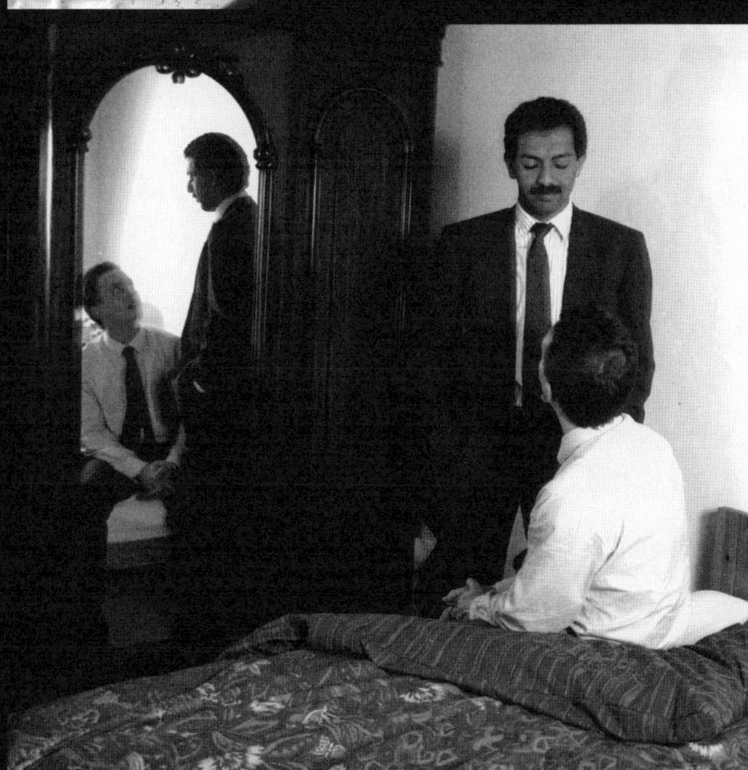

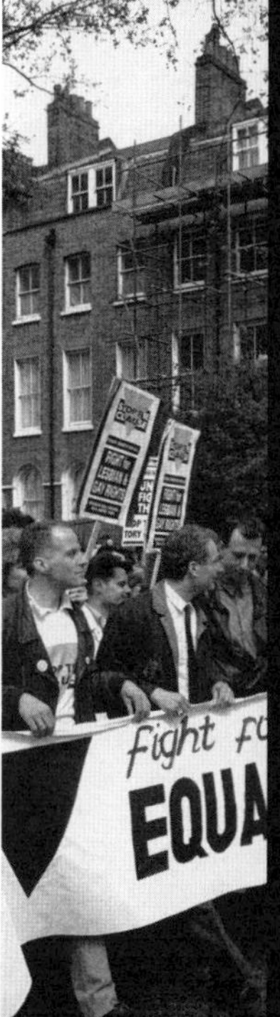

Sunil Gupta, 'Pretended' Family Relationships, 1988, photographic collage print. Courtesy Sunil Gupta / Sepia Eye New York

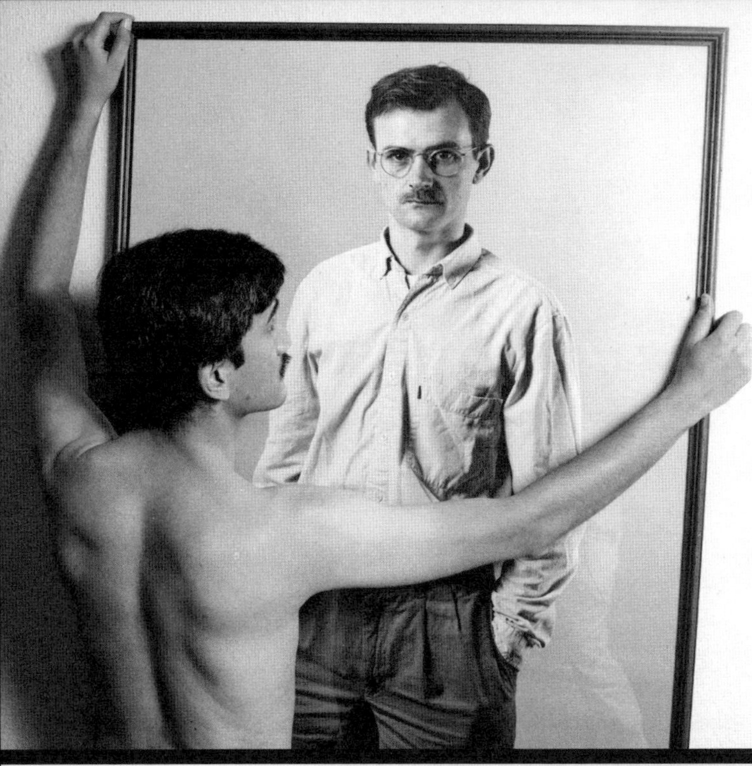

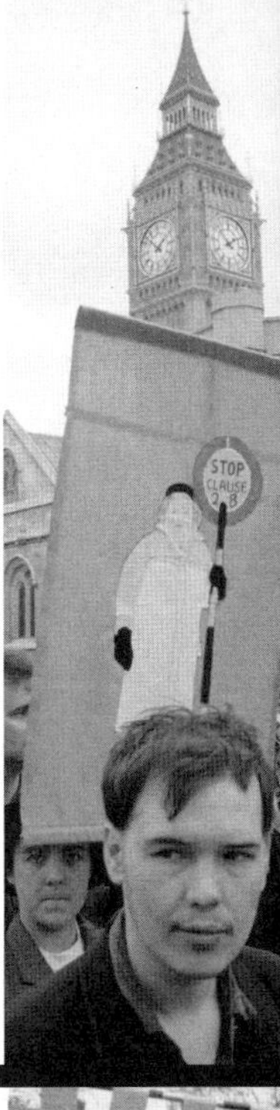

He needed
dope
to get it

up but once
it was
there he was

hooked
on it

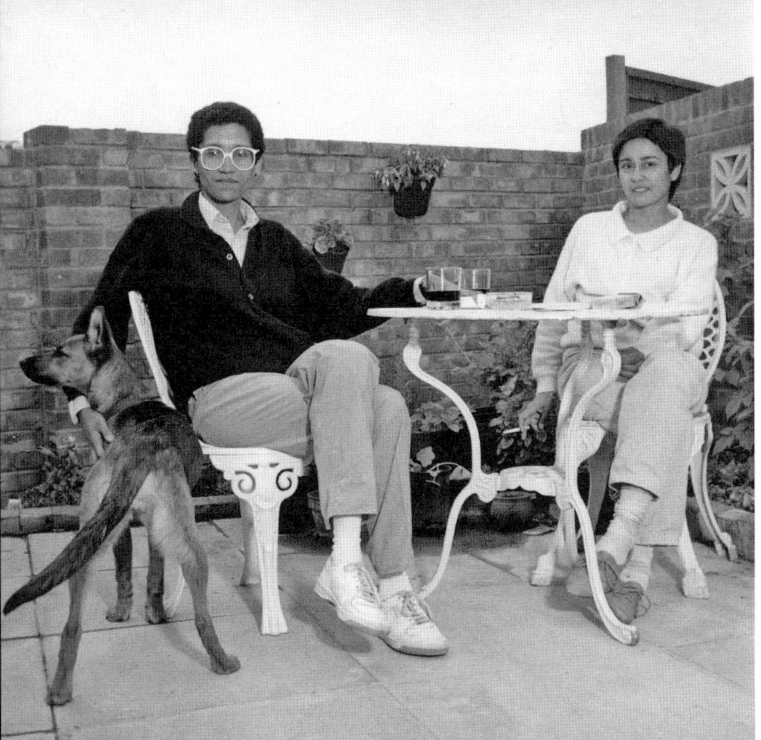

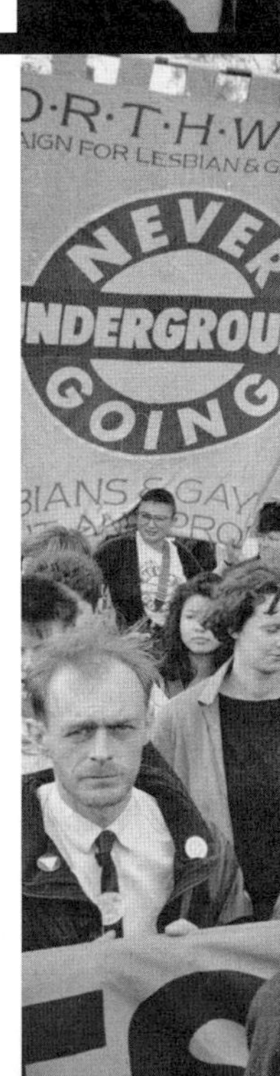

Lighting
a cigarette

You're not here

Lighting
a cigarette

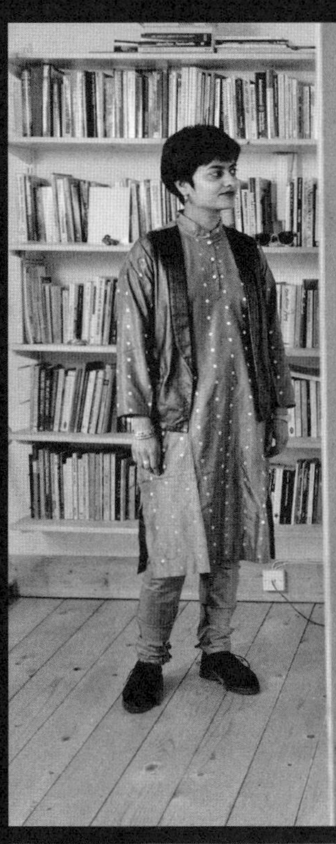
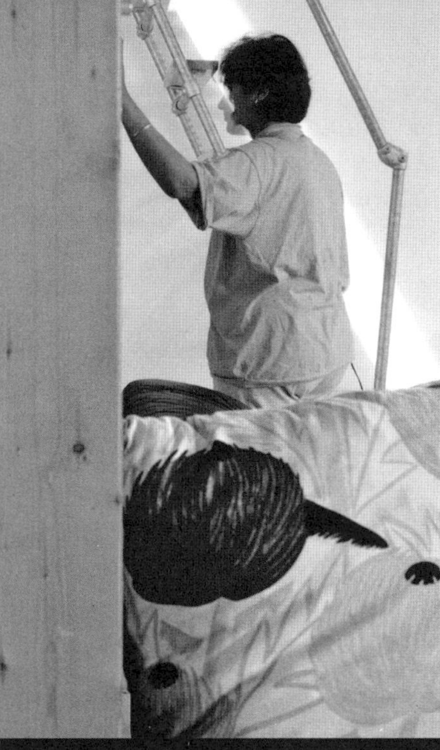
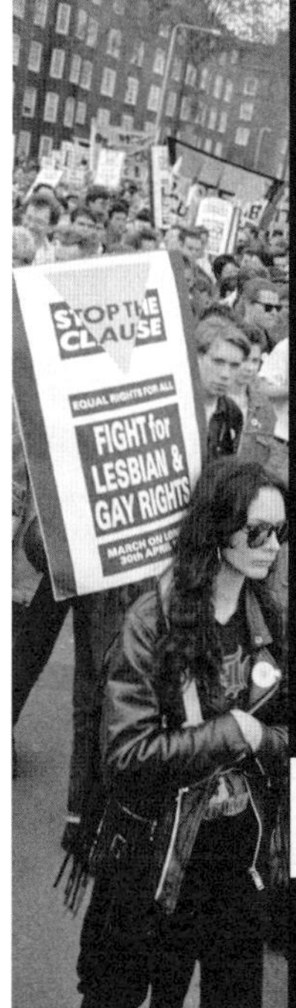

What you
got tell
me the l
ines of
your pre

tty blac
k hair

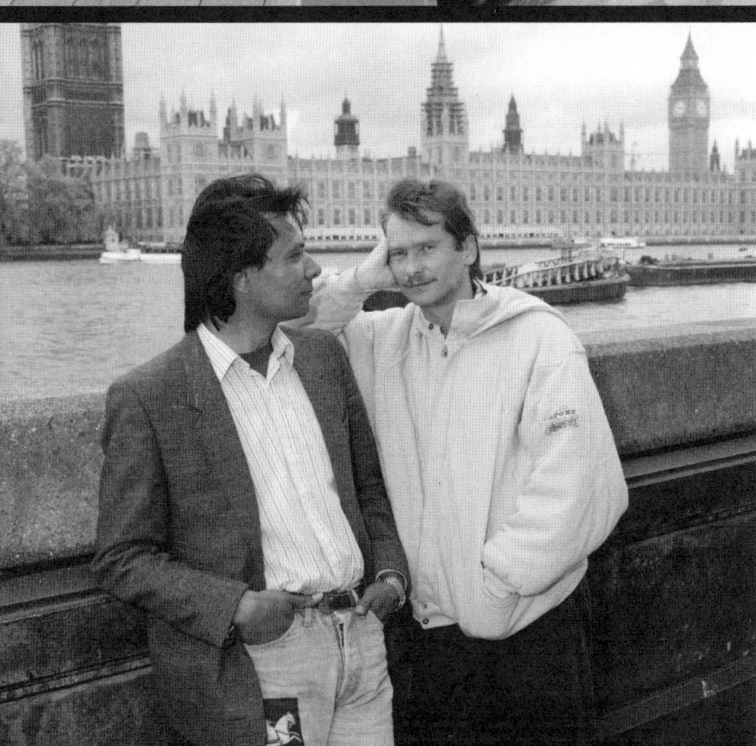
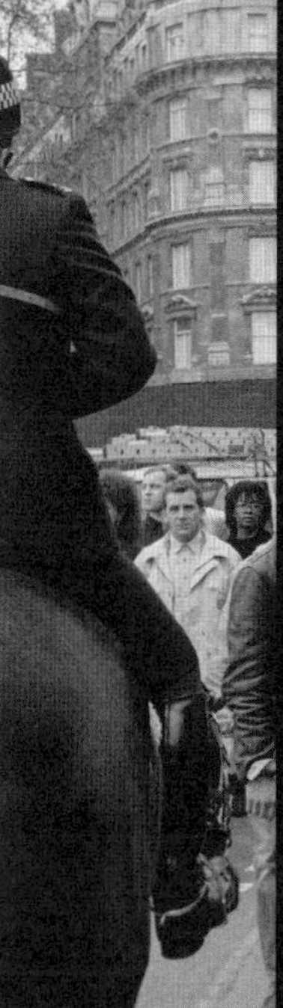

I call you
my love though
you are not my
love and it

breaks my
heart to tell you

Sunil Gupta, *'Pretended' Family Relationships*, 1988, photographic collage print. Courtesy Sunil Gupta / Sepia Eye New York

the subjects it depicts or the politics it claims to stand behind. Within the context of the rich discussions taking place amongst black photographers in Britain during the eighties — with artists such as David A. Bailey, Rotimi Fani-Kayode, Ingrid Pollard, Dave Lewis and many more, and that were chronicled in the publication *Ten 8* magazine — Gupta's series is a formative example of how the limitations of photographic image production were being put under pressure. The series asks us to consider not only who we represent — as governments, societies, subjects and artists — but also how we represent them.

In perhaps the most poignant piece in the series of 12, an Asian and a white British man sit on a bed staring at the camera. The extract for the poem reads: 'Seeing you, seeing me, all becomes clear'. To the right a man sits on a wall holding a placard that reads 'Fight'. The extract from Dodd's poem can be read as an intimate reflection between the couple. Yet, it also addresses the divide between the viewer and the works' three protagonists. It is an ambiguous recognition of both difference and similarity, at once empathetic and confrontational.

'100%'

Beatriz Herráez

Curated by Luisa López Moreno and Mar Villaespesa at the Museo de Arte Contemporáneo, Seville, in 1993, and produced by BNV, '100%' was the first exhibition in Spain to draw on the feminist perspective and to be put together with the sole participation of women artists. Villaespesa's curatorial text provocatively pointed the finger, from the exhibition title and the conviction that 'artistic languages can aspire to and signify a desire to transform society' to the necessary vindication 'of the right to a percentage of equality' in the art scene. There was a pressing need to end the overt inequality that jutted out in the history of twentieth-century Spain, characterized by the dictatorship and related to events in other contexts. A situation of isolation which generated '... a limited framework in which fostering the articulation of a theoretical corpus to form the foundations of a feminist discourse to permeate the space of plastic arts was difficult'.

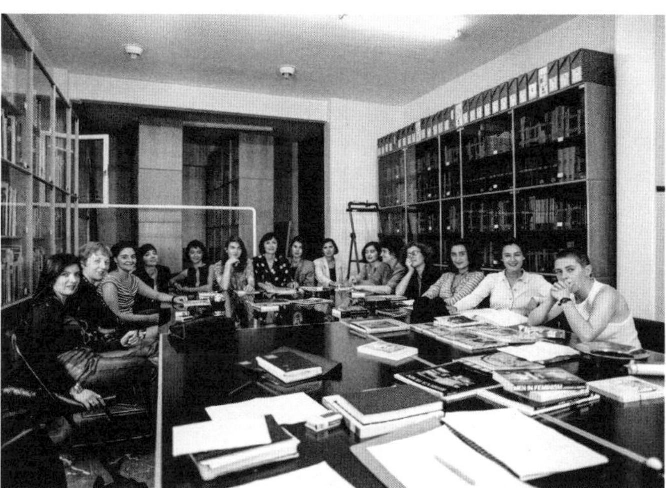

The curators and artists involved in '100%' exhibition, Museo de Arte Contemporáneo, Seville, 1993

'100%' represents a direct response to certain cultural policies which, in the nineteen-eighties, were still barely permeable to feminist thought. A case in point are the exhibition programmes promoted by publicly owned institutions and private foundations such as Spain's Ministry of Culture and Fundación la Caixa, which hoisted up a model linked to international trends, importing exhibitions and touring with exhibition series such as those organized

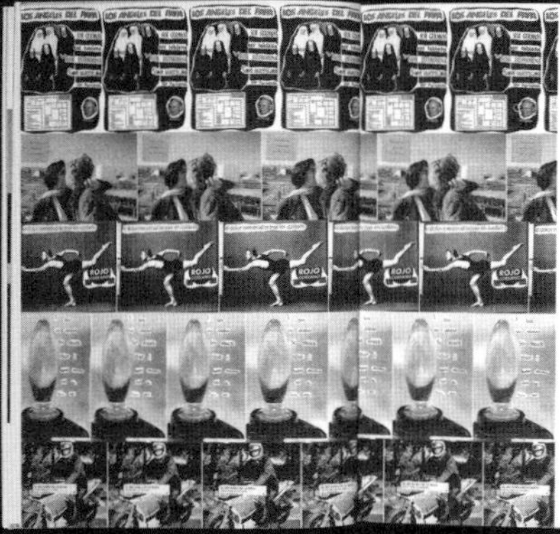

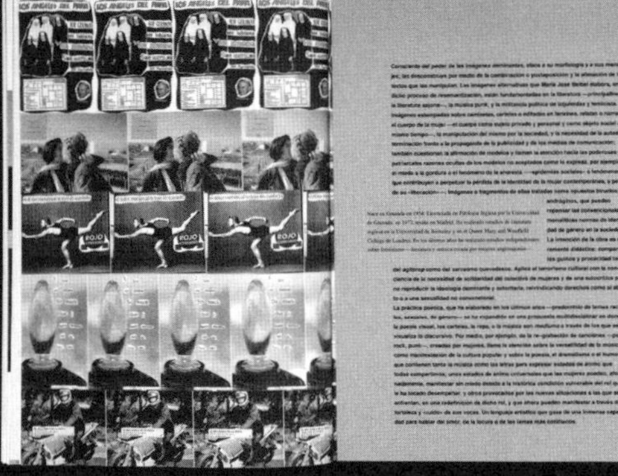

Catalogue *María José Belbel*.
Los ángeles del Papa (The Pope's Angels), 1993, poster depicted,
70×50 cm
No pienso arrugarme con los años (I Don't Intend to Wrinkle Over
the Years), 1993, poster depicted, 50×70 cm
El dolor menstrual te trae sin cuidado (Don't Give a Damn About
Period Pains), 1992, poster depicted, 50×70 cm
I love my children So much that I have decided not to have any,
1993, poster depicted, 70×50 cm
El Rey habla de la Reina: 'Doña Sofía es una gran profesional',
SOFIA (The King Talks about the Queen: Queen Sofía Is a True
Professional, SOFIA), 1993, poster depicted, 50×70 cm.
Courtesy María José Belbel, photo: Joaquín Cortés / Román Lores

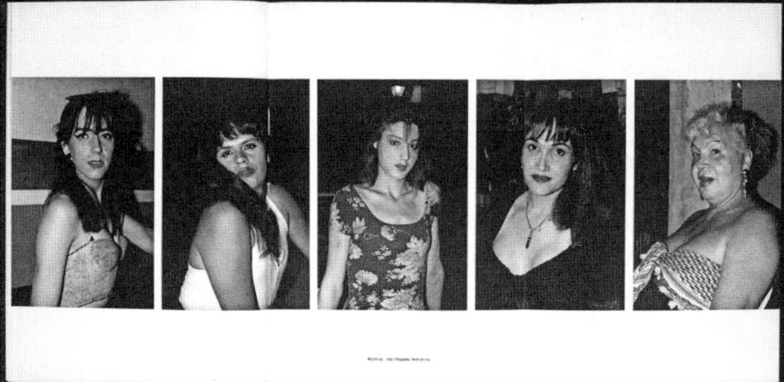

Pilar Albarracin, *Mujeres* (Women), 1993, photograph, 70×50 cm
each. Courtesy Pilar Albarracín, photo: Joaquín Cortés / Román
Lores

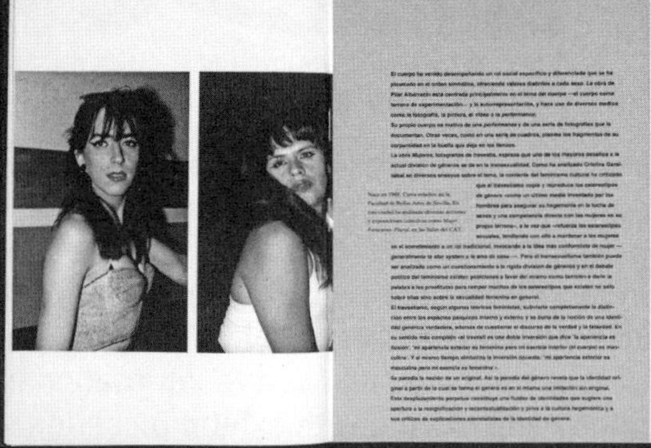

in Paris in 1987 under the title 'Cinq siècles d'art espagnol'. Their aims encompassed the design of a cultural landscape to integrate the country into the international contemporary art circuit, projecting an image of 'normality' to the outside world through the mimesis of predominant movements and the canonical discourses of the booming art market that materialized with the establishment of the ARCO Fair in 1982.

The most representative shows at the time used nation and discipline, the decade's leitmotifs, as their sole assertion and justification: 'Origen y visión. Nueva pintura alemana' (Origin and Vision: New German Paining), 'Tendencias en Nueva York' (Trends in New York), 'Transvanguardia italiana' (Italian Transavantgarde) ... Exhibitions which would be widely disseminated in the media through artists' photographs and group portraits, laying bare the continuism and the reaffirmed representation of the genial artist — a white, heterosexual male — magnified in eighties art practices. Faced with this imaginary, '100%' set forth an 'off-centre' counter-image featuring the Andalusian female artists Pilar Albarracín, Maria José Belbel, Salomé del Campo, Mercedes Carbonell, Nuria Carrasco, Victoria Gil, Nuria León, Encarni Lozano, Pepa Rubio and Carmen Sigler. Alongside their works, the exhibition catalogue compiled the writings of Mar Villaespesa and Estrella de Diego, and a compilation of key texts by feminist theorists such as Gayle Greene and Coppélia Kahn, Elaine Showalter, Nancy Miller, Janet Wolff, Kate Linker, Amelia Jones, Abigail Solomon-Godeau, Teresa de Lauretis and Elizabeth Dempster, collected by Teresa Gómez and Carmen África Vidal and translated into Spanish.

A quarter of a century later, it is outrageous to verify that the data on inequality between men and women that peppered the introduction of '100%' still applies and is documentary proof that still must be wielded when referring to the presence of women in the field of contemporary art. This is a sphere in which, accurately depicted in the '100%' catalogue, there still seems to be a need to find figures like the first female character from *Little LuLu*, the comic created in 1935 by Marjorie H. Buell, to whom the curators dedicated the show as an homage. This character fights to join a club where the maxim 'no girls allowed' still endures; a character who is able to 'beat the neighbourhood kids'.

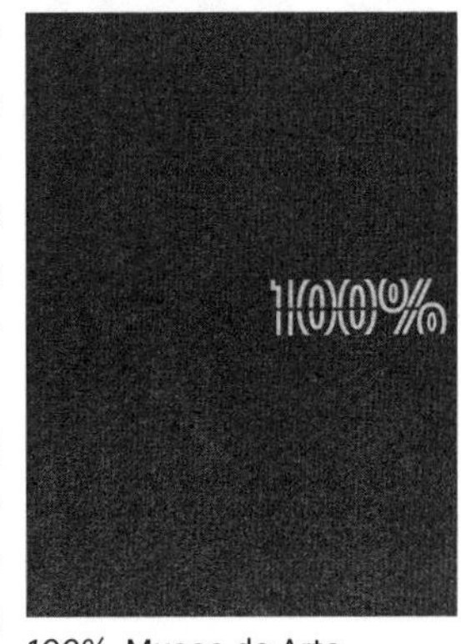

100%, Museo de Arte Contemporáneo, Seville, 1993, cover exhibition catalogue. Photo: Joaquín Cortés / Román Lores

3. PROCESSES OF

IDENTIFICATION

INTRODUCTION

Nataša Petrešin-Bachelez

In this chapter, the contributions reveal how practices wrote down history and produced theory in a social and political environment of some of the European countries in the eighties. An environment that was oppressive, patriarchal, homophobic, and racializing. The subchapters 'Hybridity and Anti-Imperialism' and 'Bodies Put Up a Fight' bring forth cases from the artistic, curatorial, activist, and other citizen practices that were constructed in a dialogue with the postcolonial political climate of contestation (Great Britain, Belgium, the Netherlands) or in opposition to the recent or ongoing history of dictatorship (Turkey, Yugoslavia, Spain). The cases in this chapter deal with theoretical premises of hybridity and its implication for the feminist social movements that enabled an embodied activism, queer politics, as well as a discussion of the importance of the changes in dealing with health issues regarding AIDS and mental illnesses.

In the first essay, Amna Malik traces the emergence of the British Black Arts movement throughout the eighties, the proliferation of the theories of race and hybridity of Stuart Hall and Homi K. Bhabha through the arts, as well as the transnational flows of Black feminism within the prevalent academic white feminism. Resonating with Malik's essay, the featured case studies offer insight into the Black women's movement in the Netherlands and the contested notion of the term 'black' in that country in the eighties, due to which the feminist movement splintered and segmented along different racial and political lines, written by Diana Franssen. She also explores the exhibition 'Double Dutch' in Tilburg, a rare initiative in the Netherlands, which aimed at countering the central position of the white Dutch artist by inviting Dutch artists to work with Dutch-based artists who were born outside Europe in an intense collaborative way. Included is also an autobiographical note on the exhibitions curated by the artist Lubaina Himid in Britain, and a contribution by Nick Aikens about Rasheed Araeen's seminal political text 'Preliminary Notes for a Black Manifesto' and about the journal *Black Phoenix* that Araeen co-directed as a prequel to the immensely influential journal *The Third Text*. The account by Chris Straetling about the artist Jef Lambrecht shows his engagement with anti-colonialist and transgressive discourses as a reaction to the Belgian colonial history.

Next, Ayşe Düzkan's essay narrates the pre-history of the second-wave feminism in Turkey which emerged following the 1980 *coup d'état* and how it was born under restrictive political and social conditions, with censorship, imprisonment, and torture of the oppositional voices, methods that were used by the government throughout the whole decade. In the light of this, the feminist movement heavily impacted on Turkish society and politics. Düzkan makes an important introduction in the racialization of the Kurdish population and identification of the Kurdish women with the Black feminism above all other social movements. Her comparison of the emancipation of women in the socialist culture of Yugoslavia, importantly shows the relation of feminism to the rise of nationalism and genocide that ravaged the country in the first half of the nineties. In relation to this essay, the case study by Tea Hvala about independent organizing, creating women-only public spaces and politicizing 'the women's question' by the new feminist groups in Slovenia and emergence of the feminist group Women in Black in Turkey, or the testimonies about two Kurdish women living in Istanbul published in *Sokak* (Street) magazine provide the reader with further details by Merve Elveren and Erman Ata Uncu.

The third essay, by Elisabeth Lebovici, begins with the sentence 'I am exposed', marking the necessity of embodiment of her personal experience in organizing and instituting AIDS activism through ACT UP and other collectives in France, by tracing the genealogy of the movement from Great Britain and US. Later on, she sums up what this chapter, entitled 'Processes of Identification', is about: 'Simply making your body manifest is to put up a fight. The vitality of bodies is a sign of struggle, when these burst into the public space.' Pepe Espaliú, who died of AIDS in the early nineties, in his performances used his sick body as an active subject of political performance, written about by Lola Hinojosa. In reference to the ongoing struggle of our contemporary global civil society with understanding either physical or mental illnesses, Bojana Piškur reflects on the new social movements in the former Yugoslavia that encompassed also the antipsychiatry movement, which engaged in practices of radically changing how society looked upon mental disorders. Yet another practice, that of the Belgian artist Hugo Roelandt, testifies to his insight that performance is an endlessly rich terrain for deconstructing the centrality of the 'I' and opposing the increasing institutionalization of performance art, by Antony Hudek. In relation to the historical crimes committed during the decades of dictatorship in Spain, Marcelo Expósito describes his video in which he accounts for recovering the memory of crimes committed during the era of Franco.

3.1 HYBRIDITY

Unity in Difference
1980s

'5 Black Women', 'Black Woman Time Now' and 'The Thin Black Line'
1983–1995

Black Phoenix
1978–1979

Black Women's Movement (ZMV)
1983

J. Lambrecht & The Belgian Institute for World Affairs in the Eighties
1982–1985

'Double Dutch'
1991

AND
ANTI-IMPERIALISM

UNITY IN DIFFERENCE

ARTISTIC PRACTICES ACROSS CLASS, SEX AND RACE IN BLACK BRITISH ART

Amna Malik

Amongst conventional left-wing thinkers the postmodernism of the eighties marked a period that displaced the old Marxist politics of class through the emergence of new subjects embodied in feminist, queer and black politics. This contributed to the commodification of the subject under globalization, corroding political solidarities of an old left based on class conflict, thus aiding its collapse.[01] However, Chantal Mouffe and Ernesto Laclau offered a rather different position. In *Hegemony and Socialist Strategy* they reconsidered Antonio Gramsci's notion of hegemony, toward a radical politics of the left in which sexuality and race marked the new political terrain. In Britain this was a significant shift, explored by Stuart Hall, and it was preceded by Indian Marxists' revision of Gramsci in *Subaltern Studies*. The latter, placing emphasis on the role of the peasantry rather than a bourgeois elite, shifted theorization and historicism of political change toward a Third World Marxism.[02] Along with Hall, Homi K. Bhabha's writings on hybridity reconsidered identity against the binary oppositions of a Hegelian dialectic underpinning colonial societies. Recent debates on inter-sectionality in the US[03] are rooted in a very different history of race than that of postcolonial Britain. During the eighties in Britain hybridity, arising from a colonial legacy, followed a different path, whereby mixed race and queer subjects challenged essentialist categories. But, as Kobena Mercer argued, hybridization was a process that affected white people as well.[04] This refusal of racial purity or cultural boundaries extended to artistic practices, with the creation of collectives, through exhibiting frameworks, and in the forging of political alliances with resonances in different parts of the world. Stuart Hall's enormously influential essay 'New Ethnicities' (1987) speaks to the commitment to view cultural identities as constantly in formation. A further example is the important 1994 ICA exhibition curated by David A. Bailey and Iniva (Institute of International Visual Arts) 'Mirage: Enigmas of Race, Difference and Desire', with an accompanying catalogue essay by Kobena Mercer, addressing Frantz Fanon's legacy for contemporary queer and feminist postcolonial debates.

Mercer's positing of a cut and mix aesthetic for Black British Art[05] offers significant links with Bhabha's theory of hybridity for a reframing of the history of art of this decade, conventionally viewed as a series of stylistic changes and based on formal innovation. When Rasheed Araeen's 'Notes Towards a Black Manifesto' first appeared, photo-conceptualism and performance were viewed as a radical left art that challenged the hegemony of modernism in their seriality and ephemerality, only to be displaced in turn by the return to painting announced triumphantly in the introduction to the catalogue for the Royal Academy's exhibition 'A New Spirit in Painting' (1981). Along with the dominance of Neo-Expressionism

01

Michael Hardt and Antonio Negri, *Empire* (Cambridge: Harvard University Press, 2000), pp. 114–159.

02

Chantal Mouffe and Ernesto Laclau, *Hegemony and Socialist Strategy: Towards a Radical Democratic Politics* (London: Verso, 1985, 2001); Stuart Hall, 'Gramsci's Relevance for the Study of Race and Ethnicity', *Journal of Communications Inquiry* 10, no. 5 (1986), pp. 5–27 and 'Gramsci and Us', *Marxism Today* June 1987, pp. 16–21; Ranajit Guha, ed., *A Subaltern Studies Reader*, 1986–1995 (Minneapolis: University of Minnesota Press, 1997).

03

For its connections with contemporary art, cf. Huey Copeland et al., 'Collective Consciousness: A Roundtable', *Artforum* 54, no. 10 (Summer 2016), pp. 266–277.

04

Kobena Mercer, 'Introduction: Black Britain and the Cultural Politics of Diaspora', in *Welcome to the Jungle: New Positions in Black Cultural Studies* (London and New York: Routledge, 1994), pp. 1–32, p. 26. The term is set out in Homi K. Bhabha, 'Signs Taken for Wonders, Questions of Authority under a Tree outside Delhi May 1817', *Critical Inquiry* 12, no. 1 (Autumn 1985), special issue 'Race, Writing and Difference', pp. 144–165, reprinted in *The Location of Culture* (London and New York: Routledge, 1994), pp. 102–138.

05

Kobena Mercer, unpublished keynote lecture 'Perforations', *Reframing the Moment: Legacies of 1982 BLK Art Group Conference*, University of Wolverhampton, 7 October 2012.

came a return of the figure of the tortured white male artist in Britain, the US and Germany. As Hal Foster defined it, two kinds of postmodernisms emerged: a critical leftist postmodernism challenging the central concepts of modernism and a conservative right-wing postmodernism that recycled the past, often classicism, in a series of parodic manoeuvres.[06] It is from the vantage point of diaspora artists in Black Britain that Mercer adopts the binary established by Foster's focus on the US, to consider a 'third' position, against such left/right positions manifested in stylistic form and choices of media.

The work of artists such as Veronica Ryan, Marlene Smith, Houria Niati, Sutapa Biswas, Zarina Bhimji, Lubaina Himid, Eddie Chambers, Keith Piper, Claudette Johnson, Sonia Boyce, Chila Kumari Burman, Said Adrus, Shaheen Merali, Tam Joseph, Kimathi Donkor, Amanda Holiday, Sunil Gupta, BAFC, Sankofa, Maxine Walker, Rotimi Fani Kayode, and many many others frequently adopted this 'third' position in relation to postmodernism's dialectic of absence and presence embedded in photo-conceptualism and performance art as form, where the seriality of the photographic image, and the temporality of the artist's body in performance, could be seen as refusals of the 'opticality' of the art object within canonical accounts of high modernism. The hybrid or 'third' position of diaspora artists deploys the dialectic of absence and presence toward other ends, by positioning it within narrative structures of art history and British history. So, on the one hand artists addressed the absence of Black subjects as creative and historic agents rather than subjects of primitivism within the modernist canon, inserting them within the language of modernism, through paintings, installation and the photographic tableau. On the other hand, in deploying the word-image juxtaposition of photo-conceptualism, for example in collage processes using newspapers and other printed material, they gave voice to the contemporary experiences of Black Britain, speaking back to the hegemony of media discourses, in which stereotypes were pervasive, and dialectically drawing attention to their absence within Britain's colonial history. Rather than adopting an either/or position, many instances of diaspora artists' work drew on both approaches in single works of art, to place emphasis on art as a space of cultural activism, thereby illuminating the fraught question of the colonial context of contemporary racism in Britain.

For women artists, such as Claudette Johnson, the question of a Black artistic practice did not preclude a dialogue with the legacy of modernism. Whilst this might distance them from Chambers and Piper, invested in a rejection of a western canon, it also marked their positions as distinctly different to those of white feminist artists for whom the explosion of media technology and

06

Hal Foster, '1984', in *Art Since 1900: Modernism, Antimodernism, Postmodernism: Volume 2, 1944 to the Present*, Hal Foster et al. (London: Thames and Hudson, 2004), p. 596.

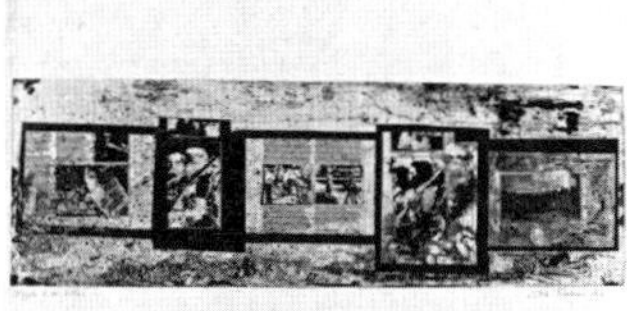

Chila Kumari Burman, *Militant Women*, 1981 etching, 101.6 × 45.7 cm

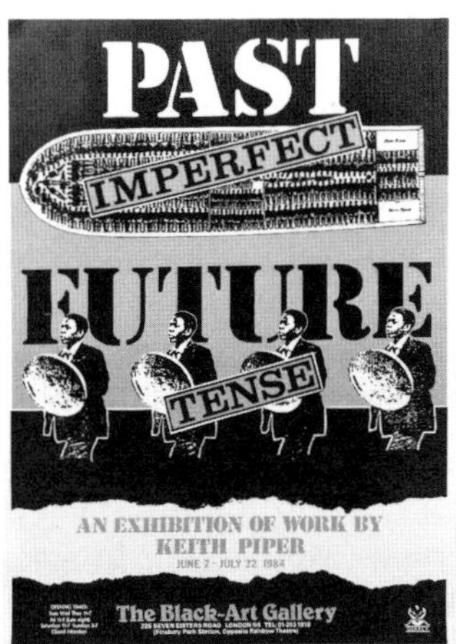

Keith Piper, *Past Imperfect, Future Tense: An Exhibition of Work by Keith Piper*, poster collage and silk-screen print, dimensions variable, 1984

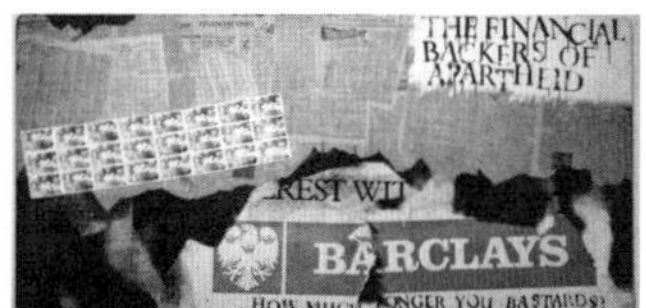

Eddie Chambers, *How Much Longer You Bastards?*, 1983, collage, 120 × 240 cm. Sheffield City Art Gallery

the subsequent objectification of both pornography and advertising had made it imperative for the body to be absented from their art. If Maud Sulter and Lubaina Himid's practices as lesbian artists did not reject heteronormative black masculinity, their positions were distinct from the critique of Black Power amongst black gay artists and theorists, who in turn forged alliances with heteronormative black feminists, of which the film collective Sankofa is an important example. Such contested positions speak to the multiplicity of difference, fought through and thought through and marked by a refusal of the pressure to occupy competing and divisive camps.

The presence of exiled artists played a significant role in the emergence of Black art, in its creative practices and political scope. Two contrasting dimensions of artistic practice can broadly be set out: one embodying what Kobena Mercer has described as 'a cut and mix aesthetic' and taking its cue from South African artist Gavin Jantjes' prints of the seventies, the other exploring the tableau as a specifically postmodern form in which the proscenium arch of classical theatre, structuring history painting in the nineteenth century, had in the twentieth entered epic film such as Eisenstein's *October* (1927). The photographs of the Iranian born artist Mitra Tabrizian, influenced by her teacher, Victor Burgin, explored this mode to a sustained degree in her important series centred on the urban alienation experienced by young black men in *The Blues* (1986–1987) created with Andy Golding. Diverse artists frequently found these two dimensions together across a range of different media. They deployed a range of sources to evoke a hybrid cultural production in which a dialogic appropriation of the dominant cultural codes[07] was undertaken to expose the complex conditions through which race, sex and class were being mobilized to refuse the stereotyping of immigrants in terms of an ethnocentrism that brought colonial conceptions of race back from the past into the present. It is noticeable that, as in Jantjes' prints of the seventies so in Tabrizian's photographic tableaux of the eighties, these artists, along with Mona Hatoum, in her many performances, were not focused exclusively or primarily on their own identities and subjectivities. They also addressed political subjects across the diverse spectrum of race and colonial history, and folded into the domestic upheavals of post-imperial Britain, the conditions of apartheid in South Africa, the genocide of Native Americans in the US, the troubles in Northern Ireland, the impact of the Arab-Israeli conflict in Lebanon or the spectacle of the veiled woman in post-revolutionary Iran.[08]

As this moment coincided with an explosion of the mass media, and contributed to a displacement of the word by the image, art with its myriad of modes of investigating the social

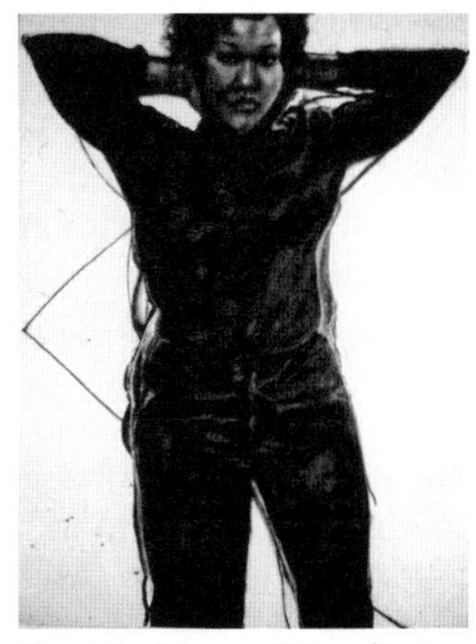

Claudette Johnson, *Trilogy (Part Two) Woman in Black*, 1982–1986, watercolour, gouache and pastel on paper, 152.5 × 122 cm

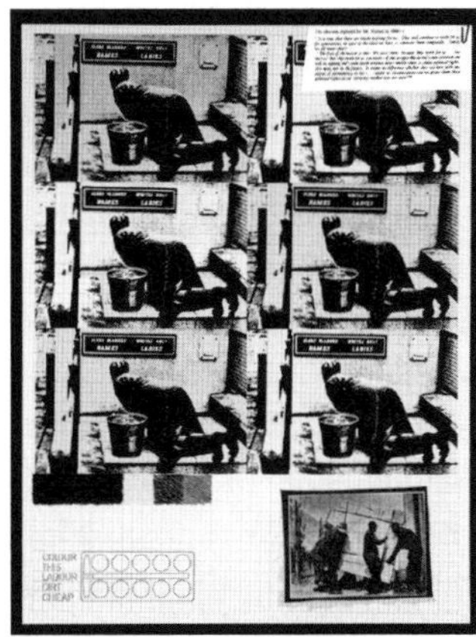

Gavin Jantjes, *A South African Colouring Book, Colour this Labour Dirt Cheap* (Part of series), 1974–1975, screen-print on card, 602 × 452 mm. Collection of Tate Britain

07

The dialogic is examined by Kobena Mercer in 'Diaspora Culture and the Dialogic Imagination: The Aesthetics of Black Independent Film Making', in *Welcome to the Jungle*, pp. 53–66.

08

Cf. Amna Malik, 'Conceptualising "Black" British Art through the Lens of Exile', in *Exiles, Diasporas and Strangers*, ed. Kobena Mercer (Cambridge and London: MIT Press, 2008), pp. 166–189.

meanings given to vision came to assume a particular value for those invested in contesting the hegemony of the nation-state. One instance of this was the emphasis on family values promoting a heteronormative and white middle class ideal, as a political unit, against the idea of community that cut across lines of sex, class and race. Against such hegemonic ideals of 'family values' the agency of the artist acquired a particularly prominent role, giving visual form to an emerging semantics of queer subjectivity that operated in, through and outside the closet, whereby the desiring gaze of black gay and lesbian subjects acquired a prominence revealing a long-standing productive agency to recode visual cultural forms against a heteronormative logic, and across racial and class differences. Such counter strategies, to challenge conservative conceptions of the subject, were emerging alongside feminist critiques of Black Power and white feminism, offering a transformed understanding of colonial and slave histories. As *Écriture féminine* emerged in the writings of Kristeva, Irigaray and Cixous, it came into collision with the work of Angela Y. Davis, bell hooks, Gayatri Spivak, Hazel Carby and Pratibha Parmar. Feminist interventions within the academy were forced into a reconsideration when faced with the lived experiences, past and present, of women whose histories were embedded in oppression. Hortense Spillers' *Mama's Baby, Papa's Maybe* (1987) transformed conventional conceptions of lack, arising from the dominance of Lacanian psychoanalysis. Her attention to the legal and linguistic absences that erased slave women from dominant accounts of this traumatic history was ground-breaking in its contribution to wider debates on counter-memory.[09] Transnational flows of Black feminism in the US were significant for political movements outside the UK. bell hooks' *Ain't I a Woman?* was cited as foundational to the Black Women's Movement (ZMV) in the Netherlands, established during International Women's Day, at Winter University in Nijmegen in 1983, to question the blindness to race amongst white feminists. Unlike the British response, the adoption of the term and rhetoric drawn from hooks of Black feminism, by ZMV as a political term for non-white Dutch women was rejected by Turkish, Indonesian and Moroccan women.

Yet, the disagreements and heated debates that characterized ZMV's various conferences and publications in eighties Britain fed productively into questions over what constitutes a politicized art practice, and what is Black art. It is noticeable that Lubaina Himid's curating of key exhibitions was premised on an interest in being inclusive of a wide range of women artists of diasporas and different sexual orientations, including the Algerian painter Houria Niati. Her hunger to engage with these women was indicative of the creative nourishment that could be had and the

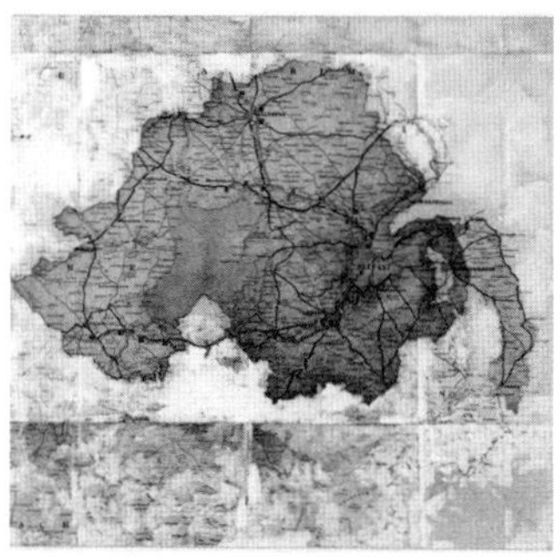

Rita Donagh, *Shadow of Six Counties*, c. 1980, graphite and acrylic on paper, 360 × 362 mm. Collection of Tate Britain

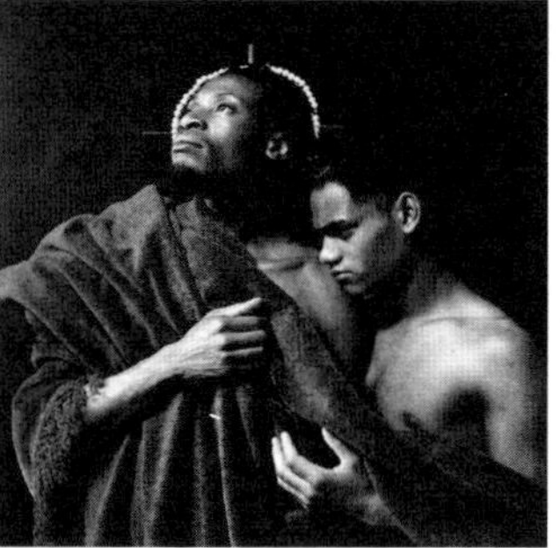

Rotimi Fani-Kayode, *Every Body Counts (Ecstatic Antibodies)*, 1989

09

Hortense J. Spillers, 'Mama's Baby, Papa's Maybe: An American Grammar Book', *Diacritics* 17, no. 2 (Summer 1987), special issue 'Culture and Counter-memory: the "American" Connection', pp. 65–81.

spaces that needed to be created, by diaspora artists, existing and working with limited resources. It is also interesting to reflect that 'The Thin Black Line' exhibition at the ICA was accompanied by discussions and events during which the participants brought along personal items of various kinds that would make this institutional space 'feel more like home'. The creation of spaces that would offer meeting places for dialogue and collaboration was the impetus towards institution building. The Africa Centre in Covent Garden provided a vital space in London in the early eighties and was the venue for the exhibition '5 Black Women at the Africa Centre' (1983), but also highlighted the need for a Black art gallery, which existed for a time in Finsbury Park, run by Shakka Dadi, and subsequently by Marlene Smith.

Such efforts at institution building also emerged in the Squatters Movement in Amsterdam, amongst whom there were many gay and lesbian activists battling the authorities at a time of enormous stigma arising from the AIDS epidemic. Parallel efforts took place in Madrid, later in the early nineties, with the collectives La Radical Gai and LSD, gay and lesbian activists. Their work across public performance, photography and activism drew attention to a confrontational language and imagery of sexuality that rejected earlier euphemisms with which queer subjects had been positioned, but was no longer tenable in a climate marked by AIDS. In Amsterdam, buildings occupied by the Squatters Movement were forcibly dismantled by the state to make way for modern new offices, drawing further parallels with hegemonic conditions of nation-states across Europe, such as Thatcher's destruction of communities in the Isle of Dogs in East London to make way for Canary Wharf. This was resisted by different constituencies across class, sex, and race, as were attempts to institute Clause 28 forbidding the discussion of homosexuality within the classroom, the focus for Sunil Gutpa's important photographic series *'Pretended' Family Relationships* (1988).

To fully understand the emphasis on solidarity across such lines in the eighties it is important to grasp the enormous challenges faced by diasporas, in the decade before in Britain because of the failures of the left, the Unions and the Labour Party to engage with the complexity of race and gender. This was brought dramatically to the fore with the strike in 1976 of labourers at the Grunwick print processing factory who were primarily Asian women, and led by Jayaben Desai. The event became a visual and political resource for subsequent critical accounts of Black Britain such as Pratibha Parmar's essay 'Gender, Race and Class: Asian Women in Resistance' (1982) which offered a detailed critical account of the use of race by white male factory workers to shame Asian women, using their cultural sensitivities to threaten their reputations within their communities, as a means to halt the strike. Parmar, as a Ugandan Asian whose family had been forced out of the country in 1972, spoke from an exilic stance and vantage of a middle class Asian family, who made up the vast numbers of manual labourers in Britain, because of the racism within the labour market, forcing women, such as her mother, into employment. She also makes the crucial point that striking women's families were financially supported by middle class Asian businesses, drawing attention to the presence of an immigrant class not generally visible within the UK during the seventies and early eighties, the association of migrants was with economic conditions and the needs of a domestic labour market.[10]

Race was seen over and above class differences because of the minimal control of this constituency over media representation, a problem brought to the fore by Rasheed Araeen in *Paki Bastard (Portrait of the Artist as a Black Person)* (1977). The interventions Araeen created in his practice at this time can be seen in the titling of his text 'The Black Manifesto' (1975) published in the journal *Black Phoenix* (1978–1979). The desire to make the complexity of class, gender and race visible across different ethnic groups emerges in different ways within different practices, and was to have a discursive dimension with many artists also writing and publishing. Araeen's involvement as a member of the British Black Panther Party and Artists for Democracy set up by David Medalla is indicative of the localized response to the rise of Black Power movements, and acknowledges the geopolitical dimensions and Marxist influences on the Black Panther movement. This was to frame his theorization of Black cultural resistance within the manifesto that engages with the long-standing hierarchies between European civilization and the deliberate underdevelopment and devaluing of the Third World, as a crucial dimension of postcolonial discourse. As we know from the presence of recent immigrants in Victor Burgin's *UK 76* (1976) and the critique of male creative privilege in John Stezaker's *Who? What? Why?* (1974) Araeen's deconstruction of the universality embedded in high modernism, canon formation, and the originality of the male artist as genius, which underpins the 'The Black Manifesto', had significant echoes amongst white male artists on the left in Britain. Araeen's experiences of exclusion from the institutions of art, and turn to conceptual art and performance has important parallels to Adrian Piper's *Mythic Being* performances (1975) as a young black man, complete with Afro and facial hair, walking through the streets of urban New York.[11]

Sankofa's many films self-consciously explored similar terrain. It is a notable dimension of Julien's film *Who Killed Colin Roach?* (1983), made for his degree show at Central Saint Martins

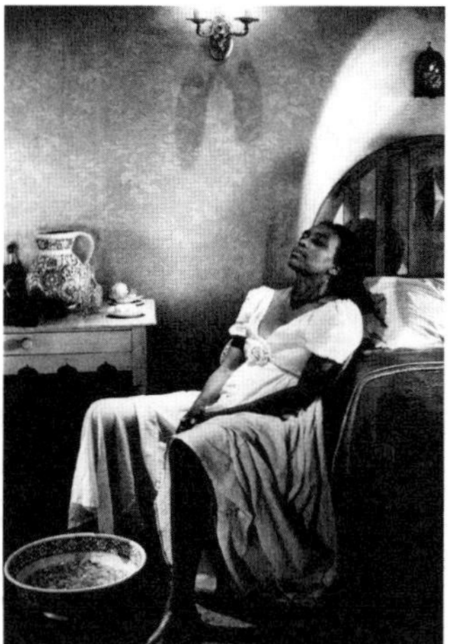
Film still from *Dreaming Rivers*

10

Pratibha Parmar, 'Gender, Race and Class: Asian Women in Resistance', in *The Empire Strikes Back, Race and Racism in 70s Britain*, ed. Andrew S. Thompson (Birmingham: Centre for Contemporary Cultural Studies; London: Hutchinson, 1982), pp. 236–275.

11

Cf. Kobena Mercer, 'Adrian Piper 1970–1975: Exiled on Main Street', in *Exiles, Diasporas and Strangers*, pp. 146–165.

prior to his work with Sankofa. Hence we see extensive archival footage of Jayaben Desai and other women strikers alongside interviews with Roach's family, in which the world of a black middle class acquires a political visibility, because of the prominence of Roach's mother in the film, as a speaking subject interviewed in her living room, drawing out a complexity of identity that was at odds with the conservative associations of this class in post-colonial discourse.[12] However, the challenges faced by artists, film-makers and photographers were not only a matter of subject mat-ter or form but also related to questions of process. A point drawn out by the Black Audio and Film Collective during the filming of a television debate for *Handsworth Songs* (1986) when technicians experienced problems capturing the faces of black and Asian audience members.[13] The 'third' position occupied by diaspora artists in engaging with rather than rejecting the medium of paint-ing or by exploring the painterly or cinematic associations of the photographic tableau can be seen as parallel to the technologi-cal problems of reproducing non-white skin within mainstream media. In all instances the seductions of the image, its beauty and our desire to look, were tied into the political question of which subjects, sexed, raced and class-based, or works of art might be given value, and by whom.

Such concerns were premised on the production of agency and identity, to make new subjects across sex, race and class vis-ible. Crucially, as these new subjects became visible they forced a reconsideration of the necessity of crossing these boundaries. Through such modes of looking, subjectivity and thereby political agency could enter the alternate public sphere of television, as signifiers of a modernity in transformation and facilitating what Mercer termed the 'hybridization' of British society.

12
Isaac Julien in conversation with Paul Gilroy, Tate Britain, 7 September, 2015.

13
Kodwo Eshun, 'John Akomfrah in Conversation with Kodwo Eshun', in *The Ghosts of Songs: The Film Art of the Black Audio Film Collective*, ed. Kodwo Eshun and Anjalika Sagar (Liverpool: Liverpool University Press, 2007), p. 133.

BLACK PHOENIX

Nick Aikens

> *Black Phoenix* is the result of a realization that we who are concerned with the cultural predicament of the Third World must stand on our own feet and speak with a unified voice, that we must collectively confront, on an international level, those forces which in the name of 'universal freedom of man' are actually causing enslavement of men and women.[01]

So reads the opening paragraph in the editorial of the first issue of *Black Phoenix: Journal of Contemporary Art and Culture in the Third World* (later renamed *Black Phoenix: Third World Perspective on Contemporary Art and Culture*) published in January 1978. The journal was due to run quarterly but only three issues emerged before it was discontinued. Edited by Rasheed Araeen and Mahmood Jamal *Black Phoenix* was a precursor to the hugely significant *Third Text*, founded and edited by Araeen, which published its first issue in 1987. *Black Phoenix* was defined by its anti-colonial position against Euro-centrism and Western cultural imperialism. The journal included lengthy opinion articles next to reviews and contributions by artists and poets.

    Issue 1 set the journal's anti-imperialist tone with Araeen's now seminal text 'Preliminary Notes for a Black Manifesto' (written in 1975), the introduction to which is reproduced here. In the text Araeen aims fire at the oppressiveness of the colonial era, the legacies of which he felt were pervasive in contemporary society. The text moves on to focus on the violent exclusion of art from outside the Western centres in the canons of art history. It culminates in Araeen demanding a form of art produced in the 'Third World' that resists the dominance of the hegemonic West, drawing on the history of Western art in the twentieth century as well as on different forms of indigenous cultures and practices, as a means to counter 'cultural imperialism'. Calling for a 'Third World Praxis' Araeen issues an open call for cultural workers to send material that will form the basis of a completed Black Manifesto.

    The editorial of issue 2, published in the summer of 1978, responded to Margaret Thatcher's infamous 'Swamped' speech, given in a TV interview when she was leader of the Conservative Party and a year before she was elected Britain's Prime Minister. In the speech Thatcher said that Britons feared being 'swamped' by migrants coming to the country, and that they might 'be rather

01

Rasheed Araeen, 'Preliminary Notes for a Black Manifesto', *Black Phoenix* 1 (Winter 1978), p. 2.

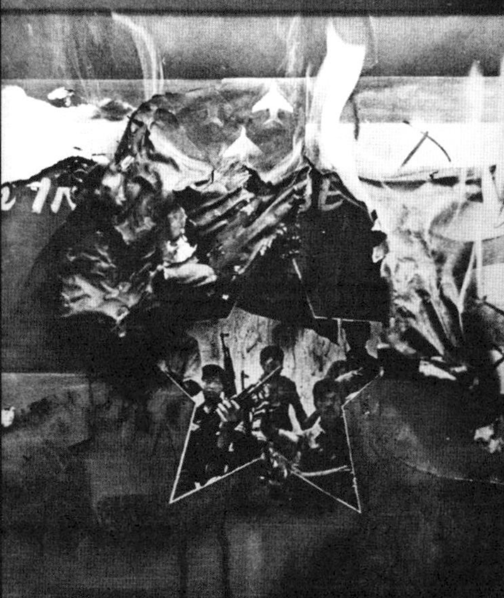

Cover of Rasheed Araeen and Mahmood Jamal, ed., *Black Phoenix. Journal of Contemporary Art and Culture in the Third World* no. 1, Winter 1978. Courtesy Rasheed Araeen

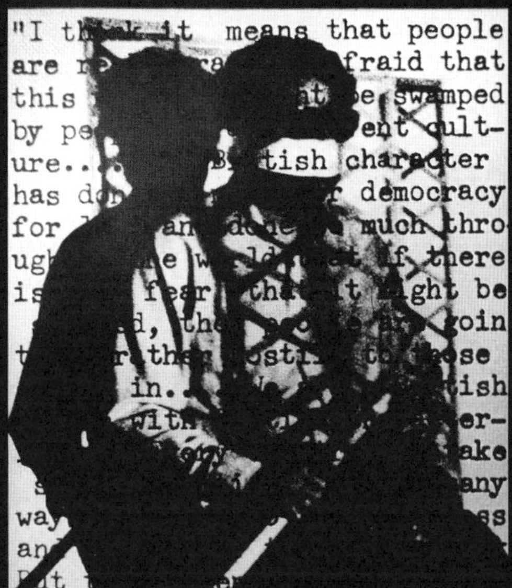

Cover of Rasheed Araeen and Mahmood Jamal, ed., *Black Phoenix. Journal of Contemporary Art and Culture in the Third World* no. 2, Summer 1978. Courtesy Rasheed Araeen

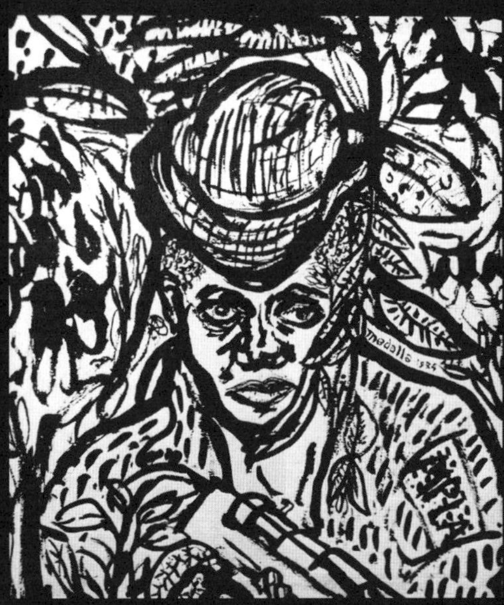

Cover of Rasheed Araeen and Mahmood Jamal, ed., *Black Phoenix. Journal of Contemporary Art and Culture in the Third World* no. 3, Spring 1979. Courtesy Rasheed Araeen

hostile to those coming in'. Indicative of the increasingly xeno-phobic, populist rhetoric in Britain in the late seventies and early eighties, Thatcher's 'swamped' speech was pounced on by *Black Phoenix*. The editorial opened: 'Swamped! Swamped! Swamped! Is the outcry. It is the lie' the editorial read. 'It is the truth. "Swamped" is the word that reveals the racist face of the British ruling class, behind the façade of humanity a vicious being.'[02] Elsewhere in issue 2 was a printed version of Araeen's 1975 performance *Paki Bastard: Portrait of the Artist as a Black Person*, with a photo from the performance adorning the cover. As art historian Courtney Martin has noted, including *Paki Bastard* — a powerful performance which saw Araeen assume the role of Pakistani immigrant artist in Britain and addressed themes of labour, immigration and vio-lence — positioned *Black Phoenix* as something more 'expansive than a periodical and something less tangible than a specific loca-tion'.[03] Such an 'expansive' approach to art, culture and politics was equally evident in Mahmood Jamal's essay 'An Introduction to Radical Urdu Poetry' published in the same issue.

After stopping the journal after its third issue due to lack of resources it would be a further nine years before Araeen would found Third Text. In comparison to the later journal, *Black Phoenix* can be seen as less academic, more militant in form and tone — its pages indicative of the rising anger and disquiet felt by a gener-ation of artists, thinkers and communities excluded by a British society that was witness to the legacies of colonial racism.

02

Rasheed Araeen and Mahmood Jamal, 'Swamped? An Art Statement / Editorial', *Black Phoenix* 2 (Summer 1978), p. 2.

03

Courtney J. Martin, 'Rasheed Araeen: Live Art and Radical Politics in Britain', *Getty Research Journal* 2 (2010), p. 19.

'5 BLACK WOMEN', 'BLACK WOMAN TIME NOW' AND 'THE THIN BLACK LINE'

Lubaina Himid

The artists who took part in '5 Black Women at the Africa Centre' (1983) were Sonia Boyce, Claudette Johnson, Houria Niati, Veronica Ryan, and me. We had never exhibited together before but this show marked the beginning of an idea to bring diasporan women artists together and make them more visible. The dominant motivation running through this show was that I was hungry to show with other black artists to see whether there was a conversation, which could be developed amongst ourselves, around presentation space and political place.

The Africa Centre was a thriving cultural hub in central London internationally known as a venue for music, performance, political exchange, literature, food and information. Lionel Ngkane, the film director and a family friend, introduced me to its delights. The response to the exhibition was encouraging; a packed opening event, a cluster of small reviews, plenty of visitors eager for rigorous debate about how the cultural mores of the African diaspora related to the contemporary art scene across Africa.

'Black Woman Time Now' was staged at the Battersea Arts Centre as part of a large festival of Black women's visual creative practice devised by Yvonne Brewster, the founding director of Talawa Theatre Company. The participating artists were Ingrid Pollard, Veronica Ryan, Claudette Johnson, Sonia Boyce, Lubaina Himid, Chila Burman, Mumtaz Karimjee, Houria Niati, Jean Campbell, Andrea Telman, Margaret Cooper, Elizabeth Eugene, Lesley Wills, Cherry Lawrence, and Brenda Agard.

The Centre itself in the eighties was rough and ready, friendly, loud and local. It had a cafe, a bar, meeting rooms and a very active performance space, as well as a small but very good gallery.

The exhibition evolved in response to a strategically friendly series of requests, politically motivated by funding obligations, from Battersea Arts Centre that needed to move toward developing diverse audiences for their events. I was given an opportunity to present a rich and multi-layered experience in which we could display a whole variety of objects we had made, revealing our different life choices and our particular philosophical narratives.

Thin Black Line, Institute of Contemporary Arts (ICA), London, 1985, exhibition catalogue. Courtesy Lubaina Himid

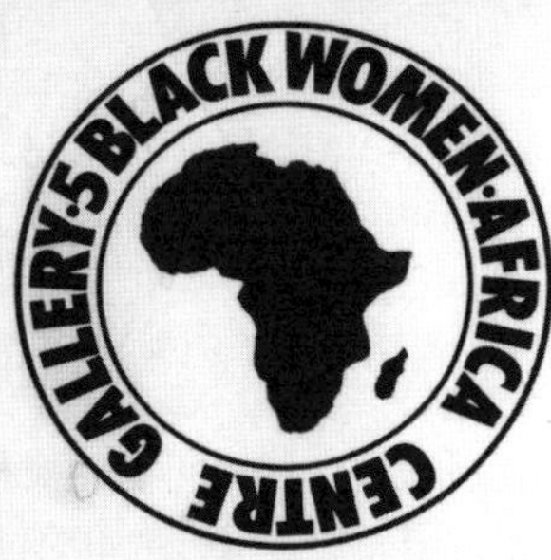

Invitation for '5 Black Women', Africa Centre Gallery, London, 1983. Courtesy Lubaina Himid

Invitation for 'Thin Black Line', an exhibition selected by Lubaina Himid, Institute of Contemporary Arts (ICA), London, 1985. Courtesy Lubaina Himid

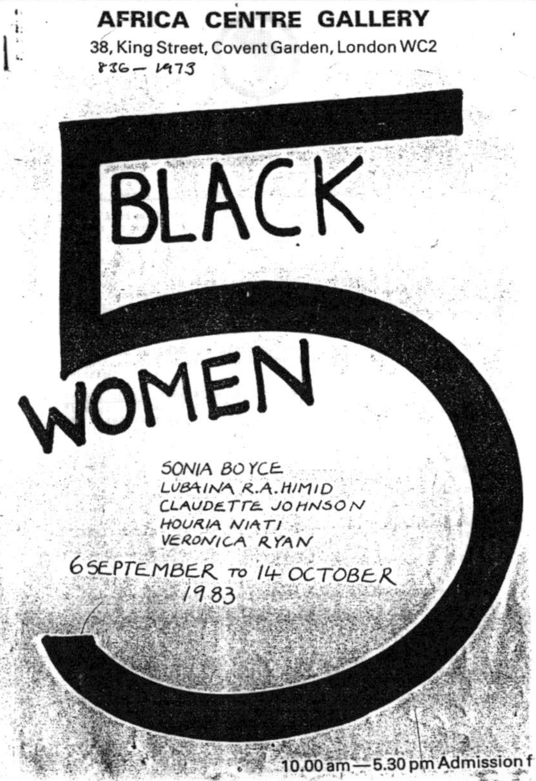

Poster for '5 Black Women', Africa Centre Gallery, London, 1983. Courtesy Lubaina Himid

The Institute of Contemporary Arts has a different kind of history from the other venues we worked with; founded in 1947, it moved to Nash House in the Mall in 1968, and was thought of by many people as the art centre of both cool and chaos. 'The Thin Black Line' exhibition came into being as a result of pressure on the ICA from funders and a strategy of dogged determination from me. The artists in the show were as follows: Marlene Smith, Veronica Ryan, Sonia Boyce, Claudette Johnson, Maud Sulter, Chila Burman, Brenda Agard, Sutapa Biswas, Jennifer Comrie, Lubaina Himid, and Ingrid Pollard. We displayed the work in the then long narrow corridor between the foyer and the cafe. We made our work in the main for other black women to engage with, in a place they rarely visited, young women like ourselves, but also for the thousands of older black women in Britain who had supported the system for decades. As well as the paintings, sculptures, photographic and print pieces we also brought favourite photographs of family, of singers, dancers and musicians, to make the space feel more like home.

We were never a movement or a group or a sisterhood or even very close friends at the time; we were a fluid flexible set of women who were not prepared to be herded into a single way of expressing ourselves.

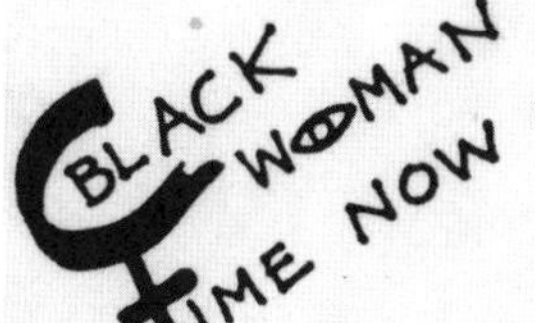

From Wed.Nov.30th – Dec.31st.

Battersea Arts Centre

Old Town Hall,
Lavender Hill,
London SW11 5TF

PREVIEW
THURSDAY 1ST. from 5-8pm.

An exhibition involving the work of fifteen black women artists.

HOURIA NIATI	JEAN CAMPBELL	ELIZABETH EUGENE
VERONICA RYAN	ANDREA TELMAN	LESLEE WILLS
CLAUDETTE JOHNSON	INGRID POLLARD	CHERRY LAWRANCE.
SONIA BOYCE	MARGARET COOPER	LUBAINA HIMID
CHILA BURMAN	MUMTAZ KARIMJEE	BRENDA AGARD.

Invitation for 'Black Woman Time Now', Battersea Arts Centre, London, 1983

BLACK WOMEN'S MOVEMENT (ZMV)

Diana Franssen

On the occasion of the International Women's Day: Winter University in Nijmegen 1983, activist Julia da Lima took the stand and defined ZMV as follows: 'With the term black women I mean women from the former and current colonies of the Netherlands, and all women that are called foreigners, allochthon, non-western, Third World, etcetera by white people'. From the outset, ZMV was conceived as a means to counter the whiteness of second wave feminism in the Netherlands and elsewhere. Throughout the eighties, some of the key figures in the movement were Mavis Carrilho, Ernestine Comvalius, Philomena Essed, Nancy Jouwe, Julia da Lima, Cisca Pattipilohy, Gloria Wekker and Mercedes Zandwijken.

Internationale Vrouwendag (International Women's Day), 1983, poster

ZMV's critique of feminism was threefold. Firstly, white women had the privilege not to be confronted with prejudices against colour or ethnicity. Secondly, studies of (anti-)racism were often carried out by white men. Thirdly, second-wave feminism at the time was being proffered by white middle-class women who had privileged access to education and professional work whereas their black counterparts mostly did not. They also resisted the principle that women would automatically be in solidarity with one another on the basis of common oppression of their womanhood.

An important influence for the Dutch black feminists were discussions taking place in America at the time. The 'Black-Conscious-Movement', black feminism, 'Black Studies' all inspired the Dutch term 'zwarte vrouwen' (black women).

bell hooks' seminal publication *Ain't I a Woman: Black Women and Feminism*[01] was an inspiration. hooks expressed the historical impact of sexism and racism on black women, the devaluation of black womanhood, the role of the media and the stereotypes they portrayed, the education system, white patriarchy, the marginalization of black women, and the disregard for issues of race and class within feminism. hooks argues strongly that white women are not more or less racist than white men and that white women should start to examine their own relationship to society, race and culture.

In the Netherlands of the eighties the term 'black' was heavily contested. Unlike in Britain or the US, where the term demarcated a political, discursive space adopted by the African, Caribbean and Asian diaspora, in the Netherlands many women did not identify as black. Turkish, Moroccan, or Indonesian women for example started their own events and discussions. In this respect the feminist movement splintered and segmented along different racial and political lines.

During the eighties, a range of activities were developed by the Black Women's Movement. One of the most heated actions happened during the conference 'Challenging Racism: theory, practice and politics' in Utrecht (organized by Studia Inter Etnica, Utrecht & Centre for Race and Ethnic Studies, Amsterdam) where protests and disagreements fed into a conference a year later called: 'Constellaties van Racisme, Seksisme en Klassisme: reproduktie, verandering en verzet' (organized by Flamboyant and CRES). Magazines were published, such as *Ashanti*, 1980–1987: a magazine especially for the women from Suriname. And *Zwarte Vrouwenkrant Umoja*, 1984–1986 (black women's newspaper) was published and on June 25, 1982 the first copy of *Vrouwenweekblad* (Women's Weekly) was published. From 1985 until 1990 Flamboyant, a meetings community and documentation centre was run by Tania Leon and Cisca Pattipilohy. After it closed, it was followed by ZAMI in Amsterdam 1992.

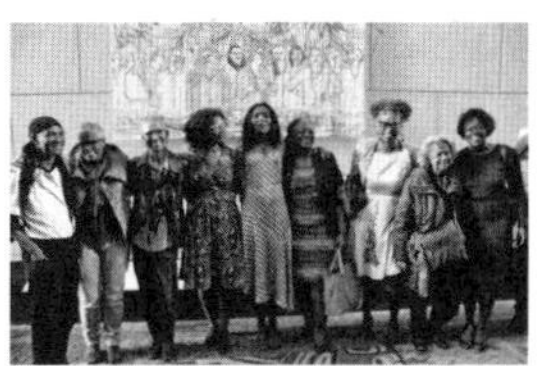

Reunion of the ZMV members, organised by Patricia Kaersenhout in the program Proud Rebels, CBK-Zuidoost, Amsterdam, 2015. Photo: Irina Popova

01

bell hooks, *Ain't I a Woman: Black Women and Feminism* (London: Pluto Press, 1981).

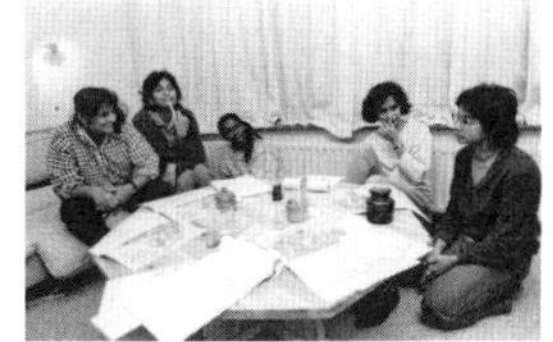

Meeting editors *Ashanti* magazine, 1985

'DOUBLE DUTCH'

Diana Franssen

'Double Dutch'[01] (1991) was an exhibition that resulted from a collaboration between initiatives from the alternative art circuit in the southern Dutch city of Tilburg and the COS.[02] Both were, at the time, engaged in different cultural projects. Such a collaboration was unusual in the eighties. The exhibition brought together Dutch artists with Dutch-based artists who were born outside Europe. The anti-colonial artist, thinker and curator Rasheed Araeen spoke at the opening. The location was an old school building in the centre of Tilburg. The artist-curator Jack Mensink expressed his intentions in the catalogue as follows: 'The work is a result of a mutual artistic openness and interest in other cultures and intensive collaboration with colleagues.' Through a direct curatorial strategy it placed Dutch and non-European artists in conversation. Nine rooms included nine pairs, creating a dialogue between their work, and by inference between their culture and aesthetic sensibility. Each pair worked in one room for two months, creating one artwork together. Beside artists from the Netherlands there were artists from, for instance, Argentina, India, Indonesia, Morocco and the Dutch Colonies. One successful integration of two cultures was the installation by the Armenian artist Krikor Momdjian and the Dutch artist Marius Boender.

Taking place in the same period as exhibitions such as 'Magiciens de la terre', the 2nd Havana Biennial and 'The Other Story', which, in different ways and with different degrees of success, sought to expand the colonial limitations of the western art world, 'Double Dutch' was a rare initiative in the Netherlands, aimed at countering the central position of the white Dutch artist.

The Tropenmuseum (Tropical Museum) in Amsterdam had been engaged in this debate for some years. In 1980, they organized 'Het eerste festival der wereldculturen' (The First Festival of World Cultures) led by Harry Leyten. Other examples are, in 1988, 'Kunst uit een andere wereld' (Art from Another World) by the Museum of Ethnology in Rotterdam and in 1987 the establishment of the Gate Foundation,[03] which aimed to forge meaningful ties between Western and non-Western art in the Netherlands. Most of these initiatives, however, operated in the realm of anthropology and ethnology with the ever luring danger of the 'exotic' and the labelling 'positive discrimination' while speaking of 'the other'.

01

'Double Dutch (transculturele beïnvloeding in de beeldende kunst / transcultural influences in the visual arts)', Tilburg, The Netherlands, Stichting Kunst Mondiaal. Exhibition 25 May 1991 throught 4 August 1991. 'Double Dutch' originated from two previous exhibitions dealing with Apartheid 'Om 'n sinkende skip blou te verf' (To Paint a Sinking Ship Blue, by Breyten Breytenbach) in 1988 Tilburg (curated by Diana Franssen) and non-western art in 'Zo ver het oog reikt' (As Far As the Eye Can See) in 1989 's-Hertogenbosch by Jack Mensink. Participating artists duos: Hugo Kaagman (NL) — Nour-Eddine Jarram (MA); Joyce Bloem (NL) — Bianca Tangande (NL); Diana Blok (UY) — Wendela Gevers Deynoot (NL); Marius Boender (NL) — Krikor Momdjian (ID); Nicolas Dings (NL) — Kunal Chatterjee (IN); Marlyn Dunker (CW) — Brigitte de Rijk (NL); André Boone (NL) — Eddie Hara (ID); Boetje Pattirane (ID) — Leo van Kampen (NL); Joseph Semah (IS) — Waldo Bien (NL)

02

Centrum voor Ontwikkelings-samenwerking (a centre for collaboration in development aid).

03

The Gate Foundation was established in 1987 in Amsterdam with the aim to stimulate the communication between western and non-western art, research into art of former Dutch

In these early initiatives, such as 'Double Dutch' the problem of diversity was restricted to aesthetic presentations, rather than a meaningful, committed and resourced process of shifting existing power dynamics. Although through the collaborative process between artists the Dutch art was still presented as the centre, non-European as the periphery. Such strategies, intentional or not, only served to reaffirm colonial power structures.[04]

colonies and transcultural art. Until its closure in 2006, the Gate Foundation had accumulated archives with documentation on more than 750 non-Dutch artists, plus a specialized library. Their archive and library is now in the Van Abbemuseum in Eindhoven.

04

Tania Canas: www. artshub.com.au/ education/news-article/ opinions-and-analysis/ professional-development/ tania-canas/diversity-is-a-white-word-252910 (accessed December 2016). To produce an artwork together takes more than just collaborating. As Canas states: 'To seek multiplicity, defies constructs that are palpable and consumable to the dominant narrative. Not working for a community but with and foremost as one. Process and production, not merely programming.'

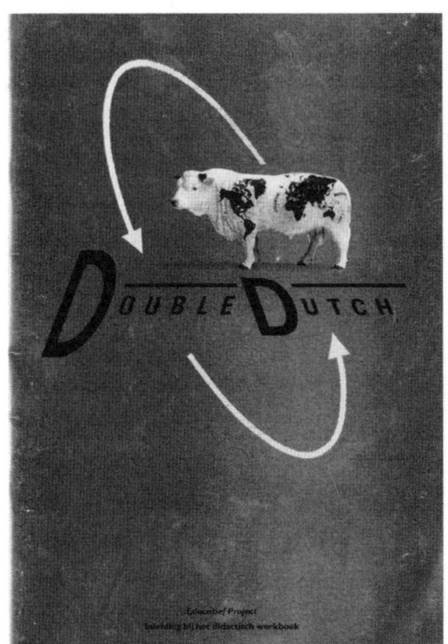

Double Dutch, 1991, catalogue cover

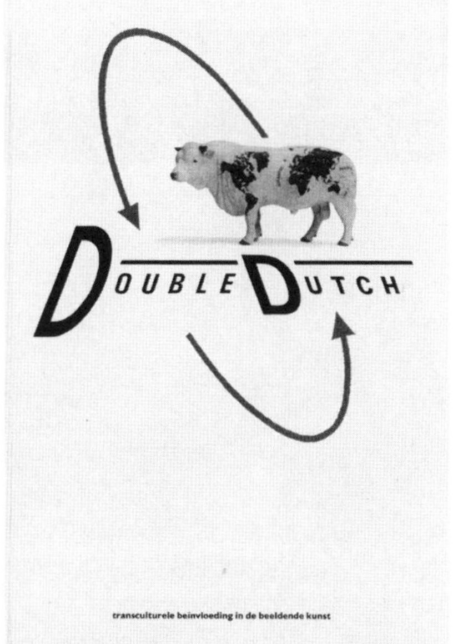

Double Dutch educational project, 1991, cover brochure

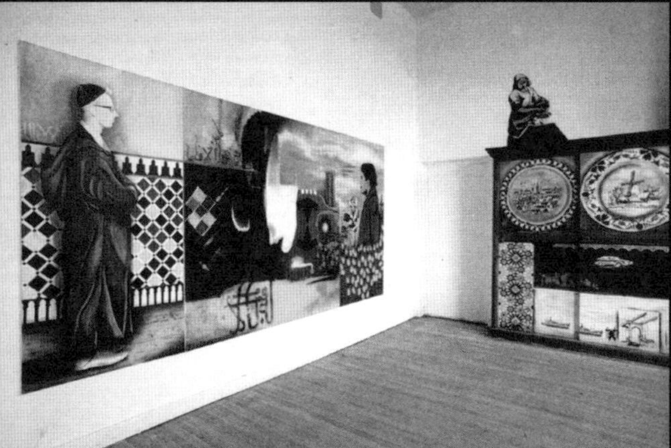

Exhibition view of Hugo Kaagman — Nour-Eddine Jarram, *Two Ways, One Purpose*, 'Double Dutch', Tilburg, 1991. Photo: Martin Stoop

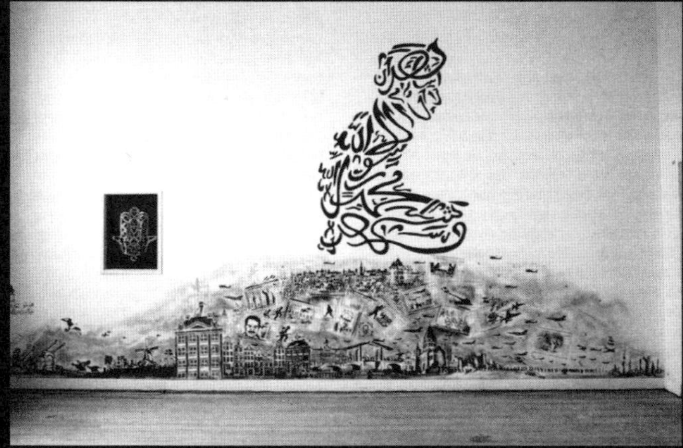

Exhibition view of Hugo Kaagman — Nour-Eddine Jarram, *Static Words, Moving Pictures*, 'Double Dutch', Tilburg, 1991. Photo: Martin Stoop

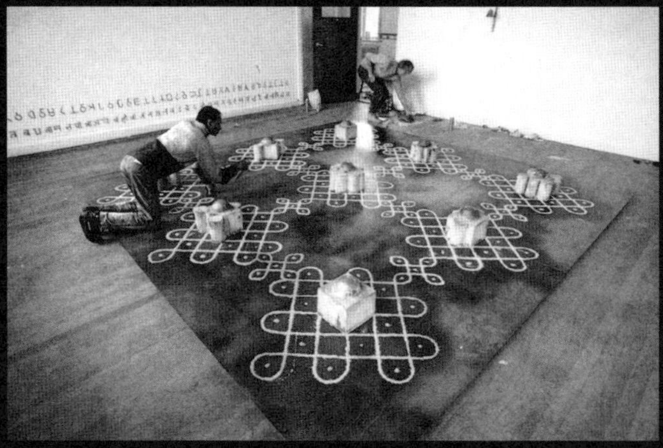

Installing Nicolas Dings — Kunal Chatterjee, *Towers of Silence*, 'Double Dutch', Tilburg, 1991. Photo: Martin Stoop

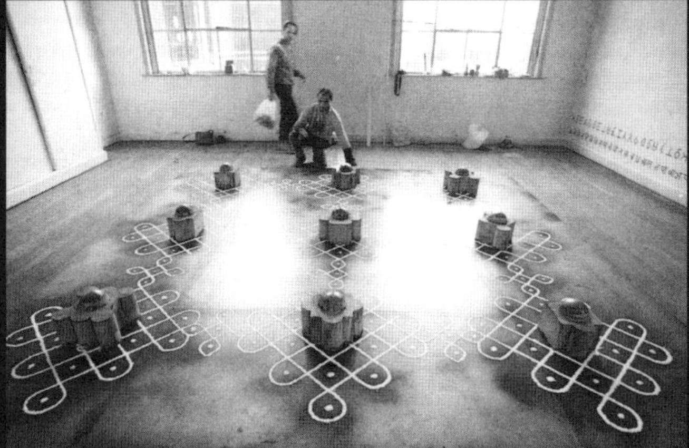

Installing Nicolas Dings — Kunal Chatterjee, *Towers of Silence*, 'Double Dutch', Tilburg, 1991. Photo: Martin Stoop

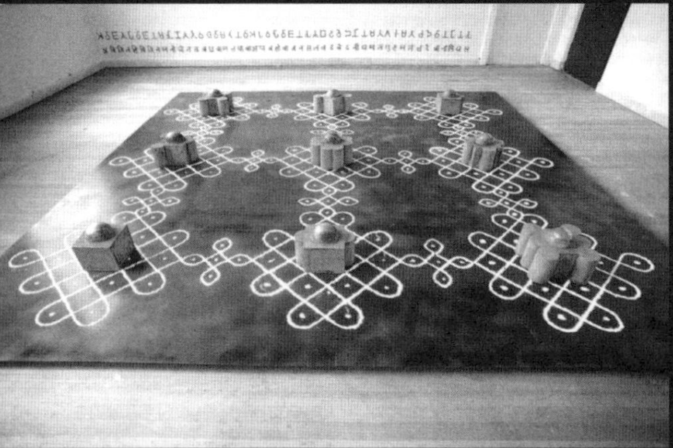

Exhibition view of Nicolas Dings — Kunal Chatterjee, *Towers of Silence*, Tilburg, 1991. Photo: Martin Stoop

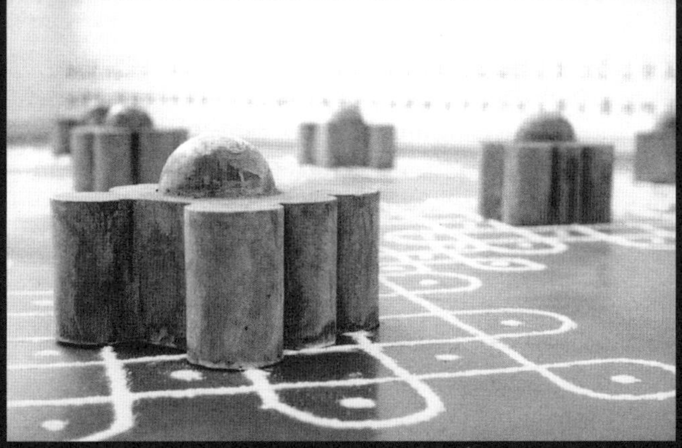

Nicolas Dings — Kunal Chatterjee, *Towers of Silence*, Tilburg, 1991, detail. Photo: Martin Stoop

J. LAMBRECHT & THE BELGIAN INSTITUTE FOR WORLD AFFAIRS IN THE EIGHTIES

Chris Straetling

The Belgian Institute for World Affairs was created in April 1982. Founders Jef Lambrecht and Karel Schoetens were young professionals working for the state broadcaster BRT at the time. Lambrecht had written his thesis on 'Anarchism in PROVO 1965–67', setting the tone of the Belgian Institute for World Affairs: on the one hand closely related to current affairs, with a thoroughness associated with investigative journalism, on the other a loose-ludicrous critical & Dadaist prankster-style approach to social situations. A Belgian identity was at that time almost non-existent: the separatist Flemish movement, disenchanted with a Walloon dependence on funds from the north, was gaining ground, heavy industries were in steep decline, growing cultural estrangement as the Flemish-French language barrier became more rigid and doubt about the central state's ability to survive both blind and politically inspired terror (the 'Bende van Nijvel', the CCC, Gladio).[01]

By proclaiming Belgium a work of art (July, 1982) and using historical references, the B.I.W.A. could address some of the issues of national identity while avoiding the then current fever involved. The call to arms to correct the misinformation disseminated internationally on cigarette packs that 'Peter Stuyvesant was the man who founded New York' came as a welcome — and comic — relief to an increasingly bitter artistic milieu. Legal steps were prepared to take the Stuyvesant tobacco company[02] to court, or at least launch a 'public prosecution' and to raise funds to retake Manhattan and correct history: the founder of the colony 'Novum Belgium' being the Walloon Pierre Minuit, who had bought part of the island in 1624 from local Indians for a purported 24 dollars. Roughly calculating inflation and current market value, the B.I.W.A. issued a bond to raise 24 000 000 000 000 000 000 000 000 US Dollars. This was part of a general artistic information campaign to raise awareness, which included actions and performances in New York City's Battery Park at the Walloon memorial, in various cities in the Netherlands and Belgium, including Ohain, south of Brussels, where Minuit's forefathers had come from. Although much of the campaign was taken in a light-hearted tongue-in-cheek vein, it was widely reported, including on the front page of the *Wall Street*

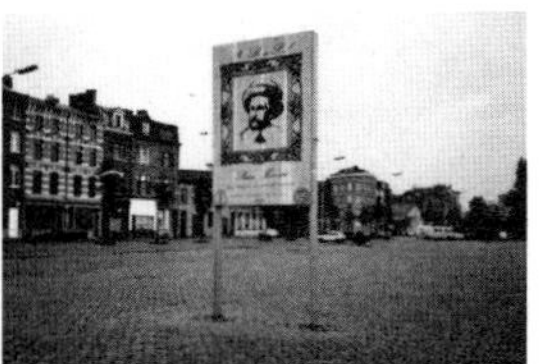

Pierre Minuit, portrait panel as presented on the filled-in docks, Antwerp, 1987

01

Bende van Nijvel (Tueurs de Brabant-Wallon) were a criminal gang that raided supermarkets, killing at will and seemingly indiscriminate — it has remained unclear who were behind it all until this very day. CCC (Cellules Communistes Combattantes), left wing urban guerrilla fashioned after the German RAF. Gladio was a secret NATO military stay-behind network that became corrupted and partially morphed into a criminal organization with right-wing tendencies (possibly linked to the Bende van Nijvel).

02

Not sure if the brand Peter Stuyvesant was then in the hands of British American Tobacco (BAT) or Philip Morris — but one may note the heavy involvement of tobacco companies in the arts at the time, see also the Stuyvesant Collection.

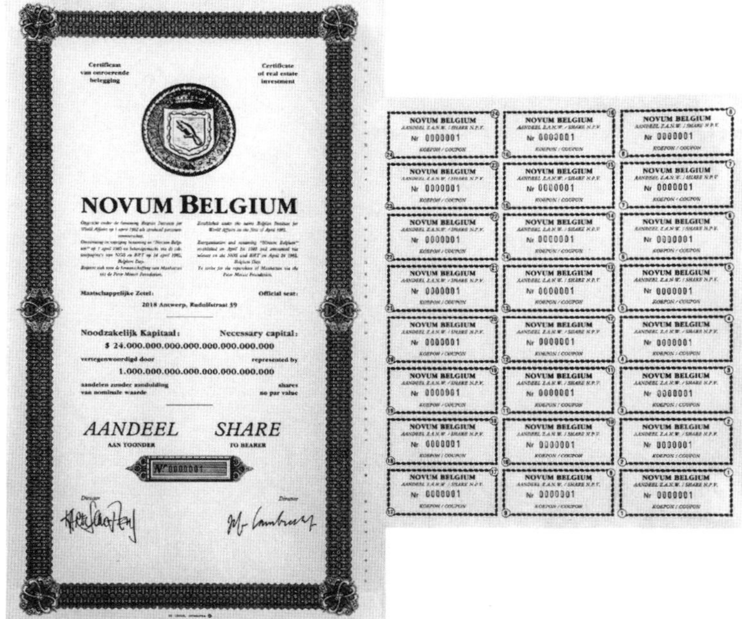

Belgian Institute for World Affairs, *Novum Belgium Share Certificate*, 1985

Journal, and this put this strange manifestation of Belgian surrealism in the limelight. Aside from regular press releases, the B.I.W.A. remained an artistic entity, using mainly ephemeral manifestations in the public space with occasional info-shows in 'alternative' venues. It had a penchant for the underdog; rooting for Belgium against all odds was in itself a manifesto of sorts.

Officially disbanded in 1985, The B.I.W.A. survived as a 'restructured' entity, reflecting the Thatcherite atmosphere of amalgamation and privatization. The B.I.W.A. became an 'umbrella organization' for more individual activities such as 'Saint Nicholas Chapter' 'Dept. Ear' or 'Feather Bros. Society'.

They teamed up for occasional B.I.W.A. projects, as in 1988–1989 during the ongoing crisis between Belgium and its former colony, Zaire, or rather its ruler, Mobutu Sese Seko concerning the waiving of debt — at a time when more African nations (or their rulers)[03] were in a clinch with their former colonial rulers. So, in order to alleviate the political log-jam the Belgian Institute for World Affairs unilaterally declared Belgium dependent of Zaire — much to the consternation of the parties concerned — leading to parliamentary questions and diplomatic notes being passed, complaining that press freedom in Belgium was out of control. In fact, the soggy document prepared by the B.I.W.A. on a dreary March morning on the river Scheldt was never accepted by the Zairian Consul to whom it was presented.[04]

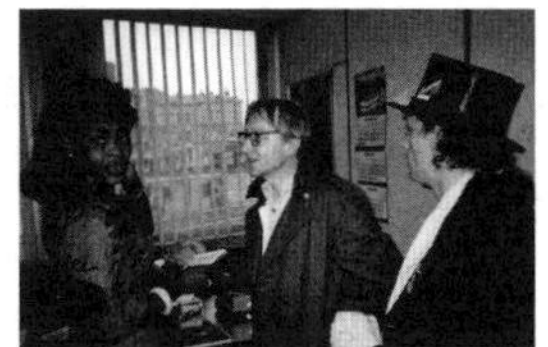

Documentation: B.I.W.A.-directors Lambrecht and Schoetens trying to convince the Zairian Consul's secretary to allow them an unscheduled meeting to submit the declaration of dependence. Courtesy Samarkand VZW

03

As earlier with the Central African Republic's Emperor Bokassa I or Uganda's Idi Amin Dada. Former colonial nations no longer had the stomach to support unsavoury despots they had more or less protected during the cold war.

04

Also see press releases in special edition of 'Lanterne de Lantin' concerning the action (ill.)

3.2 BODIES

Being There

1980s

Hugo Roelandt

Pepe Espaliú, *Carrying*,
1992, Performance

1992

143.353 (the eyes do not
want to be always shut)

PUT UP A FIGHT

'Irritating'
1984–1990

Being Called a Lunatic
Should Become a
Compliment!
1988–1989

Istanbul Kurdish
1989

Nation, Democracy and
Gender
1980s

From 'Personal is
Political' to 'Women in
Black'
1981–1989

NATION, DEMOCRACY AND GENDER

Ayşe Düzkan

Beşiktaş is one of the central districts of Istanbul, famous for its fish restaurants, market place, football team, and their fans. The office of Kadın Çevresi (Women's Circle), the first feminist collective, founded in 1984 as a commercial company to protect itself under the political conditions of the coup d'état, was located in a small building in one of Beşiktaş' busy streets.

In the office was a small desk, some DIY stools, and a library containing several feminist books in different languages, donated by visitors. On the walls were feminist posters from the USA and many European countries, and a copy of the fifth page of the prominent daily *Cumhuriyet*'s 19th of April 1935 edition, with photos of the Suffragette Conference held in Istanbul.

The women who visited that legendary office were the second-wave feminists of Turkey. Most of them were left-wing revolutionaries who would spend some time in custody or in prison during the eighties and none had heard of the first wave of feminism in their home country or of the Suffragette Conference in Istanbul. The honour of exploring the first wave of feminism in Turkey fell to a male historian, Zafer Toprak, and the copy of *Cumhuriyet* came from his personal archive. It would take some years for other historians — almost all of them women, including Serpil Çakır, Necla Akgökçe, Yaprak Zihnioğlu, and Ayşe Durakbaşa — to discover what their grandmothers had achieved. It is significant that it was the rise of the feminist movement and respective feminist policies that were increasingly becoming part of the political agenda that made this contribution to the official historical narrative possible.

By that time, the economic, political and cultural transformations that took place in the Ottoman society after the second half of the nineteenth century and the demand for 'freedom' resonated among women, especially in cities like Istanbul and Thessaloniki with their culture of political activism. Women started to express themselves through a growing body of newspapers and magazines. This period, named as the Early Women's Movement by female historians, started with letters written by women addressing problems in 1868 to the editors of the newspaper *Terakki* (Progress). The movement gained an identity with *Terakki-i Muhadderat* (Progress of Muslim Women), which was published as an appendix of the same newspaper in 1868, and matured with *Hanımlara Mahsus Gazete* (Newspaper for Ladies) (which was continuously published for 13 years between 1895–1908). The long-term women's media presence of the early period lasted until the 2nd Constitutional Monarchy.[01]

During the early period, women mainly came together around an idealism of women through their daily experiences, which they wrote up in magazines. Islam was the binding factor for these women's experiences, expressed in articles in *Hanımlara Mahsus Gazete* published by Fatma Aliye.

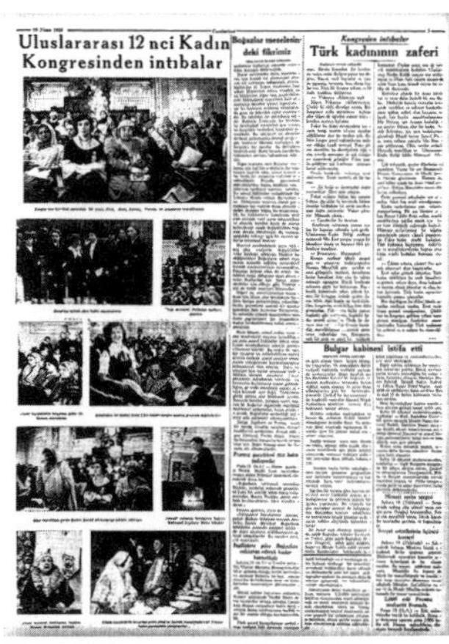

Cumhuriyet, 18th April 1935, p. 5

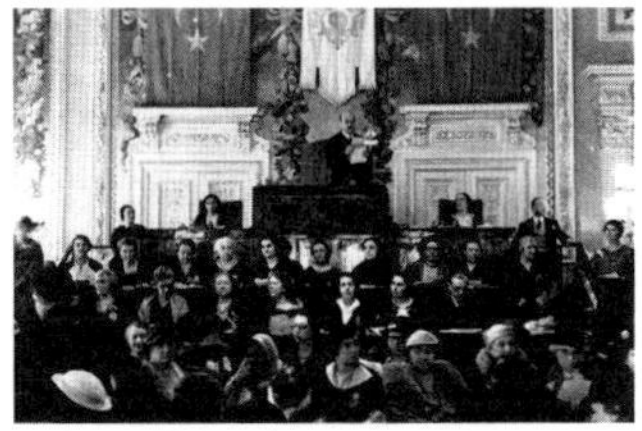

Scene at the opening of the 12th IWSA (International Woman Suffrage Alliance) Congress

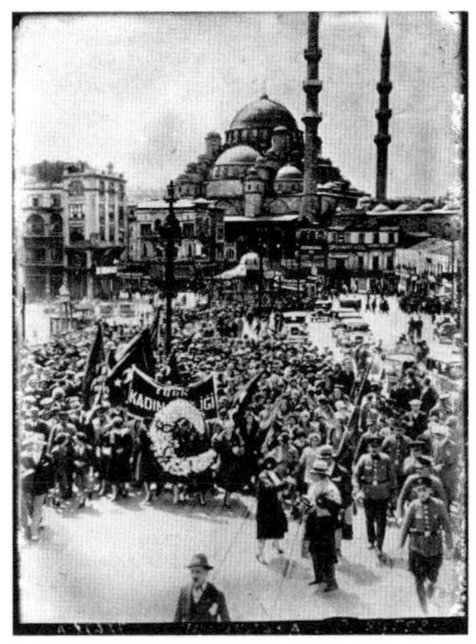

Women celebrate the introduction of women's suffrage in Istanbul

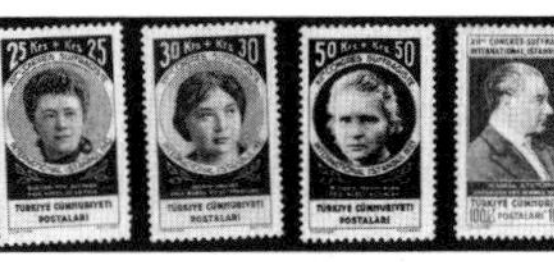

Stamps by PTT of Turkey celebrating the 12th IWSA (International Woman Suffrage Alliance)

01

Interview with Necla Akgökçe.

These first avant-gardes, who were brought up in the mansions of Ottoman Pashas, spoke many languages, allowing them to learn about the women's movement in the West. However, they differentiated themselves from their fellow comrades fighting for women's liberation in the West through the Muslim women's estate. Intellectual Ottomans demanding freedom and aspiring and working hard for modernization had 'demands such as marrying educated women and having children raised by them'[02] and these demands were in tune with a new identity for women. During the Era of Bliss, those who claimed that Muslim women were trivialized and enslaved also believed that in order to be appreciated as individuals they should be educated. They believed that Ottoman women should be teachers, nurses, i.e. have careers that suited women, and that schools for women should be opened. The Industrial School for Girls as well as English, French, household, and tailoring classes started during that time. Another characteristic of the period were the activities of female labourers. Between 1872–1907, 9 out of 50 strikes that took place in the Ottoman Empire were in sectors where primarily women worked and were organized by women workers.

The Period of the 2nd Constitutional Monarchy that started in 1908 was, in a way, a time when the outcomes of the early women's movement were being applied. Feminist historian Necla Akgökçe states that women advanced from the idea that 'women are not slaves, they are humans and valuable' to the idea 'women are also human, have rights and are equal to men and in some sense are even superior to them.'[03] 'Freedom, equality, brotherhood / sisterhood'[04] claims of the 2nd Constitutional Monarchy and İttihat ve Terakki opened the way for women's demands about equality with men. There were many women's magazines and women's associations for charity, gender equality, and women's liberation. Historian Yaprak Zihnioğlu claims that there were 40 female members in İttihat Terakki Rumeli Women's Branch when the 2nd Constitutional Monarchy was announced and most of them worked clandestinely on social projects.[05]

Female historians who reclaim the women's movement as part of the Ottoman Modernization take the year 1908 as a starting point. Yaprak Zihnioğlu believes that starting with the first days of 2nd Constitutional Monarchy Ottoman-Turkish women's demand for liberation was on the agenda. Women wanted to play a significant role in society, be seen as liberated individuals as modernity had promised them, have jobs, earn a living, and participate in political and public life.[06]

In *Kadınlar Dünyası* (Women's Word) the authors argued that women could operate in the male dominated world of politics and build a discourse about their own lives and women's rights.

02
Çakır Serpil, Osmanlı Kadın Hareketi, Metis Yayınları, Istanbul, 3rd edition, April 2011.

03
Interview with Necla Akgökçe.

04
Brotherhood and sisterhood are the same word in Turkish.

05
Yaprak Zihnioğlu, Kadınsız İnkilap/ Nezihe Muhiddin, Kadınlar Halk Fırkası, Kadın Birliği, Metis Yayınları, Istanbul, 1st edition, October 2003.

06
Ibid.

They wanted equality, yet the fight for the 'right to vote' was not a prominent demand for the Ottoman Women's Movement at the time. However, it would not be unfair to say that it was the demand for participation in public life, rather than the direct participation in political domain, that was the principal tendency of the post-1908 women's movement.[07]

The first wave of feminism in Turkey / Ottoman Empire was part of the intellectual forces that formed Turkish nationalism and the young republic. Although the official historical narrative says very little about these brave women, their contributions had a substantial effect on the daily lives of women, and their participation in the public sphere.

The second wave of feminism emerged during the eighties, under restrictive political and social conditions. The 1980 coup d'état was not just about closing down the parliament, having soldiers pace the streets, censoring the press, or putting all the leftists and some members of the fascist movement in prison where they underwent torture. For the first years, there was a midnight curfew, later extended to 2 am, meaning it was difficult to organize any political or cultural events. A generation grew up within this cultural and social climate, the so-called 'apolitical generation' of Turkey. But this was only a part of the Turkish reality. The Kurdish experience, as I shall discuss, was quite different.

The 1982 referendum on the constitutional changes took place under arms with almost transparent envelopes and blue cards for 'no' and white cards for 'yes', revealing the choice of each voter. The first elections were held in 1983 when the MDP/Nationalist Democracy Party supported by generals lost the elections and another right-wing party (ANAP/Motherland Party) won the majority of seats in the new parliament. However, very little changed after the parliament was installed; torture, injustice and violations of human rights continued. Human rights, an increasingly important issue for Turkey, was nevertheless a new concept. The Human Rights Organization was founded in 1986 in the wake of long political debates. The founders were left-wing intellectuals and relatives of political prisoners. Most of the human rights activists have been women, at first wives and mothers of political prisoners, then activists. Human rights as a political concept and criterion have remained an important part of the political debate since the eighties. For instance, Saturday Mothers, inspired by Mothers of the Plaza de Mayo and mostly organized by human rights activists, have demonstrated for their lost relatives and beloved ones since 27 May 1995. Many of these human rights activists are also feminists. In this regard feminists have contributed significantly to the democratic culture and life of Turkey.

07

Çakır Serpil, Osmanlı Kadın Hareketi, Metis Yayınları, Istanbul, 3rd edition, April 2011.

There have been opposing Kurdish groups in the Kurdish part of the country since the formation of the Republic. The Kurdish parties in Bilad el-Sham, such as the Kurdish Democratic Party and Patriotic Union of Kurdistan, had supporters in the territories of the Republic of Turkey but the formation of the Kurdistan Workers' Party (PKK) during the late seventies had a stronger impact in the region where the majority of the population is Kurdish. On 15th August 1984 the PKK raided military quarters and residences in two towns, Eruh and Şemdinli. These events marked the establishment of this newly emerging political group among Kurds. Thousands of young people took to the mountains to fight and others joined the groups in Kurdish metropoles. Women and young girls were among these new fighters. During the eighties and later, there was an enormous politicization among Kurds of all ages. Some left the country because of oppression by the state and formed a broad Kurdish diaspora all over the world. Some of them established TV channels: Med TV, Roj TV, and so on, a newspaper *Özgür Politika*, and various internet sites. Med TV (and other channels after it had been banned) that broadcasted in Kurdish and books and magazines in Kurdish have been laying the foundations of the modern Kurdish language. This has been a period of nation-building among the Kurds living in the Republic of Turkey.

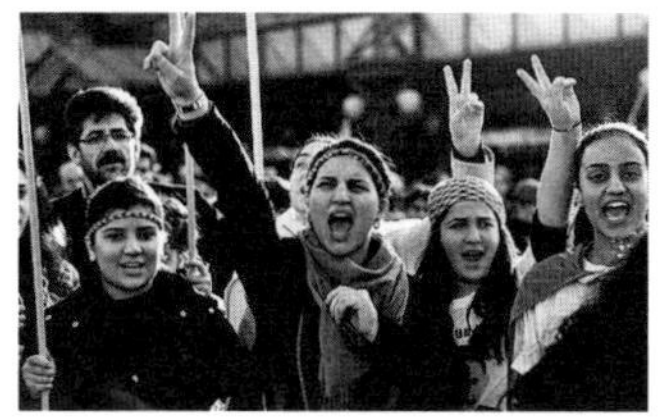

Kurdish women demonstrating in Hamburg

Every nation-building process is also a modernization process within which women play a fundamental role. This has also been true for the Kurds. But the impact of women in this process has differed from other national liberation movements, for instance in Ireland. Women were part of the nationalist struggle for Ireland since the Easter Rising of 1916. During the seventies, as the second wave of feminism emerged in Ireland, the Irish Women's Liberation Movement was formed, campaigning against the ban on abortion and contraceptives. But an amendment banning abortion on request was still recognized by the Irish Constitution in 1983. Only in 1985 did the sales of contraceptives become legal in Ireland. The constitutional prohibition of divorce was repealed in 1996. So, even though many women participated both in the legal movement and the armed struggle and women's emancipation was an important part of political discourse, it is hard to say that all the feminist demands of the time were successfully met in Ireland.

The Kurdish experience is quite different. Women in Kurdish national liberation politics have formed various structures that made them one of the major political agents of the movement. During the early nineties, women who took part in the armed struggle formed their own troops. The process that made Kurdish women fighters one of the most remarkable forces against ISIS in Syria began this way. HADEP, the Kurdish political party of the late nineties and the early two-thousands (as all Kurdish political parties are banned, their names frequently change) was one of the first political parties in Turkey that adopted affirmative action for women, with a quota of 25 percent. (At present, there is a co-presidency system, with a man and a woman sharing the authority for every post, i.e. mayors. Kurdish women try to cultivate a women's liberation ideology that they call jineology — jin meaning woman in Kurdish — which I believe is Kurdish feminism.) I think it is interesting to compare the Kurdish and Irish cases, in terms of Eurocentric prejudices. The impact of women is more limited in Ireland, a European Union member state, than among the Kurds, part of 'l'Orient'.

On the other hand, Turkish women were part of the nation and nation-state building processes of the Republic of Turkey in the first decades of the twentieth century and seven decades later, it was Kurdish women who were doing the same thing, only they were much better equipped in terms of ideology and organization.

I believe there are three main reasons for this. Firstly, patriarchal relations and patriarchal violence are stronger in the Kurdish region, not as a cultural characteristic but as a result of livestock and agricultural production, which depends on domestic unpaid labour, mainly of women. Secondly, the feminist movement emerging in Western Turkey also inspired Kurdish women. Feminists were among the first groups in solidarity with the Kurdish movement and this, I would argue, had a positive effect. Thirdly, especially since the late nineties, there has been a broad Kurdish diaspora in Western Europe and the USA and Kurdish women had contacts with feminists residing in those countries.

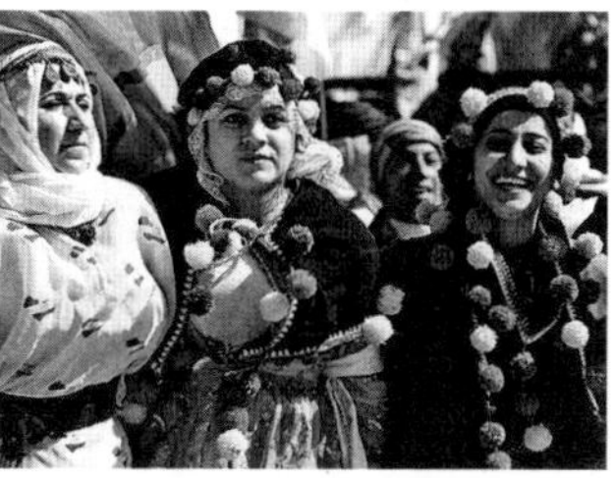

Newroz celebrations, 21 March, 2014, Diyarbakır

We may say that both Ottoman and Turkish women who took part in the formation of the Republic and the new nation were inspired by the first wave feminists, whereas Kurdish women were inspired by the second- and even third-wave feminists, with an emphasis on identity politics and black feminism. They believed that as Kurds they experienced racism and so they compared the Kurdish identity with being Black, and works of Black American feminists, namely bell hooks, inspired them a lot. Both Turkish and Kurdish women's movements have been part of the nationalist processes of nation forming and each had progressive impact on these processes.

It is also interesting to compare the situation in Turkey with feminism and nationalism in former Yugoslavia. The emancipation of women has always been part of the political socialist culture of Yugoslavia, even in the shadow of commonplace domestic violence, sexual harassment, and homophobia. Feminism emerged in Yugoslavia during the eighties. Since then there have been groups of women identifying themselves as feminists and fighting against gender-based inequality and violence. But this is not the entire story. Ethnicity has also become one of the feminist issues with the rise of nationalism, and especially, with women becoming the focus of many nationalist debates. As has often been noted, the 'ethnic war' in the Balkans should not be conceptualized as a *war between ethnic groups*, but rather as a *war that produced ethnic groups*. There were three very important things that feminist did during the war: Firstly, they condemned all the 'nationalisms' as responsible for the war, even though many writers felt and stated that Serbian nationalists bear most of the responsibility for all that happened. Secondly, rape was used as a tool for ethnic cleansing during the war. Feminists defined sexual violence and rape not as a nationalistic tool but as what it was: male violence. Thirdly, they organized practical support for women who faced sexual violence and experienced rape. Feminists in ex-Yugoslavia stood against ethnic-based nationalism, which was part of the disintegration of Yugoslavia. Their discourse was against nationalism in any form. And they were the first to stand against their own nationalism (Serbs against Serbian nationalism, Croatians against Croatian nationalism, Bosnians against Bosnian nationalism, and so on) with the legendary Women in Black demonstrating in Belgrade against sexual violence by Serbian soldiers for years.

The experiences of women living in different parts of ex-Yugoslavia and Kurdish women resonate with one another and there have been contacts through international women's organizations. In 1995, women from ex-Yugoslavia and Turkish and Kurdish women from Turkey participated in the Hippopotamus Women's Camp in Ljubljana, organized by Frauenanstiftung, a German feminist foundation, supported by the Green Party. Their experiences of discrimination, war and sexual violence, as discussed, were very similar. But while Yugoslavian women were against nationalism as a part of the disintegration of their homeland, Kurdish women were taking part in the nation-building process. So, the relation and interaction between feminism and nationalism is not stationary but reaches significance in a historical and political context.

The experience of women in Turkey is distinctive in the sense that the feminist movement heavily impacted on society and politics but also helped influence political movements and shape the changes in society at large. This was at a peak during the eighties and nineties, a period when society tried to erase the effects of the coup d'état. The tension between this effort and the persistence of mainstream politics to silence these effects is useful when looking at Turkey today.

FROM 'PERSONAL IS POLITICAL' TO 'WOMEN IN BLACK'

Merve Elveren and Erman Ata Uncu

Taking their cue from the Western feminist stance of 'personal is political', the second-wave feminists in Turkey proposed to put the oppression and rights of women at the forefront of the collective struggle for a more emancipated society.

The movement had first begun in Istanbul with 'Consciousness-Raising Meetings' that were inspired by the form of activism known by the same name. As a result of the post-coup government's continuing prohibition on public assembly, educated, urban women — the majority of whom had taken part in various political struggles of the seventies — used to gather at their homes, and would discuss forms of patriarchal relations within both private and public spheres, and the repression and discrimination they were subjected to in these contexts. First held in 1981, these spontaneous meetings developed as a reaction to centralist forms of organization, and enabled the women's movement to draw what was considered private into the public sphere. Such new structures of civil society facilitated the transition to street actions.

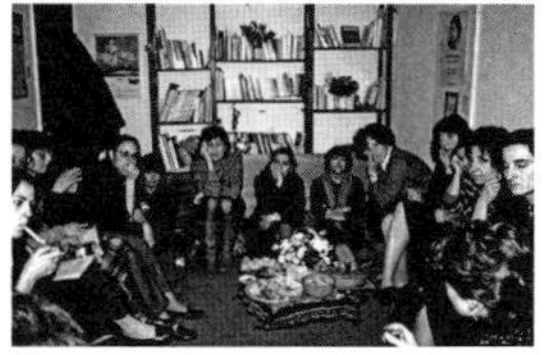

Consciousness-Raising Meeting, 8 March 1984. Archive: Füsun Ertuğ

Considered one of the first examples of civil opposition after the 1980 *coup d'état*, the rally of 'Solidarity Against Domestic Violence' (May 15, 1987) was organized by a feminist group of the period — Kadın Çevresi (Women's Circle) — within the framework of protests against a judge who repeated a common misogynistic phrase, 'Never let a woman go without a foal in her belly and a stick on her back' in a divorce lawsuit. Held in Kadıköy Yoğurtçu

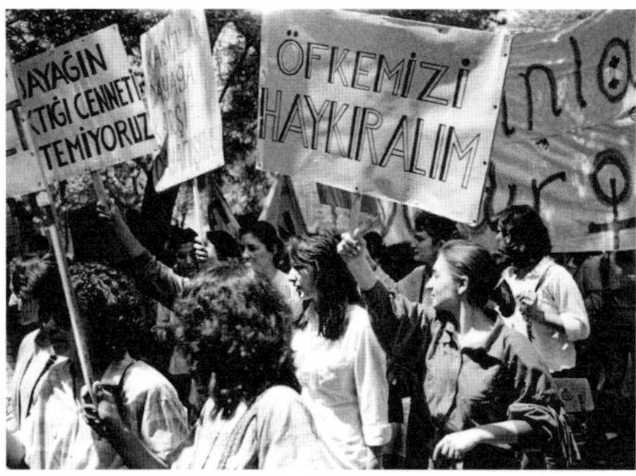

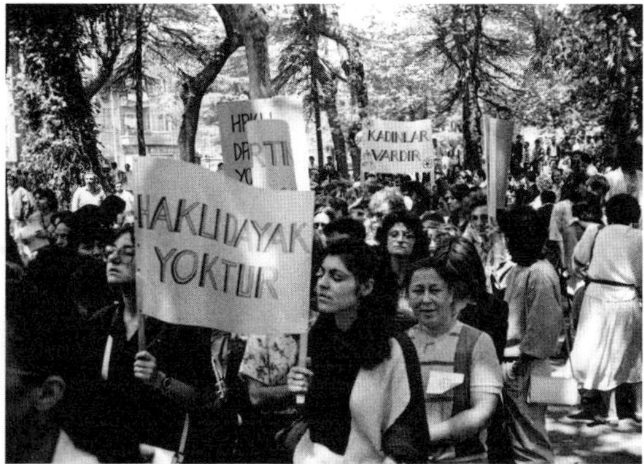

Rally for Solidarity Against Domestic Violence, 17 May 1987, Kadıköy Yoğurtçu Park, Istanbul. Archive: Murat Çelikkan

Park, the rally attracted 3,000 attendees, including the LGBTQ rights activists who were on hunger strike, protesting the police's maltreatment of transgender individuals.

In order to make the transition from private to public, feminists sought new ways of protesting in the following years. As a follow-up to the rally on May 15, an action with the same name was carried out on October 4, 1987, at the Chora Museum. This action can be considered the first of its kind as it was organized in the form of a festival. Women from different age groups and social classes attended the event, which involved talks and performances. Another event, titled 'Modern Woman Temporary Museum', took place the following year on March 3, and featured installations made of everyday objects from women's lives in order to draw attention to the lack of public visibility of women's labour.

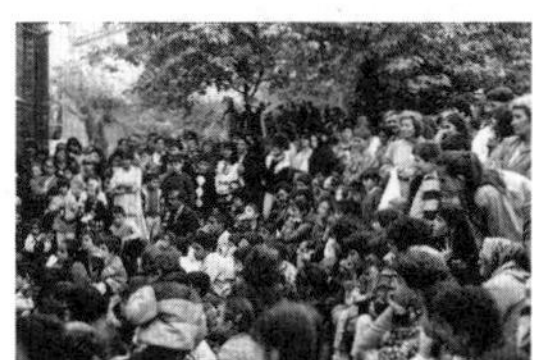

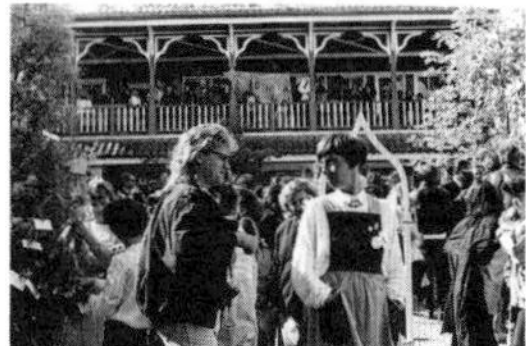

Solidarity Against Domestic Violence, 4 October 1987, Chora Museum, Istanbul, Archive: Füsun Ertuğ

Focusing solely on women's issues for the better part of the decade, second-wave feminism changed course in 1988 with the 'Circular of August 1', a set of new restrictions in prisons, issued by the Ministry of Justice of the Republic of Turkey. On August 9, 1989, in order to voice support for the hunger strikes against the Circular, a feminist group — later referred to by the press as the 'Women in Black' — blocked the traffic in Cağaloğlu Square, and read a press release. Demonstrators demanded the annulment of the August 1 Circular and called upon fellow women to wear black in order to protest the uniform regulation, and upon newspapers to print black columns. From the group that marched on August 10 in the Beyoğlu district, 11 women were detained. These women were arrested on August 12, and then referred to the State Security Court. As the 'Women's Liberation Movement' — the name they adopted in prison — they supported the hunger strikes until the end. Members of Women's Liberation Movement were released on bail at their first hearing on September 7.

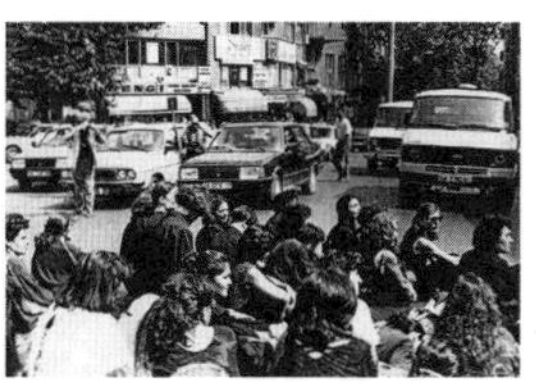

The Women in Black Protest, 9 August 1989. Archive: Murat Çelikkan

The debate on what kind of a political stance feminism should take on issues not specifically related to women was taken up in feminist circles after the action of the Women in Black. These discussions paved the way to new approaches to women's issues, such as Kurdish feminism and Islamic feminism in the nineties.

ISTANBUL KURDISH

TO BE A KURD AND A WOMAN IN THE CITY

What is your native language?

> Kurdish: 81.08%
> Turkish: 12.84%
> Both: 6.08%

Having moved from Nusaybin to Istanbul with her husband ten years ago, Habibe had a very difficult time during the first few years. Because she couldn't speak a word of Turkish. 'I was always at home with my sister-in-law', she says:

> We couldn't leave the house by ourselves. It was almost like we were prisoners. Everything was unfamiliar to us. However, what I've gone through at the hospital was the most upsetting. Accompanied by a Turkish-speaking acquaintance, I was at the Suleymaniye Hospital to give birth. She left me all alone at one point. I was petrified; I couldn't make a single noise. I could neither express myself, nor could they understand what I was suffering from. My child was stillborn.

Who is your spouse?

> Relative or from the same town: 81.08%
> Not Kurdish: 12.40%

A mother of two, 24-year-old Zeynep had moved from Batman to Istanbul ten years ago to marry her relative, whom she had only seen once. After all, he was someone she was acquainted with, not an outsider; they were going to be just fine. As luck would have it, she was wrong. Ten years into her marriage, Zeynep had still not left the house by herself.

Sokak (Street) year 1, no. 9 (22–28 October 1989)

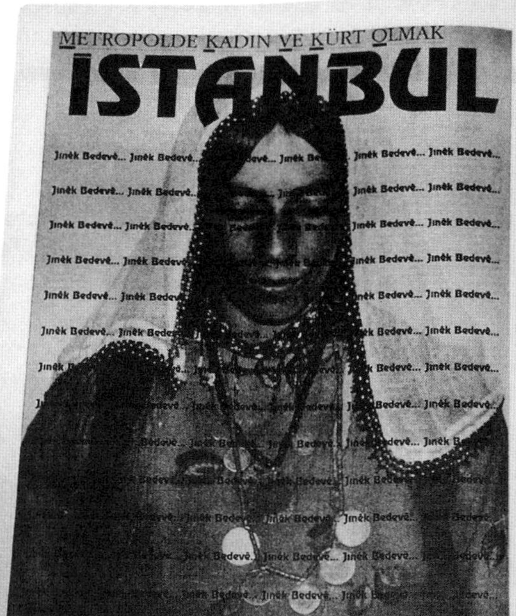
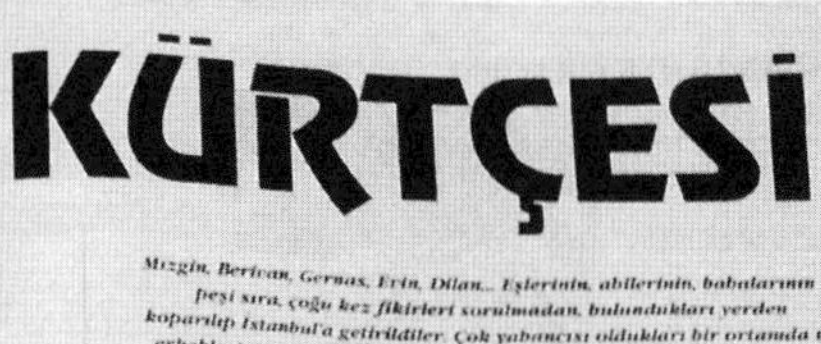
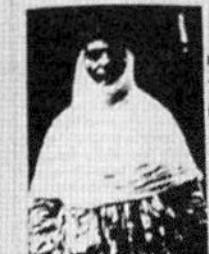
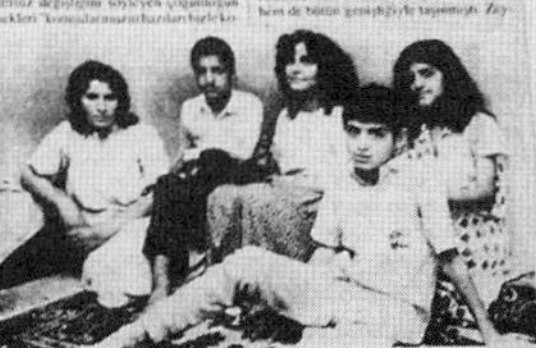

Sokak (Street) year 1, no. 9 (22–28 October 1989). Photo: Mustafa Hazneci

'IRRITATING'
NEW FEMINISM OF THE NINETEEN-EIGHTIES IN LJUBLJANA

Tea Hvala

At the end of nineteen-seventies, feminists in the Socialist Federative Republic of Yugoslavia (SFRY) began organizing separately from the state and separately from their male comrades in the oppositional new social movements. This new generation of feminists insisted on independent organizing, creating women-only public spaces and politicizing 'the women's question'. Their articulation of women's specific interests irritated both sides: Communist leadership because it demonstrated that 'the women's question' was far from being 'solved' along with 'the worker's question', and male activists because it pointed out the high levels of sexism and homophobia in the new social movements.

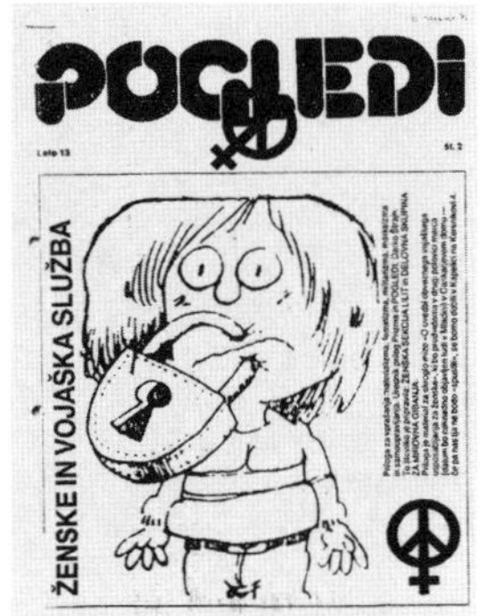

The second issue of *Pogledi* (1986), entitled 'Women and the Military Service' was prepared by Lilit and the Workgroup for Peace Movements in opposition to mandatory military training for women

State policies on women's rights in SFRY were focused on the economic and social emancipation of women as productive workers and mothers. New feminists — 'new' in relation to this Marxist-Leninist programme — believed that women's economic independence was vital for women's liberation but had to be combined with the actual (rather than symbolic) power of women in political decision-making processes and the politicization of the private sphere.

New feminists began to publicly address the political marginalization of women as well as domestic violence against women and children, the imposition of social roles of the worker and mother on women, the double burden of women's productive and reproductive labour, the gender pay gap and the barriers to women's sexual freedom, including homophobia and the legal discrimination of lesbians. State officials did not persecute them, but publicly discredited feminism as an individualistic and bourgeois ideology, imported from the West.

The earliest new feminist groups in Ljubljana, the capital of Socialist Republic of Slovenia, were the Ženska sekcija pri Sociološkem društvu (Women's Section of the Sociological Association, founded in 1984) and Lilit, founded in 1985. Lilit organized a series of women-only public events featuring lectures, discussions, exhibitions, film screenings, theatre performances and dance parties. Paradoxically, Lilit's events were most ridiculed in *Mladina*; the same oppositional weekly that published a series of supplements on feminist and lesbian politics, written by activists

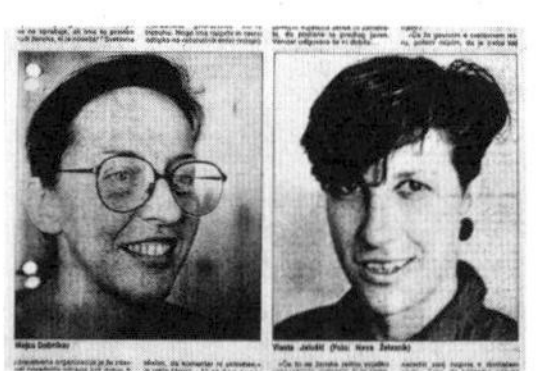

Lilit activists Mojca Dobnikar (left) and Vlasta Jalušič (right), interviewed in *Naša žena* weekly in May 1986

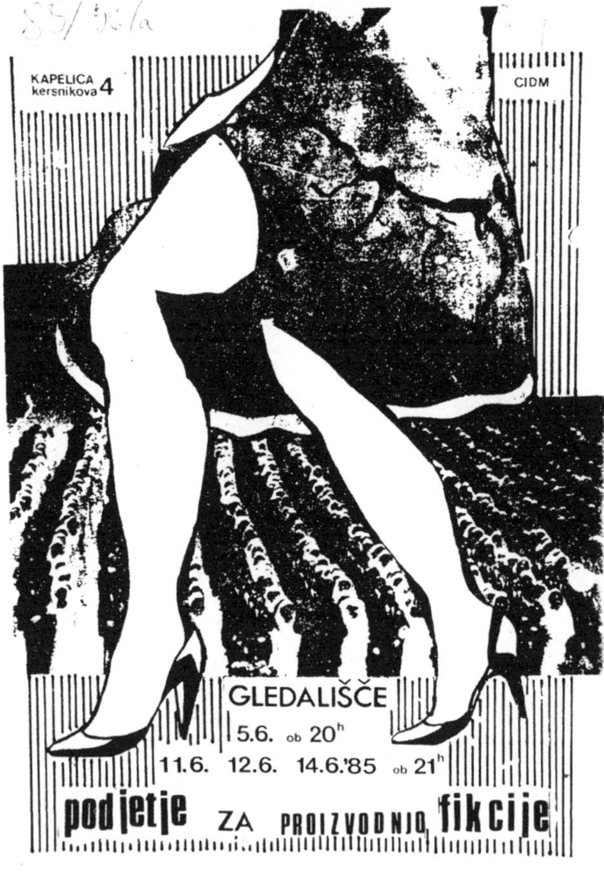

Poster for a performance by the women-only theatre group PPF, or Podjetje za proizvodnjo fikcije (Fiction Production Company, founded in 1983) at Kapelica in K4, Ljubljana on 5 June 1985. Their performance was hosted by Lilit, and according to the invitation, it featured 'an 8mm documentary on the history of the nudist movement. Fans of family films can order copies of the film which features us in the main roles and focuses on didactics, so that it is educational even for the youngest children.' Arhiv: Ženske skupine (Women's Groups Archive), Peace Institute, Ljubljana, documents 85/56a

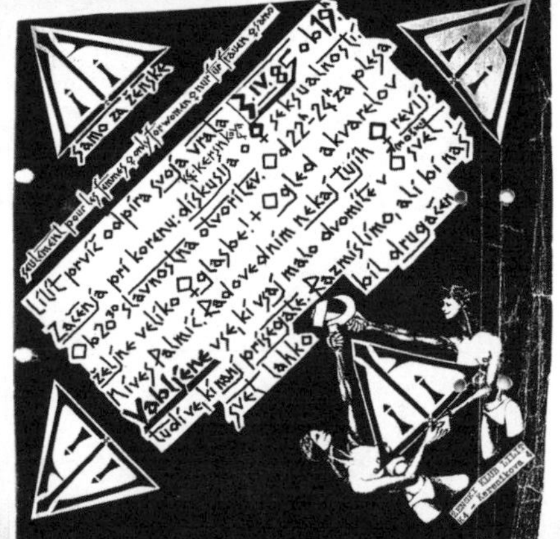

Flyer for the first women-only public event, organized by Lilit in K4, Ljubljana on 3 April 1985. It featured a discussion on women's sexuality, an exhibition of watercolours by Nives Palmić, a display of foreign feminist magazines and music for dancing. The event was open to 'all women who have at least some doubts about the world of men, and also those of you who swear to it. Let's think about whether our world could be different.' Arhiv: Ženske skupine (Women's Groups Archive), Peace Institute, Ljubljana,

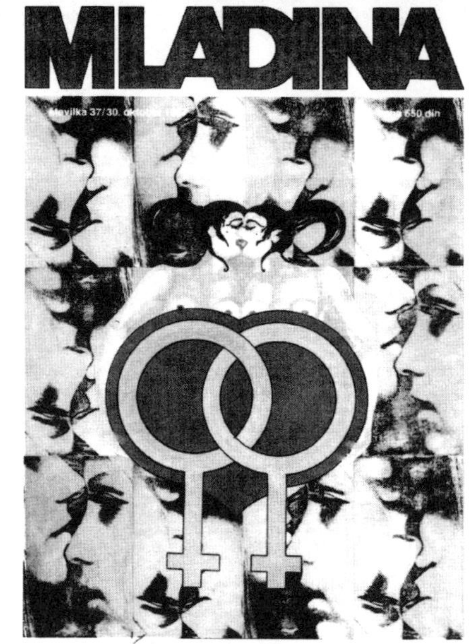

Cover of *Mladina* weekly, containing the supplement 'Ljubimo ženske: Nekaj o ljubezni med ženskami' (We Love Women: Some Words on Love between Women). The preparations for its release on 30 October 1987 encouraged the lesbian members of Lilit to form their own section, called Lezbična Lilit (Lesbian Lilit, or LL). The supplement represents the media coming out of the lesbian movement in Slovenia. Nataša Velikonja and Tatjana Greif: *Lezbična sekcija LL: Kronologija 1987–2012 s predzgodovino* (Lesbian Section LL: Chronology 1987–2012 with Prehistory) (Ljubljana: ŠKUC, 2012), pp. 72–77

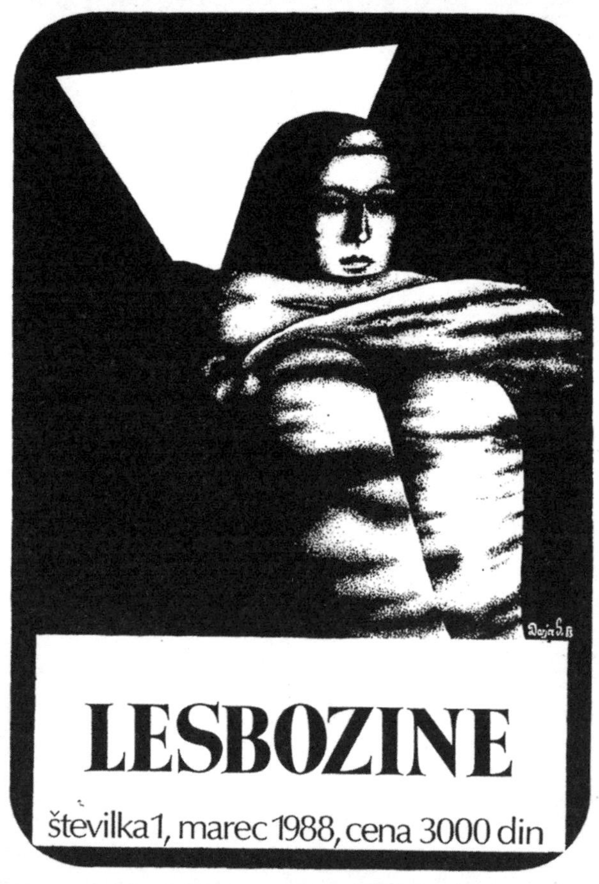

The cover of the first issue of *Lesbozine*, released in March 1988

from Lilit, Lezbična Lilit (Lesbian Lilit or LL, founded within Lilit in 1987) and other groups.

Despite the antifeminist position of the state and the ambivalent attitude of oppositional groups, the number of feminist initiatives in Slovenia grew rapidly. By 1990, there were seven political groups, an SOS phone for victims of domestic violence, a group on spirituality, a self-help group, and several women-only experimental theatre and punk music groups. Together, they formed a diverse feminist movement which — often in alliance with other sections of 'the alternatives of the eighties' — fought against mandatory military service for women, for the demilitarization of Slovenia, for the moratorium on electric power plants in SFRY, for an array of women's rights and against the increasing nationalist instrumentalization of women's reproductive ability. Ironically, abortion on demand, included in the Yugoslav constitution in 1977, was threatened in 1991 when Slovenia declared independence. It remained in the new Slovene constitution only due to the mass protests of the coalition Za izbiro (For Choice), instigated by Ženske za politko (Women for Politics, founded in 1990).

The feminist movement of the nineteen-eighties was 'irritating' and insistent enough to successfully separate women's specific interests from the general (national) interests. By opposing the idea of national unity and unity within the new social movements, it at least temporarily contributed to the 'dehomogenization of politics and the pluralisation of political arena'.[01]

Tea Hvala's text was written during her Arts & Culture Residency, provided by the Ministry of Culture of Slovenia.

01

Vlasta Jalušič, *Kako smo hodile v feministično gimnazijo* (Ljubljana: /*cf., 2002), p. 19.

SOURCES

Arhiv Ženske skupine (Women's Groups Archive), Peace Institute, Ljubljana, documents 85/11, 85/56 and 85/56a.

BIBLIOGRAPHY

Burcar, Lilijana, *Restavracija kapitalizma: Repatriarhalizacija družbe* [Restoration of Capitalism: Repatriarchalization of Society]. Ljubljana: Sophia, 2015.

Erjavec, Aleš, and Marina Gržinić, *Ljubljana, Ljubljana: Osemdeseta leta v umetnosti in kulturi* [Ljubljana, Ljubljana: The Eighties in Art and Culture]. Ljubljana: Mladinska knjiga, 1991.

Hvala, Tea, '"Iritantno": Ločeno delovanje žensk v novem feminizmu osemdesetih' ['"Irritating": Separate Women's Organizing in the New Feminism of the Eighties'], in *Osemdeseta o osemdesetih* [Eighties about the Eighties], edited by Bojana Piškur. Ljubljana: Moderna galerija, 2017, pp. 8–27.

Kako smo hodile v feministično gimnazijo [How we Attended the Feminist High School], edited by Vlasta Jalušič. Ljubljana: /*cf., 2002.

Orel, Barbara, 'Women's Perspective: The Contribution of the Ljubljana Alternative Arts Scene in the 1980s', in: *Performative Gestures, Political Moves*, edited by Katja Kobolt and Lana Zdravković. Ljubljana and Zagreb: City of Women and Red Athena University Press, 2014, pp. 79–96.

Velikonja, Nataša, ed. *20 let gejevskega in lezbičnega gibanja* [20 Years of Gay and Lesbian Movement]. Ljubljana: ŠKUC, 2004, pp. 18–19.

—, and Tatjana Greif. *Lezbična sekcija LL: Kronologija 1987–2012 s predzgodovino* [Lesbian Section LL: Chronology 1987–2012 with prehistory]. Ljubljana: ŠKUC, 2012.

BEING THERE

A VERY PARTIAL TRAVERSE OF EUROPEAN EXHIBITIONS AND AIDS ACTIVISM AT THE END OF THE TWENTIETH CENTURY

Elisabeth Lebovici

I am exposed. I must here use the representational form of the personal pronoun and then let this 'I' take on all the figures that make up a situated narrative of the HIV/AIDS epidemic, an 'exhibitional' narrative that is inseparable from emotional memory. Why? Because it appears that the HIV/AIDS epidemic, at least in its Western form of narrativization, its canonical 'beginning' stage of the eighties–nineties, is precisely that casting of a firsthand I. 'C'est ça',[01] as Louise Bourgeois said, always in French. In the context of the implementation of neoliberal financial capitalism and the advent of a liquid society (as Zygmunt Bauman characterizes the end of the twentieth century),[02] it is the advent of an individual cry, an I undone by the jitters, grief and precariousness, the experience of which — for those who survived — deconstructs authorities and composes them back together, fragmented and unwholly. This is a political I. Its matter is political. So it is in the name of this 'starred' I, the one that Barthes assigned to the 'reader', that a narration opens, a narration which can never exhaust all the other stories, but only be a vulnerable addition to them, while living in the gap between memory and history.

I am in a stupor. For several years, I was at a loss. Whether living with AIDS or not, I was living in AIDS. In its clinical version, stupor is the 'sudden annihilation of life forces, a state of decreased cognitive functioning, sensory capacity, and awareness during which one is still conscious, but only marginally so. Speaking is often difficult, if not impossible.' Such distress was manifest at the beginning of an epidemic, of which nothing was known, except its unbearable morbidity. Invisibility and silence enveloped the people, most them men and very young, disfigured by Kaposi sarcoma, blinded by Cytomegalovirus, emaciated to the bone, weakened by the fever and cough of *Pneumocystis carinii pneumonia*. Prematurity was the condition of their body. Stupor dominated in 1981 when the first articles appeared on life-threatening opportunistic infections and on a malignant 'rare skin cancer', soon called 'gay cancer' (even by the left-wing *Libération* in 1983). It persisted after the epidemic's official entry into the historical consciousness that we now know as AIDS, and even after the concurrent discovery of the causative retrovirus HIV by two teams, one French and one American, in 1983–1984. When HIV testing appeared and indicated the scale of the epidemic in 1985, the media amplified the panic caused by 'an invisible illness' carrying the fear of uncontrolled contagion. Gay men didn't only die from AIDS, they were AIDS. Sexual acts were identified with the foundations of a person's identity — whether homosexual or heterosexual — a shift which took on a heuristic value for the identification of new cases and to formulate hypotheses on the

01

'C'est ça' was the motto of Louise Bourgeois, which introduced the singing version of her poem *Otte* (recording: Brigitte Cornand, 1995).

02

Zygmunt Bauman, *Liquid Modernity: Living in an Age of Uncertainty* (Cambridge: Polity, 2000).

modes of transmission, through the binary: sexual or intravenous. It is precisely because AIDS was suspected of primarily affecting homosexuals and other already stigmatized groups (such as drug users, male and female sexual workers, foreigners, Haitians)[03] that a wave of panic spread over Northern Europe — and especially Paris, where the contamination rate was astronomical — as well as the United States and Australia, before AIDS awareness turned global. The categories defining the prevalence of the epidemic conveyed a number of biased social representations, multiplying the effects of invisibility and ignorance. 'Narratives of AIDS are always problematic, whether they arrive from science or the media.'[04]

I am suffocated. 'Homosexual panic' is an expression that Freud first described in 1920, in his theory on bisexual human development and the ulterior repression of homosexuality in a standardized heterosexual view. In 1985, Eve Kosofsky Sedgwick uses the same term to qualify the reaction that transforms strong ties between men into their opposite, an endemic state of 'homosexual panic'.[05] This panic invades everyone, 'every body' as they say in English. The denial of his HIV status by my friend Patrick Bracco. The denial of his HIV status by my friend Rudy Laurent. To say that you're HIV positive, that you're living with AIDS, is to say that you're dead, 'stripped of all power and control over the actual complex meaning and dignity of an individual's life'.[06] It is to see yourself denied all 'I' since, as Roland Barthes wrote, it is literally 'a staging of *a speech that is impossible insofar as it is speech: I am dead*'.[07] The denial of his HIV status by Michel Foucault: he remained silent until his death. It takes some time for AIDS to be spoken out and exposed, in a place of alienation where language cannot 'assume distress in its very code of distress, i.e. express it'.[08] Language is torn in a double bind between the need to fight the epidemic and the desire to preserve the gains of the seventies sexual liberation, or to keep the idea that the pursuit of sexual pleasure is a key element of self-actualization, without neglecting the care for biological life. HIV/AIDS opens up a crisis of representation. How do you visualize a crisis affecting communities that have been rendered invisible? How do you visualize people who have disappeared, in a world whose panic denies the ties that bind us to them? How do you fight the indirect visualization of HIV/AIDS through newspapers and television, which forward an iconography that isolates the socially and culturally marginalized figure of a martyr, lying down, a carrier of death and bound to die, not to live? On the one hand, a set of acronyms and imagery linked to biomedical technology focuses on the abstract rendering misdescribed as the 'AIDS virus'. A second set of images imprisons the AIDS body in the degrading category of 'victim',

03

The famous Four H: Homosexuals, Heroin users, Haitians, Haemophiliacs, to which a fifth could be added, (w)Hores.

04

David Román, *Acts of Intervention: Performance, Gay Culture, and AIDS* (Bloomington and Indianapolis: Indiana University Press, 1998), p. xix.

05

Eve Kosofsky Sedgwick, *Between Men: English Literature and Male Homosocial Desire* (New York: Columbia University Press, 1985).

06

Simon Watney, *Policing Desire, Pornography, AIDS and the Media* (London: Cassell, 1987), p. 22.

07

Roland Barthes, 'Textual Analysis of a Tale by Edgar Poe', *Poe Studies* 10, no. 1 (June 1977), 10, pp. 1–12, www.eapoe.org/pstudies/ps1970/p1977101.htm.

08

Jean-Luc Nancy, *The Inoperative Community* (Minneapolis and London: University of Minnesota, 1991), pp. 35–36, cited by John Paul Ricco, *The Logic of the Lure* (Chicago and London: The University of Chicago Press, 2002), p. 33.

which it is then only too easy to see as the visual consequence of homosexual desire. Simon Watney has described such media images as a 'diptych'.[09] This all pertains to artistic categories such as abstraction and figuration, which the art world continues to discuss, asserting through exhibitions the renewal of figuration ('A New Spirit in Painting', Royal Academy, London, 1981), the return of abstract painting ('Tableaux abstraits', Villa Arson, Nice, 1986), or 'the picture after the last picture' ('Das Bild nach dem letzten Bild', Galerie Metropol, Wien, 1991).

I am (in)visible. In Europe, the first voluntary community-based organizations are confronted with different models of action, depending on whether or not they make their community footing visible. Founded in 1982, the Terrence Higgins Trust in London asserts itself as a gay-rooted association, that offers caring and support to people with AIDS and provides a credible source of information. In France, where the so-called Republican model excludes criteria such as ethnicity, race, sexual orientation or religion, AIDES (the not-for-profit organization created in 1984 by Daniel Defert, Michel Foucault's partner, together with Frédéric Edelmann and Jean-Florian Mettetal) distanced itself on the contrary from gay and lesbian activism. The organisation models itself on the Groupe d'information sur les prisons, drawing a parallel between the moral code weighing on those who are called prisoners and the moral code weighing on those who are called the sick: both are viewed as dangerous individuals and both are prevented from speaking of their sexuality and their body. 'The sick as the new social reformers', according to AIDES. The French organization stipulates its universalism in its efforts to produce a discourse with the understanding that HIV/AIDS is not particular to a pre-specified community. So the dilemma resides in making invisible the link tying in your personal experience, activism and sexual orientation or, on the contrary, insisting on the issues that the epidemic raises for a purported homosexual community, with the risk of defining 'the gay community' as a single factitious bloc. And another observation: the invisibility of cis women (at least those who are not mothers) and of trans people when judging the effectiveness of drug development, the range of secondary effects and opportunistic illnesses, the devising of the possible interactions between therapies, or the clinical trial designs, which are then thought of in male heteronormative terms. Lesbians in particular are eradicated from prevention protocols as — this is well known — they do not fuck and do not inject drugs intravenously. It is as an act of intervention that ACT UP, created in 1987, portrays itself as a 'coalition' of diverse individuals 'united in anger and committed to direct action to end the AIDS crisis'.[10]

09

Simon Watney, 'Photography and AIDS' (1988), reprinted in *Practices of Freedom* (Durham: Duke University Press, 1994), p. 71.

10

www.actupny.org.

If visibility is at stake, then 'the profound significance of visual imagery ... largely determines most people's perceptions of all aspects of the epidemic, from health promotion to questions of discrimination, prejudice, care, treatment and service provision',[11] as the British theorist and activist Simon Watney stated in 1992. It is significant that the social function assigned to artists in the early times of AIDS is that of visionary 'shamans' or '*passeurs*' (border-guides). In 1989, 'Magiciens de la terre' gathered a globalized colloquium of 'artist-magicians' at the Centre Pompidou and the Grande Halle de la Villette. And in 1992, Kassel's documenta brought together in its nerve centre a congress of spiritual white males (David, Ensor, Giacometti, Byars), where *Wirtschaftswerte*, Beuys' backroom of economic values, took pride of place, together with the last painting of René Daniëls before he suffered a stroke in 1987. Jan Hoet's documenta delegated to younger artists a greater physicality in their interventions, be it Cady Noland, Zoe Leonard (who changed my life as a critic), Robert Gober with Christopher Wool, or Matthew Barney. In 1994 at the Tate, the British critic Stuart Morgan presented his ultimate exhibition, 'Rites of Passage', which gave visibility to artists, such as Pepe Espaliú and Hamad Butt, who had died of AIDS (Morgan himself passed in 2002). Borrowing his title from the Dutch anthropologist Arnold van Gennep, who used it to qualify critical moments in human life, Morgan's show considered the artists 'as passeurs, priests (perhaps) of that secular religion that art has become'. He devised its display as a journey through light and dark, uncovering the worrying blood red glows of the precious secretions sculpted by Louise Bourgeois.

Colour as a subject, a character, a persona. Colour against the tyranny of images. There is nothing else to see in *Blue*, the film by Derek Jarman first shown at the Venice Biennale in 1993 (same year as *Philadelphia*, the Hollywood melodrama). *Blue* is a 76-minute immersion in a blue screen that takes you to a place where all art fails. It is the story of a filmmaker who becomes blind and whose visual field then extends beyond reason, the story of the unrepresentability of AIDS, the story of a person called Blue. *Blue* is 'a film, a painting, a radio play, a soundtrack, a gay autobiography, and a book'.[12] Derek Jarman finds a form for the 'late film' idea, in the meaning that Adorno gives to 'late', that of a catastrophe, rather than a redemptive resolution.

I am angry. A 'total social phenomenon', AIDS turns society upside down with its 'postmodern' swagger and cynicism. The scientific-medical establishment is negligent. Hospitals are once again places where people end up dying, their bodies hidden from sight. Simply making your body manifest is to put up a fight.

11

Simon Watney, 'Short-term Companions: AIDS as Popular Entertainment', in *A Leap in the Dark: AIDS, Art and Contemporary Cultures*, ed. Allan Klusacek and Ken Morrison (Montreal: Véhicule Press, 1992), p. 152.

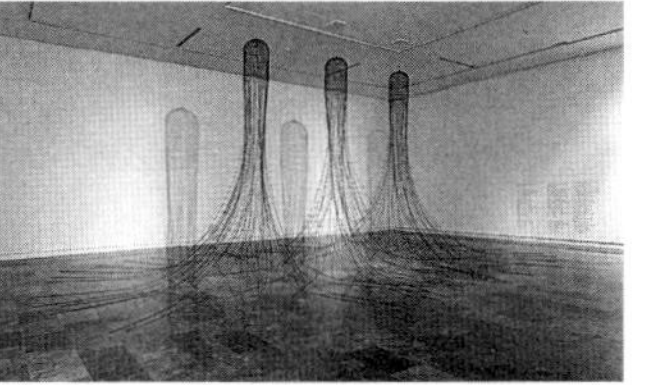

Pepe Espaliú, *Sin título (Tres jaulas)* (Untitled, [Three Cages]), 1992

12

Tim Lawrence, 'AIDS, the Problem of Representation, and Plurality in Derek Jarman's Blue', *Social Text* 52/53 (Autumn/Winter 1997), pp. 241–264, URL: www.jstor.org/stable/466743.

The vitality of bodies is a sign of struggle, when these burst into the public space. In the Autumn of 1989, in Paris, the HIV-positive members of ACT UP-Paris start running through the streets, yelling 'We don't want to die'. Grief, despair, the feeling of having nothing to lose are a unifying emotional cement and its enactment calls for empowerment: ACT UP decries all at once the havoc wreaked by a dominant organization of sex and gender, that planted the seeds of the epidemic by authorizing the inaction of the State — whether from the right or the left: in France, it is mostly the Parti socialiste which is then in power —, the reticence of the medical profession and the quasi-general indifference. AIDS politics calls attention to the dispersal of fluxes of power throughout all the cracks and crevices of the social system, that Foucault has called 'the microphysics of power'.[13] The dramatization of such politics involves insurgent bodies, intruding in governmental or supranational agencies, at drug manufacturers plants, in offices, hospitals and schools. Waking up a Minister at home to the sound of foghorns, throwing blood at an official in a department of health services, or ashes at a cocktail party of an insurance company.[14] To a gay body 'written by science' and constructed as an object, activism opposes AIDS experts claiming their knowledge and asserting their credibility through the first person.

In 1988–1989, Berlin's Realismus Studio collective gathered the pieces of anger together in an exhibition, the first in Germany and probably in Europe to fight against AIDS. 'Vollbild AIDS. Eine Kunstausstellung über Leben und Sterben' (Full-Screen AIDS. An Art Exhibition on Living and Dying)[15] is organized by the gay activist curator Frank Wagner. First it deplores the dead: the made up photographs of Rolf von Bergmann, a Berlin artist of the Junge Wilde and a close friend of Salomé (also in the exhibition); the *Portraits in Life and Death* by Peter Hujar, and the photograph of Peter Hujar on his deathbed by David Wojnarowicz. As importantly, the *membra disjecta* from the main body of the exhibition are scattered in a Berlin that is yet to be reunified. The AIDS posters of General Idea are disseminated throughout the city, while the four letters of the word RIOT, which constitute a fierce response by the collective Gran Fury, are adapted to the colours of the West German flag. In addition to the (dis)assembled artists,[16] Frank Wagner moved two 'inaugural' installations, which testify to the implication of art in the concreteness of anti-AIDS activism. The first, which occurred at the Dia Art Foundation in New York and was reinstalled in Berlin, is *AIDS and Democracy, A Case Study*, by Group Material. It transforms the exhibition space into a discussion forum, a medium that addresses on the spot both the experiences and discourses of the social crisis relating to AIDS, and the failings of its representations. 'Group Material created

13

Steven Epstein, *Impure science. AIDS, Activism, and the Politics of Knowledge* (Berkeley, Los Angeles, London: University of California Press, 1996), p. 4.

14

These actions are well described in Robin Campillo's feature film, *120 battements par minute*, 2017, Grand Prix at the Festival de Cannes 2017.

15

16 December 1988—13 February 1989. The exhibition travelled to Lausanne (Switzerland) in a revised version in 1990.

16

Thomas Bayrle, Hajo Corsten, Juan Davila, Frank Dornseif, Rinaldo Hopf, Astrid Klein, Attila Richard Lukacs, Marcel Odenbach, Martin von Ostrowski, Marcel Otto, Salomé, Jan-Michael Sobottka, Sage Sohier, Ingo Taubhorn and Rainer Wahnsinn.

"other spaces," or heterotopias, in Michel Foucault's sense of places where "real" sites of culture are "simultaneously represented, contested and inverted."'[17] In the same manner, *Let The Record Show*, another installation produced in this case at the New Museum in New York by a group of militants and artists that is not yet called Gran Fury at the time, is moved, redimensioned and updated in the window of Büchergilde Gutenberg, on Berlin's Wittenbergplatz. It shows the effigies of Ronald Reagan, Margaret Thatcher, Peter Gauweiler, and other politicians who are deemed guilty of inaction, in front of a photographic enlargement of the Nuremberg trials, under a lit neon banner with the inverted pink triangle of homosexual deportation and the equation Silence = Death. Neither depicting AIDS, nor visualizing its symptoms, this will become the image most closely associated with AIDS activism. The exhibition space, here the city of Berlin up to its wall, is thus transformed into public spaces for information, education, action and reaction. The art consists in making a public space emerge in which sexual and health-related questions become the object of debate and political issues, thereby shaping a counter-public.

I am desperate. 1991. The filmmaker Lionel Soukaz, who abandoned filmmaking when he was diagnosed HIV positive in the mid-eighties, starts his video diary *Annales* (Annals). He shoots the spread of HIV in his life, which is taken up fulltime by it, as are the lives of activists. *Annales* becomes the daily course of the actions, interventions, demonstrations, reunions, seminars, openings, and also the frolicking, that construct the I of activism. The flow of media images of AIDS is also included in the private sphere of the journal. Television in particular is shown as a paradoxical site, private in its viewing, but public in its duties and responsibilities. Soukaz films AIDS programmes on television, but he also records the gaze of his sick lover watching the screen. Nothing represents him in this fiction of a unified, consensual, national audience, which categorically excludes people who, like him, are living with AIDS. The video journal *Annales* is an archive unlike any other. It carries the intimate referent of the singular, lived experience within representations. Concomitantly, similar upheavals occur in most forms of artistic expression: the notion of intimacy (and the Lacanian notion of 'extimacy') has settled into the cultural space. As witnessed by the abundance of danced 'solos' and self-performances. As witnessed by personal diaries, which become a social phenomenon that is studied, exchanged and published.[18] As witnessed by 'house music' — the appropriated, 'sampled', mixed, computer-tinkered sounds — as the most significant sound phenomenon of the last twenty years of the twentieth century. As witnessed by the intimist images — asso-

17
Michel Foucault, 'Of Other Spaces, Heterotopias' (1967), quoted by Alison Green, 'Citizen Artists: Group Material', www.afterall.org/journal/issue.26/citizen-artists-group-material.

18
As witnessed already by the publications of Philippe Lejeune (*Le Pacte autobiographique* [Paris: Seuil, 1975]; *Moi aussi* [Paris: Seuil, 1986], etc.) and the work of Catherine Viollet — as well as by their seminars 'Literary Correspondence' and 'Genesis and Autobiography' — gathered in the ITEM research group (CNRS/ENS) since 2012.

ciated with a painstaking examination of daily life and banality — that are endemic and purulent in plastic artwork and cinema. As witnessed by the emergence of a new literary genre, labelled (in France at least) *autofiction*. As witnessed by exhibition sites that insist, as in 'Chambres d'amis' (Guest Rooms) in Ghent (1986), on the entanglement between public and private space, and as also witnessed by the blossoming of 'in apartment' exhibitions ('Pour vivre heureux, vivons cachés' [To Live Happily, Let's Live Concealed], Nevers, 1984). All these forms sketch a scenography of the intimate: as though you also need to break with the supposed neutrality of the performance place to draw up a new configuration in which the boundaries between outside and inside, and private domain and public space, are made even more porous, in line with what the HIV status and epidemic did themselves. With greater or smaller degrees of censorship and difficulty, the pathology forced out into the open space previously inadmissible words and discourses on sex and intimacy that had been kept under lock and key. Conversely, it also legitimized an ever increasing incursion into intimate and emotional relationships. Which probably explains the blossoming of a science fiction 'I', who does not know who they are, has forgotten all specific forms of life and is constructing themself within the story. It is through science fiction that this 'I' unravels all binarisms and attempts to unify and identify, in order to work on a cyborg 'I', a vampire 'I' that 'defies the stories of racialization and homophobia that still feed the pandemic nowadays'.[19]

Guillaume Dustan publishes *In My Room* in 1996.[20] The bedroom in question is not a reassuring place of one's own. It could be the dark corner of a bar, or a backroom, which become deviations from the bedroom, or deviation-bedrooms. Under the rule established by the author, the narrator is not looking so much for unity of place, as for unity of the sexual and homosexual activity that takes place there. This is what describes the plasticity of the body, since it is this activity which is the theatre of an experience of the self, in which language carries each 'blow'. Language rushes into the breach required for any utterance of the self, creating through its distortions and tensions what the philosopher Leo Bersani[21] attempted to define as the specificity of anal (gay) sex: 'Because a hole is bottomless. A hole only gets bigger.'[22] The orifice is the space of a physical impulse. Dustan's intimate disobedience is translated by indifference towards the 'safe sex' edict, which is also the edict of gay responsibility. This tension and distortion in which Dustan involves language expands in the subsequent volumes of his self-proclaimed 'auto-pornography', *Je sors ce soir* (I'm Going out Tonight) (1997), *Plus fort que moi* (Can't Help Myself) (1998), and so on and so forth.

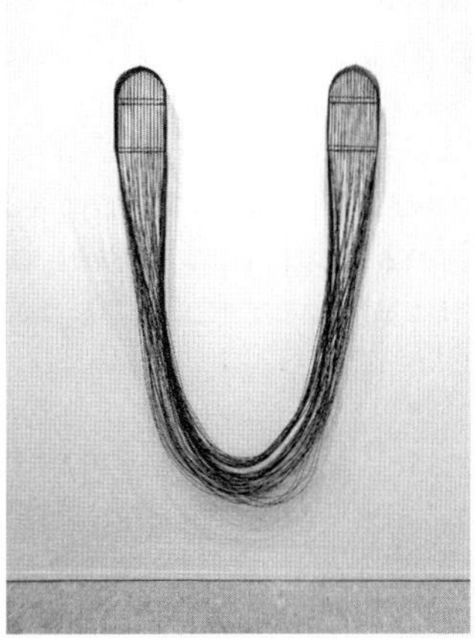

Pepe Espaliú, *Luisa II*, 1993

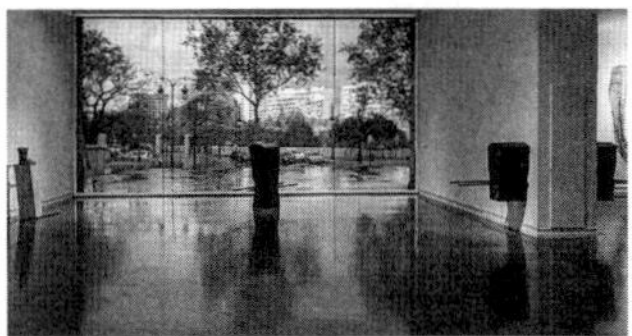

Exhibition view 'Círculo Íntimo: El mundo de Pepe Espaliú', Centro de Creación Contemporánea de Andalucía, Córdoba, 2017

19

We note the explicit vampire figure as an HIV-positive subject in a number of US series, for instance *True Blood*, created in 2008.

20

Guillaume Dustan, *Œuvres* 1 (Paris: POL, 2013); Guillaume Dustan, *In My Room*, translated by Brad Rumph (London: Serpent's Tail, 1998).

21

Leo Bersani, 'Is the Rectum a Grave?', *October* 43 (Winter 1987), special issue: *AIDS: Cultural Analysis/Cultural Activism*, pp. 197–222, and 'The Gay Outlaw', *Homos* (Cambridge: Harvard University Press, 1995), ch. 4, pp. 113–181.

22

Guillaume Dustan, *Génie Divin* (Paris: Balland, 2001), p. 236.

My practice feeds my theory: Michel Foucault is both the first public figure in France to die of AIDS, and the one whose oeuvre constitutes the most precious reference to grasp, frame and resist the disease.[23] The AIDS epidemic 'performs' a series of questions — on the government of bodies, the relation between knowledge and power, biopowers and the disciplines of standardization — which develop his thinking, from *The Birth of the Clinic* (1963) to *The History of Sexuality, Vol. 3: The Care of the Self* (1984). Similarly, those who claim allegiance to a pro-sex feminist trend, such as Gayle Rubin, Teresa de Lauretis, Donna Haraway, Judith Butler or Jack Halberstam in the United States, but also Chicana lesbians such as Gloria Anzaldúa, and black lesbians such as Audre Lorde, grant anti-AIDS activism a large part of its theory, from the *Epistemology of the Closet* to 'gender performativity', and so forth. Conversely, these authors explicitly manifest their will to link up militant theory and practice, and pay ongoing attention to the militant implications of their writings. These are replayed by Europe's 'queer multitudes', the successors of Guattari and Deleuze, and of Monique Wittig and Rosi Braidotti as well, who take inspiration from anarchist cultures to imagine a multitude of bodies: 'transgenders, men without penises, wulf dykes, cyborgs, butch women, lesbian faggots'[24] which appeal to so many political uses. However, the performative dimension of the term 'queer' seems to have become diluted with regard its capacity to reveal changes in the organization of sexual practices and the discourses that index them. In 2012, a conference was organized in Vienna, in which the circumstances of the translation, import and export of queer policies within different European spaces were examined, even calling into question the word queer itself, considered 'theoretical tofu' by some, or else an elitist, Western, or white term, or yet again, a term neglectful of power relations within sexual minorities, by others. Along with an ultimately very technical range of words in what became the discourse of the global struggle against HIV/AIDS, a language activism also developed. Experimented particularly in non-Anglo-Saxon languages, it expresses the importance of action in the area of names and naming, in order to be the actor of your own utterance, and to give free rein to your imagination while conveying a malaise vis-à-vis ordinary language and reality.[25]

I am an acronym. HIV/AIDS[26] is constructed as acronyms, a set of initials further simplified by eliminating the periods after each letter. In France, an analogous acronym, SIDA, later written sida, was created, while the Russians adopted the acronym SPID. Acronyms are everywhere. In the RH (weekly assemblies) of ACT UP (Action Coalition To Unleash Power), 'everybody talks in acronyms … with

23

Philippe Mangeot, 'sida: angles d'attaque', *Vacarme* 29 (2 October 2004), www.vacarme.org/article456.html.

24

Beatriz ('Paul B.') Preciado, 'Multitudes queer. Notes pour une politique des "anormaux"', *Multitudes* 2, no. 12 (2003), p. 17–25, www.cairn.info/revue-multitudes-2003-2-page-17.htm.

25

Marie-Émilie Lorenzi, '"Queer," "transpédégouine," "torduEs," between adaptation and reclamation, the dynamics of translation at the heart of language creations in queer feminist activism', *GLAD!* no. 2, 2017, www.revue-glad.org/462.

26

HIV: Human Immunodeficiency Virus; AIDS: Acquired Immune Deficiency Syndrome, or Acquired Immunodeficiency Syndrome.

a frenzy to bring about each week a new barbaric name, whether it is a government agency, a new coalition, a new term in the medical jargon'.[27] ART, Antiretroviral Therapies used in HAART, highly active antiretroviral therapy, such as 3TC, AZT, d4T, ddC, RTV, SQV, TDF, ZDV or INSTI, integrase strand transfer inhibitors, all come in acronyms. MSM (in French HSH), men who have sex with men, is a category coined in 1994 in AIDS epidemiology, choosing identity-free terms to reflect the idea that behaviours, not identities, place individuals at risk for HIV infection and that sexual practices cannot be interpreted as carrying fixed meanings. Electronic music counts its BPM (beats per minute).[28] In 2000, the acronym KABP, a methodology used in social science studies to measure the knowledge, attitude, behaviour and practice of specific communities in relation to HIV/AIDS, became a legendary party in Paris.

I am an archive. When you want to retranscribe, or recompose public space in the struggle against HIV/AIDS, you are inevitably confronted with the question of what remains, that is to say, the question of material culture. Originating from the bedrooms, where a few trinkets, a few souvenirs, a few images were quickly taken before the biological family of the deceased friend/lover arrived and raided the place; originating also from the boxes of the organizations or collectives in which were thrown, before a move or disbanding, the posters, stickers, flyers, badges, T-shirts, banners, newspaper clippings, magazines, photographs, videos, sound recordings, minutes of meetings, and so forth — all this flotsam that made up their daily lives; or yet again these things that were ripped off the walls, or stolen from the pavement before the passage of the dumpster truck — yes, they all make up as much the affective as the material archives of AIDS. Some were transferred to the archives of a university (The Downtown Collection, Fales Library, New York University), or a museum (Schwules Museum, Berlin; Mucem, Marseille), or else forced a national narrative to open up to countercultures (as at the Archives nationales, Paris and Pierrefitte); in other cases, spaces were built for them (ONE archives, Los Angeles, Visual AIDS, New York), or they travel around nomadically (The Museum of Transology, from the United Kingdom). Others, more frequently that you think, have been integrated into the collections of museums of modern art and are governed by the auctorial and dating logic of their inventories. Which leads to this paradoxical concern that consists in wanting to preserve their ephemeral character and their resistance to the linearity of a historical discourse, which the HIV/AIDS epidemic plunged into the realm of political emergency.

27

Didier Lestrade, *ACT UP: Une histoire* (Paris: Denoël, 2000), p. 61.

28

Cf. *120 beats per minute*, the title of the feature film retracing ACT UP-Paris' struggle against AIDS, 2017.

PEPE ESPALIÚ, *CARRYING*, 1992, PERFORMANCE

Lola Hinojosa

Art in Spain in the seventies is associated with the historiography of a kind of anti-Franco militancy, indivisible from the experimentation of mediums and the dematerialization of the art object, whereas in the eighties it appears linked to colourist and non-ideological frivolity. This paradigmatic change is intersected by the Transition and an attempt at democratic consolidation after the end of the dictatorship. The ensuing process of euphoria and disillusionment would characterize a period with a contradictory crossover of screams and silence, and the major sexual awakening of Spanish society and its cultural representation contrasted with the murky visibility of AIDS in artistic representations — even 'official' LGTB activists tepidly addressed a disease they interpreted at that early stage as a stigma that was better left in silence.

The output of artist Pepe Espaliú developed almost exclusively within the progression of the eighties due to his premature death from AIDS in 1993. This arc, albeit brief, primarily comprised a broad corpus of drawings and sculptures, with the hermetic nature of a large number of these pieces defining Espaliú as a self-engrossed artist, along the formalist lines that were predominant in that decade. Nevertheless, the conceptualisation of his artistic practice is inseparable from *Carrying* (1992), a later piece in his oeuvre which sharply contrasts with the rest of his work in both representation and conception.

Distanced from objectual production, this action was executed in a public space, in a journey through the centre of San Sebastián, whereby different sets of people, in twos, made a human chain to transport Espaliú's 'sick body' without it touching the ground. The context of the performance, so often disregarded in these analyses, is at the heart of its radicalness: the invitation to carry out a pedagogical workshop in Arteleku, an art centre which was the venue for the close-knit collaboration between the artist and attendees, who conceived the content and participated in the performance with other friends and activists. *Carrying* was repeated shortly after in Madrid, although, in contrast, the arms that carried Espaliú belonged to figures from the world of culture and politics, with a great deal of the Spanish press covering this symbolic journey.

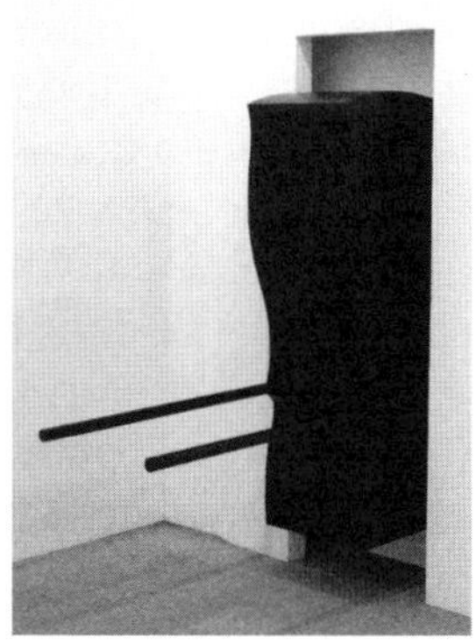

Pepe Espaliú, *Carrying XI*, 1992, patinated iron sheet, 49×51,5×140 cm. MNCARS Collection

From that point, the artist became known as an agent who managed to fight to give AIDS visibility as a disease that 'affects everyone' and who spoke out against the idleness of new democratic institutions, both in politics and health care. The contention of the work — with a vulnerable Espaliú, a self-designated artist 'deprived of hope' — built an image divested of any (homo)sexual content, helping the message to reach even the most conservative layers of Spanish society.

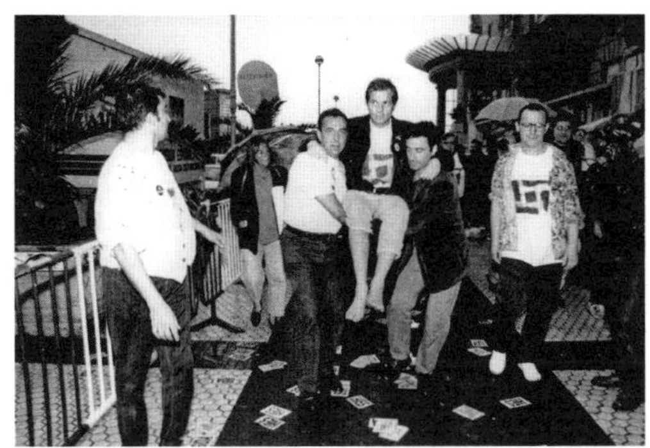

Pepe Espaliú, *The Carrying Society*, 1992, performance, San Sebastián. © Arteleku

This huge media resonance, however, had adverse effects on the understanding of the work's source. To understand the poetic scope and hybrid nature of *Carrying*, Espaliú's personal writings — a journey into withdrawal — must be considered, but without overlooking their quality as a collective piece. Espaliú's fascination with *Semana Santa* in Andalusia runs through these writings and *Carrying*, as does the iconography of lacerated saints, associated with homosexuality and the joyful and painful Barcelona of Jean Genet or the painter Ocaña, in addition to the interest towards Masotta and his 'art of the media'.

The title came into being in New York, the city where he discovered he had AIDS and heard the Hispanic collective saying 'caring' with such a pronounced 'r' sound that it seemed to allude to 'carrying'. Soon after he would make various sculptures with that name, and with a direct analogy to the subsequent action. The paradoxical contrast between the abstraction of those semi-totemic objects and the return to the real body as an active subject of performance determined Espaliú's opening out into to a new line of work that would leave its mark on the nineties. This was based on the re-politicization of the artistic context, on the resurgence of performance alluding to the genealogy of artists who politically experimented with it in the seventies, and on the rise of queer activism in the Spanish state.

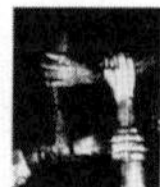

Yolanda Forcada, Juan Albin, Manu Muniategiandikoetxea, Pepa Arguiano, Jorge González, Josu Sarasua, Gabi Calparsoro, Xanti Eraso, Gemma Intxausti, J. R. Amondarain, Maite Sagarzazu, Oier Villar, Xabi Arribas, Mikel Bergara, Belén Moreno, Ander Alkorta, Txaro Fantalba, Joana Cera, Pedro Pertejo, Javier Balda, Pepe Calvo, Ricardo Catania, Mireia Sentís, Fernando Luna, Joaquín Espaliú, José Miguel Cortés, Itziar Uriasun y Cia., Garka Eizaguirre, Iñaki Rodríguez, Manel Clot, Juan Vicente Aliaga, Miguel Fernández Cid, Mª Fé, Juan Muñoz, Julián Bravo, Heike Klupman, Salah Saouli, Ute Hofritz, ACT UP, Nekane Elizondo, Miguel López, Pello Mitxelena, Josune Mateos, Jordi Riba, Juan Carrasco, Juan Fco. Murillo, Aitor Bergara, Prudencio Irazabal, Maitena Garbizu, Alberto Acha, ACT-UA, Luis Inza, Koko Rico, Koldo Aginagalde, Oscar Agüesa, Pepe Cobo, Frank Iturbe, Ismael Manterola, Argi Aizpurua, Ricardo Torre, Albaro Bazako, Javier Lizaur, Javier San Martín, Jose Gorritxo, Silvia Sanchez, Izaskun Insausti, Fer Azpitarte, Julen Atorrasagasti, Jon Mikel Uribarren, Ander Hormazuri, Esti Esteibar, Xabier Laka, Ros Garrido, Iñaki, Cristina Iglesias, Leopoldo Mª Panero, Dirk Eicken, Ute Wriss-Leader, Roswitha Paetel, Aitzpea Iribar, Ros Segues; Foto: Ricardo Iriarte

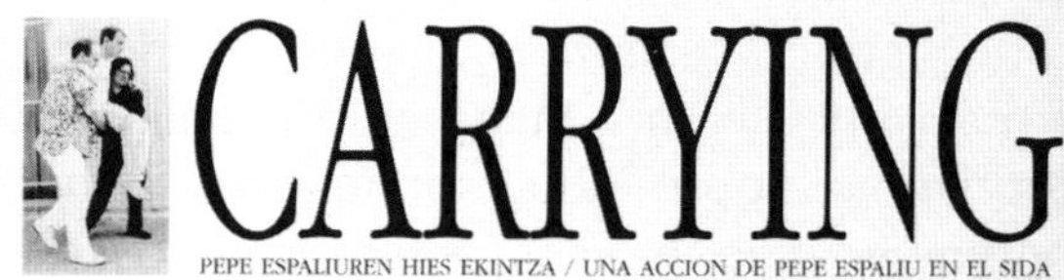

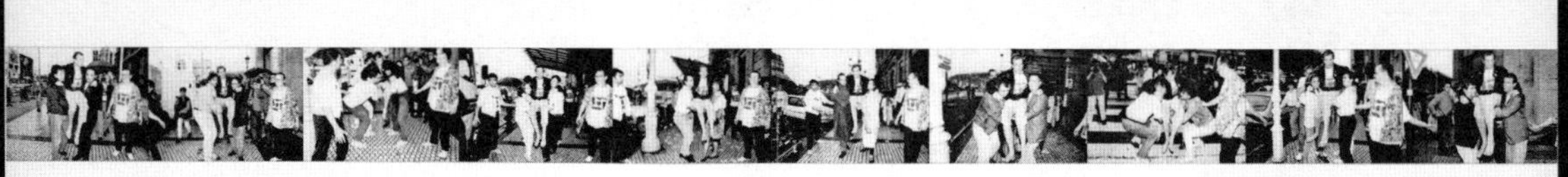

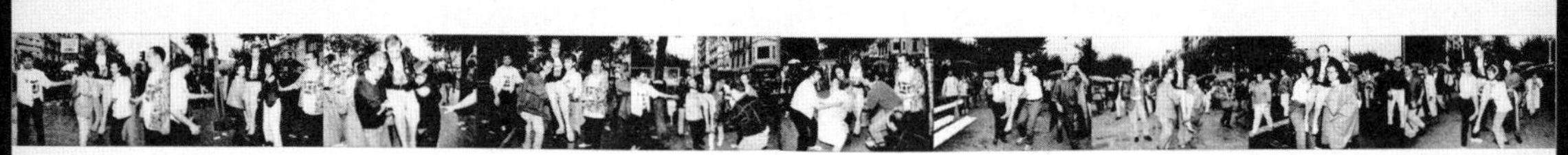

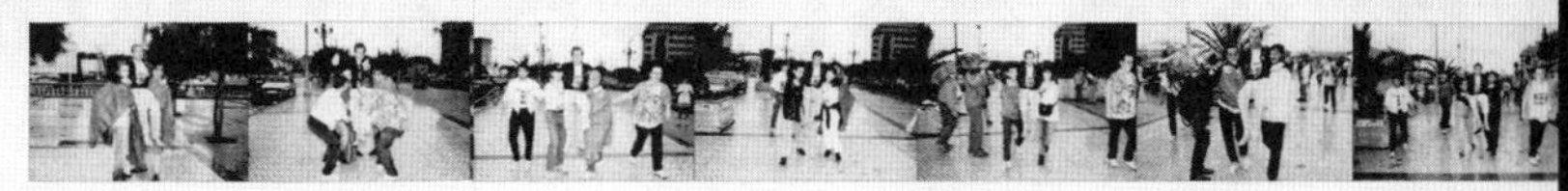

SIDA

La herida es una enfermedad de la piel
como si sólo lo que hay no bastara para hundirnos
y construir la poesía como una enfermedad de la piel

Leopoldo María Panero

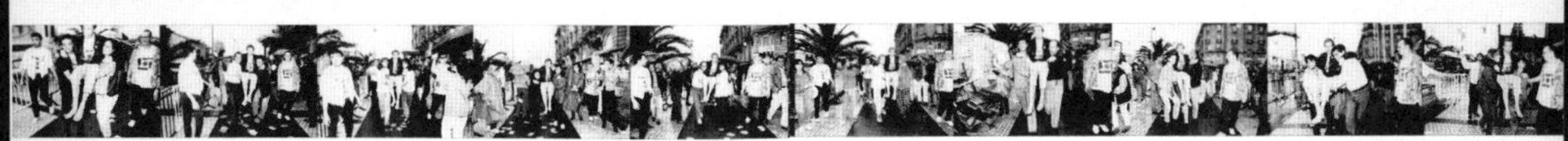

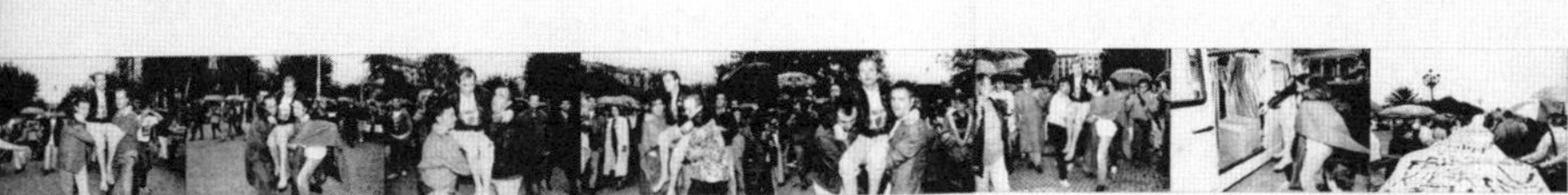

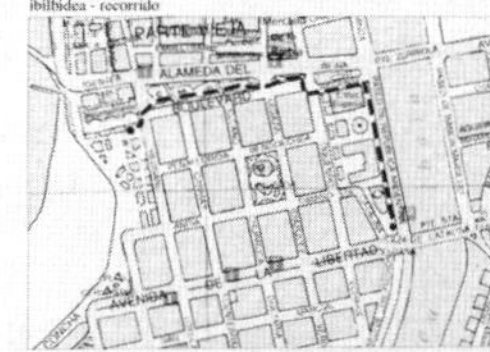

Publication edited by Arteleku (San Sebastián) on the occasion of the workshop *The Carrying Society* by Pepe Espaliú in 1992.
Photo: Joaquín Cortés / Román Lores

BEING CALLED A LUNATIC SHOULD BECOME A COMPLIMENT![01]

THE ANTIPSYCHIATRY MOVEMENT IN SLOVENIA

Bojana Piškur

In Slovenia, the eighties were a time of new radical ideas that no longer took the political, social and cultural norms for granted and were aimed at changing the overall socio-political landscape. The main protagonist in the creation of the 'new forms of sociality' (Tomaž Mastnak) was the civil society. In comparison to other Eastern European countries, the concept of civil society in Slovenia had a significantly different starting point: rather than arising from dissidence and a position of opposition, of 'the civil society against the state', it represented above all a link between different new social movements (the peace movement, the ecological movement, LGBT, the antipsychiatry movement, etc.), and the creation of institutional structures which were not merely in 'opposition' to the existing ones.

The Slovene antipsychiatry movement attempted — through a radical education of the psychiatric profession — to change society's attitude towards madness, the psychiatrists' relationship with their patients, and the hierarchical relationships themselves in psychiatric institutions in Slovenia, leaning in the process on the ideas of David Cooper, Félix Guattari and Franco Basaglia, and others. The movement connected with groups of critical humanist psychologists and social workers and it operated under the auspices of the Union of Socialist Youth of Slovenia, like many other groups in those days.

The goal of the antipsychiatry movement was deinstitutionalization, i.e. closing the institutions and substituting them with the alternative provision of community services. These ideas were articulated in Yugoslavia already in the early eighties. Lepa Mlađenović, an activist and a feminist from Belgrade, was one of the organizers of the international conference Alternative to Psychiatry held at the Student Cultural Centre in Belgrade in 1982. The conference, attended by numerous guests including David Cooper and Félix Guattari, was very influential as it articulated the ideas of deinstitutionalization — to deinstitutionalize psychiatry as an institution of violence and exclusion. However, the aims were not only closing

01

Ustanovni manifest, odbora za družbeno zaščito norosti, *Socialno delo* 27, no. 3 (1988), p. 256.

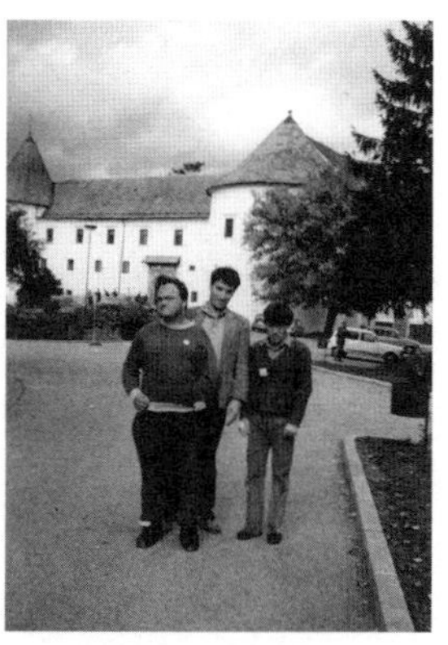

Hrastovec psychiatric asylum, 1988

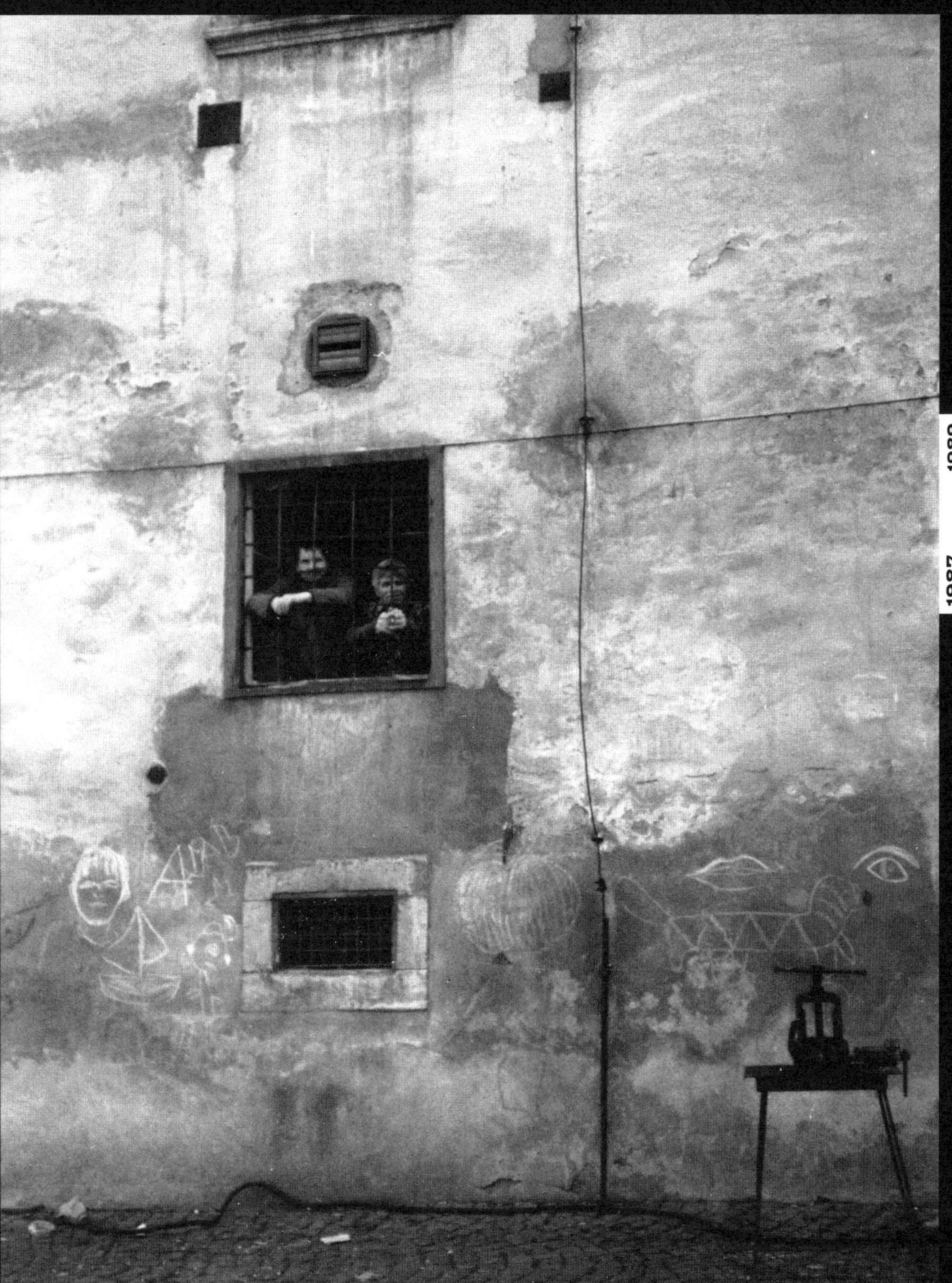

Hrastovec psychiatric asylum, 1988

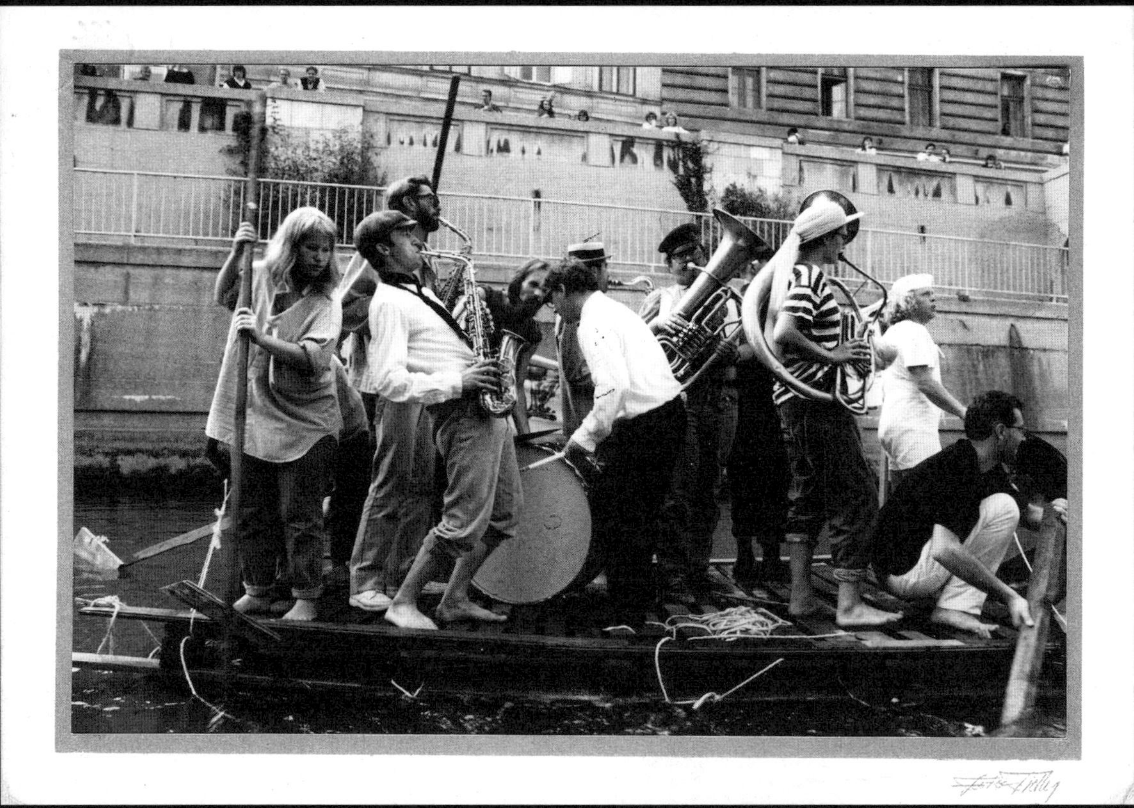

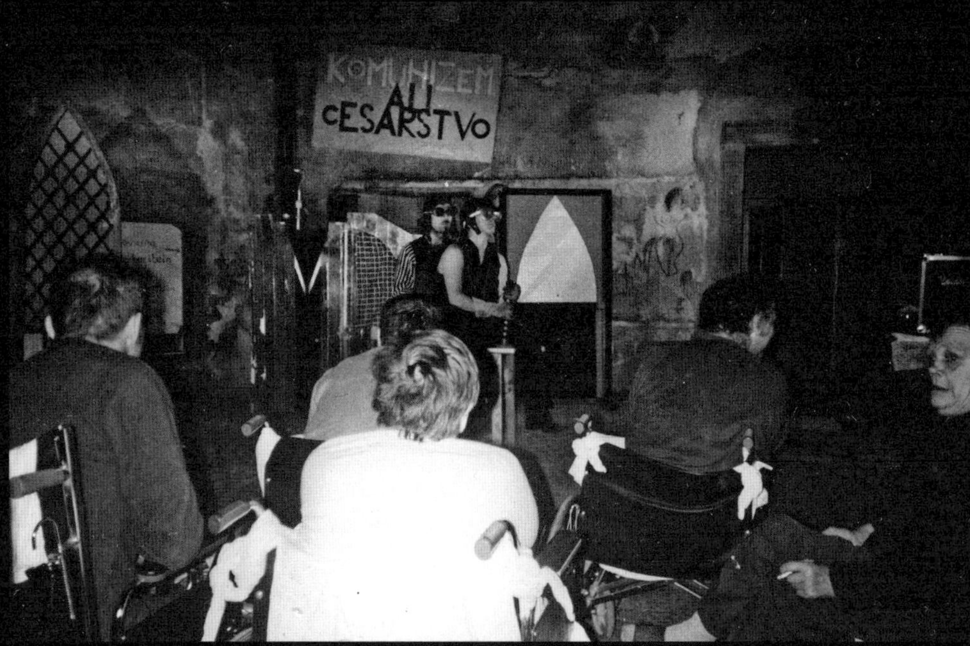

Ship of Fools, Ljubljanica river, 1989. Photo: Frenk Fidler

Hrastovec psychiatric asylum, 1988

down the institutions but an entire socio-political transformation of society, that is to say, establishing new production relations, a new ideology as well as producing new subjectivities.

But it was in Slovenia that the antipsychiatry movement actually put those ideas into practice. The movement organized two youth / student camps in the Hrastovec psychiatric asylum in 1987 and 1988 and one in Ljubljana in 1989. Hrastovec is more than an institution; it is a symbol of a total institution. The building is a castle dating from the fifteenth century. It is no coincidence that basically all psychiatric institutions were located in such buildings. The formalized and strict architectural order of those places represents authority, discipline and control. Disturbing behaviour is sanctioned; life planned and regulated, and time dictated and organized in timetables.

The Committee for the Social Protection of Madness sprang out of the second camp in Hrastovec, in 1988. Initially, it was a campaigning group for the rights of the mental health users and against the wrongs in the institutions. In their founding manifesto[02] they wrote: 'Hrastovec is the dumping ground of Slovenia's psychiatry and society as well. Society disposes of people from the margins it no longer wants in its midst by depositing them far away, so they can no longer be seen or heard of.' The group managed to raise some degree of public awareness of the problem, and its members went on to organize help and support in the community.

But the important thing was that the movement did not only problematize madness, but also society's attitude to it. Madness, the Committee wrote, was a creative principle and a driving force, and should be protected as such. It was not by chance that *Ship of Fools* was one of the symbols of the movement in Slovenia, as well as an artistic happening on the Ljubljanica River organized by the Committee in 1989.

The Committee also emphasized 'development of cultural production' — with an aim to search for various forms of madness. They organized cultural events such as theatre, circus, dance, etc. in the psychiatric institutions, in Ljubljana and Maribor as well as at demonstrations, where a slogan was: 'We do not want a madhouse, we want a civil society.' Vito Flaker, one of the protagonists of the movement wrote that the people from psychiatric institutions started to chant instead: 'We want freedom!'[03]

02

Ibid, pp. 255–256.

03

Vito Flaker, 'Hrastovec v Ljubljani', *Sub-Psihiatrične Študije* ČKZ št. 138–139 (1991), p. 57.

HUGO ROELANDT

Antony Hudek

Hugo Roelandt, who passed away in Antwerp in 2015, at the age of 65, was a visionary artist and teacher. 'Visionary' in every sense of the word: someone who saw potential where others drew a blank, and someone whose unrealized output, in the form of sketches and notes, far outweighs his realized work. His relative lack of material legacy is no doubt due to his distrust of institutions and the art market, a feeling that over the years became mutual. At the same time, Roelandt was known as a connector and collaborator, forging lasting relations over more than three decades with many friends and peers, including Marc Holthof, Roger D'Hondt, Anne-Mie Van Kerckhoven, Ria Pacquée, Luc Steels, Narcisse Tordoir and Mark Verreckt, among others. Despite these ties, Roelandt's anonymity later in his career was not surprising, in view of his intolerance of authority. In a telling episode from the nineties, Roelandt, a longstanding photography tutor at the Royal Academy of Fine Arts in Antwerp, offended the all-powerful curator Jan Hoet, who was on a jury granting degrees to Academy staff. The stakes were high — failing the test meant less salary and pension privileges — but Roelandt couldn't resist taunting Hoet, by submitting as part of his portfolio video documentation of the jury's exit following its deliberations. Roelandt transformed the academic ritual into a mock media event, thereby horizontalizing an eminently vertical hierarchical organization of authority and valorization.

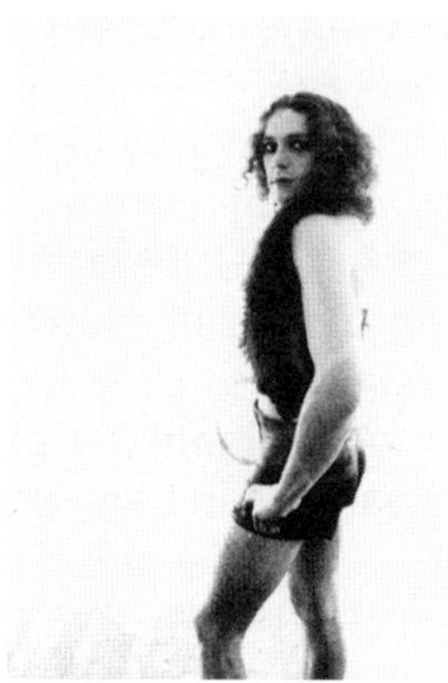

Hugo Roelandt, *Self-Portrait as Transvestite*, 1974. Photo: Estate Hugo Roelandt

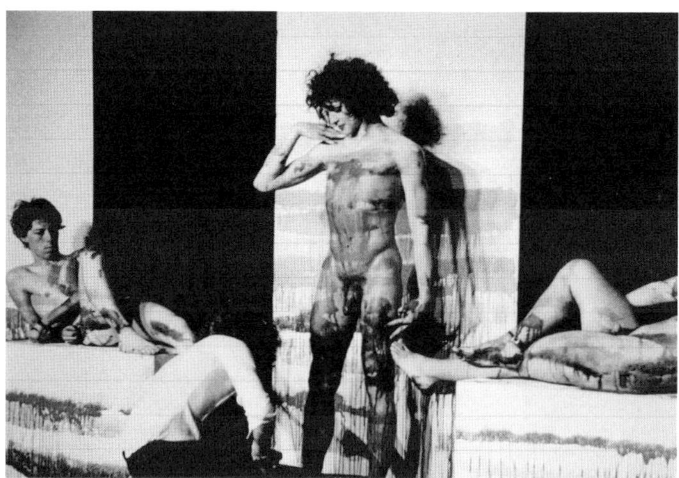

Dennis Denys painted by Hugo Roelandt, during the performance *Aesthetic Ideal*, Zwarte Zaal, Ghent, 1976. Photo: Estate Hugo Roelandt

Hidden within this anecdote are recurrent traits in Roelandt's practice: a subtle sense of humour, and an interest in tautological systems and *mise-en-abyme* — including (self-)portraiture in various guises. Among his earliest works, from c. 1972, when he had just graduated from the Royal Academy and was a partner of the then graphic designer Van Kerckhoven, is *Dag in het leven van een ster* (Day in the Life of a Star), a short 16mm film Roelandt made of two male friends acting out an ordinary domestic scene: lounging in bed, having breakfast, getting dressed in the morning. The fact that the starring couple is same-sex seems, in the matter-of-factness of its portrayal, unremarkable, yet it hints at Roelandt's ability to shift ordinary situations into something utopian. In the performance work *If you do exactly (or not exactly) what we tell you to do, you'll create your own performance* (1978), Roelandt instructed eight musicians to improvise free jazz while hanging from the ceiling of the Beursschouwburg in Brussels. Each musician was spot-lit, hovering over audience members walking on the stage underneath. Every time someone interrupted a spotlight trained on one of the musicians, the latter would start to play. The result was a complete yet playful inversion of standards of passive art viewership: the public is on stage, 'directing' the lofty musicians, but only when these lapse out of the spotlight and into darkness.

By the time of *If you do exactly (or not exactly)* Roelandt was appearing less frequently in his performances, sometimes not at all. He called his works from the late seventies and early eighties *Post Performance Projects*, seeing in them a 'reaction to the institutionalization of performance art' and a 'protest against the imposition of implicit "rules" in performance'. One such implicit 'rule' is the centrality of the embodied subject-author. Roelandt's *Post Performance Projects*, but equally his earlier portraits of himself and others, either nude or in drag, testify to his insight that performance is an endlessly rich terrain to deconstruct the centrality of the 'I'. Roelandt's representations of bodies partake of a fascination with wider apparatuses of perception, in a process one could call de-alienation ('Unverfremdung'): the familiar is not so much placed at a distance as blown up and emphasized, forcing the spectator to relate to the apparent discrepancy of the scene. This inversion of Bertolt Brecht is an open invitation to tweak the mechanisms of the world, and then, if time and resources permit, to find ways to interpret the intriguing results.

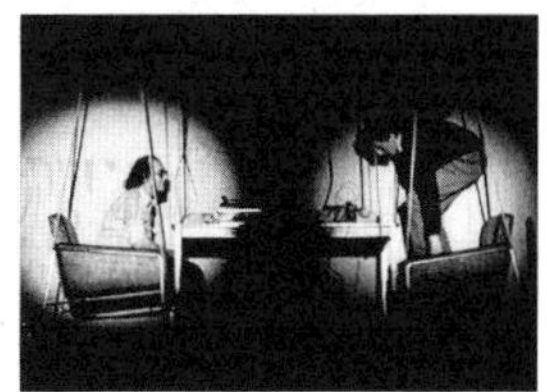

Paul Geladi and Hugo Roelandt, *Post Performance Project 2(b)*, De Warande, Turnhout, 1980. Photo: Estate Hugo Roelandt

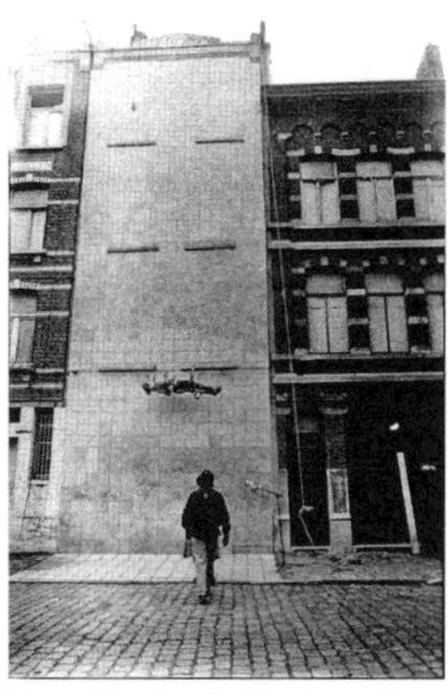

Hugo Roelandt, *Pavimenti*, performance at the opening of 'Monumenta, Sculpture in the City, Middelheim Biennial', Antwerp, 1987. Photo: Estate Hugo Roelandt

143.353 (THE EYES DO NOT WANT TO BE ALWAYS SHUT)

Marcelo Expósito

In 2008, the names of 143,353 people whose disappearance during the Spanish Civil War and in the early years of the military dictatorship could be proved were submitted to Baltasar Garzón, a judge at Spain's National Court, by the Platform for Victims of Disappearances Enforced by Francoism. However, this court case of crimes against humanity committed by the Franco Regime could not be completed after the termination of Baltasar Garzón's judicial career. The tens of thousands of disappearances form the point of departure of the video *143.353 (the eyes do not want to be always shut)*, produced in 2010.

The division of the Spanish army which revolted against the Second Republic in 1936 made use of this method of repression to far-reaching effect, pre-empting the directives of the Third Reich issued in 1941 to regulate the enforced disappearance of people who were kidnapped and killed with no record of the circumstances surrounding their murder or the whereabouts of their bodies. These directives spread terror across the territories occupied by National Socialism, and were at the root of the practice of large-scale disappearances implemented by modern dictatorships, for instance the military dictatorships which devastated Latin America in the seventies and eighties. The bodies unearthed or the mass graves found, the result of this repressive methodology, have been customarily named NN, a designation commonly attributed to the abbreviation of *Nomen Nescio*, or No Name. What isn't common knowledge, however, is the fact that the designation of NN hails from a code used by the German army to secretly refer to the 1941 directives: *Nacht und Nebel, Night and Fog*, an erudite quote from *The Ring of the Nibelung*, which alludes to the formula uttered by the despotic dwarf Alberich to become invisible by putting on a magic helmet, the Tarnhelm. *Night and Fog* was the title of a film Alain Resnais employed to rattle European consciousness in 1956, first referencing collective responsibility in executions, and later the progressive detachment of memory regarding the Holocaust:

> Who is responsible? ... Now the icy water floods the hollow of mass graves like our own bad memory ... the war dozes with one eye always open ... Who is there to warn of the arrival of

new executioners? We see images as if we could make the monster retreat into the past, to heal ourselves of the plague in the concentration camps, today ignoring scream that surrounds us and will not die down…

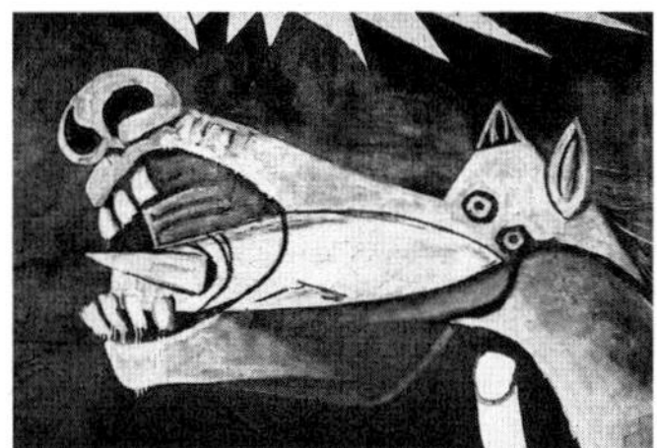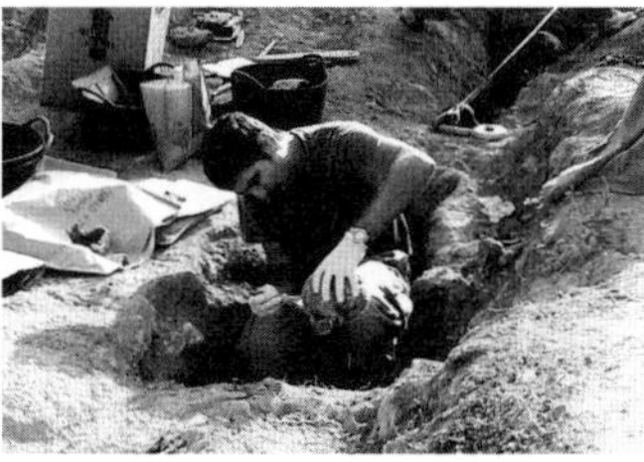

Stills from *143.353 (los ojos no quieren estar siempre cerrados)* (143.353 [the eyes do not want to be always shut]), video, colour, 117 min. Courtesy of the artists and àngels barcelona gallery

The video deploys forensic archaeology in its images to untangle the historical scope of certain archetypes of visual genocide (Saint James Matamoros, the patron saint of Spain's nationalist, discriminatory, intolerant, and repressive vision) and to excavate the historical origin of the use of images as an instrument of the catholic Counter-Reformation conceived by the Council of Trent in the sixteenth century. Yet the video also restores the history of visual interventions of politicized avant-garde movements in art (Josep Renau's poster art during the Civil War), thus drawing inspiration from Bertolt Brecht's reworking of Antigone, the cultural archetype of the political struggle against powers instituted around mourning and the ritual of inhumation. The work concludes with a thorough exploration of one of the largest exhumations of mass graves carried out by the Association for the Recovery of Historical Memory (Asociación para la Recuperación de la Memoria Histórica): 439 bodies of people who died during the war or were forcibly disappeared and recovered in Uclés between 2005 and 2007. The lack of a process of transitional justice in Spain after the death of the genocidal Francisco Franco was justified by the approval of the Amnesty Law of 1977 and the apparent de facto reconciliation instituted by the Spanish Constitution of 1978. These strands form the central theme crossing *No haber olvidado nada* (Not Having Forgotten Anything, 1997), another of my videos which featured in the exhibition 'Hard Gelatine'. Yet recovering the memory of crimes committed by Francoism today sits at the centre of political changes we are undergoing, in the form of a second transition which contests the blockades inherited from the constitutional regime of 1978. Eyes do not always want to be shut: on a day in the not-so-distant future, the right to truth, justice and reparation will also be guaranteed.

Further information

Text and script in English: https://marceloexposito. net/pdf/exposito_143353_ en.pdf

Text and script in Spanish: https://marceloexposito.net/ pdf/exposito_143353.pdf

Video: https://www.youtube.com/ watch?v=Gz6tsvs2BZY

4. NEW

ORDER

INTRODUCTION

Nick Aikens

The final section of the book borrows its title from the eponymous band, formed in 1980 by Bernard Sumner, Peter Hook, and Stephen Morris. New Order came into being following the demise of the post-punk band Joy Division and in the wake of the suicide of its lead vocalist Ian Curtis. New Order were the flagship act of the independent label Factory Records and were synonymous with its club, The Haçienda in Manchester, UK, the home of a burgeoning club and later rave culture in the eighties and nineties. Their sounds, combining synthesizers and sequencers, would usher in a new wave of electronic music. Their music, however, was being produced at the same time as different types of New Order were emerging across Europe: states, including Spain, Portugal, and former Yugoslavia were in varying degrees of transition and disintegration, the Communist bloc was in free fall and the doctrine of neoliberalism was taking hold.

Neoliberalism's cultural, social, and political effects have been pervasive and long-lasting. The emergence of the neoliberal regime and its myriad implications and ramifications for the field of culture frames the first section in this chapter 'Capital and its Crises'. As writer and theorist Boris Buden reminds us, its most visible beginnings can be traced to the election of Margaret Thatcher as British Prime Minister in 1989, even though its presence was far from limited to major Western powers in the eighties. Buden's essay 'When History was Gone' cogently argues that the emergence of the new order in the eighties that set out to weld the doctrines of neoliberalism and democracy implacably together and signal the end of history, actually served to define the opposition between the two dominant narratives of the eighties. As he surmises: 'To democratically challenge neoliberalism one must allow of the possibility that there might never be a democratic solution to its drawbacks'. As Pablo Martínez tells us, the scenes from the 1977 film *Numax presenta* bear witness to the transition from a dictatorship to a bourgeois regime in Spain following the death of Franco in 1975 and the failure of autonomous struggles to offer resistance to the new capitalist order. Elsewhere, neoliberalism's 'drawbacks' included the rampant privatization of services and land, to which artists and intellectuals kicked back, as evidenced in case studies such as the *Docklands Community Poster Project* in the UK, which Charles Esche describes. Similarly, the deregulation of markets heralded the emergence of a new form of international, de-regulated trade, premised on the free flow of goods (but not people) across borders. The example of 'KOT' or 'Muhteşem Copies' is a telling example of how a new relationship with consumer culture was being fostered in Turkey. Nav Haq shows how the artist Hussein Alpetekin was fascinated by the empty lure of the new internationalist capitalism, especially in a country that sat as the hinge between old Europe, Russia, and the soon to be emergent economies of China and the Gulf region.

Yet as Buden's text makes clear, what took place with the rise of the new, neoliberal order and the increasingly free flow of goods and vacant promises, was something more fundamental in terms of our understanding of, and relationship to, history. Francis Fukuyama would be lambasted by the left for affirming 1989 as marking the 'end of history' and the final, undeniable victory for capitalist democracy as the only game in town. In a sense, though, Fukuyama was right. As writer Luís Trindade's essay focusing on the context of post-dictatorship Portugal makes clear, the eighties signalled the arrival of an empty future, incapable of looking forward and insecure in its often ghostly relationship to the past. In the case of Portugal this meant that when freedom arrived, the expression of that freedom through pop culture was de-politicized in what Trindade calls a process of 'de-ideoligization'. Its sense of moving towards a better future evaporated: 'The eighties as the future of the sixties, did not seem to have a future itself.' What's more, Trinadas argues, neoliberalism — certainly in the Portuguese context — does not arrive as the logical outcome of what went before, but rather 'suddenly appears as the political consequence of the defeat and decomposition of the combined forces at work since the sixties'. Portugal, like states across Europe in the eighties were in various processes of radical transformation and self-definition. Aleš Mendiževec writes how in former Yugoslavia, in the context of Tito's recent death and the very visible demise of real existing socialism, the Slovenian Lacanian School spearheaded by Slavoj Žižek were, in a very different way, attempting to forge a new relationship to history and Marxist principles.

      With the explosion of excess capital came the rise of a new type of cultural world, one that had to renegotiate its relationship to both the economy and politics. Trindade sees it, in the Portuguese context at least, as a shift from politics to culture, with the latter being emptied out of the former. Art historian Corinne Diserens' text looks at the often fluid relationship formed by artists, institutions, and the world of capital. Looking at artists such as Richard Prince in New York, who drew, like Alpetekin, on the aesthetics and pull of consumer culture to Europe, and Philippe Thomas' agency, which forged a more conceptually critical, though no less slippery alliance with corporate procedures and aesthetics — a form of institutional critique that was both smart and complicit. For Diserens, Prince, and Thomas highlight 'the vertiginous rise of financial investment into the art market and its rapid accruement of value to respond to the need to find outlets for trade surplus, the alliance of museums add corporate capital ... managerial discourse, cultural engineering'. Diana Franssen examines the eventual bureaucratization of a once burgeoning scene of artist-run spaces in the Netherlands whilst the reprint of Sánchez Ferlosio's article 'Culture, That Government Invention' in Spain satirically laments the rise of the new art world in Spain, revealing a cultural system that was forever changed by money and history's alleged end.

The second section of the chapter and the closing of the book is titled '1989'. As curator Nav Haq points out, the year 1989 has become synonymous with the fall of the Berlin Wall, Tiananmen Square, the withdrawal of Soviet troops from Afghanistan, and the death of Ayatollah Khomeini. Rather than try and bring these world-shifting events directly into the book, a collection of case studies serve as markers for the various transitions different contexts and cultures were undergoing — and as signals for what the nineties might bring. Merve Elveren highlights the protests in Turkey 'We Won't Let You Kill Them', an act of solidarity to stand up for political prisoners there. In the last iterations of 'Slets', told by Bojana Cvejić, for the National Youth Day on Tito's birthday in former Yugoslavia where as if in a remarkable acknowledgement of the changing of the guard, a text adorned the mass parade of dancers saying: 'Every nationalism is equally dangerous, even ours.' In the 1989 exhibition 'Documents' in Sarajevo, as Zdenka Badovinac and Bojana Piškur chronicle, works by nearly 200 artists, all chosen for their depoliticized nature, feel like a last, failed attempt to offer a common Yugoslav art language. In Spain, 1989 saw Mar Villaespesa coin the term 'Absolute Majority Syndrome', a text reprinted here, to articulate Spanish art's worrying tendency in the eighties to become fixated with the new at the expense of historical and critical perspectives. We also see the emergence of new forms of statehood, self-understanding and self-rejection within the context of a neoliberalized Europe, as chronicled by the extraordinary examples of Sin ir más lejos (Without Going Any Further) put together for the exhibition 'El sueño imperativo' (The Imperative Dream), in Madrid in 1991 and addressed here by Rogelio López Cuenca. As Esche writes, 1989 saw the landmark exhibition 'The Other Story' in the UK curated by Rasheed Araeen, the first institutional acknowledgement in Britain's Imperial capital of the contribution of diaspora artists to post-war British art. Rave's second Summer of Love, chronicled by Nav Haq, closes the book. It was arguably the last gasp of a culturally articulated social move- ment — an attempt to offer a collective, if momentary and druginduced way out of the New Order of the decade: to use culture to escape the stifling effects of the new, privatized, individualized, neoliberal regime.

4.1 CAPITAL AND ITS

When History Was Gone
1980s

Declension
1980s

Docklands Community
Poster Project, London
1981–1991

Artists' Initiatives in the
Netherlands
1977–1995

Freedom for What?
1980s

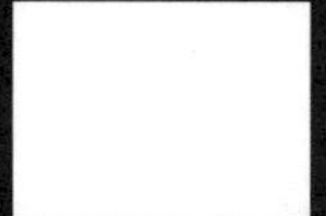

Numax presenta
1980

Culture, That
Government Invention
1984

CRISES

The Formation of the
Slovenian Lacanian
School
1980

Genuine 'KOT' or
'Muhteşem' Copies
1975–1992

Hüseyin Bahri Alptekin

WHEN HISTORY WAS GONE

Boris Buden

Neoliberalism in the eighties? That was not an issue at the time. 'Democracy' was the word on everybody's lips. One was either living it out or craving it more than anything else. Indeed, there was no alternative in the eighties — no alternative to democracy. Even then, already collapsing communism saw its future—its survival, an afterlife — in its democratic transformation. In the eighties, it seemed that nothing could stand in the way of democracy except the brute force of those who were left behind by history. Even neoliberalism, back then, looked like democracy. Hardly anyone was aware that it already had its own agenda.

A historical periodization that measures time, like here, merely by calendar — a 'decade' — only makes sense within a broader historical framework. In the eighties, this framework was clearly defined by democracy, not by neoliberalism. In fact, the eighties were the last decade of history. At the end of that period, in the summer of 1989 — the year that also stands for the fall of East European communism — Francis Fukuyama announced the end of history exactly by declaring democracy, or more precisely a Western-style democracy, as its final stage. In fact, he meant an ideological end of history: democracy as the ultimate form of human government and the finally reached *telos* of all ideological development. At the moment of the post-historical turn neoliberalism, again, is not an issue. It turned to post-history in the shadow of democracy as a final form of humanity's economic development. While it was loudly proclaimed that no political regime or system would ever again claim ideological superiority to liberal democracy, it was tacitly asserting that no alternative economic model would ever challenge neoliberal economics. This is what, at the end of the eighties, created our post-historical horizon and still determines the contours of the global order in which we live — a seemingly self-evident assumption that one cannot have democracy without its alter ego, neoliberalism, and that both are the final outcome of human history.

Of course, another narrative is also possible. It is, for instance, provided by David Harvey in *A Brief History of Neoliberalism*.[01] The breaking point that defines the broader historical framework within which we can situate the eighties as a period took place at the turn of the decade, not the end. This was the time when the first government with a clearly neoliberal agenda was installed —with Margaret Thatcher elected as Prime Minister of Great Britain in May 1979. Paul Volcker, who became the Chairman of the Federal Reserve in the summer of the same year, started the implementation of neoliberal monetary politics in the United States. The major objective was to abandon the old principles

01

David Harvey, *A Brief History of Neoliberalism* (Oxford: Oxford University Press, 2005).

of the New Deal, actually a Keynesian fiscal and monetary policy aiming at full employment and in favour of quelling inflation regardless of social consequences.[02] A year later, when Ronald Reagan entered the White House, neoliberal economic policy won full support from mainstream federal politics. Yet the turn to neoliberalism didn't take place only within the most advanced Western democracies. The first neoliberal inspired economic policy was introduced in Latin America under the dictatorship of Augusto Pinochet who, in a 1973 military putsch, overthrew the democratically elected President of Chile Salvador Allende. After the labour market was violently 'freed' from regulatory or institutional constraints such as, for instance, trade union power, the infamous 'Chicago boys' — a group of economists trained in the neoliberal theories of Milton Freedman at the University of Chicago — were called in to reverse the nationalizations and privatize public assets, open up natural resources to private exploitation, privatize social security, facilitate foreign investment and cooperate with the International Monetary Fund, for instance: take new loans, et cetera.[03] At that time a neoliberal turn also took place in one of the most closed totalitarian states of the world. With Deng Xiaoping taking power in 1979, the economic liberalization of communist China began. The famous 'four modernizations' — in agriculture, industry, education, and science and defense — which brought market forces into the Chinese economy, opened up the country to foreign trade and foreign investment, in short, enabled China's entry into the world market, which coincided with the neoliberal transformation of international trade in the eighties.[04]

According to David Harvey, the emergence of neoliberalism at the beginning of the eighties represents a revolutionary turning point in the world's social and economic history.[05] In this sense, it radically reframes the historical meaning of the eighties. Now they are not the last decade of history, which will end with the global — and eternal — rule of liberal democracy, but the first decade of the global rule of neoliberalism, whose claim to eternity is no less intrusive.

These two historical narratives are incompatible. While democracy fully subsumes neoliberalism, letting it appear as its legitimate corollary, neoliberalism itself doesn't have to pledge allegiance to the rules of democratic politics. On the contrary, it feels comfortable and sometimes thrives best where autocracy and dictatorship exert full power over individuals and where human rights are ignored or openly trampled upon. The eighties were the time when the disproportional relationship between democracy and neoliberalism was established: since then we have accepted as normal the fact that democracy is often the first to facilitate the implementation of neoliberal policies but the last to come to

02
Ibid., pp. 23–25.

03
Ibid., p. 8.

04
'The spectacular emergence of China as a global economic power after 1980 was in part an unintended consequence of the neoliberal turn in the advanced capitalist world.' Ibid., p. 121.

05
Ibid., p. 1.

people's defence when these policies result in destroying their lives. The incompatibility of the two historical narratives — the one in which democracy concludes the entire development of human history and another, which makes the neoliberal turn central to our historical experience — renders any attempt to clearly grasp the historical meaning of the eighties impossible. This is not only due to the ideological disparity of these narratives: while the first, which celebrates the happy, democratic end of history, apologetically affirms the actual historical reality, the latter, which sees neoliberalism as a cause/symptom of a historical crisis, by contrast, calls for its radical critique. In fact, the absence of a common historical ground on which these two narratives might reconcile is not what makes us unable to define the eighties. Rather, the opposite is the case: it is our inability to articulate these two narratives in a radical political opposition to each other, or more precisely, our inability or shall we say fear — to create, politically, a historical ground on which democracy and neoliberalism appear in their irreducible antagonism; a ground on which they clash with one another as open adversaries. At stake is an inability at the level of historical experience. It is an inability of socio-political subjects to totalize historical experience in terms of a mutually exclusive, binary opposition between democracy and neoliberalism.

The problem is that a historical experience, which would allow for such a radical antagonism, cannot take democracy as its ultimate horizon. In other words, for the struggle between democracy and neoliberalism to make historical sense, neither of the adversaries can take the position of history itself — not even democracy. If anything were historical about such a struggle then this would be its open outcome, one that will decide history, not the one that is decided by this history in advance. Or, to put it more clearly, a democratic struggle against neoliberalism becomes truly historical only if and when it faces the possibility that there might be no democratic exit from neoliberalism. To democratically challenge neoliberalism one must allow for the possibility that there might never be a democratic solution to its drawbacks.

MORE THAN A THEFT OF HISTORY

Now we might understand why it is so difficult to grasp the true historical meaning of the eighties. In terms of history this temporal designation is a sort of borderline case. It marks the moment at which the unity of historical time began to dissolve, making any attempt of social subjects to orient themselves within the emerging time-space dynamic of global contemporaneity illusory. In this sense we might say that there is an element of truth in defining the eighties as the last decade of history. The democratic revolutionaries of 1989 were the first to bitterly experience this in the beginning of the nineties. At the moment they toppled communist regimes in Eastern Europe, they saw themselves — and were at the same time seen by the world — as the very protagonists of history. One might say, history itself cast them into the role of history makers. This means that they were not only able to radically cut into an allegedly linear flow of historical time, dividing it into the old destined to be destroyed and the new they represented — a fundamentally modernist operation — but also to create a new historical temporality, which was, in fact, the very essence of a modern revolution. They were, at least for a moment, the embodiment of history itself.

This illusion, however, didn't last long. Soon they found themselves in a time different from the one they just created. Contrary to a naïve, common sense understanding of recent history, the democratic revolutions of 1989–1990 in Eastern Europe haven't immediately delivered what they promised — a democratic society. They didn't result, as expected, in democracy, but rather in the so-called transition to democracy, an ambiguous process of social transformation whose temporal extension was not only indefinitely open to a vague end point, but, moreover, completely out of the control of those who brought about historical change. What followed after the collapse of historical communism was not democracy proper but 'post-communism', a condition for which was claimed, from the very beginning, that it hasn't brought anything new and which was, precisely in terms of historical temporality, declared 'belated'[06] — of course, in relation to the West as the time-space of actually existing democracy. So, instead of fully consuming the hard-fought democratic freedoms, societies of the post-communist East had first to embark on an endless process of catch-up with the West. The old Cold-War divide, once pathetically epitomized in the picture of the Berlin Wall, has been replacedby a new wall composed solely of an alienated historical time.[07] The West was now more than historically ahead of the post-communist East; it was the place where history had reached its closure and where the flow of historical time had come to a standstill.

The concept through which the post-historical condition found its ideological expression was 'identity'. With the collapse of its Cold War counterpart at the end of the eighties, the West emerged as a compact identity block that claimed normative supremacy over the rest of the world. It didn't simply dislodge itself from history. Rather, it has become the very measure of historical temporality. The same applies, by and large, to democracy. Now it was no longer a historically contingent social condition, a matter

06
See for instance Jürgen Habermas, 'Nachholende Revolution und linker Revisionsbedarf. Was heißt Sozialismus heute?', in *Die nachholende Revolution* (Frankfurt am Main: Suhrkamp, 1990), pp. 179–203.

07
The turn of the eighties saw a historical revival of the temporal difference, once an effective instrument of colonial oppression deployed to project the colonized peoples in a time different from the one of the colonial powers, concretely in a non-historical time. Now, in the form of a fluid temporal border, it is used by the forces of neoliberal globalization to regulate and control the movements of capital and labour force across the world. (See Sandro Mezzadra and Brett Neilson, *Border as Method, or, The Multiplication of Labor* (Durham and London: Duke University Press, 2013), especially Chapter 5: 'In the Space of Temporal Border'). Today, as much as in the time of classical colonialism, it serves the interests of domination. This also applies to the nowadays much discussed idea of a 'multi-speed Europe'.

or cause of political struggle that forces within society could win or lose, but rather a 'property' of an identity — the identity of the West. In the normative guise of 'Western values' democracy has ascended from the social space of history to the sphere of its angelic sublimity, thoroughly purified from the dirt of real history, emphatically universal, despite its cultural (Western) particularity, and above all, timeless. It is from the higher ground of its abstract normativity that Western democracy could judge historical reality, which was now always somewhere else, not only in another non-Western place but also in another time. From the standpoint of actually existing Western democracy, real history is still taking place, yet only in the past as the temporal modus of its non-Western contemporaries. For the West, any non-Western democracy is necessarily a 'belated' one, which is why it cannot share one and the same time with it.

What the West has accomplished at the turn of the nineties was more than the theft of global history. We can describe it as a form of primitive accumulation of historical temporality, totally in parallel with the new — neoliberal — wave of primitive accumulation of capital launched after 1989 in the former communist countries. As we know, it was made possible by a radical transformation of property relations that involved the mostly criminal privatization of the state or socially owned means of production and other assets. But something similar happened in the sphere of ideology. Those who were separated from their land and factories also lost what they just created — history. The very means of their historical reproduction, a self-created historical temporality by which they alone were able to cast themselves as the subjects of history, was taken away from them. The euphoria of the democratic revolutions of 1989–1990 was short-lived and so was the historical role of their heroes. Just as they, as economically liberated individuals, were immediately surrendered to the whims of the globalized markets, so too they found themselves, as members of their transitional societies and as political subjects, running after history in a desperate attempt to catch up with its actual time. But they were always running late. History was already in foreign hands.

What we usually call post-history has nothing to do with a world in which history, having done its job, has abandoned, evaporating into another temporality that eludes historical meaning. Rather, it is a divided world, a world in which history has been expropriated — by means of an identitarian (Western) enclosure — from those who created it. What is now imposed on them as a post-historical temporality is in fact their own alienated history.[08] In the hands of its new owners, the sole rulers of the global world, it has turned into an instrument of domination and a perfect protective mechanism for the existing order. The temporal logic of

08

We could understand this transformation in terms of an identity fetishism: a relation between men and women, of which history is but temporal expression, has taken shape of a relation between identity values irreducibly separated by an objectively given temporal difference. History can happen only when human beings who enter into relationship with each other share one and the same time. This is not necessary for the relation between identities.

post-history gives the regime of the actually existing Western democracy a kind of strategic depth, a temporal buffer zone in which none of its crises can ever acquire historical meaning. However destructive or irresolvable, it will never be perceived as the terminal crisis of the system itself. Post-history is an ideological arrangement in which democracy always gets a second chance.

THE TRIPLE TURN OF THE EIGHTIES: HISTORY TO MEMORY; FUTURE TO PAST; SOCIETY TO CULTURE

In the years that followed the historical changes of 1989, history gradually abandoned the hearts and minds of the masses, which it had occupied for almost two centuries. But these hearts and minds, much like the factories of industrial modernity, from which living labour had just disappeared, were not, in fact, empty. History had left at least one of its temporal dimensions: the past.

French historian Pierre Nora argues that we live in an age of commemoration.[09] Nora has diagnosed the extraordinary rise, already in the seventies, in interest for the past. In France and elsewhere in the West, it coincided with the first serious economic crises after World War II, triggered by the huge rise in oil prices in 1974, a crisis that shattered the hitherto stable belief in progress: industrialization, urbanization and a constant growth in welfare. Secondly, the political atmosphere radically shifted following the death of General de Gaulle in 1970. The French began questioning official history, disclosing the dark side of the heroic narrative of anti-fascist resistance, the collaboration of Vichy France. But they also turned their attention to a more distant and deeper past, the history of pre-revolutionary France. 'The French Revolution is over', wrote François Furet at the end of the seventies.[10] The idea of historical time symbolically condensed around the experience of revolutionary rupture lost the prestige it had enjoyed for almost two centuries. It ceded its place to the concept of tradition. The seventies ended with what Nora describes as a 'meteoric rise of the cult of national heritage'.[11] At the same time, the French Communist party, at that point still a significant political force, started to lose its influence on both national politics and French intellectuals. The intellectual collapse of traditional Marxism was underway.

It was the historical decline of the idea of revolution that brought about radical change in the perception of history. The unity of historical time fell apart. It was kept together by the concept — a reflected historical experience as well as a prospective expectation — of a radical revolutionary rupture, which not only regulated the economy of historical loss and gain, clearly differentiating the old — consigning it to the dustbin of history — from the

09

See Pierre Nora, 'Reasons for the Current Upsurge in Memory', *Eurozine*, 19 April 2002, www.eurozine.com/articles/2002-04-19-nora-en.html (last accessed on 13 March 2017).

10

In *Penser la Révolution française (Interpreting the French Revolution)* from 1978.

11

In 1980, Valéry Giscard d'Estaing, at that time the President of the Republic, proposed to dedicate himself to the national heritage.

new that was yet to be created, but which also directed an entire historical timeline toward the future. The great beneficiary of this transformation was the past. It was, as Nora explicitly states, liberated by the disappearance of historical time oriented by the concept of revolution. In the eighties, the world was turning back to the past. Not only in France. Nora speaks of an 'ardent, embattled, almost fetishistic 'memorialism' that spread all over the world, especially after the fall of communist regimes in Eastern Europe and military dictatorships in Latin America. The key feature of this 'tidal wave of memorial concerns that has broken over the world' was the close ties between a new adoration for the past and an idea that was rapidly taking hold in intellectual and political circles: identity.

The eighties was a time when memory began to replace history both in terms of the knowledge of the past and in terms of a particular sense of temporality. It has chosen culture and not history's preference, society, as the medium of its articulation. In fact, culture established itself as the only sphere in which something like the totalization of historical experience[12] still made sense, for instance under the name of postmodernity — a cultural epoch that was first diagnosed and conceptualized at the beginning of the eighties. Then, culturally experienced time was seen as closely connected to the condition of contemporary capitalism, already affected by neoliberal policies: in 1984 *The New Left Review* published Fredric Jameson's *Postmodernism, or, the Cultural Logic of Late Capitalism*. Only a few years earlier, 1981, the same author called for us to 'always historicize!'.[13] But there was no serious answer to his call in the eighties and later it would be forgotten. It has seemed impossible to historicize in the post-historical world of neoliberal capitalism. But isn't this a reason to remember the eighties, when the trouble with history began; and a good reason to try again?

12

On the problem of cultural totalization of historical time, see Peter Osborne, *The Politics of Time: Modernity and Avant-Garde* (London and New York: Verso, 1995).

13

The famous first sentence of Fredric Jameson's, *The Political Unconscious: Narrative as a Social Symbolic Act* (London: Methuen, 1981).

NUMAX PRESENTA

Pablo Martínez

The first moving images belong to the group of workers, mostly women, leaving the Lumière factory in Lyon. That micro-story, in which life runs here, there and everywhere upon leaving work, has been repeated unceasingly throughout the history of film and marked the start, alongside the medium, of the specific relationship between cinema and the representation of work. Because, as evoked by Harun Farocki in *Workers Leaving the Factory*, cinema, just like the workers and wherever possible, has always set out to discover life outside the factory, with very few films focusing on the relationships that occur inside it. Some argue, therefore, that it becomes increasingly more difficult to construct political subjectivity and class awareness, lost as the audiovisual medium is as machinery manufacturing subjectivity for the revolutionary cause. *Numax presenta* (1979) is an extraordinary case study because it denotes a clear example of in-factory life whilst, paradoxically, showing that there is only life outside the factory walls. After nearly two hours of factory scenes, life begins in the final party, just as the factory is closing; the close of the business (from the Old English for busy, -ness) is a party, both literally and figuratively. The exploitation suffered, first via the owner and later through self-exploitation, subsequently disappears. The road to emancipation begins upon renouncing paid employment.

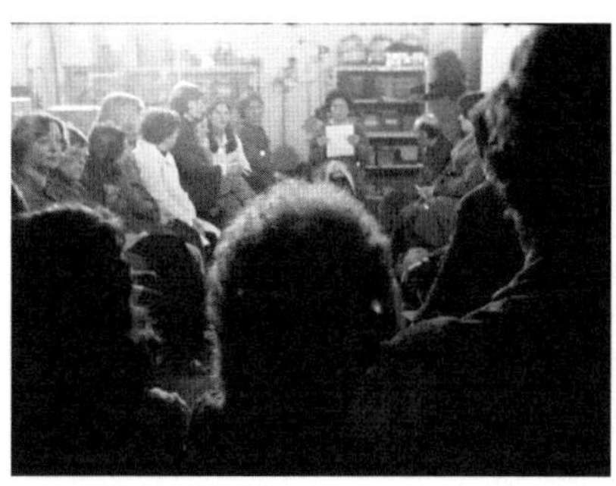
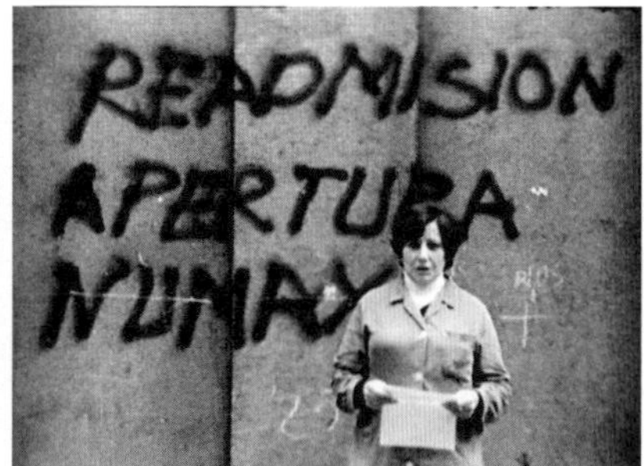

Joaquim Jordà, *Numax presenta...* (Numax presents...), 1980
Single-channel video, b/w and colour, sound, 105 min. MACBA Collection, MACBA Foundation. © The Estate of Joaquim Jordà, 2017

Numax presenta recounts the experience of workers from a small Numax S.A. electrical appliances factory in Barcelona, who, in 1977, took charge of managing production after its owners tried to force its closure. Amidst the tumultuous economic climate of the seventies in Spain, with widespread demonstrations demanding better pay disconnected from higher productivity, under the effects of the petrol crisis and immersed in the upheavals of a country emerging from a long dictatorship, the employers believed closing the factory would be more beneficial and sought to use the land for real-estate speculation. However, after two years of resistance the ongoing financial impracticality of the project made the workers decide to close the business, although not without leaving traces of their experience. With the final 600,000 pesetas from their contingency box, the Numax Workers' Assembly commissioned Joaquim Jordà to make a documentary. The Catalan film-maker was affiliated with workers' autonomy movements and, despite a ten-year hiatus away from filming, produced one of the most significant works of his career.

Numax presenta stands some distance away from any attempt to objectively represent reality, constituting a complex device in which the mix of different formal elements and experimentation in narrative production demonstrate the theatricality of social construction through the combination of re-enactments, interviews, documentary materials and representations of didactic theatre scenes which generate Brechtian effects in the narrative. The film bears witness to the capitalist transition from a dictatorship to a bourgeois democracy, which, in the same process of circulation, betrayed the aspirations of social change by a working class that was highly mobilized in the final stages of Francoism. Furthermore, it renders an account of a labour demand that becomes a fight for the conquest of personal freedom; the story of a fight which ends with the refusal to serve capital from self-exploitation and involves deceiving other workers, encouraging them to consume products unnecessarily. Yet, despite this being a film about the workers' struggle, it is devoid of any element which extols that experience, displaying instead the cracks and contradictions of a system under constant transformation, and, in the case of the Spanish state, a permutation of the industrial fabric through the development of a service economy. This is the beginning of the construction of neoliberal governmentality, placing subjectivity at the service of self-exploitation and constituting a watershed between the disciplinary past and the present of self-control, between industrial Barcelona and global capital devoted to tourist services.

DOCKLANDS COMMUNITY POSTER PROJECT, LONDON

Charles Esche

The first neoliberal regime in Europe took power under the leadership of Margaret Thatcher in 1979. Almost immediately, they began to loosen the planning and development controls that had been put in place during the years of mild social democracy in England. This push for privatization of public resources was applied to urban regeneration schemes and the London Docklands Development Corporation (LDDC) was established in 1981 as a way to exclude local democratic participation in urban development decisions and to override community objections.

Resistance to this corporate takeover of previously democratic processes centred on tenants' groups, trade unions and other community organizations. They objected to the lack of consultation and the plans to relocate most of the existing community and gentrify the area with expensive private housing. The Docklands Community Poster Project (1981–1991) grew out of this resistance and formed its cultural arm. It began as a request from community representatives to two artists, Peter Dunn and Loraine Leeson, for a small poster to alert residents about the LDDC's plans. Picking up this demand, the artists realized that a much bigger public presence was needed to compete with the visual language of the developers. The artists worked collectively with the community on developing a series of 'photo-murals' and with other artists including Sonia Boyce, Tony Minion, Keith Piper and Donald Rodney on posters and issue based exhibitions. The murals were large-scale billboards installed in the public space around the Docklands area. The billboards gradually changed over time by overlaying new images on parts of an existing poster image. The project was initially self-funded but eventually received support from the local London government and the National Arts Council.

The choice of images for the photo-murals was arrived at through discussion with the community via the Docklands Community Poster Project Steering Group and the final visual decisions were taken by the artists. This avoided watering down the final image through trying to find a consensus, while at the same time being open to input from those directly affected in the area. The steering group decided at an early stage that the main audience for the billboards should be the local inhabitants themselves,

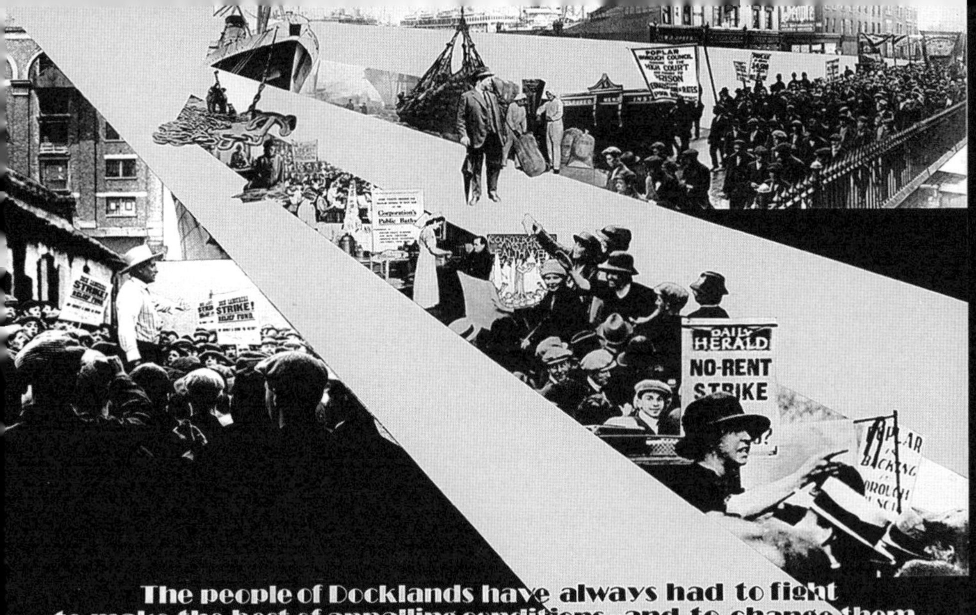

The Changing Picture of Docklands, poster. © Peter Dunn & Loraine Leeson

many of whom were not well informed about the LDDC's activities and long-term aims. The first photo-mural sequence asked the question 'what is going on behind our backs?' and made clear the opaque tactics of the LDDC. It ended with a positive and uplifting image of a future Docklands community. The second sequence focused more directly on housing, one of the most contested issues in the development/gentrification process. By linking contemporary housing issues with the historical struggle for basic democratic and civil rights, the billboards were able to tell a successful story of working-class liberation that provided a model to be repeated again in the eighties. The way the images gradually changed through the replacement of different elements of the whole billboard was one of the many innovations that the project produced. In the largely pre-digital landscape of the eighties, much of the work was done by hand and then mounted on individual wooden boards. The process became a form of slow-motion animation, both in terms of its intensive production and the final result as the narrative of the image unfolded.

Besides the billboards, the Poster Project was involved in a number of direct action campaigns including the People's Armada to Parliament, which involved mass participation by a wide cross-section of the community. While ultimately the gentrification of the Docklands went ahead, the community did win a number of important victories including keeping a city farm and cancelling a road development that would have destroyed the coherence of the neighbourhood. The intense engagement of artists in the project can be seen as exemplary in terms of giving a community a visual language through which they could speak to themselves and a wider audience, as well as serving as a model for future art activism in terms of consultation and collaboration.

GENUINE 'KOT' OR 'MUHTEŞEM' COPIES

Meriç Öner

The shift from a mixed to a liberal economy in Turkey in the mid-eighties allowed producers the right to trade in foreign currencies without ultimate supervision by the state. This was an economic novelty and complemented the infrastructure of industrialization, which had been championed by the private sector since the fifties. The booming economy manifested itself in a variety of goods, forming a visibly and materially globalized Turkey. Urban centres, the key places of this transition, provided both hand- and machine-made and local and global brands, as well as comfortable and provident lifestyle choices. Thanks to the increasing accessibility of global communication networks, international influences of the time were also readily present. The immediate images of abundance and prosperity soon hatched into promises of upgraded lifestyles. One stylized story of the transition is that of blue jeans.

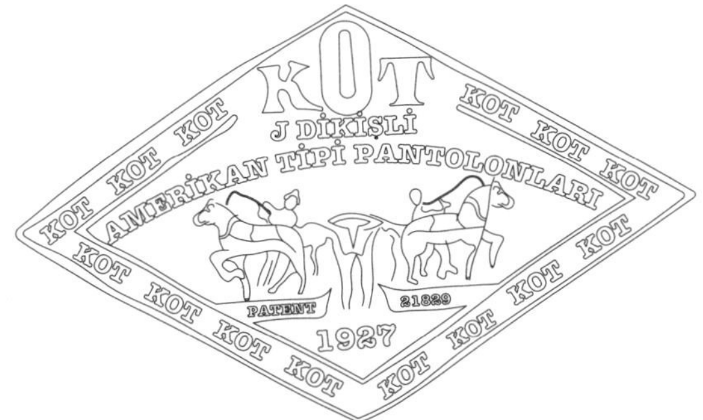

KOT original label: KOT J stitched American type trousers

Muhteşem Kot, a tradesman-tailor who produced goods for state tenders, came across a pair of Levi's during a visit to Europe in the fifties. Learning that these trousers were preferred by cowboys and farmers in the USA for their durability, he began to produce similar jeans for the Turkish market. His first products, presented in Istanbul and Ankara, used a label featuring horses pulling a pair of trousers in opposite directions, replicating Levi's. The quality of the brand was trusted because of this label and because the trousers could stand upright on their own without a mannequin, a sign of durability. The yarns in early production lacked an indispensable element of denim cloth, indigo, the organic dye of Indian

Muhteşem Kot employees, 1975, Confederation of Revolutionary Workers'
Unions, member register book

origin. Accordingly, they did not fade in the same way as their Western precedents. These dark navy trousers would only turn pale under the influence of the sunlight. In other words, the first brand of blue jeans, which gave the product the commonly used name 'kot' in Turkish, were not actual 'blue' jeans. Yet KOT was sought well after by target customers: workers and farmers mainly from rural Turkey.

KOT was registered as a trademark in 1960, two years after the death of its founder. It was a time when young urbanites became interested in denim trousers, especially with the influence of Hollywood cinema. Smuggled goods and second-hands acquired from American citizens working in Turkey were in vogue. Only in the eighties, could the local textiles producers begin to make proper denim using indigo dye, and timely so as it went mainstream just then. Unfortunately, KOT suffered severely when Europe too joined the competition of demand for denim from Turkey. Furthermore the peaking obsession with foreign brands among the consumers was met perfectly with the governmental regulations that allowed imports. KOT failed to position itself in the new market and terminated its production in 1992 without ever becoming an urban brand.

During the late eighties, when language remained a constant in making distinctions of stature and American-English was favourable to any other, it was no surprise that the term 'blue jean' (always singular) replaced 'kot' in certain circles. The reason why it could not replace it altogether is ambiguous. Yet it implicates that KOT, originating in Istanbul, enjoyed popularity as it travelled back and forth across the country. However, anyone who spent their childhood in the freshly liberalized cities of Turkey, is not likely to have heard of Muhteşem Kot. Even if they have, it is possible that they interpreted it as a denim brand and not as the name of the genuine copyist who launched the product. If one reason is that 'kot' is registered deeply in the language as a type of fabric, a second one is that its inventor's less common first name has a literal meaning worthy of an ambitious brand: 'magnificent'.

HÜSEYIN BAHRI ALPTEKIN

Nav Haq

Part of the first generation of Turkish artists to be both globally active and nationally influential, Hüseyin Bahri Alptekin (b. 1957, Izmir; d. 2007, Istanbul) is considered one of the most significant figures of the now established contemporary art scene of Istanbul. Since the mid-eighties, Alptekin focused on an artistic production that was broad in scope and included photography, sculpture, installation, neon, video, and collage. He created a 'plastic art' reflecting the prosaic material qualities of the 'global junk' that came with the flow of trans-national free-market capitalism. This kind of dislocation between object and place recurs as a thematic strand in much of his practice, analyzing how a society's representations of 'other' places conform to desires and stereotypes.

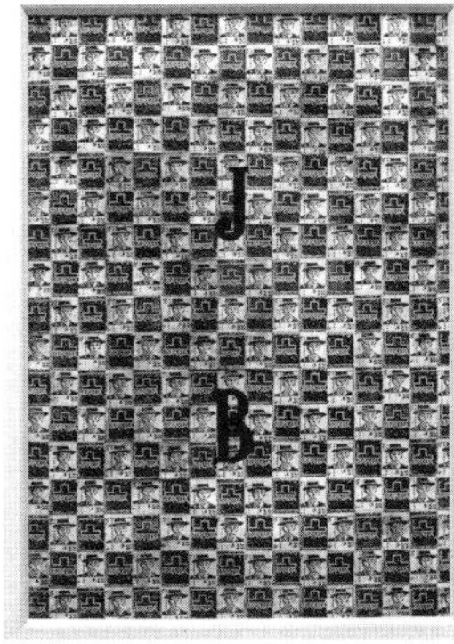

Hüseyin Bahri Alptekin, *J&B*, 1986, mixed media on paper. Collection: private collector, Istanbul. Photo: M HKA

Alptekin was fascinated by the difference between the promise of something and its banal reality. This promise could lie in the name of a cheap hotel offering the experience of a distant place, or in the branding of a mass-produced item that unconvincingly simulates luxuriousness or exoticism. As he describes in his renowned artist statement: 'I investigate the beauty and the vulgar and the relationship between them.' Alptekin was an artist who saw the profound effects of global capitalism on the everyday, observing the movement of people and products across geographies, particularly in the period following the collapse of the Soviet Union. He himself was also a traveller, a student of forms of feral capitalism surging from these places perceived as the fringes of Western modernity. It is the signifiers and remnants of all this — traces of the burgeoning effects of mobility, trade, and image circulation — that Alptekin used as the materials for his art-making, as a means to contemplate what it all represented.

His observations of an accelerated globalism began during the period in which he studied philosophy at the Sorbonne, Paris, under Jacques Derrida, and were captured in his activities around that time. *Global Digestion* (1980–2007) is a cloud-formation work Alptekin created using non-professional photographic printing. It depicts hundreds of photographs of toilets and bathrooms the artist visited during his travels. Many date back to the eighties when he was working for the photographic press agency Sipa in Paris and travelled to various African nations where he, in addition to his paid work, began photographing toilets. The eventual work was influenced by the critical theorist Slavoj Žižek's book *The*

Plague of Fantasies in which the author discusses the specificities of visiting the toilet for people of different cultures. As an artist who travelled the world during this rapid period of internationalization for contemporary art, Alptekin wanted to observe the extent to which the effects of globalization would bring homogeneity to different societies around the world. Yet, even one the most basic functions of the human body, it seems, is not a universal experience.

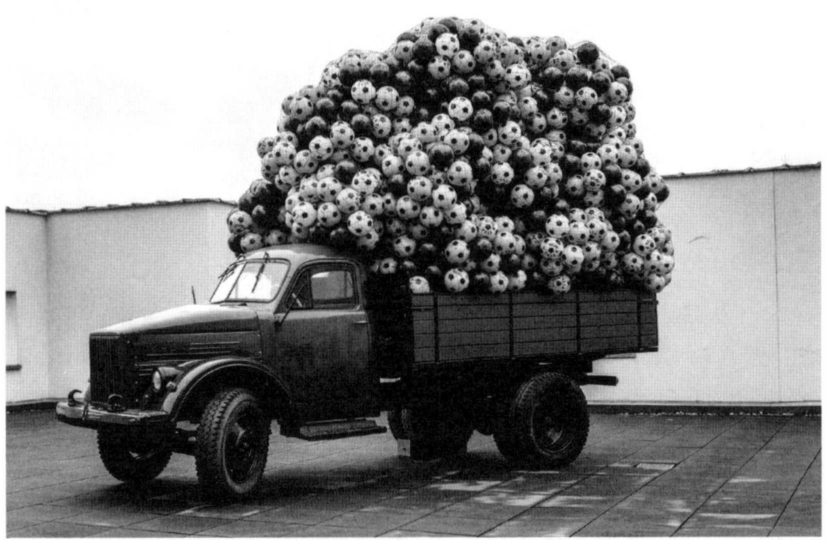

Hüseyin Bahri Alptekin and Michael Morris, *Turk Truck*, 1995, Turkish licensed red Russian made truck, plastic footballs. Courtesy The Estate of Hüseyin Bahri Alptekin, photo: M HKA

The work *Turk Truck* (1995), which Alptekin made together with Michael Morris, with whom he collaborated regularly during the eighties and nineties, reflects the influx of cheap plastic goods transported around the world. It was first created for the Istanbul Biennial in 1995, for which the artists found a truck in Izmir and drove it to Istanbul. The truck itself is typical of the vintage Russian-made trucks overloaded with goods seen on the roads in Turkey. It carries an overly large haul of coloured footballs, a cheap plastic version of balls that are normally leather. Being the most ubiquitous sport internationally as well as the prompt for much nationalistic pride, football generates such a global demand that these kinds of balls could be manufactured and transported from anywhere in the world. With the bright red colour of the truck, the work appears toy-like, yet might also be considered divisive for a 'Turk truck', as the only variety of colours for the balls available to them at that moment was the same as those of the Kurdish flag. Even seemingly innocent things can tread a fine line between the prosaic and the provocative.

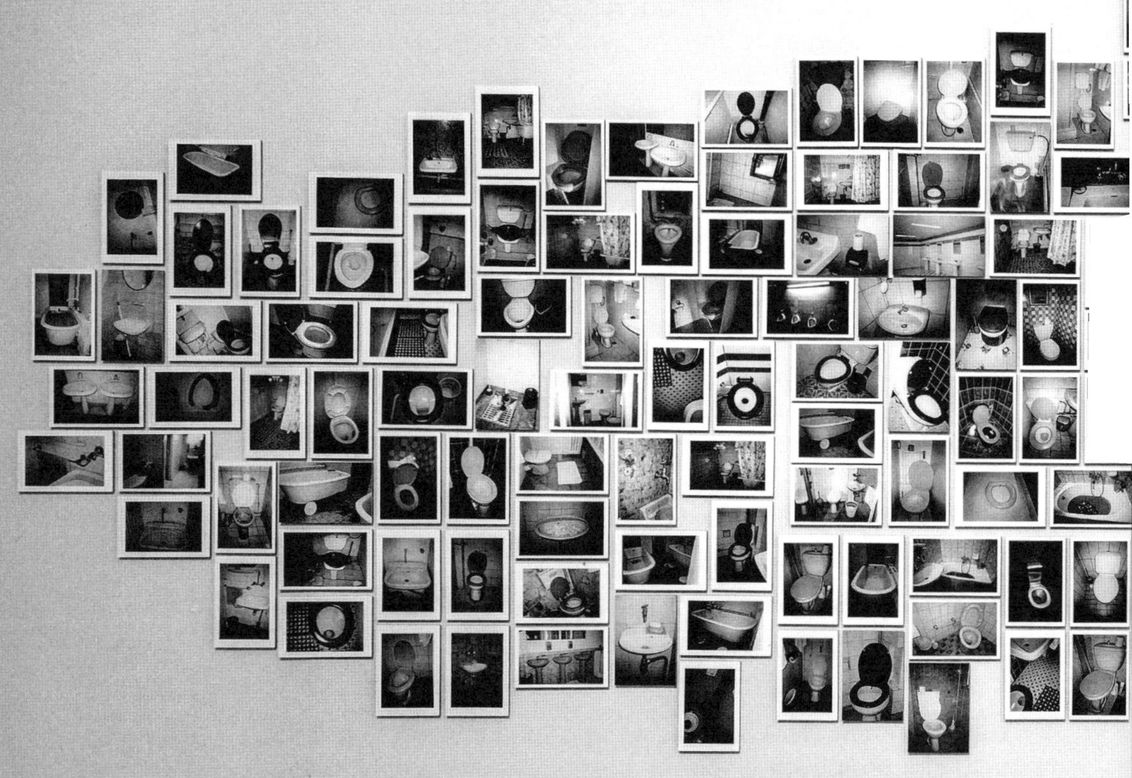

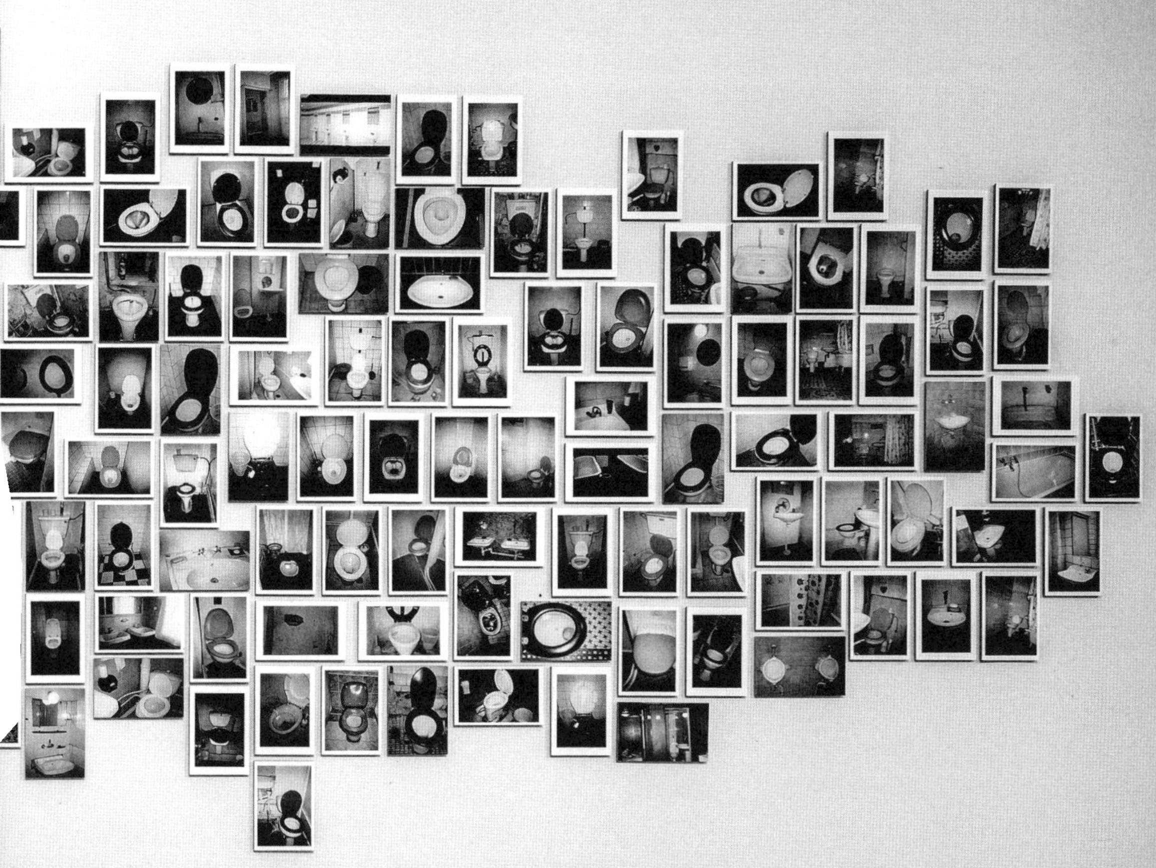

FREEDOM FOR WHAT?

THE USES OF FREEDOM, BETWEEN DICTATORSHIP AND DEMOCRACY IN PORTUGAL

Luís Trindade

Leafing through popular newspapers and magazines from fifties and sixties Portugal yields a surprising picture, quite different from what one would expect to find in the press of an authoritarian country, with its isolationist politics and censored public sphere. Portugal may have been under the rule of a conservative dictatorship, but some sectors of society — mostly the urban middle classes — are becoming increasingly familiar with a completely different world entering the country through pictures and seemingly a-political news reports: European princesses who choose 'freedom' by marrying who they love, North American politicians who show their 'democratic' spirit by using public transports, artists who claim 'freedom' is the most important aspect of creation. And, stretching it to the limit, the press could even show some sympathy for the wave of liberalism brought by Kennedy's election (at least until the new American president started to antagonize Portuguese rulers about colonialism) or for the 'freedom' marches in the USA (especially as these seemed to demonstrate that, according to the regime's ideology, some democracies were more racist than the Portuguese empire).

However, these more overtly political moments, with their inner political agenda (either criticizing the 'enemies' of Portugal or stretching the limits of internal censorship), are not really what is most decisive in this surprising familiarization of Portuguese society under authoritarianism with ideas of freedom and democracy. To start with, using these two words was itself open to contention, like when youth movements in the sixties were shown as an example of the misuse of freedom and the dangers of democracy (although the close relation between the Beatles and their fans could be seen as a positive sign of democratization). The cultural fashion of existentialism, on the other hand, could both show freedom's subversive potential when Sartre refused the Nobel Prize, or the anxieties it caused, according to the many interviews with popular singer Juliette Gréco.

These two words were signs of equalitarianism (as when Queen Elizabeth dances with the president of Ghana), markers of modernity (girls are modern, therefore they are free, or vice-versa), or anticipations of the future (freedom as a key aspect of education from nursery to university). In their almost inadvertent use we see how such a process of familiarization, or indeed banalization, seemed to not only insert Portuguese society in the cultural revolution we usually associate with the 'long sixties', but also to discreetly but decisively undermine the legitimacy of the authoritarian regime.[01]

In other words, by leaving aside for a moment not only the ideological discourses massified by the regime, but also the imaginary produced by the incipient Portuguese cultural industries

01

All these examples were taken from different issues of the popular magazines *O Século Ilustrado* and *Flama*, published in the fifties and sixties.

(strongly polarized along political lines, either celebrating nationalism or politically opposing the dictatorship), and by engaging with the wider, not necessarily political, world of communication and entertainment in circulation throughout the long sixties, we may grasp the usually overlooked processes through which the 'ideological state apparatuses'[02] — to use the period's jargon — were determining the course of historical events in ways that went beyond particular nations and their governments' policies. As Roland Barthes had already suggested in the fifties, thinking of French society — an example surprisingly close to the Portuguese case — the 'mythologies'[03] of the urban middle classes were quickly becoming universal values. In Portugal, as everywhere else in the West, at least, this meant a strong belief in modernity as a historical process marked by both progress — social and economic — and political freedom and democracy. Taking the argument to the limit, it could be said that the Portuguese dictatorship was ultimately doomed by mass culture.

If we jump ahead only twenty years, leaping over the seventies and the Carnation Revolution, to which we will have to come back later, to land in the eighties, a decade particularly associated in the social imaginary (and specially popular culture) with freedom and democracy, we are in for another surprise. Although democratization seems to be linked to a broader access to the public sphere (with both political and cultural implications) and is largely taken for granted, freedom seems to have become much more open to contention. The country's leading comedians, to give an initial example, agreed that it was much more difficult to write humour in freedom than under censorship, as the whole play with innuendo, hints between the lines and ambiguous meanings had suddenly lost its purpose when anything could be said. Some critics, on the other hand, agreed that the obstacles posed by authoritarianism and the country's isolation before 1974 had forced artists, particularly in cinema and theatre, to stick together in resistance and be much more creative than they proved being capable of when freedom arrived.

These criticisms and creative impasses did not always match what was really going on (one of the above mentioned comedians was complaining about freedom while triggering a true revolution in Portuguese humour), but do suggest a discomfort with the distance between the utopian aspirations to freedom and democracy of twenty years earlier, and the ways in which the economic crisis and political instability that affected the country throughout most of the eighties seemed to block another key aspect of the 'sixties' imaginary: the future now did not seem as promising, and the youth — the bearer of the future and its social aspirations — struggled with a decaying educational system and the perspective of unemployment.

02
Louis Althusser, 'Ideology and Ideological State Apparatuses (Notes towards an Investigation)', in *Lenin and Philosophy and Other Essays* (New York: Monthly Review Press, 1971).

03
Roland Barthes, *Mythologies* (Paris: Seuil, 1957).

It was in these circumstances that a semantic transformation occurred in the meaning of the word freedom. This is particularly visible in politicized artists to whom freedom had until very recently been a creative referent for collective transformation and who now started speaking about 'individual freedoms' and the 'freedom of our minds' as the realm of inner feelings and the expression of new attitudes. This personal, almost intimate use of freedom is not necessarily devoid of a certain sense of political statement, and even rhetoric of rebellion. If we look at two of the most emblematic and influential figures in the eighties Portuguese pop music, Pedro Ayres Magalhães and António Variações (to whom I will also return) this becomes very apparent in the way looks and fashion were not only forms of personal statement against conservatism ('when I walk in Chiado [quarter], I feel like in a straitjacket', confessed Magalhães) but also the new forms of 'freedom to do what one wants to do.'[04] António Variações, suddenly and surprisingly raised to fame for his eccentric clothes and explicit homosexual eroticism (and great pop songs) in the early eighties, summarized the change: 'I'm not a fighter, but I have a great urge of freedom and of being different from the others.'[05] A full circle had been traversed since the utopian familiarization of freedom as social aspiration and object of political mobilization in the sixties and the seventies: in the eighties, freedom not only shifted from the collective to the individual, if not indeed the intimate, but also from politics to culture, as the decisive aspect in the constitution of new subjectivities.[06]

The eighties are an important point of reference here as the decade seems to represent a closure not only of the political period that had started with the end of the Second World War, but also, and more to the point in my discussion, of a moment when popular culture, and popular music in particular, developed in parallel with the sense of historical progress pervading the whole period (and with categories of periodization such as the 'glorious thirties', 'the long sixties' or 'the long eighties'), with its permanent succession of movements and styles driven by originality as historical necessity. In this sense, the Portuguese eighties were particularly challenging because many of the country's forms of popular culture, and above all pop and rock music, despite its close alignment with the abovementioned movements and styles, were just starting. Whereas the stream of Anglo-Saxon pop/rock seemed to be heading to its end in the late eighties, early nineties,[07] the Portuguese cultural industries were finally meeting their social and economic conditions for emergence, with political democratization and the growth of mass consumerism.

Now, this challenge seems to take the form of a discrepancy between the Portuguese case and the most familiar narratives

04

Pedro Duarte, 'Heróis do Mar: "A Moda é um Prazer"', *Se7e* 25 July 1984, p. 8.

05

Cláudia Baptista, 'António Variações: "O meu êxito é uma vingança"', *Se7e*, 20 July 1983, p. 12.

06

Cf. Fredric Jameson, *The Cultural Turn: Selected Writings on the Post-Modern* (London: Verso, 1998).

07

Joshua Clover, 1989: *Bob Dylan Didn't Have This to Sing About* (Berkeley: University of California Press, 2009).

of the long sixties and, more recently, the long eighties, as recognizable forms of periodization within the Cold War. Of course, one could say that the problem is with my choice of sources, with how the use of international cultural objects (from the Beatles to Queen Elizabeth) impose on the development of Portuguese culture and its industries. And yet, I believe one could argue that to analyse all cultural artefacts in circulation within the public sphere, both national and foreign, and to move the discussion from Portuguese culture to 'culture in Portugal', not only allows us to establish closer links between the cultural and the social (as foreign forms impacted strongly in the cultural habits of growing sectors of society), but is in fact the only way to follow the emergence and the development of the Portuguese culture industries themselves, as these evolve in tandem both with international tendencies (fashions, movements, groups) and with the internal transformations of Portuguese society.

Contrasting the Portuguese sixties and eighties with what we recognize as 'the sixties' and 'the eighties' in general, is in this sense more than just establishing a comparative frame or subsuming the Portuguese case to a master narrative (in which Portugal always appears as backward). It in fact allows us to identify markers that guided the country's cultural developments to a large extent — both on the side of cultural consumption and of cultural production. It is in this context (almost a meta-context) that I believe we can identify the discrepancy, in Portugal, between the two terms we usually combine to define 'the sixties' as a cultural revolution: political radicalization and cultural and communicational massification. In Portugal, a peripheral society with late processes of urbanization and industrialization (and low rates of literacy), anti-fascist radicalization was widespread in the sixties and seventies, but the penetration of youth cultures, although dynamic and quickly increasing, was still limited to the incipient urban middle class.

What our jump from the sixties to the eighties thus shows us, is that when finally the social conditions for the emergence of a massified Portuguese pop culture seem to be in place — in the early eighties, when the youth finally constituted itself as an autonomous social and economic force — the country was already in a process of quick and deep de-politicization in a post-revolutionary context. More than de-politicization, one should probably speak of de-ideologization. In fact, the emerging pop-rock in eighties Portugal was filled with discontent that eventually constituted a local culture of angst and fury. But the lack of radical ideologies in place stopped these from materializing politically in a consistent way. In short, in Portugal, massification never met radicalization.

If we try to wrap up this exercise in periodization (thus making it clear that it is just that, an exercise) it may be suggested that the first moment, that of the long sixties spreading from the fifties to the mid-seventies, witnessed a complex process of 'class composition'[08] combining middle class expectations (which, being expectations, went well beyond the material realm of the middle classes) and both middle class and working class political radicalization. Whereas the second moment, the eighties, seemed to close the process by enveloping everything in the same 'neoliberal governmentality'.[09]

This needs to be nuanced. The strong utopian feeling pervading the last decade of authoritarianism combined two political movements within anti-fascism: economic development allowed, first, some timid signs of consumerism and the new urban phenomena associated with it to emerge (as we saw with the banal liberalism brought by foreign forms of mass culture), which, for a moment, came so close to, secondly, the ideological radicalization of the working class movement as to make them almost indistinguishable within the same explosive political process. Here, class composition, as a political process in which class struggle anticipates institutional politics, decidedly contributed to the decomposition of the authoritarian state. In line with this argument, our second moment, already after the revolutionary crisis, can be defined as that of state re-composition.

But then, in the eighties, as I also tried to suggest, the future of the sixties seemed disappointing. The anti-fascist coalition broke, with the defeat of the revolutionary process towards socialism, and eighties politics was emptied of any ideological points of reference. Or better still, anti-fascism seemed to be replaced by a youth culture that, just like the liberal middle class culture of the sixties, went well beyond the youth as such (youth became the synecdoche of democratic Portugal in the eighties), but the tone was marked by anxiety and uncertainty. The eighties, as the future of the sixties, did not seem to have a future itself. In these circumstances, these forms of anti-capitalist dissatisfaction (particularly audible in the so called 'boom' in Portuguese rock of the early eighties) were an easy prey for the then rising neoliberal governmentality based on competition and entrepreneurship. In short, sixties liberal radicalization was turned into neoliberal individualism in the eighties and state re-composition already took place under the hegemony of an anti-statist ideology.

We thus seem to have reached satisfactory versions of the Portuguese sixties and eighties, which not only accommodate the specific conditions of Portuguese society and politics during these periods, but which also — precisely by contrasting this specificity with the broader narratives associated to the con-

08

Mario Tronti, *Operai e capitale* (Milan: Einaudi Editore, 1966).

09

Michel Foucault, *The Birth of Biopolitics* (New York: Palgrave, 2010).

ceptual periodization at play in the 'long sixties' and the 'long eighties' — insert the national case in the international circulation of cultural forms more effectively. And yet, this scheme, which tries to read social and economic transformations — from sixties 'class composition' to eighties 'neoliberal governmentality' — in cultural forms, seems somehow flawed. In a word, by jumping from a moment of political radicalization to another apparently marked by de-politicization, it seems to lack a proper political narrative that is able to explain such a transformation beyond the determinism of concepts, useful as they may be, such as 'class composition' and 'neoliberal governmentality'.

The problem here seems to be that the historical narrative that links the sixties and the eighties is to a large extent yet another episode — probably the last — of a modern narrative of progress. From this point of view, the sixties represented a crisis in the Fordist model of capitalism — and the rebellions it entailed staged an uneven combination of decaying industrialization and the emerging tertiary — whereas the eighties would already be the moment of post-Fordism and its specific political and cultural forms. Now, the more one tries to think of the Portuguese case against this background, the more one feels something is missing. And the fact is that throughout this text, in order to situate the Portuguese case in our broader narrative, the Carnation Revolution, that I have been carefully trying avoid bringing into the picture, has become a true 'elephant in the room'.

Between the narrative of progress jumping from the sixties to the eighties, the Portuguese seventies come almost as an embarrassment. The truth is that the revolutionary process of 1974–1975 clarifies the two poles of the story I have been telling so far: it was both the outcome of the radical class composition of the sixties and the event eighties neo-liberal governmentality reacted against. The embarrassment with the seventies, which, in this sense, may be the key decade in this whole conceptual periodization after all, has to do with several things. To begin with, the revolution ended up in defeat of all those who engaged in its project of historical transformation. Such a defeat, on the other hand, not only explains the flaw between radicalization mounting in the sixties and the sense of backlash in the eighties, but it in fact politicizes the whole process. Neo-liberalism, rather than a sort of necessary development in the irresistible history of capitalism and civil society, suddenly appears as the political consequence of the defeat and decomposition of the combined forces at work since the sixties.[10] Moreover, and one could not fail to notice this in a discussion so deeply engaged with historical periodization such as ours, the most dramatic translation of defeat was the true reversal from future to the past in the tem-

10

Ricardo Noronha, 'A Real State of Exception: Class Composition and Social Conflict during the Portuguese Revolution (1974–1975)', unpublished article.

poral expectations of the sixties and eighties, respectively. Interestingly, the eighties, usually linked to the idea of celebration and change — or indeed to the naturalization of change[11] — seem to appear at first as a moment deeply haunted by the past, even where one would expect to find only the future: in youth culture and particularly its most progressive forms of pop music.

So, to conclude, what I propose is that we look at two icons in Portuguese pop culture of the eighties as a coming to terms with such a recent and dramatic past of transformations from dictatorship and colonialism to democracy and Europe, through revolution and socialism. For the problem to a large extent was that, when compared with the broader picture of youth culture in the long sixties (in a nutshell, 1968 and Woodstock), Portuguese youngsters in the two decades prior to the eighties seemed to be doing things they were not supposed to: fighting the colonial wars in Africa and engaging with the 1974–1975 revolutionary process, and in particular with the struggle of peasants for land reform in rural Portugal. In other words, the youth of the sixties and seventies were deeply involved with precisely those aspects of the country's past that the eighties' sense of modernity would like to see overcome: colonialism and rural life. It is in this sense that the persistence of the past in eighties pop culture can be seen as a negotiation through which this fresh memory of authoritarianism and revolution could be mourned. Now, returning to those two emblematic figures of Portuguese pop music mentioned above, Pedro Ayres Magalhães and António Variações, one hardly will fail to notice how the coincidence between the forms of modernity they articulate and those same tropes of national identity in need of mourning — Empire and agriculture — is no coincidence at all, but the accomplishment of that negotiation: Heróis do Mar, the nationalist band led by Magalhães, neutralized the ideological burden of the maritime expansion and colonialism through dance music; as for Variações, his rural origins served as a point of departure for a radical reinvention of traditional tropes through the most innovative forms in contemporary pop. Finally, if the rhythmic celebration of Heróis do Mar still met with some resistance (especially because of their use of iconography inspired by fascist propaganda), the provocative personae of António Variações and his life motto — 'from Braga to New York', that is, from isolation and underdevelopment to the world at its largest — would eventually become the ultimate definition of modernity in the Portuguese eighties.

11
François Cusset, *La Décennie: Le grand cauchemar des années 1980s* (Paris: La Découverte, 2006).

THE FORMATION OF THE SLOVENIAN LACANIAN SCHOOL

Aleš Mendiževec

The Slovenian Lacanian School (SLS) is usually understood as a theory with three sources, or elements: Marxist political philosophy, Lacanian psychoanalysis and Hegelian ontology. But as it is with Marx himself, an innovative theory cannot be reduced to its elements, for it transforms them all in the process of its own constitution. This constitutive process, which formed the SLS, happened in the eighties in Ljubljana, the capital of Slovenia. This is important in the terms of political and theoretical conjuncture: in the times of socialist social order it was necessary to at least implicitly refer to Marxist theory. And this actually was a theoretical referential field for SLS: every notion was somehow paralleled with Marxist notions such as class struggle, exploitation, and so on. However, this was not the decisive 'element' in the SLS story, for it began with Slavoj Žižek's book on Hegel (in Slovene *Hegel in označevalec*, 1980), which was subtitled 'the attempts of "materialistic turn of Hegel" in contemporary psychoanalytic theory and its meaning for historical materialism'. The materialistic turn of Hegel is Marx' critique of Hegel, which opened up a field of endless process of turning of Hegel. Žižek and Mladen Dolar — who were the main figures of the SLS in the eighties — attempted to prolong this gesture of Marx, but in a way that was critical towards Marx or rather Marxism itself (against the humanistic Marxism as promoted by the Praxis journal, which was an important theoretical and political entity in the seventies in Yugoslavia; and also against objectivistic Marxism, by which they meant Sohn-Rethel, Althusser, Kristeva, and so on). They did so via Lacan and Lacanian reinterpretation of Hegel. This is the meaning of Žižek's contemporary self-referential statements about 'the return to Hegel'.

The Lacanian theory of the lack — as promoted by Jacques-Alain Miller — was implemented into Hegel's notion of speculation and absolute knowledge: instead of emphasizing the end of history, when identity prevails, the SLS rejected the Hegelian notion of identity of identity and difference and emphasized the importance of difference, which cannot be overcome (with *Aufhebung*). History thus becomes an endless process. This is how they also reinterpreted Marx: class struggle does not mean that on the proletarian side, in the end of the revolutionary process equality between classes will prevail, or that communism can deliver a society without economic exploitation and political oppression. Class struggle, as understood by SLS, is a difference between classes that cannot be made into identity. Class struggle is transhistoric in the sense that it pushes history into a never-ending process.

Reinterpreting Hegel via Lacan also meant reinterpreting Marx. But this was a two-way process: emphasizing Hegelian and Marxist notions of the process of history meant reinterpreting the Lacanian definition of Symbolic order. The Symbolic as not static anymore, it is not a structure without history. The endless historical class struggle implies, at least formally, the possibility of a revolution against the Symbolic, which would not be a meaningless return to the same. Lacan, who was once criticized for his conservative tendencies, in the SLS gains a Marxist revolutionary charge.

So we see that the meaning of SLS cannot be reduced to its elements for it transformed them all. In the socialist times there was indeed the (at least implicit) necessity to refer to Marxism. And SLS did so — from a great distance, which was made possible by contemporary philosophy and psychoanalysis. But nonetheless they have remained Marxist through their own conceptual exigencies, which were posed by their conjunction of Hegelian ontology and Lacanian psychoanalysis, and for which they are renowned today.

DECLENSION

Corinne Diserens

On the occasion of the series of weekly discussions organized by Hal Foster in February and March 1987 at the Dia Art Foundation, Craig Owens observed in the revised published version of his intervention that

> on March 30, 1987 — one day before the Reagan administration announced protectionist trade sanctions against Japan, and Margaret Thatcher dispatched one of her trade ministers to Tokyo with the threat that she might soon take retaliatory action against Japanese banks and investments firms operating in the City of London — one of the seven paintings of sunflowers Vincent van Gogh produced in 1888 and '89 — 'to decorate a room in his house', as Tom Brokaw reminded us on the NBC Nightly News — was sold at auction in London to the Yasuda Fire and Marine Insurance Company of Tokyo for a record of 24.75 million pounds sterling',[01]

though the Yasuda company announced that upon its arrival in Japan, the painting would be exhibited in the Seiji Togo Memorial Yasuda Kansai Museum on the 42nd floor of Yasuda's corporate headquarters in Tokyo as a token of the company's 'gratitude to the Japanese people', and that the acquisition was in reality purchased to replace another version of *Sunflowers* destroyed by 'a fire' when on loan from a private Japanese collection to the Yokohama City Art Museum in 1945. In response to Robert Hughes' 'diatribe' against the traffic in paintings as public enemy number one and his fetishization of van Gogh's painting as a once-living thing, Owens argued 'that "the public" is a discursive formation susceptible to appropriation by the most diverse — indeed, opposed — ideological interests; and that it has little to do with actually existing publics or constituencies', explaining that Hughes' cultural protectionist discourse shared the same agenda as Reagan's, how AIDS became a weapon in the right's campaign against non-reproductive sexual activity, and how in the name of protection of women, of children, of *unborn* children, the campaigns against abortion, pornography and 'drug abuse', redefined as public and criminal, behaviour once regarded as private.

    This calls to mind Douglas Crimp's striking essay, 'Mourning and Militancy', published two years later in *October* about the community of AIDS activists of the time,[02] and photographer Nan Goldin's major work *The Ballad of Sexual Dependency* where she recalls:

[01] Craig Owens, 'The Yen for Art', in *Discussions in Contemporary Culture*, ed. Hal Foster (Seattle: Number One, Dia Art Foundation, Bay Press, 1987), pp. 16–23.

[02] Douglas Crimp, 'Mourning and Militancy', *October* 51 (Winter 1989), pp. 3–18.

AIDS had entered our world in 1981. By the mid-'80s a number of friends had died and others were HIV positive and working hard to survive. The glamor of self-destruction had worn off with real death among us. I found myself completely isolated and imprisoned in my Bowery.[03]

During the eighties, Nan Goldin performed live her audio-visual opera — an intimate, ambivalent, and complex narrative, made up of over 700 portraits (mainly taken indoors, in her loft on the Bowery, in bars, and clubs) that came out of her relationships, in the form of 35-mm slides constantly reedited by hand in numerous carousel trays, flashed for approximately four seconds each with two slide projectors at a time, and a changing soundtrack of songs acting as so many characters. The slideshow, whose title came from a song in Bertolt Brecht and Kurt Weill's *Threepenny Opera,* chronicles the artist's life and that of her extended family in Boston, Berlin, London, and New York's Lower East Side, 'in which there is an awareness of pain, a quality of introspection',[04] exploring sexuality, redefinition of gender roles, and behaviours beyond societal prejudices in the context of the eighties. For Goldin, this visual diary allowed her to record obsessively and to remember.

IN CERTAIN CASES, THINGS CAN BE TRUE…
THEY ARE NOT NECESSARILY RIGHT

Looking in my library for the short stories that Richard Prince published in the form of booklets in the early eighties, I came across the magazines *BOMB* and *Just Another Asshole*, the journal *Top Stories*, a forum published by Anne Turyn for non-traditional prose and narrative works, many by women authors, and books that speak strongly of their times, such as *Wild History*, published in 1985 and compiled by Richard Prince for Tanam Press, and *Blasted Allegories: An Anthology of Writings by Contemporary Artists*, an important collection of postmodern fiction and criticism published in 1987 by New York's New Museum of Contemporary Art. Edited by Brian Wallis, *Blasted Allegories* features Richard Prince's cowboy photo on the cover, chapters entitled 'A Story is Not Just a Story', 'The Order of Things', 'Discourses of Power', 'History and Memory', 'Modern Love', 'Desire, Fetish, Commodity', 'Mass Culture and the Structure of Fantasy', photographs selected by Barbara Bloom, and texts from the preceding ten years on issues of image, culture, and identity, bridging the personal, the political, and mass phenomena.[05]

Brian Wallis had previously edited *Art After Modernism: Rethinking Representation* (1984), which had a strong impact

03

David Armstrong and Nan Goldin, *A Double Life* (New York, Zurich and Berlin: Scalo, 1994), p. 10.

04

Nan Goldin, *The Ballad of Sexual Dependency* (New York: Aperture Foundation, 1986), p. 6.

05

See Robert Siegle, 'Writing Downtown', *The Downtown Book: The New York Art Scene 1974–1984*, ed. Marvin J. Taylor (Princeton: Princeton University Press; New York: New York University, the Grey Art Gallery and the Fales Library, 2006), pp. 131–153. Downtown writers such as Lynne Tillman who reworked traditional narrative from within, and Kathy Acker — whose works were among the most radical and disorienting departures in writing at the time (she had studied with David Antin) — radically altered mainstream literature, and learned to use mass culture as a mode of critique. For it was from suburbia that many of them fled into Manhattan, looking for something that was more real than what Acker called the 'nicey-nicey-clean-ice-cream-TV society'. Her work denaturalized narrative, desublimated repressed violence, and demystified power. Alluding to 'our passage through all the determining strands of cultural codes', we 'exist, like a shadow, in the interstices of argument', said Tillman.

through a selection of compelling texts by fiction writers, artists, feminist theorists, and French 'poststructuralists' (numerous new translations of European critical theory appeared in the seventies, Frankfurt School, Roland Barthes, Michel Foucault, Jean Baudrillard, Jacques Derrida, Jacques Lacan, British film theory, Continental feminist theory).[06] The publication insisted, as Wallis stated, 'on a variety of rigorous, interdisciplinary approaches, using economic, psychoanalytic, literary, and sociological theories to establish specific connections between art and social operations'. In this moment that for many Downtown artists signified the end of a period of experimentation, Wallis opened his introductory text with these words:

> beyond the more obviously symbolic overtones of 1984, the year may be remembered in the art world as that in which a debate, resulting from the loss of public funding for American art critics, revealed deep fissures and contradictions in contemporary art criticism as a whole,

and continues with an analysis that seems in hindsight to misconstrue somewhat the trans-artistic dialogues that structured the history of modernity.[07]

PRACTICING WITHOUT A LICENSE

In October 1987, the artist Philippe Thomas[08] organized the exhibition 'Sujet à discrétion (John Dogg, Barbara Gladstone, Joseph Kosuth, Allan McCollum, Philippe Thomas)' at American Fine Arts Co, a gallery located in East Village[09] and owned by Colin de Land. It included a series of identical colour photographs of the sea which were accompanied by title cards (or legitimation cards). The first image of sea was entitled 'ANONYME la mer en méditerranée (vue générale) multiple' (ANONYMOUS the sea in the Mediterranean [general view] multiple), and the second one 'PHILIPPE THOMAS autoportrait (vue de l'esprit) multiple', 1985. This amphibology proposed a self-portrait of the mind and a gaze or a mind directed out toward the sea (a view of the spirit). Each card of the other photographs preceded the mention 'self-portrait (view of the spirit)' with the name of artist John Dogg or Joseph Kosuth or Allan McCollum or gallerist Barbara Gladstone who, by their signatures, accepted to become the author.

The exhibition 'Sujet à discrétion' took place one month before the New York opening of Thomas' agency 'readymades belong to everyone®' at Cable Gallery on Broadway, transformed for the occasion into a kind of corporate lobby reminiscent of

06

The legendary 'Squizo-Culture' conference at Columbia University on November 13–16, 1975, organized in collaboration with the journal *Semiotext(e)* — a theoretical and artistic editorial space for radical thinking — had French philosophers and American writers, performers, and composers as invited guests. The conference 'began as an attempt to introduce the then-unknown radical philosophies of post-'68 France to the American avant-garde. The event featured a series of seminal papers, from Deleuze's first presentation of the concept of the "rhizome" to Foucault's introduction of his *History of Sexuality* project. The conference was equally important on a political level, and brought together a diverse group of activists, thinkers, patients, and ex-cons in order to address the challenge of penal and psychiatric institutions. The combination proved to be explosive, but amid the fighting and confusion "Schizo-Culture" revealed deep ruptures in left politics, French thought, and American culture', https://mitpress.mit.edu/books/schizo-culture.

07

Brian Wallis, 'What's Wrong with This Picture? An Introduction', in *Art After Modernism: Rethinking Representation* (Boston: New Museum of Contemporary Art, in association with David R. Godine, 1984), xi–xiii.

08

Philippe Thomas (Nice, 1951–Paris, 1995),

09

Among East Village galleries were Nature Morte, Jay Gorney Modern, 303, Pat Hearn, Cash/Newhouse, International With Monument (where Jeff Koons had his first solo exhibition in 1985), American Fine Arts Co. Even before the stock-market crash in 1987 a lot of galleries went out of business or moved to SoHo.

Marcel Broodthaers' *L'entrée de l'exposition*.[10] The French artist was as much in league with literary works by the likes of Pessoa as with conceptual art.[11] The displacement of the conceptual work, the archives of the production process and the aesthetics of administrative and legal organization,[12] from the physically experienced space of the white cube to the typographical spacing of the page, constituted, as Patricia Falguières wrote, 'one of the major issues of Philippe Thomas' work, inaugurated under the auspices of the found manuscript, the purloined letter, the lecture — the whole fictional apparatus of eighteenth-century French literature — to blossom in the form of books and publications of all kinds: catalogues, posters, leaflets, ads, postcards, and so on'.[13] The agency's ad slogan, 'art history in search of characters...', invited art lovers and collectors to invest in an ambitious artistic project to revise authorial rights, to act in the theatre of law, to 'take place' in the images, and through their archival status, in museums and collections catalogues. Thomas and his agency's exhibition apparatuses (and allegorized storage) proposed images of reality contaminated by the effects of fiction and made in such a way that each exhibition answers to the other, the end of one work heralding another, in the claim to a sort of overall cohesion taking in account reception in delay, and that may well be reminiscent of another Thomas: Blanchot's hero in whom fiction and reality was one.

Philippe Thomas' textual corpus (manuscripts, typescripts, publications, contributions in magazines, conferences, Letraset in spaces, etc.) formed the theoretical basis and the genesis of his artistic production. On March 23, 1987 in the movie theatre of Centre Pompidou (Paris), Philippe Thomas gave the lecture 'for an art of society' ('Pour un art de société. Conférence de Philippe Thomas') with the complicity of the artist Éric Duyckaerts in the audience who interrupted him at the end with a question about taking 'responsibility for an operation that will not only have been speculative in that it bet on a certain philosophy...' The text, which turned out to be a play, *Philippe Thomas décline son identité, une pièce à conviction en 1 acte et 3 tableaux* (Philippe Thomas discloses / refuses his identity, an exhibit in one act and three sets), was published with stage indications and made available at the moment the audience was leaving the theater. The collector Daniel Bosser, who granted his signature to Thomas, was credited as its author.[14] In preparation of the staging of this event, the artist wrote:

> Thus as I see it, the text — my score — is incomplete but this incompletion itself is a part of my work. It was in this way that people like Boulez and Stockhausen were important.

10

The agency readymade belong to everyone closed at Donatella Brun and Jay Chiat's, New York, in November 1993. Having given a generous grant, Jay Chiat was the main supporter of the emblematic exhibition 'A forest of SIGNS. Art in the crisis of representation', organized by Ann Goldstein and Mary Jane Jacob at The Museum of Contemporary Art, Los Angeles, May–August 1989, that looked at 'the role of originality and authorship in the production of meaning; the impact of the mass media on the individual; the investigation of truth, reality, and fiction in representation; the position of art in the art market; and the artist as a self-conscious producer of commodities' (Ann Goldstein's introduction).

11

It is worth noting that it was not until the late eighties that important overview exhibitions on Conceptual art took place in France.

12

On these aspects, see Benjamin Buchloh's textual corpus on conceptual art of the sixties.

13

Patricia Falguières, 'Codicil', in *readymades belong to everyone*, exh. cat. devoted to Philippe Thomas and the agency presented at the Museu d'Art Contemporani de Barcelona, September 27–November 26, 2000, pp. 45–46.

14

Originally published in French in 1987, a translation in English by Antony Hudek was published by Occasional Papers for *Marginalia* (Raven Row, London, December 2014–January, 2015).

In fact, when the musician arrived, he modified the score according to the audience's reactions and according to the reactions of the other musicians who performed with him / her,

thus underlining the role of the interpreter in regard to the presentation and enunciation conditions. Thomas' act of speech answered the summons made to him to appear and explain himself in a review in issue number 3 (1985) of *Public* entitled 'Philippe Thomas : sujet à discrétion ?' signed Michel Tournereau, which followed the publication of the critical edition in German of a found manuscript (*Frage der Präsentation*, Museum für Kultur, Berlin, 1982). The verb 'décliner' has double meaning in French as it can signify to disclose or give one's identity at a border as well as to take no responsibility. It constitutes both the administrative Philippe Thomas and Philippe Thomas the artist, notions that were definitely at the heart of the conception of the agency readymades belong to everyone® with the endorsement by the purchasers of becoming author of the artworks or texts proposed by the agency, disrupting but not erasing thereby conventions of collection and museum's classification systems, principles of assignation and validation, in relation to the art market and in the footsteps of a Marcel Broodthaers (defining, naming, ordering, classifying, cataloguing, categorizing). It demonstrates, 'that its (art) liturgies, administrative protocols, legal modes of identification constitute a real legitimacy apparatus through which one has to pass in order to exist as a subject',[15] and also that classifications and representations ('landmarks of our thoughts') are themselves fictional and contradictory constructions.

Brian O'Doherty (who multiplied heteronyms) is the author of the seminal book *Inside the White Cube: The Ideology of the Gallery Space*, published in 1986.[16] He never ceased to manifest that the self is not a stable identity starting with his curating in 1967 of *Aspen 5+6*, an issue of the magazine contained in a box — a white box — dedicated to Stéphane Mallarmé, opening with Roland Barthes' text 'The Death of the Author' (the original French version 'La mort de l'auteur' was published a year later) and including a recording of Marcel Duchamp reading 'The Creative Act' (1957), both contesting the authority of the author and exploring what Mallarmé (who, according to Marcel Broodthaers, unwittingly invented modern space) set to work in the space of the white page with his poem *Un coup de dés jamais n'abolira le hasard*, the uncertainty and variation principle that characterizes the public aspect of the modern work and how it is addressed to 'whomever' ('A qui veut', anybody and not everybody, in response to Leo Tolstoy's criticisms[17]).

15
Falguières, 'Codicil', p. 51.

16
Brian O'Doherty published four essays in *Artforum* between 1976 and 1981: 'Inside the White Cube: Notes on the Gallery Space', 'Inside the White Cube: The Eye and the Spectator', 'Inside the White Cube: Context as Content', and 'The Gallery as a Gesture'. *Inside the White Cube: The Ideology of the Gallery Space* (Santa Monica and San Francisco: The Lapis Press, 1986), contains the first three. A new revised edition supplemented with the fourth essay was published in 1999 by the University of California Press, Berkeley. O'Doherty was an influential member of the senior staff of the National Endowment for the Arts founded in 1965; he arrived in 1969, first as director of the Visual Arts Program and, subsequently, in 1976, as director of the Media Arts Program for a total of 27 years. He 'helped the Endowment to maintain its credibility among the most vocal and activist artists during some of the most explosive years of the Vietnam War'. (Michael Brenson, a commentator on the Arts Endowment, in *Visionaries and Outcasts: The NEA, Congress, and the Place of the Visual Artist in America*.)

17
On this subject, see Jean-François Chevrier's numerous writings.

For some artists of the 'Pictures Generation'[18] of the mid-seventies and early eighties, such as Louise Lawler, Cindy Sherman, Richard Prince, and Sherrie Levine, among others, appropriation was the formula of 'postmodern' art and their photo-based practices borrowed, quoted, copied, rephotographed, cropped; 'practicing without a license',[19] underneath each picture there was always another picture. Appropriation explores how 'representation stands for the interests of power. Consciously or unconsciously, all institutionalized forms of representation certify corresponding institutions of power'.[20] Sherrie Levine — whose works (photography, painting, sculpture), often appropriated from artworks within the modernist canon, challenge notions of originality, authenticity, and gender—positioned her art after Duchamp and Barthes, paraphrasing in 1981 his closing sentence 'the birth of the reader must be ransomed by the death of the Author', and underlining the influence of Gustave Flaubert's antiheroes Bouvard and Pécuchet:

The world is filled to suffocating. Man has placed his token on every stone. Every word, every image, is leased and mortgaged. We know that a picture is but a space in which a variety of images, none of them original, blend and clash. A picture is a tissue of quotations drawn from the innumerable centres of culture. Similar to those eternal copyists Bouvard and Pécuchet, we indicate the profound ridiculousness that is precisely the truth of painting. We can only imitate a gesture that is always interior, never original. Succeeding the painter, the plagiarist no longer bears within him passions, humours, feelings, impressions, but rather this immense encyclopaedia from which he draws. The viewer is the tablet on which all the quotations that make up a painting are inscribed without any of them being lost. A painting's meaning lies not in its origin, but in its destination. The birth of the viewer must be at the cost of the painter.[21]

If the Zurich duo Peter Fischli and David Weiss have often been likened to Beckett's characters and to cartoonist George Herriman's Krazy Kat and Ignatz Mouse (both subjects of paintings by Sherrie Levine in black casein on unpainted mahogany panels depicting Krazy Kat being struck by a brick and Ignatz throwing it), it is definitely with Flaubert's protagonists that they are associated in their desire 'to attempt the encyclopaedic and at the same time run it aground', with works such as their early *Sausage Series* (1979), the 250 small unfired clay sculptures *Suddenly This Overview* (1981) depicting historically significant and mundane scenes, the polyurethane sculptures or their alter egos — the rat and the bear — acting in their films *The Point of*

18

See the essay by Douglas Crimp, 'Pictures', *October* 8 (Spring 1979), and the recent article www.nytimes.com/2017/02/13/t-magazine/pictures-generation-new-york-artists-cindy-sherman-robert-longo.html?action=click&contentCollection=T%20Magazine&pgtype=imageslideshow&module=RelatedArticleList®ion=CaptionArea&version=SlideCard-12.

19

'Rephotographing is a technique for stealing (pirating) already existing images, stimulating rather than copying them, 'managing' rather than quoting them — reproducing their effects and look as naturally as they had been produced when they first appeared. A resemblance more than a reproduction, a rephotograph is essentially an appropriation of what's already real about an existing image and an attempt to add on or additionalize this reality onto something more real, a virtuoso real—a reality that has the chances of looking real, but a reality that doesn't have any chances of being real', www.richardprince.com/writings/practicing-without-a-license-1977/.

20

Wallis, 'What's Wrong with This Picture?'.

21

Sherrie Levine, 'Five Comments' (1980–1985), in *Blasted Allegories: An Anthology of Writings by Contemporary Artists*, ed. Brian Wallis (New York: The New Museum of Contemporary Art; Cambridge and London: MIT Press, 1987), pp. 92–93.

Least Resistance (1981) and *The Right Way* (1983), while the film *The Way Things Go* (1987) became a 'postmodern classic'.

> HE'S NOT SURE WHO HE IS WHEN HE'S THERE, OR IF IN FACT, HE'S COMFORTABLE AND WANTS TO BE THERE AT ALL. HE SAYS ONE'S IDENTITY IS EASILY CHANGED WHEN WHAT'S IN FRONT OF YOU IS REVERSED AND TRANSPARENT, DIRECTED AND PRODUCED.[22]

Richard Prince is a documentarian of the strangely ordinary whose images, objects, and texts travel the psyche of America. In 1983, he appropriated a picture published six years earlier by Playboy Press of ten-year-old child model Brooke Shields standing nude in a bathtub, the commercial photographer Gary Gross having made her up heavily to look like an older woman, and oiled her body to heighten and refract the presence of her 'he-she' adolescence. The 'stolen' perverse and controversial image, framed in gold, was exhibited at Prince's Lower East Side storefront gallery on 5 Rivington, both — the gallery and the work — being entitled *Spiritual America*,[23] after the eponymous 1923 photograph by Alfred Stieglitz, which focused on the hindquarters of a harnessed and gelded workhorse. Stieglitz saw the practice of castrating a horse to make him calmer and easier to control as symbolic of the country's repressive attitudes in general. In hanging the hotly litigated image *Brooke Shields (Spiritual America)* alone, shrine-like, Prince proposed to 'provide a counter environment'.

If Prince's counterfeit pictures gave the mass-produced, anonymously created pictures a new life assigning them an aura, a preciousness, an authority, was Thomas' agency readymades belong to everyone®, with its subversive protocols, mimetic virtuosity, and own criticality in regard to the vertiginous rise of financial investments into the art market and its rapid accruement of value to respond to the need to find outlets for trade surplus, the alliance of museums and corporate capital (with an emphasis on box-office receipts and on productivity — hence, the merchandising of everything being that museums regard 'the public' as a mass of consumers), the celebration of the return to art object as fetish commodity, in this age of gentrification, production of wealth, transnational business, international banking and stock-exchanges (including enormous debt — analysed brilliantly by Maurizio Lazzarato in *Governing by Debt*), 'entitlement' (possibility of making a *title* out of *anything*),[24] managerial discourse, cultural engineering, patronage, corporate communication strategies for enterprise,[25] and in the era of postmodernism which was, in the terms of Fredric Jameson, 'the consumption of sheer commodification as a process', and

22

Excerpt from artist's writings, back cover, exh. cat. *Richard Prince: Spiritual America* (Valencia: Aperture/IVAM, 1989). 'His way to make it new was to *make it again*, and making it again was enough for him and certainly, personally speaking, *almost* him.' (Richard Prince, 'The Velvet Well', in *Why I Go to the Movies Alone* [New York: Tanam Press, 1983], p. 63.)

23

Spiritual America is also the title of Richard Prince's 1989 artist book and solo exhibition at Centre del Carme, IVAM (Spain), and of his 2008 traveling retrospective curated by Nancy Spector. As Spector describes in the catalogue, his 'Spiritual America' 'is a dystopic nation where contradiction reigns. It is at once a country — our country — and a state of mind, in which fiction shapes reality, travesty reveals essential truths, and beauty resides in the tawdry and illicit. This psychic, yet all-too-real-place has been the subject of Prince's art for more than three decades. As chronicler of our culture's insatiable appetite for both transgression and transcendence, debasement and deliverance, Prince gives this paradox aesthetic form. Through an ever-shifting array of techniques and mediums, all grounded in the act of appropriation, he shows us what we already know about our world but have yet to really see. He excavates the 'normal', borrowing content from advertising imagery, off-color jokes, retro car design, motorcycle clubs, pulp fiction, and even art history, to expose the inner mechanics of desire—how it is framed, sold and perpetuated in our mass-cultural consciousness. This desire exceeds the mere lust for material goods or sexual fulfillment to include an obsession with recognition that borders on the desperate.' *Richard Prince: Spiritual America* (New York: Solomon R. Guggenheim Museum, 2008), p. 14.

the reflex and the concomitant of yet another systemic modification of capitalism itself ..., [when] such lexical neoevents, in which the coinage of a neologism has all the reality impact of a corporate merger, are among the novelties of media society which require not merely study but the establishment of a whole new media-lexicological subdiscipline, ...

was the agency then anticipating the definitive death of the rebellious, creative downtown scene of the seventies (and its eccentric singularities and shared sensibilities) that had fallen into obscurity and broken down with the return of the medium-specificity, disciplines, and auratic values of the art object, elaborating a complex commentary on the analogies between media and market that may be located in the form itself, as proposed at the time by Jameson when he wrote:

> This is the place at which we need to return to the theory of the image, recalling Guy Debord's remarkable theoretical derivation (the image as the final form of commodity reification). At this point the process is reversed, and it is not the commercial products of the market which in advertising become images but rather the very entertainment and narrative processes of commercial television, which are, in their turn, reified and turned into so many commodities?[26]

If the exhibition with its curatorial apparatus and the work's procedures and modes of address have long been questioned in the wake of a legacy of institutional critiques (Duchamp, O'Brian, Broodthaers), for Thomas, it is the site for a public staging where images are experienced as the production of a narrative which contextualizes and organizes through a web of resonances the reading of his own work (in particular in the case of the fascinating exhibition 'Feux pâles' (Pale Fires, from Nabokov's singular to Thomas' plural) which opened in December 1990 at the CAPC in Bordeaux,[27] and the subsequent production *Un cabinet d'amateur*, 1991, a sort of *Boîte-en-valise* and, as such, an instance of legitimation). At the heart of his practice was an institutional perturbation, 'a misprint in the text of the history of art' (Thomas) in which Freud figured,

the Freud of *Jokes and Their Relation to the Subconscious*, which enabled Thomas to deliver an updated version of the Roussellian *Comment j'ai écrit certains de mes livres* (*How I Wrote Certain of My Books*): *The Joke* treated as a practical manual, the key concept of *figurability* as method, the

24

The differential calculation not of 'values', but of the risks of variation in the equivalency rates of these values amongst themselves... About values and titles, see Falguières, 'Codicil', p. 50.

25

'Spirit of enterprise to set the grinding cogs of the bureaucratic machine into motion ... patronage is a powerful and sophisticated new communications tool, which obeys precise principles of functioning that have to be strictly respected', Alain-Dominique Perrin (Chief Executive Officer of Cartier), *Mécénat français: Rapport général*, Ministère de la Culture, Mission sur le Mécénat, 1986.

26

Fredric Jameson, *Postmodernism, or, The Cultural Logic of Late Capitalism* (Durham: Duke University Press, 1991), p. 276.

27

Produced with the support of the agency readymades belong to everyone®, it was structured in 11 sections: 'Inventories of the Memorable'; 'Collector's Cabinets'; 'The Art of Using Up Leftovers'; 'The Museum Without Object'; 'Modernity's Liability'; 'The Flesh is Dreary, Alas, and I Have Read All the Books'; 'Respect for Etiquette. Interest of the Title-Card'; 'The Reflected Museum'; 'Measure for Measure'; 'Lot for Sale'; 'The Index'. See Daniel Soutif, 'Feux pâles: Souvenirs', in exh.cat. *Philippe Thomas: readymades belong to everyone* (Barcelona: MACBA/ Actar, 2000), pp. 109–139.

condensation and the displacement, the *Witz* as economic models in the elaboration of the *Souvenir-écran* (screen memory) whose amended dialogue of institutional men provides us with virtuoso and farcical exegesis.[28]

28
Falguières, 'Codicil', p. 48.

Both Richard Prince and Philippe Thomas shared photographic processes that reintroduce photography to the play of narrative and emancipate the images from their signifying original environment with the use of the series, the detail, the enlargement, the focus and out-of-focus, the close-up, extracting a kind of photographic unconscious, spotlighting the sameness with difference, and rendering them almost unrecognizable to the point of becoming abstract or holding hallucinatory and uncanny qualities determined by the photographs ability to project a sensation of normalcy and by the suasion of images.

The exhibition 'Sujet à discrétion' presented 'self-portraits' of the gallerist Barbara Gladstone who started to represent Richard Prince's work the same year, of Joseph Kosuth, the conceptual artist, influenced early on by Ad Reinhardt's work and Ludwig Wittgenstein's *Tractatus Logico-Philosophicus*, and credited with initiating appropriation strategies, and language-based pieces in the sixties, of Allan McCollum, whose *Perpetual Photo* was then included in Thomas' *Pale Fires*' chapter 'Modernity's Liability' along with Gerhard Richter's *Gray* painting, and of John Dogg, East Village artist invented by Richard Prince and the late charismatic Colin de Land. Prince published a text piece based on what he says to be a transcription from recorded conversations between John Dogg and the author from March to June 1985, with reproductions of Dogg's works supplied by Prince from his own collection. The title of this text, 'In propria persona', 'means, to act in one's own defense'[29] (remaining the summons made to Thomas to take responsibility...).

29
Exh. cat. *Richard Prince: Spiritual America*, pp. 328–333.

This text is an edited short version of an unpublished essay.

ARTISTS' INITIATIVES IN THE NETHERLANDS

Diana Franssen

The desire of artists to side-step the official art circuit was expressed by German artist Dieter Hacker on the poster for the opening of the 7. Produzentengalerie in Berlin in 1971: 'Tötet Eure Galeristen. Kollegen! Gründet Eure eigene Galerie' (Kill Your gallery owners! Colleagues! Start Your own gallery). It was a call for artists to collaborate outside the art market and to self-organize. The values of decentralization, participation, self-organization and networking were at the heart of these early initiatives. Hacker's proclamation was a call to take action from the bottom up.

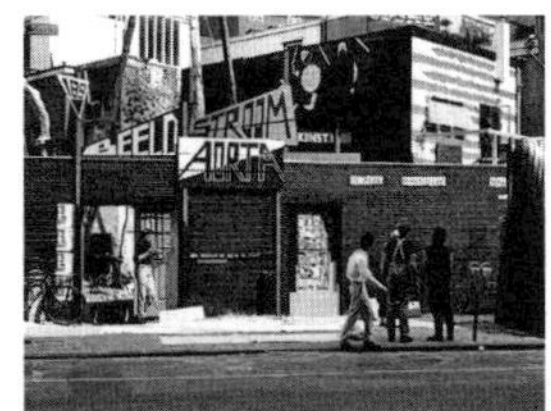
Aorta artist space, Amsterdam, c. 1980

This appealed to the early eighties artists' initiatives, which had close ties to the squatters movement in the Netherlands. People in the squatters movement often had artistic ambitions as well, with squats hosting concerts and other cultural activities. Out of these informal activities a number of new artist-led initiatives emerged to create spaces for new forms of art — performance, video, television and installations — to be shown. These practices were largely ignored by the museum collections, which were focused more on the status of the art object and the legacies of modernism.

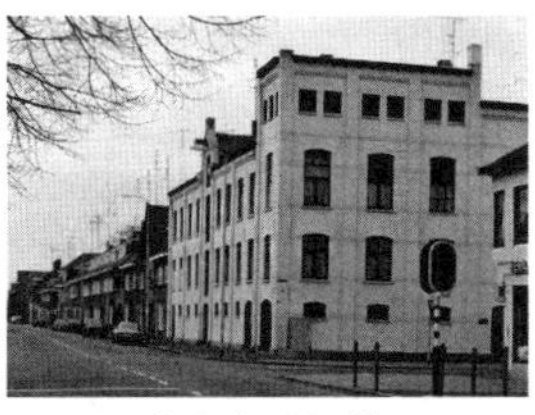
Het Apollohuis, Eindhoven, 1980

The history of De Appel in Amsterdam is interesting in this regard. It started as a self-organized space funded largely by founder Wies Smals. As its reputation grew, the City of Amsterdam began to support it but there was always a struggle between bureaucratic government pressure to become an institution and the wish to uphold the idealism of the initiative. It was only after Wies Smals' tragic early death that her successor Saskia Bos fully professionalized the operation and built a serious art world institution

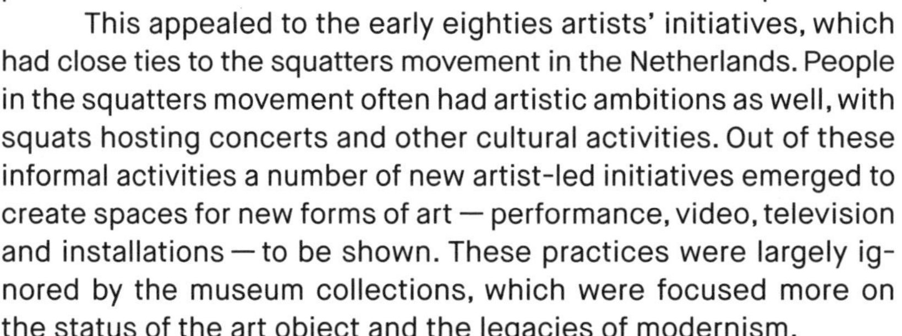

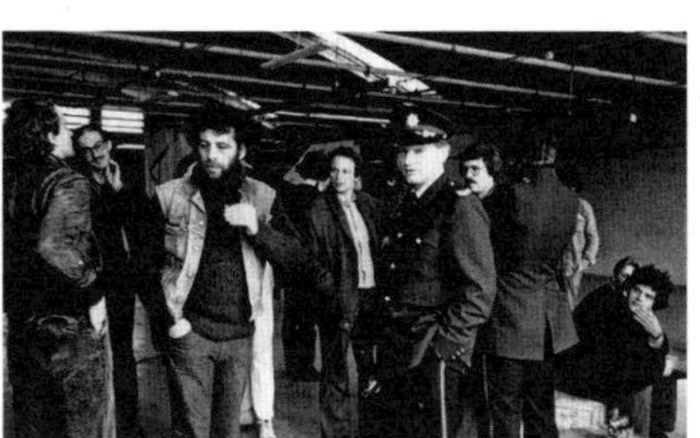
Squatting De Fabriek, Eindhoven, 31 March 1980. Photo: Peter Cox

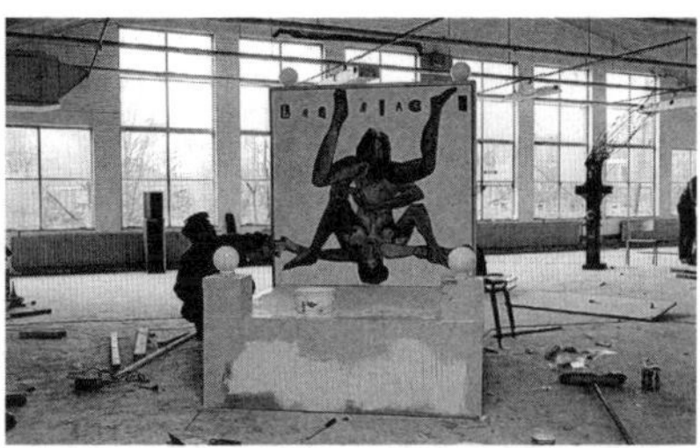
Veld van eer, zand erover, De Fabriek 1984, installation view with Rob Scholte, Martin van Vreden, Harald Vlugt, Ronald Heiloo, Aldert Mantje. Photo: Peter Cox

that conformed to the expectations of its funders. V2_ was another such project, emerging out of the alternative culture and squatting circuit of 's-Hertogenbosch, that developed in a less conformist, institutional way. It remained focused on media and video experimentation throughout the decade but remained somewhat marginalized within the mainstream art world of the time. By moving to Rotterdam they became institutionally more recognized.

The aesthetic of punk-like aggression and DIY attitude was shown through the explosive growth of bands (Soviet Sex and Blue Murder by Maarten Ploeg), record companies and magazines. Fanzines such as *Koekrand* (1978–1980) were published by the artists Hugo Kaagman and Diana Ozon, appearing in stencil or photocopy. The magazine was published under different names many times, underlining the unwillingness to be framed. Some of these, such as the magazine *De Angst* (1983) by Dirk van Weelden, Rob Scholte, Edzard Dideric, and Martin Bril only published two editions. In many ways the spirit of the eighties speaks through the poems, cartoons and essays produced. *Zien* magazine by artist Gérald Van Der Kaap was intended to be a work of art, in which typography played an important role.

After 1984, the growth in artists' initiatives stagnated as the role of artist-organizer became increasingly difficult; alongside increasing institutionalization and bureaucratization, government grants also played an important role in the Netherlands, at first allowing experiments to occur, then creating a climate of financial dependency and accountability. Some of the 'alternative' spaces that flourished in the eighties became recognized institutions, for example V2_ Institute for the Unstable Media (Rotterdam), De Appel Foundation (Amsterdam), BAK, Institute for the contemporary (Utrecht) or Casco (Utrecht).

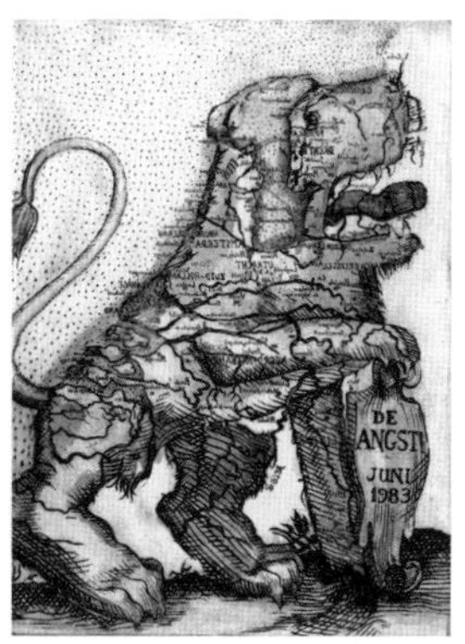

De Angst! (The Fear) nos. 1 and 2, 1983, magazine edited by Rob Scholte, Martin Bril, Edzard Dideric, Dirk van Weelden

By the late eighties, a new generation of alternative spaces emerged. Under the shadow of recession, the collapse of the art market and the bleak financial position of young artists, they focused on discourse and on creating conditions in which art could be presented on their terms. These new initiatives combined the ideas and achievements of previous generations whilst being more pragmatic in their goals. They increasingly imitated the art world: walls were painted white and they mimicked the mechanisms of the established circuit, to which they now only offered symbolic resistance. Conversely, 'alternative' methodologies were increasingly drawn into the realm of the 'official', like, for instance, site specific installations, forms of process art or the collecting of Performance Art by museums. The difference between alternative and mainstream became hard to discern.

CULTURE, THAT GOVERNMENT INVENTION

Rafael Sánchez Ferlosio

The Socialist Government,[01] possibly through its mechanical and short-sighted obsession with disassociating itself wherever possible from the nazis, seems to have adopted a cultural policy which has, in its heavy-handed ineptitude, taken a shine to the polar opposite of Goebbels' definition. Indeed, if Goebbels said, 'every time I hear the word *culture* I cock my gun', the socialists act as if he'd said, 'Once I hear the word *culture*, I hand a blank check to the messenger'. On a human level, it goes without saying that the socialist government's attitude is preferable; yet culturally I'm not sure which is worse.

Matters are hardly helped by the fact that such opinions are so widely imitated: by the opposition, regional governments, savings banks, state-owned organizations, etc. I must admit, this morning writing with due serenity is perhaps beyond me, but I've just been handed the final straw: a letter whose unhappy author is going to suffer, because of me, the injustice of being a scapegoat. To demonstrate the misery I'm talking about, I feel there is a need to get it down on paper. It's from the head of a state-owned organization (maybe I'm wrong in not naming names), whom I don't know from Adam and who, with overfamiliarity, writes:

> Dear friend, I'm writing to invite you to participate with one of your pieces, (*sic* the comma) in an exhibition catalogue, that we want to be a little different. It's a show featuring current painters, who, instead of painting on canvas will paint on fans. That said, it won't be an exhibition of 'fans' (*sic* the speech marks) it's just the support won't be canvas. Therefore they will be large-scale fans and the painters will have absolute freedom to paint, break and play around with them as they wish. We have acquired these supports from China and Japan, and some other smaller ones from Valencia. If you accept we would like you to send us, (I'd already decided to stop putting *sic*) a two/three-page text, agreed to be paid at 50,000 pesetas. We've invited the foremost prose writers and poets, whose contributions we feel would be of particular interest, and among whom you will find numerous friends. We would like to have the text by the beginning of February. As is customary, we would like

01

The PSOE (the Spanish Socialist Workers' Party) remained in government from 1982 to 1996 under the presidency of Felipe González, who won four straight general elections.

to make express mention of the opening ceremony and we hope the presentation of the show, at the beginning of May, will have a festive and refreshing feel. Take care, NN.

Let's get to it: If I, someone who knows very few people, should find 'many friends' among those 'foremost prose writers and poets' and all of them are going to cost fifty grand per head, then how much is that royal joke of a catalogue alone going to cost? On top of that, there are probably even higher fees to be paid to the artists for screwing around with the 'supports' — smearing them, breaking them and playing around with them with *carte blanche*, as the project foresees — the printing costs of the catalogue — in *full colour*, I presume — the cost of organizing and programming, the cost of postage and propaganda, and whatever else, the price of the supports, with their shipping and customs duties, from China and Japan, no less, and, finally, the splurge on nibbles and booze for the 'opening act', which the entity in question is delighted to highlight and 'as is customary (for them), (we) would like to make express mention'; and to boot, the cost of the bill for this 'festive', 'refreshing', obscene and revolting cultural clown fest.

The author of the letter jumps on the fact that these so-called intellectuals, with that perk of the profession of respecting nothing and no one, cannot feel one jot of respect towards themselves, nor, therefore, are they going to take offence at seeing their names on such a letter, as members of any another profession would. Yet that is not really the issue; it's more about the insult of the widespread custom of such splurges to the Budget and tax payer, not to mention the bad example set and the decadence which, for any idea of culture, entails the proliferation of similar monstrosities, of which the current Ministry of Culture — possibly preceded by certain socialist town councils — is the biggest and keenest standard-bearer. However, even though intellectuals are excluded from the right to feel insulted by anything and anyone, they can feel personally affronted by having their own nullity verified, and nothing so resoundingly confirms that as the "unconditional support of the signature" characterising the present uses of cultural trafficking. How many times recently have I had to bite my tongue when I hear: 'Not much, just two or three pages on anything, whatever you want, whatever springs to mind... Come on, you're not telling me that if you sit in front of the typewriter...!' No one ever requests anything specific, the development of something concrete they feel you hit the target with in one of your texts and, more to the point, no one ever stipulates that your submission be interesting and pertinent. And you see what you had thought about and written, and hereinafter what you think and write, boil down to nothing, with the crude and brazen public trading of your signature the only thing to remain standing, without even the most disgraceful drivel being able to diminish that trade. You come away with the clear impression that whatever you put above your signature stands for absolutely nothing.

No one ever turns to so-called intellectuals taking them seriously, aptly demonstrated by those who require them, not to gainfully parade around their mere names, but to ask them to render some kind of anonymous and free service (and no government could have dreamed of a greater willingness to collaborate as the current one in October 1982!). But they aspire to little more; no need for their potential use to be valued at what it should be — they're maybe even a nuisance — just the decorative non-validity of their standing and signature. It's enough to harbour the suspicion that there is some kind of subliminal instinct encouraging intellectuals to be reduced to the status of cocktail drunkards, paid-for honorary boozers, there to add sheen to events with the hollow sound of their names, wholeheartedly fulfilling the clairvoyant prophecy of the *chotis* dance: 'In Chicote a high-class celebration/with the *crème* of intelligentsia.' Such confusion between spirituality and spirits means that a truly expressive audit of the current concept of culture would not be carried out by an accountant itemizing, in pesetas, the various entries of cultural squandering; instead it would be the remit of a hydraulic machine measuring the hecto-litres in the rivers of alcohol supplied. Sometimes physical presence is scarcely required; a name inside in the programme often suffices. An organic intellectual from the University of Menéndez Pelayo, in charge of a seminar on bullfighting in Seville, spent a couple of months scheduling conferences for me (at least five) to attend, and no matter how much I told him I had no intention of going, as well as the fact that I took a dim view of Menéndez Pelayo's inability to spend public money on a more serious cause (I was imagining an alcohol-imbued flamenco coven on the same old fallacies and twaddle of play, myth, earth, the vernacular, charisma, ritual, ancestry, ceremony, sacrifice, funerals... stoppp!!!), he kept on insisting with an attitude almost verging on personal disdain — this time he was an acquaintance of mine — with my explicit refusal being completely ignored, practically falling on deaf ears. He kept on saying: 'Yeah, man, if you come, you'll see how much you like it once you're here', until, in the end, whether I wanted to or not, and despite my refusal and absence, he ended up putting my name in the programme. It would appear, though, that the name was the only thing that mattered — its presence and continuity in the printed pamphlet, like a graduation hat-and-scroll photo. The only true function of cultural events is their having taken place, their pamphlet everlasting proof.

If in the origin of the passion for events, cultural or not, an eagerness we could call 'eventmania', lies the intrinsic motivation of bureaucratic mentorship — given that the number and calibre of events held is always somewhat visible and conspicuous in the 'hereby' section on any bureaucrat's CV — then worse still, to my clear understanding, is the spirit of publicity. And that influence is laid bare in everything we deem cultural. Look no further than the straightforwardness of accepting a congenial advertising word like 'promotion': people talk of 'patriotic events', but 'patriotic promotion' jars. By contrast, 'cultural promotion' is much slicker. And the aforementioned unconditional support for the signature could signal how prevailing cultural uses imitate the value system of advertising, in which a Name is always a Name; for instance, what Gene Kelly is to the advertisers of a Catalan champagn — even if he appears coated and dusted in talc and takes two or three stumbling dance steps (comparable to the two or three pages 'on anything' requested to acclaimed signatures), he will always be, unconditionally, that Geneee... Kelly!!! We all know he hardly gets paid peanuts for saying '*kahrtah nevahdah*'. This 'eventmania' has permeated, culturally, through the spirit of advertising to such an extent that it has now adopted economic forms of advertising management: at certain cultural celebrations in Navarra, of which I was a part this past summer, I discovered, to my utter amazement, that the whole commotion of 'events', funded by the Government of Navarra and the Príncipe de Viana Institution, has been fully entrusted to the management of a 'professional agency' 'specialized' in staging culture. For cultural promotion now has 'agencies', similar to 'advertising promotion'. The breadth of the example involving Spain's current Ministry of Culture — specifically in reference to the Menéndez Pelayo Summer University, its most dazzling and evasive 'trumpet-blower' — envied and imitated in the homologous department of regional governments, municipalities, state entities, banks, savings banks and any other institution with a cultural 'budget', looks out, resolutely, across a horizon where culture, and with it the same concept and meaning, is fully substituted by its own campaign of advertising promotion. Culture will gradually become more exclusively concentrated into the pure celebration of the 'cultural event'. It will be identified by its strict presentation of propaganda, just as the author of the letter transcribed at the beginning of this article expressly declared with such brazen naivety: 'As is customary, we would like to make express mention of the opening ceremony.'

The same degenerative and reductive concept of culture is behind the successful but embarrassing slogan 'culture is a party', of which Santiago Roldán, the dean of the University of Menéndez Pelayo, is, by all accounts, a cordial and convinced addict. The prestige of the 'party' and 'festivities' seems to have become as untouchable today, as big a taboo, as the prestige of the 'people' and the 'popular'. It's all but an iron-clad code of silence which prevents any attempt to reveal the dark, obscurantist side of parties, the repressive immemorial pact in them, between desperation and conformism, and which, to my knowledge, could account for the fact that in the festive syndrome lies precisely the compulsion to destroy property or just simply squander. If this assumption is accurate then I leave the reader with the choice to pursue a reflection on what, for the internal content of the matter, this total identification between culture and party could mean and harness. I personally will still be here clasping the outermost angle.

Therefore, as if the mimicry of the advertising mentality belonging to the biggest brands wasn't enough, in this Trimalchio's Supper of socialist culture, mere expenditure in and of itself ends up, without further ado, ratified as a certain attribute of decorum, even an ingredient of quality, combining at the same time through the recognition of culture as a party, the compulsion towards squandering without leftovers, perhaps grounded in the most baleful and oppressive encumbrance of this suspect festive spirit. Another factor, an almost inevitable natural companion, normally bringing with it such a festive and party-going inclinations towards cultural activities, is the imperative of culture's 'popularity'. In his splendid article 'La política cultural "socialvergente"' (Cultural Policy of 'Social Vergence', *El País*, 17 February 1984), in reference to the atmosphere in Catalonia, Félix de Azúa highlighted the almost identical practice of guidelines between the cultural policies of the Convergència i Unió and the Socialist Party in Catalonia. I'll focus on a few sentences from the article:

> The cultural policies of the Catalan socialists lean towards populism of the worst idealistic kind. This involves, so they say, 'eliminating elitism' ... or 'promoting popular art'. They are walking blindly towards Max Caliner and the cultural policy of Convergence ... . In this consideration there are a couple of mistakes. The first and biggest is in the term 'popular'. Which people? ... . The second mistake refers to neutrality and the fear of cultural control. This is pure deceit. As long as funding exists there will always be cultural control. Yet the Left try to cover up a bad conscience with the story of 'popular culture'. Promoting cinema that flatters the most brutal and leader-

less areas in society (for instance *Locos, locos carrozas*) or funding performances verging on pathological (for instance the near entirety of the theatre shown in Barcelona), with the excuse that they're 'popular', hides the impotence of civil servants to put on an intelligent production. They endeavour to avoid criticism from the Left through the figment of the 'people' or 'Catalan popular tradition', whilst offering attendance figures ..., figures which could be multiplied by ten if there were a decision to finance a public execution — the most popular show ever. (Hitherto, Félix de Azúa).

Lastly, I'll synthesize with an example: given that, on one side, culture is a party—and parties are under the obligation to be expensive—inexpensive theatre staging, for instance chamber theatre, would come up against the resistance of promotors because of the typically vulgar fear that performance could be branded penurious or even indecent. And, given that, on the other side, culture doesn't have to be elitist but popular, the use of chamber theatre again would be rebutted through the serious imperfections in its elite character.

Consequently, chamber theatre, the most splendid formal invention by the old avant-garde, via the dual affliction of being neither popular nor expensive but, conversely, cheap and elitist, would be ostracized by the current cultural promotors as something doubly undesirable, even coming to represent a paradigm of what, in their view, *mustn't* be done.

Yet these socialist leaders sometimes proclaim themselves fans of the poet Antonio Machado without regularly visiting Juan de Mairena's[02] classroom, or having little or no memory of it. When Mairena put forward his ideal teaching centre, he clearly countered a possible, regrettable 'Advanced School of Popular Knowledge' against a possible, desirable 'Popular School of Advanced Knowledge'. Therefore, what Mairena advocated could be narrowly deemed as 'cheap elitism', whereby, through affecting cheapness merely in the activity of teaching, not taught knowledge, such a school could be allowed to conceive the aspiration of someday making that knowledge the majority. The cultural policies of this government are the exact opposite of Mairena's 'cheap elitism': expensive, or, more to the point, exorbitant and extortionate elitism. Yet still 'festive and refreshing', all the more so if wine and spirits are included in the concept of 'refreshments'.

[02] Juan de Mairena is a fictional character — a professor of rhetoric — created by Antonio Machado (1875–1939).

This article 'La cultura, ese invento del Gobierno' by Rafael Sánchez Ferlosio was originally published in the newspaper *El País* on 22 November 1984.

1984

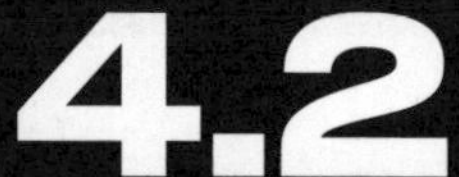

4.2

'The Other Story: Afro-Asian Artists in Post-War Britain'
1989

1989 – The Second Summer of Love
1988–1989

Sin ir más lejos
1991

Absolute Majority Syndrome
1989

1989

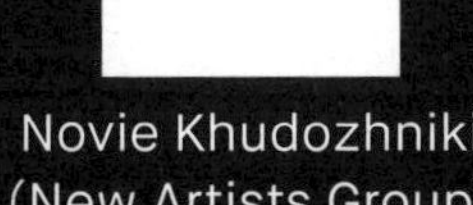

Novie Khudozhniki
(New Artists Group)

1982–1991

Mass Dancing and the
Political (Un)Conscious

1987–1989

'Yugoslav Documents '89'

1989

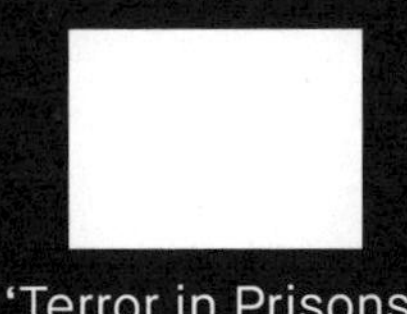

'Terror in Prisons'

1989

'TERROR IN PRISONS
WE WON'T LET YOU KILL THEM'

Merve Elveren and Erman Ata Uncu

Issued by the Ministry of Justice of the Republic of Turkey in 1988, the 'Circular of August 1' brought a set of restrictions to prisons, such as compulsory uniforms, reduction of the time period in which convicts were allowed to remain in the common area, use of only Turkish as a language during visits, and the surveillance of communication with the outside world through letters or telegrams. Signalling the first steps to a system of isolation in prisons, the circular started country-wide hunger strikes in more than twelve prisons. The death of two convicts on hunger strike (after they were transferred from Eskişehir Special-Type Penitentiary to Aydın Penitentiary) caused great uproar and led to nationwide protests.

     Intellectuals Aziz Nesin, Mîna Urgan, Rasih Nuri İleri, Mehmet Ali Aybar, and Emil Galip Sandalcı embarked on a symbolic 48-hour hunger strike at the Istanbul Pera Palace Hotel; a group of second-wave feminists, referred to by the press as 'Women in Black', made a call 'for women to protest against these murders, demand the annulment of the Circular of August 1, wear black in order to protest the uniform regulation, and for newspapers to print black columns'; the Istanbul branch of the Human Rights Association organized the 'Human Rights Now, Not Tomorrow!' concert and started a petition signed by 10,000 people; a group of writers painted their books black in front of the AKM (Atatürk Cultural Centre); *Sokak* (Street) magazine contributed to the protests with the page 'Terror in Prisons: We Won't Let You Kill Them' and called for the legislators of the Circular of August 1 to resign and for public protests. From June 29 to August 19, 1989, nearly 1,500 convicts participated in the hunger strike.

TERROR IN PRISONS
WE WON'T LET YOU KILL THEM

The State has clearly declared war on prisoners. We ask: Where has the State obtained such authorization? What official positions are occupied by the murderers who take the decision to transfer prisoners who are on the brink of death as a result of hunger strikes?

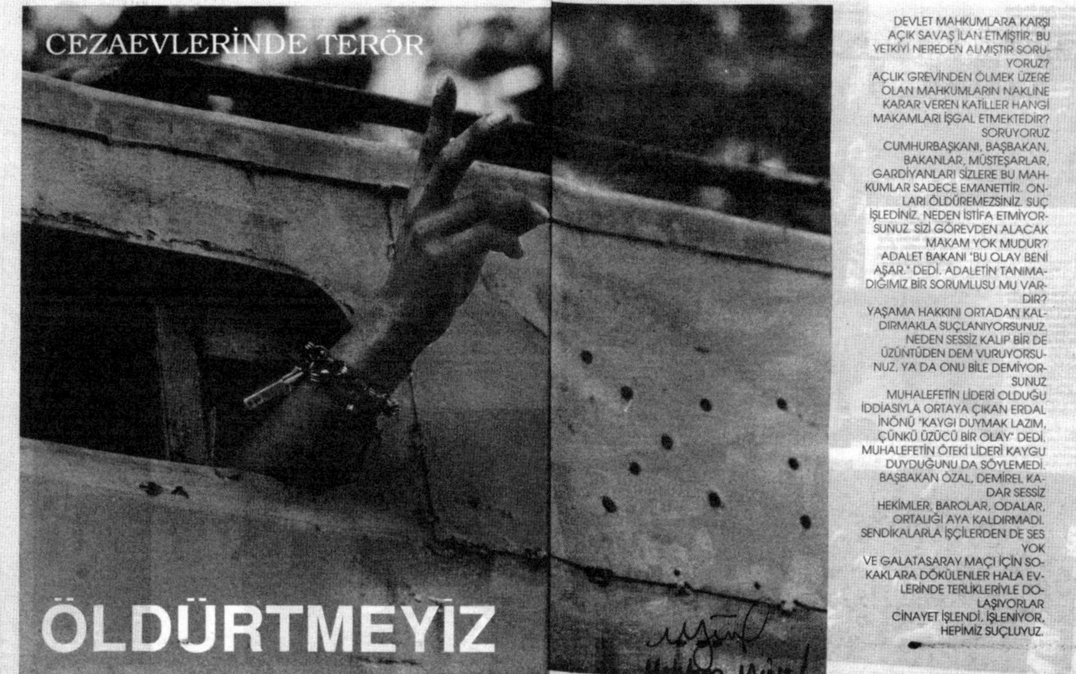

Sokak (Street) year 1, no. 1, 27 August–3 September 1989. Photo: Mehtap Yücel. Archive: Tuğrul Eryılmaz, Murat Öneş and Nilgün Öneş

We are asking you: President, Prime Minister, Ministers, Undersecretaries, guardians! These prisoners are merely in your custody. You are not authorized to kill them. You have committed a crime. Why are you not resigning? Is there no authority that will relieve you of your duty? The Minister of Justice has said, 'This incident exceeds my authority.' Is someone we do not know responsible for justice?

You are accused with violating the right to life. Why do you remain silent, yet speak of your sadness, or fail even to mention that? Erdal İnönü, who claims to be the leader of the opposition, has said, 'One must be concerned, because this is a saddening incident.' The other opposition leader did not even express concern. Prime Minister Özal is as silent as Demirel. Doctors, bar associations, and professional chambers have not stood up in protest. Unions and workers are nowhere to be heard either, and those who pour onto the streets for Galatasaray's football game are still slouching around at home in their slippers. A murder has been committed, murders continue to be committed, we are all culpable.

Sokak (Street), year 1, no. 1, 27 August-3 September 1989. Photo: Mehtap Yücel.
Archive: Tuğrul Eryılmaz, Murat Öneş and Nilgün Öneş

MASS DANCING AND THE POLITICAL (UN)CONSCIOUS

Bojana Cvejić, Marta Popivoda and Ana Vujanović

The genealogy of mass dancing in communist parades has a kind of political consciousness. In the period immediately after the October Revolution, the Proletkult movement in Russia organized mass spectacles where lessons of the revolution were rehearsed. In these spectacles, the events of the October Revolution, French Revolution and the Paris Commune were re-enacted at authentic-looking historical sites, using a mix of amateurs and professional performers. Alongside this tradition, we can find counterparts to mass dancing in German *Freikörperkultur* and *Festkultur*, in the USSR (*fizkultura*), and in Czechoslovakia (*Sokoli*, the falcons), whereby the New Soviet Man was celebrated or pan-Slavic nationalism was built.

In the second era of communist Yugoslavia, formed under Tito's leadership after WWII, the same mass celebrations were practiced on several occasions (May Day, the Five-Year Plan, and so on) and a peculiar place is occupied by *Slet*, the youth parade in honour of Tito's birthday, held every 25th of May. *Slet* consisted of carrying the relay baton of youth (*štafeta mladosti*) from the extreme northwestern point to the southeastern point of the country, while youths from six republics and two provinces passed it on. On May 25, thousands of youths, pioneers (elementary school pupils), and students of the military army performed mass choreographies in the largest stadium in the capital, Belgrade. The spectacle displayed the roles of workers, youth, children, sportsmen, and soldiers in mass ornaments such as the flag, the five-pointed star, crops as the emblem of peasants, the factory as the emblem of workers, and so on. A special act in the dramaturgy of the event was the climactic moment when an elected youth, typically an excellent student, handed over the relay baton to Tito, wishing him a happy birthday.

The social choreography of *Slet* staged a triangular bond between the people performing and watching the performance, the revolution as the object of the mass movement, and the leader whose honour was a moral and political pledge of revolutionary zeal.[01] The political consciousness ... was a method of building and preserving state ideology. The ideology of the state didn't only involve socialism, but also 'brotherhood and unity' among the ethnically varied peoples and minorities that constituted Yugoslavia.

01

This interpretation originates from a conversation with Marta Popivoda as part of her research for the documentary archive film *Yugoslavia: How Ideas Moved Our Collective Body*.

In 1987, seven years after his death, *Slet* was still performed in homage to Tito, whose place was thereafter taken by the political delegates of the six republics. The then President of the Young Communist League of Yugoslavia, Hašim Redžepi, received the baton in Tito's place. The second to last celebration[02] began to hint at a breakdown. The recording of the broadcast event on Radio-Television Belgrade shows signs and warnings of the upcoming collapse of Yugoslavia, but these signs are displayed choreographically: an eclectic mix of folk dances and generic dances to Yugoslav pop and rock music, confusion among dancers about the ornament they are supposed to make, sloppy dance routines, and close-ups on an overall sense of inertia, arbitrariness, and lazy indifference felt among thousands of bodies. The real symptom of the ideological deregulation is evidenced by a scene which deviates the farthest from the mission of *Slet*, … in which, as a commentator explains, two hundred and fifty particular characters from European history (members of all classes, from medieval knights to noble gentlemen and butlers) … form a fragmented multitude which has nothing to do with the history of Yugoslavia, its state symbolism, or socialism. The discrepancy between the choreographic and the ideological is confirmed in the textual messages projected on a screen in the stadium, such as 'every nationalism is equally dangerous, even ours'. These were remarked on by the TV commentators, who wondered, for example, why one dance split into eight different folk dances.[03]

The *Slet* from 1987 not only evinces signs of the collapse of the state ideology of brotherhood and unity, it also shows how its logic of political consciousness allows it to narrate a message of warning about the political disunity.

This text was adapted from Bojana Cvejić and Ana Vujanović, *Public Sphere by Performance* (Belgrade: TkH; Berlin: bbooks; Paris: Les Laboratoires d'Aubervilliers, 2012), pp. 68–70.

02

In the subsequent two editions, the genre of mass choreography dissolved along two lines: solo accompanied by a mass chorus (1988) and decentralized multiple smaller-scale youth gatherings in many Yugoslav cities (1989) in lieu of one grand stadium spectacle.

03

'It seems like we are not as united as we should be… This is a warning about the current political situation, albeit in a playful, dancy message…'

1989

1987

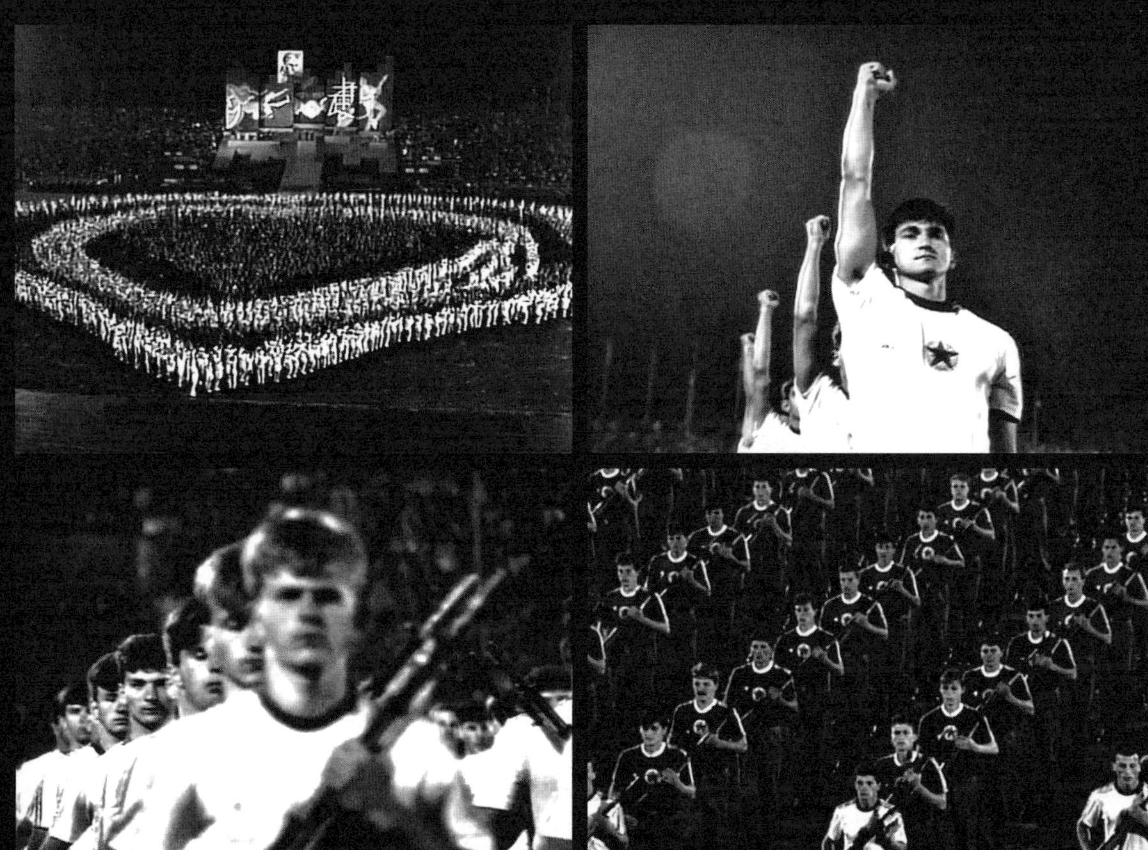

Mass Ornament #1 by Marta Popivoda and Ana Vujanović, 2013–2014, video still

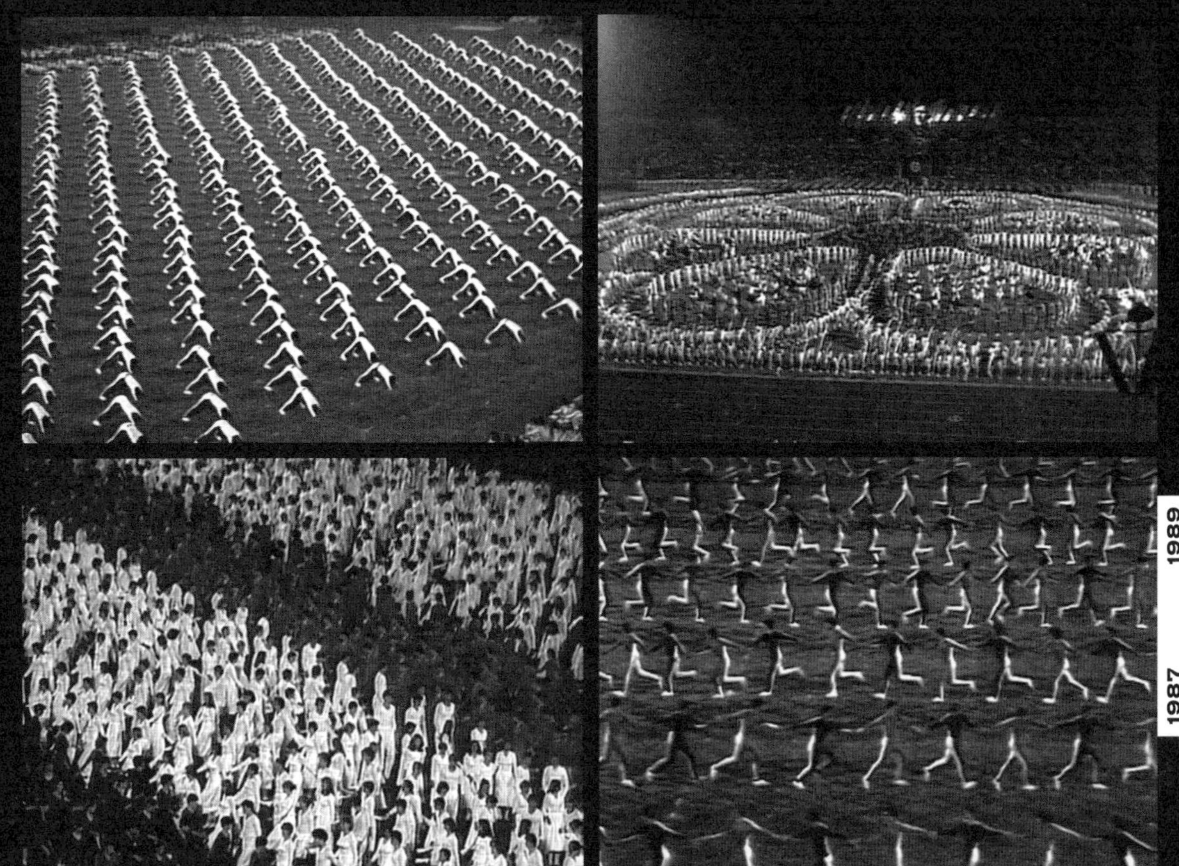

Yugoslavia: How Ideology Moved Our Collective Body by Marta Popivoda, 2013, documentary film still

'YUGOSLAV DOCUMENTS '89'

Zdenka Badovinac and Bojana Piškur

The genealogy of the 'Jugoslavenska dokumenta' (Yugoslav Documents) goes back to 1984, when three artists and friends from Sarajevo, Jusuf Hadžifejzović, Saša Bukvić and Rade Tadić, decided to organize a series of solo exhibitions of contemporary artists they thought highly of, in an attempt to give the Sarajevo public a unique opportunity to see the works of their fellow artists from across Yugoslavia. According to Hadžifejzović, the selection concept was based on *druga linija*, 'the other line', a term coined by Ješa Denegri. In the broadest sense, the term illustrates a direction, i.e., accepting the most topical and up-to-date principles in art and radically rejecting the mainstream system of art thinking. The three organizers were given a 25 m² wall at their disposal in the club of the Collegium Artisticum, located in the underground Skenderija centre, to put up the works of the invited artists. The exhibitions were staged between 1984 and 1987 without any budget, in a self-organized manner, and with each exhibition usually lasting a week. The first exhibition was by Boris Demur; in total there were almost 80 of them.

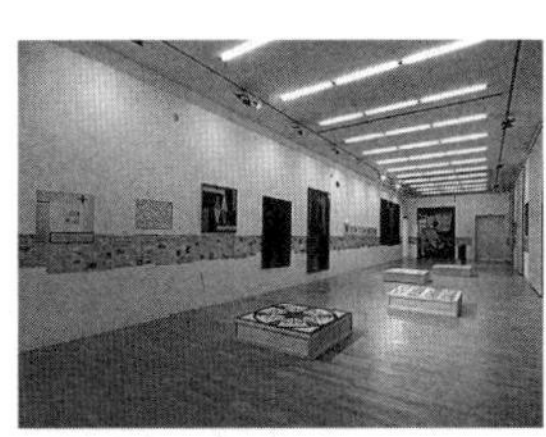

Exhibition view 'The Heritage of 1989. Case Study: The Second Yugoslav Documents Exhibition', Moderna galerija, Ljubljana, 2017. Photo: Matija Pavlovec

A significant change occurred in 1987, when 'Yugoslav Documents' transformed into a biennial event curated by Hadžifejzović and Tadić under the organizational auspices of the ZOI'84 Olimpijski centar Skenderija. The second biennial 'Documents', in 1989, became more ambitious in terms of organization and financial support, the selection of works and concepts, and the number of invited artists and foreign guests. It had a clear vision of positioning itself and Yugoslav art in the wider international context. It was also an attempt to make Sarajevo the fourth artistic centre in Yugoslavia (besides Ljubljana, Zagreb and Belgrade). The exhibition was held in Skenderija on 8,000 m² and was sponsored by some cultural organizations from the republics and various labour organizations (i.e., socialist companies). The opening on 1 July 1989 was attended by more than 6,000 people, including politicians from Bosnia-and-Herzegovina; it was broadcast live on Yugoslav television.

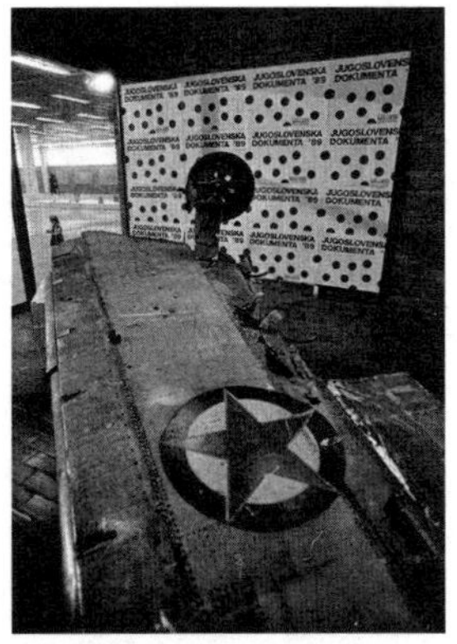

Installation view of work by Jadran Adamović, 'Yugoslav Documents '89', Olympic Center Skenderija, Sarajevo, 1989. Photo: Jane Štravs

'Yugoslav Documents '89' was one of the last large-scale 'Yugoslav' exhibitions before the breakup of the country. It featured 189 artists, who were chosen by 16 committee members from all republics and an organization committee. The members of the selection committee were free to propose any kind of art, according to their preferences. As a consequence, the selected works were in a variety of styles and techniques, including extended media and performance, in the typical spirit of postmodernist pluralism ('pluralism is the only ism') of the late eighties. However, more emphasis was given to contemporary works and artists that were influenced by older avant-garde movements. Questions such as 'What is contemporary Yugoslav art?' were raised at the accompanying conference. Also, an extensive catalogue was published on the occasion, with texts by various theoreticians and colour reproductions of the artworks.

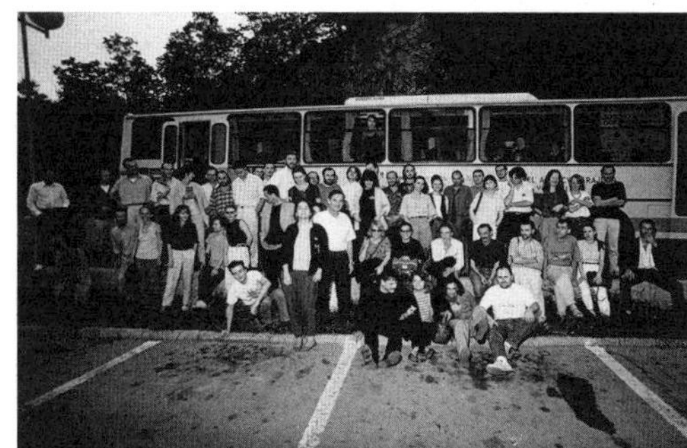

Group portrait of artists participating at the 'Yugoslav Documents '89', Sarajevo, 1989. Photo: Jane Štravs

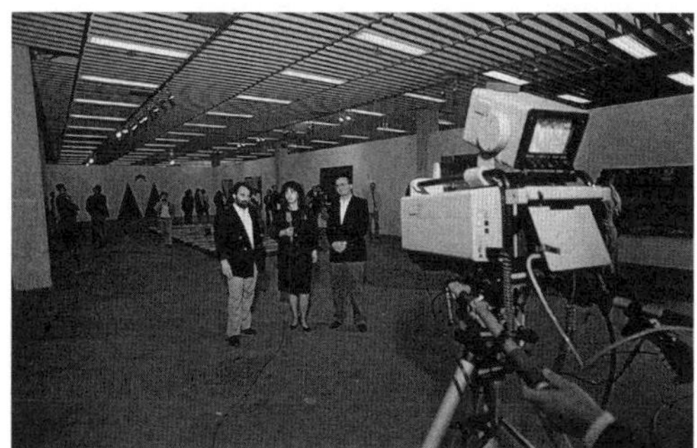

Exhibition view 'Yugoslav Documents '89', Olympic Center Skenderija, Sarajevo, 1989. Photo: Jane Štravs

Although some of the works referred to the social and political context of the eighties in some way, the exhibition was in general emphatically apolitical, with the organizers trying to avoid any kind of political debate. This is even more significant in view of the fact that in 1989, Yugoslavia had already started to break up. From today's perspective and in light of the subsequent events of the nineties, the exhibition was perhaps the last desperate attempt to preserve a common Yugoslav art space, the numerous artistic friendships, cultural networks and the feeling of *raja*[01] that was so specific to the pre-war Sarajevo.

01
Raja signifies a community based on acceptance, comradeship and hospitality.

NOVIE KHUDOZHNIKI (NEW ARTISTS GROUP)

ST. PETERSBURG IN THE EIGHTIES

Nav Haq

It was the generation of the Non-Conformist artists' movement during the last decade of the Soviet Union from which the Novie Khudozhniki (New Artists) group was formed. Founded in 1982 with artist Timur Novikov as its figurehead, the group included Sergei 'Afrika' Bugaev, Oleg Kotelnikov, Evgenij Kozlov and Georgy Guryanov amongst numerous other affiliates. They emerged as some of the foremost artistic protagonists during the optimistic transition to *glasnost* (openness) during the *perestroika*-era (reforms), through to the dissolution of the Soviet Union towards the end of 1989, and beyond.

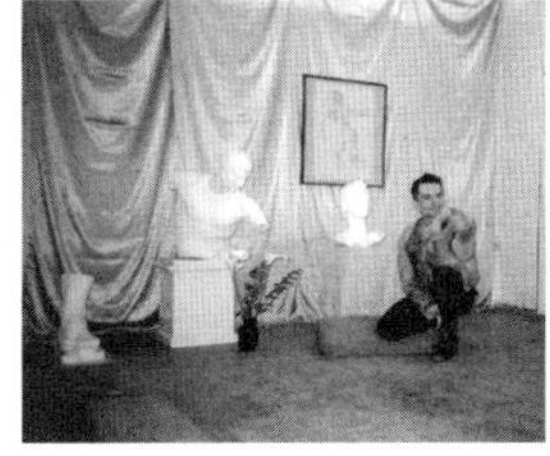

Timur Novikov at an exhibition of drawings by Alexander Samokhvalov at the New Academy, St. Petersburg, 1994. Courtesy Agnès & Jean-Pierre Rammant-Peeters

The New Artists created an eclectic postmodern mix of avant-garde practices, incorporating visual art, music, fashion, actions and cinema. Their visual art, inspired by Expressionist paintings, Primitivism and Pop Art alike, also emphasized an intrinsic communitarian approach through the organization of concerts, parties and exhibitions. Using domestic spaces such as flats to work in, they practiced in a deeply collaborative way, with this distinct interdisciplinarity that removed the distinctions between art and subculture. The group even organized the first mega-parties or electronic music rave events in Russia in 1990 and 1991, including the infamous Gagarin Party in Moscow, becoming themselves DJs, designers of the visuals and posters, and attracting international guests to perform.

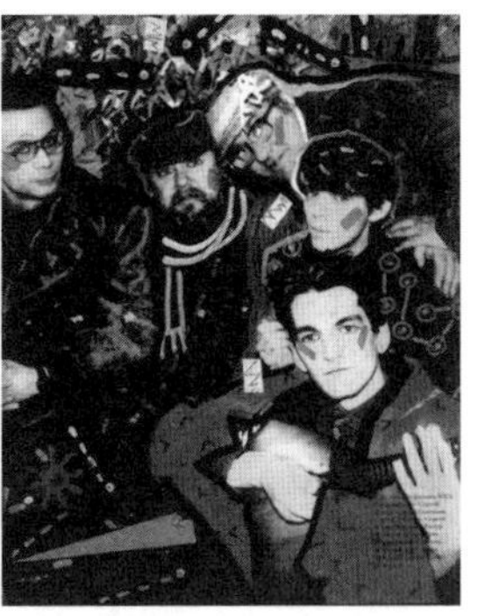

Sergey Shutov, Sergei Soloviev, Pavel Lebeshev, Sergei Bugaev and Timur Novikov on the set of the film *Assa*, Yalta, 1987, director: Sergei Soloviev. Courtesy Sergey Shutov

As the core protagonist, Novikov also started two other avant-garde initiatives during this period, which embodied this new and unbridled pop optimism. Firstly, this was through experimental rock and New Wave with the music group Novie Kompozitory (New Composers) for which he even created new instruments for their experimental sounds. Later in 1989, this was followed by the Novaya Akademia (New Academy) which, through a certain ironic position, looked towards a return to the classical ideals of perfection and beauty in the culture of ancient Greek antiquity. Its philosophy of 'Neo-Academicism' involved a master-and-apprentice type pedagogy as part of its anti-Modernist approach. The group were also involved in film projects in various roles, whether as actors or set designers, receiving acclaim for their contribution to the cult crime movie *Assa* (1987), directed by Sergei Solovyov.

The fluidity of their work as a group extended beyond mere aesthetics and into notions of the self. The New Artists were typically incorporating representations of homoeroticism as well as sexual and gender fluidity into their artistic practice, the kind that if took place today might be oppressed or censored as 'homosexual propaganda' in Russia. During the later Novaya Akademia years, Novikov helped set up the video network Pirate TV as an artistic appropriation of MTV-style popular formats. Its main presenter was the performance artist Vladislav Mamyshev-Monroe, who became a central figure in the gay scene, taking on different characters through cross-dressing and the openness of his sexuality. In rather homespun style, Monroe dressed up as different historical figures, from Marilyn Monroe to Charlie Chaplin.

Friendship was the central element of the New Artist group, providing it with such momentum that it became perhaps the most influential movement for the Russian artist scene of the Post-Soviet era. With an emphasis on the 'New' of 'New Artist', it is the sense of unbridled creativity, openness and desire for self-determined understandings of culture and selfhood that we can take from this group — a true moment grasped where art, politics an identity were all up for grabs.

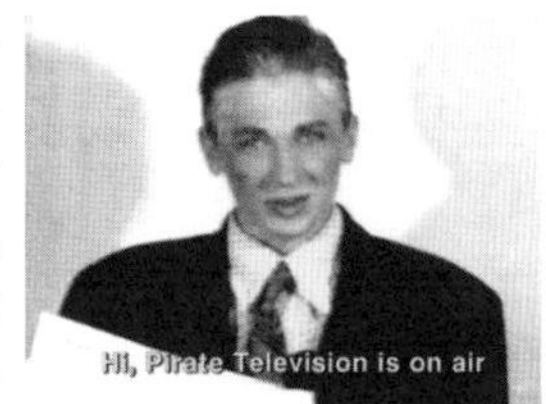

Vlad Mamyshev-Monroe presenting an episode of *Piratskoye Televideniye* (Pirate TV), 1991–1994, video still. Courtesy M HKA

1991

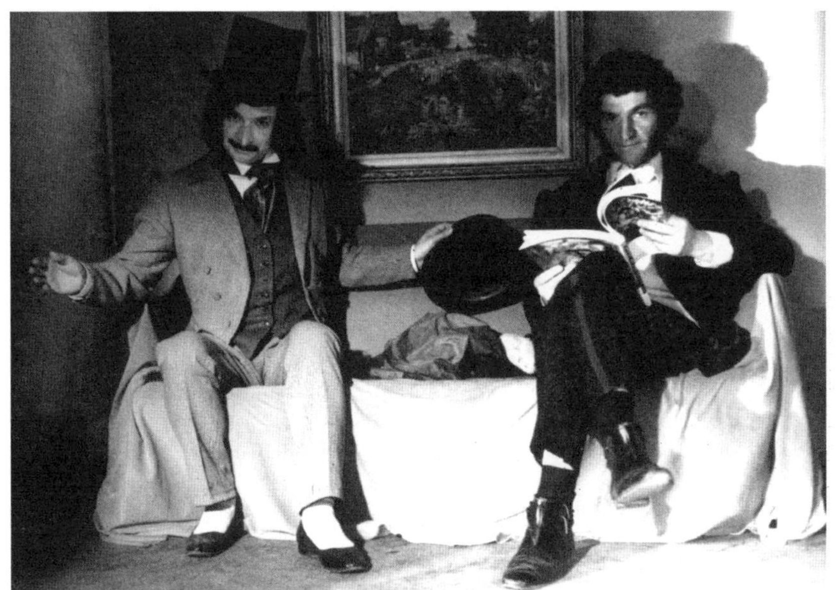

Filming *The Manifesto of Neo-Academism* directed by Olga Tobreluts, c. 1993
Andrei Khlobystin as Gogol and Timur Novikov as Pushkin. Courtesy Agnès & Jean-Pierre Rammant-Peeters

1982

ABSOLUTE MAJORITY SYNDROME

Mar Villaespesa

This text was originally published in *Arena* magazine of which art critic and independent curator Mar Villaespesa was director.

ABSOLUTE MAJORITY SYNDROME

MAR VILLAESPESA

Generally a great problem now in Spanish art is the self-helpful adoption of foreign models. It is a question of imitating the winner of the race. When one does not want to face the *"Here and Now"* situation, it suggests the lack of critic conscience concerning our collective memory; not to face it with nostalgia but rather face it as an instrument and reference point which will firmly place us in a reality world and determined context.

Active and healthy symptoms in the international art panoramas at the end of the 70's and beginning of the 80's have been the recovery and new vision of some ignored moments of history or at least members scorned until nowadays, e.g. the Italian Transvanguard recovered some artists adjacent to the *"official"* protagonists of movements such as futurism or metaphysical painiting. In the same way for instance, the paintings by German artists start to recover some of the classical expressionists and some inmediate predecessors like Beuys and Polke, the same as the Americans exert themselves in a new vision of Pollock or the Pop Art.

At the same time, the point of view of the generation debates ideas as it also rebuilds the past, transforming history in a dynamic and open platform, rather than in a stable and cramped values hierarchy.

In Spain, the history of the last forty years had a structure established parallel to the power, which means that it was static, hierarchic and unshakeable. Any kind of totalitarian state can use this model and thus justifies it making it be permanent, taking apart relationships with their momentaneous present and thus avoiding a critical and dialectical thought through the conversion of the present int a destiny. By being clearly conscient of the immedite past, even if it is not such a pleasant feeling, one avoids the denial of destiny and can assume present as a continuous action platform.

This denial of destiny has been one of the seeds that, with a non alarming desire, bloomed at the very beginning of the decade in view of the national strate of euphoria because of its recently elected democracy. The obsolete abstraction of the univeral feeling of the pro-Franco slogans: *"Spain is a destiny unity in the universal idea"* has been substituted by another may be more up to date abstraction, but which finally carries out the same structural function, which is namely the international phenomenon

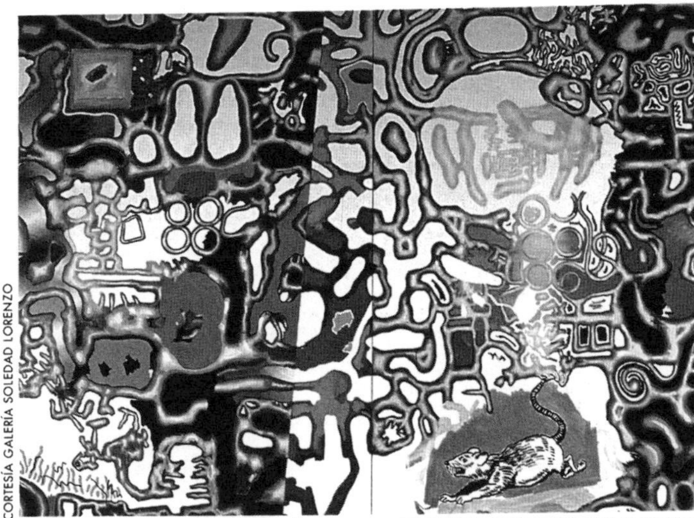

CORTESÍA GALERÍA SOLEDAD LORENZO

LUIS GORDILLO. TODO OÍDOS. ACRÍLICO, PAPEL, MADERA/ACRYLIC, PAPER, WOOD. 1987. 144×158 cm.

as a common plan. So it has been a diagram of an inherited behaviour more than an ideological fact, and surprisingly, at the same time, it represents the lack of some intellectual minorities, presumably critical, that did not doubt about the reason of such a situation. In concern of us, this debate should have been given by the artists.

LACK OF CRITICAL CONTEXT

What does Spanish art answer to? What kind of questions does it ask society? What sort of connection does our art of the 80's answer to, or how does it answer to the problems of the refered years? Not the artists or the art community, because they are not conscious of their environment, remain enclosed in an absolute aestheticism in the elegant and wonderful blind alley of the right behaviour feeling? It is that the 80's paintings and sculptures are a reaction to the latest vanguards, or a strategy to renew

their significance, or a continuity, may be, of the mere act of painting and building? Is it just wondering whether it is possible to assume a postmodern conscience without having been aware of a conscience of the end of Modernity? I think the lack of a crisis context provoked a thought of some obsolete means of doing art; this thought being masked in many cases, not of innocuos lirism any more, but a fashionable appearance.

It is not a question of doing on absolute generality concept since there exist exceptions, but the exceptions do not generate reality; and that is why the vanguard is not based on exceptions, but on theorical facts. Though we probably would have to think about the *"exception"* phenomenon so typical in the Spanish culture. Some of the artists having been considered as *"exceptions"* of the XXth centuary, like Picasso, Dalí, or Miró, were part of avant-garde movements such as cubism, surrealism, but always far from our borders...

The common project of cubism or surrealism

occurs in the center of Art —Paris. May be in Spain was the following generation, known here as the generation of 1927, with idiosyncracy and surrealist characteristics (Buñuel, Lorca, Óscar Domínguez...), which has been shortened by the civil war, by the time when a global artistic project of international vanguard was laying the foundations of modernity in our country. The loose of the concept of the present reality provoked the fact that from the 40's until nowadays, the artistic projects have been considered and analysed through valid models in other contexts, rather than having been answering to a reality, and analysed for their capacity of critical answer to the refered reality. This is why any innovation project was forgotten by the non efficiency of the answers of the context where it happened, though it was present in its protagonists' intuition and minds.

Do the exceptions go on being the cultural axis of the Spanish art by the end of the 80's? Does not it prove the absence of an authentic avant-garde or postmodernism spirit, characterized by the general projects rather than the concrete artists?

In Spain, everything was working thanks to individualities, exept in the case of some group situations, in which individualism also reigned (for example, in the 60's, the New Generation Group or the Constructivists Group composed by Gordillo, Teixidor, Alexanco, E. Asins, Lugan...; in the 70's, the Conceptuals in Madrid: Luis Muro, Paz Muro. N. Criado...; or in Barcelona: García Sevilla or C. Pazos...; the abstraction of the *"Trama"* Group: Broto, Grau...; the abstraction in Sevilla: Delgado, Suárez, Bermejo, Tovar..., and the *"Madrid Figuration"*: Pérez Mínguez, Alcolea, C. Franco, Cobo, Pérez Villalta, Quejido, the sculptor M. Navarro...). We should analyse and strictly discuss which of these groups respond to a pragmatic agreement or a common project, and knows by intuition a rupture desire, not only with the previous Spanish groups, but also concerning the lineality uses and the relevant Art means of these times; or we should try to think if, on the contrary, these groups somehow reply to a pursuit of the vanguard courses of the moment.

Whatever the conclusion would be, it is clear that most of the times, the individuals, as well as the groups disappeared, or ill interpreted each other because of a lack of genealogy, context and critical answer.

THE 80's

Actually, art, during the Franco period had deep context problems; the 80's art still has the same problem, though it begins to be solved, due to the increase of cultural space (a regular circulation of international exhibitions has started in galleries and institutions, at the same time than Spanish art begins to travel regularly beyond the border of our country; the Arco Fair is getting more important, as well as the activities of public and private entities such as the Reina Sofía Art Center or the Caixa; also art

workshops are created as for example the Círculo de Bellas Artes, etc.).

The art of the 80 (the *"pos-trans/avant-garde movida"*, the new sculpture, the *"Sevilla Figuration"*...) has unfortunately been reasessed due to its character as a representative or ambassador of the Spanish democratic euphoria, inside and outside our country. The boom of the *"international"* is considered as a *"reason to be"* and it gives rise to the great success topic, including the historical success beyond our borders. These customs constantly appear in all the rules of our society with such an unusual than understandable euphoria in many aspects. We should wonder about the propaganda, about the official control and about some critical sectors than confuse criticism with journalism and art with social phenomena to the detriment of the artist's works. This fact leads to the illusion of the birth of an ex-nihilo art which does no have any connection with the rather inmediate past, nor with a determined reality. On another hand, this momentary illusion finally begins to.

Everything ran parallel to a critical and theoretical emptiness, while the artists's projects have been recognized according to foreign or commercial models resumed in the device: *"Tell me where you exhibit, I shall tell you how important you are"*. The value criteria have been intervined by the art and international market propaganda. The hierarchy of the values reply to merchandise criteria rather than social needs criteria. Neither the Modernity or the avant-garde nor the post-modernity, though it is supposed to be less *"strict and moralist"* have converted the market —an instrument— in the only goal of art.

To give an excessively positive vision of the 80's would mean to betray the critical thought and furthermore to open the way to a wellbeing and euphoria propaganda, that even if it is evident, is built on a blowed up reality with a view to a serie of socio-political and economical contradictions that we constantly feel. But to behave negatively would also falsify some realities which start to be palpable. Finally the artists and the critics as well as the general Spanish culture are offered the option to distinguish from quantitative changes of reality and qualitative ones answering the inner reality of society but not foreign models. For instance, Spanish art needs museums —which does not only mean physical spaces— but it obviously would be necessary to be up to the contradictions of the models we follow —whether European or American.

SPANISH ART REVISION

It is important to revise Spanish asrt history because it would be arduous to analyse what Art has been in the running decade without knowing what it has been in the past. The revision must include the arguing of the history context and situating it in an international outline, to be able to calibrate its reach. But the attempts to do so, which proliferated in recent exhibitions (Feito, Viola, Aspectos de una década...) only insisted on the historical aspects and the museum character.

Obviously the revision cannot assume the

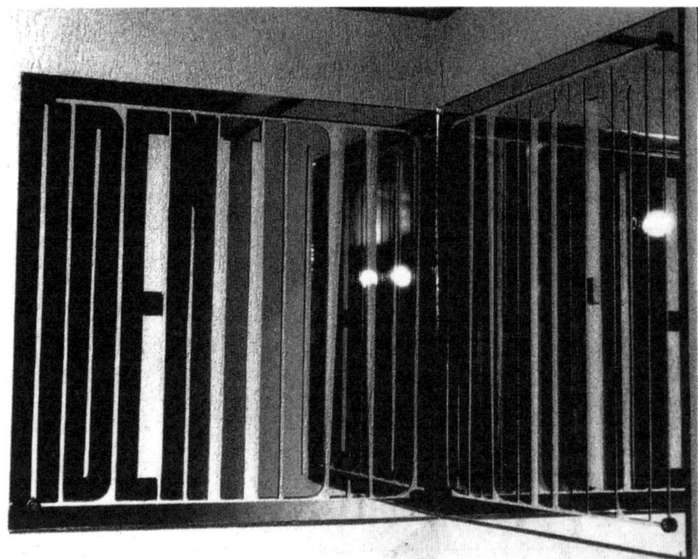

NACHO CRIADO. IDENTIDAD. INSTALACIÓN/INSTALLATION. 1977.

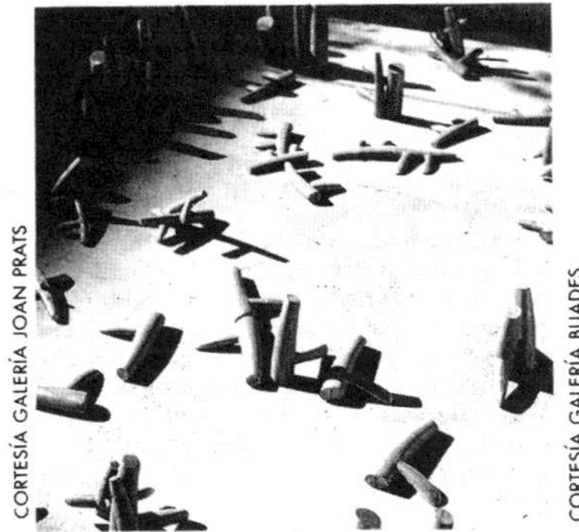

MIQUEL NAVARRO. ORGÁNIC. PLOMO/LEAD. 1987.

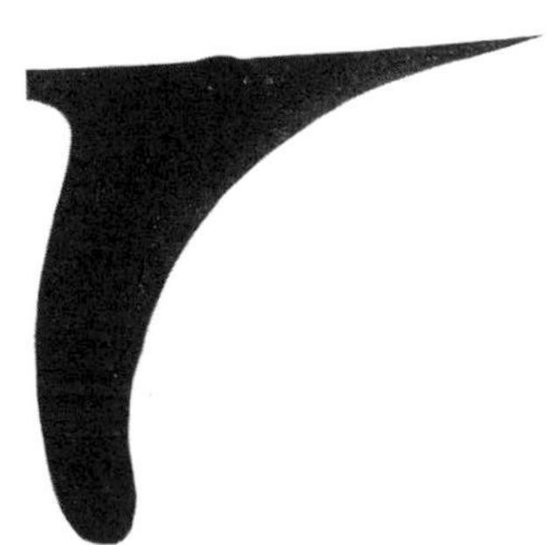

SCHLOSSER. SIN TÍTULO/UNTITLED.

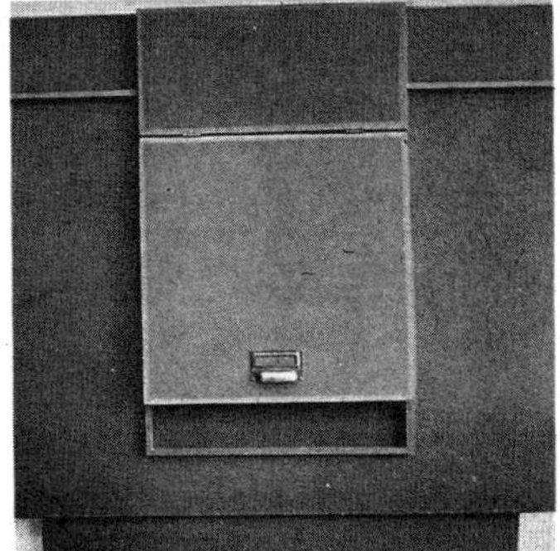

TEIXIDOR. POSIBILIDAD EN EL ROJO. 1967.

1989

nationalist settled mind without falling into the hypocracy of justifing its own state of victim. But we cannot forget that the fact of converting the artists into simple representative of Spanish art into the international panorama, can be dangerous too, because the protocol established image has got nothing to do with the real problems of our society, and to which art has to answer in a critical way. In many exhibitions, the problem of Spanish art has been reduced to a protocol image (remember the **Five centuries of Spanish art** exhibition in Paris in 1987).

Art must not frame the power but reply to the community problems. This is the only way of avoiding the most innocuo lyricism and mimicry: doble axis of the Spanish art problems as a global unity.

The euphoria hymn and consecration of some artists konwn along the 80's decade (Barceló, Sicilia...) and the desire of including others from last decade in art history (Pérez Villalta...), without arguing their work by the time it reaches maturity, has a been a backwards step concerning past situations. Let us hope that other artists in similar situations will be luckier and that their art —not themselves— will have the oportunity of being argued before it is included into the art history and before they receive national prizes (like S. Solano, J. Muñoz, Paneque...).

Finally a scenery takes shape the euphoric energy of some images fade, we withness the continuity of projects already initiated by other artists in the past decade (Schlosser, Lootz, S. Sevilla, Zush, M. Navarro, C. Franco, Quejido...). At the same time, glimpses of incipient necessity of references or starting points, as well as connections to confront answers and common ideas are noticed, coinciding with the revision of conceptual and objective proposals that will help to revise the recent history of Spanish conceptual art (Equipo Crónica, Torres, Muntadas. E. Balcells, P. Noguera, F. Abad, C. Pazos, N. Criado, Zaj...). Once established, there will be a renewal of the art language and the significance of art and the artist himself or herself according to our society (Pedro Romero, Agustín Parejo, School...). The regularity of the exhibitions thus may erase the clumsy and topical barrier of art *"before and after Franco"* created in such a way to ignore the past, instead of arguing about it.

ART AND POLITICS

There has been an interrelation between art and politics over the past decade which may present a sympton of vitality and connection with reality, a concept that Spanish art was missing. The problem is that the art and the supposed vitality have run at the same speed with the power euphoria, at the expenses of democracy. Nevertheless, this collaboration is the golden dream of any dictatorship.

In 1982, the socialist government won the elections with an absolute majority, giving rise to prepotency and demagogic situations, for with energy has been wasted, and also used to monopolize the decisions of political and social life. As far as art is concerned, it has been centred as a propaganda tool rather than a tool to educate (the basic problem of lack of up to date programs in art schools is alarming). The parallelism between art and the political course appeared recently to be more encouraging: an incipient reply and critical awareness expressed in the political field through the General Strike of past december 14th.

The euphoria of what we could qualify as an absolute majority syndrome within the political world, is reproduced in the art world by a syndrome of being discovered. This sould be replaced by the aim of self-determination and self-discovery. It will then be possible to start a dialogue which must not be the self-helpful continuity of different generations, but a critical dialogue in which the starting point of young artists could question and resert the aesthetic and ethical projects of the artists that have been chosen as a reference. This would be the refreshing part to be acheived by the young artists (definitively the protagonists of the 80's Spanish panorama), and which should be different from the one they have been assigned, converting them in a center of attention, demand and propaganda. In other words, it would be like forcing a situation, which, in most of the cases, hardly results to be bearable. ▲

Translation: SYLVIE IMBERT

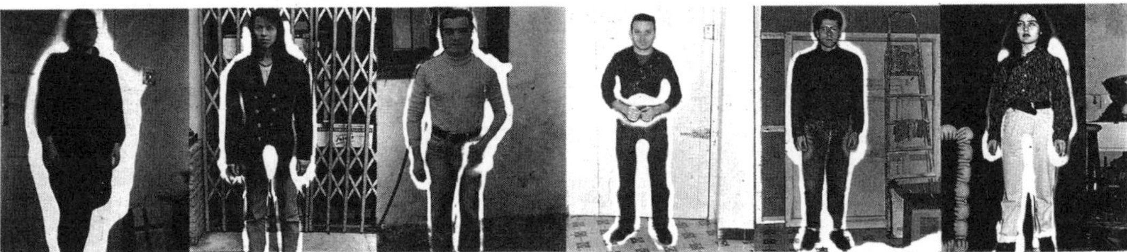

SIN IR MÁS LEJOS

Rogelio López Cuenca

Sin ir más lejos (Without Going Any Further) was put together for the exhibition 'El sueño imperativo' (The Imperative Dream), curated by Mar Villaespesa at Madrid's Círculo de Bellas Artes in 1991.

Sin ir más lejos unfolded across two planes, inside the gallery in which it exhibited, in a series of display cabinets, an ensemble of handwritten posters used by anonymous people to beg in the streets. These posters, largely cardboard and acquired from their owners and creators, were displayed along with prints of virgins and saints, interspersed with postcards reproducing images of the major cultural events Spain was organising for the following year: the Universal Exposition of Seville (Expo '92), the Fifth Centenary of the Discovery of America, the Olympic Games in Barcelona, and European Capital of Culture, which went to Madrid in 1992.

Furthermore, a set comprising six offset printed posters reproducing different photos on a frieze with official logos of these events was stuck around the streets of Madrid.

The *Sin ir más lejos* posters put forth an ironic and critical re-reading of the hegemonic narrative which presented these events as definitive proof of Spain's rise to the first division of Western democracies.

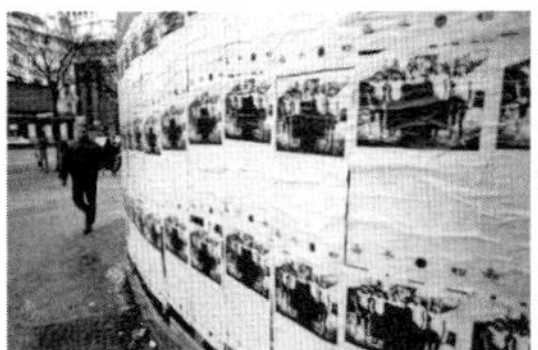

Sin ir más lejos (Without going further) posters, 70 × 40 cm, Madrid, 1991. Photo: Javier Andrada

On one of the posters, President Felipe González, who had held office in successive terms since 1982, appeared with special glasses to view projections in 3D; glasses to see with complete clarity: grey-brown nocturnal felines evoking Deng Xiaoping's lauded and poetic maxims of Chinese pragmatism: 'It doesn't matter whether a cat is white or black, as long as it catches mice.'

On another, a group of indigenous Americans (from the Amazon, judging from the styling — as they said at the time — of the haircuts) posed in front of the objective: Anthropology? Police? Science? Missionary? Tourist? Beautician? At any rate, it was Eurocentric and colonial: our gaze. A polysemic and ambiguous, yet always unsettling, sign of a cross, red, was also superimposed over the image.

Another poster featured a photograph of the cover of the record *Vigo 92*, by the Galician rock group Os Resentidos: a scathing and acerbic condemnation of the obscene channelling and concentration of public investment which prompted a macro-event like the Olympics to be held. The photograph depicts five gypsy children in the shanty town where they live, each one holding an old bicycle wheel to form the philanthropic emblem of the Olympic rings.

The manipulation, expropriation and exploitation of the cultural expression of a historically marginalised community, such as the gypsy community, sets the focus of another poster. A striking image of a woman dressed as a flamenco dancer ('as a gypsy', to put it another way) on a background with a Nazi flag. It is not staged, either, but a real photo taken in Málaga in 1939.

A flag once again appears in a photograph of the astronaut Buzz Aldrin taking his first steps on the moon in 1969. Yet, in this instance, the stripes do not accompany the stars. On this occasion it's Catalonia's national flag, in the midst of such an Olympic moment — Do you remember, Catalans? — the zenith.

A scene from the bitter-sweet *Bienvenido, Mr Marshall* (Welcome, Mr Marshall, 1953) illustrates another of the posters, cruelly mirroring the embarrassing atmosphere leading up to 1992 and its related events.

And, to finish off, Baron Thyssen's passionate swing dance, in celebration of who knows what, or at least we didn't know what; we'll never know with any certainty, although we do have our suspicions.

The most unsettling part is that these posters don't seem like they're reflecting a bygone time twenty-five years ago, a quarter of a century ago. They are talking about the here and now.

'THE OTHER STORY:
AFRO-ASIAN ARTISTS IN POST-WAR BRITAIN'

Charles Esche

'The Other Story' was a significant milestone in the recognition of non-white, non-European artists by the cultural authorities in London and an important attempt by British state institutions to deal with the cultural and artistic consequences of imperialism and migration. The exhibition was held at the Hayward Gallery in London in 1989, a British establishment venue that is part of the enormous South Bank arts complex, programmed at the time by the national Arts Council. As well as programming the Hayward, curators were responsible for an extensive programme taking modern art out into the British provinces. To that end, 'The Other Story' went on tour to museums in Wolverhampton and Manchester, after its London showing.

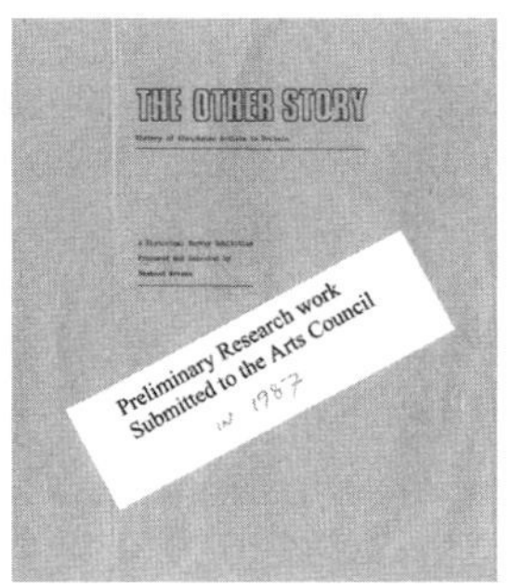

'The Other Story: Preliminary Research Work submitted to the Arts Council', 1987. Courtesy Rasheed Araeen and Asia Art Archive

The exhibition was organized and curated by Rasheed Araeen, a Pakistani artist, curator and writer based in London who was a seminal figure in the emergence of the Black and Asian Arts movement in England. Araeen had already established two important magazines, *Black Phoenix* and *Third Text*, and helped set up what became Black Umbrella, a visual art resource for Afro-Asians. He was also an active artist, showing in England and internationally. Despite these substantial achievements, the road to 'The Other Story' was a long one. The idea was first brought up in 1978 and was repeatedly rejected by various guardians of British cultural policy until 1986. In 1987, the Hayward Gallery finally agreed to the principle of the show — that it should be a show by and about Black and Asian artists — and the curatorial production process was financed and set in motion.

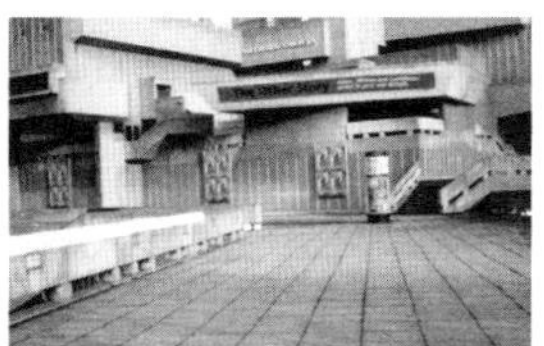

'The Other Story: Afro-Asian Artists in Post-War Britain', Hayward Gallery, Southbank Centre, London, 1989. Courtesy Rasheed Araeen and Asia Art Archive

Opening in late 1989, 'The Other Story' roughly coincided with two other landmark international exhibitions 'Magiciens de la terre' at the Centre Pompidou, Paris and the 3rd Havana Biennial in Cuba. In very different ways, all three of these events marked a substantial shift in the politics of exhibition making and were the first steps towards a wider inclusion of works and voices within the dominant narratives of modern art. Such inclusion was Araeen's hope when he first proposed the exhibition and he certainly understood his project as starkly opposed to the search for authenticity and indigenous culture promoted by 'Magiciens de la terre'. In contrast, Araeen's focus was on the legacies of British imperialism and on

BLACK PHOENIX

Third World Perspective on Contemporary Art & Culture

████████████████████████,
London NW6 3PJ

28 October 1978

Andrew Dempsey,
The Arts Council of Great Britain,
105 Piccadilly,
London W1V OAU

Dear Andrew Dempsey,

Just to suggest that the Arts Council of Great Britain should now look into the possibility of organising a survey exhibition of the works of <u>black artists in Britain</u>. Although I'm aware of the pitfalls in approaching art from a point of view that may lead to separate groups based on sex, race, etc., the separateness already exists and it is not of our own making but a result of the attitude of the society. Moreover there doesn't seem to be any choice for us except in asserting now our historical presence here separately, till the cultural institutions of the country come to terms with the multi-racial aspect of this society by fully recognising the equal abilities of all peoples irrespective of colour and race.

I would therefore like to propose a study project which should look into what has actually been produced by black artists in Britain for the last thirty or so years, by placing them in their socio-historical context, and then making this information available to public. This could take the form of a book as well as become a basis for a comprehensive exhibition.

This information is crucial at this particular time when the progressive forces of the country are moving towards recognising the fact that black people are here to stay and they shall, and will, become permanent part of British society. It is important therefore for the people to know that black people constitute not only those who by their hard work have been contributing to the material prosperity of the country but also those who have been engaged in artistic and cultural activities.

The ignorance of the work of professional black artists in this country is in fact responsible for the lack of incentive among the younger generation of blacks (40% of them are born here) to enter the field of visual arts. The situation now requires an urgent redress and this cannot be achieved by merely providing new opportunities, nor by pigeonholing black people into various ethnic categories and then placing them in the context of the countries of their origin, but by fully recognising their past achievements in this country. The presence of black artists in Britain is part of recent British history, as well as the world at large, and this aspect of the history must be brought to surface if we as black people are expected to contribute positively towards the development of this society into a truly multi-racial society.

I would therefore like to know if the Arts Council is prepared to consider this proposal. However I shall be away in Pakistan for the next six weeks and this will give you enough time to think and discuss the matter with your collegues. I shall be back in London sometime in the middle of December and then, if you wish, we can discuss the matter further and, if possible, give the proposal a concrete framework.

With regards,

Rasheed Araeen

addressing the disappointment and rejection of post-1945 immigrants to Britain, to the imperial centre, who were not embraced in the way the propaganda of empire implied.

The exhibition largely traced artists working within modernist and conceptual art traditions in the broadest sense. It featured artists with roots in Africa, the Caribbean, the Indian subcontinent, Japan, China and the Philippines. The oldest artists, such as F N Souza or Frank Bowling had arrived in England just after the Second World War from different British colonies and fought for recognition as black artists working in an autonomous, modernist style. Araeen, who was younger but more politicized, included himself, a number of his contemporaries and the younger generation of Black and Asian artists, such as Sonia Boyce, Eddie Chambers, Lubaina Himid and Keith Piper, who all developed their work in the context of what came to be known as the Black British Art Movement of the eighties.

It is worthwhile noting that the more commercially successful black artists at the time, such as Anish Kapoor, refused to take part in the exhibition for fear that it would reduce their work to statements of identity. Of the three generations covered in the show, only the youngest had any female representatives, something that was criticized at the time. The British establishment's response to the show in the media and art world was hostile, though with important exceptions. Despite their eager dismissal, however, 'The Other Story' has become a historical exhibition that pushed the issue of Black and Asian artists to the forefront and confronted a major British state institution with its racism and cultural exclusiveness for the first time.

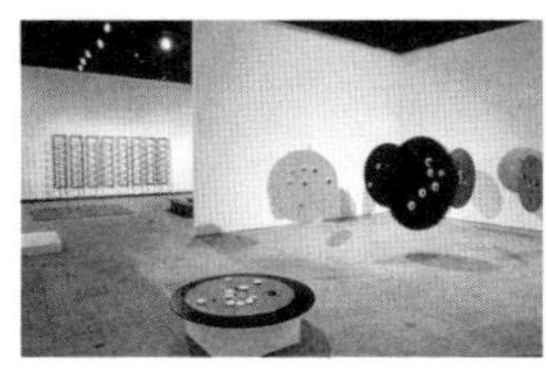

Exhibition view of works by Li Yuan-chia and Rasheed Araeen, 'The Other Story: Afro-Asian Artists in Post-War Britain', Hayward Gallery, Southbank Centre, London, 1989

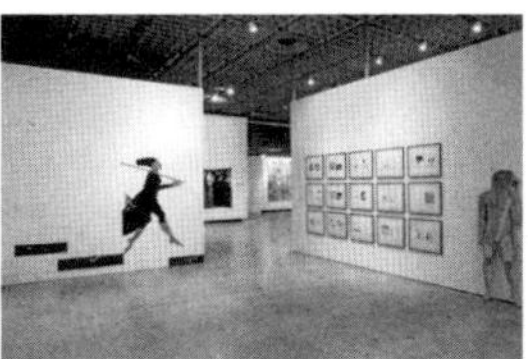

Exhibition view of work by Lubaina Himid, 'The Other Story: Afro-Asian Artists in Post-War Britain', Hayward Gallery, Southbank Centre, London, 1989. Courtesy Rasheed Araeen and Asia Art Archive

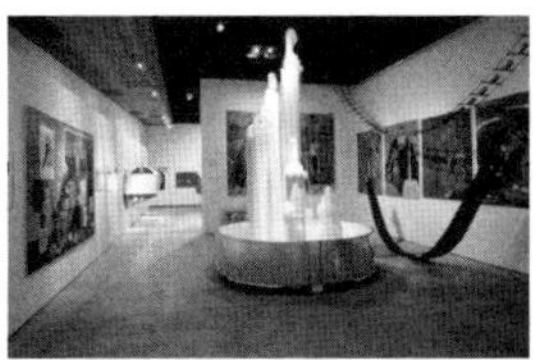

Exhibition view of work by David Medalla, 'The Other Story: Afro-Asian Artists in Post-War Britain', Hayward Gallery, Southbank Centre, London, 1989. Courtesy Rasheed Araeen and Asia Art Archive

1989—THE SECOND SUMMER OF LOVE

Nav Haq

1989 was a year of major geopolitical events around the world. Not only did the Soviet Union collapse, it was also the year in which, for example, the Soviet military withdrew from Afghanistan. It was the year that the Solidarność (Solidarity) movement was legalized in Poland and thus allowed to take part in free elections. It was the year that the student-led Tiananmen square protests were taking place in Beijing. It was the year in which Ayatollah Khomeini, founder of the Islamic Republic of Iran following the revolution he had led a decade earlier, died. Yet, in a Great Britain still coming to terms with deep recession and the impact of Thatcherism, young people it seemed were preoccupied with a cultural revolution of their own. Rave.

The first pinnacle of the rave movement in the United Kingdom is seen as 1988–1989, and was dubbed the 'Second Summer of Love', despite actually spanning two summers. In being described as this, it became linked to previous historic cultures of psychedelia, particularly the hippy movement and its Summer of Love two decades earlier, in 1967. A lifestyle revolution ensued for youth culture, as acid house moved from Ibiza to the British underground and rapidly graduated to the mainstream of British clubland and the after-hours party scene, first in Manchester with clubs such as The Haçienda, and then in London with clubs such as Shoom. The unlicensed free party and warehouse party scene also ensued, all fuelled by the popularity of the new drug ecstasy arriving from the continent. A battle between a mass youth movement lifestyle and the authorities was to ensue.

Slowly losing grip on power, then Prime Minister Margaret Thatcher made 35 changes to her cabinet throughout 1989, including the controversial sacking of Foreign Secretary Geoffrey Howe due to their disagreements over Britain's place in Europe. Weakened, Thatcher even took a holiday (to Salzburg), something she would never normally want to do. She would resign the following year. One of the hottest summers on record in Western Europe, the then Home Secretary Douglas Hurd had commented that 'a long heatwave meant trouble', aware of preceding events of the same era such as the Battle of the Beanfield at Stonehenge in 1985, and of the further growing nationwide youth movement. Perhaps

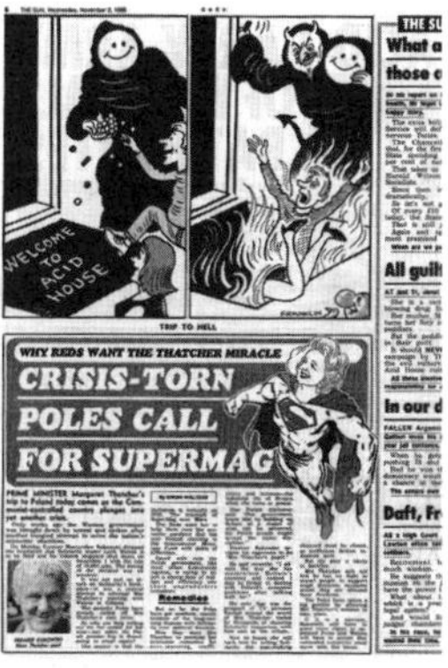

Welcome to Acid House, comic strip by Franklin from *The Sun* newspaper, 2 November 1988. Courtesy Dan Gilson

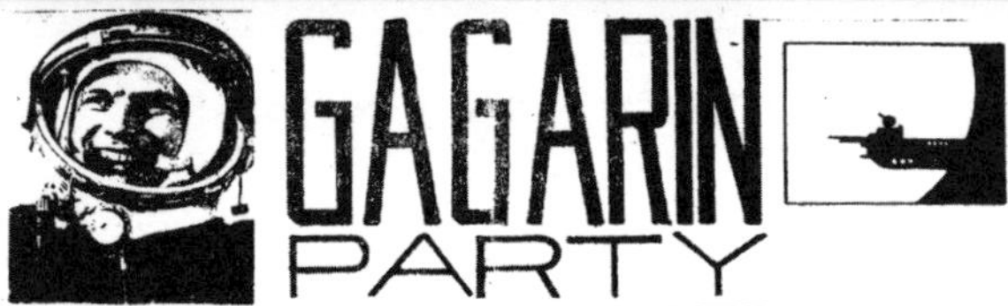

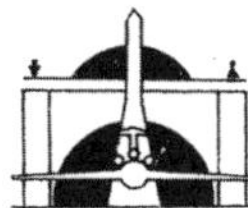

Flyer for Gagarin Party, Moscow's first rave, 14 December 1991. Courtesy Sergey Shutov

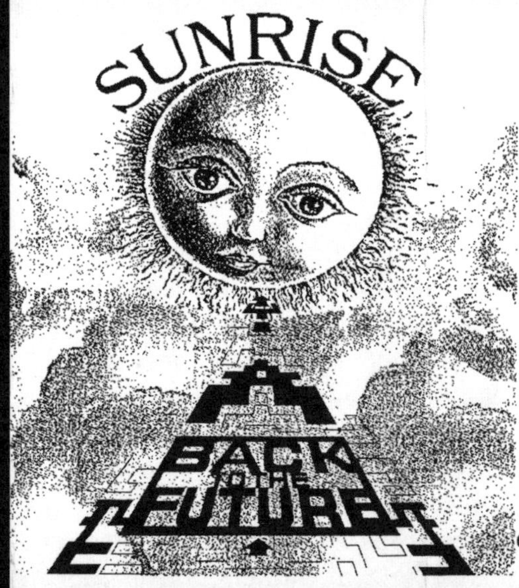

Flyer for Sunrise / Back to the Future rave party, 12 August 1989. Courtesy M HKA

themselves conscious of an impending clampdown on rave culture, party organizers Sunrise organized the biggest outdoor rave yet, the Sunrise/Back to the Future acid house party, at Longwick, Buckinghamshire, on 12 August that year. It attracted over 20,000 people, and naturally a media controversy followed.

Events such as the Battle of the Beanfield, the 1989 Sunrise party and then the infamous week-long Castlemorton rave of May 1992 in the Malvern Hills, which is reported to have had up to 40,000 attendants, were all unlicensed manifestations that ultimately paved the way for the criminalization of rave, most conspicuously through the Criminal Justice and Public Order Act of 1994. A second pinnacle of rave took place around 1992, yet 1989 was when the combination of moral panic and neoliberalism began to take a grip, tightened further through the nineties, on the possibilities of such a sporadic and largely unlicensed youth movement continuing and growing. With other nations in Western Europe adopting similar legislation to prohibit such autonomous social and creative organization, the question arises as to how society in late-capitalism might find a space for new forms of culture, organization and lifestyle.

CONTRIBUTORS

NICK AIKENS (born 1981) is a curator at the Van Abbemuseum, Eindhoven, since 2012. Recent exhibition projects include 'The 1980s. Today's Beginnings?', Van Abbemuseum, Eindhoven, 2016 (co-curated with Diana Franssen), 'The Place is Here', Nottingham Contemporary (co-curated with Sam Thorne), Middlesbrough Institute of Modern Art and South London Gallery, 2017 and 'Rasheed Araeen: A Retrospective', Van Abbemuseum, Eindhoven, 2017 (and touring to MAMCO, Geneva, BALTIC, Gateshead, and Garage Museum of Contemporary Art, Moscow through 2019). He is the co-editor of *What's the Use? Constellations of Art, History and Knowledge* (2016) and a number of artist monographs, most recently *Rasheed Araeen* (2017) and *Too Much World: The Films of Hito Steyerl* (2015). He is a Research Affiliate of the CCC Research Master Programme, HEAD, Geneva School of Art and Design, and a member of the editorial board for L'Internationale Online. He is a course leader at the Dutch Art Institute (since 2012) and was recently a tutor at the Design Academy Eindhoven (2014–2016).

HENRY ANDERSEN (born 1992) is an artist whose projects typically centre on written text and evolve through open-ended collaborations with friends. Andersen is interested in poetry, architecture, and erotica. He has presented work at a number of festivals, exhibitions, and other platforms including Kunstenfestivaldesarts and La Loge (both Brussels), Perth Institute of Contemporary Arts (AU), 2017 Pune Bienale (IN), and Bâtard Festival (Brussels). He recently released a record of spoken text, *Stanzas or the Law of the Good Neighbour*, with the Belgian label KRAAK. Since 2016, he has a founding member of Slow Reading Club.

Henry Andersen lives in Brussels.

ZDENKA BADOVINAC (born 1958) is a curator and writer, who has served as Director of the Moderna galerija in Ljubljana since 1993. Since 2011, Moderna galerija has two locations: the Museum of Modern Art and the Museum of Contemporary Art Metelkova. In her work, Badovinac highlights the difficult processes of redefining history alongside various avant-garde traditions within contemporary art.

Badovinac's first exhibition to address these issues was 'Body and the East: From the 1960s to the Present', 1998. She also initiated the first Eastern European art collection: Arteast 2000+. One of her most important recent projects is 'NSK from *Kapital* to Capital: Neue Slowenische Kunst: The Event of the Final Decade of Yugoslavia', Moderna galerija, 2015. Badovinac was Slovenian Commissioner at the Venice Biennale from 1993 to 1997, 2005 and 2017, and Austrian Commissioner at the São Paulo Biennial in 2002 and the President of CIMAM, 2010–2013.

BARIŞ GENÇER BAYKAN (born 1978) is an academic. Baykan holds a Master's degree in Political Sociology from the University of Paris X Nanterre (FR) and a PhD in Sociology from the University of Kent (UK). He is currently working as an Assistant Professor of Public Administration at the University of Yeditepe, Istanbul, where he teaches social movements, urbanization and environmental policy. His research interest are social movements and anti-GMO movement, climate movement, green parties and green political thought.

Baykan's recent publications include *Effect of Materialism and Environmental Knowledge on Environmental Consciousness among High School Students: A Study Conducted in Istanbul Province* (2015, co-edited with Ahu Ergen and Seda Gökçe Turan).

Baykan lives and works in Istanbul.

HAKIM BEY (born 1945) is an American political writer, essayist, and poet, known for first proposing the concept of the Temporary Autonomous Zone (TAZ), based in part on a historical review of pirate utopias. He has worked with the not-for-profit publishing project Autonomedia in Brooklyn, New York, and has written essays on such diverse topics as Tong traditions, the utopian Charles Fourier, the Fascist Gabriele D'Annunzio, alleged connections between Sufism and ancient Celtic culture, technology and Luddism, and Amanita muscaria use in ancient Ireland. He writes regularly in publications such as *Fifth Estate* and the NYC-based *First of the Month*.

MANUEL BORJA-VILLEL (born 1957) has been the director of Museo Nacional Centro de Arte Reina Sofía (MNCARS) in Madrid since 2008.

Previously, he was the director of the Fundació Antoni Tàpies and the MACBA / Museu d'Art Contemporani de Barcelona. Together with searching for new forms of institutionality, an important part of his programme in the MNCARS is centred on the development and reorganization of the collection, changing the method of presentation of works. Recent exhibitions he has programmed include: 'Pity and Terror in Picasso's Path to Guernica' (2017), 'Marcel Broodthaers: A Retrospective' (2016), 'Territories and Fictions, Thinking a New Way of the World' (2016), 'Not Yet, On the Reinvention of Documentary and the Critique of Modernism' (2015), 'Really Useful Knowledge' (2014), and 'Playgrounds, Reinventing the Square' (2014).

ROSI BRAIDOTTI (born 1954) is a philosopher and Distinguished University Professor at Utrecht University. She holds a BA from the Australian National University; a PhD from the Université Panthéon-Sorbonne in Paris and Honorary Degrees from Helsinki and Linkoping. She is a Member of the Australian Academy of the Humanities and the Academia Europaea. In 2005 she was awarded a Knighthood in the Order of the Netherlands Lion. Her books include *Nomadic Subjects* (2011), *Nomadic Theory* (2012) and *The Posthuman* (2013). In 2016 she co-edited with Paul Gilroy: *Conflicting Humanities*. www.rosibraidotti.com

BORIS BUDEN (born 1958) is a writer and cultural critic. He studied philosophy in Zagreb and received his PhD in cultural theory from Humboldt-Universität in Berlin. Buden is permanent fellow at the European Institute of Progressive Cultural Policies in Vienna. His essays and articles cover the topics of philosophy, politics, cultural and art criticism. Recent publications include: *Transition to Nowhere* (forthcoming 2018); *Zone des Übergangs* (2009); *Der Schacht von Babel* (2004).

Buden lives and works in Berlin.

CRISTINA CÁMARA (born 1975) is an art historian and cultural manager. Since 2006, she is the curator of Film and Video Collection at the Museo Nacional Centro de Arte Reina Sofía where she has been part of the curatorial team of exhibitions such as 'Territories and

Fictions: Thinking a New Way of the World', 2016–2017, and 'Minimal Resistance: Between Late Modernism and Globalization: Artistic Practices during the 80s and 90s', 2013–2014. Her research focuses on the moving image: history, collection and exhibition. Her last curatorial work was 'Val del Omar: The Mechanical Mysticism of Cinema', MEIAC, Badajoz; CGAC, Santiago de Compostela, and Laboral, Gijón, 2015.

Cámara lives and works in Madrid.

JESÚS CARRILLO (born 1966) was Lecturer of Contemporary Art History at the Universidad Autónoma de Madrid, Head of the Cultural Programmes Department of the Museo Nacional Centro de Arte Reina Sofía from 2008 to 2014 and General Director of Cultural Programmes of Madrid City Council from 2015 to 2016. He combines the analysis of contemporary culture and cultural institutions with a critical reading of historical narratives of art. He has published: *Arte en la Red* (2004), *Naturaleza e imperio* (2004) and *Tecnología e imperio* (2003), and as editor: *Modos de hacer: Arte crítico, esfera pública y acción directa* (2001), *Tendencias del arte, arte de tendencias* (2003), *Desacuerdos: sobre arte, políticas y esfera pública en el Estado español* vols. 1, 2, 3, 4 and 8 (2004–2007), *Douglas Crimp: Posiciones críticas* (2005), and *Martha Rosler: Imágenes públicas* (2008).

BOJANA CVEJIĆ's (born 1975) work spans philosophy, theatre and performance education. She is the author of several books on performance theory and philosophy: *Choreographing Problems* (2015), *Public Sphere by Performance* (2012) (with Ana Vujanović), and *Drumming & Rain: A Choreographer's Score* (2013) (co-authored with A.T. De Keersmaeker). She has collaborated as a dramaturge in a number of choreographies (by X. Le Roy, Eszter Salamon, Mette Ingvartsen, Anne Teresa De Keersmaeker. De Smedt). As a co-founding member of TkH/Walking Theory editorial collective and performing arts theory magazine, Cvejić has engaged in theoretical-artistic research projects, currently *Performing the Self in the 21st Century*, with Ana Vujanović and Marta Popivoda. In 2013, Cvejić curated the exhibition 'Danse-Guerre', Musée de la danse, Rennes. In 2014, she devised a choreography and lecture programme titled 'Spatial Confessions' for Tate Modern's Turbine Hall. Cvejić is Associated Professor of Dance and Dance Theory in KHIO Oslo and has been a long affiliate teacher at P.A.R.T.S. Brussels, where she is currently coordinating Research Studios.

LUC DELEU (born 1944) set up T.O.P. Office (the Turn-On Planning Office) in Antwerp in 1970, just after earning his degree in architecture. It can be described as an interdisciplinary urban planning firm. In 1970 Deleu also had his first solo exhibition, 'Luc Deleu Says Farewell to Architecture' at the self-organized gallery Vacuum voor nieuwe dimensies (Vacuum for New Dimensions) in Antwerp. Yet to date he has given up neither architecture nor art. He sees them as closely related manifestations of thinking. What he once said of himself is still true: 'I am an artist because I am an architect.'

Deleu lives in Antwerp.

DIEDRICH DIEDERICHSEN (born 1957) has been Professor for Theory, Practice, and Communication of Contemporary Art at the Institute for Art History & Cultural Studies at the Academy of Fine Art, Vienna since 2006. From 1998 to 2007 he was Professor for Aesthetic Theory/Cultural Studies at Merz-Akademie, Stuttgart. He writes for several magazines, dailies and journals in the German speaking world (*Texte zur Kunst*, *Theater heute*, *Cargo*, *Spex*, *Die Zeit*, *tageszeitung*, *Süddeutsche Zeitung* and many others). In the eighties he was an editor and/or publisher of music journals in Hamburg and Cologne (*Sounds*, *Spex*).

Since 1992 he has curated exhibitions in Zürich, Stuttgart, Los Angeles, Berlin, Graz and elsewhere, currently together with Anselm Franke as director of 'Love & Ethnology: Hubert Fichte', a global literature/exhibition project with shows in Lisbon, Salvador de Bahia, Rio de Janeiro (2017), Santiago de Chile, Dakar, New York (2018) and Berlin (2019) with Haus der Kulturen der Welt and several curators and institutions.

Most recent books include: *Körpertreffer: Zur Ästhetik der nachpopulären Künste* (2017); *Über Pop-Musik* (2014); *The Whole Earth: California and the Disappearance of the Outside* (2013).

Diederichsen in Berlin and Vienna.

NAZIM HIKMET RICHARD DIKBAŞ (born 1973) is an academic and an artist. Dikbaş holds a Master's degree in Continental Philosophy at the University of Warwick. He is currently teaching 'Creativity and Dissidence' at the Cultural Management Postgraduate Programme at Istanbul Bilgi University. He is also a member of the music group Zen and art collective Hafriyat.

His recent exhibitions include 'Outside the Sentence There Was a City', SALT Ulus, Ankara, 2016; 'Unprogressive Soul', Öktem&Aykut, Istanbul, 2014; 'Untitled', 12th International Istanbul Biennial, 2011; 'New Forms of Rest and Entertainment', Galeri Non, Istanbul, 2011; 'Expecting Pleasure to Solve Problems', Galeri Splendid, Istanbul, 2009. In addition, he has translated works by Vladimir Nabokov and Flannery O'Connor into Turkish, and Orhan Pamuk and Hrant Dink into English.

Dikbaş lives and works in Istanbul.

CORINNE DISERENS was the curator of Taipei Biennial 2016 (Taiwan), the director of Erg – higher art & research academy, Brussels between 2011 and 2016, and the jury chairwoman of the Akademie Schloss Solitude, Stuttgart. From 1989 to 1993, Diserens was curator at IVAM–Institut Valencià d'Art Modern, and between 1996 and 2008 she directed the Musées de Marseille, the Musée des beaux-arts de Nantes, the opening of the new Museo d'arte contemporanea in Bolzano, and organized international coproductions for MACBA, Barcelona. She has curated seminal artist's retrospectives, biennials, thematic exhibitions, monographs and catalogues as well as directed numerous publications, researches, symposiums, and workshops. She studied art history at Université Panthéon-Sorbonne, Paris, and was Fellow at the Whitney Museum of American Art, Independent Study Program, New York.

AYŞE DÜZKAN (born 1959) is a writer, journalist, editor and activist. She writes for www.artigercek.com, *Özgürlükçü Demokrasi* and works as an editor at Güldünya Yayınları, a collective feminist publishing house. She has worked for various media, including *Özgür Gündem*, *Radikal*, *Milliyet*, *Pişmiş Kelle*, *Kırmızı Alarm*. She was one of the founders of two feminist magazines, *Feminist* and *Pazartesi*.

She has written three books and was one of the 1000 women nominated for the Nobel Peace Prize in 2005.

MERVE ELVEREN (born 1985) is the Senior Programmer of Research and Programs at SALT in Istanbul and Ankara. Her research focuses on intersections of memory, visual culture and politics.

Recent exhibitions include: 'How Did We Get Here', SALT Beyoğlu and Galata, Istanbul, 2015, realized within the framework of L'Internationale's five-year programme 'The Uses of Art: The Legacy of 1848 and 1989'; 'A Promised Exhibition', a comprehensive exhibition of Gülsün Karamustafa, SALT Beyoğlu and Galata, Istanbul, 2013 (co-curated with Duygu Demir).

Elveren lives and works in Istanbul.

CHARLES ESCHE (born 1963) is director of Van Abbemuseum, Eindhoven; professor of contemporary art and curating at Central Saint Martins, London, and co-director of *Afterall* journal and books. He teaches on the Exhibition Studies MRes course at CSM, and at the Jan van Eyck Academie, Maastricht. He (co-) curated 'Le Musée Égaré', Kunsthall Oslo, 2017; 'Printemps de Septembre', Toulouse, 2016; Jakarta Biennale 2015; 31st São Paulo Bienal, 2014; U3 Triennale, Ljubljana, 2011; RIWAQ Biennale, Palestine, 2007 and 2009; Istanbul Biennale, 2005; Gwangju Biennale, 2002, and other international exhibitions. He is chair of CASCO, Utrecht. He received the 2012 Princess Margriet Award and the 2014 CCS Bard College Prize for Curatorial Excellence.

MARCELO EXPÓSITO (born 1966) is an artist, writer, and cultural producer, currently Member of Parliament for En Comú Podem and Third Secretary in the Spanish Congress. For twenty years he has been an activist in political movements against neoliberalism, such as the anti-globalization movement and the EuroMayDay. He has collaborated with militant research networks in Europe and in Latin America such as the Universidad Nomada, the Red Conceptualismos del Sur and the European institute for progressive cultural policies (eipcp). He has written, edited and translated relevant contributions in the debate on the relations between artistic avant-garde, cultural activism and political practices, including *Walter Benjamin, productivist* (2013) and *Conversación con Manuel Borja-Villel* (2015).

BOŽIDAR FLAJŠMAN (born 1956) is a teacher of art with a PhD in art pedagogy, a theoretician of social and political visual communications, essayist, artist, photographer, editor and environmental activist. His work was presented in the exhibition: 'Low-Budget Utopias', Museum of Contemporary Art Metelkova, Ljubljana, 2016.

His publications include: *Podobe časa, Metlika na razglednicah* (Images of Time, Metlika on Postcards) (2015); *Likovna dejavnost in ekološko ozaveščanje* (Art and Ecological Awareness) (2009); *Five Minutes of Democracy* (with Mojca Drčar Murko, Boris Vezjak and Darko Štrajn) (2008); *Vizualna ekologija: ekološki nagovori vidnih sporočil* (Visual Ecology: Ecological Aspects of Visual Communications) (2006).

Flajšman lives and works in Ljubljana, Slovenia.

ANNIE FLETCHER is currently Chief Curator at the Van Abbemuseum, Eindhoven. She also tutors at De Appel, Amsterdam, the Dutch Art Institute Arnhem and the Design Academy Eindhoven. She recently worked on the museum's retrospective of Qiu Zhijie and the ten-day caucus project called 'Becoming More', in 2017. Other projects include 'El Lissitzky: the Artist and the State' at IMMA Dublin, and a 'Republic of Art' at the Van Abbemuseum in 2015–2016. She was Van Abbe's lead contributor to the 'Museum as Hub' collaboration led by the New Museum in New York from 2006–2014 and is part of the on-going collaborative team that developed the 'Museum of Arte Util' with Tania Bruguera in 2013 and continues to develop the Association of Arte Util today. She curated 'After the Future' at Eva Ireland's International Biennial of Visual Art in 2012. Other projects include solo exhibitions or presentations with Ahmet Ogut, Hito Steyerl, Sheela Gowda, David Maljkovic, Jo Baer, Jutta Koether, Deimantas Narkevicius, Minerva Cuevas, and the long-term projects 'Be(com)ing Dutch' (2006–2009) and 'Cork Caucus' (2005) with Charles Esche. She was co-founder and co-director of the rolling curatorial platform 'If I Can't Dance, I Don't Want To Be Part Of Your Revolution', with

Frederique Bergholtz and Tanja Elstgeest. With Sarah Pierce she developed the Para Education Department at Witte de With, Rotterdam, in 2004. As a writer she has contributed to various magazines and publications.

DIANA FRANSSEN (born 1954) is curator and head of research at the Van Abbemuseum, Eindhoven. Her aim is to provide a broad public with access to modern and contemporary art and in doing so encourage critical reflection on the relationship between art and wider social conditions.

Recent exhibitions include: 'YOU'VE GOT 1243 UNREAD MESSAGES', Latvian National Museum of Art, Riga, 2017; 'Positions III: Rossella Biscotti, Duncan Campbell, Maryam Jafri, Natasja Kensmil', 2016; 'The 1980s: Today's Beginnings?', 2016 (with Nick Aikens); 'A Republic of Art', Van Abbemuseum, Eindhoven, 2015 (with Annie Fletcher).

Diana lives and works in Eindhoven.

GEORGE&HARRISON are the designers of this publication. George&Harrison is an Eindhoven-based graphic design studio, founded by Martijn Maas and Maarten Stal in 2013. The studio, a small team of people from diverse backgrounds, specializes in publications, digital media and visual identities, working on commissioned projects in the fields of art, culture, and commerce. The design practice of George&Harrison focuses on combining clean, strategy-driven solutions and powerful aesthetics. Context, research and dialogue are key to George&Harrison's approach. www.georgeandharrison.nl.

JUNE GIVANNI (born 1950) is a film curator, currently developing the June Givanni Pan African Cinema Archive (JGPACA), after three decades in the industry. She ran the BFI's African Caribbean Unit; programmed Planet Africa at TIFF; and programmed at film festivals and art institutions in five continents over three decades. She specializes in African and African diaspora cinema with Black British Cinema at its core.

JGPACA recent exhibitions include: 'The Place is Here', Nottingham and London, 2017; 'Pan African Film Lounge Installation', Autograph, London, 2015; 'Movements', Cookhouse Gallery, London, 2014.

Publications include: 'A Curator's Conundrum', in *The Moving Image: The Journal of the Association of Moving Image Archivists* (Spring 2004); *Symbolic Narratives: African Cinema* (1997); *Black Film Bulletin* (1993–1996) (with Gaylene Gould); Black Film and Video List (1988, 1990).

June Givanni lives and works in London.

LISA GODSON (born 1970) is Director of the MA Design History and Material Culture programme at NCAD in Dublin, a Visiting Research Fellow at Trinity College Dublin and formerly Tutor and Fellow at the Royal College of Art, London. She is a graduate of the Royal College of Art (PhD, MA) and Trinity College Dublin (BA).

Recent and forthcoming publications include *Making 1916: the Visual and Material Culture of the Easter Rising* (2015) (co-edited with Joanna Bruck); *Religious Architecture in Ireland, Germany and Beyond: Influence, Process and Afterlife since 1945* (2018) (co-edited with Kathleen James Chakraborty); *Understanding Uniform: Clothing and Discipline in the Modern World* (2019) (co-edited with Jane Tynan); *'How the Crowd Felt': Ritual and Affect 1922–39* (author) (2018). She lives and works in Dublin.

TERESA GRANDAS (born 1963) is an art historian. She studied History of Art and Philosophy at the University of Barcelona and is curator at MACBA, Barcelona. She is focused on research projects on art and counterculture practices, and Spanish art.

Selected exhibitions: 'Poetry Brossa', MACBA, 2017 (with Pedro G. Romero); 'Hard Gelatin: Hidden Stories from the 80s', MACBA, 2016–2017; 'Video-nou', Van Abbemuseum, Eindhoven, 2016; 'The Passion According to Carol Rama', MACBA, 2014–2015, (with Paul B. Preciado) Musée d'Art Moderne de la Ville de Paris, 2015, EMMA, Espoo, 2015–2016, Irish Museum of Modern Art, Dublin, 2016, GAM-Galleria Civica d'Arte Moderna e Contemporanea, Turin, 2016–2017; 'Eulàlia Grau: I Have Never Painted Golden Angels', MACBA, 2013; 'Utopia is Possible: ICSID: Eivissa, 1971', MACBA, 2012, Museu d'Art Contemporani d'Eivissa, 2013 (with Daniel Giralt-Miracle); 'The Museum of the Affects', Moderna Galerija, Ljubljana, 2011-2012 (as part of curatorial team with Bart de Baere and Bartomeu Mari,

Bojana Piškur and Leen de Baar); 'Àngels Ribé: En el laberint', 1969–1984, MACBA, 2011; 'Parallel Benet Rossell', MACBA, 2010–2011 (with Bartomeu Marí).

NAV HAQ (born 1976) is Senior Curator at M HKA–Museum of Contemporary Art Antwerp. He was previously Exhibitions Curator at Arnolfini, Bristol, and curator at Gasworks, London. Haq has curated monographic exhibitions with artists such as Hassan Khan, Cosima von Bonin, Shilpa Gupta, Imogen Stidworthy and Otobong Nkanga. Group exhibitions include: 9th Göteborg International Biennial of Contemporary Art, 2017; 'Energy Flash: The Rave Movement', 2016; 'Don't You Know Who I Am? Art After Identity Politics', 2014 (with Anders Kreuger); 'Superpower: Africa in Science Fiction', 2012; 'Museum Show: A Historical Survey of (Semi-fictional) Museums Created by Artists', 2011; 'Contour Biennial 2007', Mechelen (BE); and 'Lapdogs of the Bourgeoisie: Class Hegemony in Contemporary Art', 2006–2009 (with Tirdad Zolghadr). In 2012 he was the recipient of the Independent Vision Award for Curatorial Achievement, awarded by Independent Curators International, New York.

BEATRIZ HERRÁEZ is an art historian. She has worked as curator at the Collections Department at Museo Nacional Centro de Arte Reina Sofía, Madrid, from 2012–2016, and as Chief Curator at Montehermoso Kulturunea (Basque Country) from 2007 to 2011. She has co-curated exhibitions organized by Museo Reina Sofía such as 'Territories and Fictions. Thinking a New Way of the World', 2016–2017; 'Minimal Resistance. Between Late Modernism and Globalization: Artistic Practices during the 80s and 90s', 2013–2014; and the solo project 'Erlea Maneros Zabala', 2016. Her curatorial works include 'Je, je... luna: María Luisa Fernández: Works Produced between 1979 and 1997', 2015–2016; at AZ zentroa, Bilbao, and Marco, Vigo, 2015–2016; 'What I See: Susan Hiller' at Montehermoso, Vitoria-Gasteiz, 2010; 'Soy el final de la reproducción', Sculpture Center, New York, and 'castillo/corrales', Paris, 2007–2008. She currently works on the upcoming solo exhibitions of the artists Julia Spinola at CA2M, MAdrid, and Itziar Okariz at Tabakalera, Donostia-San Sebastian, scheduled for 2018.

LUBAINA HIMID, MBE (born 1954) is an artist and professor of Contemporary Art at the University of Central Lancashire. In her artistic, academic, and curatorial work, Himid brings forth and celebrates the lives and histories of people of the Black diaspora. Himid has exhibited work in a number of major institutions such as Badischer Kunstverein, Karlsruhe; South London Gallery; Spike Island, Bristol; Modern Art Oxford; Nottingham Contemporary and Walker Art Gallery, Liverpool. Forthcoming solo exhibitions include Musée régional d'art contemporain Occitanie/Pyrénées-Méditerranée, Sérignan, and Frans Hals Museum, Haarlem. Her work is held in several public collections, including National Museums Liverpool; Tate, London; Museum Ludwig, Cologne; Arts Council Collections, Rhode Island School of Design, Providence; Middlesbrough Institute of Modern Art, and the Victoria & Albert Museum, London. She is a nominee for the 2017 Turner Prize.

LOLA HINOJOSA (born 1979) is Head of Performing and Intermedia Arts Collection at the Museo Nacional Centro de Arte Reina Sofía, Madrid. When she joined that institution in 2006, she collaborated in the creation of the Film and Video Collection Department. Her main fields of study are performance, moving images and gender theory. She has been part of the curatorial team of exhibitions organized by Museo Reina Sofía, such as 'Territories and Fictions: Thinking a New Way of the World', 2016–2017; 'Minimal Resistance: Between Late Modernism and Globalization: Artistic Practices during the 80s and 90s', 2013–2014; 'Encounters with the 30s', 2012–2013.

She lives and works in Madrid.

ANTONY HUDEK (born 1976) is a writer and curator based in Antwerp. He is currently director of the postgraduate Curatorial Studies program at KASK—School of Arts, Ghent. Before, he was research curator (Tate Liverpool, 2013–2014), curator and deputy director of Raven Row, London (2014–2015), and director of Objectif Exhibitions, Antwerp (2015–2016). For M HKA, the Museum of Contemporary Art Antwerp he edited the catalogue *Joseph Beuys: Greetings from the Eurasian* (2017). In parallel, he continues to co-run Occasional Papers, a non-profit press founded in 2008, devoted to histories of art and design.

TEA HVALA (born 1980) is a writer and radio maker. She holds BA degrees in Sociology of Culture and Comparative Literature, and an MA degree in Anthropology of Gender. Her work is focused on grassroots feminist activism and art, independent media and science fiction. At Radio Študent, she co-authors *Sektor Ž*, a monthly radio show on feminism. She co-organizes the Deuje babe festival and co-edits the spol.si website.

Recent publications include: *Skrivna bolnišnica* (Secret Hospital) (2017) (co-authored with Špela Oberstar); *Podzemlje* (The Underground) (2016); *Razkorak* (Discord) (2015). Tea Hvala lives and works in Cerkno, Slovenia.

GAL KIRN (born 1980) holds a PhD in political philosophy from the University of Nova Gorica (2012). He was a researcher at the Jan van Eyck Academie in Maastricht (2008–2010), and a research fellow at ICI Berlin (2010–2012). He received a fellowship at the Akademie Schloss Solitude in Stuttgart (2015) and was a postdoctoral fellow of the Humboldt-Foundation (2013–2016). He has been teaching courses in film, philosophy, and contemporary political theory at the Freie Universität Berlin, at Justus-Liebig-Universität Gießen and University of Primorska.

Kirn published *Partizanski prelomi in protislovja trznega socializma v Jugoslaviji* (Partisan Ruptures and Contradictions of Market Socialism in Yugoslavia) (2015). He is a co-editor (with Marian Burchardt) of *Beyond Neoliberalism: Social Analysis after 1989* (2017) (with Peter Thomas, Sara Farris, and Katja Diefenbach), *Encountering Althusser* (2012) (with Dubravka Sekulić and Žiga Testen) and of *Yugoslav Black Wave Cinema and its Transgressive Moments* (2012). He is also editor of *Postfordism and its Discontents* (2010). At the moment he is starting to write a manuscript for Brill Publisher on the topic of partisan counter-Archive.

He lives in Berlin and holds an Open Topic Position at TU Dresden.

NEŽA KOGOVŠEK ŠALAMON (born 1978) is a lawyer and a researcher. She studied at the University of Ljubljana, Faculty of Law, and University of Notre Dame Law School in the US. She works as Director of the Peace Institute–Institute for Contemporary Social and Political Studies. In her work she specializes in human rights from the perspective of constitutional law, international law, and administrative law. She is a member of a number of professional networks in her research fields. Recently she has been nominated as a representative of the Republic of Slovenia in the European Commission against Racism and Intolerance at the Council of Europe. Her research fields include asylum, migration, citizenship and non-discrimination law.

Recent publications include: *Challenges of the Constitutional Law in the 21st Century: Liber Amicorum Ciril Ribičič* (2017) (co-edited with Matija Žgur and Boštjan Koritnik); *Lgbt People as Refugees and Immigration Rights* (2017); *Asylum Seekers and HIV/AIDS: Legal Issues, Well-Being and Fundamental Rights* (2016); *Asylum Institutions in the Western Balkans: Current Issues* (2016); *Razor-Wired: Reflections on Migration Movement through Slovenia in 2015* (2016) (co-edited with Veronika Bajt); *Erased: Citizenship, Residence Rights and the Constitution in Slovenia* (2016); *Traits of Homophobia in Slovenian Law: From Ignorance towards Recognition* (2012); *Migration Law: Slovenia* (2011).

Kogovšek Šalamon lives and works in Ljubljana, Slovenia.

ANDERS KREUGER (born 1965) is a curator and writer. He is Senior Curator at M HKA, the Museum of Contemporary Art Antwerp, and one of the editors of the London-based journal *Afterall*.

Recent exhibitions at M HKA include 'A Temporary Futures Institute', 2017 (co-curated with Maya Van Leemput); 'Robert Filliou: The Secret of Permanent Creation'; 'The Welfare State', 2015.

Recent essays in *Afterall* include: 'Ethno-Futurism: Leaning on the Past, Working for the Future' (#44); 'The Gely Korzhev Retrospective in Moscow: Why Him? Why Now?' (#42); 'Ion Grigorescu: My Vocation Is Classical, Even Bucolic' (#41).

Anders lives and works in Antwerp, Belgium.

ELISABETH LEBOVICI (born 1953) PhD in Aesthetics, University of Paris 10, is an art historian and art critic. Since 2006, she co-curates the seminar 'Something You Should Know: Artists and Producers' at the Ecole des Hautes Études en Sciences Sociales (EHESS, Paris).

She was an editor at the arts and culture department of the daily newspaper *Libération* (1991–2006) and a chief-editor of *Beaux Arts* magazine (1987–1990). As a freelance writer, she has contributed to many publications. Her most recent publication: *Ce que le sida m'a fait: art et activisme à la fin du XXe siècle* (2017).

ROGELIO LÓPEZ CUENCA (born 1959) is an artist and independent researcher, whose work — focused in media images analysis, construction of collective identities and cultural criticism — is carried out through publications, courses, workshops, exhibitions, intervention in public spaces, TV or the Internet (www.malagana .com), blending procedures from visual arts as well as from literature or social sciences.

His more recent works deals with the manipulation of history and collective memory: *Los bárbaros* (2016); *Valparaiso White Noise* (2013); *Saharawhy* (2012); *Ciudad Picasso* (2011); *Mapa de Mexico* (2010); *Mappa di Roma* (2007); and *Malaga 1937* (2007).

López Cuenca lives and works in Málaga.

GEERT LOVINK (born 1959) is a Dutch media theorist, internet critic and author of *Uncanny Networks* (2002), *Dark Fiber* (2002), *My First Recession* (2003), *Zero Comments* (2007), *Networks Without a Cause* (2012) and *Social Media Abyss* (2016). In 2004 he founded the Institute of Network Cultures at the Amsterdam University of Applied Sciences. His centre organizes conferences, publications and research networks such as Video Vortex (online video), Unlike Us (alternatives in social media), Critical Point of View (Wikipedia), Society of the Query (the culture of search), MoneyLab (internet-based revenue models in the arts). Recent projects deal with digital publishing and the future of art criticism. He also teaches at the European Graduate School (Saas-Fee (CH)/Malta) where he supervises PhD students.

AMNA MALIK (born 1969) is an art historian and Senior Lecturer in History and Theory of Art at the Slade School of Fine Art, UCL. She specializes in twentieth-century and contemporary art and diaspora and has published a number of essays on African American, Black British, South Asian and Middle Eastern artists in Europe and the US. Malik is currently working on a book that examines aesthetics and art practices across diasporas from Africa, Asia and the Middle East.

PABLO MARTÍNEZ (born 1983) is Head of Programming at MACBA, Barcelona. His research focuses on educational work with the body and the potential of images for constructing political subjectivity. He was Head of Education and Public Activities at CA2M (2009–2016), and Associate Professor of Contemporary Art at the Faculty of Fine Arts of the Complutense University of Madrid (2011–2015).

He is Editorial Secretary of the journal of art and visual culture *Re-visiones* and a member of Las Lindes, a research and action group working on education and cultural and artistic practices. He has co-edited, with Yayo Aznar, *Arte actual: Lecturas para un espectador inquieto* (2011) and was editor of *No sabíamos lo que hacíamos. Lecturas para una educación situada* (2017). He curated solo shows of *Werker Magazine* and Adelita Husni-Bey.

LOURDES MÉNDEZ is Chair of Anthropology of Art at the University of the Basque Country. She studied Social Anthropology at the Université Paris 8. After completing her PhD, she joined the Faculty of Fine Arts at the University of the Basque Country as a lecturer. Her research covers the analysis of the field of visual arts from the perspective of materialistic feminism; the problems deriving from the design and application of cultural policies at a local and EU level; and the consequences of institutional policies based on the assumption of the so-called 'gender perspective' in feminist research.

Her most recent books and essays include: *Exclusionary Genealogies* (2016); *From the Trap of Difference to That of Excellence* (2014); *Antropología del campo artístico: Del arte primitivo ... al contemporáneo* (2009); *Galicia en Europa: El lugar de las artes plásticas en la política cultural de la Xunta; Antropología feminista* (2008); and *Cuerpos sexuados y ficciones identitarias: Ideologías sexuales, deconstrucciones feministas y artes visuales* (2004).

ALEŠ MENDIŽEVEC (born 1987) is a philosopher, studying at the Faculty of Philosophy at the University of Ljubljana. He is doing his PhD on the philosophy of Louis Althusser, mainly his aleatory materialism through practical philosophy.

Recent publications include: 'Transformacija materializma: Althusserjev Rousseau od praznine koncepta h konceptu praznine' (The Transformation of Materialism: Althusser's Rousseau from the Void of Concept to Concept of the Void), *Problemi* 3–4 (2016).

Mendiževec lives in Ljubljana and works as an editor for culture and humanistics on Radio Student.

ANA MIZERIT is a curator, graduated in social studies and art history at the Faculty of Arts at the University of Ljubljana. She works as Research and Assistant Curator in Moderna galerija, Ljubljana, where she collaborated on a number exhibitions, including 'NSK from Kapital to Capital: Neue Slowenische Kunst: An Event of the Final Decade of Yugoslavia', 2015. Her recent exhibitions include: DRAUGHT|PLATEAURES-IDUE', 2018; 'Mladina 80s', 2017 (with Robert Botteri); 'DRAUGHT|Peter Rauch: Pavillon', 2017.

Ana Mizerit lives and works in Ljubljana.

ALEXEI MONROE (born 1969) is a cultural theorist specialized in the work of the Slovene arts groups Laibach and NSK and the post-Yugoslav group Autopsia. Other interests include industrial and electronic music and culture, and the Stag as a cultural symbol. He was programme director of the First NSK Citizens' Congress, 2010, and a member of the organizing committee of the 2nd NSK Folk Art Biennale, 2016.

MERIÇ ÖNER (born 1979) is a trained architect and Director of Research and Programs at SALT. Focusing mainly on Turkey and its surrounding geography after 1950, she develops material culture research with a comprehensive and progressive approach. Her work circulates in forms of print and online publications, exhibitions, and public programmes. Recent exhibitions include 'One and the Many', SALT Galata, Istanbul, 2016; 'SUMMER HOMES: Claiming the Coast', SALT Beyoğlu, Istanbul, 2014, and 'Modern Essays 4: SALON', SALT Galata, Istanbul, 2012.

Recent publications include *Tracing Istanbul (From the Air)* (2009) and *Mapping Istanbul* (2009) (with Pelin Derviş).

Öner lives and works in Istanbul.

NATAŠA PETREŠIN-BACHELEZ (born 1976) is an independent curator, writer and editor. Among the projects and exhibitions she curated are 'Show Me Your Archive and I Will Tell You Who Is In Power', KIOSK/KASK School of Arts, Ghent (with Wim Waelput); 'Let's Talk about the Weather', Sursock Museum, Beirut, 2016 (with Nora Razian and Ashkan Sepahvand); 'Resilience. U3 Triennial of Contemporary Art in Slovenia', Moderna galerija, Ljubljana, 2013; transmediale.08, HKW, Berlin, 2008; 'Our House is a House that Moves', Living Art Museum, Reykjavik, 2006. In France she curated: 'On Becoming Earthlings. Blackmarket for Useful Knowledge and Non-Knowledge #18', Musée de l'Homme, Paris, 2015 (with Alexander Klose, Council, Mobile Academy); 'Tales of Empathy', Jeu de Paume, 2014; 'The Promises of the Past 1950–2010', Centre Pompidou, Paris, 2010 (with Christine Macel and Joanna Mytkowska); 'Société anonyme', Le Plateau/ FRAC, Ile-de-France, 2007 (with Thomas Boutoux and François Piron). She is curator of the project 'Not Fully Human, Not Human At All', Kadist, Paris, 2017–2020 (with other institutions), co-curator of 'Defiant Muses. Delphine Seyrig and feminist video collectives in France (1970s-1980s)', LAM, Lille and Museo Nacional Centro de Arte Reina Sofía, Madrid, 2019 (with Giovanna Zapperi), and curator of the Contour Biennial 9: 'Coltan As Cotton', Mechelen, 2018–2020.

Between 2010 and 2012, she was co-director of Les Laboratoires d'Aubervilliers and co-founder of the network of art institutions Cluster. She is a co-organizer of the seminar 'Something You Should Know' at EHESS, Paris (with Elisabeth Lebovici and Patricia Falguières), and a member of the research group Travelling Féministe, at Centre audio-visuel Simone de Beauvoir. She was the chief editor of the online platform L'Internationale Online (2014–2017), and the chief editor of the *Manifesta Journal* (2012 and 2014).

BOJANA PIŠKUR is a writer and curator at the Moderna galerija in Ljubljana. Her research focuses on political issues and how they relate to or are manifested in the field of art, looking specifically at the regions of former Yugoslavia and Latin America. She has contributed to numerous publications and lectured extensively on topics such as post avant-gardes in the former Yugoslavia, radical education, cultural politics in self-management, and the Non-Aligned Movement.

She lives and works in Ljubljana, Slovenia.

MARTA POPIVODA (born 1982) is a filmmaker and video artist. Her work explores concerns with the discursive power structures of the contemporary (art) world, intersections between performance and film, and the Yugoslav socialist project, through the production of films, video installations and performance. Her work has been part of exhibitions and programmes at Tate Modern, London; MoMA, New York; M HKA, Antwerp; Q21/MuseumsQuartier and 21er Haus, Vienna; Garage Museum of Contemporary Art, Moscow; HOME, Manchester; McaM, Shanghai; Beirut Art Center; Musée de la danse, Rennes; Moderna galerija, Ljubljana; Arsenal and SAVVY Contemporary, Berlin; Forum des Images, Les Laboratoires d'Aubervilliers and Khiasma Gallery, Paris, etc. Her first feature documentary *Yugoslavia: How Ideology Moved Our Collective Body* premiered at the 63rd Berlinale and was later screened at a large number of festivals worldwide. Recently, she received the Berlin Art Prize for the visual arts by the Akademie der Künste Berlin and the Edith-Russ-Haus Award for Emerging Media Artist.

CARLOS PRIETO DEL CAMPO, a militant in European social movements, has a degree in Law and a PhD in Philosophy from the Complutense University of Madrid, and is an expert in accounting and public sector auditing after having worked as a civil servant for the Spanish Ministry of Economy and Finance between 1989 and 2010. He is also an independent editor and activist in the field of culture, and has been editor of the Spanish edition of *New*

Left Review since 2000, and director of the publishing projects 'Cuestiones de antagonismo' (1999–2012) and 'Prácticas constituyentes' since 2013. He has held various management posts in Spain's public sector and was rector of the Quito Institute of Higher National Studies (2013–2014) and an adviser to the Ecuadorian government in 2010 and in 2012–2013 and in 2014–2015. He is currently Director of the Study Centre at Museo Reina Sofía and is a member of the editorial board of L'Internationale Online.

PEDRO G. ROMERO (born 1964) has been active as an artist since 1985. His current work involves two major apparatuses in Archivo F.X. and Máquina P.H., and he also participates in UNIA arteypensamiento and PRPC (the Platform for Reflection on Cultural Policies) in Seville. In 1999, he published *El trabajo* in the project *Almadraba*, developed in Tangiers, Tarifa and Gibraltar, and between 2008 and 2010 he curated the project *...de rasgos árabes* in Mexico, Argentina, Chile, Brazil and El Salvador. Furthermore, he has curated 'Tratado de Paz' for Cultural Capital DSS2016, the exhibition 'Poesía: Brossa', MACBA, Barcelona, 2017–2018 (with Teresa Grandas), and the exhibition 'Aplicación Murillo: Materialismo, charitas y populismo', Sevilla, 2018 (with Luis Montiel). He was also a participating artist at documenta14 Athens/Kassel.

RAFAEL SÁNCHEZ FERLOSIO (born 1927) is a writer and essayist. Widely regarded as one of the finest prose writers in the Spanish language, he is the author of the novels *Industrias y andanzas de Alfanhuí* (1951), *The River: El Jarama (Dedalus Europe 1992–2004)* (1955) and *El testimonio de Yarfoz* (1986). Moreover, his numerous articles and essays place him among the greatest thinkers and polemicists in late modernity, and he was awarded the Cervantes Prize in 2004 and the National Award for Spanish Literature in 2009.

IGOR ŠPANJOL (born 1972) studied Sociology of Culture and Art History at The Faculty of Arts, Ljubljana University. He works as a curator at the Moderna galerija, Ljubljana with a focus on curating of contemporary art exhibitions. Recent exhibitions include: 'Vadim Fishkin: No Magic', 2015; 'Tadej Pogačar & the P.A.R.A.S.I.T.E.', 2014, 'Hills and Valleys and Mineral Resources', 2014; Marko Pogačnik, 'The Art of Life—The Life of Art', 2014.
Španjol lives and works in Ljubljana, Slovenia.

CHRIS STRAETLING (born 1960) is an artist and occasional curator. He studied at NSCAD and Dalhousie University, Halifax, Nova Scotia. He currently runs a project office 'Bureau Gruzemayer' after having (co-)founded various alternative exhibition spaces (Inexistent, AK-37, Factor 44, all in Antwerp, since 1986.)
Recent exhibition projects include 'Buktapak-top in Berlin', Grüntaler 9 & GlogauAIR, Berlin, 2016; 'Ramble', FeliXart Museum, Drogenbos (BE), 2014.
Recent publications include *Observatoire des Simple et des Fous*, 2015 (co-authored with Lise Duclaux); *Salon Rouge*, 2015 (co-authored with Patrick Morarescu); article in *Emergency Index #5*, 2016.
Straetling lives and works in Antwerp.

LUÍS TRINDADE (born 1971) is a cultural historian who teaches Portuguese history and culture at Birkbeck, University of London. He is currently working on a research project on the history of audiovisual culture in Portugal during the second half of the twentieth century. Recent publications include: 'What shall I do with this sword? Narrative, speech and politics in the Carnation Revolution', in *Cultural and Social History* (2017); *Narratives in Motion: Journalism and Modernist Events in 1920s Portugal* (2016).
Trindade lives and works in Lisbon and London.

ERMAN ATA UNCU (born 1977) is an art writer. After graduating from Mimar Sinan Fine Arts University's Sociology Department, Istanbul, he received his Master's degree in Film Studies from the University of Amsterdam. Currently he is working as the editor of Sabancı University's Sakıp Sabancı Museum.
Recent exhibitions include: 'How Did We Get Here', SALT Beyoğlu and Galata, Istanbul, 2015 realized within the framework of L'Internationale's five-year programme 'The Uses of Art: The Legacy of 1848 and 1989'.
He was a senior reporter for the daily *Radikal* and contributed to publications such as *Art Unlimited, Istanbul Art News* and *Milliyet Sanat*.
Uncu lives and works in Istanbul.

VALIZ is an independent international publisher on contemporary art, design, theory, critique, typography and urban affairs, based in Amsterdam. Our books offer critical reflection, interdisciplinary inspiration, and establish a connection between cultural disciplines and socio-economic, political questions. Our programme consists of two components:
— theory and texts on art and visual culture;
— books that are conceived and elaborated in close collaboration with artists, designers and art institutes.

Apart from publishing Valiz organizes cultural projects in which certain topics in contemporary art, politics and culture are investigated.
www.valiz.nl

JELENA VESIĆ (born 1974) is an independent curator, writer, editor and lecturer. She is co-founder of Prelom Collective and co-editor of *Red Thread* — journal for social theory, contemporary art and activism. She has published numerous essays exploring the relations between art and ideology in the fields of geopolitical art history writing, experimental art and exhibition practices. Her recent essay book *On Neutrality* (2016) (with Vladimir Jerić Vlidi and Rachel O'Reilly) is a part of the Non-Aligned Modernity edition, dedicated to exploring different cultural-political cases of the Non-Aligned Movement.

Her most recent exhibition 'Story on Copy' was presented at the Akademie Schloss Solitude, Stuttgart, 2017.

MAR VILLAESPESA has worked as an art critic and independent curator since the eighties. She was previously the director of the magazine *Arena* and has curated, in collaboration with BNV producciones, 'El sueño imperativo', 'Plus Ultra', '100%', 'Word$Word$Word', 'Érase una vez…', 'Além da Água', 'Almadraba', 'Ghuraba' and 'Estancias', among other projects. From 2000 to 2015, she was a member of the UNIA arte y pensamiento team, directing *Pensar la edición*, *Transacciones*, *Sobre capital y territorio*, and 'Atravesando fronteras: realidad y representación en el Mediterráneo', and edited the newsletter *Desacuerdos*, *Feminismos*. She has recently worked alongside Laurence Rassel to curate the Esther Ferrer retrospective at the Museo Nacional Centro de Arte Reina Sofía in Madrid.

VLADIMIR JERIĆ VLIDI is media researcher and editor with a MA degree in Culture of Global Media from the Faculty of Media and Communication, Belgrade. Associated with various different local initiatives he is or was a part of Prelom Kolektiv, TEDx Belgrade, Reconstruction Women's Fund, Darkwood Dub, Creative Commons Serbia and more. He is a member of the editorial board of *Red Thread* journal for social theory and author of a number of independent projects. Currently engaged with research and production of critical texts and translations from the fields of media theory, social theory and artistic practice.

ANA VUJANOVIĆ (born 1975) is a freelance cultural worker in the fields of contemporary performing arts and culture and holds a PhD in Theatre Studies. She is a member of the editorial collective of TkH (Walking Theory), a Belgrade-based theoretical-artistic platform, and editor-in-chief of the TkH *Journal for Performing Arts Theory*. A particular commitment of hers has been to empower independent scenes in Belgrade and former Yugoslavia. She has lectured at various universities and educational programmes throughout Europe, was a visiting professor at the Performance Studies Dpt. of the University Hamburg, and teaches at HZT Berlin. Since 2016 she has been an associate team member and mentor of fourth-year students at SNDO–School for New Dance Development in Amsterdam. She participates in art projects in the fields of performance, theatre, dance, and video/film, as a dramaturge and co-author.

She has published a number of articles in journals and collections and authored four books, most recently *Public Sphere by Performance* (2015) (with Bojana Cvejić). Currently she is working on an independent research project *Performing the Self in the 21st Century*, with Bojana Cvejić and Marta Popivoda, and editing a book *A Live Gathering: Performance Performance and Politics*, with L.A. Piazza.

Wills, Lesley   253
Wilson, Harold   32
Wittgenstein, Ludwig   353
Wittig, Monique   19, 290
Wojnarowicz, David   287
Wolff, Janet   233
Wool, Christopher   286

X

Xiaoping, Deng   316, 378

Y

Yande, Claude   80
Yuan-chia, Li   382

Z

Zacharoloulos, Denys   134
Zahl, Peter-Paul   95
Zandwijken, Mercedes   256
Železnik, Adela   14
Zelter, Angie   147
Zihnioğlu, Yaprak   267, 268
Žižek, Slavoj   106, 308, 330, 342

ACKNOWLEDGEMENTS

This publication extends the discussions that begun during eleven exhibitions, two conferences, two publications and one MA seminar. It draws on the accumulated knowledge and speculations of the many artists, curators, writers, and institutions involved. The editors would like to give a warm THANK YOU to the contributors of *The Long 1980s* and the projects listed below, and all the people who made their realization possible. We are incredibly grateful, inspired and energized by your ideas and dedication.

'Minimal Resistance. Between Late Modernism and Globalisation: Artistic Practices During the 80s and 90s'
Exhibition and public programme Museo Reina Sofía, Madrid, Spain
16 October 2013–5 January 2014

Curators: Manuel Borja-Villel, Beatriz Herráez, Rosario Peiró
  Curatorial assistants: Cristina Cámara, Lola Hinojosa

Artists: Ignasi Aballí, Pep Agut, Txomin Badiola, Ángel Bados, Georg Baselitz, Lothar Baumgarten, Dara Birnbaum, Cabello/Carceller (Helena Cabello, Ana Carceller), Miguel Ángel Campano, Guy de Cointet, Jordi Colomer, René Daniëls, Hanne Darboven, Moyra Davey, Jiri Georg Dokoupil, Marlene Dumas, Diamela Eltit, Erreakzioa-reacción, Pepe Espaliú, Estrujenbank (Patricia Gadea, Juan Ugalde, Dionisio Cañas, Mariano Lozano), Harun Farocki, María Luisa Fernández, Peter Fischli, Peter Friedl, Patricia Gadea, Radical Gai, Dora García, José María Giro, Jack Goldstein, Leon Golub, Dan Graham, Guerrilla Girls, Federico Guzmán, Candida Höfer, Jenny Holzer, General Idea, Cristina Iglesias, Pello Irazu, Joaquim Jordá, Mike Kelley, Martin Kippenberger, Louise Lawler, Pedro Lemebel, Mark Lombardi, Rogelio López Cuenca, LSD, LTTR, José Maldonado Gómez, Allan McCollum, Isidoro Valcárcel Medina, Miralda, Juan Luis Moraza, Reinhard Mucha, Matt Mullican, Juan Muñoz, Antoni Muntadas, Paz Muro, Itziar Okariz, Ulrike Ottinger, Marc Pataut, Raymond Pettibon, Sigmar Polke, Preiswert, readymades belong to everyone®, Pedro G. Romero, Helke Sander, Agustin Parejo School, Allan Sekula, Cindy Sherman, Fernando Sinaga, Jo Spence, Hito Steyerl, Thomas Struth, Rosemarie Trockel, Juan Ugalde, Juan Uslé, Eulàlia Valldosera, Marcelo Expósito/Arturo Rodríguez/Gabriel Villota, David Weiss, James Welling, Franz West

'NSK: From Kapital to Capital. An Event of the Final Decade of Yugoslavia'
Exhibition and public programme Moderna galerija, Ljubljana, Slovenia
11 May–16 August 2015

Curator: Zdenka Badovinac

Artists: Neue Slowenische Kunst: Laibach, IRWIN, Scipion Nasice Sisters Theatre, New Collectivism, Department of Pure and Applied Philosophy, Retrovision, Film, Builders

Conference
19–21 June 2015, auditorium MG+, Moderna galerija, Ljubljana, Slovenia
 Concept: Zdenka Badovinac and Eda Čufer
 Conference participants: Zdenka Badovinac, Izidor Barši (Neteorit), Barbara Borčić, Eda Čufer, Mladen Dolar, Charles Esche, Former artist known as Adrian Kovacs, Anthony Gardner, Boris Groys, Marina Gržinić & Jasmina Založnik, Lev Kreft, Tomaž Mastnak, Rastko Močnik, Alexei Monroe, Katja Praznik, Daniel Ricardo Quiles, Igor Vidmar, Alexei Yurchak

Publication: *NSK from Kapital to Capital: Neue Slowenische Kunst –an Event of the Final Decade of Yugoslavia*
 Editors: Zdenka Badovinac, Eda Čufer and Anthony Gardner
 Published by Moderna galerija and MIT press (Ljubljana / Cambridge, MA, 2015)
Contributors: Bojan Anđelković, Inke Arns, Zdenka Badovinac, Barbara Borčić, Dominic Boyer, Eda Čufer, Mladen Dolar, Goran Đorđević, Anthony Gardner, Gediminas Gasparavičius, Boris Groys, Marina Gržinić, Chrissie Iles, Jana Intihar Ferjan, Taras Kermauner, Željko Kipke, Jela Krečič, Lev Kreft, Dejan Kršić, Dušan Mandič, Tomaž Mastnak, Rastko Močnik, Alexei Monroe, Stojan Pelko, Tone Peršak, Katja Praznik, Daniel R. Quiles,

Dimitrij Rupel, Sylvia Sasse, Stevphen Shukaitis, Lilijana Stepančič, Darko Štrajn, Igor Vidmar, Catherine Wood, Alexei Yurchak, Slavoj Žižek, Jaša L. Zlobec

'How did we get here'
Exhibition and public programme SALT Beyoğlu & SALT Galata, Istanbul, Turkey
3 September–29 November 2015

Curators: Merve Elveren, Erman Ata Uncu

Artists: Halil Altındere, Serdar Ateşer, Aslı Çavuşoğlu, Barış Doğrusöz, Ayşe Erkmen, Esra Ersen, and Hale Tenger.
 Archives of: Serdar Ateşer, Nakiye Boran, Murat Çelikkan, Gülizar Çepoğlu, İbrahim Eren, Füsun Ertuğ, Tuğrul Eryılmaz, Gençay Gürsoy, Sadık Karamustafa, Esen Karol, Vasıf Kortun, Murat Öneş, Nilgün Öneş, Gülnur Acar Savran, Yücel Tunca, Amnesty International Turkey, Aziz Nesin Archive, Pozitif Group, SALT Research–Harika-Kemali Söylemezoğlu Archive and IFEA Archive.

'1980s — The Multiple Origins of Contemporary Art in Europe Today'
Lecture series, KASK School of Arts University College, Ghent, Belgium
January–June 2016

Coordinators: Nataša Petrešin-Bachelez, Steven ten Thije, Erwin Wittevrongel

Participants: Nick Aikens, Carles Ametller, Jozef Devillé, İştar Gözaydın, Teresa Grandas, Nav Haq, Amna Malik, Antoni Muntadas, Carlos Prieto, Erman Ata Uncu, Borut Vogelnik, Adela Železnik

'The 1980s. Today's Beginnings?'
Exhibition and public programme Van Abbemuseum, Eindhoven, the Netherlands
16 April–9 September 2016

Programme curators: Nick Aikens and Diana Franssen

Exhibition Chapters 'The 1980s. Today's Beginnings?':

'Talking Back. Counter Culture in the Netherlands'

Curator: Diana Franssen

Artists: Catrien Ariëns, Hans Breeder, Daniel Brun, Miguel-Ángel Cárdenas, Ulises Carrión, René Daniëls, DEDO-Harry Heyink, Sandra Derks, Jaap Drupsteen, David Garcia & Annie Wright, General Idea, Heiner Holtappels, Patricia Kaersenhout, Jouke Kleerebezem, Bertien van Manen, Raul Marroquin, Mariano Maturana, Rob Scholte, Lydia Schouten, Joost Seelen, Servaas, Sluik/Kurpershoek, Stansfield/Hooykaas, Moniek Toebosch

'NSK: From *Kapital* to Capital. An Event in the Final Decade of Yugoslavia'

Curator: Zdenka Badovinac

Artists: Laibach, IRWIN, Scipion Nasice Theatre, Cosmokinetic Theatre Red Pilot, Cosmokinetic Cabinet Noordung, New Collectivism, Department of Pure and Applied Philosophy, Builders, Retrovision, Film

'Thinking Back. A Montage of Black Art in Britain'

Curator: Nick Aikens

Artists: John Akomfrah, Rasheed Araeen, Black Audio Film Collective, Sonia Boyce, Chila Burman, Eddie Chambers, Rotimi Fani-Kayode, Mona Hatoum, Lubaina Himid, Gavin Jantjes, Claudette Johnson, Isaac Julien, Keith Piper, Ingrid Pollard, Donald Rodney, Marlene Smith, Maud Sulter

  Archives: Blk Art Group Research Project, African-Caribbean, Asian & African Art in Britain Archive (Chelsea College of Arts Library, University of the Arts), The June Givanni Pan African Cinema Archive (including films by Imruh Bakari and Amani Naphtali), Making Histories Visible Archive (Centre of Contemporary Art at the University of Central Lancashire), The Stuart Hall Library, Iniva (Institute of International Visual Arts), London

'Video-Nou / Servei de Video Comunitari, a case study in Spanish transition'

Curator: Teresa Grandas
Artists: Video-Nou / Servei de Video Comunitari

'How did we get here. Turkey in the 1980s'

Curator: Merve Elveren

Artists: Aslı Çavuşoğlu and Barış Doğrusöz.
  Archives of: Yücel Tunca, Aziz Nesin Archive, Füsun Ertuğ, Gençay Gürsoy, İbrahim Eren, Gülnur Savran, Murat Öneş, Nilgün Öneş, Tuğrul Eryılmaz, Murat Çelikkan, Serdar Ateşer

'Archivo Queer? Screwing the system (Madrid 1989–1995)'

Curator: Fefa Vila Núñez

Artists: Archivo Queer? is comprised of material drawn from collective production in the late eighties and nineties by activists who collaborated with LSD and Radical Gai.

'Energy Flash – The Rave Movement'
Exhibition and public programme Museum van Hedendaagse Kunst Antwerpen (M HKA) Antwerp, Belgium
17 June–25 September 2016

Curator: Nav Haq

Artists: Jacques André, Irene de Andrés, Cory Arcangel, George Barber, Jef Cornelis, Jeremy Deller, Denicolai & Provoost, Rineke Dijkstra, Aleksandra Domanović, Andreas Gursky, Dan Halter, Henrik Plenge Jakobsen, Ann Veronica Janssens, Martin Kersels, Mark Leckey, Daniel Pflumm, Matt Stokes, Sergey Shutov, The Otolith Group, Walter Van Beirendonck

Publication: *RAVE: Rave and Its Influence on Art and Culture*
  Published by M HKA Museum van Hedendaagse Kunst Antwerpen & Black Dog Publishing (Antwerpen/London, 2016)
  Editor: Nav Haq
  Contributors: Irene de Andrés, Jeremy Deller, Kodwo Eshun, Mark Fisher, Nav Haq, Walter Van Beirendonck, Renaat Vandepapeliere, Wolfgang Voigt

'The Eighties – A Decade of Extremes'
Exhibition and public programme Museum van Hedendaagse Kunst Antwerpen (M HKA), Antwerp, Belgium

17 June–18 September, 2016
Curator: Leen De Backer

Artists: Georg Baselitz, Guillaume Bijl, Jean-Marc Bustamante, Club Moral (Danny Devos & Anne-Mie Van Kerckhoven), Jef Cornelis, René Daniëls, Thierry De Cordier, Anne Teresa De Keersmaeker, Wim Delvoye, Bernaded Dexters, Lili Dujourie, Jan Fabre, GAL, Robert Gober, Rodney Graham, Keith Haring, Jenny Holzer, Jörg Immendorff, Per Kirkeby, Jeff Koons, Barbara Kruger, Robert Mapplethorpe, Paul McCarthy & Mike Kelley, Allan McCollum, Cady Noland, Ria Pacquée, A.R. Penck, David Robilliard, Martha Rosler, Rob Scholte, Thomas Schütte, Cindy Sherman, Walter Swennen, Jan Vercruysse, Franz West

'One and the Many'
Exhibition and public programme SALT Galata, Istanbul, Turkey
6 September–13 November 2016

Curator: Meriç Öner
Research team: Meriç Öner, Dilek Himam, İlhan Ozan, Cem Kaya, Ayşe Coşkun Orlandi, Baron von Plastik, Asya Ece Uzmay, Emirhan Altuner, Merve Dokumacı, Özüm Yelkencioğlu.

Artists: Ahmet Altekin, Atilla Argat, Hraç Aslanyan, Yahşi Baraz, Davut Beresi, Başak Gürsoy, Ali İhsan İlkbahar, Fatoş İnhan, Hüsnü Karagözoğlu, Sami Kariyo, Yıldırım Kaymal, Aytaç Kot, Jan Nahum, Adil Öztoprak, Baron von Plastik, Nalan Sakızlı, Hasan Subaşı, Arman Suciyan.
   Archives of: Adel, Arçelik, Bingo, Dalin, Evyap, Fatoş Toys, Ford Otosan, Gorbon Tiles, Hotiç, İGS, İnci Deri, Istanbul Toy Museum, Izmir University of Economics, Faculty of Fine Arts and Design, Jumbo, Kelebek, Migros, Mudo, Oyak Renault, Paşabahçe, Penti, Pınar, SEK, Selpak, TAMEK, Tofaş, Tofaş Bursa Anatolian Cars and Carriages Museum, Ülker, Vakko

'New Spaces, New Images. The 1980s through the Prism of Events, Exhibitions, and Discourses'
Exhibition and public programme Moderna Galerija, Museum of Modern Art, Ljubljana, Slovenia
14 October 2016–1 January 2017

Curators: Asta Vrečko, Martina Malešič
Artists: Jani Bavčer, Mirsad Begić, Dušan Benko, Emerik Bernard, Bogdan Borčić, Željko Borčić, Janez Boljka, Eta Sadar Breznik, Dragica Čadež, Tone Demšar, Ivan Dvoršak, Damjan Gale, Bojan Gorenec, France Gruden, Marina Gržinić, Herman Gvardjančič, Andrej Hrausky, Zdenko Huzjan, IRWIN, Boris Jesih, Janez Kališnik, Sergej Kapus, Dušan Kirbiš, Marjan Kocjan, Nino Kovačević, Metka Krašovec, Janez Lenassi, Miljenko Licul, Lojze Logar, Evita Lukež, Živko Marušič, Ranko Novak, Nuša in Srečo Dragan, Matjaž Počivavšek, Franc Purg, Vojteh Ravnikar, Andraž Šalamun, Duba Sambolec, Davorin Savnik, Peter Savnik, Peter Skalar, Peter Škerlavaj, Jože Slak - Đoka Mojca Smerdu, Janez Suhadolc, Tugo Šušnik, Dušan Tršar, Vinko Tušek, Branko Uršič, Jernej Vilfan, Mitja Visočnik, Lujo Vodopivec, Jože Vrščaj, V.S.S.D. (Veš slikar svoj dolg / Painter, Do You Know Your Duty?), Božo Zadravec, Boris Zaplatil, Milan Zornik

'Hard Gelatin. Hidden Stories from the 80s'
Exhibition and public programme MACBA Museu d'Art Contemporani de Barcelona, Barcelona, Spain
4 November 2016–19 March 2017

Curator: Teresa Grandas

Artists: The exhibit included feature films, documentaries, television programmes, magazines, comics, fanzines, artworks, exercises in anti-art and other materials. 5QK's (Alfonso de Sierra, Luis Escribano, Ramón Massa, Ces Marti, Enric Bentz), Francesc Abad, Agustín Parejo School, Marcel·lí Antúnez Roca, Tere Badia, Txomin Badiola, Cecilia Bartolomé, José Juan Bartolomé, Antonio Beneyto, Miguel Benlloch, Bartomeu Cabot, Tino Calabuig, Alán Carrasco, Colita, Octavi Comeron, Pepe Espaliú, Marcelo Expósito, David Fernández de Castro, Miguel Gallardo, Angustias García, Daniel García Andújar, Joan Gelabert, Ricardo González, Eulàlia Grau, Isaías Griñolo, Federico Guzmán, Joaquin Jordà, Lluís Juncosa, Manolo Laguillo, Rogelio López Cuenca, Laia Manresa, José Luis Marzo, Antoni Muntadas, Nazario, Ocaña,

Joan Palou, Anton Patiño, Carlos Pazos, Pere
Portabella, Preiswert, Manolo Quejido, Joan
Rabascall, Arturo-Fito Rodríguez, Montse
Romaní, Pedro G. Romero, María Ruido,
Fernando Ruiz Vergara, Pepe Sales, Mireia
Sentís, SIEP (Col·lectiu artístic), Llorenç Soler,
Albert Subirats, Carlos Taillefer, Taller Llunàtic
(Bartomeu Cabot and Josep Albertí), Andreu
Terrades, Steva Terrades, Francesc Torres,
Adrià Trescents, Guillermo Trujillano, Isidoro
Valcárcel Medina, Jordi Valls, Ventura Pons,
Vídeo-Nou, Gabriel Villota, Jaume Xifra, Zush
Catalogue contributors: Teresa Grandas, Pere
Portabella and Servando Rocha

'The 80s Against the Grain'
Conference MACBA Museu d'Art Contemporani de Barcelona, Barcelona, Spain
14 December 2016

Organized by Public Programmes Department
MACBA

Participants: Nick Aikens, Alberto Berzosa,
Marta Echaves, Merve Elveren, Equipo
Palomar, Diana Franssen, Nav Haq, Luis López
Carrasco, Fefa Vila

**'The Heritage of 1989. Case Study: The
Second Yugoslav Documents Exhibition'**
Exhibition and public programme Moderna
galerija, Museum of Modern Art, Ljubljana,
Slovenia
26 April –17 September 2017

Curators: Zdenka Badovinac and Bojana
Piškur

Artists: Jožef Ač, Jadran Adamović, Tome
Adžijevski, Azra Akšamija, Nada Alavanja,
Mrdjan Bajić, Jože Barši, Aleksandar Saša
Bukvić, Jovan Čekić, Lana Čmajčanin, Danica
Dakić, Radomir Damnjan Damnjanović,
Vlasta Delimar, Boris Demur, Slobodan Braco
Dimitrijević, Vladimir Dodig Trokut, Nuša and
Srečo Dragan, Marija Dragojlović, Sandro
Đukić, Bojan Gorenec, Zoran Grebenarović,
Herman Gvardjančič, Jusuf Hadžifejzović,
Zdenko Huzjan, Bora Iljovski, IRWIN, Nina
Ivančić, Sanja Iveković, Anto Jerkovič, Željko
Jerman, Olga Jevrić, Sanjin Jukić, Dušan Jurić,

Anto Kajinić, Narcis Kantardžić, Segej Kapus,
Laslo Kerekeš, Željko Kipke, Julije Knifer,
Adrian Kovacs, Ivan Kožarić, Tomaž Lavrič,
Zmago Lenardič, Branko Lepen, Roman Makše,
Markovačič (Marko Kovačič), Milovan DeStil
Markovic, Vlado Martek, Dalibor Martinis,
Mladen Materić, Slobodan Era Milivojević,
Marko Modic, Marjan Molnar, Petre Nikoloski,
Edin Numankadić, Dušan Otašević, Neša
Paripović, Milija Pavićević, Slobodan Peladić,
Goran Petercol, Matjaž Počivavšek, Tadej
Pogačar, Marjetica Potrč, Mileta Prodanović,
Dubravka Rakoci, Retrovizija, Duba Sambolec,
Jože Slak Đoka, Damir Sokić, Mladen Stilinović,
Sven Stilinović, Vlado Stijepić, Gabrijel Stupica,
Aneta Svetieva, Škart, Ilija Šoškić, Jane Štravs,
Jovan Šumkovski, Tugo Šušnik, Radoslav Tadić,
Talent (Vladimir Perić), Matej Taufer, Goran
Trbuljak, Emir Tulek, Dragomir Ugren, Gergelj
Urkom, Branka Uzur, Verbumprogram, V.S.S.D.,
Xhevdet Xhafa

**'Show Me Your Archive and I Will Tell You Who
is in Power'**
Exhibition and public programme KIOSK,
KASK / School or Arts Ghent, Ghent, Belgium
27 April–16 June 2017

Curators: Nataša Petrešin-Bachelez and Wim
Waelput

Artists: Marwa Arsanios, Saddie Choua,
Françoise Dasques, Amandine Gay, Kapwani
Kiwanga, Alex Mawimbi (Ato Malinda), Eva
Olthof, collective Study Group for Solidarity
and TransActions, archives of Chantal De Smet
   Public programme participants: Paola
Bacchetta and Françoise Vergès, Mara
Montanaro, Amandine Gay and Po B.K. Lomami,
Kapwani Kiwanga, Chantal De Smet and Jacqui
Goegebeur, Fatma Arikoglu, Nella van den
Brandt, Samira Saleh, Sophie Withaeckx

COLOPHON

Editors
Nick Aikens, Teresa Grandas,
Nav Haq, Beatriz Herráez,
Nataša Petrešin-Bachelez

Co-editors
Merve Elveren, Adela Železnik

**Assistant editorial coordination
for Museo Reina Sofía**
Sara Buraya Boned

Contributors
Nick Aikens, Henry Andersen,
Zdenka Badovinac, Barış Gençer
Baykan, Hakim Bey, Manuel Borja-
Villel, Rosi Braidotti, Boris Buden,
Cristina Cámara, Jesús Carrillo,
Bojana Cvejić, Luc Deleu, Diedrich
Diederichsen, Nazım Hikmet
Richard Dikbaş, Corinne Diserens,
Ayşe Düzkan, Merve Elveren,
Charles Esche, Marcelo Expósito,
Božidar Flajšman, Annie Fletcher,
Diana Franssen, June Givanni,
Lisa Godson, Teresa Grandas,
Nav Haq, Beatriz Herráez,
Lubaina Himid, Lola Hinojosa,
Antony Hudek, Tea Hvala, Gal
Kirn, Neža Kogovšek Šalamon,
Anders Kreuger, Elisabeth
Lebovici, Rogelio López Cuenca,
Geert Lovink, Amna Malik, Pablo
Martínez, Lourdes Méndez, Aleš
Mendiževec, Ana Mizerit, Alexei
Monroe, Meriç Öner, Nataša
Petrešin-Bachelez, Bojana Piškur,
Marta Popivoda, Carlos Prieto del
Campo, Pedro G. Romero, Rafael
Sánchez Ferlosio, Igor Španjol,
Chris Straetling, Luís Trindade,
Erman Ata Uncu, Jelena Vesić,
Mar Villaespesa, Vladimir Jerić
Vlidi, Ana Vujanović

Translation
Phillipa Burton (Elisabeth Lebovici);
Gökcan Demirkazık (Merve Elveren,
Erman Ata Uncu, 'From "Personal
is Political" to Women in Black',
Merve Elveren, Erman Ata Uncu,
'Sokak'); Nazım Hikmet Richard
Dikbaş (Merve Elveren, Erman Ata
Uncu, 'Istanbul Kurdish: To Be a
Kurd and a Woman in the City',
Merve Elveren, Erman Ata Uncu,
'Know Your Rights', Merve Elveren,
Erman Ata Uncu, 'No to Compulsory
Military Service', Merve Elveren,
Erman Ata Uncu, 'Petition of
Intellectuals', Merve Elveren,
Erman Ata Uncu, 'Terror in Prisons:
We Won't Let You Kill Them'); Neil
Fawle (Cristina Cámara, Jesús
Carrillo, Marcelo Expósito, Teresa
Grandas, Beatriz Herráez, Lola
Hinojosa, Rogelio López Cuenca,
Pablo Martínez, Lourdes Méndez,
Carlos Prieto del Campo, Pedro G.
Romero, Rafael Sánchez Ferlosio);
Sylvie Imbert (Mar Villaespesa);
Tamara Soban (Božidar Flajšman,
Ana Mizerit); Alice Tetley-Paul
(Diedrich Diedrichsen); Graham
Tomson (Manuel Borja-Villel)

Text editor
Leo Reijnen

Proofreading
Els Brinkman

Index
Elke Stevens

Graphic design
George&Harrison
www.georgeandharrison.nl

Typefaces
Druk Text Wide
Maison Neue

Production
Valiz: Pia Pol, Astrid Vorstermans

Paper inside
Munken Print White, 100 g/m²

Paper cover
Imitlin Neve Tela, 125 g/m²

Lithography
Mariska Bijl, Wilco Art Books,
Amsterdam

Printing
Bariet-Ten Brink, Meppel

Binding
Wilco, Amersfoort

Publisher
Pia Pol, Astrid Vorstermans / Valiz,
Amsterdam in cooperation with
L'Internationale

Partners
L'Internationale
is a confederation of six
major European modern and
contemporary art institutions:
Moderna galerija, Ljubljana,
www.mg-lj.si
Museo Reina Sofía, Madrid,
www.museoreinasofia.es
MACBA Museu d'Art Contem-
porani de Barcelona, Barcelona,
www.macba.cat
Museum van Hedendaagse
Kunst Antwerpen, www.muhka.be
SALT, Istanbul and Ankara,
www.saltonline.org
Van Abbemuseum, Eindhoven,
www.vanabbemuseum.nl

L'Internationale proposes a space
for art within a non-hierarchical
and decentralized internationalism,
based on the values of difference
and horizontal exchange among
a constellation of cultural agents,
locally rooted and globally
connected.

This publication is part of the
programme 'The Uses of Art:
The Legacy of 1848 and 1989',
co-financed by the Culture
Programme of the European Union
and developed by L'Internationale
together with KASK School of
Arts University College Ghent,
Liverpool John Moores University,
Middlesbrough Institute of
Modern Art and the University of
Hildesheim.

This publication was made possible through the generous support of

L'Internationale
www.internationaleonline.org

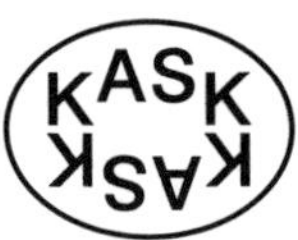

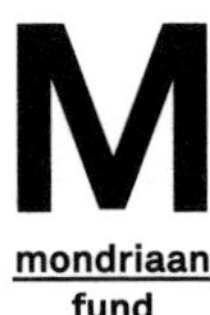

KASK School of Arts
University College Ghent
www.schoolofartsgent.be

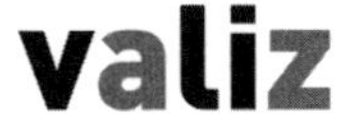

HoGent

Mondriaan Fund
www.mondriaanfonds.nl

M

mondriaan fund

www.valiz.nl

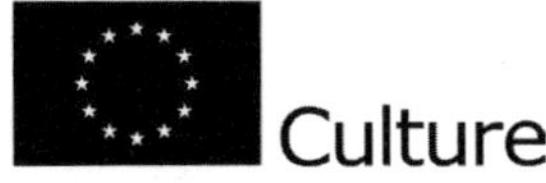

European Union,
Culture Programme

Culture

This project has been funded with support from the European Commission. This publication reflects the views only of the authors, and the Commission cannot be held responsible for any use which may be made of the information contained therein.

The editors, authors and the publisher have made every effort to secure permission to reproduce the listed material, illustrations and photographs. We apologize for any inadvert errors or omissions. Parties who nevertheless believe they can claim specific legal rights are invited to contact the publisher.

Distribution
BE/NL/LU: Centraal Boekhuis, www.cb.nl

GB/IE: Anagram Books, www.anagrambooks.com

Europe/Asia: Idea Books, www.ideabooks.nl

Australia: Perimeter Books, www.perimeterbooks.com

USA: D.A.P., www.artbook.com

Individual orders: www.valiz.nl; info@valiz.nl

ISBN 978 94 92095 49 7
Printed and bound in the EU
Valiz, Amsterdam, 2018